# American Immigrant Cultures

# Editorial Board

# AMERICAN IMMIGRANT CULTURES

## Builders of a Nation

*Edited by*

DAVID LEVINSON
MELVIN EMBER

**Volume 2**

MACMILLAN REFERENCE USA
Simon & Schuster Macmillan
NEW YORK

Simon & Schuster and Prentice Hall International
London   Mexico City   New Delhi   Singapore   Sydney   Toronto

*American Immigrant Cultures* was prepared under the auspices and with the support of the Human Relations Area Files at Yale University. HRAF, the foremost international research organization in the field of cultural anthropology, is a not-for-profit consortium of twenty-three sponsoring members and three hundred participating member institutions in twenty-five countries. The HRAF archive, established in 1949, contains nearly one million pages of information on the cultures of the world.

Simon & Schuster Macmillan
1633 Broadway
New York, NY 10019

Printed in the United States of America

Printing Number
  3 4 5 6 7 8 9 10

**Library of Congress Cataloging-in-Publication Data**

American immigrant cultures: builders of a nation / David Levinson
    and Melvin Ember, editors in chief.
        p.    cm.
    Includes bibliographical references and index.
      ISBN 0-02-897214-7 (vol. 1: alk. paper) — ISBN 0-02-897213-9
    (vol. 2: alk. paper) — ISBN 0-02-897208-2 (set: alk. paper).
        1. Minorities–United States.    2. Ethnicity–United States.
    3. Immigrants–United States.    4. United States–Ethnic relations.
    I. Levinson, David.    II. Ember, Melvin.
    E184.A1A63448   1997
    305.8′00973–dc21                                                97-17477
                                                                        CIP

This paper meets the requirements of ANSI-NISO Z39.48-1992 (Permanence of Paper).

# KALMYKS

The ethnonym "Kalmyk" is also spelled Kalmuck and Kalmuk. The self-appelation of Kalmyks is Khal'mg (Qal'mg). They were referred to as *qalmaq* or *qalmuq* in the sixteenth and seventeenth centuries by their Turkic-speaking neighboring peoples and tribes; hence the Russian spelling Kalmyk. This ethnicon must have come into use at the end of the sixteenth or at the beginning of the seventeenth century. It is not used in Central Asia, however, where the Kalmyks are commonly known among their closely related various Mongolian nationalities as Idjil Monggol (the Volga Mongols), Öröd (Oirats), or Dörwn Öröd (Four Oirat tribes). The latter are Torgud, Dörböd, Khoshud (Qoshud), and Khöd (Qöd) or Qoyid. The fourth member of this Oirat confederation has been variously referred to as Qöd (Qoyid), Dzungar or Djungar (Zün gar), or Tsoros.

The Kalmyks are closely related to all the Oirats of Central Asia. (Inner Asia is another toponym used in scholarly publications.) The latter are found in Dzungaria, which is now the northern half of Sinkiang Province in northwestern China; in Tsinghai Province (Kuku-Nur), north of Tibet; and in the western part of Mongolia. The ancestors of the present-day Kalmyks inhabited Dzungaria until the early seventeenth century.

## Unique Ethnicity

The Kalmyks occupy a unique place in the United States as well as in Europe (including the European part of Russia) from the standpoints of ethnicity, language, religion, and anthropology. They constitute the only concentrated ethnic group in the United States who practice Tibetan Buddhism or Lamaism, speak a Mongolian language, and physically typify the distinctive Mongoloid race.

The Kalmyks constitute the western branch of the Mongolian race and as such are regarded as the western mongols or the Mongols of the West. They are closely related to Mongols and Buriats (Buryats). The former, frequently referred to as the Khalkha (Qalqa) Mongols, eastern Mongols, or Mongols proper, live in Mongolia and in China, principally in Inner Mongolia, Sinkiang, Tsinghai, and Manchuria. The latter constitute the Buriat Republic in Russia and are ordinarily classified as northern Mongols.

The close kinship among the Kalmyks, Buriats, Mongols, and other lesser Mongolian nationalities is quite evident from the well-established fact that they all (1) belong to the same distinctive Mongoloid race, (2) speak languages characterized by their close linguistic affinity (they are all Mongolian languages, which constitute an important branch of the Altaic family of languages), (3) adopted the Tibetan version of Buddhism (Lamaism), which has played such a significant role in the religious, cultural, and political life of the Mongol peoples, and (4) maintained many identical or similar customs and traditions throughout the centuries in spite of their far-reaching migrations, forced dispersion, and the centuries-long close intercourse with the Chinese, Turkic peoples, and others who adhered to alien customs.

The Kalmyk people are historically divided into several long-standing tribal subgroups. The major ones are the Torgud, Dörböd, and Khoshud (Qoshud). The Torgud have constituted the majority of the Kalmyk nation in Russia from the seventeenth through the twentieth centuries. The Dörböd tribe is subdivided into Iki (Greater) and Baγa (Lesser) Dörböd. Iki Dörböd inhabited an *ulus* (a large-scale territorial nomadic unit ruled by a prince or a lesser noble) of their own in Stavropol Province until the end of the Russian Civil War in 1920–1921, whereas the Baγa Dörböd have been occupying the Kalmyk steppe in Astrakhan Province. For various reasons, primarily on account of the authoritarian rule of some of the Kalmyk khans, chiefly Ayuki Khan, a significant number of the Torgud and Dörböd broke away and fled westward to the Don Cossacks. Over time they became known as the Buzāva or Don Kalmyks. All of them, except for the Qoshud, are represented in the United States.

## Immigration History

In the 1620s, a considerable number of the ancestors of the Kalmyks, mostly Torgud, migrated westward to the lower Volga region of Russia. In January 1771, approximately 169,000 people fled Russia to Dzungaria to avoid being completely subjugated to imperial Russian domination. They left behind, on the west bank of the Volga, one-fifth of their kinsmen, who had to recognize the authority of the central Russian government. Some Kalmyks sided with the Bolsheviks during the Russian Civil War of 1917–1920, while many others supported the anti-Bolshevik forces. The latter fled Russia in 1920 and settled in France, Yugoslavia, Bulgaria, and Czechoslovakia. The rapid advances by Soviet armies into southeastern and central Europe from the fall of 1944 to the spring of 1945 caused the uprooting and flight of the Kalmyk émigrés from Bulgaria and Yugoslavia (September 1944) and Czechoslovakia (April 1945) to Austria, Germany, and France.

After the war, approximately eight hundred Kalmyks found themselves in various displaced-persons camps in Munich and other parts of Bavaria under the aegis of the United Nations Relief and Rehabilitation Administration (UNRRA) and the International Refugee Organization (IRO). The political and economic uncertainties of early postwar Europe, coupled with their fear of Soviet military aggression, led the Kalmyk refugees to consider moving to any suitable country outside Europe. Even though the United States had passed the Displaced Persons Act of 1948, the Kalmyks were at first termed inadmissible, since they were regarded as Orientals and thereby excluded under the Oriental Exclusion Act of 1922. Section 303 of the U.S. Nationality Act of 1940 prohibited the immigration of people of a nonwhite race. All attempts at immigrating to the United States, Canada, Australia, and even to places as widely scattered as Paraguay, Ceylon (Sri Lanka), Abyssinia (Ethiopia), and Madagascar failed on racial grounds because the Kalmyks were not regarded as Caucasians. After fifteen months (April 1950–July 1951) of repeated appeals to the Board of Special Inquiry and Board of Immigration Appeals of the U.S. Immigration and Naturalization Service, counsel for the appellants, Mr. and Mrs. Dorji Remilev, at last convinced the Board of Immigration Appeals that the Kalmyks were members of the white or so-called Caucasian (European) race, despite their Asian origin. The matter of the

Samson and Dorji Remilev at the time of their decisive test case concerning the race classification of Kalmyks. (Arash Bormanshinov)

cosponsors, the Church World Service of the National Council of the Churches of Christ, and the Tolstoy Foundation, both headquartered in New York City, to carry out this undertaking.

The first group of Kalmyk immigrants arrived in New York City on December 25, 1951, followed by several more, with the last significant group arriving on February 22, 1952. They were sent by their sponsors to two different communities: New Windsor, Maryland, and Parvin Park, near Vineland, in southern New Jersey. By late spring and early summer 1952, the Kalmyks were able to relocate, with the assistance of their two principal cosponsors, to Philadelphia; to Freewood Acres in Howell, New Jersey; and to Paterson, New Jersey. In the late 1950s yet another community came into existence in New Brunswick, New Jersey. The Kalmyk population of Paterson has decreased ever since that time.

During the 1950s and 1960s, more Kalmyks from West Germany, France, and Belgium immigrated to Philadelphia, New Jersey, and New York City, thus increasing the overall Kalmyk population to 950 or more. (No attempt has ever been made to conduct a separate census of the Kalmyk population in the United States.)

## Settlement Patterns

From the very beginning of their life in the United States, the Kalmyks followed a clear pattern of settlement—toward segregation, concentrated settlement, and against dispersion. This helped them to maintain close contact with one another in a new country whose language and customs were unfamiliar. In Philadelphia, for example, during the initial ten to fifteen years, most of the Kalmyks lived in their own brick rowhouses not far from one another, generally within ten city blocks to the north and south of Girard Avenue, in the lower part of the northeastern section of Philadelphia. Since the mid-1960s, however, most of the Kalmyks have been moving out of that area to more affluent sections in the upper part of northeastern Philadelphia, north of Roosevelt Boulevard, resulting in noticeable geographical

Remilevs constituted a decisive test case, since a positive finding on the racial eligibility of both appellants was absolutely essential to the admission of the Kalmyk refugees to the United States. On July 28, 1951, the Kalmyks were ruled eligible for U.S. naturalization, thus ending more than ten years of the Kalmyks' ordeal in war-torn and postwar Europe.

All Kalmyks eligible for immigration arrived in the United States between late December 1951 and late February 1952. Most came from West Germany; a few came from Austria. Approximately 650 Kalmyk refugees entered the United States by late February 1952.

In 1951, the IRO allocated funds for the transportation of the Kalmyks and an additional $182,000 for their subsequent resettlement in the United States. These funds enabled the two main dispersion. The other large group, that of Howell, New Jersey, has been able to maintain its original pattern of concentrated settlement.

An ever-increasing number of college- and professionally trained Kalmyks brought about a new phenomenon in geographical mobility—a tendency toward dispersion. Thus, since the 1970s, small emerging groups have settled in or near Washington, D.C., San Francisco, Los Angeles, and New York City. In due course, this trend toward more dispersion—necessitated by job opportunities—will most likely continue and play not an insignificant role in matters related to the maintenance of Kalmyk ethnicity.

## Language Maintenance

Kalmyk and various Oirat dialects spoken in Central Asia make up the western branch of the Mongolian language group, an important division of the Altaic family of languages. Modern Kalmyk is divided into three dialects: Torgūd, Dörböd, and Buzāva. The latter is quite close to Torgūd and is spoken by the Don Kalmyks, who before the 1920s used to inhabit the Sal district of the Don Cossack region. In general, all Kalmyk dialects are very close to each other.

Perhaps the most difficult and disturbing aspect of Kalmyk life is the fact that the overwhelming majority of the children and grandchildren of the Kalmyk immigrants speak their mother tongue either poorly or not at all. As a rule, most children speak Kalmyk at home, if their parents speak it or if their grandparents live in the same household, until they enter kindergarten. Once they are enrolled in public schools, however, they soon forget their mother tongue and adopt English. It is also known that some parents deliberately speak English with their children to improve their own ability to speak passable English. English has thereby become the principal language of both spoken and written communication and a lingua franca among them, their parents, and people their age. The prospect of becoming part of a monolingual, English-speaking society is a grim and unavoidable reality for the Kalmyk community.

## Economic Adjustment

From an economic standpoint, the Kalmyks have fared fairly well. For most of them, the language barrier during the early and mid-1950s was a formidable obstacle, particularly for those beyond middle age. Moreover, only a very few Kalmyks had a professional background and held university degrees. In Philadelphia and Paterson they entered the job market as laborers and assembly-line workers, while the majority of women were absorbed by the vast garment industry. In Howell most of the young and middle-aged men quickly learned the house building trade and became subcontractors and construction workers, jobs they have been performing ever since. Today, Kalmyk Americans earn their livelihood in a variety of occupations. The American-born generation has acquired different skills, trades, or obtained college and/or graduate and professional degrees.

## Community Organization

Intergroup or interethnic relations are almost nonexistent. The Kalmyks have not been active politically. Although some of them are probably registered Democrats or Republicans within their own states, they have not supported any political party as a group. The only known exception is an insignificant number of Kalmyks who are active in local Republican affairs in Howell. Strangely enough, there are no contacts between the Kalmyks and the neighboring Russian community in Lakewood, New Jersey, nor are they active in Don Cossack affairs locally or nationwide. A similar situation prevails in Philadelphia.

Shortly after their arrival in the United States, the Kalmyks organized themselves into three societies: one in Philadelphia and two in New Jersey. The membership in these two societies in New Jersey reflects the centuries-old tribal subdivision and territorial separation of the three ethnic components of the Kalmyks. As a consequence, the Torgud and the Lesser Dörböd as well as the Greater Dörböd, who lived in certain areas of the Astrakhan and Stavropol provinces of Russia, have jointly set up their own social organization in Howell, while the Buzāva or Don Kalmyks have established a similar society a couple of miles farther south. The Philadelphia society consists only of Buzāva Kalmyks.

## Religion

The Kalmyks have been fervent and faithful Buddhists, following the faith of their forefathers. Buddhism has become a more important factor than ever in the life of the Kalmyk communities in the United States. It contributes toward group solidarity. The Kalmyks adhere to the Tibetan form of Buddhism, or Lamaism, and have always recognized His Holiness the Dalai Lama as their highest spirtual leader. The first Kalmyk Buddhist temple in the United States was dedicated in 1955. Three more were also erected in Howell: in 1958,

1970, and 1977. In these temples the three major religious holidays of the lunar year—Tsagan sar (New Year), Ürüs-Ovā (Festival of Spring), and Zul (Feast of Lights)—as well as other religious festivals and rites are celebrated. Temples are also the places where all Kalmyk marriage formalities take place, memorial services for the deceased are conducted, and so on. All the native Kalmyk monks who came with their coreligionists in 1951–1952 have since passed away. Their successors are natives of Inner Mongolia and Tibet who were brought in from their refugee residences in India.

## Assimilation and Cultural Persistence

Until their resettlement in the United States, the Kalmyks were able to maintain their distinct ethnic identity. Intermarriages were almost unheard

A Kalmyk Buddhist temple built in 1977 in Howell, New Jersey. (Arash Bormanshinov)

of, unless there were no Kalmyk counterparts around. Conversion to Christianity or any other religion was nonexistent. The Kalmyk language was spoken by everybody. However, since about 1960, an inevitable, steadfast process of loss of national Kalmyk identity due to various socio-economic and other factors has taken place. The number of marriages between Kalmyks of both sexes and non-Kalmyks has been progressively growing. The majority of boys and girls of marriageable age, however, continue the traditional pattern of marrying Kalmyk counterparts. While divorce in cases of endogamous (in-group) marriages is rare, the divorce rate in exogamous (out-of-group) marriages has become noticeable.

The period since the arrival in 1951 of the first Kalmyk immigrant group in the United States can be characterized as one of material prosperity and educational progress. But this very same progress has been achieved at the cost of an irreversible loss of pride in the Kalmyk ethnic heritage. Old customs, traditions, and religious holidays are not always faithfully followed by the second generation. A noticeable and inevitable increase in exogamous marriages has also become one of the contributing factors for the continuous process of assimilation and integration into American society.

To combat and correct this situation, Kalmyk-language schools for public-school-age children were first set up from 1954 to 1956 by the Society for the Promotion of Kalmyk Culture in Philadelphia and in 1974, 1975, and 1976 in New Brunswick, Howell, and Philadelphia, respectively. The latter schools were sponsored and supervised by the Kalmyk Mongol Studies Council, founded in June 1975. From 1974 to 1975, weekly classes in Oirat and Kalmyk history and Kalmyk grammar were conducted on the campus at Rutgers University in New Brunswick.

## Conclusion

It is too soon to tell whether the numerically small Kalmyk minority group can continue to preserve a distinct ethnic identity in the United States. It is equally hard to predict whether the third and ensuing generations will withstand a menacing trend leading toward complete assimilation, dissolution, and disappearance into the American mainstream.

## Bibliography

Bormanshinov, A. (1961). *Kalmyk Manual*. New York: American Council of Learned Societies.

Bormanshinov, A. (1963). "The Kalmyks in America, 1952–1962." *Royal Central Asian Journal* 50:149–153.

Bormanshinov, A. (1988). "The Kalmyks in the United States 35 Years Later." *The Mongolia Society Newsletter* 5:2–13.

Bormanshinov, A. (1990). *The Kalmyks: Their Ethnic, Historical, Religious, and Cultural Background*. Howell, NJ: Kalmyk American Cultural Association.

Bormanshinov, A. (1990). "Some Problems of Cultural Assimilation of the Kalmyks in the United States and Europe." *Ural-Altaische Jahrbücher* 9:225–235.

Halkovic, S. A. (1985). *The Mongols of the West*. Bloomington: Research Institute for Inner Asian Studies, Indiana University.

Howorth, H. H. ([1876] 1964). *History of the Mongols from the 9th to the 19th Century*, Part 1: *The Mongols Proper and the Kalmuks*. New York: Burt Franklin.

Khodarkovsky, M. (1992). *Where Two Worlds Met: The Russian State and the Kalmyk Nomads, 1600–1771*. Ithaca, NY: Cornell University Press.

Krader, L. (1963). *Social Organization of the Mongol-Turkic Pastoral Nomads*, Chapter III: *Volga Kalmuks*. The Hague: Mouton.

Riasanovsky, V. A. ([1929] 1979). *Customary Law of the Mongol Tribes (Mongols, Buriats, Kalmucks)*, Part III: *The Customary Law of the Kalmucks*. Westport, CT: Hyperion Press.

Romney, A. K. (1965). "Kalmuk Mongol and the Classification of Lineal Kinship Terminologies." In *Formal Semantic Analysis*, edited by E. A. Hammel. *American Anthropologist* 67(5), Special Publication, Part 2.

Rubel, P. G. (1967). *The Kalmyk Mongols: A Study in Continuity and Change*. The Hague: Mouton.

Scheffler, H. W. (1980). "Kalmuk Mongol Kin Classification." *Anthropological Linguistics* 22(6):233–247.

ARASH BORMANSHINOV

# KASHUBIANS

The Kashubians are a Slavic ethnic group emanating from the Baltic seacoast in Europe. They are closely related to the Poles, who live to the south and east, but have become partially assimilated to the Germans bordering on the west. They are known by several ethnonyms: Kashubs, Kaszubi (Polish), Kaszëbë (Kashubian), Cassubians, and Slovincians (a western subgroup).

The contemporary European Kashubians, numbering approximately 150,000, inhabit the Gdańsk, Koszalin, and Bydgoszcz provinces of Poland. They are the last remnant of the Pomeranian (from Slavic *po*, along, and *morje*, the sea) Slavs who once inhabited the Baltic coast between the Vistula and Elbe rivers as far west as Kolberg, Germany. At the beginning of the twentieth century, the Kashubian area extended thirty-seven miles farther west than it does today, stretching to the southern shore of Lake Gardno. Although they were Kashubians, inhabitants of that territory spoke a distinct dialect, called themselves Slovincians, and professed the Lutheran faith, which stands in sharp contrast to the Catholic majority of surviving Kashubians. The Slovincians have since died out, having lost their ancestral language and their ethnic consciousness.

## Language and Culture

Both Kashubian as a separate language and Kashubian culture as distinct from Polish culture have been contested for political, religious, and scholarly reasons. Kashubianisms first appeared in early fifteenth century Polish texts, and a few religious tracts were translated from German during the Protestant Reformation of the sixteenth and seventeenth centuries, but original works were not written in Kashubian until the second half of the nineteenth century, during an ethnic awakening led by Florian Ceynowa at the very time when immigration to America was reaching its peak.

Linguists differ in their classification of Kashubian depending on their time perspective. From a diachronic or historical point of view Kashubian is considered to be a separate Slavic language as the last surviving remnant of Pomeranian. From a synchronic or contemporary point of view Kashubian is seen as a highly differentiated dialect of Polish. Neither during the Reformation nor during the nineteenth century did the attempts to establish a Kashubian literary language receive sufficient popular support for a successful separatist movement. Yet, during the Reformation the use of Kashubian religious texts was the means by which German Lutheran missionaries were able to convert central Pomeranian Kashubians (such as the Slovincians) from Catholicism and bring about their eventual Germanization. Though the Kashubian literary activity that began in the nineteenth century has persisted for more than a century, each author writes in his own regional dialect. First in 1919 (Friedrich Lorentz) and again in 1981 (Edward Breza and Jerzy Treder), attempts were made to establish a normative grammar of literary Kashubian, but it remains to be seen if the latest attempt will succeed, since there are no more than a hundred Kashubian intellectuals in Poland who write in Kashubian. Consequently, Kashubian literary activity during the 1990s functions as regional literature in contemporary Poland. Had a more ardent nationalism arisen among the Kashubians in the past, there is no reason why they could not have established their own nation with its independent Slavic literary language as did the Sorbs, Macedonians, Belarusans, and Slovaks. Thus in Europe contemporary Kashubian culture functions as a subset of Polish culture, with some remnants of Pomeranian culture that are lacking in Polish culture. The resulting blend has acquired a cohesive and unique quality that allows the differentiation of Kashubian culture from Polish culture. Nevertheless, it is somewhat misleading to speak in terms of a culture that is specifically Kashubian, since Polish elements tend to predominate.

## Immigration Patterns

The history of Kashubian immigration to the United States is one of temporary Polonization for most, temporary Germanization for some, and ultimate Americanization for all. The sources for this history are scant. What does exist is embedded in Polish immigration history, which is traditionally divided into four periods: (1) 1608 to the American Revolution—mostly adventurers and religious refugees; (2) the American Revolution to 1854—political refugees; (3) 1854 to World War I—economic refugees; and (4) World War I to the 1990s—various types. In the first period there is only one Kashubian immigrant recorded. Having emigrated from Koszalin, Pomerania, in the 1640s, Daniel Litscho settled in New Amsterdam (later to become New York), where he became a prosperous tavernkeeper. By the end of the American Revolution, Poland no longer existed as an independent state. It had been divided into Prussian, Russian, and Austrian sectors. The Kashubian area devolved to the Prussian sector, and it is from Prussia that the Kashubians emigrated during the second period. Their emigration began in 1848, a year of widespread European unrest, and continued for approximately forty years. The bulk of Kashubian emigrants came from poor farming areas in southern West Prussia and Pomerania, especially the Kościerski, Chojnicki, Człuchowski, and Bytowski districts. During the first dozen years of this exodus the Hamburg Maritime Navigation Company attracted thousands of southern Kashubians to America by providing free ocean passage. This flow of emigration continued well into the third period, with the result that between 1860 and 1890 more than half the population of Bytów had left for America. From Gdańsk (German name, Danzig), 64,000 departed between 1871 and 1880, and 120,000 more between 1881 and 1890. Most sailed to the United States, but others left for eastern Canada and southern Brazil. During this same period a few hundred Slovincian families emigrated from the Słupsk district. The bulk of Kashubian immigration to America had been completed by the end of World War I. There has been little immigration during the fourth period, mainly limited to the brief period between the end of World War II and the establishment of Communist Poland and the German Democratic Republic.

These more recent immigrants came in smaller numbers and tended to settle in cities, whereas their predecessors had mostly settled on farms. Consequently the assimilation of the later immigrants has proceeded much more rapidly.

The great majority of Kashubians who immigrated to the United States were farmers or fishermen. Many found work in factories, but rarely did they seek employment in the mines. Although Kashubians have dispersed throughout the United States, sizable enclaves exist in the following states (listed in order of decreasing magnitude): Illinois, New York, Minnesota, Michigan, South Dakota, Missouri, Pennsylvania, Maryland, and Massachusetts. Specific settlements of varying sizes were established in the following cities and counties, listed here alphabetically by state: Chicago (near Noble and Division streets and St. Józefat Catholic Parish, where they are from Weyherowo); Brighton, Iowa; Baltimore, Maryland; Webster, Massachusetts; Detroit (St. Kazimierz and St. Wojciech Catholic parishes), Parisville, and Poznań, Michigan; Pine Creek, Independence, Sturgeon Lake, Little Falls, Florian, and Greenbush, Minnesota, plus the St. Stanisław Catholic Parish and Marshall, Kittson, and Roseau counties; St. Louis and Hermann (Lutheran Slovincians), Missouri; Trenton (Holy Cross Catholic Parish), New Jersey; Buffalo (mostly Catholics, but some became affiliated with the Polish National Catholic Church), New York, and New York City; Warsaw, Minto, and Fried, North Dakota; Pittsburgh, Pennsylvania; Puck (near Waubay) and Grenville (from Puck and Wejherowo), South Dakota; Milwaukee, Jones Island (mostly fishermen), Stevens Point, Wisconsin, and Portage County. At the beginning of the twentieth century the total Kashubian population of these settlements was estimated at approximately 100,000, some 7,000 of whom were Slovincians. At the close of the century their descendants had increased two and a half fold.

## Religion and Assimilation

The motives for immigration to the United States were mixed. Religious persecution certainly played a role, approaching that of economic hardship. As a disenfranchised Catholic minority in Lutheran Prussia, the Kashubians focused their ethnic identity on the Roman Catholic Church and its attendant religious and social institutions. It is not surprising, then, that U.S. Kashubians never developed any sizable secular ethnic organization. During the course of their more than a century of living in the United States, the vast majority of Kashubians have centered both their spiritual and their social life on the Catholic Church. Their folklore too has a strong admixture of Catholic religious elements. This close tie of Kashubian culture to the church has enabled the Kashubian folklore imported from Europe to flourish in the United States for at least four generations. But with the fifth generation, assimilation has accelerated to near completion. Contributing factors are the exodus of the younger farm generations to cities, fracturing the cohesive socioreligious ethnic unit, as well as the midcentury changes in ritual and practice of the Catholic Church, removing it as a buttress for folk culture. Gone are the *dyngus*, a children's Easter ritual; the *wupji*, a vampire demon; and the *radgba*, a rhymed wedding invitation chant. The Kashubian language itself is fast fading in the minds of the older generations. Fortunately, however, the United States was beneficiary of the Kashubians' most renowned poet, Hieronim Derdowski, of Wiele in the district of Chojnice, who immigrated to the United States in 1885. Having settled in Winona, Minnesota, then considered the Kashubian capital of the United States, he became the publisher of *Wiarus*, a Polish-American newspaper in which he occasionally inserted short works in Kashubian. His greatest work, *O panu Czorlińscim, co do Pucka sece jachoł* (Concerning Mr. Czorliński, Who Drove to Puck in Search of a Fishing Net), remains the acknowledged gem of Kashubian literature.

*See also:* POLES

## Bibliography

Breza, E., and Treder, J. (1981). *Gramatyka Kaszubska*. Gdańsk, Poland: Zrzczenie Kaszubsko-Pomerskie.

Lorentz, F.: Fischer, A.; and Lehr-Spławiński, T. (1935). *The Cassubian Civilization*. London: Faber & Faber.

Neureiter, F. (1991). *Geschichte der Kaschubischen Literatur*. Munich: Verlag Otto Sagner.

Perkowski, J. (1966). "The Kashubs—Origins and Emigration to the U.S." *Polish American Studies* 23(1):1–7.

Perkowski, J. (1969). *A Kashubian Idiolect in the United States*. Bloomington: Indiana University Press.

Perkowski, J. (1972). *Vampires, Dwarves, and Witches Among the Ontario Kashubs*. Ottawa: National Museum of Man.

Perkowski, J. (1973). "Kashubian Folklore in America." In *American Contributions to the Seventh International Congress of Slavists*, Vol. 2: *Literature and Folklore*, edited by V. Terras. The Hague: Mouton.

Perkowski, J. (1983). "Twentieth-Century Kashubian Literature." In *Encyclopedia of World Literature in the 20th Century*, Vol. 3, edited by L. S. Klein. New York: Frederick Ungar.

Stone, G. (1993). "Cassubian." In *The Slavonic Languages*, edited by B. Comrie and G. Corbett. London: Routledge.

Topolińska, Z. (1974). *A Historical Phonology of the Kashubian Dialects of Polish*. The Hague: Mouton.

Topolińska, Z. (1980). "Kashubian." In *The Slavic Literary Languages*, edited by A. M. Schenker and E. Stankiewicz. New Haven, CT: Slavica.

JAN L. PERKOWSKI

# KHMU

One of the smaller ethnic communities in North America, with about four thousand members in the 1990s, the Khmu (also known as Kmhmu and Kammu) nevertheless take great pride in their distinct language and culture. In their homeland—the mountainous region of northern Laos and neighboring areas of northern Thailand, northwestern Vietnam, and southwestern China—the Khmu number some half a million persons.

In that region of tremendous ethnic diversity, the Khmu are the largest group of highlanders speaking a Mon-Khmer language (related to the national languages of Vietnam and Cambodia). Their lowland neighbors are Lao, Thai, or Vietnamese, and in the mountains they live alongside the Hmong, Mien, highland Tai, and various Tibeto-Burman groups.

Historical and linguistic evidence indicates that the Khmu homeland centered anciently in the region of Meuang Chvaa, the site of modern-day Luang Phabang, Laos. As Lao, Thai, and other Tai groups migrated into Meuang Chvaa over the past millennium, the Khmu were displaced, fleeing into mountainous retreats. Until the middle of the nineteenth century, Khmu probably remained within what are now the borders of Laos, but during the latter half of the century they expanded into the provinces of Chiang Rai, Nan, and Chiang Mai in Thailand; the provinces of Son La and Lai Chau in northwestern Vietnam; Nghe An Province in central Vietnam; and the Sipsongpanna region of Yunnan Province in China.

The first Khmu arrived in the United States in 1975, when the establishment of the Communist government of the Lao Peoples Democratic Republic (PDR) led many of those who had been allied with the former, Pro-Western, Royal Lao Government to flee their country. Other Khmu followed throughout the late 1970s and early 1980s, establishing communities in several U.S. states.

## Language and Identification

The Khmu language is the largest member of the Khmuic branch of the Northern Division of Mon-Khmer. From centuries of contact with Tai-speaking neighbors, the Khmu language includes quite a bit of vocabulary borrowed from Lao, Thai, and related languages. More recent contact with English is evident in the speech of many U.S. Khmu.

In their own language, "Khmu" means simply "human, person," but people often use the word as an ethnonym, to distinguish members of the Khmu ethnic group from those of other ethnicities. In the past, Khmu were known to others as "Khaa," a pejorative term in Lao-Thai languages referring to

"slave, servant" and to those of Mon-Khmer ethnicity. They were also known by the less pejorative term "Phou Theung" or "people of the midlands," as well as by a profusion of other names, both respectful and insulting.

By 1950, the Royal Lao Government was using the term "Lao Theung" as a collective term to denote the Khmu and other Mon-Khmer-speaking peoples, and this name was taken up (along with "Lao Soung" for the Hmong and Mien, and "Lao Loum" for the lowland Lao) by the Communist Neo Lao Hak Xat and made official by the Lao PDR. In the 1995 Laotian Census, the Lao government abandoned the collective terms in favor of specific names for each group (in U.S. censuses, Khmu are simply Asian Americans, so the U.S. population can only be estimated).

## Cultural Characteristics

In the ethnographic mosaic of culturally diverse northern Indochina, the Khmu are distinguished from others by their language, history, religious practices, and rich traditions of music, song, and folklore. Their material culture generally resembles that of their non-Khmu neighbors, and in many cases is indistinguisable.

Khmu clothing, for instance, is usually like that of others: Older women may wear a handmade blouse and skirt patterned after those of their Lao-Thai neighbors, while younger women, children, and men wear purchased clothes of Western cut. In the United States, Khmu wear traditional clothing only on the special occasion of a New Year celebration or a family ceremony.

Within the local economies of their homeland, Khmu were renowned for their great skill with bamboo and rattan basketry, which they traded with other groups for knives, tools, clothing, and other goods. For those Khmu living in the United States, bamboo is a precious commodity, and the pressures of work and school leave little time for basketry or other crafts.

Although there are no water buffalo in northern California that can be ritually sacrificed, Khmu in the United States are able to preserve important elements of their traditional religious beliefs, even if in attenuated form. The Khmu traditionally believe in a pantheon of spirits (most important of which are the *hrooy gaang,* or family-household spirit, and the *hrooy kung,* or village spirit) that are the focus or rituals of respect and appeasement. Each person also has a soul-spirit or *hrmaal,* which is inclined to flee the body at times of stress, illness, or transition. Ceremonies are frequently held to call the spirit back into the body or to prevent the soul-spirit from leaving by binding it with strings tied around the wrist. At death, the soul-spirit must be guided to its resting place with a special song. For those Khmu who have immigrated to the United States, it is often difficult to find the time and materials with which to honor the spirits, and many now adhere to Catholic, Protestant, or Mormon faiths (some had converted in Laos, others in refugee camps, and still others after arriving in the United States). Except among the most strictly fundamentalist Christians, however, many elements of the traditional practices can be maintained in altered or reduced forms, even if important aspects of the supporting beliefs underlying those practices have been abandoned or forgotten.

Similarly, Khmu in the United States preserve only a few elements of their rich traditions of verbal artistry, storytelling, song, and music. The special bamboo needed for flutes or reed pipes is simply not available, and even though ingenious elders have substituted PVC pipe for bamboo, or plastic bottles for the resonating chamber of a flute, these are poor substitutes.

More crucial are the changes in social context and life routines: Khmu in Texas or in Washington State are more likely to be found gathered together in front of a television than in front of a cooking fire. U.S. Khmu no longer walk for hours from their mountain rice fields to their village homes, so they have no occasion to play the special percussion instruments that would have been used for amusement along the way. In addition, life in the United States proceeds at a very different pace than in a highland village; for most Khmu Americans, school and work consume most of their time year-round, while in Southeast Asia the year alternates periods of intense and backbreaking agricultural work with periods of time available for crafts, ceremonies, music and song, and leisure pursuits.

## Settlement

More than half of all U.S. Khmu live in California. During the process of refugee admission and resettlement, Khmu managed to reestablish coherent communities of people from specific regions in Laos—even in some cases replanting villages within a complex of garden apartments.

The largest U.S. community is located around San Francisco Bay, in cities including San Rafael, San Pablo, Richmond, and Oakland. Khmu there are almost all from the regions of Nam Tha, Houei Sai, and Pak Beng in northwestern Laos, and they speak several dialects distinguished from Khmu elsewhere by vocabulary and because words are spoken with either a high or a low tone.

Smaller communities from the same regions of Laos are found in Seattle and the Greater Boston area. The second largest U.S. community, that in Stockton, California is made up of Khmu from Luang Prabang Province of north-central Laos. Their nontonal dialects are similar to those spoken by Khmu from Xieng Khouang Province in northeastern Laos, who have settled in Santa Ana and Fresno, California; Oklahoma City; and Fort Worth.

## Life in the United States

Many Khmu have flourished in the United States, like a once-stunted seedling from which a heavy rock has been lifted. In their homeland they previously had few opportunities for education, employment possibilities were limited, and Khmu had no political voice. Perhaps more so than other Indochinese refugees, Khmu therefore welcomed the opportunites offered by life in the United States, and many have taken the fullest advantage of those new possibilities. Khmu point with great pride to those who have now graduated from college, ranging from community colleges to top-ranked universities including Harvard, the University of California at Berkeley, and the University of Washington.

Despite their own past difficulties, Khmu have a strongly ingrained notion of community service, as evidenced by their work as teachers, teacher aides, social workers, medical translators, and in similar positions. In Stockton, a Khmu-led social service agency celebrated its tenth anniversary of funded services to Vietnamese, Cambodian, and other Laotian refugees in 1995, and Khmu there and elsewhere participate actively in organizations of the Laotian community or of the Indochinese and Asian-American communities more broadly.

The transformations experienced within their lives by today's Khmu Americans are striking. Those born in bamboo houses atop a mountain ridge, with little knowledge of or connection to the outside world, now sit behind a desk with computer, fax, and phone, administering programs or running businesses and communicating by e-mail to friends around the world.

The Khmu experience in the United States is not, however, a uniformly successful one: Many families encounter unmanageable stresses and pressures, as elders may find their knowledge and skills irrelevant or forgotten. Children may never have opportunities to see their parents or grandparents display that knowledge, or if it is displayed, the children may attach little value to it in comparison with what they see on television or among their peers. Families with the strongest foundations in Khmu tradition usually adapt most readily to modern technology, while parents whose knowledge of traditional life and belief is not as deep are more likely to see problems among their children and to experience difficulties themselves in adapting to their new way of life.

*See also:* LAO; THAI; VIETNAMESE

## Bibliography

Center for Research in Social Systems. (1970). *Minority Groups in Thailand.* Washington, DC: U.S. Department of the Army.

Dang, Nghiem Van. (1973). "The Khmu in Viet Nam." *Vietnamese Studies* 36:62–140.

Halpern, J. M. (1964). *Economy and Society of Laos: A Brief Survey.* New Haven, CT: Southeast Asia Studies, Yale University.

Lindell, K.; Lundström, H.; Svantesson, J.-O.; and Tayanin, D. (1982). *The Kammu Year: Its Lore and Music.* London: Curzon Press.

Lindell, K.; Swahn, J.-O.; and Tayanin, D. (1977–1995). *Folk Tales from Kammu,* 5 vols. London: Curzon Press.

Proschan, F. (1989). *Kmhmu Verbal Art in America: The Poetics of Kmhmu Verse.* Ph.D. diss., University of Texas at Austin.

Proschan, F. (1992). "Fieldwork and Social Work: Folklore as Helping Profession." In *Public Folklore,* edited by N. Spitzer and R. Baron. Washington, DC: Smithsonian Institution Press.

Smalley, W. A. (1961). *Outline of Khmu Structure.* New Haven, CT: American Oriental Society.

Suwilai Premsrirat. (1993). *Thai-Khmu-English Dictionary.* Salaya, Thailand: Institute of Language and Culture for Rural Development, Mahidol University.

Tayanin, D., and Lindell, K. (1991). *Hunting and Fishing in a Kammu Village.* London: Curzon Press.

FRANK PROSCHAN

# KOREANS

Of Mongolian racial origin, Koreans share physical characteristics with Chinese and Japanese. Until the beginning of the twentieth century, China had a strong cultural influence on Korea, particularly through Confucianism. Koreans had depended on Chinese characters for many centuries, but in the fourteenth century Great King Sejong created the Korean alphabet, *hangul.* Historically Korea had a strong cultural influence on Japan, but Japan invaded Korea several times. Most recently, between 1910 and 1945, Korea was under Japanese colonial rule. Because of this, there are still strong anti-Japanese sentiments in Korea.

As soon as Korea was liberated from Japanese rule in 1945, it was divided into two halves because of internal political conflicts on the one hand and U.S.-Soviet ideological conflicts on the other. South Korea has been under the strong influence of the United States, whereas North Korea maintained close political and military ties with the former Soviet Union and China until the early 1990s. The division of Korea led to a civil war, known as the Korean War, in 1950, in which the United States and other anti-Communist allies supported South Korea, and the former Soviet Union and China supported North Korea. Although the Korean War ended in 1953, Korea has been permanently divided into two opposing political and economic systems, with millions of family members separated between North and South. The Cold War period ended with the unification of Germany in 1990 and the dissolution of the former Soviet Union in 1991, yet Koreans still suffer their national division, a legacy of the Cold War.

The United States began to influence Korea culturally at the end of the nineteenth century, when American Protestant missionaries established Christian schools and modern hospitals there. However, it was during the Korean War that the United States came to maintain close political, military, and economic ties with South Korea. The United States sent more than half a million soldiers to South Korea during the Korean War and has maintained sizable military forces—approximately 45,000—in South Korea, many of whom have brought Korean wives to the United States. The presence of U.S. servicemen, with a U.S. television station (AFKN), in Korea also has exerted a strong American cultural influence there. In turn, this cultural influence encouraged many Koreans to immigrate to the United States when the U.S. immigration law was relaxed in 1965.

Taking advantage of cheap labor, South Korea has followed a course of export-oriented economic development since the late 1970s. This development has been a great success. South Korea achieved gradual economic growth through the 1980s but has experienced an "economic explosion" since then. In 1994, South Korea had a $10,000 per capita income. The great economic improvement and the replacement of military dictatorship by a popular government in South Korea since the late 1980s have boosted Koreans' sense of national pride, which has contributed to a moderate level of anti-American sentiment in South Korea. South Korea still is one of the strongest U.S. political allies, and most Koreans remain friendly to the United States. Yet, many Korean college students and intellectuals feel that South Korea has depended on the United States too much and that the presence of U.S. military forces in South Korea hinders Korean unification.

## Immigration History

The approximately seventy-two hundred Koreans who moved to Hawaii to work on sugar plantations between 1903 and 1905 constituted the first wave of Korean immigrants to U.S. territory. The Hawaiian plantation owners' need for cheap, nonwhite laborers was the pull factor for the immigration of Koreans at the beginning of the twentieth century, whereas economic difficulty caused by droughts, floods, and the ensuing famines in Korea was the push factor. Nevertheless, this early immigration of Koreans to Hawaii might not have been possible without the work of Horace Allen, then U.S. minister to Korea. Ninety percent of the 1903–1905 Korean immigrants to Hawaii were unmarried young males, with children constituting only a small proportion. Approximately 40 percent of the pioneer immigrants had converted to Christianity in Korea, and the majority attended Christian churches in Hawaii. Many Korean Christians decided to immigrate to Hawaii for religious freedom as well as for a better economic life.

Although Korean labor immigration ended in 1905, approximately two thousand additional Korean immigrants arrived in Hawaii and California between 1906 and 1924: "Picture brides," invited by pioneer bachelor immigrants by exchanging pictures; and political refugees and/or students. Japan made Korea a protectorate in 1905 and then colonized it in 1910. Many Korean intellectuals and politicians engaged in anti-Japanese agitation after this annexation. Under surveillance by the Japanese police, many Korean anti-Japanese patriots moved to the United States via Shanghai, most helped by American missionaries. These people constituted the core of Korean community organization in Hawaii and California, directing organizational activities toward Korean independence and the anti-Japanese movement.

The 1924 U.S. immigration law, commonly known as the national origins quota system, included a provision that banned all Asian immigration, thus cutting off Korean immigration to the United States.

Korean immigration to the United States steadily increased between 1950 and 1964. The McCarran-Walter Act of 1952, modifying the Asian exclusion, allowed an annual quota of one hundred immigrants from each Pacific and Asian country. This moderation of Asian exclusion partly contributed to the increase in Korean immigration in the 1950s. However, a more important factor for the assumption of Korean immigration during this period was the close U.S.-Korean relationship associated with the Korean War. Korean wives of

U.S. servicemen constituted the largest category of Korean immigrants during this period. During and after the Korean War, a large number of U.S. soldiers stayed in South Korea. Many of these servicemen married Korean women and brought them to the United States. Korean children adopted by U.S. citizens constituted another major category of Korean immigrants admitted to the United States between 1950 and 1964. Finally, Korean students who arrived in the United States for further study and who later changed their status to permanent residents were the third major category of immigrants in the intermediate period between 1950 and 1964.

The Immigration Act of 1965 abolished discrimination in immigration quotas based on national origin. More important for the immigration of Asians, the new immigration law abolished the Asian exclusion provision, which had been in effect to a greater or lesser degree since 1924. This liberal immigration law has led to drastic changes in source countries of immigrants, from European to non-European. It has affected Korean immigration significantly as well as that of other Asian countries. Annual Korean immigration numbered

Korean-language signs identify the Korean stores located in Koreatown in Flushing, New York. (Chong-Gwon Park)

a few thousand in the middle 1960s, but the number gradually increased in the late 1960s and early 1970s. It passed thirty thousand in 1976 and maintained an annual flow of more than thirty thousand in the 1980s. Korea was the third-largest source country of U.S. immigrants in the 1980s, following Mexico and the Philippines.

Conceding a great undercount of Koreans in the 1970 U.S. Census (69,130), the Korean population in 1970 may not have reached the 100,000 mark. However, nearly 700,000 Koreans immigrated between 1970 and 1993. The Korean-American community has consequently witnessed a radical population growth. The 1990 U.S. Census estimated the Korean-American population to be close to 800,000, and that total was probably more than one million in 1995. One million Koreans in the United States constitute 20 percent of approximately five million overseas Koreans. Korean Americans make up the fourth-largest Asian ethnic group in the United States, after Chinese, Filipinos, and Indians. The 1990 U.S. Census showed that only 27 percent of Korean Americans were born in the United States.

Lack of economic opportunity, social and political insecurity, and the difficulty of sending children to higher educational institutions pushed many Koreans to immigrate to the United States in the 1970s and early 1980s. However, economic, political, and social conditions have been substantially improved in South Korea since the late 1980s. The social and political insecurities that pushed many South Korean intellectuals to the United States have been reduced. In addition, South Korea had a popular presidential election at the end of 1987, ending a sixteen-year military dictatorship. In 1992, they elected Kim Young Sam as their first civilian president since Syngman Rhee was ousted by a student uprising in 1960.

The significant improvements in economic, social, and political conditions in South Korea on the one hand and the increasing publicity of Korean immigrants' adjustment difficulties in the United States on the other have mitigated the influx of Korean immigrants since the late 1980s. The annual number of Korean immigrants has gradually decreased since 1988, falling to below twenty thousand in 1992. In contrast, the numbers of Filipino, Chinese, Indian, and Vietnamese immigrants have increased greatly since the late 1980s. This reverse trend in Korean and other Asian immigration patterns is likely to continue until the current immigration law is revised. This means that the Korean population will be an increasingly smaller proportion of the Asian-American population in the future. As the annual number of Korean immigrants has gradually decreased, the proportion of Korean Americans born in the United States has increased substantially. Major Korean communities are gradually experiencing generational transitions as descendants of post-1965 immigrants reach adulthood.

## Settlement Patterns

Like other Asian immigrants, Korean immigrants before 1965 were heavily concentrated in Hawaii and West Coast states, particularly in traditional Asian enclaves such as Honolulu, San Francisco, and Los Angeles. However, post-1965 Korean immigrants are more widely scattered. The 1990 U.S. Census showed that California had the largest share of the Korean population (33%), followed by New York (12%) and Illinois (5.2%). New Jersey has become an increasingly popular destination for Korean immigrants; it had the highest growth rate (200%) in the Korean population between 1980 and 1990. The New York–New Jersey metropolitan area has emerged as the second-largest Korean center, next to the Los Angeles–Orange County area. Greater New York is attractive to other Asian immigrant groups as well; in fact, it is the capital for Chinese and Asian Indian Americans.

Los Angeles County has the largest number of Koreans, with about 200,000. The presence of Koreans in Los Angeles is more clearly discernible in Koreatown, three miles west of downtown Los Angeles. Koreatown covers approximately twenty-five square miles and is the residential and commercial center for Los Angeles Koreans. About thirty-five hundred Korean-owned businesses with exotic Korean-language signs are located in Koreatown, where coethnics find Korean food, groceries, books, magazines, and other services with distinctive cultural tastes. Koreatown is also the social and cultural center for Los Angeles Koreans. The L.A. Korean Association, several Korean business associations, dozens of Korean social service agencies, and other Korean social and cultural organizations are located there. Korean ethnic organizations hold meetings at Korean restaurants and offices in Koreatown at night. Koreans all over the Los Angeles–Orange County area visit Koreatown to eat traditional Korean food and celebrate important family affairs at Korean restaurants. Several Korean motels in Koreatown accommodate many Korean tourists from Korea and other parts of the United States. During the 1992 Los Angeles riots, many Korean stores in Koreatown were burned and/or looted.

## Economic Adjustments

Probably the most interesting aspect of Korean immigrants' adjustments in the United States is their occupational concentration in small business. Korean immigrants in Los Angeles, New York, and other major cities have found economic niches in several business specialities such as grocery/liquor retail; produce retail; dry cleaning service; and retail sales of Asian-imported manufactured goods such as bags, hats, and other clothing. Surveys suggests that nearly half of Korean workers in Los Angeles and New York are self-employed in small businesses and that another 30 percent are employed in coethnic businesses. Thus, Korean immigrants are highly segregated economically, with about 80 percent working in Korean businesses as owners or employees.

Korean immigrants choose to start small businesses mainly because they have disadvantages for employment in the general labor market in terms of language and job information. Korean immigrants with a college degree have more language barriers than college-educated Filipino and Indian immigrants, who spoke English in their native countries. In addition, Korean immigrants' strong networks and their middle-class background help them to establish and operate small businesses. The pioneer Korean merchants in the 1970s lacked business capital, information, and training; thus, it took them several years to get ready to own their own businesses. In contrast, Koreans who have immigrated since the late 1980s have been able to establish their own businesses faster, many within one year of immigration, because they have brought a greater amount of money from Korea and have been able to get business information and training easily through employment in coethnic businesses.

Earlier, Jewish and Italian merchants ran businesses in low-income black neighborhoods such as Harlem in New York and Watts in Los Angeles. Korean merchants have largely replaced these white merchants in low-income black neighborhoods. Surveys reveal that Korean immigrants own the majority of businesses in many black neighborhoods in South-Central Los Angeles and Brooklyn, New York. The relationship between business owners and customers is inherently stressful. When business owners and customers are separated along racial or ethnic lines, the relationship is even more stressful. The Korean-black relationship has involved serious conflicts. Korean merchants in New York have encountered several long-term black boycotts. The 1990–1991 black boycott of two Korean produce stores in Brooklyn that lasted a year and a half attracted international media headlines. The hostility of black residents toward Korean merchants culminated in the 1992 Los Angeles riots, during which approximately twenty-three hundred Korean-owned stores in South-Central Los Angeles and Koreatown were burned and/or looted by rioters.

Members of a group maintain in-group solidarity when they encounter threats from the outside; black hostility toward Korean merchants via boycotts, arson, and destruction of stores during riots have solidified the Korean community. For example, during the 1990–1991 boycott of the two Korean produce stores in Brooklyn, not only Korean merchants but also nonmerchant Koreans donated money to help "the victims of black rac-

Mayor David Dinkins, on February 22, 1992, visits the owner of Red Apple, the Korean grocery store that was the target of a boycott that lasted one and a half years. (Chong-Gwon Park)

ism." In September 1990, Koreans in New York also organized a demonstration in front of City Hall to show their dissatisfaction with Mayor David Dinkins's "lukewarm effort" to terminate the boycott. Approximately seven thousand Koreans all over the New York–New Jersey area participated in the demonstration. The victimization of Korean merchants during the Los Angeles riots, a more serious threat to Korean immigrants' economic survival than the boycott, solidified the Korean community to a greater extent than the Brooklyn boycott. Koreans all over the United States participated in fund-raising drives to help Korean riot victims and raised approximately $4.5 million. Three days after the riots, the Korean community in Los Angeles held a peace and solidarity rally in Koreatown in which thirty thousand Koreans participated. Also, Korean riot victims staged daily rallies in front of City Hall for one month, making several demands to Mayor Tom Bradley to protect their economic interests.

Korean grocery/liquor, produce, and fish retailers play a "middleman role" in that they distribute products made by white corporations to low-income, minority customers. Conflicts of Korean middlemen with white suppliers also have enhanced the Koreans' solidarity and contributed to improvements in their lobbying skills. Through their regional and national organizations, Korean grocery/liquor retailers have negotiated with white suppliers and manufacturers prices of grocery and liquor items. Korean produce retailers in New York have demonstrated against and/or boycotted white suppliers several times to make the suppliers improve their services to Korean merchants.

## Gender Role Changes and Marital Relations

Confucianism has had a powerful influence on Korean culture, particularly on the Korean family system. One of the important aspects of Confucianism is a patriarchal ideology that assigns a lower status to women and emphasizes a clear role differentiation between husband and wife. In traditional Korean society, the husband exercises complete authority and power over his wife and children. The husband is the primary breadwinner and decision maker in the family, whereas the wife is expected to obey him, devotedly serve him and his parents, and perpetuate her husband's family lineage by bearing children. Despite a high level of industrialization and economic development during recent years, much of the traditional gender role differentiation has been preserved in South Korea. A relatively small proportion of married women—approximately one-third—participate in the labor force in South Korea. The gender gap in education has been significantly reduced, and many women attend college, but even most college-educated women give up their careers for marriage.

Probably the most significant change in the family system brought about by Koreans' immigration to the United States is a radical increase in the labor force participation rate of Korean women. Surveys show that approximately 70 percent of Korean immigrant women who are married work outside the home, a higher labor force participation rate than even white married women in the United States. Newly immigrated Korean women usually find employment in coethnic businesses as cashiers or salespersons. Many Korean immigrant women work with their husbands in family stores. A small number of Korean immigrant women run their own businesses, independent of their husbands. Manicure service is one of the major Korean businesses in New York City, and typically a woman runs a Korean nail salon.

The contribution of the wife to the family economy usually increases her marital power and status. Korean immigrant wives exercise greater marital power than their counterparts in Korea partly because of their increased economic role. However, since a Korean working wife is generally helping her husband in the family business, her contribution to the family economy does not always provide the kind of economic independence that many employed American wives enjoy. Moreover, the fact that most Korean workers—both husbands and wives—are segregated in Korean-owned stores, with little interaction with non-Korean coworkers, does not help them change their traditional gender role orientation. For example, Filipino immigrant workers, more than 90 percent of whom are in the general labor market, with much interaction with non-Filipino, white coworkers, are likely to adjust to more egalitarian marital relations faster than Korean immigrant workers. In addition, although most Korean immigrant wives work long hours outside the home, they are responsible for almost all housework, causing them to suffer from overwork and double burdens.

## Child Socialization

Another important feature of Confucianism is its emphasis on children's education. Under the impact of the Confucian cultural tradition, Koreans have great faith in children's education and respect educated persons. Koreans' deep faith in education is well reflected in the fact that "You are an uneducated person" is one of the worst curses you can receive in Korea. Parents in South Korea —mothers in particular—measure their success largely based on their children's educational success. Therefore, parents try to do everything pos-

sible to give their children a good education. Colleges and universities in South Korea can accept only a small proportion of candidates from high schools. They accept freshmen largely based on scores in the competitive entrance examinations that put great weight on mathematics, English, and the Korean language. Parents shoulder heavy financial burdens to send their high school children to private institutions or hire tutors to prepare them for the college entrance examinations. Children in South Korea have a lot of pressure outside as well as inside the school—for good students, to get admitted to a good university, and for average students, to get admitted to any college.

Korean immigrants have transplanted their child-rearing practices that emphasize children's education to the United States. Korean immigrants usually make initial settlements in working- or lower-middle-class neighborhoods where there are many Korean residents. However, many of them move to suburban middle-class areas where there are good public schools. Many Korean immigrant parents of junior or senior high school students send them to private institutes after school and on weekends to prepare them for admission to specialized high schools or prestigious colleges or universities. Several dozen private institutes that specialize in math and English have mushroomed in Los Angeles, New York, and other communities with large Korean populations.

Korean immigrants' faith in their children's education and their various activities in support of it contribute to their children's success in school. Both Los Angeles and New York City school districts have specialized high schools that admit students based on results of competitive examinations in English and mathematics. Koreans make up a large proportion of students in such schools in the two cities, although the Korean population in each city is less than 2 percent. Many Korean-American students win major academic prizes at graduation ceremonies and in various academic contests every year. Most important, Korean-American students are admitted to prestigious universities in large numbers. In fact, Asian Americans are overrepresented in several schools of the University of California system and at Ivy League universities in the East. Korean students are the second-largest Asian group, after Chinese, at most of these prestigious universities.

Although many Koreans have made exceptional achievements in school, many others, particularly new immigrants, have problems in school and are involved in a variety of delinquent behaviors. Gang-related crimes have become the most serious juvenile problem in the Korean community. The Los Angeles and New York Korean communities have several Korean gang organizations. Recruited largely from immigrant children who have language barriers and difficulty with schoolwork, gang members engage in such criminal activities as group fighting, murder, armed robbery, burglaries of Korean homes, kidnapping, and extortion of Korean businesses. The number of Korean children affiliated with gangs is very small, but many other Korean children have less serious forms of juvenile problems, such as truancy, fighting, and running away from home. Language barriers, cultural differences, and a sense of alienation and discrimination in school are just some sources of Korean children's problems. Yet Korean immigrant families are more responsible for their children's problems than the school system. Value conflicts combined with the language barrier have created an unbridgeable distance between Korean parents and their adolescent children. Most Korean parents put great pressure on their children to excel in school and advance to a good college, which further alienates children from their parents. Finally, Korean immigrant parents' lack of time to play with and supervise their children at home because of long work hours also contributes to their children's delinquency.

## Community Organization

The Korean community has more ethnic organizations than any other Asian immigrant community; thus, Korean immigrants are actively involved in ethnic networks. There are many different types of ethnic organizations: Korean churches, alumni associations, business associations, professional associations, sports and recreational organizations, social service agencies, cultural organizations, and political organizations. Ethnic churches, alumni associations, and ethnic media play a central role in uniting Koreans.

Christians, the vast majority of whom are Protestant, make up about 25 percent of the population in South Korea. However, Christians are overrepresented among Korean immigrants in the United States. Surveys reveal that more than 50 percent of Korean immigrants attended Christian churches in Korea. Moreover, many Korean immigrants who did not attend Christian churches in Korea go to Korean immigrant churches for practical purposes. As a result, approximately 75 percent of Korean immigrants regularly go to Korean churches. Each Korean community has a large number of Korean churches, and the vast majority of Korean churches are of Presbyterian or other Protestant denominations. For example, there are approximately five hundred Korean churches, with a population of 150,000, in the New York–New Jersey Korean community.

Korean churches serve several important social functions for Korean immigrants: providing social services and fellowship, and maintaining the Korean cultural tradition. Many Korean immigrants who were non-Christians in Korea attend ethnic churches for these practical purposes. Korean churches provide various services for their members: job referral, information about businesses and children's education, health clinics, family counseling, and ethnic education for children. Also, Korean churches provide Korean immigrants with places to meet coethnics for fellowship and recreational activities. Separated from their relatives and friends, most new Korean immigrants feel a sense of alienation in a foreign environment. Association with coethnic members is essential to cope with this alienation. All Korean immigrant churches have a fellowship hour after the Sunday service, with snacks or free lunch provided, during which church members associate. In addition, Korean churches help Koreans maintain the Korean cultural tradition by providing Korean-language instruction for younger-generation Koreans and by sponsoring many cultural activities.

Next to churches, alumni associations play an important role in tying Korean immigrants together. The 1994–1995 *Korean Directory of Southern California* listed more than 160 alumni associations. Approximately one-third of them are college based; the others are high school based. Alumni associations usually hold outdoor picnics in the spring and fall. The gatherings feature Korean food, and alumni and their families enjoy recreational activities. All alumni associations have a major party for members and their families, usually in a hotel ballroom, at the end of the year. Several university alumni associations in New York have prepared year-end parties for alumni members' children who attend college, to facilitate children's mate selection by providing them with an opportunity to get together. Each alumni association is further divided into subgroups based on year of graduation. Members of each subgroup maintain strong friendship networks and aid one another beyond formal organizational activities.

They often organize rotating credit associations for mutual benefit.

As previously noted, Koreans in Los Angeles created Koreatown close to downtown Los Angeles, and Koreans in New York also established a similar Korean enclave in Flushing. However, the vast majority of Korean immigrants in the two cities as well as those in other cities live outside the Korean enclave; they are integrated into the Korean community based on social networks. The ethnic media play a central role in integrating geographically dispersed Korean immigrants by keeping them informed of what is going on in the local community. The media also draw attention to their homeland by supplying daily news from Korea. There are three Korean-language dailies in southern California and four dailies in the New York–New Jersey metropolitan area. All the newspapers, as branches of major dailies in Korea, duplicate articles published out of their headquarters in Seoul. They also include a Korean-American section, which carries news about the Korean community and the larger American so-

A Korean dancer performs during a festival sponsored by the Korean Produce Association of New York to celebrate Korean Thanksgiving Day. (Chong-Gwon Park)

ciety. There are several Korean television and radio stations in Los Angeles and New York. Two Korean television stations in each community offer Korean programs for twenty hours a day and provide news edited by the Korean Broadcasting Station in Seoul. Korean immigrants have an advantage over other Asian immigrant groups for establishing homeland-language media because they have only one language. Since Filipino and Asian Indian immigrants have several different languages, they have difficulties creating native-language ethnic media programming.

## Bibliography

Abelmann, N., and Lie, J. (1995). *Blue Dreams: Korean Americans and the Los Angeles Riots.* Cambridge, MA: Harvard University Press.

Choy, B. Y. (1979). *Koreans in America.* Chicago: Nelson-Hall.

Hurh, W. M., and Kim, K. C. (1984a). "Adhesive Adaptation of Korean Immigrants in the U.S.: An Alternative Strategy of Minority Adaptation." *International Migration Review* 18:188–214.

Hurh, W. M., and Kim, K. C. (1984b). *Korean Immigrants in America: A Structural Analysis of Ethnic Confinement and Adhesive Adaptation.* Madison, NJ: Fairleigh Dickinson University Press.

Hurh, W. M., and Kim, K. C. (1990). "Religious Participation of Korean Immigrants in the United States." *Journal of the Scientific Study of Religion* 19:19–34.

Kim, I. S. (1981). *New Urban Immigrants: The Korean Community in New York.* Princeton: NJ: Princeton University Press.

Kim, K. C., and Hurh, W. M. (1988). "The Burden of Double Roles: Korean Wives in the U.S.A." *Ethnic and Racial Studies* 11:151–167.

Light, I., and Bonacich, E. (1988). *Immigrant Entrepreneurs: Koreans in Los Angeles, 1965–1982.* Berkeley: University of California Press.

Min, P. G. (1988a). *Ethnic Business Enterprise: Korean Small Business in Atlanta.* Staten Island, NY: Center for Migration Studies.

Min, P. G. (1988b). "The Korean American Family." In *Ethnic Families in America: Patterns and Variations,* 3rd edition, edited by C. Mindel, R. Habenstein, and R. Wright Jr. New York: Elsevier.

Min, P. G. (1991). "Cultural and Economic Boundaries of Korean Ethnicity: A Comparative Analysis." *Ethnic and Racial Studies* 14:225–241.

Min, P. G. (1992). "The Structure and Social Functions of Korean Immigrant Churches in the United States." *International Migration Review* 26:1370–1394.

Min, P. G. (1996). *Caught in the Middle: Korean Communities in New York and Los Angeles.* Berkeley: University of California Press.

Park, I. H.; Fawcett, J.; Arnold, F.; and Gardner, R. (1990). *Korean Immigrants and U.S. Immigration Policy: A Predeparture Perspective.* Honolulu: East-West Population Institute, East-West Center.

Patterson, W. (1987). *The Korean Frontier in Hawaii: Immigration to Hawaii, 1896–1910.* Berkeley: University of California Press.

Yoon, I. J. (1993). *The Social Origins of Korean Immigration to the United States from 1965 to the Present.* Honolulu: East-West Population Institute, East-West Center.

Yu, E. Y., and Phillips, E. H., eds. (1987). *Korean Women in Transition: At Home and Abroad.* Los Angeles: Center for Korean-American and Korean Studies, California State University.

Yu, E. Y.; Phillips, E. H.; and Yang, E. S., eds. (1982). *Koreans in Los Angeles: Prospects and Promises.* Los Angeles: Center for Korean-American and Korean Studies, California State University.

PYONG GAP MIN

# LAO

The Lao-American immigrant community can be understood to include either all of those whose birthplace was the nation of Laos (officially, the Lao Peoples Democratic Republic), or all of those whose ethnolinguistic identity is Lao. These two groups overlap without being identical. The first group, referred to in this entry as Laotian, includes not only the lowland Lao ethnic group but also highland groups such as Hmong, Mien, and Khmu, as well as smaller groups such as Lahu, Lua, Phou Thai, Thai Lue, and Thai Dam. The second group, referred to in this entry as Lao, includes the majority population of Laos as well as several million people in neighboring areas of Thailand. (The English language can make the distinction easily between Laotian and Lao, while in the Lao language this can only be done with compound expressions.) Within Laos, as within the Laotian-American community, the lowland Lao constitute approximately one-half of the population, with the various highland minorities comprising the other half. In the United States, people who are ethnolinguistically and culturally Lao but were born within the borders of Thailand are more likely to identify themselves as Thai or Thai Isaan (i.e., Northeastern Thai) than as Lao.

The Lao Peoples Democratic Republic recognizes more than forty distinct ethnolinguistic groups, almost all of whom are represented in the United States, even if their numbers are very small. The minorities who constitute sizable communities in the United States are from various regions of Laos, primarily the north. The Khmu and Hmong are found throughout northern Laos, with Mien concentrated in the northwest. The Thai Dam are speakers of a language closely related to Lao; most of the two thousand or so in the United States first fled to Laos from the Dien Bien Phu region of northwestern Vietnam after the French defeat in 1954 and then to Thailand in 1975. The one thousand Lua, also known as Tin, Thin, Pray, or Mal, are speakers of a Mon-Khmer language from the province of Sayaboury in western Laos. The Lahu number fewer than five hundred in the United States, and they speak a language in the Tibeto-Burman family of languages. It is dificult to estimate the United States population of Phou Thai (Highland Thai) from the southern provinces of Laos, Thai Lue from the northwest, or Thai Deng from the northeast (all of whom speak dialects closely related to Lao) because they are generally assimilated into Lao culture and do not constitute distinct publicly identified communities.

## Demographics

The Laotian-American community, including all of those regardless of language or ethnicity who trace their ancestry to the nation of Laos, numbered 250,000 people in the 1990 U.S. Census. Of these, slightly more than half were Lao, with the remainder being members of various Laotian minority groups. Three-quarters of the Laotian-American population were foreign-born immigrants to the United States; this will change as the number of immigrants remains fixed while the number of children born in the United States increases. (The census statistics are difficult to reconcile for various reasons. A child born in a refugee camp in Thailand to Hmong parents, for example, may be counted as either Laotian or Hmong by nativity and have either Laos or Thailand listed as place of birth, depending on how the parents understood and completed the census form. In those statistics, the term "Laotian" has a somewhat different scope than in this entry; in census materials, it refers to all non-Hmong natives of Laos and includes both Lao and non-Hmong highlanders. In the census material, the term is also used, quite inaccurately, as the name of the language properly known as Lao.)

Virtually all of the foreign-born Laotian-American community entered the United States as refugees, following their flight from their homeland in the wake of the Communist victory in the second Indochina War (1954–1975) and the establishment in 1975 of the Communist-governed Lao Peoples Democratic Republic. Those who fled were often people who had been employed by the United States or the Royal Lao Government, or they had been soldiers in regular or irregular armed forces resisting the Communists. Initially, those who left Laos for refugee camps in Thailand included two large groups: Hmong highlanders allied militarily with the United States, and lowland Lao who were primaily residents of the larger cities along the Mekong River. However, most

A woman in ceremonial clothing celebrates the Laotian New Year in Seattle, Washington. (Kevin R. Morris/ Corbis)

people of all ethnic groups remained within Laos, adopting a wait-and-see attitude and finding comfort in the restoration of peace after decades of warfare. In 1978 and 1979, as Laos faced a severe drought, the government implemented an onerous policy of agricultural collectivization; together these hardships encouraged large outflows of refugees, both Lao and minorities. The number of refugees fleeing to Thailand was highest in this period, tapering off by the mid-1980s. By 1990, those who left Laos were no longer presumed by international authorities to be political refugees eligible for U.N. protection and resettlement in a third country; most were instead considered economic migrants and the numbers decreased sharply.

Those who left Laos in 1975 and 1976 were rapidly resettled in the United States, France, and other countries of final resettlement. Of those who left a few years later, most of the Lao and non-

Hmong highlanders had only brief stays in Thai refugee camps. Many Hmong residents of the camps, however, were reluctant to seek resettlement in the United States and thus languished in the refugee camps for years, even decades, cherishing hopes of returning to Laos. Roughly 20 percent of the Lao and 24 percent of the Hmong who entered the United States as refugees arrived before 1980 as part of the first wave. In the early 1980s, the tide of arrivals was predominantly Lao and other non-Hmong Laotians; in the late 1980s, arriving refugees were increasingly Hmong. (During the 1990s, the overwhelming majority was Hmong, as hardly any Lao or non-Hmong highlanders remained to be resettled in the Thai camps by 1990.)

There has been virtually no return migration of Laotian Americans to their homeland, although by the late 1980s the Lao government had moderated its policies, and a number of those who had left as refugees felt comfortable returning as visitors. Some became partners or investors in Lao-American joint ventures, taking advantage of economic reforms implemented by the Lao Peoples Democratic Republic beginning in 1985. Others, particularly young men, who reached adulthood in the United States visit Laos to find a marriageable partner who will return with them to live in the United States.

All Laotian immigrants are far less likely than Vietnamese immigrants, for example, to become naturalized U.S. citizens, regardless of their length of stay in the United States; foreign-born Hmong are only half as likely as foreign-born Lao to become naturalized U.S. citizens. However, because of the much higher birthrate of Hmong in the United States compared to other Laotians, the proportion of the Hmong-American population that has U.S. citizenship (both native and naturalized) is higher than the proportion of the Lao-American population that has U.S. citizenship. For the same reason, the number of Hmong born in the United States is increasing rapidly and the proportion of immigrants-to-natives is decreasing; the proportion of Hmong within the total Laotian-American population is also increasing.

## Settlement in the United States

Government resettlement policy encouraged dispersion of refugees to scattered locations throughout the United States, but Laotian immigrants rapidly coalesced in several areas through secondary migration. In 1990, about 45 percent of the population resided in California, with other sizable concentrations in Wisconsin, Minnesota, Texas, Washington, and Massachusetts. Of the non-Lao minorities, the Thai Dam community are centered in various Iowa cities, while Lahu are primarily concentrated in Visalia, California. Most Lua live in Santa Rosa and Stockton, California, while Thai Lue are found in Seattle, Washington, and the East Bay of northern California. Fresno and other cities in the San Joaquin Valley of California are home to large concentrations of Hmong, while Mien live in the East Bay, Portland, and Seattle. Khmu have settled in the East Bay, Stockton, Santa Ana, Seattle, and Boston. The Lao are found throughout California and other states.

Family members may live close together (indeed, entire villages have even been transplanted to given locations), or they may be dispersed across the country, gathering together only at weddings, holidays, or other occasions. For the most part, Laotian immigrants have settled in small- and medium-sized cities and their suburbs, avoiding the largest metropolises (except for those in southern California) and generally not seeking small town or rural locations. In urban and suburban areas, Laotians tend to live in rented garden apartments or homes; increasingly they have purchased their own homes. Rarely do they live in concentrated mono-ethnic neighborhoods of Laotian families; more often one finds Lao, Hmong, other Laotian minorities, Cambodian, Vietnamese, Mexican, black, and European-American families living alongside one another. From outside appearance there is usually little to distinguish a Lao or Laotian home from that of their American neighbors, except perhaps a backyard garden in which traditional vegetables are carefully cultivated. Indoors, however, people convert Western-style houses or apartments into Lao homes through items of decor and through practices such as the obligatory removal of shoes before entering the house. Indeed, the most visible indication that a dwelling is inhabited by Lao Americans is the array of shoes and sandals on the front porch or stoop.

## Language

The Lao language is a member of the Southwestern branch of the Tai family of languages, closely related to the national language of Thailand as well as regional languages spoken in Thailand, Vietnam, Burma, and China. There is great dialectal variety within Lao itself, so that speakers of Lao can easily determine by their pronunciation whether someone is from Luang Prabang in the north, Vientiane in the center, or Pakse in the south. Lao is designated as the official language of Laos, and members of highland ethnic minorities generally learn the national language in school, the military, or the marketplace. There are far more speakers of the Lao language in northeastern Thailand than within the borders of Laos; Lao is also used in parts of Cambodia, Vietnam, and China as a market language and lingua franca. The national language of Thailand—Thai or Siamese—is understood by most Laotians who have been exposed to it through radio, television, videos, and popular music. In present-day Laos, indeed, there is concern that Thai may soon supplant the Lao language, especially among younger residents of urban areas. Many Lao adults, whether in Laos or the United States, can readily read the Thai language, although within the U.S. community the ability to read or write Thai is more common among those who reached adulthood in Laos. Younger Lao Americans may now find themselves studying Thai in college, since few universities offer instruction in the Lao language.

The Lao language nevertheless remains an important medium of communication for Lao Americans of all generations, even though children rarely learn to read and write the language and their use of Lao often diminishes in favor of English once

they begin school. Among Laotian highlanders, however, children typically speak their mother tongue and English; the only members who speak Lao are those who learned it while in Laos or in refugee camps. An active if small Lao-language press provides news of the Laotian-American community and events in Laos. Perhaps more important in preserving fluency in Lao among younger Lao Americans are cassettes of Lao popular songs, recorded in Laos, Thailand, or the United States. The Lao language maintains its central role in the sphere of religion, where Buddhist temples serve as classrooms for language instruction, and religious ceremonies and teachings are conducted in Lao.

## Religious Practices and Beliefs

For lowland Lao in the United States, Theravada Buddhism continues to play a central role in the social and cultural life of the community (this is not the case for Hmong and other highland Laotian). Dozens of cities with sizable Lao populations are home to Buddhist temples, some newly built in a modernized Lao style and others simply rehabilitated American-style houses. As it had in the homeland, Buddhism provides an underlying ethical and moral orientation toward life that may be overlain with folk Buddhist practices, or with Christianity. Especially at times of major seasonal Buddhist rituals—such as the New Year (celebrated in mid-April), Visakha Bousa (commemorating the birth, enlightenment, and death of Buddha, in mid-May), Khao Phansa (marking the so-called Buddhist Lent, in July), and Ok Phansa (the end of the rainy season and the Buddhist Lent, in October)—families and entire communities join together at the temples for religious observances and festivities. Temple parking lots typically overflow as celebrants attend from far and wide, with grandparents and elders performing ritual obligations while teenagers join in games, sports, and courtship. Such festive celebrations are also the time for Lao community arts groups to perform traditional music and dances, as well as modernized rock-influenced popular music and social dancing.

At other times, the Buddhist temples are quieter, but they remain important in the lives of many, especially older Lao immigrants. The Buddhist monks offer counseling and guidance and dispense folk remedies for ailments both physical and mental. Buddhism also provides a system of charity and benevolence that provides a social safety net for the community. Adherents seek to gain merit through charitable contributions and other good deeds, and those in need can always find support and succor at the temple. The monks or laypeople also provide lessons in the Lao language and culture, and in Buddhist belief. In Lao tradition, a young man was obliged to enter the temple for a short period as a religious adept, thereby gaining merit for himself and honoring his parents and ancestors. In the United States, this tradition has been attenuated, but it is still observed sometimes upon the death of a parent, or during a period of emotional trouble when the calming influence of the Buddhist practices of meditation and contemplation are valued to restore people to the proper path.

Many Lao in America have become adherents of Christianity. For some this began in Laos, or during their stays in Thai refugee camps, where religious organizations often provided relief or education. Others converted to Christianity in connection with their resettlement; arriving refugees were often sponsored by members of a religious congregation and sometimes reciprocated the hospitality by adopting the religion of their hosts. From the perspective of most Buddhists, religion can be additive, with newly found Christian beliefs and practices supplementing without supplanting traditional Buddhist ones. Similarly, for Catholics and many other denominations, Christianity does not require the wholesale abandonment of Buddhist beliefs and practices, even if some are deemed to be superstitious or need to be adapted to be compatible with Christian belief. For many fundamentalist and evangelical denominations, however, Buddhism is the devil's work and adherents are obliged to renounce completely their sinful ways. In many Lao communities, and even within families or across generational lines, serious

Lao Americans participate in a religious ritual. (Mukul Roy)

conflicts can arise between practitioners of Buddhism and fundamentalist Christians. Such conflicts are even more common among non-Buddhist Laotian highlanders, whose folk religious practices are condemned by fundamentalist Christians as satanic worship.

## Family and Home Life

Like many other immigrant communities, Laotian Americans face substantial stresses that are often focused within the family. Elders have few opportunities to demonstrate their traditional cultural competence and knowledge in the novel contexts of American life, and children may consequently grow up with little respect for their parents and grandparents. The hard-won knowledge and wisdom possessed by many members of the older generations are unrecognized by the American community and often have little immediate survival value in urban life, where knowing about agricultural practices or the natural environment of Laos is irrelevant. Mass media and U.S. institutions do not encourage Laotian-American young people to honor their elders, instead devaluing them as superstitious or old-fashioned. Within Laotian tradition, respect for elders is obligatory and automatic, and immigrant parents may find it difficult to conceive that their children would not simply inherit this pattern of behavior.

These generational gaps are reinforced when Laotian Americans come into contact with institutions of the larger U.S. community. Because children gain English language skills more readily than adults, they are often called upon to take responsibility for contacts with schools, hospitals, and police; this inversion of traditional lines of authority can often create difficulties. These inverted relations—with youngsters sometimes having greater authority than their elders and elders garnering little respect from the younger generation—create and reinforce stresses within families and communities. However, it seems that the families that adjust most successfully to life in the United States are not necessarily those where the parents are the most "modern" or adapted to urban

life, and the most successful children are not always those whose parents are most flexible in responding to American ways. Parents and elders who are confident of their own knowledge and value their own traditions most strongly—often those who are strictest and most culturally conservative with their children—usually are better able to raise children who can reconcile cultural gaps and social displacements than parents who are insecure about their own cultural heritage.

For Laotians of all ethnic backgrounds, marriage is traditionally a relationship involving entire families and even communities, rather than simply the man and woman at the center. Marriages are arranged between families, but there is much opportunity for the principals to exercise their own choice in the matter. Typically, a wedding involves several successive rituals of betrothal and marriage. At the betrothal or engagement ceremonies, parents and elders from both families negotiate the arrangements for the wedding and the value of the brideprice. This usually occurs only after the future husband and wife have decided together to ask their parents to begin the process; in some cases, negotiations begin even when the two are relative strangers to one another, but they each have the right to refuse or withdraw from the match. Rather than a dowry, Laotian Americans maintain the tradition of the brideprice—valuables and money given by the man's family to the woman's family. The negotiations for the brideprice are steeped in tradition, and in the United States they may still be carried out in terms of how many water buffaloes and how many bronze drums will be provided to the bride's family; once the terms are mutually agreed the value will be converted into dollars since water buffaloes are hard to come by in suburban America. The marriage ceremonies follow the betrothal by some days, weeks, or even months. Most often, the couple officializes the marriage in a civil ceremony or church ceremony, but there is also a house ritual in which the gathered families and friends ratify the match through blessings and a wrist-tying ceremony. Following the wedding, the newly married couple will often live in the home of the bride's parents for some time before establishing their own home.

The wrist-tying ceremony, known in Lao as *basii* or *sou khouan*, is ubiquitous among Laotian of all ethnicities. In many Laotian-American communities, Saturdays and Sundays are filled with such ceremonies. The wrist-tying is intended to bind a person's spirit to the body, since the spirit is apt to flee during moments of stress, transition, or adversity. The assembled guests join together in blessings and prayers, and then each ties a cotton thread around the wrist of the honoree, murmuring a blessing while tying the knot. The strings are left on the wrist for three days, when all but one are cut off; the remaining thread may remain tied until it falls apart. These ceremonies mark almost every important event in the life of a Laotian: birth, death, marriage, sickness, recuperation, departure for a trip, arrival as a guest, safe return home, beginning a new job, graduation, and so on. The ritual itself is always followed by a shared meal featuring traditional specialty foods. Wrist-tying is practiced by highlanders whose religion is animism and by Lao lowlanders who are devout Buddhists. Among those who have converted to Catholicism the ceremony continues even if the prayers now invoke the Christian pantheon, but among some fundamentalist Protestants the threads are condemned as "devil strings," and believers are enjoined from participating.

## Economics and Education

Laotian Americans are quite diverse in their pre-immigration backgrounds and similarly diverse in their accomplishments and attainments in the United States. The community includes members of elite urbanized families who were educated at universities in France or the United States before 1975, as well as members of rural highland minorities who have had no formal education. There are former jet pilots and former cabinet ministers as well as former farmers and fisherfolk. Not surprisingly, some members of the Laotian-American community have prospered and succeeded in the United States while others have encountered substantial difficulty and frustration. These differences do not necessarily coincide with ethnic lines; there are lowland Lao in college alongside Hmong and Khmu, just as they may share a cell in a youth facility or prison. Generally, members of the first wave of immigrants (those who entered the United States before 1977) have adjusted best to their new home and have most successfully acculturated themselves to American life. These first-wave immigrants were typically better educated, more prosperous, and more experienced in Western ways than those who came later.

For people of rural and highland backgrounds, acculturation to life in the United States has often been more difficult. Parents may not attach great value to formal education, encouraging their children to start a family and get a job rather than pursue protracted studies. Children (especially those born outside the United States) often find that schools fail to meet their needs, and there is no apparent value to education. In many areas, the dropout rate for Laotian Americans of all ethnicities is quite high; the incarceration rate for juveniles is often correspondingly high. At the same time, many Laotian Americans attain great achievements in schools and colleges, entering universities of the highest national rank and prospering there.

As with education, there is great occupational and economic diversity among Laotian Americans. Many are employed as social workers, teachers, teacher aides, interpreters, or other paraprofessional occupations. In many California cities, Laotian Americans are valued as dependable and careful employees in electronics assembly plants or other high-technology or light-industry factories. In the Midwest, Laotian Americans are recruited to work as meatcutters. A few have established themselves as truck farmers, usually growing speciality vegetables sold at Asian-Americans groceries and farmers' markets. In many cities, Lao operate small grocery stores and video rental shops, providing the special foods and entertainment that allow Laotian Americans to make their new homes more like their old ones. A sizable proportion of immigrants have nevertheless not managed to find employment; they depend on public assistance for their livelihood.

## Community Identity

Questions of personal and cultural identity are often complicated for members of the Laotian-American community. A single person may identify himself or herself sometimes as Lao and sometimes as American; today as a member of the Lao ethnic group and tomorrow as a person of Laotian ancestry; on occasion as a devout Buddhist and otherwise as a practicing Christian. Increasingly, Laotian Americans who come to maturity in the United States are intermarrying with members of other Laotian ethnicities and with Americans of diverse ethnic background, further complicating questions of self-identity. Among some natives of Laos, ethnic identity increasingly takes precedence over national identity, so that Hmong-American children may speak only Hmong and English and never learn to speak the national language of their parents' homeland, Lao. Similarly Thai Dam are reestablishing contacts with relatives in Vietnam, turning their attention more to their ancestral homeland than to their temporary home in Laos, where they lived between 1954 and 1975. In view of the availability of Thai videotapes, popular music, and magazines in the United States, many Laotian Americans increasingly identify with a transnational Thai-Lao culture. On other occasions

A young boy holds a sign with two American flags to celebrate his mother at her naturalization ceremony after her immigration to the United States from Laos. (Dean Wong/Corbis)

Laotian Americans find they have common causes and shared problems with Vietnamese Americans and Cambodian Americans.

Just as the personal identities of Laotian Americans are dynamic and evolving, so the community identities are shaped and reshaped by local, national, and international factors. For Lao, Hmong, Khmu, and other highland minorities now living in the United States, internal and external relations and interactions will continue to contribute to an evolving identity as Laotian Americans.

*See also:* HMONG; KHMU; MIEN; THAI

## Bibliography

Donnelly, N. D. (1994). *Changing Lives of Refugee Hmong Women.* Seattle: University of Washington Press.

Knoll, T. (1982). *Becoming Americans: Asian Sojourners, Immigrants, and Refugees in the Western United States.* Portland, OR: Coast to Coast Books.

Krulfeld, R. M. (1992). "Cognitive Mapping and Ethnic Identity: The Changing Concepts of Community and Nationalism in the Laotian Diaspora." *Selected Papers on Refugee Issues* 1:4–26.

Lewis, J., ed. (1992). *Minority Cultures of Laos: Kammu, Lua', Lahu, Hmong, and Iu-Mien.* Rancho Cordova, CA: Southeast Asia Community Resource Center, Rancho Cordova Unified School District.

Nguyen-Hong-Nghiem, L., and Halpern, J. M., eds. (1989). *The Far East Comes Near: Autobiographical Accounts of Southeast Asian Students in America.* Amherst: University of Massachusetts Press.

Proudfoot, R. (1990). *Even the Birds Don't Sound the Same Here: The Laotian Refugees' Search for Heart in American Culture.* New York: P. Lang.

Rynearson, A. M. (1996). "Living Within the Looking Glass: Refugee Artists and the Creation of Group Identity." *Selected Papers on Refugee Issues* 4:20–44.

Savada, A. M., ed. (1995). *Laos: A Country Study.* Washington, DC: Federal Research Division, Library of Congress.

Van Esterik, P. (1992). *Taking Refuge: Lao Buddhists in North America.* Tempe: Program for Southeast Asian Studies, Arizona State University.

FRANK PROSCHAN

# LATINOS

*See* ARGENTINEANS; CALIFORNIOS; CHILEANS; COLOMBIANS; CUBANS; DOMINICANS; ECUADORIANS; HONDURANS; MEXICANS; NICARAGUANS; PANAMANIANS; PERUVIANS; PUERTO RICANS; SALVADORANS

# LATVIANS

Latvians in the United States originate from Latvia, one of the three Baltic states on the eastern shore of the Baltic Sea. To the north of Latvia is Estonia, then Finland; to the northwest, across the Baltic Sea lies Sweden; Lithuania is to the south, then Russia (the portion comprising the former East Prussia) and Poland; and to the east is Russia. Comprising an area of 24,946 square miles, Latvia is slightly larger than West Virginia. Latvians have inhabited their homeland since 2000 B.C.E.

In its crossroads position between eastern and western Europe, Latvia or parts of it have, over the centuries, been under the domination of Teutonic Knights, Sweden, Poland, or Russia. In 1918, Latvia declared independence; by 1921, its statehood was recognized by the Western nations, and Latvia was admitted as an equal member to the League of Nations. This period of independence lasted until June 1940 when, as the result of the secret agreement between Joseph Stalin and Adolf Hitler (the Molotov–von Ribbentrop Pact of August 23, 1939), Latvia was attacked, occupied by, and annexed to the Soviet Union. The following year, known as the "year of terror," brought political reprisals, executions, and mass deportations to slave labor camps in Siberia. On June 22, 1941, Nazi Germany attacked the Soviet Union, and within a few weeks Latvia became occupied by German troops. By 1945, the German Army retreated, and the Soviet forces once more occupied Latvia. Fearing the return of the atrocities of the previous Soviet occupation, 10 percent of the nation's population fled to the West for refuge. By the end of 1961, about forty thousand of the refugees had found homes in the United States. Latvia regained its independence in August 1991.

The language of the Latvians is Latvian (Lettish in older reference materials) and belongs, together with Lithuanian, to the Baltic branch of the Indo-European language family. It is a conservative, highly inflectional language.

## Emigration from Latvia to the United States

The first individuals and small groups of Latvians immigrated to the United States as early as the seventeenth century, some via Tobago, where a colony of the Kurland Duchy was established (1640–1690) by Duke Jacob of Kurland. These early immigrants settled in Delaware, Pennsylvania, and Boston. In the middle of the eighteenth century, some Latvian iron ore miners and cannon forgers lived in Riga Hill, Connecticut. In the early and middle nineteenth century, Latvian seamen and missionaries arrived; the best known of the latter was George Heinrich Loskiel, associated with the Moravian Church of Bethlehem, Pennsylvania, noted for his work with Native Americans and the author of more than four hundred hymns.

Most of the nineteenth-century immigration to the United States was for personal and economic reasons. Many were young men from Kurzeme, the western part of Latvia; without English-language skills they worked on railroad construction, in the quarries, and as lumberjacks. They were followed by individuals and families of varied occupations, religions, and political convictions. Data about these immigrants are sketchy, found mostly in Latvian and American periodicals of that time. In the immigration documents they are classified as Russians, or occasionally as Lithuanians or Poles, since officially they all were subjects of czarist Russia. Many jumped ship illegally. Political immigrants hid their nationality for fear of persecution. Often their names underwent spelling changes; sometimes completely new names were assumed, making it difficult to trace the origins of many of them. Most settled in Boston, New York, Philadel-

phia, and Baltimore. The official statistics cite 4,309 Latvians in the United States by 1900; the number of illegal immigrants was much larger. In August 1888 Jekabs Zibergs (Sieberg) founded the first Latvian colony, including an association and parish, in Boston; one of the earliest Latvian organizations, established in 1892, was the Association for Free Latvians in Philadelphia.

In the years 1901–1910, the number of Latvian immigrants doubled. Some of the newcomers were young men who were avoiding being drafted into the Russian Army for participation in the unpopular Russo-Japanese War (1904–1905). The largest group, however, comprised the first wave of organized refugees. They were political immigrants, fleeing persecution for participating in the revolution of 1905. It is estimated that after the suppression of the revolution about four thousand Latvians immigrated to the United States.

In the 1930 U.S. Census, 20,673 persons were registered as being born in Latvia; together with those born in the United States and identifying themselves as Latvians, the number was 38,091. A total of 60 percent of those born in the United States had become U.S. citizens. From 1930 to 1935, 956 Latvians immigrated to the United States and 298 repatriated. During Word War II immigration was greatly hampered; nevertheless, 638 Latvian citizens entered the United States. From 1946 to 1949, immigration visas were obtained by 4,275.

After World War II, about 120,000 Latvian refugees were placed in displaced persons camps in Germany. Under the auspices of the 1948 Refugee Act that allowed families from the displaced persons camps to enter the United States, about 37,500 Latvian refugees were admitted by 1951, comprising the second and by far the largest and most significant Latvian immigration wave. To enter the United States the immigrants needed sponsors to guarantee work and lodging. Initially most of the sponsors were church organizations; later the new immigrants themselves sponsored relatives and friends. Organizations such as Latvian Relief in New York, founded in 1940, provided sixteen thousand sponsorships. Some selfless individuals spared no effort to enable larger Latvian groups to immigrate together. A notable example is the Rev. Janis (John) Laupmanis, of Latvian descent, whose efforts enabled an entire Latvian choir, Dziesmu Vairogs, together with their relatives, to immigrate to Kalamazoo and Grand Rapids, Michigan, in the early 1950s and laid the basis for one of the most active Latvian communities.

Most of these political refugees or exiles were well educated, more than 80 percent having held professional, educational, or managerial positions. In the United States, however, with a few exceptions, they were engaged as unskilled or farm laborers, or domestic help. A physician could be found tending hospital grounds, a mathematics professor working as a school janitor, a composer and opera director in a print shop. A project to establish a large agricultural colony in Mississippi with laborers from the displaced persons camps drew 694 Latvians in 1948–1949. They settled near Senatobia, founded a parish, and built a church; however, after a few years most had moved North. Harsh labor conditions, low pay, a strange climate, and a desire to be closer to relatives and acquaintances caused almost all who were sponsored for work on farms to move to cities after their initial year of servitude. In the 1960s, the largest Latvian centers were in New York (8,000); Chicago (6,000); Boston (3,000); Milwaukee, Cleveland, and Minneapolis-St. Paul (2,000 each); Seattle-Tacoma and Los Angeles (1,500 each); Philadelphia (1,300); Indianapolis (1,200); and Kalamazoo and Grand Rapids (1,000 each). Large groups of Latvians also lived in Iowa, Delaware, South Dakota, Colorado, the District of Columbia, Connecticut, Maryland, Nebraska, and Oregon. As of the mid-1990s, about 102,000 Latvians, most of them U.S. citizens, lived in the United States. A unique Latvian community is developing near Three Rivers, Michigan, where a sizable number of retired Latvians have bought lots and built houses. They have named their streets after place names in Latvia, and the whole development bears the name Latvijas Ciems (Latvian Village).

## Social and Psychological Structure

The World War II political refugees and their descendants constitute the major part of Latvians in the United States. Differing from immigrants who moved to the United States for personal, economic, or religious reasons, they held, as a group, a sense of mission: to preserve their language and culture and to do their part to help Latvia shake Soviet Russian rule and occupation. To this end they established and maintained educational, cultural, and political organizations besides the usual religious and social ones. Their values were passed on to the second and third generations.

After the first years of menial labor, most of the younger immigrants supplemented their professional skills with English, sometimes changing their fields, or completed their interrupted higher education, and resumed or started careers as physicians, dentists, scientists, engineers, lawyers, architects, librarians, professors, or health workers. In 1953, about five hundred studied in U.S. colleges or universities. Others worked in offices, in manufacturing plants, or in sales. The older generation, less agile in language acquisition and, being responsible for their families, often including parents, unable to take off from work to reeducate themselves, most often continued to labor in factories, mills, or hospitals or as janitors or office workers. However, they were determined to provide higher education for their children, and almost all of them sent their children to college. By 1975, 4,755 Latvians were known to have graduated from U.S. colleges or universities. In 1995, about 80 percent of the Latvians in the United States had obtained higher education.

In the 1950s, most of the new Latvian immigrants found spouses within the Latvian community; in each new generation the number of marriages with people of other nationalities increases. In most cases the mixed marriage means at least partial distancing from the Latvian community, since the language in the family is almost exclusively English, whereas the language of most Latvian community events, including church services, was still Latvian in the mid-1990s.

In the 1990s, except for the very old, Latvians have adapted well to American social and professional life and are productive members in all areas of American society. The young immigrants and their children have served faithfully in the U.S. military forces; Latvian names are found in the killed-in-action lists of both the Korean and Vietnam wars.

## Religious Organizations

The first organizations most often were church congregations. Since most of the immigrants came from western Latvia, where Lutheranism was predominant, there is one or more evangelical Lutheran parish in every Latvian community where sermons are held in Latvian. In 1995, there were more than fifty such parishes. Many own their churches, paid for by dues and donations and often using the skilled labor of the parishioners. Some smaller congregations share the pastor, who may travel several hundred miles to serve a remote parish. Most operate Sunday schools; some sponsor Boy and Girl Scout troops; and all have a ladies' auxiliary which tends to the needs of older and impaired parishioners, supports church activities, and organizes programs and fund-raising events. In Boston, Chicago, Cleveland, Grand Rapids, Indianapolis, Milwaukee, Philadelphia, and St. Paul there are Latvian Catholic congregations; Baptist parishes exist in Chicago, Cleveland, Grand Rapids, and Philadelphia.

## Schools and Education

Given the unique character of the post–World War II Latvian immigrants group, high priority was given to Latvian language and culture preservation and teaching. Almost all Latvian communities established so-called Latvian Saturday schools, where children from kindergarten through the twelfth grade learned the language, literature, folklore, traditions, geography, and history of Latvia. The schools flourished in the 1950s through the 1970s. In the 1990s, there are twenty-seven such schools. In 1980, four- and six-week summer high

schools were organized in Pennsylvania, Washington State (Shelton), and Michigan (Three Rivers). Students come from all fifty states, Canada, and (since 1991) from Latvia. The curriculum consists of intensive language study supplemented with literature, folklore, culture, and history lessons. Many of the instructors are professional teachers or even university professors who dedicate their summer vacations to these schools. In 1995, about 150 students attended the Latvian summer high schools.

At the university level, Latvian courses have been offered at the University of Pennsylvania, Kent State University, Stanford University, and Western Michigan University. From 1981 to 1992, Western Michigan University offered a full minor and major program in Latvian, drawing students not only from the United States, but also from Canada, South American, Europe, and Australia. The program was sponsored and financially supported by the American Latvian Association and, in the later years, by the Latvian Studies Center, Kalamazoo, Michigan. The program was phased out a year after Latvia regained its independence and it became possible for students from the United States to study at the University of Latvia.

The Latvian Studies Center (established and built in 1982 to meet the needs of Western Michigan University's Latvian students and paid for by donations from Latvian organizations and individuals in the United States, Canada, and Venezuela) served the students as a dormitory and cultural center, including the largest Latvian library in the United States, from 1982 to 1992. From 1993 to 1996, it housed exchange students from the Baltic states. Its 22,830-volume library has, over the years, added music, video, and art collections. Until the summer of 1995, the center's library was served by a full-time professional librarian; in 1996, with the organization searching for operational funding, the collection was managed by volunteer workers.

To provide a nonacademic cultural setting, there are annual week-long seminars for young adults and families. They are organized by dedicated individuals and groups and take place at various recreational camps during summer or Christmas vacations. The activities include lectures, discussion sessions, and practical instruction in Latvian handicrafts, such as folk costume weaving and embroidery, jewelry making, pottery, woodwork, and Latvian dishes. For children there are Latvian summer camps, usually in Latvian-owned camp properties, notably Latvian Church Camp, the "Catskill Camp," Elka Park, New York; Latvian Center Garezers, Three Rivers, Michigan; and West Coast Latvian Educational Center, Shelton, Washington. Children come from all parts of the United States to these camps, where Latvian language usage and enhancement are focal points.

## General Organizations

In each Latvian community there is at least a local Latvian association; in the larger communities there are chapters of the global Latvian Relief Organization Daugavas Vanagi, credit unions, Girl and Boy Scout troops, Latvian fraternity and sorority chapters, hunters' and fisherman's clubs, musical ensembles, theater troupes, and handicraft clubs. Most of the organizations are members of the American Latvian Association in the United States, Inc. (Rockville, Maryland), whose Latvian Institute supports various cultural endeavors. Its education section coordinates the Latvian Saturday and summer school work, and throughout the Soviet occupation of Latvia it kept Latvia's plight visible to the American government and people (the United States never recognized Latvia's forceful annexation by the Soviet Union). Since 1991, the American Latvian Association has also helped to coordinate aid to Latvia. The seat of the global World Federation of Free Latvians is also in Rockville, Maryland.

## Culture and the Arts

The cultural foundations of the American Latvian Association and of the World Federation of Free Latvians support various music, art, and other cultural activities with grants, scholarships, and awards. Latvian Foundation, Inc., established in 1970 for the express purpose of funding cultural and educational projects that otherwise would not materialize, by 1995 had paid-in grants of more than $900,000. The General Goppers Foundation (Detroit, Michigan), established in memory of the general and Latvian Boy Scout leader who was executed by the Soviets in 1941, each year awards prizes for literary, music, and other works created for children and young adults and supports the Latvian Studies Center library.

In the field of music, following a hundred-year tradition, a Latvian Song Festival is organized every four to five years. About fifty choirs, with more than one thousand voices and dressed in the ancient ethnic costumes, participate in the main concert. During the three- to five-day festival, there are singing competitions, folk-dance performances, solos, ensembles, instrumental and orchestral concerts, art and ethnographic exhibits, poetry and prose readings, organizational meetings, and other activities. The place of the song festivals rotates among major U.S. cities. In the Latvian communities there are frequent choir and solo concerts coordinated by performing arts associations. In the 1990s, a number of musicians from Latvia visited Latvian communities in the United States. In 1988, there were sixty-four choirs or musical ensembles in the United States with 1,188 singers. In 1995, there were more than sixty active professional Latvian musicians—composers, instrumentalists, vocalists, or music professors—in the United States.

In art, the major event is the annual exhibit, organized by the American Latvian Association Culture Foundation. Often an artist of this exhibit is selected to receive the annual Culture Foundation Honorary Award ($1,000). There are regular art exhibits in various local Latvian houses or centers; moreover, many Latvian artists regularly exhibit their work in galleries in New York, San Francisco, and other places. The American Latvian Artists Association supports the interests of Latvian artists in the United States. A large permanent collection of Latvian art (eight hundred items) is housed at the Latvian Studies Center in Kalamazoo.

Latvian folk art is supported by the Latvian Applied Arts Association, most of whose members dedicate themselves to studying and furthering the ancient ethnographic traditions. Other members of the association develop modern applied arts skills. To preserve many examples of original folk art and to introduce the younger generations and others to it, there are four Latvian ethnic museums in the United States: in the Bronx, New York; Rockville, Maryland; Chicago; and Three Rivers, Michigan.

In the 1950s and 1960s, there were theater troupes with professional directors and actors in Boston, New York, Washington, D.C., San Francisco, and Los Angeles. As of 1995, only the San Francisco and Los Angeles troupes were active. In some Latvian communities there are local theater enthusiasts who occasionally stage a play.

### The Ethnic Press

From 1950 to 1996, four major Latvian publishing houses—Grāmatu Draugs, Brooklyn, New York; Tilta Apgāds, Minneapolis; Upeskalns, Shippenville, Pennsylvania; and Gauja, East Lansing, Michigan—as well as a large number of smaller publishing companies or individuals issued more than four thousand books in Latvian. Besides belles lettres, the books include folklore, literary criticism, history, music, art, philosophy and religion, educational books, cookbooks, and others. Some U.S. Latvian authors have published their work also in Latvian publishing houses in Stockholm and elsewhere.

The major Latvian newspaper *Laiks,* published in Brooklyn since 1949, is issued twice a week and serves about ten thousand subscribers. Monthly or quarterly periodicals are published in Chicago, Three Rivers, Los Angeles, and San Jose. Many parishes and local associations periodically publish their newsletters. Two notable annual journals are published in Kalamazoo: *Latvju Māksla* (Latvian Art) and *Latvju Mūzika* (Latvian Music), with contributors from three continents. From 1959 to 1992, the Latvian children's magazine *Mazputniņš* was published successively in Kalamazoo, Chicago, Boston, Cleveland, and again in Kalamazoo. The journal *Labietis* is devoted to Latvian ethnography, folklore, and the revived ancient Latvian religious beliefs; *Treji Vārti* is a magazine of general interest. The photo journal *Tilts* (1949–1976) documented Latvian social and cultural life. Latvian authors are contributors to journals and newspapers published in Canada and Europe.

### Bibliography

Bilmanis, A. (1977). *A History of Latvia.* Westport, CT: Greenwood Press.

Karklis, M., and Streips, L. (1974). *The Latvians in America, 1640–1973.* Dobbs Ferry, NY: Oceana.

Rutkis, J., ed. (1967). *Latvia: Country and People.* Stockholm: Latvian National Foundation.

Simanis, V. V., ed. (1984). *Latvia.* St. Charles, IL: The Book Latvia.

Spekke, A. (1957). *History of Latvia.* Stockholm: M. Goppers.

ARNOLD SILDEGS

# LEBANESE CHRISTIANS

Lebanon is a mosaic of religious communities. A larger proportion of Christians to Muslims live in Lebanon than in any other Arab country. A 1943 census indicated that Christians constituted slightly more than half of the population. While it is unlikely that Christians outnumber Muslims today, Lebanon remains a Christian stronghold in the Middle East.

Maronite Christians were the followers of St. Maron, a monk who lived in northern Syria at the end of the fourth century. A theological dispute separated his followers from the Byzantine Christians. At the end of the seventh century, persecutions by the Byzantines forced the Maronites to leave Syria for the safety of Mount Lebanon, though they spread to other parts of the Middle East as well. In the twelfth century the Roman Catholic Church accepted the Maronites into its fold, although the Maronites were permitted to retain their distinctive rituals and practices.

Other groups of Lebanese/Syrian Christians include various branches of the Eastern Orthodox churches as well as the Melkites. The latter group had been Orthodox but became affiliated with the Roman Catholic Church, although also retaining their distinctive practices. In addition, Armenian Christians immigrated to the United States from Lebanon. However, most were latecomers to Lebanon, and their history is such that they are classified separately from other Lebanese Christian groups.

The Ottomans instituted a system of governance, known as the millet, in which authority was delegated to community and religious leaders in the various non-Muslim communities. Under the millet system the Christians of the empire maintained some autonomy and were exempt from military service. The Maronites of northern Mount Lebanon were able to be relatively free of Ottoman control and developed a warlike social and political structure interwoven with religious identity. Orthodox Christians and Melkites were more likely to reside in cities and towns and became successful entrepreneurs when Europeans introduced manufactured goods into Lebanon.

However, their economic condition seriously deteriorated when silkworm production, a staple of the nineteenth-century Lebanese economy, was

A Syrian/Lebanese immigrant in New York City in the early 1900s sells cool drinks from the ornate metal container he carries on his back. (Library of Congress/Corbis)

ruined by periodic droughts, famines, and insect blights. Adding to the problem were severe overpopulation and the collapse of the Ottoman Empire, during which time the people suffered greatly from lawlessness and overtaxation. Intercommunal violence between the Maronites and the Druze resulted in massacres of the Maronites in 1860. During this time Lebanon was considered part of Greater Syria, which included Palestine, modern-day Syria, and Lebanon; there was no clear-cut distinction made among these peoples. However, the vast majority of people who emigrated from Greater Syria to the United States were from Mount Lebanon. For this reason the people discussed in this entry will be termed "Lebanese," although the people did not refer to themselves by this appellation until 1930. In fact, religion and kinship traditionally have been the bases of ethnic identity for Lebanese Christians rather than a sense of loyalty to a state.

## Immigration

The deplorable conditions in the Levant in the nineteenth century, along with the famine that accompanied World War I, drove the Lebanese from their homeland. The promise of economic opportunity attracted them to the United States. In 1878, the first family from the region arrived in America, but immigration did not begin in earnest until about the 1890s. Between 1900 and 1910, about five thousand people a year immigrated to the United States, with the peak period being 1913—1914, when nine thousand arrived.

Once in the United States, the Lebanese proved to be industrious. Pack peddling was adopted as the major, though hardly the sole, means of earning a living. Historian Alixa Naff has noted that Syrian/Lebanese pack peddling became a multimillion-dollar business. Those who did not become peddlers often found themselves supplying goods to the peddlers. Christian women, not as restricted in their movement as traditional Muslim Lebanese women, joined in this occupation, along with their children. The women also sewed clothing, made other items for the men to sell, and helped run small shops. The most illustrious of these early immigrants was the poet/philosopher/artist Kahlil Gibran, who arrived in Boston in 1895 with his mother and siblings. Gibran grew up in the Lebanese-Syrian enclave of Boston's South End and was desperately poor, but his talent drew the attention of a group of wealthy Bostonians, who supported and promoted his work. Gibran wrote in both English and Arabic, and his book *The Prophet* (1923) was a best-seller in America.

The entrepreneurial spirit for which the Lebanese are famous served this community well. A large proportion rapidly moved into the middle class. Not uncommonly, in a single generation, members of this group became professionals, owners of their own businesses, and involved in other occupations requiring specialized skills. By the 1940s their prosperity gave them wider contact with American society as they took on the values of middle-class American culture. Moving to prosperous suburbs, they have dropped the outward symbols of their ethnicity and give the appearance of being totally assimilated into the American melting pot. Anglicizing their names and wearing no distinctive clothing, they are quite indistinguishable from other Americans.

A remarkable number of children of first-generation peddlers and suppliers have become highly successful; some have even become celebrities. Comedian Danny Thomas; international businessman and the father of Queen Nur of Jordan, Najeeb Halaby; senior White House correspondent Helen Thomas; and leading consumer advocate Ralph Nader are just a few of these Lebanese-American success stories.

Many Lebanese of the Eastern rite churches began attending "American" churches, again reinforcing the image of a totally assimilated population. The Maronites and the Melkites joined Latin Catholic churches, while the Orthodox saw themselves easily aligned with the Episcopalians. However, these adaptations can be misleading, as there is an identifiable Lebanese Christian community in the United States.

## Maintaining an Identity Through Churches

The 1990 U.S. census indicates that there are about 400,000 people in the United States of Lebanese Christian descent, spread out fairly evenly in the Northeast, Midwest, and South. Struggling to define a clear identity for themselves has not always been easy. Finding channels to maintain this identity is equally difficult. In fact, Lebanese Christians have been referred to as one of America's "hidden minorities." In spite of the departure of so many Lebanese Christians to "American" churches, the Eastern rite churches have been strong repositories of Lebanese culture in America. There are estimates that about half of the first- and second-generation Lebanese Christians have worked to maintain the Eastern rite in their religious traditions, and in so doing have helped maintain Lebanese identity. All the religious groups have built their own churches. Even in remote places in the United States, one can find beautiful Lebanese Christian churches ornately decorated with their characteristic icons. For example, St. Mary Church, of the Antiochan Orthodox rite, stands in Iron Mountain in Michigan's Upper Peninsula, a town with a population of about ten thousand. Church rituals and social life as well as kinship networks give cohesion to this community of descendents of Lebanese immigrants.

During the earlier years of immigration, Lebanese Christian clergy were often greeted with hostility by Roman Catholic priests of the Latin rite, since the former were permitted to marry. The Latin rite clergy gained control of the Eastern rite churches until Vatican II in the 1960s, when the pope gave all the Eastern rite Catholic groups in the United States the right to govern themselves according to their own disciplines. For example, the pope began to permit the patriarchate of the Melkite Church the right to nominate its own bishops.

Also in the aftermath of changes brought about by Vatican II, Bishop Francis Zayek from Lebanon became the first bishop of the Maronite Diocese of America in 1972. The United States was divided into two Maronite dioceses in the 1990s, with about fifty churches throughout the country. Following the dictates of Rome, Maronite priests in the United States are not allowed to marry. If a married priest comes from Lebanon, he is entitled to perform the rituals of the church but may not became a parish priest. At St. Maron Cathedral in Detroit, long the center of the single American Maronite diocese, the congregation is still largely of Lebanese descent, although Maronites from other parts of the Middle East also attend, as do converts who are mostly spouses of original members. One Mass is said in English, with the consecration being in Aramaic; the other is said in Arabic and Aramaic, while the sermons are always in English. Lebanese Christians have not tended to maintain the Arabic language in America. Aside from their strong inclination to assimilate, they also tended to use French in their homeland as a result of long-standing French influence, especially among Christians, in the region.

Even though the Maronites and the Melkites are affiliated with the Roman Catholic Church, there are differences in ritual practices, such as in the dispensing of sacraments. For example, the Maronites combine baptism and confirmation. The Melkites, while submerging a child in the baptismal font, also administer first communion and confirmation at the same time. Priests for the Eastern rite churches are still imported from the Middle East. However, the Melkites have opened seminaries in the United States, and even men of non-Arabic descent have become priests. In some areas, such as in Texas, Eastern rite churches are changing and expanding to reach beyond the traditional constituency.

Attempts to have children marry within the community have met with mixed results. In the early days, social networks, including traveling priests, were established to assist in matchmaking efforts to help ensure in-group marriages. In the first couple of generations the Maronites had been the most successful of all the groups in this regard. One of the net effects of this marriage pattern has been the perpetuation of the Middle Eastern-style patriarchal family structure. However, the pattern of marrying within the religious/ethnic background, even among the Maronites, appears to be breaking down and, no doubt, this will affect family structure. Melkites have been far less successful in marrying their offspring to other Melkites. Instead they tend to marry other Roman Catholics. This is probably due to the fact that the Melkites were viewed as so different from other Christians in America that they thought it to be to their advantage to change their rite and traditions to fit the Roman Catholic model. Melkites, then, were thrust into the ranks of Roman Catholic society. Although it is becoming increasingly common for Lebanese-American Christians to marry non-Lebanese Christians, it is still unusual for them to marry people from other Lebanese Christian groups (e.g., Melkites still do not marry Greek Orthodox).

Both the people and their priests consider it a great challenge to retain the interest of their young in their churches and religion. The problem is intensified by the fact that, in inner-city areas, parents prefer to see their children attend parochial schools, which are run by Roman Catholic churches. Either through necessity or preference, people enroll in the churches that are attached to the schools, thus detracting from the population of the Eastern Christian churches.

## Efforts at Political Organization

Although churches serve to create a sense of religio-ethnic cohesion, definitions of identity have been particularly narrow. Lebanese Christians have resisted using the term "Arab" to define themselves because "Arab" had become associated with "Muslim." While there are examples of Lebanese-American Christians and Muslims living harmoniously and cooperatively, such as when the émigré newspaper *Muraat al-Gharb* called for aid for all U.S. Syrian/Lebanese during the Great Depression, alliances between the groups have been fragile. For example, Lebanese Muslims and Christians of Quincy, Massachusetts, attempted to form a social club in 1931. However, a dispute broke out over

whether to use a flag with the cedars of Lebanon or not. The Christians, in favor of the French mandate forming the separate entity of Lebanon, as distinct from Syria, favored the term "Lebanese" and the cedars of Lebanon flag. The Muslims, seeing France and other European countries as interfering in the Arab world, disapproved of Lebanon's creation. Therefore, Christians today generally refer to themselves as Lebanese (or, more commonly, Lebanese Americans).

This situation changed somewhat after the 1967 Arab-Israeli Six-Day War. After this war there was an effort in the United States to unite the Arabic-speaking peoples to take a stand against the Israelis who had, during the war, taken a large amount of Arab land, leaving tens of thousands of Palestinian Arabs either homeless or under foreign occupation. Many Palestinian refugees fled to Lebanon, forcing the Lenanese to at least speak out against the State of Israel. There are organizations that reflect this Arab identity, such as the American-Arab Anti-Discrimination Committee, founded by Senator James G. Abourezk in 1980. Such unification efforts have been difficult to maintain, however, because the Lebanese Civil War, beginning in 1975, turned Palestinians and Maronites, among other groups, into bitter enemies.

While some organizations in America include both Christian and Muslim Lebanese, the divisions between not only Christians and Muslims but also among the various sectarian groups remain strong. Even in the small community of Lebanese/Syrian descendants of various denominations in Rhode Island, the Lebanese Maronites have not joined with the other groups in social, cultural, and philanthropic organizations but instead have formed their own organization, the Lebanese-American Club, in North Providence. On the other hand, people of various Arabic backgrounds did unite as an ethnic group in promoting the election of political figures during the 1960s. Still, the tendency has been factionalism rather than a united Arab-American effort. Jimmy Carter had a "Lebanese-American Committee" during his 1976 presidential campaign, but a broader-based "Arab-American" support group quickly failed. Actions taken by Lebanese Americans sympathetic to Phalangists, a militia consisting of certain factions of Maronites in Lebanon, led to the demise of this organization.

In 1982, during the invasion of Lebanon by Israel, there seemed to be hope that not only Lebanese of various persuasions, but Arab Americans in general, could become a united front for political action. However, efforts at unification had limited results, largely because Lebanese Phalangists were among those responsible for killing Palestinians in the refugee camps of Sabra and Shatilla outside Beirut. The alliance of some Lebanese Christian groups with the State of Israel has had negative repercussions for intergroup alliances with other Lebanese or with other Arab communities.

Lebanese Christians, though differing among groups, have tended to have a particular strategy for adapting to America while maintaining at least some of their unique identity. While the general ethos has been to assimilate into American society, church membership and activities, a strong preference for Lebanese-style food, and festive social gatherings have helped maintain a degree of cultural identity that might otherwise have been obliterated.

See also: LEBANESE MUSLIMS; SYRIANS

## Bibliography

Ahdab-Yehia, M. (1980). "The Detroit Maronite Community." In *Arabic-Speaking Communities in American Cities,* edited by B. C. Aswad. New York: Center for Migration Studies.

Bragdon, A. L. (1989). "Early Arabic-Speaking Immigrant Communities in Texas." *Arab Studies Quarterly* 11:83–101.

Doche, V. (1978). *Cedars by the Mississippi: The Lebanese Americans in the Twin Cities.* San Francisco: R&E Research Associates.

Gibran, J., and Gibran, K. (1991). *Kahlil Gibran: His Life and World.* New York: Interlink Books.

Gibran, K. (1994). *The Beloved: Reflections on the Path of the Heart,* trans. J. Walbridge. Ashland, OR: White Cloud Press.

Hagopian, E. C., and Paden, A., eds. (1969). *The Arab Americans: Studies in Assimilation.* Wilmette, IL: Medina University Press International.

Haiek, J. R., ed. (1975). *The American Arabic-Speaking Community 1975 Almanac.* Los Angeles: The News Circle.

Kayal, P. M. (1980). "Religion in the Christian "Syrian-American Community." In *Arabic-Speaking Communities in American Cities,* edited by B. C. Aswad. New York: Center for Migration Studies.

Naff, A. (1985). *Becoming American: The Early Arab Immigrant Experience.* Carbondale: Southern Illinois University Press.

Orfalea, G. (1988). *Before the Flames: A Quest for the History of Arab Americans.* Austin: University of Texas Press.

Orfalea, G. (1989). "Sifting the Ashes: Arab-American Activism During the 1982 Invasion of Lebanon." *Arab Studies Quarterly* 11:207–225.

Rizk, S. (1943). *Syrian Yankee.* Garden City, NY: Doubleday.

Smith, M. K. (1981). "The Arabic-Speaking Communities in Rhode Island: A Survey of the Syrian and Lebanese Communities in Rhode Island." In *Hidden Minorities: The Persistence of Ethnicity in American Life,* edited by J. H. Rollins. Lanham, MD: University Press of America.

LINDA S. WALBRIDGE

# LEBANESE MUSLIMS

Lebanese Muslims and their descendants constitute the largest group of nonindigenous Muslims in the United States. They are divided into Sunni Muslims, the majority Muslim sect in the world, and Shi'ite or Shi'i Muslims, or simply the Shi'a. Sometimes outsiders call them Metawala, but this is a derogatory term. Though the Shi'a constitute only about 10 percent of all of the world's Muslims, they far outnumber Sunnis in Lebanon.

After the death of the Prophet Muhammad in the seventh century C.E. in Arabia there was a dispute over leadership in the Muslim (or Islamic) community. The majority accepted the leadership of a close companion of the Prophet, Abu Bakr. After Abu Bakr's death, other companions of the Prophet assumed the role, either through appointment or election. Those who accept their leadership are known as Sunnis. Those who refer to themselves as Shi'a believe that the Prophet appointed his cousin and son-in-law, Ali ibn abi Talib, to succeed him and, after him, certain male descendants of Ali and his wife, the Prophet's daughter Fatima. The Shi'a believe that Abu Bakr and all subsequent Sunni leaders have been usurpers, and relations between Sunnis and Shi'a have generally been hostile.

The reasons why Shi'a outnumber Sunnis in Lebanon can be found in Lebanese geography and history. Over the centuries, persecuted religious minorities—Muslim and Christian—have fled to Mount Lebanon to escape their oppressors. Among those minorities were the Shi'a. Conflicts with neighboring religious communities led the Shi'a to move to other regions of what was then known as Syria, namely Jabal Amil (southern Lebanon) and the Bekaa, both of which are away from the coastal urban centers. Until the end of World War I this area was part of the Ottoman Empire. Under the French mandate following World War I the political boundaries of Lebanon were formed and the linking of religious sectarianism and political identity was solidified.

The Shi'a, while large in number, were the lowest-ranking of all religious groups in Lebanon. The Sunnis, on the other hand, dominant in the coastal cities of Beirut and Tripoli and surrounding villages, had access to the economic and social benefits of Lebanese urban life, as did many of their Christian neighbors. Lebanon's large Christian population benefited from close ties with certain European nations, even while under Ottoman rule. Lebanese Sunnis had the advantage of sharing the same religious affiliation with their Ottoman Turkish overlords, giving them a relatively privileged position in society. The Shi'a, on the other hand, had no advantageous connections and were in an inferior political and economic condition.

As the Ottoman Empire slowly collapsed, the pressures on the peoples of Lebanon/Syria became overpowering. Extreme poverty, overpopulation, famine, oppressive taxation, and fear of the conscription that almost invariably involved permanent removal from one's family and friends made life in the region unbearable for many. Since about 1880 Lebanese Christians had been immigrating to America. Fear of a hostile reception by American non-Muslims prevented most Sunni and Shi'a Muslims from doing the same. However, at the beginning of the twentieth century a small group of Muslims began to test the waters and traveled to America. Still, of the approximately thirty-nine thousand Syrian/Lebanese who entered the United States between 1909 and 1914, only about 10 percent were Muslim. Faced with mass starvation in the wake of World War I, Muslims had no choice but to emigrate if they were to survive. The United States was but one of their destinations.

## Settling in America

It is difficult to ascertain exactly how many Lebanese were among the early Muslim immigrants to America. One of the problems is that Lebanon was viewed as Greater Syria, and the people referred to themselves as Syrians. Adding to the confusion was the U.S. immigration practice of labeling these immigrants "Turks." Although the Lebanese/Syrian Muslim immigrants were Ottoman citizens, they were ethnically Arab, not Turkish.

Early Lebanese/Syrian Muslim immigrants were mostly men and frequently were illiterate or poorly educated. Following the example of their earlier Christian conationals, some took up peddling wares throughout the United States, ultimately collecting in such places as Ross, North Dakota, and Cedar Rapids, Iowa. However, Muslims were more likely to gravitate to industrial cities, including Detroit, Pittsburgh, and Michigan City, Indiana. While there were Islamic centers and standing buildings converted into mosques in most of these cities, Cedar Rapids has the distinction of being the first community to build from scratch a mosque with a minaret and dome, which it did in 1935. In the 1990s, Cedar Rapids had approximately two hundred Muslims from Arab backgrounds, many of them Lebanese.

In the first half of the twentieth century there were so few Muslims in the United States that differences between Sunni and Shi'a were minimized, though not completely obliterated; being Muslim in a Christian country was a sufficient unifying force. Also, the Lebanese Shi'a were not religiously sophisticated. The Lebanon from which they originated was a backwater area of the Shi'a world. Their clerics, the *ulama,* have been described as "obscurant, timid, and conservative," emphasizing incredible stories of superhuman feats of Shi'a heroes. Also, the Shi'a before the 1960s practiced *taqiyya* (dissimulation) for fear of persecution by Sunnis. Lebanese Shi'a in the early days of their arrival to the United States lacked political consciousness and were accustomed to hiding their unique rituals and beliefs from Sunnis. Therefore, joining with Sunnis in shared Islamic holidays and customs was not difficult. Furthermore, they saw it as being in their best interest to assimilate into American society, so that obvious markers of Islamic identity, let alone Shi'a identity, were eliminated or de-emphasized. All of the early Muslim communities, including Highland Park, Michigan; Des Moines, Iowa; and Ross, North Dakota, had a large proportion of Lebanese Muslims.

## Developments in the Community

A Sunni-Shi'a split began to occur in the 1960s. While it did not affect all Muslims in America, it was very conspicuous in Dearborn, Michigan, the home of the largest Arab Muslim community in the United States. Immigrants from all over the world have been drawn to this town, which borders on Detroit, through kinship networks and by the opportunities for employment at the huge Ford River Rouge plant. Until the 1960s, the Lebanese Shi'a in Dearborn shared their religious life, and a mosque, with not only Lebanese Sunnis but also Muslims from other parts of the world. However, in the 1960s, encouraged by the

efforts of a Lebanese cleric, the Lebanese Shi'a of the Dearborn-Detroit area built their own mosque just over the border from Dearborn, in Detroit. Although the trend was to differentiate themselves religiously from non-Shi'a, they still appeared assimilated in American society. For example, in the 1960s and much of the 1970s, women did not cover their hair, either inside or outside the mosques. Parties and weddings were held in the mosques, something unheard of in the Middle East. Also, the most elaborate Shi'a rituals were not carried out in the mosques.

Changes in the U.S. Muslim community have been and continue to be reflections of events in the Middle East. During the 1960s, an *alim* (religious cleric) named Musa Sadr had gone to Lebanon to teach the Shi'a about their religion and to elevate their position in society, causing a religious awakening among the Shi'a.

Even more dramatic, though, were changes in the late 1970s and 1980s. The Lebanese Civil War starting in 1975, the Iranian Revolution of 1979, and the invasion of Shi'a areas of Lebanon by Israel in 1982 had effects in America. The largest wave of Lebanese immigrants were escaping warfare in their country. Between 1975 and 1985, approximately thirty-nine thousand entered the United States. Thousands of them arrived from the parts of southern Lenanon predominantly populated by Shi'a and now controlled by Israel. Fighting among Shi'a factions and bombings by Israel also have caused Shi'a to flee the Bekaa region.

Although not highly educated, this later wave of immigrants, arriving often as families, have been relatively successful economically, their entrepreneurial skills serving them very well. Religious fervor in Lebanon, encouraged by the success of the Iranian Revolution, continued to increase through the 1980s. Lebanese Shi'a concentration in particular American cities such as Dearborn and Toledo, Ohio, and the Lebanese Muslims' economic prosperity have drawn new clerics to the United States. These clerics have been trained in the holy cities of Qom in Iran and An Najaf in Iraq. The tendency has been for the clerics to expect increasing conformity with Islamic law and to emphasize those aspects of the religion peculiar to Shi'ism. The Lebanese Shi'a do not have a uniform opinion about how strictly they should adhere to religious laws. The community consists of people who are as religiously observant as ultra-Orthodox Jews and as lax in attention to religious laws as Reform Jews.

Sunni Lebanese, numbering far fewer than Shi'a, have generally joined with other ethnic groups in forming religious communities. Among the Sunnis coming from Lebanon are Palestinians, who, though they may have spent their entire lives in Lebanon, do not consider themselves Lebanese.

## Intergenerational Problems

There have been pronounced tensions between assimilated first-wave immigrants and their children, on the one hand, and second-wave immigrants, on the other. The religious and cultural practices of the later immigrants, who far outnumber the earlier immigrants and their descendants, have been sources of continued friction. Earlier immigrants had largely assimilated into American society. Even in Dearborn, where there was an early Sunni-Shi'a split, the Shi'a were not encouraged to appear conspicuous or to be alienated from their neighbors. Most of these people spoke English — if not always in the home, then certainly in public.

The immigrants of the 1970s and 1980s, on the other hand, left Lebanon under duress, and with no burning desire to become Americans. Maintaining their Arabic language and customs is of paramount concern, as is perpetuating religion in their children's lives. The old wave of immigrants complain that the newcomers confuse religion and Lebanese life.

The children arriving in this most recent wave of immigration were raised in conditions of warfare. Aside from the trauma many of them experienced, they also did not come with the multilingual backgrounds that so characterized Lebanese education prior to the outbreak of civil war. This group of children has been raised almost exclusively with Arabic and have required ESL

(English as a second language) classes. Once they master enough English, they tend to do well in school, as the general attitude of Lebanese parents toward education is positive. However, parents prefer that their children go into practical and lucrative fields rather than studying the humanities or social sciences. While many girls are still expected to marry young, increasing numbers of parents are eager for their daughters to at least go through high school and, increasingly, through college. It is not uncommon to find a family in which an older sister married in her midteens and a younger one has waited to marry until she has finished college. A limited number of occupations are seen as acceptable for women, however. The ones usually cited are education, pharmacy, and medical technology.

## Community Life

Family bonds in Lebanon are very strong. Although the Lebanese Shi'a complain that loyalties are breaking down among them in America, this is difficult to discern from the outside. Sons and daughters remain at home with their families until marriage, if not later. When an unmarried son is employed, he will generally turn the money earned over to his parents, frequently the mother, as it is often she who manages the household finances. Families regularly pool capital, employ relatives, jointly start businesses, or buy real estate for rental, so that individuals who arrive in the United States virtually penniless often prosper within a few years.

As in Lebanon, marriages remain a family affair. Young people who are interested in marriage do not talk about falling in love; rather, they want to find someone who is suited to them. Practical considerations are foremost. Marriage within a family is still valued, so that parents might arrange for a relative to come to the United States to marry a son or daughter. Not surprisingly, offspring of marriageable age sometimes protest this arrangement. Many young people who have grown up in the United States do not wish for their parents to interfere in choosing a partner for them. However, this is certainly not a universal sentiment. Children raised in a strong religious environment and who are eager to sustain their religious beliefs are likely to defer to their parents' opinions. However, even less religious young people may prefer the traditional style of arranging a marriage because they wish to maintain family sodidarity, the most important basis of their culture. Young people who form romantic alliances outside the religious/ethnic community are generally compelled to break off such relationships and marry within the group.

Social life revolves around family. Family visiting is the most common form of entertainment. During these visits, refreshments are continually served. During the earlier wave of immigration, Islamic proscriptions against alcohol were breaking down. The religious revivalism that has affected the later wave of immigrants has reversed this pattern. Lebanese Muslims may own liquor stores, but liquor is rarely found in their homes.

Weddings are the most important social functions of the community. However, most Lebanese weddings are the equivalent of an American wedding reception and are held at a rented hall. The actual contract between the man and the woman is generally signed at the time the couple becomes engaged. The engagement is a binding agreement in which matters of the dowry (in Islam, the man pays the bride a designated amount) are clearly established. While the engagement may be a public affair, it is not as lavish as the wedding, at which perhaps hundreds of guests attend. Live music, traditional dancing, and dinner always constitute the program. However, the most religious members in the community object to such events. They believe that vibrant music and dancing are un-Islamic and so opt for quiet weddings, often at local mosques.

While an educated and fairly assimilated minority of Lebanese Muslims join national organizations such as the Arab-American Association or the Islamic Society of North America, it is uncommon for the more recent immigrants to become involved in activities outside the family and, perhaps, the local mosque. Their being Shi'a rather than Sunni also places them in the position of being different from the majority of Arabs and other Muslims and subject to prejudice, especially by organizations influenced by Saudi Wahhabis.

Lebanese Muslims are rarely involved in local politics, though they do understand that such involvement is important. In Lebanon they were not accustomed to participating in political and social activities outside their own group. Also, they are generally busy making a living. Men, who are generally the breadwinners in the family, tend to work long hours to support their families. The other reason that they are not involved in activities of the larger society has to do with attitudes toward them by the non-Muslims who surround them. Since they come from a part of the world that is generally portrayed in negative terms by the media, and since many of them adhere to Islamic dress codes, speak Arabic, and have customs alien to the larger culture, they are ridiculed and insulted. Therefore, they avoid contact with outsiders except when doing business.

In large communities the Lebanese Muslims are largely self-sufficient and able to enjoy many of the aspects of the life they had in Lebanon, including Lebanese-owned shops and restaurants. In areas with large concentrations of Arabs, such as southeastern Michigan, cable television plays an important part of Lebanese-Muslim life, as there are programs in Arabic, many of which come directly from Lebanon. Members of families either singly or as a group return to Lebanon as frequently as possible, and, not uncommonly, people continue to purchase land in Lebanon. All of these factors help maintain strong ties to the home country. Because of these ties and because Muslims tend to congregate in neighborhoods in cities, they are able to preserve their culture and religious life to a considerable degree. Children are urged to speak Arabic in the home and to remember that they are Lebanese (or Arab) and Muslim. While accommodation to American society is occurring largely because Lebanese tend to own businesses that often do business with Americans, assimilation is not evident. However, the children of immigrants raised in the United States refer to themselves as "Arab Americans" and are strongly affected by American culture, although many of them still wish to maintain their Arabic and Islamic identities.

*See also:*   LEBANESE CHRISTIANS; SYRIANS

## Bibliography

Abraham, S., Abraham, N., and Aswad, B. (1983). The Southend: "An Arab Muslim Working-Class Community." In *Arabs in the New World: Studies on Arab-American Communities*, edited by S. Y. Abraham and N. Abraham. Detroit: Center for Urban Studies, Wayne State University.

Abu-Laban, S. McI. (1991). "Family and Religion Among Muslim Immigrants and Their Descendants." In *Muslim Families in North America*, edited by E. H. Waugh, S. Abu-Laban, and R. B. Qureshi. Edmonton: University of Alberta Press.

Ajami, F. (1986). *The Vanished Imam: Musa Al Sadr and the Shi'a of Lebanon*. Ithaca, NY: Cornell University Press.

Aswad, B. (1991). "Yemeni and Lebanese Muslim Immigrant Women in Michigan." In *Muslim Families in North America*, edited by E. H. Waugh, S. Abu-Laban, and R. B. Qureshi. Edmonton: University of Alberta Press.

Eisenlohr. C. J. (1988). "The Dilemma of Adolescent Arab Girls in an American High School." Ph.D. diss., University of Michigan.

Haddad, Y., and Lummis, A. T. (1987). *Islamic Values in the United States*. New York: Oxford University Press.

Naff, A. (1985). *Becoming American: The Early Arab Immigrant Experience*. Carbondale: Southern Illinois University Press.

Norton, A. R. (1987). *Amal and the Shi'a: Struggle for the Soul of Lebanon*. Austin: University of Texas Press.

Orfalea, G. (1988). *Before the Flames: A Quest for the History of Arab Americans*. Austin: University of Texas Press.

Walbridge, L. S. (1994). "The Shi'a Mosques and Their Congregations in Dearborn." In *Muslim Communities in North America*, edited by Y. Y. Haddad and J. I. Smith. Albany: State University of New York Press.

Walbridge, L. S. (1996). *Without Forgetting the Imam*. Detroit: Wayne State University Press.

Wigle, L. D. (1980). "An Arab Muslim Community in Michigan." In *Arabic-Speaking Communities in American Cities*, edited by B. C. Aswad. New York: Center for Migration Studies.

LINDA S. WALBRIDGE

# LITHUANIANS

Although records exist of Lithuanians in the United States prior to the Civil War, their numbers were small and their presence left no lasting impact on the ethnic landscape of the country. Lithuanians began arriving in the United States as a significant immigrant group in the latter half of the 1860s. This wave of immigration reached a peak in the second decade of the twentieth century and continued until the Immigration Act of 1924 essentially stemmed the flow. During this sixty-year period, Lithuanians in America established vibrant communities incorporating religous, economic, social, and political activities. These communities served as the core for the second and third waves of Lithuanian immigration—those arriving after World War II and those arriving after the reestablishment of Lithuanian independence in 1990. Thus the picture of Lithuanians in America is a fairly complex one. Being "Lithuanian" has different meanings, depending on the wave of immigration to which one can trace ancestry.

## History

The motivations for emigration from Lithuania to start the first significant wave were many, but the ultimate reasons were economic. Both the United States and Europe were in the midst of the Industrial Revolution, which, while creating new opportunities for work, also created massive shifts in population. For Lithuanians the more immediate effect was the abolition of serfdom by imperial Russia in 1861. Prior to this, the Lithuanian serf was essentially bound to the land, with little freedom of movement, and was under the control of the landowner. Under these conditions the serfs' social mobility was limited. Serf status was marked by use of the Lithuanian language, while that of the landowner was marked by use of Polish or Russian. Schooling was nearly impossible, since the serf was tied to demands of farming.

Thus the abolition of serfdom gave the former serf a measure of self-determination, but it also brought many hardships. In the ensuing land reform, the former serfs tended to receive the poorest arable land, often in plots too small to be economically productive. Managerial skills were likewise limited among the former serfs after two hundred years of bondage. Land fragmentation through inheritance created further pressures on the newly freed serfs. Land plots, small to begin with, often reached the limits of productivity. Under these conditions new patterns of inheritance emerged in which only one of the offspring would inherit the land in its entirety, often "buying out" the other siblings, thus freeing more peasants from the land and creating more seekers of economic opportunity. Finally, many young Lithuanian men opted to leave their homeland rather than face being drafted into the Russian Army.

All this created an emigration whose early trickle in the late 1860s grew to a virtual tidal wave by 1900. For the early immigrants, conditions in America were especially severe. Generally lacking education and skills, they had to accept what work was available. Since these early immigrants tended to be young, single men, they joined railroad construction crews. Later, as the young men married, they pursued a more stable lifestyle, most often in Pennsylvania, in the coal mining industry. An important consequence of this shift in occupations was the establishment of Lithuanian communities. Lithuanians sought out one another as a means of social adaptation to the new life. Voluntary associations for burial insurance, for sickness benefits, and for education were the first to be established. From these, religious associations arose to help in building churches. Parishes then created schools, which themselves became the foci of other ethnically based activities. Thus,

true communities emerged that determined the shape of ethnicity for succeeding generations.

The earliest of such communities were in the southern anthracite coal region of Pennsylvania and included Shenandoah, Shamokin, and Mount Carmel. Toward the end of the nineteenth century, northern communities were established, the most significant in the Scranton and Wilkes-Barre area. In this way, Pennsylvania became the "capital" of Lithuanians in America in the early part of immigration.

Although railroads and coal mines provided initial opportunities for the early immigrants, manufacturing offered safer and more secure work. Communities grew where opportunities were most favorable. In the New England states, communities such as Boston, Worcester, Lowell, Waterbury, and New Britain were based on various forms of textile and leather manufacturing. In western Pennsylvania, Pittsburgh drew Lithuanians for its bituminous coal mines and its then growing steel industry. Other communities were established westward along the principal trading routes of America; Cleveland, Detroit, Cincinnati, Dayton, and Grand Rapids all housed sizable numbers of Lithuanians. By far the most important of these western centers was Chicago, where fourteen thousand Lithuanians had already settled by 1900. The number and scope of voluntary associations were proportionately high. In addition to the types mentioned above, which were found in most Lithuanian communities, Chicago offered societies that catered to specific interests such as theater production, militarism, and politics. By the turn of the century Chicago had become the foremost center of Lithuanian cultural activity, replacing the Pennsylvania anthracite region. Even today Chicago has the greatest concentration of Lithuanians outside Lithuania.

The massive flow of Lithuanians into America was slowed by World War I and effectively stopped by the National Origins Act of 1924. Second- and third-generation Lithuanians became the core of the established communities, and assimilation pressures put a significant strain on their survival. Educational advancements allowed for greater

A baker arranges loaves of rye bread in a Lithuanian bakery in Pittsburgh in 1943. (Library of Congress/ Corbis)

social and physical mobility, and core communities began experiencing shrinkage.

The end of World War II brought the onset of the second major wave of Lithuanian immigration into the United States. The major distinction between the first and the second waves was in motivation. The first wave tended to be economic immigrants. Post–World War II immigrants were refugees fleeing what they belived to be a future of oppression from the invading Soviet Union. Many fled Lithuania with the express purpose of organizing resistance to Soviet occupation. At the end of the war these refugees were repatriated to various nations, but the majority, about thirty thousand, were admitted to the United States as displaced persons (DPs). To be admitted, the DPs had to have sponsors willing to guarantee their livelihood, which Lithuanians already in America readily agreed to do. Thus in the initial period of this repatriation, DPs settled wherever there were existing communities—that is, where their spon-

sors lived. Soon, however, DPs tended to gravitate to larger communities, leaving the smaller ones to continue the process of assimilation. Notably, small Pennsylvania mining communities such as Forest City and Mahanoy City, which at one time were centers of intense Lithuanian activity, continued dissipating.

The reasons for DPs avoiding permanent settlement in smaller, established communities is not difficult to ascertain. This was a sociologically different set of Lithuanians. Whereas the first wave tended to be of peasant background, the DPs tended to be middle to upper-middle class. They tended to be well educated, and had held professional positions in prewar Lithuania. Thus they faced a wholly different set of circumstances than earlier immigrants. They were not forced to follow the labor market. They had the freedom of geographic mobility. Coupled with the desire to work for the liberation of their homeland, DPs congregated in larger cities with existing Lithuanian communities, where they could find others of like thinking. The largest number ultimately settled in Chicago, but New York, Boston, Baltimore, Philadelphia, Cleveland, and Detroit also drew substantial numbers. Some smaller cities such as Rochester, New York; Worcester, Massachusetts; Waterbury, Connecticut; and Elizabeth, New Jersey, attracted proportionately smaller numbers.

The creation of voluntary associations is an important step in the adaptation process of any immigrant community. First-wave Lithuanians set a top priority for the establishment of churches and other local associations, religious and otherwise. The focus of the associations was community service to the new immigrants, who exhibited a far different approach. Because of their overriding desire to return to the homeland, the subsequent need to maintain language, customs, and political consciousness, and because of the generally small and dispersed nature of this population, the primary emphasis was in the establishment of intercommunity associations rather than locally oriented societies. No new churches were built by the newcomers, for example, and likewise few locally oriented associations were organized.

Where the need existed for local associational benefits, the new immigrants joined already established groups. Thus the DPs were connected to each other not only through personal, familial, and local associational ties, but also via a vast network of national and even internatonal relationships. Those who chose to maintain their Lithuanian DP identity could opt to belong to a number of associations, each having local, regional, and national activities that brought together Lithuanians from all parts, serving to integrate this wave of immigrants in a manner not generally available to the original group. Herein lies the essential difference between the two waves: First wave Lithuanian immigrant ethnicity tended to be locally oriented, while post–World War II Lithuanian immigrant ethnicity included national and international as well as local ties. For the early immigrant, Lithuanian identity was determined largely by local circumstance. For the DP, Lithuanian identity was predetermined; its basis rested on language, and through language the knowledge of Lithuanian culture. Thus the DPs almost immediately established ethnic schools to promote the language, and national organizations to reinforce cultural association.

Whether this difference in associational orientation gave the latter group an edge in maintaining ethnic identity is problematic. Associational activity continues, and language schools ("Saturday schools") are still in operation, at least in the larger communities. But even here the pressures of assimilation are apparent. Members of adult-oriented associations tend to be in older-age categories. Youth-oriented associations are declining in enrollment, as are enrollments in the Saturday schools. The language of use in these youth organizations is shifting gradually from Lithuanian to English. Even in the Saturday schools, Lithuanian is beginning to be taught as a foreign language, not as the primary one. In effect, the same patterns of assimilative change seem to be affecting the second wave of Lithuanians in America as they did the first.

The heightened freedom of movement allowed to Lithuanians before and after the restoration of Lithuanian independence in 1990 has again increased the flow of new immigrants to the United States. Little is known about the social characteristics of these new arrivals. They seem to be economically oriented in the same category as the first wave of immigrants, thus putting themselves somewhat at odds with the second wave of immigrants. But the numbers are still comparatively few, and it remains to be seen whether they will have a significant impact on the Lithuanian-American ethnic landscape.

## Factionalism

Lithuanian communities in America are complex entities. In addition to differentiations due to the time of arrival, further factionalism centered on conflicts over language, religion, and ideology, reflecting similar developments in the native country. The shape of Lithuanian-American communities was in large part determined by the resolution of these conflicts.

Conflict over language has to do with the historical circumstances of Lithuanians in Europe. Lithuania was created as a medieval state in the thirteenth century by bringing together tribes of Baltic-speaking peoples. As the state expanded, it incorporated an ever larger proportion of non-Lithuanian-speakers. Lithuanian rulers readily accepted non-Lithuanian cultural patterns as a helpful method of maintaining social and political order. Grand Duke Algirdas, for example, accepted orthodoxy, married into Slavic families, and used Slavic languages in official state documents. While this tolerance of non-Lithuanian influences certainly helped to establish Lithuanian hegemony, it also had the ultimate effect of relegating Lithuanian culture and language to the lower social strata of the nation. During the period of alliance and union between Lithuania and Poland, the upper classes in Lithuania avoided the Lithuanian language and associated cultural characteristics. A "high culture/low culture" situation developed, with Polish preferred for the upper classes.

The period of Russian imperial occupation of Lithuania (1795–1918) futher complicated the issue of identity. Resistance to the occupation was generally led by Polish-speaking nobility and by the Catholic Church, likewise dominated by Polish-speaking clerics. Thus, for some Lithuanians, Polish was not only the language of the "high culture" but also was the language of resistance. At the same time, Lithuanian-language ascendancy was fueled by the fires of nationalism then sweeping Europe. Lithuanians began seeing use of the language not as a liability but as a source of cultural pride. Tensions between proponents of the two approaches to language use were considerable. Immigrants to America reflected these tensions. Early communities often were divided along Polonophile/nationalist lines. A case in point is the oldest Lithuanian church in America, St. Casimir's in Shenandoah, Pennsylvania. It was built by Lithuanians and staffed by a Lithuanian missionary. After three years, the missionary left. As is the norm in the Catholic Church, a replacement was named by the bishop of the diocese. This priest was Polish. When he refused to conduct services in Lithuanian, a group of Lithuanians blocked his way to the church in July 1877. The new pastor called the police. A number of Lithuanians were arrested, and in the ensuing trial it was discovered that the deed did indeed list St. Casimir's as a Polish church. Apparently local authorities who drew up the deed did not distinguish Lithuanians from Poles. Lithuanians themselves were for the most part illiterate and not sophisticated enough to note this obvious mistake. Polonophile Lithuanians favored the use of Polish in the liturgy and supported the Polish pastor, thus creating strong fractures in the community. Ultimately the Lithuanian faction split from St. Casimir's and established another wholly Lithuanian parish, St. George's.

Other communities experienced similar tensions, at least in the early years of their formation. Most of the disputes centered on control of religious property and liturgy, as it did in the Shenandoah case. In effect, people had to choose their identity. The exact number of those who chose either Polish identity or who believed in Polish-Lithuanian institutional unity will probably never be known. But it was large enough to support a separate newspaper, *Saule*, which ceased publication only in 1959, and it was strong enough in the early days of immigration to mount serious challenges to emergent Lithuanian nationalism.

The religious institution provided a source of both comfort and tension. Most Lithuanians are Catholic, and the new immigrants of the first wave sought security and guidance from the Catholic Church. Church construction was a high priority for any sizable new community; churches provided for spiritual needs, for meeting places, and especially for "culture brokers" in the form of educated priests to help them in their adaptations. However, the very structure of the Catholic Church also engendered a degree of factionalism. The Catholic hierarchy provided no support for building churches. Immigrant communities had to provide all the funds for such construction. Yet church rules required that new buildings be deeded to the diocese before parishes be assigned priests. Many in the communities objected to such a procedure. They argued that control over church properties should rest with those who financed their construction. An extension of this argument was that parishioners should choose parish priests. Yet, once the deeds were signed over, parishioners effectively lost all official control over parish operations. Disaffection in immigrant communities over such issues was compounded by the fact that in the late nineteenth century the church hierarchy consisted primarily of persons of Irish origin. Some believed that many of the official church directives had at their base an attempt to disenfranchise Lithuanians as an ethnic group. This led to further divisions. Some Lithuanians chose to remain loyal Catholics, supporting the church in all its decisions; some became secularized and even anti-Catholic; while others, under the influence of nationalism, opted to create independent churches. Most of these nationalistic religious groups ultimately merged with their counterparts among Polish Americans in the Polish National Catholic Church. At the height of this activity, about 1930, there were thirteen such Lithuanian parishes. This had fallen to only two active parishes by the 1990s.

Protestantism was never a dominant force in Lithuanian religious life. The initial successes of Protestantism in the early days of the Reformation were blunted by the effectiveness of the Counter-Reformation in Lithuania. Thus the number of Protestant Lithuanians in America is small and their institutions are limited.

Ideology is yet another source of factionalism among Lithuanians in America. In general these differences mirrored those found in the mother country. Among the first wave, for example, the two emergent forces of nationalism and socialism interacted within the boundaries of the immigrant communities to create numerous organizations to which Lithuanians could devote their allegiance. Even the religious community was torn within its own ranks by dissension between those who wanted to blend Catholicism with nationalism and those who believed that Catholicism superseded all other ideologies. Susivienijimas Lietuviu Amerikoje (Association of Lithuanians in America) and Lietuviu Romo Kataliku Susivienijimas Amerikoje (Lithuanian Roman Catholic Association in America) are cases in point. In 1886, the first attempt to unite the many existing local associations in the scattered immigrant communities in the United States centered on Susivienijimas Visu Lietuvininku Amerikoje (Association of All Lithuanians in America). Its organizers were a group of nationalists called *ausrininkai* (dawnists). But its basic weakness was that it did not have the support of the Lithuanian clergy, who believed that the leaders of this new association were essentially anticlerics. This spurred the Catholic faction to organize an association of its own, Susivienijimas Visu Draugystiu Katalikisku Lietuvisku Amerikoje (Association of All Catholic Lithuanian Societies in America). The first association failed. While the second attempted to placate some of the fears of members by renaming itself Susivienijimas Lietuviu Amerikoje (Association of Lithuanians in America), basic tensions remained. It became polarized into the Catholic faction, which was thought to be ruled by despotic clerics by the other side, and the nationalist freethinkers, who in turn were thought to be atheists by the Catholics. In 1901, these tensions led to a hostile split, resulting in two separate associations. After a long court battle, the nationalists were allowed to keep the name and some of the symbols of the former association, while the clerical faction retained most of its financial assets and renamed itself Susivienymas Lietuviu Rymu Kataliku Amerikoje (Association of Lithuanian Roman Catholics in America). While the latter association's unity was to preclude further internal upheavals, the former, composed now of those who would not or could not belong to the Catholic association, underwent yet another severe ideological battle. This centered around the rise of socialism.

At the beginning of the twentieth century, socialists formed a relatively small proportion of the total number of Lithuanians in America, yet they found a fertile ground for recruitment among the working class. Their insistence on the overthrow of the Czarist regime in Lithuania coincided with feelings of nationalism prevalent in Lithuanian communities. Indeed, the first Lithuanian-American socialists were nationalists. After the failed 1905 uprising in Lithuania, internationalist socialists immigrated to America, where they gradually replaced the nationalists in existing organizations. In 1919, the prime socialist association, Lietuviu Socialistu Sajunga (Lithuanian Socialist Alliance), allied itself to the Communist movement in the United States. Thus in one stroke the socialists were now connected with the Communists through the Lithuanian Communist Alliance, which in turn was tied to the Communist Party of America. Internationalist ideology was formalized, especially the belief that class ties superseded all nationalist ties. In 1930, in Chicago, the Communists attempted an organizational coup of the Association of Lithuanians in America. It failed, but the Communist elements pulled out of the organization, founding the Lithuanian Workers' Alliance, and drew three thousand members away from the original association.

This process of separation at the national level was simply a mirror of conditions locally. There, especially in larger cities, parallel institutions appeared in the areas of mutual assistance, schools, choirs, and the like. It was not uncommon to find, for example, three "social halls" in the larger communities: the church hall; the nationalist hall; and the Communist, or "progressive" hall. This ideological diversity strained the communities financially and socially. With the establishment of Lithuanian independence in 1918, the strains between the church faction and the nationalist faction abated. At the same time, however, the international orientation of the Communists during the independence period further isolated them from both other ideologies, and hence from the majority of Lithuanians in America.

After 130 years, the strongest surviving institution formed by the first-wave Lithuanian immigrants is the Catholic Church. Many of the parishes have been closed or transformed to nonethnic status. Nevertheless, those that remain continue to be centers of Lithuanian activity. The nationalist associations, on the other hand, have experienced a long period of decline. The Association of Lithuanians in America continues to operate, but at a much diminished level, with the membership aging and not being replaced by younger generations. This is more pronounced for the Communist-oriented associations, which are now nearly extinct.

However, while the social associations of the first wave of immigrants have been generally in decline, the ideologies have not; both nationalism and the church received a strong boost from the Lithuanians America received after World War II under the Displaced Persons Act of 1948. These displaced persons were sociologically very different from their first-wave counterparts and exhibited a different pattern of adaptation. First, they were not economic immigrants but political repatriates, with the immediate goal of returning to a freed homeland. Second, they tended to be educated, propertied, and in positions of power in Lithuania before the war. In a word, they were middle class. In America they mostly avoided small cities with a substantial manufacturing base, common settlement points of economic immigrants of the first wave. After an initial dispersion due to requirements of sponsorship, which the first-wave immigrant communities generously provided, they concentrated in larger communities, where middle-class opportunities were greater. Thus, cities such as Chicago, New York, Detroit, Boston, and Cleveland saw substantial increases in their Lithuanian populations. Small communities, on the other hand, did not benefit from their numbers. With the exception of Philadelphia, few post–World War II immigrants settled in Pennsylvania, which was often considered the center of Lithuanian activity for the first wave of immigrants.

Even in the larger cities, the DPs established their own unique associational ties, focused on maintaining Lietuvybe (a Lithuanian national consciousness). These associations were for the most part intercommunity based. They transcended local affiliations and local ties. Some were politically based, such as Vyriausias Lietuvos Islaisvinimo Komitetas (Supreme Committee for Lithuanian Independence). Others were more socially oriented, such as Lietuviu Bendruomene (Lithuanian Community). Still others focused on the socialization of the young, such as the Lithuanian Scouting Association and Ateitininkai (Futurists). Intracommunity associations geared specifically to the DPs were relatively few. Most DPs joined already existing local groups fostered by the first-wave community. No new Catholic church building has been constructed by the DP communities.

Thus, those who choose to manifest their Lithuanian DP identity may belong to a number of different organizations, each having local, regional, and national gatherings. Since the fall of the Soviet Union and the reestablishment of the independent Lithuanian state, even associational ties with the homeland are now possible.

Although the overlay of national ethnic ties beyond the local community has given the DPs a hedge against the pressures of assimilation, they are not immune. Ethnically homogamous marriages, once the focal point of the maintenance of Lietuvybe, have substantially declined. Language and culture classes, so-called Saturday schools, now incorporate the teaching of Lithuanian as a second language to the young. The use of Lithuanian as the vernacular language in church services has also declined.

These trends toward greater assimilation into American culture may be offset somewhat by the arrival of more immigrants from Lithuania since the reestablishment of independence in 1990. If they continue the patterns set by the two previous immigration waves, they should join the local communities and invigorate their ethnic character. It is simply much too early, however, to make such conjectures.

## Demographics

The question of the total number of Lithuanians in the United States is difficult to answer. As the historical overview indicates, there have been a number of migratory periods, each of which has been subjected to the assimilative pressures characteristic of all ethnic groups in the United States. The question becomes, in effect, one of ethnic identification. Are third- and fourth-generation descendants of immigrants who arrived in 1870 just as much "Lithuanian" as the children of those who arrived in 1950? The latter would probably say no; the former would most likely say yes. The U.S. Bureau of the Census solves this problem by simple self-ascription. In this method, a person is assigned a given identity if that identity appears either solely or in combination with another.

Using the above criterion, the 1990 U.S. Census shows 526,089 persons claiming Lithuanian ancestry in the United States. Most tend to be concentrated in the urban centers of the Northeast, the Midwest, and California. Southern areas of the United States were traditionally avoided by Lithuanians. However, the warmer climate has attracted substantial retirees, and new ethnic communities have arisen in Arkansas, Arizona, and especially Florida.

Of the total number of Lithuanians in the United States, 34,523 as foreign-born. Most of this number were presumably born in Lithuania. Of these foreign-born, 2,142 entered the United States between 1980 and 1990. The majority of these immigrants arrived in the latter half of the decade, when controls on physical mobility in the former Soviet Union were somewhat relaxed.

This newest group of immigrants follows the general pattern of economic immigrant sex ratio, with 56 percent of the new arrivals being male. They are a well-educated group, with 58 percent of them holding bachelor degrees or higher. This probably accounts for the fact that their income level surpasses that of all other categories of Lithuanians in America, with a per capita income of $28,089, comparecd to $22,507 for U.S.-born Lithuanians, and $25,549 for Lithuanian imigrants arriving in the United States before 1980. Thus, while this group can be labeled economic immigrants, their characteristics set them apart from the first wave of economic immigrants, who tended to have low educational levels and who thus occupied low-paying, low-status jobs. Yet they also differ from the refugees of the post–World War II wave who, although also well educated, tended to occupy lower-status positions, partially as a result of poor language preparation.

## Assimilation and Cultural Retention

Like most other European ethnic groups, Lithuanians in America are exposed to substantial assimilative pressures from the greater society. While first- and second-generation immigrants tend to maintain significant associational ties, third- and fourth-generation descendants tend to lose the cultural markers that identify ethnicity. For Lithuanians, one of the most important of these markers is knowledge of the language. First-wave immigrants were able to promote language use through sheer masses in their communities and by establishment of language schools for children. However, as the educational level of the immigrant communities increased, so did both social and physical mobility. As these third- and fourth-generation members moved, language schools faced ever-increasing difficulties, having fewer students and fewer teachers competent and willing to teach. Social and physical mobility also was a prime cause in increasing rates of ethnically heterogeneous marriages, which in turn placed further pressures on language maintenance. Over time, the ethnic vitality of the early communities has all but disappeared. As mentioned earlier, all that remains in many of the numerous communities scattered throughout the eastern United States is often the church building. And even here the parishioners may be of different groups, reflecting more recent sources of immigration.

This process also seems to be operating with the post–World War II immigrants. In a study conducted in the mid-1970s of the Los Angeles refugee community, more than half of all Lithuanian marriages were ethnically mixed. The same study noted that the use of language as an identity marker was deemphasized over the years. In short, the refugee population seems to be succumbing to the same assimilation effects as did the first wave.

All this is not to say that Lithuanian ethnicity has disappeared. Organizational activity in both populations continues. The church remains a focal point of ethnic awareness and activity. Well over one hundred churches still operate as ethnic parishes. Most larger communities continue to maintain parishes in which Lithuanian-language services are offered. The Knights of Lithuania, one of the oldest Lithuanian associations and one whose activity played important roles in the restoration of Lithuanian independence in both 1918 and 1990, provides an opportunity for those whose language skills in Lithuanian may be minimal. Associations organized by the post–World War II immigrants continue to operate, albeit in a changed mode. The ethnic press continues to publish both periodicals and books. In the early 1980s there were two daily, three weekly, three biweekly, and three monthly newspapers. In the same period twenty-three academic and specialized periodicals were published.

With the restoration of independence, there has been an increase in the free flow of information from Lithuania. This, along with the growing number of postindependence immigrants, may have the same effect on Lithuanian communities as the post–World War II immigrants had on the first wave, a revitalization of ethnicity and ethnic behavior.

## Bibliography

Baskauskas, L. (1985). *An Urban Enclave: Lithuanian Refugees in Los Angeles.* New York: AMS Press.

Budreckis, A. (1976). *The Lithuanians in America, 1651–1975.* Dobbs Ferry, NY: Oceana.

Fainhauz, D. (1991). *Lithuanians in the USA.* Chicago: Lithuanian Library Press.

Gedmintas, A. (1989). *An Interesting Bit of Identity: The Dynamics of Ethnic Identity in a Lithuanian-American Community.* New York: AMS Press.

Gerutis, A., ed. (1969). *Lithuania: 700 Years.* New York: Manyland Books.

Green, V. (1975). *For God and Country: The Rise of Polish and Lithuanian Ethnic Consciousness in America.* Madison: State Historical Society of Wisconsin.

Jonitis, P. P. (1985). *The Acculturation of the Lithuanians of Chester, Pennsylvania.* New York: AMS Press.

Kucas, A. (1975). *Lithuanians in America.* Boston: Lithuanian Encyclopedia Press.

Suziedelis, S., ed. (1970–1978). *Encyclopedia Lituanica.* Boston: Lithuanian Encyclopedia Press.

Van Reenan, A. (1990). *Lithuanian Diaspora.* Lanham, MD: University Press of America.

Wolkovich-Valkavicius, W. (1991). *Lithuanian Religious Life in America.* West Bridgewater, MA: Corporate Fulfillment Systems.

ALEKSANDRAS GEDMINTAS

# MACEDONIANS

"Macedonian" is a geographically based identity correlating to an ancient civil and military state in the strategic region of the central Balkans. This was the realm of Alexander the Great, which has never fully regained an autonomy it lost to Rome in 164 B.C.E. Slavic tribes dispossessed the original inhabitants in the sixth and seventh centuries C.E., assuming the territorial designation. They settled into a feudal peasant society that came under manipulation by diverse groups and nations who pressed for their integration into foreign spheres of influence. The Ottoman Turks gained ultimate control of the Balkans at the end of the fourteenth century and held sway in Macedonia into the early twentieth century. Macedonians were largely unmoved by nationalist developments that roused their Serbian, Greek, and Bulgarian neighbors, groups more easily self-defined and externally sanctioned as nations and contestants for Macedonian territory and identity. This history circumscribes Macedonian settlement in North America, where they emerge as an indeterminate if not invisible people despite their substantial population (estimated 140,000 foreign-born and 250,000 American-born). They use this public imperception to their advantage to the extent that it is a major element of their ethnicity.

## Migrant to Immigrant

Migration emerged as the Macedonian peasant's primary means of modifying intolerable economic and sociopolitical pressures imposed by external nation-states. A limited regional process of migration known as *pechalba* exploded with extension to North America in the late nineteenth century. Males, most of whom were between sixteen and forty-five years of age and unskilled, left their villages in droves to join a foreign wage-labor economy. They subordinated themselves and their society to a circular pattern of temporary labor abroad, usually three years, and equally temporary leisure at home. Migrants could take advantage of the host society without needlessly committing themselves, their families, their identities, or their scant resources to the vacillating demands of a foreign society where they had no control.

A wave of more politically indoctrinated émigrés followed in the wake of the abortive Ilinden Uprising of 1903, a Bulgarian-incited rebellion against Turkish control of Macedonia. Turkish reprisals forced flight to North America, mostly from the heavily hit southwestern region near Kostur and Lerin. Reliable figures place the number of Macedonians in North America by 1908 at fifty thousand—economic migrants and political refugees alike. Their major center was Granite City, Illinois, and other towns surrounding St. Louis, Missouri, where some ten thousand worked in the rolling mills and foundries. Others labored on the railroads, in the meat-packing houses of Chicago and Toronto, and in the burgeoning automobile industry in Detroit. They found jobs in the coal fields and steel foundries of Pennsylvania and western New York as well as in the industrial cities of Indiana and Ohio.

The dream of the political partisans to foster a second Ilinden Uprising ended abruptly. The 1912–1913 Balkan Wars drove the Turks out of the Balkans and unceremonially divided Macedonia as spoils among Greece, Serbia, and Bulgaria. World War I sanctified this division, with Bulgaria losing large portions of its new Macedonian domain to Greece and Serbia in retaliation for allying with Germany. As Bulgaria's command of Macedonian territory in the Balkans diminished, its control of Macedonian identity in North America increased.

The Bulgarian Orthodox Synod sent a mission in 1907 to preserve religious and nationalist aims among émigrés against the encroachment of Greek, Serbian, and American Protestant institutions. The mission formed its first core of churches in Granite City in 1907; in Steelton, Pennsylvania, in 1908; in Toronto in 1910; and in Indianapolis, Indiana, in 1915. A second surge of church construction began in the 1920s and continued for the next two decades as enclaves institutionalized around Bulgarian parishes and language schools. Bulgaria effectively secured the allegiance of Macedonian expatriates by sanctioning a new church-enclave identity: Macedono-Bulgarian. This identity, introduced as official policy in 1918 to safeguard Bulgaria's interests in North America during World War I, also served to define and consolidate a new Macedonian immigrant identity after the war ended.

## Immigrant Culture

The Johnson-Reed Act of 1924 severely restricted alien entry into the United States, although Canada remained a backdoor entrance, especially at the Windsor-Detroit corridor. Macedonians funneled into the auto industry, and Detroit emerged as the largest Macedonian immigrant hub before World War II, with a population of seven thousand. A scarcity of jobs during the Great Depression forced many migrants to return to the Balkans. Approximately twenty thousand resolved to remain as immigrants and repatriated their families to ethnic national enclaves. There they could find ready mechanisms of adaptation and support in a world of dwindling resources. The enclave provided a market for entrepreneurs who established restaurants, groceries, butcher shops, and bakeries for an available ethnic clientele. The businesses in turn furnished jobs to a captive labor supply, at low wages but with access to a fund of knowledge on how to operate in the host society.

Some Macedonian immigrants elected to identify with Serbians and Greeks where that offered the best return and easiest entrance into the appropriate enclave communities. The majority joined Bulgarian enclaves and accepted a Bulgarian-mitigated identity. Macedono-Bulgarian enclaves provided Macedonians with a stable ethnic and national identity but could not protect them from complications at home and abroad. The postwar Bulgarian state became increasingly reactionary, imposing restrictions on the Macedonian minority in its midst and in the diaspora. This brought the émigrés and their associations into friction with the state's political messages. The primary immigrant association was the Macedonian Political Organization (MPO), created in October 1922 in Fort Wayne, Indiana. It had chapters in all Macedonian centers, catered to by a newspaper founded in 1927, *Makedonska Tribuna* (Macedonian Tribune), which published in Bulgarian. The MPO sought Macedonian autonomy in concert with Bulgarian interests, forging an uneasy alliance with a state it could not restrain and policies it did not always endorse.

The MPO leadership's selective strategy of appeasing the Bulgarian state brought it into open conflict with extremists within its midst. In 1928, these radicals left the MPO and formed the Macedonian People's League with their vision of an independent Macedonia within a Balkan Soviet Union. During World War II, the league emerged as the key Macedonian organization, as the MPO had excessively identified with Bulgaria, which had joined the Nazi cause. The Macedonian People's League dissolved in 1948 when branded a Communist-front organization at the outset of the Cold War. The MPO revived, but its pro-Bulgarian perspective became increasingly vulnerable in a changing world. On the losing side in both world wars, Bulgaria went astray again in the postwar period when it became not only avowedly Communist but stubbornly Stalinist as well. Macedono-Bulgarian identity lost its vitality in America as a result. It would be shattered by a postwar influx of Greek and Yugoslav-Macedonian immigrants who were less amenable to a singularly Bulgarian version of Macedonian identity.

## Greek Option

In contrast to the political incompetency of Bulgaria, Greece fared better in the postwar world. It emerged as a staunch Western ally and celebrated defender of democracy, first against the Nazis and then against the Communists. The Greek Civil War of 1946—1949 divided Greece between Western-supported forces and those sanctioned by the Soviet Union and satellite regimes in Yugoslavia and Bulgaria. The Communists promised Macedonia its independence, gaining them the favor of Macedonians throughout the world, including the MPO. The Communists lost the war, however, forcing many Macedonians to flee Greece for the neighboring states of Yugoslavia and Bulgaria. It also led to a rush of emigrants seeking permanent salvation in North America.

The enhanced status of the Greek state allowed Greek immigrant institutions greater host society sanction to co-opt Macedonian identity, made easier because of Bulgarian failures. The MPO's support of Bulgaria during World War II and the Greek Civil War resulted in its harassment by American authorities, who questioned its political motives. The MPO timidly reemerged in 1952 under the less odious title of the Macedonian Patriotic Organization, emphasizing its Macedonian identity, opposition to communism, and loyalty to American ideals. The organization remains powerful but conservative and married to an untenable vision of Macedonia in Bulgarian times.

Macedonian emigration from northern Greece increased dramatically after the Civil War, incited by a state only too glad to be rid of a troublesome minority. Although the actual numbers are hard to divine, an approximate population of seventy-five thousand Greek Macedonians entered North America as whole villages were evacuated. In the Detroit area alone it resulted in a postwar Macedonian population of thirty thousand. This glut of people might have added to the old Macedono-Bulgarian institutional order or to a new Greek-Macedonian enclave identity. Instead, it resulted in a deemphasis on national identities and related ethnic community structures.

Entering as Greek nationals, the new immigrants could not be Greeks according to the stringent doctrine of the Greek state and its ethnic representatives in North America. Neither could they identify openly with the Bulgarian-Macedonian community, which was dangerously "Red" by implication. Any untoward involvement with Bulgarian institutions might draw the undue attention of American officials or interfere with the emigration or life chances of family members left behind in Greece. Such were the obstacles that many found it easier to enter Canada, where in Toronto, they established the largest Macedonian immigrant settlement (more than 100,000). Macedonians in North America increasingly had to learn when it was safe to be Macedonian and safer to be Greek, Bulgarian, or even Yugoslav.

## Yugoslav Option

In 1944, the Macedonian People's Republic emerged as part of the Yugoslav Federation. This substate, a fragment of Macedonia proper, advanced an unprecedented Macedonian national identity, supported for the first time with a literate language (able to be read and written), Orthodox church, and a general cultural, media, and educational system. Large-scale Yugoslav-Macedonian immigration did not begin until the early 1960s, and eventually forty thousand immigrated to North America imbued with a nationalist vision and the sanction of the only state — Yugoslavia — recognizing "Macedonian" as a legitimate designation. Bulgaria had deemphasized Macedonian, insisting on a generic Slavic or precise Bulgarian identity via such state-sponsored associations as the Slav Committee or the later Committee for Bulgarians Abroad. Greece, represented by the Pan-Macedonian Association, pressed a Hellenic definition of Macedonian and denied the existence of a Slavic minority in its midst, admitting only to "Slavophones" — Slavic-speaking Greeks.

The Yugoslav Macedonian Republic became the only consistent purveyor of a Macedonian national identity. Operating through the Matica for Macedonians Abroad, it established Yugoslav-Macedonian churches and language schools in all areas of Macedonian settlement in North America. These institutions competed with Bulgarian and Greek churches, language schools, and expatriate organizations and had the advantage of promoting a singular Macedonian identity that caught the attention of both the immigrant community and the host society. Yet, just as many Macedonians appeared ready to commit to this new public stance, it dissolved within their grasp with the breakup of the Yugoslav state.

The Macedonian nation that rose from the debris of Yugoslavia gained its autonomy in 1991 and little else. It was accepted into the United Nations, after long and rancorous debate, not as "Macedonia" but under the obscure title of "The Former Yugoslav Republic of Macedonia." Because of opposition, it was the first member whose flag was not ceremonially raised and flown outside U.N. headquarters. It remains uncertain whether this small, poor state can survive the animosity of its neighbors. In contrast, the immigrant community is far more affluent and resilient at a time when foreign states do not offer reliable patronage for Macedonian identity.

## Subgroup Identity

The anarchic complexity of postwar sociopolitical conditions served to divide the extranational loyalties of Macedonians in North America. This led them into dangerous public confrontations over identities they could not control. The old national enclaves and identity structures broke under the impact, unsalvageable with revised models of the nation (or a little nation in enclave resident). Although many people still pursue a Macedonian national course, others have accommodated to adjacent ethnic communities and identities — Greek, Bulgarian, or Serbian, or identities as disparate as Hungarian and Czech. The majority withdrew from the public forum of the nation-state and ethnic group and turned their efforts toward private options that they could more readily control.

The inadequacy of the nation has been replaced by the powerful metaphor of the village (*selo*) in the old country (*stari kri*). This new symbol is a mechanism of exclusive and inclusive identity in a world where dangerous identities abound. It reforms a face-to-face community in back-to-back North America. This subgroup identity is based on an extended corporate household and a bilateral kinship model couched in village idiom and creating a unit of recruitment, finance, and socioeconomic mobility.

Each subgroup unit creates its own symbolic and interactionist sense of being Macedonian in North America that does not measurably interfere with other subgroups. It brings together politically incompatible individuals into an agreeable alliance, creating a homogeneity of membership without the need to access national ideologies. It provides a system each member can control and define free from the imposed conditions of nations that degrade their identity and minimize their existence.

North American Macedonian identity is now often more consistently expressed in archaic village terms (e.g., Prekopantsi, those from the village of Prekopanna) than national or ethnic typologies. This allows placement as *nashi* (ours) versus *ne se nashi* (not one of ours, one who does not have integrative knowledge of the multiplex relationships of the subgroup). Individuals who do not fit the model receive national designations such as Amerikantsi (Americans), Ghertsi (Greeks), or even Makedontsi (Macedonians). These are pejorative labels recognizing those without valid subgroup connections and likely to be dangerous.

## Women's Roles

When males left on their migratory excursions, they abandoned their villages, demarcated roles, and the font of kinship to female management. Women responded by modifying the strict patrilineal kinship model and inserting elements of the matrilineal model to create a bilateral kinship system. When women followed the men to North America they entered with command of the kinship system and its implicative power that they did not relinquish to the men. They used this social monopoly to restructure and maintain the village subgroups when states began to lose their legitimacy. The women keep the subgroup values, implant its oral dialect to the children, and establish its resident culture. The women prepare the ritual food items and minister to the dead at funerals and ancestor worship ceremonies, invigorating kinship obligations among the living. Through their command of kinship and the subgroup, Macedonian women were able to gain more equality and power than normally allowed by male-dominated ethnic institutions.

What the subgroup could not supply, Macedonian women found in host institutions, having quickly learned the dominant language and customs of American society. This was in contrast to the more restricted experiences of other Balkan and Mediterranean women. Despite integration into American society, in-group marriage (endogamy) is high among Macedonians. They do not condone marriage to Amerikantsi, a synonym for social irresponsibilty. Even Greeks, enemies on a national level, can be acceptable marriage partners to Macedonians. Also admissible are those from communities with a similar peasant value system respecting hard work, property accumulation, and family, such as Italians. The most valuable marriage partner is another Macedonian, one who will willingly accept the standards of the subgroup and will not disrupt its social, economic, or linguistic order.

## Linguistic Diversity

Macedonians speak a South Slavic language akin to Bulgarian and Serbo-Croatian. In North America such a statement becomes arbitrary, as there is no longer any simple linguistic correlation to nationalism. Many in the community speak Greek exclusively and see themselves justifiably as Macedonian; others speak Slavic and refuse to call themselves anything except Greek. This paradox can be explained by Macedonian retention of a dual or multiplex linguistic structure.

Linguistically, Macedonian is an oral tradition. It is the dialect of the village, learned from parents and grandparents. Its use in America continues to be unconditional, nurturing, and limited to the informal needs of the subgroup. Although original words have vanished (unnecessary in a foreign urban environment), the dialect mode remains as a sanction of subgroup membership. Macedonian is not dissolving into transitional forms, an indication of loss, anymore than the use of literate forms is an indication of ethnic strength. With the increased use of English loanwords and grammatical transferences, new dialects emerge that sustain Macedonian subgroup identity.

The strength of the oral tradition is balanced by an often capricious literate language. Sociopolitical developments define the literate form, which may emerge as Serbian Macedonian, Bulgarian, Greek, myriad other languages, or a combination thereof. In America English has become the primary literate form, the linguistic mate to oral Macedonian. Literate languages do not define a single Macedonian identity (if they ever did), but they do add to a repertoire of identities.

## Situational Identity

In North America, Macedonians no longer have a direct link to national identities not otherwise amended by forces beyond their ability to control. This is not to deny national correlations. Rather, they become aspects of public presentations allowing a portrayal as Greek, Bulgarian, Serbian (Yugoslav), or others, without the impediments. Ethnic nationals, after all, do not "own" their identities but "borrow" them from the state or lease them from state-based immigrant institutions. Macedonians borrow identity without having to acknowledge states or associated institutions. They need only approximate identity within a given situation of limited function. When Macedonians took the lead in the restaurant industry in Detroit and Toronto, they retained Greek identity over the counter to manage the occupation and not upset the fixed perspective of their host society customers.

The audience for Macedonian identity has decreased. If recognized by host society members it is as a remnant of already sanctioned national categories—the same as or opposite to—but rarely as a category unto itself. This paradox allows Macedonians to manipulate the rules of overt identity. It permits them to move between identities with remarkable ease, needing only to supply data adequate to the public situation and the needs of circumstance. Their polyglot capacity, acquired through varied migration experiences and imposed national options, adds to their situational skill in impersonating others. In a world that has chaotically destroyed their primary public identity, the number of identities they may access has increased while the requirements for support have decreased, allowing them a greater series of quasi-identities.

## Conclusion

External ethnic boundaries no longer adequately define Macedonians or their social reality. A group seemingly on the verge of breakdown, they are no less cohesive because of conflicts over their identities and national distinctions. Issues that divide the group are also issues that sustain personal ethnic boundaries. They strengthen the attachment of each member, family, and subgroup to a personal vision of Macedonian identity. Public conventions protect a singular private concept of Macedonian that cannot be readily threatened by outsiders, even fellow Macedonians. This is the ultimate definition of Macedonian, of existence despite external pressures and imposed conventions. It is an identity that is more likely to survive in North America than in Macedonia itself.

*See also:* BULGARIANS; GREEKS; SERBS

## Bibliography

Abbott, G. (1909). "The Bulgarians of Chicago." *Charities and the Commons* 21:653–660.

Brailsford, H. N. (1906). *Macedonia: Its Races and Their Future.* London: Methuen.

Bulgarian Academy of Sciences. (1978). *Macedonia: Documents and Material.* Sofia: Author.

Christowe, S. (1976). *The Eagle and the Stork.* New York: Harper's Magazine Press.

Herman, H. V. (1978). *Men in White Aprons.* Toronto: Peter Martin.

Jelavich, B. (1983). *History of the Balkans.* New York: Cambridge University Press.

Petroff, L. (1994). *Sojourners and Settlers: The Macedonian Community in Toronto.* Toronto: University of Toronto Press.

Sakelliariou, M. B., ed. (1983). *Macedonia: Four Thousand Years of Greek History and Civilization.* Athens: Ekdotike Athenon.

Vasiliadis, P. (1989). *Whose Are You? Identity and Ethnicity Among the Toronto Macedonians.* New York: AMS Press.

Wilkinson, H. R. (1951). *Maps and Politics: A Review of the Ethnographic Cartography of Macedonia.* Liverpool: Liverpool University Press.

PETER VASILIADIS

# MAHARASHTRIANS

The ethnic group identified by the name "Maharashtrian" in North America is similarly identified in India, the nation-state of its origin. Maharashtrians are residents of the state of Maharashtra in western India. While the majority speaks Marathi, the state's official language, many residents of the state speak other Indian and foreign languages. Despite the presence of such minority linguistic groups, the terms "Marathi-speakers" and "Maharashtrians" are generally treated as synonymous. During British rule in India Maharashtrians were also referred to as "Marathas" or "Marattas" by the British administrators and were so called in other regions of India. In Maharashtra itself the term "Maratha" refers to a caste cluster.

## Historical Background

Maharashtra is the most industrialized state in India, with Bombay (renamed Mumbai, a Marathi name, in the 1990s) as its capital. According to the 1991 Indian Census the population of the state is seventy-nine million. The 1991 figure for Marathi-speakers is not available, but taking into account annual population growth and the 1981 Indian Census figure for Marathi-speakers, it can be estimated that Marathi is spoken by more than sixty million people and that Marathi-speakers constitute almost 80 percent of the population of the state.

The cultural and historical tradition of Maharashtrians is rich and old. The region was inhabited almost three thousand years ago, and many Hindu and Buddhist kings ruled the region during the ancient and classical periods. Buddhist caves and monuments scattered throughout Maharashtra indicate that Buddhism was brought to Maharashtra by Emperor Ashoka in 300 B.C.E. Many temples were built by the various Hindu dynasties that ruled the region during the first eleven centuries C.E. Maharashtra was periodically ruled by various Muslim dynasties, including the sultanates and the Moguls, for the following five centuries.

In the middle of the seventeenth century, there arose a local political movement of Hindu resistance to Muslim rule that eventually resulted into the establishment of what is called the Maratha kingdom. Shivaji Bhosale, the initial leader of this movement, was crowned in 1674 as king of the Marathas. In the systematic expansion of his rule, Shivaji built many forts throughout Maharashtra. (There are more forts in Maharashtra than in any other region of India.) The Maratha kingdom lasted 150 years and at its peak ruled most of India and brought the Moguls and other Muslim rulers under control. The city of Pune, eighty miles east-southeast of Bombay, was the capital of the Maratha kingdom. The political power of the Maratha kingdom diminished toward the end of eighteenth century as the British gradually brought all of India under their control.

## Marathi Literature

The Marathi literary tradition goes back to the thirteenth century, during which many religious, philosophical, and biographical texts in prose and verse were written by the Mahanubhavas, a religious sect. Then followed Hindu devotional literature by Maharashtrian saint-poets, among whom Dnyaneshwar is the best known for his *Bhāvārth Dipikā* or *Dnyāneshwarī*, a commentary on the Sanskrit religious and philosophical text *Bhagavad Gītā*. Dnyaneshwar was followed by other saint-poets such as Namdev, Eknath, Janabai, Chokhamela, Tukaram, and Ramdas, who composed devotional poetry in the meter form *abhanga* in praise of the Hindu Maharashtrian deity popularly known as Viṭṭhal. These saints established the most popular Hindu religious sect in Maharashtra, the Vārkarī Panth, centered around the temple of Viṭṭhal in the town of Pandharpur. This devotional literature touched the hearts of the masses because the saints preached equality in the worship of God and protested against the existing rigid caste system characteristic of Hinduism.

During the reign of the Maratha kingdom evolved the popular folk genres of *povāḍā* (ballad) and *lāvṇī* (poetic composition of love), which became major entertainment for the masses. The ballads eulogized the conquests of the Maratha rulers, describing the various battles they fought. The lāvnī literature, on the other hand, focused on the erotic aspects of love. There emerged a folk performance genre known as *tamāshā* (entertainment). Tamāshā performers were touring groups of singers and dancers who used both the povādā and lāvnī compositions in their dancing, singing, and comedy, the latter being woven around the themes of the childhood antics of the epic hero Krishna and *gopīs* (milkmaids) of his birthplace, Vrindavan. Tamāshā continues to be a popular entertainment form for the masses.

Much of the literature in the pre-British period was religious in orientation except the ballads. With British rule firmly established in India there began to develop nonreligious Marathi literature in the second half of the nineteenth century, first through translations of various literary works in English and later by way of independent works in literary genres such as the novel, short story, essay, play, travelogue, biography, and autobiography. At present, Marathi literature is rich, diverse, and extremely popular.

## Maharashtrians in North America

Since Maharashtrians do not constitute a separate entry in the United States and Canadian censuses, but are subsumed under the category "Asian Indians," their exact number is difficult to determine, and only a rough approximation can be made. According to the estimate provided by Brihan Maharashtra Mandal, a North American umbrella organization of Maharashtrians, there are between thirty to forty thousand Maharashtrians in North America. There were very few Maharashtrians in North America before 1950. Their number increased substantially during and after the

Participants in the Indian Independence Day celebrations in San Francisco include the Maharashtra Mandal float, which depicts the crowning of Shivaji, the founder of the Maratha kingdom. (Maharashtra Mandal – Bay Area)

1960s because of liberal immigration policies in the United States and Canada.

*Settlement Patterns and Religious Background.* Maharashtrians are scattered in all regions of the United States and Canada and generally are concentrated in major cities such as New York, Chicago, Los Angeles, San Francisco, Toronto, Vancouver, Dallas, Houston, Washington, D.C., and Atlanta. A small number of families also live in midsize cities and towns. The largest concentration of Maharashtrians is in the New York–New Jersey area, followed by Chicago and vicinity.

Maharashtrains are a highly educated ethnic group. Most men and women have college and/or university degrees, either from India or from North America. Many arrived in North America as students of higher education and after receiving their degrees decided to remain rather than return to India. Many then brought over members of their immediate and extended families, taking advantage of the liberal immigration policies. More recently, however, the inflow of Maharashtrians to North America has slowed due to increasing immigration restrictions.

Maharashtrian men and women are in such diverse professions as medicine, engineering, computer programming, architecture, higher education (especially the natural science disciplines in universities), business consulting, plant and corporate management, investment and banking, research in medicine and natural sciences, chartered accounting, federal and state employment, and insurance. Many work for big corporations in various capacities such as chemists, technicians, pharmacologists, and hardware and software experts. Quite a few have their own business, wholesale and retail, in such areas as clothing, design, electronics, restaurants, and export-import. By some estimates engineering is the profession in which a high number of Maharashtrians are engaged.

*Religion.* The majority of Maharashtrians in North America are Hindus, although there are Christian, Muslim, and Jain Maharashtrians. There is considerable variation in the religious practices of Hindu Maharashtrians, and many tend to be nonorthodox and reformist. However, most celebrate the major Hindu festivals, which they consider to be part of the Maharashtrian culture. Along with other Hindu Indians, Marharashtrians provide financial and other kinds of support for construction and maintenance of Hindu temples in major cities in North America. Many cultural activities are centered around temples or other worship centers, which also serve as community centers for all Indians.

*Marriage, Family, and Kinship.* Arranged marriage is the norm among Maharashtrians, though there is a growing trend toward love marriages. Maharashtrians generally prefer to marry other Maharashtrians of their own caste, although the number of intercaste, interregional, and North American–Maharashtrian marriages is increasing. Maharashtrians are ambivalent about mixed marriages.

A common practice among unmarried men and women is to convey their desire to be married to their parents, who either place matrimonial advertisements in various English- and Marathi-language newspapers and magazines in North America and Maharashtra, or spread the news through their social network. Matrimonial advertisements invite correspondence, with photographs from parents of eligible young men and women, and after some preliminary negotiations, a meeting between prospective bride and groom is arranged. If they like and approve of each other and if other negotiations work out, a marriage is planned.

Married men tend to arrive in North America by themselves at first and bring over their wives and children once they are settled in suitable jobs, although a later trend is for both husband and wife to arrive together. While it is difficult to know with any degree of accuracy the rate of divorce, it is increasing among Maharashtrians. Most Maharashtrian families are nuclear, although one or both grandparents, who generally live in India, often make long visits in North America. Maharashtrians in North America also make frequent trips to India for holidays and to visit their parents and other relatives.

## Cultural Activities

*Voluntary Organizations.* Maharashtrians are anxious to maintain their cultural heritage, and they have undertaken a variety of cultural activities. In major North American cities there are voluntary organizations, usually called Maharashtra Mandal (Maharashtra Association), which plan numerous activities such as lectures, plays, annual picnics, and celebrations of Hindu festivals. These organizations have a formal structure, and officers are elected at regular intervals. There is an annual membership subscription, and donations are always welcome. The general practice for organizing an event is to hire an auditorium at a local high school and send invitations to members. Refreshments are served at every cultural event. A directory of Maharashtrians, published in 1995 by the Brihan Maharashtra Mandal, listed forty-three associations of Maharashtrians throughout North America.

The first convention of Mahrashtrians in North America was held in 1980 in Chicago under the auspicies of the Brihan Maharashtra Mandal. Conventions are held biennially, during the July Fourth weekend. These meetings provide a unique opportunity for Maharashtrians to exchange ideas concerning various issues facing them. The planning of the meeting is handled by a local committee in cooperation with the national committee. The chief guest and keynote speaker is generally a prominent political leader or a literary figure from the home state in India. The convention lasts three days and includes several panels, workshops, speeches, competitions for the younger generation, and numerous entertainment programs, including a full-length play, musical performances, and individual talent shows. The convention also serves as a venue for contact and cooperation among Maharashtrian businesses from India and North America. Attendance at these meetings increased steadily and reached more than 3,000 in 1995, resulting in an imposed upper limit of thirty-five hundred for the 1997 convention. Those wishing to participate in the convention are encouraged to register as early as possible.

A youth organization specifically aimed at first-generation Maharashtrian young men and women and called Maharashtrian Association of Indian Youth Together Representing America (MAIYTRA) was established in 1993 and also has biennial conventions.

In 1978, the Maharashtra Foundation, a charitable organization, was established by a Maharashtrian, Yashwant Kanitkar. Its principal aim is to provide financial support for worthwhile social and economic projects in Maharashtra and neighboring states in India. For example, it has provided support for village improvement, education, medical assistance to village communities, and protection of the environment in rural areas. It gave $500,000 to the victims of an earthquake in Maharashtra in 1993. The foundation also donates to ongoing projects in the United States. It has three categories of membership: patrons, who pay $1,000 for life membership; life members, who pay $500; and subscribing members, who pay an annual subscription of $20. The foundation publishes an annual newsletter, which lists members and money disbursed to various projects.

*Theater.* Maharashtrians take a great interest in theater. The modern theatrical tradition in Maharashtra is about 150 years old. Contemporary Marathi theater in India is varied, controversial, vigorous, and very popular. It has many manifestations, such as folk theater, children's theater, historical theater, and Dalit theater ("theater of the downtrodden," a term of self-reference used by the untouchables in Maharashtra). Humor is one of its most significant attributes, and Marathi comedies are extremely popular.

Maharashtrians in North America miss participation in Marathi theater back home and compensate in various ways. A popular activity of the voluntary organizations, especially those in big cities with a large concentration of Maharashtrians, is the production of one-act and/or full plays. When such performances are successful, they are taken on the road on weekends for a few additional shows in nearby cities and states, depending on the enthusiasm and spare time available to those involved. Local Maharashtrian organizations enthusiatically provide financial and other kinds of support for these performances. The first Marathi plays in North America were produced in the New York–New Jersey area and the Chicago vicinity in 1972 and have since become an annual event. Since 1988, plays are produced annually in the Chicago area. All involved in these productions do so in their spare time, since all hold a full-time job. From time to time theater groups from Maharashtra are invited to tour North America to perform the most popular plays. The most anticipated event at the biennial convention of Marathi-speakers in North America is the play performance. In June and December 1995, Kalābhavan, an amateur theater group from Philadelphia, went on a tour in Maharashtra to perform a folk drama.

*Music.* Maharashtrians are very fond of Indian music, especially North Indian classical music. The Maharashtrian tradition of classical music is rich, with many past and present well-known musicians. The most popular singers and dancers frequently tour North America and give concerts in major cities. Many first-generation boys and girls learn classical music and visit India for additional training. Raga Mala Performing Arts of Canada, founded by Jagannath Wani, a Maharashtrian professor at the University of Calgary, organizes tours of Indian classical musicians and dancers to North America and has published a yearly magazine called *Bansuri* (Flute) since 1984. It also holds an annual competition for a scholarship award of $2,000 to students of Indian vocal or instrumental classical music, classical dance, or theory and/or history of Indian music or dance.

*Literary and Journalistic Activities.* A major part of maintaining cultural identity is the dissemination of news from the home region in India and provision of opportunities for the creative literary talent of individuals in the immigrant population. The first goal has been fulfilled by the successful operation of a monthly newsletter, *Brihan Maharashtra Vritta* (Greater Maharashtra Newsletter), printed in the Devanagari script in which the Marathi language is written. It began publication in January 1981 in Chicago. Originally it was handwritten and was distributed free to those who wanted it. Now it is computer-produced, and there is an annual subscription of $15 in the United States and $18 in Canada. A significant portion of the newsletter is devoted to political and cultural news in Maharashtra. Articles on social and cultural issues as well as news items of local activities of numerous Maharashtrian organizations also appear. The editorial board is selected on a rotating basis, and the offices generally move to the city of the editor. A special annual issue on the occasion of the Festival of Lights is published in November. It includes literary contributions by Maharashtrian authors in North America.

A Marathi quarterly literary magazine, *Ekata* (Unity), devoted to both fiction and nonfiction, began publication in 1978. It provides an opportunity for the creative talents of Maharashtrians in North America. Each issue has several short stories, essays, travelogues, and articles on social and cultural issues relevant to the lives of Maharashtrians in North America. The annual subscription is $15. Some publishers in Maharashtra have published novels, short-story collections, autobiographical experiences and life stories of Maharashtrian writers in North America.

In 1993, Sunil Deshmukh, a Maharashtrian from America, established an endowment for annual literary prizes to the best works written in Marathi in such major literary genres as the novel, short story collection, play, autobiography, essay, literary criticism, and sociopolitical commentary. Two committees were established, one in Maharashtra and the other in North America, to evaluate all literary publications for the final selection.

## Conclusion

Maharashtrians in North America are a vibrant community. While many have become American citizens and participate in many mainstream activities, they also are anxious to maintain their cultural traditions and pass them on to the next generation. The various activities described in this entry indicate their determination in this endeavor.

*See also:* JAINS

## Bibliography

Apte, M. L. (1976). "The Political Novel in Marathi." *Contribution to Asian Studies* 6:75–85.

Apte, M. L. (1992). *Humor and Communication in Contemporary Marathi Theater.* Pune, India: Linguistic Society of India.

Basham, A. L. (1954). *The Wonder That Was India.* New York: Macmillan.

Fisher, M. P. (1980). *The Indians of New York City.* New Delhi: Heritage.

Gargi, B. (1966). "Tamasha." In *Folk Theater of India,* edited by B. Gargi. Seattle: University of Washington Press.

Gordon, S. (1987). *The Marathas, 1600–1818.* New York: Cambridge University Press.

Jenson, J. M. (1988). *Passage from India: Asian Indian Immigrants in North America.* New Haven, CT: Yale University Press.

Joshi, S., ed. (1982). *Shivaji and Facets of Marathi Culture.* Bombay: Marg.

Ministry of Information and Broadcasting, Research and Reference Division. (1993). *India: A Reference Manual.* New Delhi: Ministry of Information and Broadcasting, Publication Division.

Raeside, I. (1968). "Early Prose Fiction in Marathi, 1828–1885." *Journal of Asian Studies* 27:791–808.

Saran, P., and Eames, E., eds. (1980). *The New Ethnics: The Case of East Indians.* New York: Praeger.

Schulberg, L. (1968). *Historic India.* New York: Time-Life Books.

Zelliot, E. (1982). "Marathi: An Historical View of the Maharashtrian Intellectual and Social Change." In *South Asian Intellectuals and Social Change,* edited by Y. K. Malik. Columbia, MO: South Asia Books.

Zelliot, E., and Engblom, P., eds. (1982). "A Marathi Sampler: Varied Voices in Contemporary Marathi Short Stories and Poetry." *Journal of South Asian Literature* 17 (full issue).

MAHADEV APTE

## MALAYALAM SPEAKERS

Among the many communities who have immigrated to North America from various parts of India are Malayalam speakers from the state of Kerala. It was estimated in 1991 that there were 34 million Malayalam speakers worldwide, of whom 22 million lived within India. Kerala, with a population of 29 million in 1992, is one of India's smaller, more scenic states and is its most densely populated. It was formed in 1956 following the reorganization of India (after the country became independent in 1947) along linguistic lines. Kerala incorporates areas in southwestern India where Malayalam, a language derived primarily from Sanskrit and Tamil, is spoken by a majority. Kerala borders the states of Karnataka to the northeast and Tamil Nadu to the east.

Immigrants from Kerala and/or those whose mother tongue is Malayalam are referred to as either Keralites or Malayalees. While an intriguing and interesting group, Malayalees are rarely treated as a distinct community in research on and analyses of American immigrant cultures. This may be because Asian Indians themselves have only been recognized as a separate U.S. Census classification since 1980 and because Malayalees comprise a small proportion (approximately 10%) of that larger group. The Asian Indian community was estimated by the U.S. Census as 387,223 in 1980; 525,600 in 1985; and 815,000 in 1990. Malayalees, like many other Asian Indians, are a somewhat new group of immigrants to the United States. They are also, like many others from the Eastern Hemisphere, beneficiaries of the Immigration and Nationality Act of 1965, which ended an earlier system based on national quotas. The 1965 act focused on job skills needed in the United States and the reunification of family members as criteria in awarding immigration visas. Similar legislation passed in Canada in 1967 also contributed to Malayalee immigration there.

Most Malayalees in the United States are likely to live in the larger states of New York, California, Illinois, New Jersey, or Texas. Although large concentrations do not exist in any particular part of the country, their residences are generally close to or in major metropolitan areas such as New York City, Los Angeles, Chicago, Houston, or Dallas. However, in the late 1980s and 1990s and because of economic shifts, Malayalees have begun to move away from these traditional "ports of entry" to other parts of the United States.

Linguistically, Malayalam and its rich (though compared to other Indian languages relatively recent) literary and artistic heritage represent a tremendous source of pride and a common bond among these immigrants. High literacy levels in Kerala also have contributed to the growth of the language. Consequently Keralite immigrants are well educated. However, as with other American immigrant communities, there undoubtedly has been erosion in the primacy and use of Malayalam among the second and third generation. Concerned Malayalees have attempted to counter this trend with periodic family visits to Kerala and exposure to Malayalam language and arts in a variety of formal and informal settings.

## History and Cultural Relations

As noted earlier, literacy rates among both males and females have been historically high in Kerala, reportedly reaching 100 percent in the early 1990s. This has led to progressive social views (e.g., high rates of participation in family planning) and behavior (e.g., a series of leftist governments, far-reaching land reforms, a sex ratio that favors females). However, Kerala's high education levels and population density have also led to continued movement out of the state in search of employment. (The plight of educated unemployed youth is a constant theme in Malayalam literature and movies.) In the early part of the twentieth century, the search for suitable employment resulted in large numbers of Malayalees moving to other parts of India (where they are found in a variety of governmental agencies, the military, industry, and health care) and to Malaysia and Singapore (where they historically occupied lower supervisory and clerical positions in plantation agriculture and commerce). In the 1970s and 1980s, many Malayalees immigrated to oil-rich Middle Eastern countries, such as Saudi Arabia and the United Arab Emirates, as well as

to the United States and Canada. Unlike some other Asian Indian groups, only a few Malayalees have settled in the United Kingdom or Australia. Although many continue as permanent residents of the United States or Canada, an increasing number of Malayalees have become citizens of these countries. Citizenship effectively shifts their status from that of "sojourners" who intend to go back to Kerala to that of "settlers" who are tied to their new country socially and economically.

## Economy

Although general patterns of Malayalee immigration to the United States are similar to those of other Asian Indian groups, there are some specific economic differences. While there has been no estimate of their relative proportion, unlike for other Indian groups, a considerable number of the post-1965 first-generation immigrants were women, who arrived in the United States as nurses and brought their husbands and families with them. Others, who were single, went back to Kerala to get married and were joined by their husbands later. In India nursing was and continues to be a profession that attracts many Keralite Christian women. Shortages in related fields in the United States during the 1960s and 1970s resulted in the recruitment of nurses from India. Later immigrants tended to be in skilled professions (physicians, engineers, professors, scientists, computer scientists) or were students who stayed on as technical or managerial professionals after changing their immigration status. As in other Asian Indian groups, and given participation in professional and technical occupations, household incomes among Malayalees have tended to be higher than the national average. In the 1980s and early 1990s, the earlier waves were joined by somewhat less skilled parents, siblings, and other relatives. Their lower educational and occupational profiles, along with shifts in the American economy, are likely to lead to some erosion in above-average household income levels.

## Kinship, Marriage, and Family

In Kerala marriages are arranged primarily within religious and caste groups, with emphasis on the suitability of the family (in terms of wealth and reputation or "character") of the proposed partner. Given their small numbers in America, it is difficult if not impossible for families to arrange marriages in the traditional way. As a result, parents are likely to be resigned to intercaste (for Hindus), interdenominational (for Christians), or interreligious marriages to other Malayalees as well as to other Asian Indians. They may be less accommodating about marriages outside the Malayalee or larger Asian Indian communities. Needless to say, significant differences exist between first- and second-generation Malayalees regarding dating as a form of mate selection.

In Kerala, Malayalee family patterns are also likely to vary according to religion, and among Hindus, according to caste. Gender role norms and interaction are more egalitarian in Malayalee families. There is, for example, a long though currently eroded tradition of matrilineal descent and inheritance (being traced through the female side) among the Nayars, a Hindu community who in the past dominated Kerala politically. In addition, there has been strong support for the education and employment of females outside the home. These "liberal" patterns carry over among Malayalee immigrants and find additional support in the Western setting. Therefore, in mate selection and in other family issues, females and males tend to have more of an equal say in comparison to other Asian Indian immigrant groups. Malayalees, like other Asian Indian groups, attempt to foster in their children a sense of duty to family and relatives. Conflicts may result among family members and between different generations, centered on the dilemma of family obligations versus individual choice and freedom (emphasized by the dominant culture). One specific issue that may spark conflict is the advisibility of divorce as a solution to marital conflict. In fact, cases of divorce among this group are rare, and divorcing couples are viewed with disdain by first-generation Malayalees.

As a result of earlier immigration patterns, most Malayalees often have relatives and friends in other parts of India, the Middle East, and Southeast Asia. The same is true with regard to America due to family reunification provisions of immigration law. Thus, Malayalees are likely to be enmeshed in extended family and kinship networks of aunts, uncles, nieces, nephews, and cousins that stretch across many parts of the world. Other Malayalees are regarded as friends and likely to be welcomed into the family as such. American Malayalees seek to strengthen family connections through frequent visits to relatives in and out of Kerala, generally coinciding with summer vacations. The consequence is a cosmopolitan worldview and outlook that is rooted at the same time in a Malayalee identity.

## Sociopolitical Organization

Given the proportionate smallness of their population in India, Malayalees are not a strong or cohesive political force there. At the all-India level they are often loyal lieutenants to the powers that be. Kerala itself is a microcosm of national politics, with every group and subgroup represented by a plethora of political parties, often splitting off from and jockeying with each other for power. One common thread in these various groups is a leftist bent. The world's first freely elected Communist government was formed in Kerala in 1957, and a series of leftist or left-center governments have held office subsequently. The political economy is distinctly pro-labor, and many observers have viewed Kerala as a viable alternate model of economic develoment (compared to a capitalist one) emphasizing human development and distributional equity.

Therefore, Malayalee immigrants are likely to have liberal-progressive views and a keen interest in electoral politics. They appear to have accommodated themselves to the narrower political and ideological spectrum of North America. Given their relative prosperity, they are frequent financial contributors in the United States to the Democratic party and, to a lesser extent, the Republican party.

Other forms of interest and participation in American politics vary according to whether individuals are permanent residents or citizens.

Internally, the tendency of Malayalees to form separate organizations does carry over, with several metropolitan areas boasting more than one Keralite association claiming to represent all Malayalees. At the local and regional levels Malayalee organizations participate, with varying levels of enthusiasm, in umbrella groupings of Asian Indians that often tend to be dominated by non-Malayalees. The organization that unites all Malayalee groups is the Federation of Kerala Associations of North America (FOKANA), which, beginning in 1983 in New York City, has held large national conventions every two years during the summer. FOKANA is decidedly apolitical, and its major activities are social and cultural. It also has contributed to charitable and educational projects in Kerala.

It is difficult to say if Malayalees in America face prejudice and discrimination because of who they are. They tend to be lumped along with other Asian Indians who themselves are rather new to the dominant culture's consciousness. In the 1980s, there were attacks on Asian Indians in New Jersey carried out by a group generally known as the Dotbusters (named after the beauty mark worn by many Indian women on their foreheads). Malayalees were concerned about such incidents, though not to a degree greater than other Asian Indians.

## Religion and Expressive Culture

Malayalee immigrants represent a range of religions that have coexisted in relative harmony in Kerala. Traditionally the majority of people in Kerala have been Hindus; their temples and religious practices, it has been argued by some, show lingering traces of Buddhist influence. Christianity is reputed to have been brought to India by one of Jesus Christ's twelve disciples, St. Thomas. Until the middle of the twentieth century, a number of Jewish families and places of worship also flourished in Kerala. This long-standing religious harmony is unique when compared to the rest of India.

The immigrant Malayalee community includes strong contingents of Christians, Hindus, and Muslims. Among Christians (often thought to constitute the vast majority of North American Malayalee immigrants) there are Roman Catholic, Syrian Orthodox, Pentecostal, and other Protestant denominations who have origins specific to Kerala, such as the Church of South India. Given the relative newness of this community in North America, religious practices by Malayalee immigrants tend to follow those brought by the first generation from Kerala. Religious observances often begin rather informally, with periodic gatherings at the homes of like-minded believers. Over time these may be continued along with or incorporated into more formal structures and places of worship.

Hindu Malayalees have joined with other Asian Indian groups to contribute to the building of temples (e.g., in Pittsburgh and Houston). As a result of such participation some American temples have incorporated a deity, Ayyappa, generally identified with Kerala Hinduism, as one of the objects of devotion. Many Christian Malayalee immigrants have a choice of participating in existing American churches or forming their own. In the 1980s and 1990s, with the exception of Roman Catholics, followers of other Kerala Christian denominations established their own prayer groups or churches and conducted services in Malayalam, often with ministers from India. Even among the Roman Catholics, some occasions are marked with special services for Asian Indians, most of whom are Malayalees. Muslim Malayalees, who are not large in number, tend to join with others of similar faith for mosque-related religious activities. Malayalees outside Kerala, regardless of religion, come together to celebrate Onam (the traditional harvest festival, which also has Hindu mythological connotations) and Christmas. Such celebrations are often sponsored by local Malayalee organizations and involve cultural performances and feasting.

The arts and literature have an important place in Malayalee culture. Although distinct Malayalee artistic traditions are relatively recent, there are a disproportionate number of all-India award-winning novelists, dancers, poets, playwrights, singers, filmmakers, and actors from this tiny state. Malayalee immigrants also keep in touch with developments in various artistic fields in Kerala through Malayalam magazines and movies on videotape, which are widely available in ethnic Asian Indian stores. Many Kerala associations in North America sponsor performances by artists from Kerala. In addition, they attempt to develop knowledge of and interest in the community's culture and heritage among members of the next generations; this is achieved through conferences, cultural performances, and publications.

Although still strong in Kerala, medical practices rooted in Hindu (Ayurvedic) and Muslim (Unani) traditions are rarely sought by Malayalee immigrants. In part this is the result of a significant proportion of the immigrants working in medical settings in America, and the prestige associated with Western (allopathic) medicine in India itself.

Finally, beliefs about death and the afterlife are conditioned by the religious preferences of individual Malayalees. For example, Hindus have their dead cremated and, if needed, carry the ashes back to India for immersion in a body of water. Both practices are in keeping with Hindu traditions. However, it would be safe to say that given the relative "youth" of most Malayalee immigrants, issues regarding deaths and funerals have yet to be dealt with systematically and often generate ad hoc solutions.

*See also:*  SOUTH ASIAN CHRISTIANS

## Bibliography

Helweg, A. W., and Helweg, U. M. (1990). *An Immigrant Success Story: East Indians in America.* Philadelphia: University of Pennsylvania Press.

Pais, A.; Bhaskar, B.; and Kurian, P. (1989). "Malayalees in North America." *India Abroad* 19(38):12–14.

Unnithan, N. P. (1994). "Nayars: Tradition and Change in Marriage and the Family." In *Portraits of Culture: Ethnographic Originals,* edited by M. Ember, C. Ember, and D. Levinson. Englewood Cliffs, NJ: Prentice Hall.

Williams, R. B. (1988). *Religions of Immigrants from India and Pakistan.* Cambridge, Eng.: Cambridge University Press.

N. PRABHA UNNITHAN

# MENNONITES

Anabaptism was a sixteenth-century European religious movement, and the term "Anabapist" identified the people in the movement who refused, among other things, infant baptism and military service. The term "Mennonite" was first used during the Protestant Reformation in the sixteenth-century Netherlands, where it referred to the Anabaptist followers of Menno Simons, a disaffected Roman Catholic priest. Beginning in the seventeenth century, Mennonites were one of three (the other two being the Amish and the Hutterites) Anabaptist groups that emigrated from Europe to the United States. Mennonites include urban, rural, conservative, and progressive religious groups and communities. An emphasis on decentralized authority and church congregations, combined with pressures to assimilate, have contributed to the formation of various Mennonite groups; for example, Beachy Amish Mennonite, Church of God in Christ, Mennonite (Holdeman), Conservative Mennonite, Evangelical Mennonite Church, Old Order Mennonites, and Old Order River Brethren. Most, however, prefer to identify with one of two large church conferences, the Mennonite Church General Assembly or the General Conference Mennonite Church. Through evangelism and migration other Mennonite communities, congregations, and denominations have been established throughout the world.

Sixteenth-century European Anabaptists faced the combined and hostile forces of feudalism, emerging capitalism, and the Roman Catholic Church. They were among other Protestant Reformation groups that sought religious, political, and economic change. Unlike mainstream reformers, however, Anabaptists rejected the notion of a state church; they refused infant baptism and called for a community of believers or "rebaptizers" (thus, Anabaptists)—those who subscribed to the practice of adult baptism upon the confession of faith. Collectively they formed independent *Gemeinden* (church communities), each of which claimed to represent a "true" Christian way of life. Through baptism, adults made a voluntary commitment not only to the church but also to a closed community of believers. Mennonites used the threat of banishment, strict rules of endogamy (in-group marriage), control of language, regulation of dress, and related social practices to distinguish themselves from other groups.

The church was to be a voluntary association of believers who chose freely, but obediently, to submit to the community. The church, they argued, must remain separate from the state and secular or worldly affairs. Thus special emphasis has been given to the ethical teachings of the New Testament, and in particular the Sermon on the Mount. Christians were to gather in communities; reject the outside world, war, and violence; and refuse to take oaths. Life in the community was to be simple, and individual differences in wealth and status were to be deemphasized. Mennonites, however, rejected the more radical Anabaptist teachings on the "community of goods." Instead, they believed that followers should voluntarily limit their private property (unlike their cousins the Hutterites, who stress communal property) insofar as it undermined the common aims, faith, and practices of the community; individual self-interest was to remain subordinate to the interests of the community. Mennonites interpret the Bible to mean that Christians may possess property, but it must be recognized that all things come from God, the one and only proprietor of goods. All that one can hope to do is practice effective "stewardship."

A violent backlash (the Counter-Reformation) combined with the rapidly emerging capitalist economy resulted in their persecution and dispersion. For nearly three centuries—in Poland, Prussia, Russia, and the United States—Mennonites negotiated with feudal lords and emergent nation-states for land, religious freedom, and various kinds of military exemptions. Thus, central to the identity of Mennonites is the knowledge that they have existed in opposition to institutions of state, education, church, market, and the military.

## Immigration and Settlement History

Mennonites have been on the move for nearly four hundred years; the largest concentrations are not in their countries of origin. Elaborate mutual aid practices have always facilitated and made successful their many migrations. Faced with unfriendly political foes or economic conditions, Mennonites have continuously searched for new land where government officials would assure religious freedom and military exemption. The first

A Mennonite woman sells apples at a farmers' market in Lititz, Pennsylvania, in 1942. (Library of Congress/Corbis)

community of Mennonites in the United States (1683, in Germantown, Pennsylvania) was established by a group from Krefeld, Germany. In 1710, Swiss and South German Mennonites established the largest colonial settlement in Lancaster County, Pennsylvania. As land in Pennsylvania became scarce and expensive, prosperous Mennonites, as well as those seeking to escape economic hardship, moved to the frontier. Further movement of individuals and families from Pennsylvania in the nineteenth century led to the establishment of communities in Virginia, Maryland, Ohio, Illinois, Indiana, Iowa, Missouri, and Kansas. In general, before the twentieth century, they settled in rural areas and farmed.

Throughout the nineteenth and early twentieth centuries, Mennonites continued to leave Prussia (later Germany), Switzerland, Poland, and Russia to join relatives in the United States. A second wave of Mennonite immigration occurred in the 1870s, when twelve thousand Mennonites arrived from Russia. These Russian Germans settled almost entirely in the Middle West. Pennsylvania and Kansas are home to the largest Mennonite groups; however, their churches are found in every state and in most large cities.

Due to the dispersion of Mennonite communities and their missionary activities, linguistic affiliation is diverse. Some American communities use Plattdeutsch (Low German) in daily conversation and German for religious rituals. Often English is the only language, especially in progressive communities. Only the more conservative groups use German to conduct religious services.

## Cultural Distinctions

Though their "plain" dress, Anabaptist teachings, and other social practices helped to distinguish Mennonites in the New World, their settlement patterns in Pennsylvania encouraged interaction with other groups. Cultural isolation was not among the central tenets of Mennonite belief; indeed, in the early settlement years (1683–1800) they often shared educational resources (teachers and school buildings) and

church ideology with Quakers and Lutherans. Their philosophy of nonresistance (pacifism) was also similar to those espoused by Quakers. Mennonites in the colonial era were not easily distinguished from other German settlers. Thus, for Mennonites, cultural separation was in large part produced by their centuries-long unyielding opposition to war, government, and the forces associated with modernity (e.g., urbanism, public education, materialism, fashionable dress, and public drinking). The Mennonites' experience of discrimination has usually come as a result of public reaction to their refusal to participate in the institutions of state (e.g., taxation, schools, or military service). Mennonites in the United States have not suffered economically due to their immigrant status and cultural peculiarities; they easily entered the economic mainstream. By exercising their right to vote and by discouraging members from holding political office — as opposed to discriminatory political forces shutting them out of formal office — for most of their history (exceptions have occurred in recent times) they have *chosen* to avoid officeholding.

Cultural and religious distinctions for the Mennonites began with three eighteenth- and nineteenth-century concerns: war, urbanism, and the Industrial Revolution. These issues have sharpened the cultural boundaries. The Revolutionary War and Civil War were major tests of Mennonite belief and identity. How do pacifists prohibit military service and at the same time remain good citizens? During World Wars I and II, and more recently during the Korean and Vietnam wars, these questions have repeatedly confronted Mennonites. At each political juncture, then, negotiating military exemptions have sometimes contributed to internal group division, personal intimidation, and discrimination. During the Revolutionary War and the Civil War, Mennonites provided horses, cattle, and wagons to the military. There were discussions about the potential contradictions involved in assisting war efforts, yet refusing direct military service. Some Mennonite groups adopted a conservative stance and opposed all contributions to war efforts. Others assumed a

Members of the congregation attend a church service at the Alexandervohl Mennonite Church in Goessel, Kansas. (Philip Gould/Corbis)

more progressive position and consented to offer auxiliary supplies. In the twentieth century, in lieu of military service, most have negotiated conscientious objector status and worked as volunteers in hospitals, schools, and national parks. During World Wars I and II, the Korean War, and the Vietnam War, many Mennonites, opposed to all types of collaboration, were imprisoned. In some cases (especially World War I) they were forbidden use of the German language, parochial schools were closed, and their barns were painted yellow.

Among Mennonite groups, internal controversies — such as those created by military service — have often led to the formation of new churches and communities. Dissension over nonresistance, however, was not the only external force producing the conditions for schism and change. Over the past three centuries Mennonites have unevenly adopted modern ways; this includes the use of technology; urban life; commercial activities; and most important, rejection of public schools. Dissenting opinions have often resulted in fragmentation and the formation of splinter groups. Traveling in Lancaster County, Pennsylvania, for example, one discovers groups variously demarcated by religious practices and beliefs; for example, the absence or presence of foot washing, baptism by immersion, and a professional as opposed to a lay ministry. Conservative splinter churches might separate themselves from other

Mennonites by strict adherence to particular clothing styles, buggies, or automobiles. Though such distinctions may appear trivial, they are fundamental to the understanding of Mennonite identity. For example, Old Order Mennonites responded to twentieth-century technological change by proscribing the use of automobiles, televisions, radios, and telephones. As a consequence, use of horse and buggies set them, like the Amish, apart from their urban counterparts who own businesses, enter various professions, and adopt modern technologies.

The Swiss and German Mennonites in Pennsylvania, Ohio, Indiana, and Kansas have lived on scattered private farms. Those in Germantown, Pennsylvania, and some in Kansas lived briefly in village settlements. Throughout the twentieth century, increasing numbers have settled in urban areas. Among the more than 250,000 Mennonites in the United States, less than one-third live on farms; one-third in rural communities (but non-farm); and more than one-third in large, urban areas. From their beginnings, Mennonites have been known for their agricultural, craft, and artisanal skills. In the Netherlands and Prussia, they drained swamps and built and maintained sophisticated canal systems. The Swiss Mennonites breed exceptionally productive dairy cattle. In eighteenth-century Russia, Mennonites became known for their dairy herds, merino sheep raising, and orchards and were pioneers in the production and marketing of the famous hard winter (turkey red) wheat that later brought them to the attention of land agents in the United States. In the United States, they were recognized not only for grain production but also for processing and storage. Most have become wage laborers, successful entrepreneurs, educators, or professionals, while only a minority earn a living from farming. Though their communities have often been extensively involved in commercial activities, they have also been quite self-sufficient. Conservative groups have strongly discouraged wage labor or commercial occupations, and in some cases, churches proscribe members from earning interest or purchasing insurance.

In the past, Mennonites were forbidden to marry non-Mennonites and, in some cases, members of other Mennonite groups. Now only the more conservative limit marriage to group members. Marriage is strictly monogamous, and historically, families negotiated the conditions of marriage; only conservative Mennonites participate in selection of marriage partners. Liberal denominations, however, continue informal marriage arrangements through church-sponsored events and organizations (camps, retreats, and institutions of higher education). The marriage ceremony in all groups is taken as seriously as baptism and is a ritual centered in the congregation and performed by church elders or pastors. The Swiss Mennonites, unlike those descended from the Russian-German wing, have historically conducted the marriage ritual in the home. Though most conduct church weddings, they tend to be simpler than many Protestant ceremonies. Small extended families (grandparents, parents, and children) were once common; today the nuclear family predominates.

Children were and continue to be raised according to strict codes of conduct. Among some groups, dress codes are strictly enforced for all ages. Many insist on providing their own educational institutions, and some withdraw children from school beginning in the eighth grade. Most parents, however, encourage offspring to remain in school and continue with postsecondary education. Though many Mennonite groups have held tenaciously to parochial schools, state bureaucracies have often pressured them to concede partial control. Many, though not all, Mennonites have believed that children should not receive education beyond reading, writing, and arithmetic. Life in agrarian communities was, according to these teachings, potentially jeopardized by knowledge of "worldly" affairs. Though conservative Mennonite groups retain control of their educational institutions, the majority use public schools. In fact, at the level of postsecondary education, many have distinguished themselves. There are several major Mennonite colleges and Bible institutes throughout the world, and their historical archives are among the finest.

## Social Institutions

Two social institutions—church and education—have played dominant roles in Mennonite life. The church or congregation was the most powerful institution: It sanctioned marriage, negotiated with secular authorities, and established codes of conduct (ordnung). Male church elders were the ultimate authorities, and no secular agency could rule on matters pertaining to community life. In fact, not until the twentieth century were women, in some denominations (and congregations), permitted or encouraged to assume the roles of church elder (aeltester), bishop, minister, or teacher.

Emphasis on the strict separation of church and state meant that members could not participate in political organizations outside the community. And within the community, a hierarchical distribution of power was highly suspect; nevertheless, a three-tiered ministry emerged. The highest and most revered was that of elder, who was elected by community members and who, among other things, had exclusive authority to ordain new elders. In addition to elders there were preachers and ministers (dienaren), who were also chosen by the congregation. Deacons were appointed by the congregation to serve the poor and care for widows, the elderly, and orphans. A professional clergy is, for the most part, a modern practice, though conservative groups still insist on the importance of a lay clergy.

In addition to the ceremonies found in most Protestant religions, Mennonites give special consideration to the rituals of baptism and foot washing at communion. The rite of entrance into the community is symbolized by baptism and foot washing (often the cause of some controversy). The latter practice was a means of symbolizing that no one person was better than another. Access to heaven is not predetermined; one is assured an afterlife only after having been a disciplined member of the community. Historically some have given emphasis to the community in their mortuary tradition by burying members in the order of dying, deemphasizing family membership.

*See also:* AMISH; GERMANS; HUTTERITES

## Bibliography

Bender, H. S., ed. (1955–1959). *The Mennonite Encyclopedia*, Vols. 1–4. Hillsboro, KS: Mennonite Brethern Publishing House.

Dyck, C. J. (1981). *An Introduction to Mennonite History.* Scottdale, PA: Herald Press.

Dyck, C. J., and Martin, D. D., eds. (1990). *The Mennonite Encyclopedia*, Vol. 5. Scottdale, PA: Herald Press.

Juhnke, J. C. (1989). *Vision, Doctrine, War: Mennonite Identity and Organization in America, 1890–1930.* Scottdale, PA: Herald Press.

Kraybill, P. N. (1984). *Mennonite World Handbook.* Lombard, IL: Mennonite World Conference.

Loewen, R. K. (1993). *Family, Church, and Market: A Mennonite Community in the Old and the New Worlds, 1850–1930.* Urbana: University of Illinois Press.

MacMaster, R. K. (1985). *Land, Piety, Peoplehood: The Establishment of Mennonite Communities in America, 1683–1790.* Scottdale, PA: Herald Press.

Schlabach, T. F. (1988). *Peace, Faith, Nation: Mennonites and Amish in Nineteenth-Century America.* Scottdale, PA: Herald Press.

Smith, H. C. (1981). *Story of the Mennonites.* Newton, KS: Faith and Life Press.

JEFFREY L. LONGHOFER

# MEXICANS

Mexicans immigrating into the U.S. Southwest are moving into territory that was once part of Mexico. Many Mexican Americans (Americans of Mexican descent, also called Chicanos) can trace their roots to settlements in the U.S. Southwest as early as 1595. For these Mexican Americans, the history of immigration included the movement of U.S. citizens into Mexican territory, resulting in the eventual loss of that territory after the Mexican War (1846–1848). Immigration of Mexicans into what was now U.S. territory began shortly after 1848 but did not emerge as a major movement until the twentieth century. In the latter half of the nineteenth century, the United States relied on immigrants from Europe, China, and Japan to satisfy the growing demand for immigrant labor in its rapidly expanding industrial and agricultural economy. However, resentment toward these immigrant groups grew, leading to dramatic restrictions on their immigration in the early part of the twentieth century, after which Mexican immigrants became an even more important source of labor in the economy of the United States.

## The Roots of Mexican Immigration

An understanding of contemporary Mexican immigration requires a brief history of its origins. Porfirio Díaz, president of Mexico from 1876 to 1911, laid the groundwork for both the Mexican Revolution and Mexican immigration to the United States. One of Díaz's goals was to modernize Mexico. To accomplish this he invited foreign investment from Europe and the United States and separated the Mexican *campesino* (peasant) from the land, thus creating a mobile labor force for capitalist development. By the time his presidency came to an end with the revolution, five million rural Mexicans had lost their rights to land. In villages and towns across the Mexican countryside, upwards of 98 percent of the farmers had no land to farm. During this time, the railroads were built, with U.S. financing, connecting the interior of Mexico with U.S. and European markets. The railroads also provided the rural labor force with a cheap means of transportation to Mexico's growing urban-industrial centers and to the northern border.

The growing demand for labor in the American Southwest was attractive to Mexicans. In the early part of the twentieth century, New Mexico, Arizona, Colorado, and Oklahoma needed workers for their booming coal and copper mines. In California, the deserts of the Central and Imperial valleys were being transformed into rich, labor-hungry, agricultural lands. A growing population and economy

A customs inspector in El Paso, Texas, in 1916 searches a Mexican who has just crossed the bridge from Juarez, Mexico. (The National Archives/Corbis)

meant large-scale construction in expanding cities throughout the Southwest, but especially Los Angeles, San Diego, San Francisco, and Denver.

In its search for a labor force to meet these new labor demands in the Southwest, the United States turned to international sources. Chinese immigrants were brought to work in the agricultural fields and mines and on the railroads. Their immigration was virtually stopped with the Chinese Exclusion Act of 1882, a response to the "Yellow Peril" campaigns against the Chinese. The Japanese followed, but they, too, were characterized as a competitive threat due to their success in farming, fishing, and other economic endeavors. The "Gentlemen's Agreement" with Japan in 1907 closed the door on their immigration.

In the early 1900s, Mexicans became a preferred alternative labor force in the Southwest for a number of reasons. Mexican culture was not so different from American culture, relative to Asian cultures. U.S. employers already had experience with Mexicans through their investments in Mexico. And Mexicans had a long history in the area; their presence was not new or exotic. In addition, Anglo Americans commonly characterized Mexicans as indolent, passive, noncompetitive, inferior "half-breeds" who lacked ambition and who were satisfied with their lot in life, or at least believed there was little they could do to alter their future (they were, in other words, fatalists). They were portrayed as people who would not become economic competitors with their employers. And finally, Mexicans were viewed as the quintessential temporary immigrants who would return like "homing pigeons" to Mexico rather than stay permanently in the United States. With such characteristics, Americans viewed Mexicans as providing ample labor at little cost.

So pervasive were these perceived characterizations of Mexicans that in 1911 the Dillingham Commission, which was established to study the immigration issue, argued that Mexican immigration should be promoted as the best solution to the Southwest's labor needs. It even went so far as to exempt Mexicans from the head tax for immigrants that was established under the immigration laws of 1903 and 1907. With the higher wages offered in the United States compared to Mexico, and with active recruitment campaigns by American employers, Mexicans with few opportunities in Mexico became attracted to jobs in the United States.

By the 1920, a pattern of immigration had been established, and the stage was set for the first large immigration of Mexicans to the United States. The postrevolutionary years in Mexico were chaotic and violent, especially in the countryside. Across the border, the United States needed labor. The American economy was growing, but perhaps more important for Mexicans, the United States shut the door to low-skilled labor from Europe. The immigration laws of 1921 and 1924 severely restricted the immigration of southern and eastern Europeans. Once again, Mexicans became a suitable alternative for America's labor-hungry agricultural fields and factories. American businesses often sent recruiters to Mexico in search of laborers for work in the Midwest, including Chicago, where the communities they established continue today.

Immigration from Mexico and the rest of the world came to a virtual stop during the Great Depression of the 1930s. In fact, many Mexicans returned to Mexico—some willingly, others unwillingly. Anti-immigrant, especially anti-Mexican, sentiments flourished during the early 1930s. President Herbert Hoover even blamed the Depression on the presence of Mexican immigrants, providing another example of scapegoating of immigrants during difficult economic times. As a consequence, the U.S. Immigration and Naturalization Service (INS) routinely rounded up Mexicans and repatriated them to Mexico, forcing them to take their American-born children, who were U.S. citizens, with them. Close to 500,000 Mexicans were repatriated during the Depression.

Although Mexicans were eschewed during the 1930s, the 1940s witnessed a renewed recruitment of Mexican labor. World War II ushered many American men and some women out of the labor force and into military service. Many other women entered the workplace, but a labor shortage still existed. The United States turned to Mexico for unskilled and semiskilled laborers who would work in the United States on a contract basis for a few months. Beginning in 1942, this program became popularly known as the "Bracero Program," *bracero* meaning "arms" in Spanish. Although the Bracero Program was to last only during the war years, its advantages as a ready source of cheap labor, especially in agriculture, proved irresistible. The program continued until 1964.

During the course of the twenty-two-year Bracero Program, hundreds of thousands of Mexicans were recruited to work in the United States. Mexican workers came from many states, but principally from the highly populated central

Migrant workers from Mexico recruited in 1943 by the Farm Security Administration to harvest and process sugar beets under contract with the Intermountain Agricultural Improvement Association. (Library of Congress/Corbis)

states of Jalisco, Michoacán, Zacatecas, Querétaro, Guanajuato, and Puebla. While in the United States, bracero workers learned about opportunities in the American labor market and they established contacts with American employers. When the Bracero Program ended in 1964, the demand for the labor these workers provided did not vanish. Employers still needed the workers in their fields and on their ranches, only the workers could no longer immigrate to work legally as braceros. Not surprisingly, the number of illegal immigrant workers rose dramatically after the termination of the Bracero Program. The system of employer-employee contacts, immigration routes, and social networks continued to operate, only clandestinely. The same Mexican states that supplied workers for the Bracero Program are the principal source of most Mexican immigration today.

Since the 1960s, use of Mexican labor has diversified, especially in the Southwest. Once working primarily in agriculture, undocumented Mexicans are now found in many urban and suburban jobs, performing work that pays low wages and offers few benefits and that therefore is not generally attractive to U.S. citizens.

## A Demographic Profile

The Mexican-American population has grown rapidly. Between 1980 and 1990, Mexican Americans increased by approximately 7.75 million persons, a 54.4 percent increase over the decade. The dramatic growth in the Mexican-American population is, to a significant degree, due to immigration. Between 1980 and 1988, a total of 625,690 Mexicans legally immigrated to the United States, more than from any other Latin American country. In 1981 alone, 101,268 Mexicans legally immigrated, almost double the numbers of the year before and after. Since 1984, the number of legal Mexican immigrants entering the United States has continued to rise steadily, with a new peak reached in 1988, when 95,039 Mexicans legally immigrated. Mexicans accounted for 14.8 percent of the 643,025 immigrants admitted in 1988.

The years of 1989 and 1990 were unusual due to the large numbers of Mexicans admitted as legal immigrants under the legalization program authorized by the 1986 immigration law—the Immigration Reform and Control Act (IRCA). Fully 405,172 Mexicans were admitted as legal immigrants in 1989, and another 679,068 in 1990.

Legal Mexican immigrants live in similar geographic areas as Mexican Americans generally. California alone absorbs at least half the total flow of legal Mexican immigrants, averaging about 67,000 legal immigrants per year since 1981. Looking at one year provides a good example of where Mexican immigrants intend to reside. More than half (56.4%, or 53,622) of the 96,039 legal Mexican immigrants in 1988 chose California as their state of intended residence. Mexican immigrants that year also intended to reside in Texas (23.9%), Illinois (6.2%), Arizona (3.6%), New Mexico (1.8%), and Colorado (1.2%). Therefore, most (80.7%) legal Mexican immigrants in 1988 intended to reside in one of the southwestern states of California, Texas, Arizona, New Mexico, and Colorado. Thus the Southwest is both the region with the largest Mexican-American population and the area that attracts most legal Mexican immigrants. Almost 90 percent of Mexican immigrants choose to reside in a metropolitan area. The municipality of Los Angeles–Long Beach attracted one out of three (33.6%) legal Mexican immigrants in 1988. Other key urban destinations for Mexicans included Chicago, San Diego, El Paso, and Houston.

The traditional picture of the Mexican immigrant was of a young, single, male agricultural worker who immigrated for a few months and then returned home. This characterization was an accurate reflection of many Mexican immigrants during the early part of the twentieth century, and well into the 1940s, 1950s, and 1960s, when thousands of men immigrated as temporary contract laborers under the Bracero Program. Although men may have predominated in those earlier immigration flows, Mexican women also immigrated, both legally and illegally, to the United States, where they helped establish Mexican communities throughout the Southwest and Midwest. In 1988, women made up 43.9 percent of the legal immigrants from Mexico.

In the past, the immigration literature characterized women as appendages to their immigrating husbands; women immigrated to reunite with their husbands who were already in the United States. Today, single women from Mexico immigrate to the United States for economic as well as social reasons. They immigrate to find "a better life," seeking employment in the rapidly growing service sector, especially in domestic work. They often have family remaining in Mexico who rely on the money they send back. Some Mexican women are single parents who leave their children with parents or siblings when immigrating to the United

States. In some cases these women may have intended to work in the United States for a short time, but their stay became extended. Thus, they often bring their children from Mexico to join them in the United States. If current trends persist, women will continue to make up a significant proportion of the Mexicans who immigrate to the United States well into the twenty-first century.

## Undocumented Immigration

Many people immigrate to the United States without documentation from the INS. Popularly called "illegal aliens," these undocumented immigrants often are in the United States for relatively brief periods. Some, however, do settle and add to the existing population. Because undocumented immigrants are a clandestine population, making accurate estimates of their numbers is difficult. Some reasonable assessments are, however, available. For example, data from the 1980 U.S. Census were used to estimate the number of undocumented immigrants in the country during the early 1980s at between 2.5 million and 3.5 million. This number was dramatically reduced by the approximately 3 million undocumented immigrants legalized under the 1986 immigration law, about 75 percent of whom were Mexicans. On average, between 200,000 and 300,000 undocumented immigrants settle in the United States each year, a range that has been consistent for many years.

Undocumented immigrants come from many countries, such as China, Ireland, and Colombia. Mexicans, however, make up a large proportion of the undocumented population. For example, Mexicans made up about 70 percent of the undocumented population in 1988. Undocumented Mexicans tend to be relatively young—most are eighteen to thirty-four years of age. Historically, most undocumented immigrants were males, but the proportion of females has increased to more than 40 percent. Undocumented Mexicans on average have six to seven years of education.

California attracts the largest proportion of undocumented immigrants of all nationalities. For example, California had approximately half (1.74

A family crossing into the United States illegally waits by a Tijuana River estuary at low tide. (Raymond Gehman/Corbis)

million) of the nation's undocumented immigrants in 1987. Although undocumented immigrants accounted for only 1.4 percent of U.S. residents in 1980, they made up 6.3 percent of California's total population. Not surprisingly, about half of the approximately 100,000 undocumented Mexican immigrants entering the United States each year choose California as their state of residence. Although many undocumented immigrants are attracted to California, they also reside in many other states, including Washington, Texas, Illinois, New York, and Florida.

## Families and Immigration

Families play an important role in the immigration process. Family networks extend well beyond the immediate household, often linking family members across national borders. Although the availability of jobs in the United States may fuel Mexican immigration, it is the transnational links of Mexican families that make immigration possible. Because of the extensiveness of these transnational social networks, established immigrant families often serve as landing pads for later immigrating family members, especially females. New immigrants turn to family for a place to live while they get settled, information about jobs in the local area, and insights into the cultural norms of the community. Therefore, Mexican immigrant households often consist of extended family members. Undocumented immigrants who have formed a family in the United States face additional pressures that contribute to their household composition. Having other adults in the household helps undocumented immigrants survive despite low wages, high rents, child-care needs, and sudden absences from the family due to apprehension by the INS.

Families form the key links in what is known as "chain migration." Countless examples exist of this process. Typically, a pioneer from a Mexican community immigrates to work in the United States. He or she then helps relatives and friends immigrate, who then help others. The reproduction of community in this way means that many

friends and family from the same community or region in Mexico soon come to live near each other in the United States. As this process unfolds over time, Mexican immigrants develop a multiplicity of ties to other families, friends, and societal institutions in the United States. These ties create a sense of community among Mexican immigrants that both emerges from and fosters family settlement rather than return migration to Mexico.

Mexican women are particularly apt to desire to settle in the United States, often in contrast to their male counterparts. Why this is so has to do with many factors. First, Mexican women often immigrate once and then stay in the United States, whether they originally arrived to join husbands or were on their own. Mexican men, on the other hand, have often made many trips to the United States. Mexican immigrant women typically get year-round jobs in domestic work, hotels, restaurants, or manufacturing. In addition, undocumented women often fear recrossing the border clandestinely. Crossing the border at night, over hillsides and through ravines, is a dangerous undertaking, one that many undocumented women would rather avoid, even if it means not returning to Mexico as often as they would like. Moreover, the experience of working for wages, which they may not have done in Mexico, may lead to changes in women's relations with their fathers and husbands. Their independent earnings and contributions to their family's welfare increase their sense of independence and often lead to a greater role in the family's decision making. All these factors lessen traditional family patriarchy — male dominance — and contribute to Mexican women's reluctance to return "back home" permanently. Finally, if Mexican immigrant women form a family in the United States, either by having children or bringing their children from Mexico, they are more likely to desire to stay in the United States. Add to this the increasing sense of community felt by Mexican women as they develop friends among their neighbors, some of whom may be relatives or friends from Mexico, and the reasons for gender differences in desires for return migration and settlement become apparent.

## Legalization and Citizenship

Many Mexicans immigrate to the United States legally. For undocumented immigrants, however, acquiring legal resident status is an important step toward working and living in the United States in relative security. Many undocumented immigrants manage to acquire legal resident status — that is, to become legal immigrants. They do this in a number of ways. For example, a relative who is a citizen of or legal resident in the United States can sponsor an undocumented immigrant's application for legal resident status. An employer can sponsor an undocumented worker if the work he or she performs qualifies and proves not to affect U.S. citizen job seekers negatively. An undocumented immigrant might also qualify for a government-sponsored legalization program such as that created by the 1986 immigration law. Finally, an undocumented immigrant might marry a U.S. citizen who then sponsors his or her application for legal residence. Given these various opportunities for legalizing one's immigration status, an undocumented immigrant may not be stuck in that status indefinitely.

Members of the same family can acquire legal resident status at different times, which often leads to families of mixed immigration status. The following scenario is typical of such families. The pioneer immigrant in the family, the one with the most time in the United States, acquires legal resident status through an employer or relative who has become a U.S. citizen. He or she then brings his or her spouse to the United States along with any children. Finally, he or she has a child born in the United States, making the child a U.S. citizen. The family now consists of one parent who is a legal immigrant, one parent who is an illegal immigrant, children who are undocumented immigrants, and a child who is a U.S. citizen. In all likelihood, the undocumented immigrants in the family will also one day find a way to become legal residents.

With legal resident status comes the opportunity to naturalize and obtain U.S. citizenship. Mexicans historically have had low naturalization rates, for several reasons. Mexican immigrants often believe that gaining U.S. citizenship would place obstacles to their dream of returning to Mexico someday, possibly to retire. For others, it is the emotional issue of nationalism, of losing one's national identity.

Over the years, however, larger numbers of Mexicans have sought U.S. citizenship. Between 1979 and 1988, there was an increasing trend in the number of Mexicans who became naturalized citizens, reaching a peak in 1986 and then decreasing somewhat before stabilizing and then increasing again in 1995 and 1996. These results reflect a positive movement toward becoming a U.S. citizen, perhaps a result of the efforts of groups such as the Southwest Voter Registration Program. The negative portrayal of immigrants that has characterized much of the public debate since the late 1970s may also have raised interest among Mexican immigrants to acquire the benefits of U.S. citizenship.

## Cultural Continuity and Acculturation

Mexican immigration during the last half of the twentieth century has changed the profile of the Mexican-American, or Chicano, population. Eighteen percent of the Mexican-American population in the United States was foreign-born in 1970. In 1990, in contrast, 33 percent of the Mexican-origin population was foreign-born. Because of immigration, the proportion of immigrants among Chicanos in the nation almost doubled during the 1970s and 1980s. In California, Mexican immigrants accounted for 41.7 percent of the Mexican-American population in 1990. Mexican immigrants bring with them the Spanish language, values, and behavior that reinvigorate Mexican-American culture in communities in the Southwest and throughout the United States.

Without immigration, Chicanos would retain some of the immigrant generation's cultural beliefs and behaviors. By the third generation, however, the overwhelming majority of Mexican Americans born in the United States are dominant in English rather than Spanish. Immigration from Mexico and

A Mexican wearing a sombrero and blanket celebrates Cinco de Mayo in St. Paul, Minnesota. (Richard Hamilton Smith/Corbis)

other Latin American countries keeps Spanish alive. Mexican immigrants also bring with them values of family solidarity, religion, and hard work that sometimes stand in sharp contrast to American values of individualism and secularism. Behavior patterns among Mexican immigrants are also relatively healthy. For example, only 5 percent of the babies born to Mexican immigrant mothers were of low birthweight despite having risk factors such as low levels of education, low income, and lack of medical insurance. Positive birth outcomes have been attributed to low consumption of alcohol and other drugs and low use of cigarettes by recent immigrant women. Moreover, they are particularly unlikely to use drugs during pregnancy. Mexican immigrants continue behaving in these ways in the United States, but eventually fall victim

to acculturation. Moreover, there is growing evidence that this is also true for attitudes about education. Mexican immigrant children bring with them positive attitudes toward and respect for education, only to have them erode into the cynicism found in the urban youth culture in the United States. In short, it appears that acculturation may be bad for immigrants' health and educational attainment.

Mexican immigrants have also added creatively to the cultural life of the communities they settled in. As they mixed with other members of American society, the result has often been the production of ways of life that have become "American" rather than "Mexican." In the nineteenth century, the Mexican *vaquero* became the American cowboy, who retained much of the basic material culture and language of the vaquero (the saddle, the lasso, the rodeo). Mexicans in southern Texas borrowed the accordion and polka rhythms of their German immigrant neighbors and created *Norteño* music. This music continues as a popular musical form throughout the U.S. Southwest and Mexico, but for many Americans it was unknown until the murder of the popular Texas singer Selena. Spanish-language television and radio are extremely popular throughout the Southwest. Still, much of the musical and artistic production of Mexican immigrants and their descendants remains outside the American mainstream. Mexican Americans are not well represented in national television and movies, nor is there much variation in the presentation of thematic issues surrounding their lives. The dramatic range rarely extends beyond a gang and drug lifestyle.

*See also:* CALIFORNIOS; MEXICANS OF THE SOUTHWEST; PUNJABI MEXICANS; SPANIARDS

## Bibliography

Allen, J. P., and Turner, E. J. (1988). "Where to Find the New Immigrants." *American Demographics* 9:23–60.

Borjas, G. J., and Tienda, M. (1993). "The Employment and Wages of Legalized Immigrants." *International Migration Review* 27:712–747.

Cardoso, L. A. (1980). *Mexican Emigration to the United States, 1897–1931.* Tucson: University of Arizona Press.

Chavez, L. R. (1992). *Shadowed Lives: Undocumented Immigrants in American Society.* Fort Worth: Harcourt Brace Jovanovich.

Cornelius, W. A.; Martin, P. L.; and Hollifield, J. F. (1994). *Controlling Immigration: A Global Perspective.* Stanford, CA: Stanford University Press.

Craig, R. B. (1971). *The Bracero Program: Interest Groups and Foreign Policy.* Austin: University of Texas Press.

Donato, K. M. (1993). "Current Trends and Patterns of Female Migration: Evidence from Mexico." *International Migration Review* 27:748–771.

Hoffman, A. (1974). *Unwanted Americans: Mexican Americans in the Great Depression, Repatriation Pressures, 1929–1939.* Tucson: University of Arizona Press.

Hondagneu-Sotelo, P. (1994). *Gendered Transitions: Mexican Experience of Immigration.* Berkeley: University of California Press.

Massey, D. S.; Alarcon, R.; Durand, J.; and Gonzalez, H. (1987). *Return to Aztlan.* Berkeley: University of California Press.

Mendoza, I.; Ventura, S.; Valdez, R.; Castillo, R.; Saldivar, L.; Baisden, K.; and Martorell, R. (1991). "Selected Measures of Health Status for Mexican-American, Mainland Puerto Rican, and Cuban-American Children." *Journal of the American Medical Association* 265:227–232.

Portes, A., and Bach, R. L. (1985). *Latin Journey: Cuban and Mexican Immigrants in the United States.* Berkeley: University of California Press.

Suárez-Orozco, C., and Suárez-Orozco, M. (1995). *Transformations: Immigration, Family Life, and Achievement Motivation Among Latino Adolescents.* Stanford, CA: Stanford University Press.

LEO R. CHAVEZ

# MEXICANS OF THE SOUTHWEST

For generations, Mexicans have been traveling the road north to the southwestern United States even before it became the United States. It is probable that the earliest movements of ideas and human populations from the northern edges of Mesoamerica to southwestern North America probably were rather frequent since about 700 C.E., if not earlier. Much earlier than this, various types of important seeds of corn, beans, squash, and chili seemed to have originated in the central Mexican area and then grew in the southwestern United States by 1500 B.C.E. Whether these were carried by persons, blown by the wind, or traveled serendipitously along riverain systems is not known.

It is known that in the state of Arizona there are more than 189 Mesoamerican ball courts, upon which was played a ball game called ule, which can only have originated much farther south, probably in the fringes of Mesoamerica. There are other indications that there were south-to-north trading exchanges by various peoples so that there were probably three main lines of trade and exchange between the peripheries of Mesoamerica along the west coast of Mexico, up through the Sierra Madre corridor, and along the Gulf of Mexico into what is now the southeastern United States.

The central idea is that these routes in pre-European times were well traveled by traders, merchants, and others willing to take risks to exchange such sumptuary and ritual items as red scarlet macaws from southern Tamaulipas, mosaic mirrors from central Mexico, copper bells from Zacatecas, and perhaps pottery. In exchange, to the peripheries of Mesoamerica were sent seashells from the California and Mexican Pacific coasts and the Sea of Cortez, and turquoise was carried from Los Cerrillos, New Mexico, just north of present Sante Fe, and perhaps buffalo hides from the Plains.

These same trails, of course, were used in the sixteenth century by Spanish explorers to establish later colonies of the Kingdom of New Spain (Mexico) in present-day New Mexico, Texas, Arizona, California, and southern Colorado. This early colonization process was responsible for most of the town settlements such as Tucson, Arizona; San Antonio, Texas; Sante Fe, New Mexico; and from San Francisco to San Diego, which were all established by migrating Hispano/Mexicanos between 1605 and 1821, the latter year marking the independence of Mexico and its northern provinces from Spain.

Many of these migrating populations were agropastoralists, laborers, farmers, and craftspersons; few were part of the landed aristocracy. First known as Hispano/Mexicanos in the sixteenth century, these colonists for the most part were small working farmers and cattle and sheep ranchers and "working class" construction workers, adobemakers, carpenters, blacksmiths, and plasterers who worked in difficult and trying environmental and ecological circumstances. This migration of populations continued through the Mexican period (which began in 1821), the Mexican War (1846–1848), and beyond, with most of the population growth for the region basically consisting of migrating families from what is now northern and central Mexico into the southwestern United States. This expansion, for example in Texas, was primarily the result of migration from the northern and central Mexican provinces with adults making up two thirds of the population in Texas and 68 percent of the population of San Antonio over a sixteen-year period. Most were Hispano/Mexicano migrants from Saltillo, Camargo, Monterrey, Monclova, and Rio Grande, but they also came from such places in central Mexico as Querétaro, Mexico City, and Guadalajara.

During the Mexican period, the population of Hispano/Mexicanos became citizens of the new Republic of Mexico and therefore "Mexicano" or "Mexicans," but the self-reference was primarily the colonial one of Hispano/Mexicano.

## Immigration in the Early Twentieth Century

These processes of population movement from south to north were never interrupted, even by the aftermath of the Mexican War, in which half of Mexico, including the present U.S. southwestern states, were turned over to the United States. In fact, the California Gold Rush resulted in the first large-scale migration of twenty-five thousand Mexican *gambusinos* (prospectors) in 1848 from northern Sonora, when Arizona was still part of that Mexican region.

What is significant in this movement is that it set the stage for many following ones due to great changes of economy and production throughout the southwestern region and influenced Mexican migration throughout the United States. Thus, following this initial movement, the development of industrial agriculture, the expansion of the railroad, the development of large-scale ranching, and the large-scale development of copper mining stimulated large-scale labor movements from many parts of the border areas and central Mexico, which are the major sources of migrants to what became the United States.

Historically Mexican migration has not been unidirectional and at different periods has been cyclical, depending on economic conditions in Mexico itself. From the earliest migrations of the nineteenth century to the present, there has always been the pattern for cohorts of immigrants not only to return physically but also to send remittances to relatives who remain in Mexico. These remittances were used for reinvestment in agricultural lands in their points of origin.

Mexican migration to the United States in the twentieth century can be divided into two major demographic transitions: 1900 to 1929, and 1960 to the present. Between 1900 and 1929, a total of one million Mexicans migrated across the border as the aftermath of two processes. First, there were internal demographic changes in Mexico between 1876 and 1900, which increased the Mexican population by 40 percent, part of whom began to migrate to the Southwest prior to 1910. Second, there was a political upheaval created by the Mexican Revolution from 1910 to 1926 that was followed by a major depression in 1929.

However, this movement of the Mexican population found ready acceptance in the labor market, especially in agriculture, as the aftermath of the Chinese Exclusion Act of 1882 and the "gentlemen's agreement" of 1907, both of which excluded Asians from agriculture. This induced the agricultural industry to create labor contracting offices along the border and even in Mexico to recruit Mexicans to work in the citrus fields of California, the sugar beet areas of Colorado, Michigan, Minnesota, and Ohio, and the cotton fields of Texas, California, and Arizona. Coupled with great labor demands by the growth of industrial mining, the development of construction industries, and railroads, Mexicans moved into Kansas, Illinois, New York, and Pennsylvania.

The Southwest gained the greatest number of Mexicans for the 1900–1929 period, with Texas receiving more than 65 percent of all new immigrants, followed by Arizona, and then California. For migration to Arizona and Texas, the most important element that drove thousands across the border was the violence of the Mexican Revolution, which killed more than one million Mexicans.

The movement of Mexicans involved many of the social strata of Mexico, rich and poor, educated and uneducated, literate and illiterate, so that the border areas of Texas, Arizona, California, and

New Mexico were forever changed by the presence of a very heterogeneous population. They joined family members living in those states in cities such as Tucson, Albuquerque, El Paso, San Diego, and as far north as San Francisco; all of these cities were founded between the sixteenth and eighteenth centuries. They brought with them ideas and institutions that coincided with those already established, and in fact for most Mexicans it was as if they were stepping from one neighborhood to another rather than from one country to another. It was not until 1929 that visas were required of Mexicans crossing into the United States.

This population referred to themselves as Mexicanos in Texas, Manitos in New Mexico, Sonorenses in Arizona, and Californios in California, but all were categorized as "Mexicans" by non-Mexicans as a word of opprobrium in the Southwest. Although this negative definition emerged

A barber stands in front of his shop in the Mexican section of San Antonio, Texas, in 1939. (Library of Congress/Corbis)

out of the Mexican War and racist perceptions carried by southern Anglo settlers to Texas in the 1830s, the word "Mexican" became reinforced as a negative during the 1900–1929 period with cheap labor, ignorance, and even more negative characteristics such as thievery, dishonesty, and stupidity.

Mexicans migrating to Tucson from the adjoining Mexican state of Sonora would settle in neighborhoods already inhabited by other Mexicans whose descendants had fought Apache warriors only fifty years before. The newly arrived would probably get jobs through their resident kin networks in construction, the railroad, lumberyards, county maintenance, and in mostly blue-collar and service employment, while on Sundays they would attend San Agustin's Catholic Church. They joined mutual aid societies and read the *El Fronterizo* newspaper in Spanish, while their children attended Ochoa elementary school, passed through *quinceñeras* (religious puberty ceremonies), and became what was to become known as the Mexican-American generation. This generation, born of Mexican parents in the 1920s and early 1930s, joined with others to fight in World War II and Korea, and upon their return from these wars they refused to permit the rampant discrimination against them to continue on their jobs, in the schools, and in residential locations.

Abruptly, however, migration to the Southwest slowed to a trickle after 1929, with only 23,000 Mexicans migrating in a decade, compared to 450,000 in the previous ten years. From 1929 to 1937, during the Great Depression, repatriation and deportation measures were instituted in the United States and 500,000 persons of Mexican origin were "voluntarily" deported or forced to return to Mexico. One-third were American citizens, mostly teenagers who had been born in the United States. However, these teens, already greatly acculturated and dissatisfied, returned sometimes surreptitiously to their place of birth in the United States in time to join the armed services for World War II, where they received twelve Medals of Honor (four posthumously).

## The Bracero Period

Between 1930 and 1950, only eighty-three thousand Mexicans legally migrated to the United States, yet added to this number were five million agricultural workers, most of whom were recruited for World War II agricultural labor known as the Bracero Program. At the same time, relatively large-scale illegal migration also occurred. Many of those who had been temporary agricultural workers in fact became "illegal" when they overstayed their original labor contract and chose to live in the United States. During this period Mexicans also became known as "wetbacks," a word of opprobrium referring to the Rio Grande crossing between Texas and Mexican border states.

By 1954, a second large-scale deportation movement, called "Operation Wetback," resulted in more than one million arrests of illegal Mexican migrants. However, this number may not be precise since the same individual may have been arrested more than once. However, one unexpected outcome of this second expulsion was large-scale unrest in many Mexican neighborhoods. Many times immigration raids were indiscriminate, with border patrol agents sweeping into neighborhoods and illegally searching homes, workplaces, recreational centers, and stores, and even waiting outside Catholic churches on Sunday mornings after Mass. In addition, bakeries, restaurants, bars, public parks, swimming pools, Mexican movie theaters, and bus stops were all fair targets for the "sweeps" of heavily armed and aggressive border patrolmen.

Often men would be hidden by relatives in back rooms, garages, or packing sheds. Sometimes men wandered about the countryside, where they were easily identified and arrested. Later, these same men would turn up, again in the same places where they had been previously arrested. This pattern was to be repeated many times in the post-1960 period.

## The Chicano Generation

By 1960, however, 55 percent of Mexicans in the United States were native-born, down from

Migrant workers in Delano, California, demonstrate behind a bunch of white grapes in 1966 as part of the strike (which lasted five years) organized by Cesar Chavez. (Ted Streshinsky/Corbis)

more than 50 percent foreign-born in 1950. The increase in the number of native-born was due to high birthrates. There were an estimated five million Mexicans, both native-born and foreign-born, in the United States in 1960, a figure that had almost tripled by 1990.

Mexicans have always preferred to settle in the Southwest. In 1910, only 5.7 percent of the Mexican population lived outside of that region, but that figure had increased to 12.8 percent by 1960. This trend of concentration has continued and varied slightly, with 87 percent of the Mexican population living in the southwestern states in 1970, a slight drop to 83 percent in 1980, and 83.6 percent in 1990. Illinois, particularly Chicago, has been the preferred place outside the Southwest since 1970.

Especially after 1960, the Mexican population of the United States became urban. By 1990, the Mexican population was more than 90 percent urban, concentrated especially in southern California in the Los Angeles–Anaheim–Riverside area; in the northern California San Francisco–Oakland–San Jose area; in central and southern Texas in the Houston–Dallas–San Antonio–El Paso–McAllen areas: and then followed by Phoenix, Arizona. Other metropolitan cities with large Mexican populations include Albuquerque, San Diego, Tucson, and Chicago.

In 1994, native-born and foreign-born Mexicans comprised more than seventeen million, or 65 percent of the total U.S. Hispanic population of more than twenty-six million. It is highly likely that Mexicans will more than triple their total by the year 2050; their population increased by more than 50 percent between 1980 and 1990, and it had increased a further 20 percent by 1994. However, there is controversy as to whether the 1970 to 1980 increase of 93 percent is accurate or may instead be closer to 63.3 percent.

Of these increases, less than half was due to legal and illegal migration; the rest was due to high fertility rates during the 1960s and before. In 1970, 82.1 percent of the U.S. Mexican population was native-born, but the native-born had decreased to 74 percent by 1980 and to 67 percent by 1990. Yet this masks the fact that more than half of the Mexican foreign-born entered the United States between 1980 and 1990; of these, the great majority were legal migrants. Thus between 1980 and 1990 a little more than 2.2 million Mexicans were legally admitted to the United States, of whom 630,000 were admitted legally between 1980 and 1988, while 406,000 Mexicans were admitted legally in 1989, and another 680,000 in 1990.

These large numbers are in reality a reflection of the legalization program authorized by the Immigration Reform and Control Act of 1986 and not actually numbers of persons physically entering the United States. However, such numerical increases, whether by natural birth or by migration, do suggest a tripling of the Mexican population by 2050.

## Social, Economic, and Educational Characteristics of Mexicans in the United States

*Labor Force Characteristics.* In 1980, only 22.5% of the Mexican labor force in the U.S. Southwest was in upper white-collar and upper blue-collar occupations; the largest percentage (75%) was concentrated in the secondary and tertiary labor sectors: low white-collar (21.3%), low blue-collar (32.5%), service (15.5%), and farm workers (5.8%). In 1994, a total of 25% were in upper white and upper blue-collar occupations, while the rest were in low white-collar (26%), low blue-collar (23%), service (21%), and small-farm

labor occupations (6%). The significance of these differences is that in fourteen years, low-paid service occupations increased significantly while there were modest increases in upper white-collar and upper blue-collar occupations. Mexicans in low blue-collar occupations diminished. This is congruent with changes in the broader economy toward more service-oriented occupations.

Such occupational participation is reflected in per capita income. In 1980, the ratio of Mexican to non-Hispanic white per capita income was 0.55, and of mean household income, 0.78. In 1994, the per capita income ratio dropped to 0.44 and the median household income to 0.70. Therefore Mexican individuals earn less than half as much income as Anglos, and Mexican households have less than three-fourths as much income as Anglo households.

In Tucson, the mean per capita income in 1980 for 76 percent of the Mexican population was $5,202, and for 24 percent of the Mexican population, it was $8,398. For the Anglo population, the percentages were almost exactly reversed, with only 25.5 percent earning $5,202 and 74.5 percent earning $8,398. In comparing mean household income, 76 percent of the Mexican population earned $14,488 while 24 percent earned $21,994. Only 25.5 percent of the Anglo population earned $14,488 while 74.5% earned $24,245.

*Income Implications.* In 1992, a total of 27.4 percent of all Mexican families were in poverty, in comparison to 22.5 percent ten years earlier. Anglos had only 7.6 percent of all families below the poverty line. Slightly more than 13 percent of all Mexican households earned $50,000 or more, while the median was $22,477. When compared to Anglo populations these figures show the same disparity of income as that in 1980 but accentuated in 1992, with Anglos having only 10.2 percent of all such families below the poverty level, 28.4 percent of households earning $50,000 or more, and with a median household income of $32.311. In mean income, Mexican families earned only $27,968, while Anglos earned $46,715. Whether compared by "family" (which includes two or more persons who are related) or "household" (which includes all persons who occupy a housing unit), the results are the same: Mexicans are in poverty more than twice that of Anglos; more than twice as many Anglos earn more than $50,000; and the average income of Anglo families is almost twice that of Mexicans. For the most part, most Mexican households derive their income from working-class occupations, with only slightly more than 12 percent occupying managerial or professional positions, in comparison to 29 percent of Anglos in the same categories. Thus 78 percent of employed Mexican men and women are mostly engaged in low blue-collar, service, low white-collar, and agricultural labor, with only 3.1 percent in upper blue-collar occupations. Income is also derived from employment by several household members, members having two jobs, and the use of scarce resources in innovative and creative ways. Also, more Mexican households contain more adults than non-Hispanic white households and thus have potentially more earners per household. This advantage, however, is offset by a larger number of children per household; greater unemployment than among the non-Hispanic white population; and, probably for the first ten years of a household cycle, intermittent employment. In addition, one in five households is largely part of the primary labor sector in income, stability, and security of employment.

However, there are some significant gender differences that may provide insight into the manner in which patriarchy may be distributed within the households. First, 51.6 percent of Mexican women are in the labor force, which is only 7 percent less than for Anglo women. Second, 14 percent of Mexican women in the labor force are in upper white-collar occupations as managers or in a professional capacity, while only 9.3 percent of Mexican males are similarly employed. Almost 30 percent of employed Anglo women and 29 percent of Anglo men are managers or professionals. A total of 16.7 percent of Mexican women and 28.4 percent of Mexican men earned $25,000 to $50,000, while 2.1 percent of Mexican women and 3.8 percent of Mexican men earned more than $50,000.

The differences in the percentages of Mexican females and males earning less than $25,000 is significant, with slightly more than 82 percent of females and slightly less than 68 percent of males earning less than the amount. Among Anglos, the difference between females and males is more significant, but at lower percentages: 62.4 percent and 35.1 percent respectively. In terms of distributed income at this level, the totals for Mexican males are more like those for Anglo females, but both are significantly higher than for Mexican women; however, none approaches the low percentage distribution of Anglo males. From these data it is not obvious that at the upper end of the occupational scale patriarchy affects the labor force participation of Mexican women. And, given the unequal percentage of labor force participation between Mexican women and Mexican men (51.6% to 80.5%), the difference in the percentage of Mexican women earning more than $50,000 is 44 percent lower than that of males (2.1% to 3.8%).

The basic conclusions that can be reached, however, are that a higher percentage of both U.S. Mexican males and females earn less than $25,000 compared to Anglo males and females but that U.S. Mexican women are much more highly represented as a percentage than Mexican males, Anglo females, or Anglo males. This factor is quite important in ferreting out a steady but continuous development of the process of the feminization of poverty, in which larger and larger groups of women are overrepresented within the poverty sector.

However, poverty has been highly concentrated in the southern counties of the U.S. border region, so that the probability of higher income is greatest in the western coastal counties but decreases consistently as one moves east toward the lower Rio Grande valley in Texas, such as in Starr County, where the percentage of families in poverty was 45 percent in 1980 and rose to 60 percent in 1990. Yet for the most part such poverty areas are rural; the pattern of poverty is very much a consequence of the organization of industrial agriculture.

*Income and Education.* For Mexicans there is a direct correlation between income and education, so that lower income distribution is associated with lower educational attainment, and in part, lack of attained education is related to age, since the population as a whole is so young. Nevertheless, in 1994, of Mexican adults twenty- five years or over, only 6.3 percent had attained a bachelor's degree or more, while 24.3 percent of Anglos had reached that educational level. Similarly, only 46.7 percent of the Mexican population had attained a high school education or more, while 91 percent of Anglos had reached that level. At the bottom end of the educational spectrum, 5.7 percent of Mexicans had less than a fifth-grade education, while Anglos had only 0.8 percent at this level. Coupled with dropout rates of 50 percent or more from secondary schools, ladders for achievement and even entry into above-the-minimal-wage jobs are not available to an important part of the Mexican population.

## Family and Language Characteristics

*Household Structure.* Mexican households, whether of the recently arrived or not, will be structured around the search for and maintenance of work in metropolitan or semimetropolitan areas. Fewer than 10 percent of all Mexicans reside in rural areas, including rural farm and nonfarm regions, such as rural enclaves in northern New Mexico and southern Colorado and mining towns in the copper belt of southeastern Arizona and New Mexico. Even Mexican populations who have worked the various agricultural migrant streams from the 1920s to the present have a tendency of "settling in," so that there are Mexicans living in Wisconsin, Michigan, and Illinois as largely urban or semiurban dwellers but who originated as immigrant farmworkers. Seasonal or migrant farmworkers account for a very small part of the Mexican population. Probably no more than 10 percent of the Mexican population works as farm laborers; of these, most were not born in the United States.

A young girl dressed in a traditional costume dances in Market Square in San Antonio, Texas. (Sandy Felsenthal/Corbis)

Thus for Mexicans, the single most important value is to "settle in" and create house and hearth for themselves and future progeny. But a typical Mexican household's structure will vary according to generation, education, location, income, and when the analysis occurs during the development cycle. All households go through a developmental sequence, and Mexican households are no different, with one exception: There will usually be more persons present, especially more children, and at one time during the lifetime of the founders they will be in residence and will form the core to a cluster of other households. At this stage it is not unusual for grandparents to be caretakers of grandchildren from their own children's homes, which usually are within a mile of the core household. This clustered effect is especially present when nearby lots and houses are modestly priced, so that over time many of the original founding generation's children will live nearby with their own children and form satellite households, which over the developmental cycle will become core households themselves.

Such clusters of relations are built around the idea of reciprocity and mutual trust (*confianza*), and these have a tendency to radiate out from each household, multiply over time, and then be used in a variety of ways. A single core household that itself was a satellite will have a number of horizontal, thick relations with other core households of the same generation. These will form networks of exchange between them as well, so that siblings of the same generation who were part of satellites will transition into becoming cores as children and grandchildren are born.

These networks of exchange of approximately the same generation radiate into nonneighborhood and nonfamilial settings such as schools, businesses, small-scale institutions, churches, and other community settings such as doctors' offices, restaurants, lumberyards, and service settings such as social service and assistance offices. Each network that penetrates these settings creates "friends of friends" with those not related, so that the totality of relations for each household may run into the hundreds and seem like a very large web of connections that may be called on at particular times.

More than 60 percent of Mexican households at one time will have been a "satellite" and eventual "core," so this pattern of evolution and attendant expanding characteristics seems to be usual. Certainly census material points in that direction: Mexican households in 1990 had twice as many persons living within the household, made up of subfamilies and relatives, as did non-Mexican and non-Hispanic households, even though these numbers do not include the cluster of relations outside the immediate physical context of the household itself.

*Language Characteristics.* A high level of Spanish-language maintenance is importantly asso-

ciated with these household clusters, since grandchildren will more than likely have access to one or more generations of persons who speak the language, as well as relatively recent arrivals. In 1990, a total of 65 percent of Mexicans born in the United States spoke a language other than English, and 21 percent did not speak English well. This means that 79 percent did speak English, of whom a large percentage spoke Spanish as well. On the other hand, 96 percent of foreign-born Mexicans spoke a language other than English, and 71 percent did not speak English well. Thus most of the monolingual Spanish-speaking persons were foreign-born while most of those born in the United States were bilingual.

Foreign-born Mexicans residing in the United States are at a much greater disadvantage economically and occupationally than are U.S.-born Mexicans, in part because of lack of English-language skills. The dominance of English over Spanish in the United States is unquestionable, since for most children, English is the spoken and instructional language. This has created what can be termed "literacy fracturing." In studies conducted in Tucson, for example, only 68 percent of the sample read Spanish "well or very well," with an equal percentage writing in Spanish "well or very well." Since most schools are conducted in English, the ability of parents to participate in their own children's literacy *in Spanish* is "fractured"; the process, possibility, and practice of literacy activities in Spanish are hindered within Mexican households, even those where Spanish is the dominant language.

This educational situation does not permit the extended development of Spanish literacy and comprehension in reading and writing, so that disuse after one generation guarantees only an oral tradition transmission. However, language maintenance is directly associated with two important factors: proximity to the border and urban living. The closer to the border, the greater the tendency for language transmission and its maintenance. However, in the Southwest there is a tendency for both language loss and language replacement, especially due to the increased migration rates since

1970; most of these migrants will settle in urban areas.

## Community Life, Religion, and the Ritual Cycle

Since Mexicans in the United States are primarily urban dwellers, many of the advantages and disadvantages of urban living will also be part of their life. Myriad ritual activities and voluntary associations are important parts of the Mexican life cycle, whether urban or not.

Although more than 70 percent of Mexicans in the United States were Roman Catholic in 1990, there is an important movement to other religious groups, and some Mexicans have become Pentecostals, Baptists, Seventh-Day Adventists, or Mormons. The attraction of these churches seems to be associated in part with dissatisfaction with the manner in which the Catholic Church has responded to the needs of newly arrived migrants. First-generation Mexican Americans seem to be attracted to less structured fundamentalist groups, while second- and third-generation Mexican Americans seem to be attracted to the Mormon religion, with its emphasis on family life.

However, regardless of religious orientation, it is probable that much of community life will be structured by the many rituals in which Mexicans participate, which can be termed the "ritual cycle." Throughout the year, a series of major and minor rituals punctuate the daily and weekly life of Mexicans. Two mandatory participatory rituals divide the yearly cycle: the celebration of Christmas and Easter. In addition, secular and religious rituals such as weddings, baptisms, funerals, anniversaries, high school and university homecoming celebrations, and birthdays fill the ritual cycle. For the most part such events incorporate newer generations in very tangible and recognizable ways. In a sense each new generational member is provided a historical glimpse of the past in different secular and ritual forms and is made part of the same process by his or her participation.

These, then, form the bases of community life, provide a kind of "cultural glue" to the sense of community and identity, and ease the problems of undereducation, poverty, and low income.

## Conclusion

The Mexican population in the United States is a heterogeneous one of varying generations, backgrounds, points of origin, and class cultures. Yet Mexicans share in common a strong sense of familial connection and an unfailing desire to work and succeed, and they have served honorably when called to arms. Nevertheless, part of the population suffers from undereduction, modest income, and overrepresentation in the nation's wars. Demographically, it is a growing population whose language extends back in history to the sixteenth century and forward to the present with the most recent arrivals. It has developed highly adaptive patterns of familial life and religious beliefs, and it continues to search diligently for occupational security, protection, and success. Given the rates of the population's growth neither the problems nor the successes will soon abate.

*See also:*   CALIFORNIOS; MEXICANS; PUNJABI MEXICANS; SPANIARDS

## Bibliography

Bean, F., and Tienda, M. (1987). *The Hispanic Population of the United States.* New York: Russell Sage Foundation.

Campa, A. L. (1979). *Hispanic Culture in the Southwest.* Norman: University of Oklahoma Press.

Chavez, L., and Martinez, R. G. (1995). "Mexican Immigration in the 1980s and Beyond: Implications for Chicanos." In *Chicanos: The Contemporary Era*, edited by I. Ortiz and D. Maciel. Tucson: University of Arizona.

Clark, B. M. (1976). "Mexican Migration to the United States." In *Mexican Migration*, edited by T. Weaver and T. Downing. Tucson: Bureau of Ethnic Research.

Garcia, J. M. (1993). "The Hispanic Population in the United States: March 1992." *Current Population Reports, Population Characteristics.* Washington, DC: U.S. Department of Commerce.

Grebler, L.; Moore, J. W.; and Guzman, R. C. (1970). *The Mexican-American People, The Nation's Second Largest Minority*. New York: Free Press.

Swadesh, F. L. (1974). *Los Primeros Pobladores: Hispanic Americans of the Ute Frontier*. Notre Dame, IN: University of Notre Dame Press.

Tjark, A. V. (1979). "Comparative Demographic Analysis of Texas, 1777–1793." In *New Spain's Far Northern Frontier: Essays on Spain in the American West*, edited by D. J. Weber. Albuquerque: University of New Mexico Press.

U.S. Bureau of the Census. (1993). "Persons of Hispanic Origin in the United States: August 1993." *Current Population Reports*, 1990 CP-3-3. Washington, DC: U.S. Government Printing Office.

Vélez-Ibáñez, C. G. (1996). *Border Visions: The Cultures of Mexicans of the Southwest United States*. Tucson: University of Arizona Press.

CARLOS G. VÉLEZ-IBÁÑEZ

# MIDDLE EASTERN JEWS

*See* JEWS, MIDDLE EASTERN

# MIEN

The Mien (Iu Mien, Yao, Man, Dzao) are a tribal people of the mountains of East and Southeast Asia. They have for centuries survived on the periphery of Chinese civilization, selectively absorbing aspects of Chinese culture while resolutely maintaining indigenous language, ritual, and social organization. There are about five million Mien, most of whom continue to live in remote areas of southern and western China. Significant Mien populations are also found in the northern tier of Southeast Asia, in Burma, Laos, Thailand, and Vietnam.

As a distinct tribal minority, the Mien have always been forced to adjust to the demands of larger political entities and dominant cultures.

Mien villages are typically situated in high mountain ranges where farmers grow rice, vegetables, and selective cash crops. The immigration of Mien from China to Southeast Asia is thought to have begun only in the mid-nineteenth century. Expanding ethnic Chinese populations displaced Mien minority communities from valuable upland valley lands, forcing refugees to search for new farmland across the southern Chinese border.

The Mien population of Vietnam (where they are termed "Dzao" and are subsumed under fourteen different subgroups) is thought to number about half a million people. (The Mien are often referred to as "Yao" in older writings and continue to be called Yao in China.) Approximately fifty thousand Mien were known to reside in Laos at the beginning of 1975. It is from this group, formerly resident in the provinces of Nam Tha and Sayaboury, that Mien immigrants to the United States derive.

## The Indochina Conflict

Between 1960 and 1975, the U.S. government was deeply committed to supporting the neutralist government of Laos. The Laotian monarchy was sympathetic to the American cause in Vietnam and lent its assistance to American efforts to arm irregular guerrilla forces employed to provide intelligence on and harass the movement of supplies for Communist Vietnamese forces in South Vietnam. These supplies were moved by truck along the Ho Chi Minh trail, which coursed through the mountains of western Vietnam, at times entered central Laos, and also branched into eastern Cambodia. During the Indochina conflict American airplanes flew thousands of combat sorties over Laos, the U.S. government provided hundreds of millions of dollars of assistance to the Laotian government, and tens of thousands of Laotian soldiers were recruited, trained, and maintained by American funds.

The most effective of the Laotian soldiers were those recruited from the northern hill tribes of this rugged, landlocked Southeast Asian nation. The most numerous of these guerrilla soldiers were recruits from the Hmong ethnic group (thought to number 350,000 in Laos in 1975). The second-largest group involved in the American War effort in Laos were the Mien. Situated near the Chinese border at Nam Tha and Muong Sing in northwestern Laos, the Mien in the late 1950s were initially recruited to conduct cross-border reconnaissance operations in southwestern China. In the mid-1960s Mien soldiers fought as pro-American guerrillas under the leadership of Hmong General Vang Pao.

In 1975, pro-American governments in South Vietnam, Cambodia, and Laos collapsed. Succeeded by hard-line Communist regimes, the new governments moved quickly to neutralize, disarm, and sometimes imprison former pro-American allies. "Reeducation camps" were established in both Laos and Vietnam to instruct defeated representatives of the failed pro-American governments in the philosophy and practice of Marxism. In this context more than one million refugees from Cambodia, Laos, and Vietnam fled their homelands to find refuge in the United States between 1975 and 1995. Among the hundreds of thousands of refugees from Indochina were approximately 150,000 tribal people from Laos as well as approximately 110,000 Hmong, 20,000 Mien, and a mélange of smaller groups, including Lahu, Khmu, and Akha, and Vietnamese minority peoples such as the Rhade, Koho, and Cham from southern Vietnam.

## Mien in America

Mien refugees were initially resettled in diverse locales across the United States, including Alabama, New Mexico, and Minnesota, but most Mien relocated to the West Coast, in cities such as Long Beach, San Francisco, Portland, and Seattle. Almost all Mien-Americans resided in West Coast venues in 1996. California supports the largest Mien community in the United States. Sacramento is home to approximately six thousand Mien. The San Francisco Bay Area (especially Oakland and Richmond) supports a population of similar size. Other major communities exist in Redding (seat of Shasta County, where Laotian Americans comprise

the largest ethnic minority group) as well as a string of California central valley towns, including Stockton, Merced, Fresno, Visalia, and Porterville.

Mien refugees have not easily adjusted to life in the United States. The educational level of Mien adults brought to America in refugee airlifts was the lowest of all the groups admitted from 1975 to 1995. Mien adults over age twenty-five were typically illiterate in Lao much less in French or English. Moreover, the vast majority of Mien adults had never been exposed to even a minimal level of elementary schooling in Laos. Because the plurality of Mien refugees entered the United States from 1979 to 1981, before coherent orientation and English-language programs were established in refugee transit centers, very few Mien were prepared for the adaptation challenges they would face in the United States.

A Mien priest in Richmond, California, summons ancestral spirits to pass through the house portal by tapping on a water buffalo horn. (Eric Crystal)

Numerous Mien families who deplaned at West Coast airports carried rice and vegetable seeds and core agricultural implements. Some began to plant corn in November and December 1980 in front-yard gardens in West Oakland, where they were initially resettled by voluntary agencies. A great many middle-aged and older Mien women arrived in America wearing their traditional folk costumes (black embroidered turbans, homespun tunics, and elaborately embroidered trousers). Transported from a familiar Southeast Asian cultural environment to an alien American world in just a few hours, the Mien were immediately forced to deal with many unfamiliar aspects of daily American life, including door locks, glass windows, private cars, compulsory education, banks, and welfare requirements.

## Independence in the Mien Experience

Prior to their arrival in Thai refugee camps beginning in 1975, almost all Lao-Mien were independent owner-operators of family farms. They resided in houses they built and owned and farmed fields that for all intents and purposes were their own property. Family nutritional requirements were met by the farm. Income was derived from the sale of produce and also from wages remitted by Mien soldiers employed by the Royal Lao Army. Refugees arriving in California immediately qualified for refugee cash assistance, funds administered by the Department of Social Services.

When federal cash assistance expired, almost all Mien subsequently qualified for domestic transfer payments (under the Aid for Families with Dependent Children, Supplementary Security Income, or General Assistance Programs). Within a few months many Mien families quickly established a pattern of dependence on transfer payments. Although modest by American standards, these payments enabled Mien refugees to enjoy amenities such as electricity, running water, and private transportation unknown in their home communities.

Typically settled in the poorest urban neighborhoods, many Mien families soon became victims of crime and random violence. Tensions between Mien and their largely African-American and Mexican-American neighbors was often exacerbated by lack of ability in the early years to communicate effectively in English. For Mien refugees resettled in the United States, arrival signified a radical break with the past. Most disturbing of all the new challenges confronted by the Mien community has been a growing gap between parents and children, whose life experiences have differed so radically.

## Generation Gap

Mien students educated beginning in kindergarten in American schools have inevitably developed significantly different worldviews, social attitudes, and values from their parents. Most of their lives have been spent in the least desirable urban neighborhoods. They have studied in the most impoverished urban schools. Exposed to media depictions of upper- and middle-class American life yet relegated to the unique underclass the welfare system has created, many of these young Mien have become involved with the criminal system, have failed to finish high school (and in more than a few cases have not completed junior high school), and face bleak prospects in the job market. Parental expectations and youth aspirations often have clashed. Such value confrontations are nowhere more apparent than in the case of marriages, where parental pressure on young girls to marry early sometimes conflicts with the girls' desire to remain in school. In traditional Mien farming culture, early marriage, and the production of many children constituted economic advantage. Mien marriage ceremonies are elaborate—occasions for community celebration and the cementing of cross-clan family ties. But the relationship between marriage and effective economic independence has not been stressed in the Mien community, leading in many cases to a second generation on welfare dependence.

The Mien from Laos arrived in the United States as a traditional, culturally coherent, relatively classless society. Almost all Mien shared the same traditional religious and cultural values; possessed equivalent skills as village farmers; and cooperated as members of coherent, mutually supportive village communities. In many California communities today, 60 to 70 percent of Mien adults remain dependent on transfer payments. The remainder are gainfully employed in a range of occupations, from certified schoolteacher to automobile mechanic to industrial factory worker. For those who have been employed, consistent saving and family loan networks have facilitated the purchase of homes and full participation in the "American dream." For those who have remained on welfare and whose sons and daughters may also be dependent, the promise of America remains a distant dream, the independent farming life of far-off Laos a fading memory.

## Mien Culture at the Crossroads

The very rich and integral tapestry of Mien traditional culture has inevitably faded and become tattered in the resettlement context. It is virtually impossible to maintain the values and life ways of an independent mountain farming people in the context of urban American life. The Mien arrived in the United States with more than 90 percent of their population committed to the traditional religion of their ancestors, Ley Nyey. An amalgam of archaic Chinese Taoist and Southeast Asian animist belief and practice, traditional Mien religion presents a coherent array of ceremonial practices designed to link the living with the world of the ancestors, to cure the sick, and to assure prosperity in the future. During the time that Mien have been residing in America they have been subject to vigorous Protestant evangelical activity organized by missionary groups who made little impact on this group in Laos until the situation in Thai refugee camps proved to be somewhat more fertile ground for conversion.

Today, approximately half of the Mien population in Seattle is Christian, and 20 to 30 percent have converted in California. Such conversions inevitably generate intracommunity tensions as Christians forbid marriage of sons and daughters

A Mien child in Oakland, California, wears a traditional cap to provide protection from malevolent spirits. (Eric Crystal)

with traditional believers. Christian converts are urged to destroy any and all objects considered sacred in the traditional faith. Heirloom books of genealogy and ritual, and implements of ritual practice of ebony, pewter inlay, or silver are oftentimes crushed or burned at conversion ceremonies. Children of traditionalist parents frequently are estranged from ritual practice even if they do not opt for conversion. The sometimes day-long rituals command the attention of older people but often fail to attract younger community members, who might prefer to play volleyball, socialize, or watch television. Conversion rates have dropped off in California in recent years as the split between Christian and non-Christian Mien has stabilized. Yet the future of Mien traditional religion, cohesive community interaction, and even Mien language in America remains in question as successive generations become increasingly removed from the roots of Mien traditional farming adaptation and community life.

## The Future of the Mien Community

Approximately twenty thousand Mien reside in the United States. Almost all Mien live in California, Oregon, or Washington State. Twenty families also live in Alaska. As Mien families are consistently large and the rate of outmarriage has remained low, the size of the Mien community will undoubtedly grow. Achieving economic independence is the most significant issue facing the Mien community. Mien adults have probably been the least successful in adapting to American economic conditions of any discernible Southeast Asian refugee group. Recalling the educational and cultural background of the Mien, their problems in adapting to American life should not be considered surprising. Today scores of Mien students are enrolled in four-year colleges and universities. A number of Mien have graduated and are working as professionals in school systems and other local government offices. A handful of Mien have successfully opened private business ventures (such as garages, gas stations, or local food stores) across California. No immigrants to the United States have ever been asked to bridge a greater gap in education, culture, or economics than have the Mien from Laos.

*See also:* LAO

## Bibliography

Butler-Diaz, J. (1981). *Yao Design in Northern Thailand*, revised edition. Bangkok: Siam Society.

Hanks, L. M.; Hanks, J. R.; and Sharp, L., eds. (1965). *Ethnographic Notes on Northern Thailand*. Ithaca, NY: Southeast Asia Program, Cornell University.

Lewis, J., ed. (1992). *Minority Cultures of Laos*. Rancho Cordova, CA: Southeast Asia Community Resource Center.

Lemoine, J. (1982). *Yao Ceremonial Paintings*. Bangkok: White Lotus Press.

McKinnon, J., and Bhruksasri, W., eds. (1983). *Highlanders of Thailand*. Kuala Lumpur: Oxford University Press.

Walker, A. R., ed. (1975). *Farmers in the Hills: Upland Peoples of North Thailand*. Pinang, Malaysia: Phoenix Press.

ERIC CRYSTAL

# MONTENEGRINS

Montenegrins immigrated in substantial numbers to the United States in the late 1800s and early 1900s from the rocky area they consider to be their homeland, a region that lies above the Adriatic seacoast in present-day Yugoslavia and just to the north of Albania. While Montenegrins often settled in places that attracted other Serbian immigrants, they have remained a distinct ethnic subgroup. Today there are tens of thousands of Americans of Montenegrin descent.

## Ethnic Definition

Although Montenegrins consider themselves to be Serbs, and Serbs also consider Montenegrins to be Serbs, there are some distinctive differences. For one thing, Montenegrins speak the *jekavski* dialect of Serbo-Croatian, while Serbs speak *ekavski*. Montenegrins have their own special cultural heroes as well as their own tradition of heroic epics, which includes many shorter songs about sheep-stealing or raids with head-hunting. Whereas Serbian folk music is melodic and lyrical, similar to the music of western Europe, Montenegrin village music is based on a different tonal scale entirely and contrasts driving bass voices of males with the shrill, plaintive timbre of females. In dancing, rural Montenegrins still emulate eagles, leaping grandly into the air. These cultural differences, in combination with great differences in political history, social organization, and world-view, distinguish a formerly tribal people living in Old Montenegro and mountainous southern Hercegovina from all other Serbs.

As a distinctive ethnic group Montenegrins define themselves partly in terms of being from a particular region, but even more in terms of a unique history of four centuries of successful armed rebellion against the Ottoman Turks. This protracted struggle enabled them to remain politically autonomous when the other Christians all around them, mostly Serbs, were politically enslaved. Their name for themselves in the Serbian language is Crnogorci (People of the Black Mountain). The Venetians used the Italian term "Montenegro." Montenegrins consider themselves to be Serbs primarily because of their religion and use of the Cyrillic alphabet. As Christians they are members of the Eastern Orthodox Church, and like other Serbs they hold a special feast annually, the *slava*, for the clan's patron saint. Serbs are the chief Eastern Orthodox Christians who do this; the slava is believed to contribute to the welfare of the household and clan.

Montenegrins were a highly unique ethnic group not only in the former Yugoslavia but also in Europe as a whole. They had a genuinely "nonliterate tribal" culture as recently as the latter part of the eighteenth century, and aside from a small cadre of Eastern Orthodox clergy, they were without reading and writing until 1851. In the present Republic of Montenegro there are still several dozen tribes (*plemena*), and until 1850, each was, in effect, a sovereign mini-nation. In 1851, a small, politically centralized tribal kingdom was formed, and it sometimes played a significant role in Balkan and world affairs.

## Historical Context

Montenegrins are extremely conscious of their history and of their cultural uniqueness as Europeans who, for centuries, were largely isolated from civilization. They consider themselves to have been warrior heroes who were crowded together in a stony refuge area that was eminently

defensible, where a life of continual violence was forced on them. They were attacked frequently because the Ottoman Empire knew these Serbian warriors might ignite a general insurrection of the enslaved Christians in the Balkans, and the Russians were always there to help their brother Serbs throw off Muslim control.

Montenegrins are quite conscious of their past as tribal warriors who went raiding for badly needed provisions and took human heads as trophies. Their strong sense of ethnic identity is heightened by the glory of having been the only people to resist the Ottoman Empire as early as they did and for such a long period of time. In modern times Serbs in Belgrade stereotype Montenegrins as being "clannish," hyperpatriarchal, and "lazy." In truth they are preoccupied with having sons and proclaim the importance of males, as do other warrior societies. However, the "laziness" ascribed to the males is based partly on cultural misunderstandings. In the old days men were either out raiding or occupied with feuding much of the time, so the custom developed that women did much of the heavy labor.

A typical tribe consisted of several thousand people whose means of reckoning descent and inheriting property was patrilineal, and in the older tribes it was believed that all clans were linked to a common ancestor. Basically, Montenegrins lived in communal households consisting of a patriarch, his sons, and various women from other clans who married his sons. After several generations such a household might become quite large, with a group of male first or second cousins living communally and referring to one another as "brother." Eventually, because arable land was so scarce and scattered in small plots, Montenegrin communal households had to split. However, membership in the clan continued to be important because the clan was also the unit of feuding.

Each household owned a plot of land in the winter village, while during the summers all the households of a tribe shared use of the tribe's extensive high mountain pastures, where most of the people went to herd sheep and goats and process milk products. Montenegrins lived on cheese, milk, yogurt, salt butter, occasional meat, and vegetables grown in the winter village. Because Montenegro was an overpopulated refuge area, another important part of the household economy was raiding. The season lasted approximately half the year, and men would go out in groups of up to thirty on stealthy forays. Targets were local Muslims — actually Serbs who had Islamicized for economic advantage — but also neighboring Christian Serbs or Albanians who lived under the domination of Ottoman lords. Montenegrins still sing heroic epics about these raids, and the prizes included not only livestock but also Muslim brides and human heads. A typical raiding tactic was to sneak into a corral at night and cut the bell from the ram that led the herd, then draw the sheep away by gently sounding the bell.

If Montenegrins have a distinctive "ethnic personality," this is due to their practice of raising their sons to be warriors and because they define male and female roles so divergently. The tribes regularly went to war against Ottoman armies (who had been sent to subjugate, punish, or tax the tribes) and often did so when heavily outnumbered. The tribesmen who became free earliest were those of Old Montenegro, around the small town of Cetinje, just inland from the Adriatic coast south of Dubrovnik. Their rugged terrain was mostly unfit for agriculture, providing only the occasional fertile basin in the midst of all but barren limestone hills and mountains, but it was eminently defensible. There were no proper roads, but numerous defiles, cliffs, and passes, which made it possible for a few thousand warriors to defend.

These tribesmen were extremely egalitarian. No man was willing to take orders or acknowledge ranking lower than another. The tribal leader, while highly respected and necessarily a good warrior, was obliged to gather the entire tribe whenever there was a decision to be made. Likewise, when all the tribes temporarily united into a military confederation to resist a massive Turkish attack, the supreme leader of the confederation was without any real power even though he was chosen for his bravery and wisdom. Normally this

was a *vladika*, or bishop of the Eastern Orthodox Church.

In 1850–1851, Montenegro underwent radical political and cultural changes. Danilo II asked the tribal council if he could become a secular leader so he could marry the daughter of a rich Venetian merchant, and the council assented. A ruthless man, Danilo proceeded to subvert what remained of the egalitarian tribal society that persisted in Montenegro and created a despotic kingdom. He accomplished this by collecting taxes by force, and all the tribes fell in line once he had beheaded several hunded people, many of them noncombatants, in the powerful Kuci tribe. At that point the tribes of Old Montenegro had been joined with the Sedmoro Brda, the seven large tribes in southeastern Hercegovina, and this mighty tribal confederation was quickly turned into a small nation with a police force, army, and elementary schools (for males only).

The Turks attacked in force, laying siege to Montenegro as a serious threat to their empire, but the new tribal dukedom held out. Danilo was assassinated in 1860, and his nephew, Nikola Petrovic (who later granted a constitution in 1905 and was given the title of king in 1910), carried the struggle forward. The peace of 1878 saw Montenegro gaining political recognition as a nation and large amounts of territory in Hercegovina at Ottoman expense, but the price of recognition was emigration. Whereas the overpopulated Montenegrins in their stony refuge area has always managed to live fairly well by raiding their more affluent neighbors, the price of becoming a "modern" nation with guaranteed frontiers was that raiding was stopped. People began to starve.

## Immigration and America

Hungry Montenegrins had always emigrated. A few went to Istanbul and became water-carriers. Others emigrated from Montenegro to various parts of Serbia. However, after full recognition of nationhood was achieved in 1878 the hunger was pervasive and America beckoned, along with South America. A stream of males directed itself toward the United States. In the 1830s, Montenegrins from the Bay of Kotor had already formed a colony in New Orleans (working as fishermen), and with the end of raiding many came to Chicago in the mid-1800s. After the California Gold Rush Montenegrins settled in San Francisco, Sacramento, Fresno, Los Angeles, and San Diego. In 1880, the pattern of emigration changed, and it was Montenegrins from the mountains rather than the coastal areas who immigrated to America. Their target was the industrial heartland with its coal mines and steel mills, including Pittsburgh.

In the early 1900s, there were more than a quarter of a million Montenegrins in Montenegro, and perhaps 10 percent of that number had immigrated to the United States, mostly men from nineteen to twenty-four. These immigrants remained very bound to their culture of origin and most of them sent home substantial amounts of money. They also remained emotionally tied to their homeland and its political fortunes. In 1911–1912, King Nikola started the First Balkan War by attacking Turkish Albania, and this led to a series of smaller wars that led directly to World War I. All across America, Montenegrin immigrants rushed to board special trains that carried them to the East Coast, where they embarked to fight the "Turks," who were actually Islamicized Albanians just as "tribal" as the Montenegrins had been. Were it not for this First Balkan War, there probably would be twice as many Montenegrins in the United States today.

In 1916, the Austrians defeated the Montenegrins, and King Nikola fled to Italy, where his daughter had married into the royal house. Montenegro as an independent nation was finished, and the peace made in 1920 integrated Montenegro into a Slavic kingdom dominated by Serbia. Many of the American immigrant returnees perished in Austrian prison camps, but now reimmigration was difficult because U.S. immigration laws enacted in the early 1920s placed quota restrictions on Serbian entry into the United States. Subsequently, the Great Depression made America less attractive for Montenegrins facing poverty at home, and basically the survivors were stuck where they were. Although modest immigration began after World War II, the bulk of Montenegrins in America arrived before 1911. After World War II, many Montenegrins immigrated to Serbian centers such as Milwaukee, Chicago, Detroit, Cleveland, and New York, and as political rather than economic refugees many of them were more educated than the earlier immigrants. They also were more involved with politics back home, some being monarchists and some simply anti-Communists.

Montenegrins in America continue to view themselves as Serbs with a very special history and culture. As Eastern Orthodox Christians who practice the slava, they associate with other Serbs religiously and through cultural organizations, but their distinctive history and worldview continue to stand them apart as a separate and very proud ethnic entity.

*See also:*  SERBS

## Bibliography

Boehm, C. (1983). *Montenegrin Social Organization and Values: Political Ethnography of a Refuge Area Tribal Adaptation*. New York: AMS Press.

Boehm, C. (1986). *Blood Revenge: The Enactment and Management of Conflict in Montenegro and Other Tribal Societies*. Philadelphia: University of Pennsylvania Press.

Cvijic J. (1918). *La Peninsule Balcanique*. Paris: Geographie Humaine.

Djilas, M. (1958). *Land Without Justice*. New York: Harcourt, Brace.

Djilas, M. (1966). *Njegos: Poet, Prince, Bishop*. New York: Harcourt, Brace, & World.

Durham, M. E. (1928). *Some Tribal Origins, Laws, and Customs of the Balkans*. London: George Allen and Unwin.

Milic, Z. (1995). *A Stranger's Supper*. New York: Twayne.

Ranke, L. von. (1853). *The History of Servia, and the Servian Revolution*. London: Henry Bohn.

Simic, A. (1967). "The Blood Feud in Montenegro." In *Essays in Balkan Ethnology*, edited by W. G. Lockwood. Berkeley, CA: Kroeber Anthropological Society Special Publications.

Vialla de Sommieres, L. (1820). *Voyage Historique et Politique au Montenegro.* Paris: Alexis Eymery.

Wilkinson, J. G. (1848). *Dalmatia and Montenegro,* Vol. I. London: John Murray.

Wyon, R., and Prance, G. (1903). *The Land of the Black Mountain.* London: Methuen.

CHRISTOPHER BOEHM

# MUSLIMS

*See* AFRICAN MUSLIMS; BANGLADESHIS; BOSNIAN MUSLIMS; CHAM; EGYPTIAN MUSLIMS; IRANIANS; IRAQI MUSLIMS; ISMAILIS; JORDANIANS; LEBANESE MUSLIMS; PAKISTANIS; PALESTINIANS; SYRIANS; TURKS; YEMENIS

# NEPALESE

Nepalese immigrants in the United States comprise a comparatively small community but reflect the diversity of Nepalese ethnic backgrounds. Culturally, these encompass the three geographical areas of Nepal, popularly known as the Himal (high, mountainous region bordering the Tibetan autonomous region of China), the Pahad (the middle hills), and the Tarai (the southern flat area bordering India). Despite their geographic, linguistic, and ethnic diversity, Nepalese immigrants in the United States are collectively known by the single group name "Nepali" which stands for both the people and the lingua franca of present-day Nepal, a country situated between the two giants of Asia: China and India.

The common traits of Nepalese immigrants are classified by their original Nepali nationality, languages, and cultures. The physical features of Nepalese immigrants vary according to their geographical and ethnic origins. Nepalese of Bhotia origin (Himalayan highlanders) are considered ethnically Mongoloid. Their physical features are very similar to those of Tibetans, and they are also known as Tibeto-Mongolians. This community comprises different subgroups, such as Sherpa, Gurung, Tamang, Kirati, Magar, and other people of Himalayan origin.

The people representing the Pahad are basically Bahun-Chhetris and Newars. Among them, Newars are mainly from Katmandu Valley. This community comprises both Hindus and Buddhists by religious belief and Indo-Aryan and Mongoloid by physical features, although the Newars are a highly syncretized group with their own language, popularly known as Newari. Anthropologists believe the Bahun-Chhetris belong to the Caucasoid Indo-Aryan family. They are physically similar to North Indian people. The Tarai people, also known as Madheshe, are from the southern tropical plains known as Tarai or Madesh. They are physically and culturally very similar to the Indians of Bihar and Uttar Pradesh.

## Immigration and Settlement History

The history of Nepalese immigration to the United States is a recent phenomenon compared to that of most other Asian and South Asian countries. The first Nepalese obtained permanent U.S. residence in 1952. A gradual increase in the number of Nepalese immigrants began only after 1956—

1957, but even as of the mid-1990s, the total number of Nepalese in the United States is relatively small.

The main deterrents for earlier Nepalese immigration to the United States were: (1) the Nepalese government's internal restrictive policy, (2) the absence of diplomatic relations between Nepal and the United States until 1947, and (3) Nepal's lack of access to Western material culture and languages.

Nepal's difficult geopolitical situation has determined the scope and nature of the country's foreign policy and foreign contact through the ages. Thus, the further causes for the late arrival and small number of Nepalese immigrants in the United States can be identified as Nepal's economic disadvantage, poor literacy rates, lack of compulsory education, the physical distance, and cultural and linguistic disparities. The requirement of a high school diploma or occupational skills or experience still prevents common Nepalese from obtaining an immigrant visa.

Effectively, Nepalese were directly prevented from immigrating to the United States by the U.S. immigration and naturalization policy. The past policy of immigration quotas by continents prevented Nepalese from entering the United States in considerable numbers, since the Asian limit was largely filled by émigrés from larger Asian countries, such as India, China, Pakistan, Philippines, and Korea. Because the initial Nepalese immigrant community in the United States was so small, the number of relatives allowed entry under the Immigration Act of 1965 was also limited. Therefore, the new system favoring family reunification was favorable only for those countries that had already created large immigrant communities in the United States before 1965.

In the United States, Nepalese immigrants are mainly centered in or near large cities and where renowned universities are located. States such as California, New York, Maryland, Illinois, Texas, Michigan, and New Jersey, as well as metropolitan Washington, D.C., have relatively large numbers of Nepalese immigrants. The major portion of the Himalayan-origin Nepalese have settled almost exclusively in large cities such as New York, San Francisco, and Seattle.

Since only a few Nepalese Americans and permanent residents of the first generation are now close to retirement age, there is no existing evidence of circular and return immigration, but it is expected. Second-generation Nepalese Americans pursuing higher education or beginning professional work do not in general consider returning to Nepal. They are accustomed to the American way of life and material facilities. In addition, there is no infrastructure for economic development in Nepal that would attract such sophisticated individuals born, educated, and trained in a much more technologically advanced country.

## Demographics

Nepalese constitute only about 0.05 percent of the total number of Asian and about 0.4 percent of the total number of South Asian immigrants in the United States. Nepal has not been included as a separate nation in the U.S. Immigration and Naturalization Service (INS) yearbook since 1993. A total of 2,433 Nepalese were admitted to the United States as permanent residents between 1952 and 1993. The rate of Nepalese immigration has increased more steadily in the 1990s under a U.S. lottery quota. A total of 860 Nepalese were admitted as permanent residents between 1990 and 1993. Projecting these data through 1995, there are about 3,000 Nepalese in the United States as permanent residents or naturalized citizens. About 47 percent of them are female. But the total estimated number of Nepalese in the United States (including legal and illegal workers, students, scholars, exchange visitors, tourists, business people, international job holders, and so on) is about 18,000.

Nepalese immigrants in the United States can be categorized in five tentative sub-groups: Bahun-Chhetri, Newar, Tibeto-Mongoloid Himalayan, Tarai or Madhese, and other. The Bahun-Chhetri is the largest group, constituting about 45 percent of the total Nepalese immigrant population in the United States. The Newar community from Kat-

TABLE 1   Nepalese Immigrants Admitted to the United States, 1952–1993

| Year | Number | Year | Number |
|------|--------|------|--------|
| 1952 | 1  | 1973 | 46  |
| 1953 | 0  | 1974 | 43  |
| 1954 | 0  | 1975 | 56  |
| 1955 | 0  | 1976 | 68  |
| 1956 | 1  | 1977 | 80  |
| 1957 | 5  | 1978 | 68  |
| 1958 | 0  | 1979 | 79  |
| 1959 | 4  | 1980 | 95  |
| 1960 | 4  | 1981 | 83  |
| 1961 | 5  | 1982 | 97  |
| 1962 | 5  | 1983 | 105 |
| 1963 | 3  | 1984 | 75  |
| 1964 | 7  | 1985 | 63  |
| 1965 | 4  | 1986 | 86  |
| 1966 | 8  | 1987 | 78  |
| 1967 | 9  | 1988 | 106 |
| 1968 | 19 | 1989 | 134 |
| 1969 | 32 | 1990 | 184 |
| 1970 | 25 | 1991 | 174 |
| 1971 | 40 | 1992 | 206 |
| 1972 | 39 | 1993 | 296 |
|      |    | Total | 2,433 |

Source: U.S. Immigration and Naturalization Service (1993).

older than seventy. In total there were only 56 Nepalese immigrants prior to 1968, but as a result of changes to immigration law in the 1960s, the number of Nepalese acquiring permanent residency has increased from 19 in 1968 to 296 in 1993, for a total of 2,433 Nepalese immigrants. Although there is no separate yearly data available after 1993, using the tentative total estimate of Nepalese immigrants (covering the available data from 1956 through 1993 plus rough estimates for 1994 and 1995), the average ratio of yearly admittance can be calculated as no less than 71 individuals.

## Language

Although Nepalese in the United States have different ethnic, lingual, and cultural backgrounds, Nepali is their primary language of communication. Most Nepalese whose native language is not Nepali can still understand, speak, read, and write it, since most of them had at least a high school education in Nepal, where a certain level of fluency in writing and reading Nepali is required in the schools. Nepali is the mother tongue of Nepalese of Pahad origin, whereas the native language of other Nepalese is different. For example, most of the Newars from Katmandu Valley speak Newari as their mother tongue, and the Nepalese of Tarai origin speak Maithili, Bhojpuri, Avadi, or Tharu as their mother tongue. Similarly, those of Himalayan Mongol origin use different Tibetan dialects, such as Sherpa, Gurung, Tamang, Magar, and Kirat (Rai and Limbu).

Although they continue to use ethnic native languages, some Nepalese immigrants prefer to use English or to be bilingual and in some cases trilingual, using, native language, Nepali, and English. Most Nepalese Americans speak both Nepali and English fluently. Nepalese professionals educated in Western schools use English as their primary language. Similarly, second-generation Nepalese Americans employ English as their first language, and it is likely that use of Nepali and the ethnic languages will diminish in subsequent generations. A good number of Nepalese families speak exclusively English from the time of their

mandu Valley is about 40 percent of the total Nepalese population in America. Until the late 1980s the third-largest group was the people from the southern plains of Nepal, the Tarai or Madhese. But the number of immigrants from the Himalayan highlands, people of Bhotia origin, has increased quite rapidly in the 1990s, and they have become the third-largest Nepalese immigrant population, at 10 percent of the total, with the Tarai or Madhese group at 5 percent.

Most Nepalese-American families are first-generation since many arrived in and after the 1980s, and most are still under age fifty. Those who arrived before that time are also generally not arrival in the United States. In most cases, Nepalese Americans are developing a demeaning attitude toward Nepali and other native ethnic languages of Nepal; in general, they do not feel pride in maintaining their languages. This is due to the small size of the Nepalese community and the lack of professional and social use for Nepali and the other ethnic languages of Nepal in the United States. Unfortunately, no decisive programs have been developed to maintain and promote the ethnic languages of Nepal (except for a weekly class that has been conducted in Columbus, Ohio, since 1995 to teach beginning Nepali to Nepalese children). Nor have the Nepalese immigrants established their own ethnic press. However, some Nepalese organizations are planning to open a Nepalese cultural center to conduct Nepali language and cultural classes. A Nepali literary association—the International Nepali Literary Society—has been established in the Washington, D.C., area to promote Nepali language and literature; it also publishes a bimonthly literary journal, *Antardrishti*. Similarly, publications, such as *Kurakani* (published by the America-Nepal Friendship Society), *Chautari* (the newsletter of the Society of Nepalese Students in New York), and *Diyalo* (the magazine of the Nepalese Community Network of Canada) include Nepali essays, poems, and other news and views in both Nepali and English. The Alliance for Democracy and Human Rights in Nepal also publishes a newsletter in New York.

## Cultural Characteristics

*Economy and Housing.* Because they are still in the first generation, Nepalese immigrants in the United States have not yet established large businesses and industrial enterprises. A major portion of early Nepalese immigrants hold white-collar jobs, including technical, educational, or other professional and semiprofessional positions. They are engineers, doctors, horticulturists, agroeconomists, geologists, geographers, professors, lawyers, economists, and technicians. Some established Nepalese individuals run small businesses such as consultancy and engineering firms, health clinics, travel agencies, food stores, restaurants, and Oriental craft imports. Approximately, 80 percent of Nepalese immigrants who arrived prior to the mid-1980s have comfortable lifestyles, owning apartments or houses. Some also own other properties or have other investments along with considerable savings.

However, unlike the earlier immigrants, the majority of Nepalese who arrived after the mid-1980s are not well educated or qualified professionally. More than 60 percent of later immigrants—as opposed to 20 percent of earlier arrivals—are unskilled workers who earn subsistence wages. There is no record of homeless Nepalese in the United States.

*Religion.* Hinduism and Buddhism are the dominant religions of Nepalese in America. Hinduism is the national religion of Nepal; about 90 percent of Nepalese are Hindu. In America, about 80 percent of Nepalese are Hindu Bahun-Chhetris and Newars. Most of the people from Nepalese Tarai also believe in Hinduism. A portion of the Newar population and most of the Himalayan-origin Tibeto-Mongolian Nepalese follow either Buddhism or the Tibetan Bon type of shamanism. Although there are some Theravadins, the majority of Buddhist Newars are followers of Mahayana Buddhism.

Nepalese Hindus in the United States celebrate their religious festivals both collectively and in individual households. Although Nepalese communities do not have their own Hindu temples, most Nepalese frequently visit Hindu temples founded and run by different Indian communities. Nepalese in America, under the leadership of the Nepalese American Council, are planning to establish a cultural center and a Hindu temple in the Washington, D.C., area. A Nepali Hindu religious association, Sanatana Dharma Seva Samiti, which was established in New York City in 1992, organizes events for some of the main religious pujas (festivals) each year.

*Worldview.* As in Nepal, there are two basic worldviews within the Nepalese communities in the United States, reflecting their Hindu and Bud-

Nepalese Americans worship Shivalingam in the Teej Festival in New York City in 1994. (Ramesh K. Dhungel)

dhist orientations. Hindus believe that the universe is undergoing an eternally repeated cycle of creation, protection, and destruction, represented by their three major deities, Brahma, Vishnu, and Maheshvara, respectively. The Hindu universe is comprised of three popular *lokas* (worlds): *svarga*, an immortal world that could be compared with heaven; *martya*, a mortal world (the earth); and *patala* or *naraka*, which could be compared with hell. Hindus believe that every human being according to his or her *karma* (action) as a mortal on Earth would either get a place in *svarga* or in *naraka* after death. They also believe in *punarjanma* (rebirth) and *moksha* (salvation) from mortal life.

For Buddhists in general, the mortal world is a place of suffering, but they also believe that such suffering can be transcended through attaining wisdom and by good action. In addition, they believe in the theory of karma and the countless *bhuvanas* (realms). The Vajrayanists of Nepal believe in the *adibuddha vajradhara* (spiritual Buddha) as an absolute controller of the universe, which includes thirteen kinds of worlds popularly known as *trayodasabhuvana*. The Mahayanists believe that every being in the world is empty or devoid of self-nature (*sunyata*) and always needs help from a bodhisattva (one whose essence is enlightened), especially to become enlightened to achieve bodhisattvahood or *nirvana* (emancipation) from worldly sufferings.

*Marriage, Family, and Kinship.*   In most cases, Nepalese immigrants were married in Nepal before immigration to the United States, or they return to Nepal to get married. There is also a growing tendency among second-generation Nepalese males to return to Nepal to find an appropriate partner. Because of this trend, second-generation Nepalese women may have difficulty obtaining a Nepalese husband. Consequently, there is also a growing tendency among young Nepalese women to marry an American or a man of other nationality. Usually, Nepalese young men do not want to marry a Nepalese woman raised and educated in an American environment. In some cases, parents of such Nepalese women try to sponsor suitable Nepalese men to immigrate to the United States to marry their daughters.

Nepalese society is bound with a strong tradition of class hierarchy, which has become a sensitive issue in Nepalese communities in America. Nepalese Americans are more likely to accept international matrimonial relationships than an inter-caste marriage within their own Nepalese community. Dozens of Nepalese men in America have already married American and other international women.

Thus, because the Nepalese-American community is small, multiethnic in origin, and still strongly bound by religion, marriage practices among second-generation Nepalese in America may become complex and problematic. Even so, because of these traditional factors the marriage life of Nepalese Americans is highly successful with a divorce rate of less than 1 percent.

As is common among Hindus and Buddhists generally, a hierarchy-based gender and seniority prevails in Nepalese society, the senior male member of a family having authority in family affairs. Family life is very important to the Nepalese, and a sense of mutual respect and understanding is very strong. Every member of the family holds a special place and position having respect and recognition under Hindu and Buddhist family traditions.

*Community Institutions, Organizations, Festivals, and Functions.*   Nepalese in America strive to maintain unity by establishing Nepalese organizations on various bases, including geographic region, ethnicity, student affairs, religion, culture and literary development, academic activities, mutual friendship, politics, and human rights. This trend, which started in the early 1980s, increased in popularity in the 1990s. The Nepalese American Council was established in 1991 as an umbrella association for Nepalese organizations in America. Other associations related to Nepal and the Nepalese are Association of Nepalese in Americas; Association of Nepalese in Midwest America; America-Nepal Society (Washington, D.C.); American-Nepal Society of California; America-Nepal Friendship Society (New York); Nepal Association of Northern California; Nepalese Association of Southeastern America; Florida-Nepal Association; Greater Boston Nepali Community;

Association of Nepalese in Canada; Nepalese Community Network of Canada; International Nepali Literary Society (Washington, D.C.); Nepal Forum at Columbia University (New York); Society of Nepalese Students in New York; Nepalese Women's Association (New York); Alliance for Democracy and Human Rights in Nepal (New York); United Sherpa Society (New York); Nepalese and Friends Association (Arizona); Nepa Pasa Pucha Americaye (Washington, D.C.); Phoolbari Club (Washington, D.C.); Nepali Youth Organization, USA (Washington, D.C.); and Sanatana Dharma Seva Samiti, New York.

Through these organizations, the Nepalese in America celebrate their social, cultural, religious, and Nepali national festivals. To share common experiences and ideas, they organize conventions, seminars, meetings, religious pujas, speeches, cultural programs, and community picnics from time to time. These organizations publish newsletters as well as literary and other publications. In addition to those titles mentioned earlier, Nepali publications include *Nepal Update, Dabu, Samjhana,* and *The Horizon* (all in the Washington, D.C., area), as well as *View-Points* (in Ohio), *Sagrmatha Times* and *Namaste* (from the Midwest), *Samachar-Vichar* (in Boston), *Yati* (in Georgia), and *Laligurans* (in Canada). In addition, Nepalese have developed their own information home pages and programs on the Internet.

## Social and Cultural Assimilation

Although the Nepalese community is very small, there has been a deliberate effort to participate in local and national political decision-making processes. Particularly, Nepalese Americans think that changes in Nepal will affect only their psyche, but events in the United States will affect the very foundations of their existence. However, a Nepalese identity seems to remain very strong among Nepalese, although they have been attracted by American culture and lifestyles. Thus, in reality and in anthropological definition, Nepalese immigrants in America can also be defined as "marginal people" who face a dilemma in their attempt to adopt to the sociocultural norms of the host society.

Some researchers have also observed a Nepalese-American tendency to avoid American sociocultural organizations and activities in particular to preserve their original self-identity. However, perhaps because of their knowledge of English, a number of Nepalese have become involved quickly in community affairs, and some Nepalese have been honored by city government, such as that of Boston, for their active participation in social work.

Despite the diligent efforts of their parents, most Nepalese youths born and raised in the United States are not particularly serious about maintaining Nepalese ethnicity, language, religion, and culture, which does not bode well for the preservation of Nepalese identity in the United States.

Interethnic integration among the Nepalese seems more effective in America than in Nepal. Sociocultural associations of Nepalese immigrants have served an important role in this regard.

Because Nepalese Americans are few in number and scattered in residence, there has not been much violence against them. However, there is a deep feeling of discrimination among the Nepalese educated elite and unskilled workers, both on the job and in finding a job, with cultural and racial differences as the bases.

*See also:* BUDDHISTS

## Bibliography

Bista, D. B. (1967). *People of Nepal.* Kathmandu: Nepal Department of Publicity, Ministry of Information and Broadcasting.

Harris, G. L.; Giddens, J. A.; and Lux, T. (1973). *Area Handbook for Nepal, Bhutan, and Sikkim.* Washington, DC: U.S. Government Printing Office.

Lyman, S. M. (1977). *The Asian in North America.* Santa Barbara, CA: ABC-CLIO.

Shrestha, M. N. (1995). "Nepalese in America: A Historical Perspective." In *Nepalese American Perspectives,* edited by M. N. Shrestha. Cincinnati: Association of Nepalese in Midwest America.

Upadhyay, P. (1991). "The Social Assimilation of Nepalese Immigrants in the United States and the Role of Their English-Language Training in This Process." Ph.D. diss., University of Connecticut.

Upadhyay, P. (1995). "Social Life of Nepalese Immigrants in the United States." In *Nepalese American Perspectives*, edited by M. N. Shrestha, Cincinnati: Association of Nepalese in Midwest America.

U.S. Bureau of the Census. (1980). "Foreign-Born Immigrants in the United States." *1980 Census of Housing and Population* 1-245. Washington, DC: U.S. Government Printing Office.

U.S. Bureau of the Census. (1993). *Statistical Abstract of the United States,* 113th ed. Washington, DC: U.S. Government Printing Office.

U.S. Immigration and Naturalization Service. (1993). *Statistical Yearbook of the INS, 1992.* Washington, DC: U.S. Government Printing Office.

U.S. Immigration and Naturalization Service. (1993). *Immigrants Admitted to the United States 1954–1993* (Computer File, ICPSR 6449). Washington, DC: U.S. Department of Justice.

Vaidya, K. L. (1996). "Nepalese in America." *Chautari* 2(2): 8–9.

RAMESH K. DHUNGEL

# NICARAGUANS

The Nicaraguan community in the United States is highly concentrated in three urban areas. According to the figures reported in the 1990 U.S. Census, there were 168,659 Nicaraguans living in the United States. Of these nearly 43 percent lived in Florida, primarily in the Miami area. Approximately 35 percent reported living in California, mostly in or around Los Angeles, and an additional 7 percent were registered in the New Jersey–New York City metropolitan area.

Nationally, the Nicaraguan community is financially better off than most other Central American immigrant groups. In 1990, the median household income for the Nicaraguan community, which is young and mostly female, was $25,171, ranking it ahead of all Central American national groups except Costa Ricans. Individually Nicaraguans also fare better in the United States than most other immigrants. The per capita income for Nicaraguan immigrants of $8,030 is the highest of any group except Costa Ricans.

These national indicators mask the significant regional differences existing in the Nicaraguan communities. The most affluent community is located in the New York–New Jersey area, and the poorest is found in the Miami area. Because of these regional discrepancies, there is evidence that many families live a precarious existence in the United States. Approximately 20.1 percent of the families, and 22.9 percent of the individuals, register incomes below the poverty level. Research in southern Florida showed that approximately eight thousand Nicaraguan families relied on welfare benefits in 1995.

The settlement pattern of the Nicaraguan community and its poor economic situation are two of the few points on which the different demographic sources agree. For example, the statistical year-books of the Immigration and Naturalization Service (INS) report a higher number of Nicaraguans living in the United States than does the U.S. Census. The 1995 yearbook, which covers immigrant registrations up to 1993, reports that approximately 250,000 Nicaraguans live in the United States and approximately 50 percent of them (roughly 125,000) live in the Miami area.

The figures published in the INS statistical yearbooks are preferred by some analysts and policy makers for a variety of reasons. The most obvious reason is that the U.S. Census seems unable to overcome chronic problems of under counting minority populations and immigrant communities. Many Nicaraguans are unclear about the requirements of becoming a legal resident, and the fear of deportation has kept them away from the agencies that provide official counts. In addition, the large majority of Nicaraguans believe that they can apply for refugee status in the United States and therefore, upon arrival, file a request for political asylum. These applications are recorded by the INS at sixty-five offices throughout the country, so the INS numbers provide a broader coverage than do the U.S. Census samples often used to estimate minority populations.

## Waves of Immigration

According to INS figures, 23,261 Nicaraguans were admitted as permanent residents in the United States between 1976 and 1985, while 75,264 were admitted as permanent residents between 1986 and 1993. Before the 1970s, Nicaraguan immigration to the United States was minimal. While there was some northward movement after the beginning of the Somoza era in 1937, most of the Nicaraguan population in the United States immigrated after the 1979 victory of the Sandinistas. Approximately 75 percent of the foreign-born Nicaraguan population in 1990 had arrived in the United States after 1980.

Between 1980 and 1982, a large number of Nicaraguans fled the country as a direct result of the Sandinistas' victory and the subsequent restructuring of the social, political, and economic systems. The first of these immigrants were refugees associated with Anastasio Somoza, his family, or the National Guard. The top elite of the country also fled. Nicaraguan capitalists, who feared reprisals and were overwhelmed by the amount of international support received by the Sandinistas, moved their resources outside the country.

Between 1983 and 1990, the professionals and members of the middle class left Nicaragua in increasing numbers. The primary push factors during this period were the mandatory military service requirement instituted by the Sandinistas in 1982 and the nationalization of foreign companies that employed many of the top professionals. Throughout the 1980s, an increasing number of Nicaraguan immigrants to the United States filed political asylum applications to obtain refugee status (13,377 in 1987; 16,170 in 1988; and 35,431 in 1989). As a result, the U.S. government began to review the cases more carefully because of the belief that economic, rather than political, reasons might be behind the rising number of immigrants.

The defeat of the Sandinistas in the 1990 elections generated a third wave of immigration to the United States, and a total of nearly sixteen thousand Nicaraguan immigrants were admitted as permanent U.S. residents in 1991 and 1992. After the election of Arnoldo Aleman to the Nicaraguan presidency in 1996, however, a pattern of reverse migration seems to have started developing. Ethnographic data signals a return of business people and professionals (many of whom are legal residents of the United States) to Nicaragua. Similarly, some Nicaraguan immigrants who live near the poverty level in the United States seem to be considering a return to Nicaragua. In fact, officials from the Nicaraguan Immigration Office claim that close to fifteen thousand families living abroad returned to Nicaragua following the defeat of the Sandinistas in 1990.

## Acquiring Legal Permanent Residence

Nicaraguans who arrived before January 1, 1982, obtained their permanent residency status through the amnesty authorized by the Immigration Reform and Control Act (IRCA) of 1986. IRCA allowed two groups of illegal aliens to become temporary and then permanent residents of the United States: (1) legalization applicants, aliens who have been in the United States unlawfully since January 1, 1982, and (2) special agricultural worker applicants, aliens who were employed in seasonal agricultural work for a minimum of ninety days between May 1985 and May 1986. In 1988, Nicaraguans submitted 15,530 applications for legalization under the IRCA program.

Nicaraguan and Cuban exiles march through Miami's Little Havana in 1985 to raise support for freeing Nicaragua from Communism. (UPI/Corbis-Bettmann)

Substantial differences in naturalization rates occur among Nicaraguans in different occupational categories. In general, people in highly skilled occupations, particularly medical professionals and engineers, have the highest naturalization rates. People without a substantial attachment to the labor force, such as homemakers or retired persons, have low naturalization rates. Persons in their late teens and twenties, on the other hand, have a high propensity to naturalize; this rate, however, declines gradually as age increases. Overall, the 1990 U.S. Census figures report that 15 percent of Nicaraguan immigrants had become U.S. citizens. In 1993, INS estimated that there were still approximately seventy thousand undocumented Nicaraguans in the United States.

## Cultural Characteristics

The Nicaraguan community in the United States is comprised of three culture groups: the Creole peoples of the southern Atlantic Coast, the mestizos of the Pacific Coast, and the Miskito population of the Rio Coco and the Puerto Cabezas area.

The Creole population is considered to be the oldest Nicaraguan population in the United States. Most Creole immigrants are professionals—nurses, teachers, accountants—and many entered the United States as students as early as the 1950s. Like other Caribbean rim populations, Creoles are a mixed-race people. Creoles find it relatively easy to adjust to U.S. culture, as American influence in Nicaragua through trade and missionary work has historically been long standing. Institutions such as baseball, Boy Scouts, and Girl Guides constituted an established part of Atlantic Coast town life in the Nicaragua of the 1930s.

The mestizo population is the largest Nicaraguan population in the United States, but most mestizos only arrived in the United States after the 1979 revolution in Nicaragua. In southern Florida, mestizos are concentrated in the middle- and upper-class neighborhood of Sweetwater and in the more working-class areas of Little Havana and Hialeah. Most cultural organizations are run by professionals and business owners, as the demanding American work schedule generally prevents working-class individuals from participating in cultural activities.

The Miskito population, considered to be of more recent arrival, immigrated to the United States after repeated repression by the Sandinistas in the 1980s. Some Miskitos are professionals, but most work as janitors, cleaning women, and guards in hotels and restaurants. Although Miskitos are an indigenous people of Nicaragua, they are typically of mixed blood and quite Westernized in their living habits. Ever since their first contact with Europeans, Miskitos have interacted with cultural outsiders, trading their labor for foreign goods or wages in a variety of commercial ventures.

Primary genres of Nicaraguan folklife include music, patronal festivals, church celebrations, and foodways. Nicaragua is a predominantly Catholic country, and patronal festivals, which are processional in nature, constitute the major folk expression of this religiousness. The festivals also provide a context for artistic practices of all kinds and for the expression of local identity. The major patronal festivals still celebrated in the Nicaraguan communities of southern Florida include San Sebastian, Santa Ana, Santo Domingo de Guzman, San Jeronimo, La Purisima, and La Griteria.

## Conclusion

The Nicaraguan community in the United States is growing, and those immigrants who obtain permanent residency are quick to naturalize. Nonetheless, the exile community watches carefully the events unfolding in relation to the economic and social crisis affecting Nicaragua. Those who lack a permanent immigration status fear a forced departure to a country where nearly 60 percent of the population is unemployed or underemployed. In the face of such a grim future, it is likely that most Nicaraguans in the United States will remain and that a new generation of Nicaraguan Americans will become established in the cultural, political, and economic environments of U.S. cities.

## Bibliography

Cortazar, J. (1989). *Nicaraguan Sketches*. New York: Norton.

Cuadra, P. A. (1976). *El Nicaraguense*. San Jose: Editorial Universitaria Centroamericana.

Helms, M. (1971). *Asang: Adaptations to Culture Contact in the Miskito Community*. Gainesville: University of Florida Press.

Pena Hernandez, E. (1986). *Folklore de Nicaragua*. Guatemala City: Editorial San Piedra Santa.

U.S. Bureau of the Census. (1993). *Census of Population, 1990: Ancestry of the Population in the United States*. Washington, DC: U.S. Government Printing Office.

U.S. Immigration and Naturalization Service. (1994). *Statistical Yearbook of the Immigration and Naturalization Service, 1994*. Washington, DC: U.S. Government Printing Office.

GUILLERMO J. GRENIER

# NIGERIANS

*See* IGBO; YORUBA

# NORWEGIANS

Norwegian immigrants to the United States are a distinctly homogeneous group. They come from Norway, the westernmost country on the Scandinavian peninsula. Norway is bordered on the north by the Barents Sea, on the west by the Norwegian Sea, and on the south by the North Sea. Norway, a constitutional monarchy, is 125,181 square miles, slightly larger than New Mexico. Norway shares an eastern border with Sweden, Finland, and Russia. Svalbard, a group of islands off the northern coast, and the approximately 150,000 islands along the 12,000-mile coastline of fjords, inlets, and bays facing westward, belong to Norway. Most Norwegian immigrants came primarily from the rural and western districts. While Norwegian immigrants have averaged only 1 to 2 percent of the American population, heavy concentrations, especially in the Midwest, have had a strong influence in their adopted communities. The Saami, or Lapps, also inhabit the northernmost districts of Norway and represent a separate subgroup, ethnically and linguistically distinct from other Norwegians. Immigration patterns to the United States are not documented separately for the Saami as an ethnic group because they maintain Norwegian citizenship. Norwegians, also known from 800 C.E. as Norsemen in Britain and Normans in northern France (Normandy), refer to themselves as Nordmenn ("men of the North") or Norsk ("Norwegians") literally "of the northern way").

## Immigration History

Westward immigration of Norwegians has a long history, beginning with the Vikings. Norwegians were established in Iceland, Greenland, and the Faeroe Islands before 1000 C.E. However, scholars have long disputed that Leif Erickson discovered North America in about 1000 C.E. or that Norse settlements were established as far west as North Dakota in the thirteenth and fourteenth centuries. In the seventeenth century, Norwegian seamen joined the crews of Dutch ships bound for New Netherland (New York State). Most settled farther west, in Rensselaerwyck colony (Albany, New York); some settled in New Amsterdam (New York City). Their descendants remain in these areas, and Brooklyn at one point boasted 40,000 Norwegians, claiming the title of fourth-largest Norwegian city. Sustained immigration to North America began in the nineteenth century, when economic conditions in northern Europe became increasingly harsh. More than 863,000 Norwegians immigrated to the United States between 1820 and 1993. Letters home to relatives became a significant conduit to Norway and increased interest in the United States. The greatest periods of immigration occurred from 1866 to 1872, 1880 to 1893, and 1900 to 1910.

Descendants of Norwegian immigrants pose in 1925 beside the Restauration, the sloop on which their ancestors sailed to America. (Minnesota Historical Society/Corbis)

Economic conditions and religious freedom were major factors for the first pioneers. Immigration to the United States began in earnest with the sailing of the sloop Restauration from Stavanger in southwestern Norway on July 4, 1825. There were fifty-two men, women, and children on board, primarily from Tysvaer and the surrounding Rogaland and Hordaland *fylker* (counties) in southwestern Norway. The sloopers were met in New York Harbor on October 15, 1825, by Cleng Peerson. They were aided by American Quakers in relocation to Kendall Township, in northern New York State, on the shores of Lake Ontario. Peerson, a fellow native of Tysvaer, had preceded them in 1821 and established initial contact with the

Quakers. The Kendall settlement served as a way station for future westward migrations to the Midwest, especially to the settlements in Fox River Valley in northern Illinois and to southern Wisconsin. Peerson also established settlements in Shelby County, Missouri, and Bosque County, Texas. The State of Texas gave Peerson a ranch, where he died, for his pioneering contributions. His work was continued by other pioneers. Hans Barlien spent two years trying to establish a "New Norway" at Sugar Creek in southeastern Iowa in 1840. Twelve years later the renowned Norwegian violinist Ole Bull financed a new colony that was named New Norway in September 1852, and later renamed Oleana. It did not last a year due to lack of financial resources and inability to sustain the settlers.

By the beginning of the twentieth century, Norwegian communities stretched across the northern United States from New York to Seattle. Chicago and Minneapolis became the major midwestern urban hubs for Norwegian immigrants. The immigrants, primarily farmers from western Norway, settled among groups from their native areas, working on established farms and in lumber mills throughout Wisconsin, Iowa, Minnesota, and the Dakotas. By the end of the nineteenth century, the Midwest no longer presented sufficient opportunities for land ownership and employment. New arrivals began to move farther west, to Oregon, Washington, British Columbia, and Alaska. During the first quarter of the twentieth century, Seattle had the highest concentration of Norwegian immigrants in the West. The Pacific Northwest drew them to the fishing, lumber, and shipbuilding industries. A few immigrants early found their way to unlikely places such as the Texas prairie. Although these settlements did not rival those of the Midwest or Pacific Northwest, during the last quarter of the twentieth century the oil industry created more opportunities for exchange, bringing a new generation of Norwegians to Texas to work and live. Although they can now be found in all fifty states, the heaviest concentration of Norwegian natives and descendants continues to be centered in the Midwest and Pacific Northwest. More than 32,000 Norwegians in America returned to Norway during the Great Depression. In O. S. Lovoll's *The Promise of America* (1984), official Norwegian statistics from 1891 to 1940 show as many as a quarter of all immigrants who arrived in America after 1881 returned and permanently resettled in Norway.

## Demography

The U.S. Immigration and Naturalization Service (INS) has recorded total numbers of Norwegian immigrants on an annual basis since 1861. From 1820 until 1861, numbers for Swedes and Norwegians were combined. The reports show that numbers of Norwegian immigrants documented from 1820 to 1993 began modestly, swelled to a high point in the first decade of the twentieth century, then began a downward trend. Official numbers for Norway and Sweden combined in the 1820s show that 90 Norwegians and Swedes immigrated to the United States; the 1830s, 1,201; the 1840s, 13,903; and the 1850s, 20,931. Beginning in 1861, the number of Norwegians was isolated and demonstrated a significant increase each decade until 1911. Norwegian immigrants in the 1860s numbered 71,631; the 1870s, 95,323; the 1880s, 176,586; and the 1890s, 190,505—the peak decade of Norwegian immigration. Numbers began dropping by the 1900s with 95,015, the 1910s with 66,395, and the 1920s with 63,531, marking the end of mass waves of Norwegians to the United States. Although immigration to America remained strong until 1931, Norwegian immigration was never as intense as in the period from 1860 to 1930. The drop in subsequent decades reflected improved conditions in Norway as well as changes in U.S. immigration policy and quotas. The 1930s brought 4,740 Norwegians to the United States. The total in the 1940s increased slightly, to 10,100. Figures rose again, to 24,513, from 1950 to 1959. From 1960 to 1969, this level was nearly maintained, at 18,411. A sharp decline occurred from 1970 to 1979, with 4,070 Norwegian immigrants. From 1980 to 1989, there were 3,780 Norwegians admitted to the United States, and the first part of the 1990s showed a continuation of this trend, with 524 immigrants in 1990, 486 in 1991, 665 in 1992, and 608 in 1993.

## Language

When the first immigrations began in the 1820s, the linguistic scene in Norway was beginning a tumultuous period that continued to the end of the twentieth century. Norway was first under Danish rule from the fourteenth century until 1814, when the end of the Napoleonic Wars placed Norway under Swedish rule. Independent, rural Norwegian peasants, especially in the western counties, refused to relinquish their native dialects and lose their national identity, partially realized by language choice. By the mid-nineteenth century, nationalistic fervor was given validity in the form of a new language called *landsmål* ("the people's language"), later changed to *nynorsk* ("New Norwegian"). Nynorsk, a compilation of rural dialects mainly from the western coast of Norway, was the dialect of the majority of the immigrants. Nynorsk, an artificial, written form (as adherents generally retain their native spoken dialects), stood in direct opposition to Dano-Norwegian, first called *riksmål* ("language of the realm"), and, since 1929, renamed *bokmål* ("book language"). For a country of only a few million speakers, the Norwegian language situation was complex.

The significance of the language situation in Norway had important ramifications for Norwegian immigration, because the major immigration coincided with the language conflict in Norway. Language use and attitudes in America were affected. The first immigrants were western rural natives who spoke dialects on which nynorsk was based. The rural peasants' insistence on using their own indigenous dialect, coupled with official status sanctioning it, reflected the independence and tenacity of the Norwegian character. This resistance was also a factor in settlement patterns in the United States, as dialect groups were motivated to move to areas with other speakers of their own dialect. High mountain ranges, bodies of water, and vast, uninhabited stretches of land had contributed to the rise of approximately twenty-two identifiable dialects in Norway, many not mutually intelligible. It was not until after World War II that English became common in the Norwegian school curriculum and brought new immigrants with significant knowledge of English to the United States. More than a century of Norwegian immigrants arrived in the United States with little or no education or fluency in English. The situation increased their desire to settle among Norwegian-speakers, especially those from the same dialect region. The Norwegian language was maintained in communities in several strongholds—the

Lutheran Church and social organizations such as the Sons of Norway and the regional *bygdelags* (groups representing areas of origin). In the mid-nineteenth century, schools established by early immigrants at first taught in Norwegian but gradually switched to English. St. Olaf's College in Northfield, Minnesota, was established in 1886, originally as a seminary. St. Olaf has remained a focal point for Norwegian language and related studies for more than a century. Other institutions, such as the University of Washington, the University of Minnesota, Pacific Lutheran College, and the University of Wisconsin, also maintain strong Norwegian-language programs.

Waves of immigrants throughout the twentieth century kept the Norwegian-American community infused with new Norwegian-speakers. Independent development of the original dialects spoken by the early arrivals resulted in a modified code, mutually intelligible with but distinct from Norwegian spoken contemporaneously in Norway. The relative ease of mixing English and Norwegian based on close proximity of codes led to the development of a variety of American Norwegian somewhat foreign to Norwegian-speakers from Norway.

As assimilation occurred, tolerance for linguistic variation did not pose a significant obstacle based on linguistic history. Linguistic variation also had been compounded by the development of Scandinavian communities in the Pacific Northwest and the Midwest where Norwegian, Swedish, and Danish were spoken; the three languages are closely related, but mutual intelligibility varies. As the immigrants did begin to switch to English, the close proximity of English and Norwegian as members of the northern branch of the Germanic language family lessened the difficulty in learning English. Norwegian and English share many cognate vocabulary items as well as a strong syntactic similarity, especially in word order and morphemic structure.

Another factor in easing the transition from Norwegian to English was that Norwegians have maintained one of the highest literacy rates, in the high 90 percentiles. Traditionally Norwegian are avid readers and lead the world in highest number of books read per capita. High concentrations of Norwegians in certain areas such as the Dakotas, Minnesota, and Wisconsin made bilingualism easy to maintain. Use of Norwegian began to lessen after World War I, when personal sentiments and social acceptance in the United States stressed the importance of being "American." In addition, arrivals to the United States after World War II were fluent in English, by then a staple in the Norwegian school curriculum. Generational differences are evident, with the newer immigrants speaking a Norwegian from the homeland that has undergone independent change from the American Norwegian spoken in the United States. True to the egalitarian nature inherent in Norwegians, there are no gender differences in the Norwegian spoken either in the United States or in Norway. The upper midwestern dialect of English became heavily influenced by Norwegian, especially in Minnesota.

Widely scattered communities, political activism, and high literacy rates encouraged the establishment of a press for the settlers. In 1847, the first newspaper, *Skandinavia*, was published in New York, and the weekly *Nordlyset* (Northern Lights, 1847–1850) began in Muskego, Wisconsin. *Emigranten* (The Emigrant, 1852–1892) was published by pastors of the Norwegian Synod in Madison, Wisconsin, and so was the church magazine *Maanedstidende* (Monthly Times, 1850–present, published in English since the 1940s). Nearly six hundred different publications, mostly short-lived, followed. The most successful publications have been the *Minneapolis Tidende* (Minneapolis Times, 1887–1935), later absorbed by the *Decorah-Posten* (Decorah Post, 1847–1972) in Decorah, Iowa; the *Western Viking* (1889–present), based in Seattle; and the *Nordisk Tidende* (Norway Times, 1891–present), published in Brooklyn. The *Western Viking* and the *Nordisk Tidende* publish articles in both Norwegian and English.

A Norwegian flag flies above the participants in a Seattle Seafood Fest. (Jim Corwin/Corbis)

## Cultural Characteristics

*Economy.* When Norwegians first arrived in the United States in the 1820s, they represented primarily unskilled and semiskilled laborers working on farms and in the lumber, fishing, and shipbuilding industries. Since that time, with education in university, college, vocational-technical, and apprenticeship programs, they work in all major industries, such as education, entertainment, publishing, law, medicine, environment, computers, and manufacturing. Although they occupy all economic brackets, the majority are firmly rooted in the middle class. General values of thriftiness, environmental concerns, conservation of resources, hard work, simplicity, and quality of life issues characterize their attitude toward maintaining a stable, comfortable lifestyle. Their basic orientation to hard work, respect for rules, and aversion to conspicuous consumption has eased assimilation into the general population.

*Kinship, Marriage, and Domestic Unit.* Norwegian kinship is established primarily through the male line, with families increasingly choosing their own place of residence rather than living with the father's relatives. Norwegian kinship terminology reflects members' matrilineal and patrilineal relationships (bifurcate collateral), for example, *mormor* (mother's mother) and *farmor* (father's mother). Basic Norwegian kinship terminology among monolingual English-speakers is still recognized beyond the second generation. American and Norwegian domestic patterns display a high level of similarity, and assimilation was relatively simple. Marriages are monogamous, with free choice of mate selection by the individual. Marriages in the first decades after arrival included Norwegians and other Scandinavians but quickly moved to include other ethnic groups as assimilation occurred. The domestic unit tends to be nuclear (married pair and children) or stem (married pair, children, and spouse's parent or parents). Women's rights are respected; Norwegian women traditionally have been included as decision makers and, in 1913, were the first in Europe given the right to vote. Increased mobility in the twentieth century has often taken them farther from their original settlements, but families maintain their extended family contacts, including ties to family in Norway.

*Interpersonal Relationships.* Norwegian Americans are typically straightforward, stoic, hardworking, disciplined, and generally quiet and introverted, although they can be said to "work hard and play hard." To outsiders they maintain a friendly but impersonal distance that is quickly dismissed upon entry into personal space. Social responsibility and environmental issues are a natural outcome of their personal worldview of thrift, hard work, and quality-of-life issues. Their social relationships reflect their respect for, ties to, and pride in their heritage. They tend to maintain membership in service organizations promoting social assistance and educational programs supporting their youth. Social and heritage organizations such as the Sons of Norway continue to maintain strong memberships, especially in the Pacific Northwest and the Midwest.

*Religion.* Norwegian Americans have traditionally been Lutherans. A significant factor in the initial immigrations to the United States was the search for religious freedom. Quakers and Mormons were responsible for their initial westward movement. Some joined the Mormon Church when they moved with them to the West. Disputes among the various synods in the Lutheran Church resulted in a splintering. Intermarriages, as well as intellectual expansiveness and freedom of expression, began to lead some into various other Protestant camps.

*Arts and Sports.* Norwegian immigrants are represented in all the arts and have inherited a strong literary heritage from their homeland. They are also particularly gifted in design and graphics. Industrial arts of rosemaling (handpainted designs on wood), knitting, crochet, woodworking, and carpentry are practiced. Literary clubs, *leikarringen* (folk dance), and male chorus groups enjoy strong membership and success. Norwegian Americans excel in sports, especially in the Nordic winter sports of skating and skiing. They also participate actively in football, soccer, and track. Norwegian immigrants inherited a great love of nature and enjoy the outdoors as active hikers, runners, and cyclists.

## Assimilation and Cultural Persistence

Compatibility of cultures has allowed assimilation to take place without negating heritage. Discrimination against Norwegian immigrants has been minimal, and rejection of heritage was not necessary for social acceptance into the mainstream American society. Relations with other Scandinavian groups, particularly Swedes, Danes, and, to a lesser extent, Finns, have been fostered. Norwegians have continued to look toward Norway for innovations and guidance, particularly in social and welfare issues. Traditions and holidays continue to be observed, particularly the Norwegian Independence Day (May 17). This is observed in almost every Norwegian community in the United States with a parade or picnic to commemorate and celebrate values mutually held by both Americans and Norwegians. Traditions are maintained in the home with visible signs of Norwegian culture such as rosemaled decorations, Norwegian flags, plaques with prayers and expressions in Norwegian, and family heirlooms. Families continue to prepare traditional foods, especially during holidays, and the original names and recipes are maintained by monolinguals beyond the second generation.

Although widespread, cultural assimilation is by no means complete. While close linguistic, sociocultural, and attitudinal factors have made assimilation into the American mainstream relatively effortless, pride in heritage, high concentrations of descendants, and continued maintenance of relationships within the Norwegian-American communities and with family in Norway have prevented obliteration of Norwegian heritage in the United States.

*See also:* ICELANDERS; SWEDES

## Bibliography

Andersen, A. W. (1975). *The Norwegian Americans.* Boston: Twayne.

Bergmann, L. N. (1950). *Americans from Norway.* Westport, CT: Greenwood Press.

Bjork, K. O. (1958). *West of the Great Divide: Norwegian Migration to the Pacific Coast, 1847–1893.* Northfield, MN: The Norwegian-American Historical Association.

Blegen, T. C. (1931). *Norwegian Migration to America, 1825–1860.* Northfield, MN: The Norwegian-American Historical Association.

Blegen, T. C. (1940). *Norwegian Migration to America: The American Transition.* Northfield, MN: The Norwegian-American Historical Association.

Haugen, E. (1966). *Language Conflict and Planning: The Case of Modern Norwegian.* Cambridge, MA: Harvard University Press.

Haugen, E. (1969). *The Norwegian Language in America: A Study in Bilingual Behavior,* 2 volumes. Philadelphia: University of Pennsylvania Press.

Lovoll, O. S. (1984). *The Promise of America.* Minneapolis: University of Minnesota Press.

Norlie, O. M. (1973). *History of the Norwegian People in America.* New York: Haskell House.

Schultz, A. R. (1994). *Ethnicity on Parade: Inventing the Norwegian American Through Celebration.* Amherst: University of Massachusetts Press.

Semmingsen, I. (1978). *Norway to America: A History of the Migration.* Minneapolis: University of Minnesota Press.

Zempel, S. (1991). *In Their Own Words: Letters from Norwegian Immigrants.* Minneapolis: University of Minnesota Press.

KAARIN LILLEHEI-BAKHTIAR

# OKINAWANS

Uchinaa is the native term for Okinawa, and the Okinawans are a distinct minority within Japan. At various times in its history Okinawa has been called Liu-chi'iu, Loochoo, the Great Loochoo, Lequio Major, Gores, Lequios, the Nanto, Nansei shoto, and Ryukyu retto, as well as by the poetical term Uruma.

The first Okinawan immigrants to the United States did not set out to take up permanent residence. The intention of the majority was to work hard, save money, and return home with the means to improve their lot in life. However, in the course of events they decided to make the United States their new home.

Okinawans in the United States present a society divided for the most part into West Coast mainland and Hawaii communities. The two groups differ in their paths of settlement in and acculturation to their adopted land. Mainland Okinawans, free immigrants, are perceived to be outgoing, individualistic, more educated, urban, commercial, loosely knit, freely marrying outsiders, and well integrated into the Japanese community. Hawaii Okinawans, initially contract laborers, are seen as inward-looking, less educated, rural, and agricultural. They tend to marry within their group and to be tightly knit, and they are constantly battling segregation from the larger Japanese community.

## West Coast Okinawans

Okinawans began to arrive, sporadically and in small numbers, on the West Coast of the United States in 1889. From the beginning they were free immigrants. Ultimately there were more Okinawans, who transshipped from Hawaii. In 1902, the first Okinawan association was founded in San Francisco. In 1906, about thirty Okinawans moved from Mexico to Los Angeles. That same year, survivors of the great San Francisco earthquake resettled in Los Angeles. From about this time, Los Angeles became the center of Okinawan settlement in the United States. There was no active antagonism by the *naichi* (non-Okinawan) Japanese. Nevertheless, many Okinawans were reluctant to display their Okinawanness, as if it were something of which to be ashamed. Marriage outside of the Okinawan community was not at all uncommon. Many Okinawans flocked to urban areas in the relatively early stages of their life in the United States.

The Nanka Okinawa Kenjinkai (Southern California Okinawan Association) was founded in

A young Okinawan dancer in a colorful *bingata* (red patterns) costume performs to Okinawan music. (Dave Au/United Okinawan Association of Hawaii)

1901 and lasted until about 1925. In the aftermath of World War I and the emergence of the Communist party in Russia, some young Okinawans got together to study social issues, which quickly led to formation of the socialistic Reimeikai (New Dawn Society) in 1921. They antagonized the mainstream faction of the Nanka Okinawa Kenjinkai, who consequently helped organize the Zaibei Okinawa Seinenkai (Association of Young Okinawans in America) to counterbalance the Reimeikai. In another move, the semi-official Okinawa Kaigai Kyokai (Association of Overseas Okinawans) was established in Okinawa in 1924, followed by the opening of its southern California branch in 1925, which replaced the Nanka Okinawa Kenjinkai.

In 1932, the Third Communist International, held at Long Beach, was raided by police. Among those arrested were ten Japanese, of whom five were Okinawans. This shocked the Okinawan mainstream, represented by the Okinawa Kaigai Kyokai branch of southern California, which opposed the Nanka Okinawa Kenjinkai for harboring Communists. Five Okinawans were expelled to the Soviet Union in 1932. In addition, Miyagi Yotoku, who returned to Japan in 1933, engaged in espionage for the Soviet Union (the Richard Sorge case); he was arrested, and he died in prison.

Because the Japanese authorities cracked down harshly in response to the Red scare, most Okinawans in the United States sought protection in joining the aforementioned government-affiliated Okinawa Kaigai Kyokai and lived as loyal overseas Japanese citizens. As an indication of the extent to which Okinawans became integrated into the Japanese community, in December 1941,

Nakamura Gongoro, an Okinawan and a graduate of the UCLA Law School, was serving as the president of the Nanka Chuo Nihonjinkai (Central Association of Japanese in Southern California) representing the entire Japanese community.

The outbreak of war in the Pacific in December 1941 saw the general disbanding of Japanese organizations, including those of Okinawans, followed by the mass evacuation of the entire Japanese populace from the West Coast to detention camps in February 1942. After the war ended on August 15, 1945, the evacuees returned to Los Angeles. Okinawans were stunned by the extent of the devastation suffered by Okinawa. Their ancestral land was severely scarred by the last, bitter battle of World War II. Zaibei Okinawa Kenjinkai (Association of the People of Okinawa Prefecture in America), dormant during the war, was galvanized into action to help Okinawa. Immediately, the Okinawa Kyuen Renmei (League for Assisting Okinawa) was organized for emergency operations. It was later developed into the Okinawa Fukko Renmei (League for the Reconstruction of Okinawa) to continue to offer aid.

Zaibei Okinawa Kenjinkai changed its name to Hokubei Okinawa Kurabu (Okinawan Club of North America), dropping the word "prefecture" because many members were uncomfortable with the term. It may be symbolic of the maturity and the independence from Okinawa of Okinawans in the United States. Though still suffering the aftereffects of detention, Okinawans in the United States found that everything in their relationship with their ancestral country had changed. Namely, they found themselves in a position to offer help to Okinawa in everything, tangible and intangible, from dollars to democracy. Still, on the home front, they found it difficult to pick up where they left off in 1942, when they were rounded up for detention camps.

In 1959, there was a discussion between club leaders and young, second-generation Okinawans on the future direction of the Hokubei Okinawa Kurabu. It was unanimously agreed that the young Okinawans would continue to participate in the club's activities, but they would not assume leadership positions. However, they would actively participate in the larger regional communities.

In 1955, the Okinawan *issei* (Okinawa-born) population in the United States was 1,369. They were engaged in twenty-nine kinds of occupations, including agriculture, sewing (work as a seamstress), and operating boardinghouses or restaurants. Their sons and daughters were engaged in fifty-five kinds of occupations. The largest group was students, followed by other white-collar occupations. They worked as secretaries, teachers, lawyers, dentists, and government officials, occupations clearly indicating a strong shift from rural to urban and from nonskilled to skilled. They lived mainly in southern California, around Los Angeles, but they also spread out to San Francisco, Fresno, Frolin, and Oakland, as well as Arizona and Colorado. They also settled in New York, Washington, D.C., and Chicago. Shokan Shima, a prominent old leader, remarked, "There is no longer a need for us to stick together; we are now able to stand on our own feet and defend ourselves wherever we may choose to live."

However, partly because of the influence of the nationwide awakening of minorities and partly because of the need of each generation to live their own lives and find their own identity, young Okinawans eagerly organized cultural activities such as seminars, publication of their own history, and ethnic exhibitions.

## Okinawans in Hawaii

Okinawans immigrated to Hawaii in tightly knit groups organized by their own leaders or by immigration companies. Immigration officially started in 1900, with the arrival of 26 agricultural contract laborers (contract labor was abolished in April 1900). The number quickly rose to a peak of 4,467 new arrivals in 1906.

By 1925, a total of 36,535 Okinawans had arrived, a little more than 10 percent of the entire Japanese population in the state. The 1996 Okinawan American population is said to be roughly 40,000.

Large numbers of villagers were transplanted from Okinawa to Hawaii, planning to earn money and return home. Therefore, they saw no need to adapt to the new environment. They identified themselves with their home village communities in Okinawa. There were some educated professionals, too, but their number was small.

Japan's rapid modernization began in 1868 and was practically completed by 1900. Yet, the reforms in Okinawa lagged behind until about 1921. This is significant in that most Okinawans arrived in Hawaii before 1926. Thus they came from the old Okinawa characterized by numerous isolated consanguinous village communities. Consequently they identified first and foremost with their villages, and only secondarily and legally to the entity called Okinawa, much less to Japan. In fact, they owed little to the new Okinawa or Japan except hardships such as taxation. It was probably these hardships that forced them to leave their ancestral villages in the first place. Thus the history of Okinawans in Hawaii is that of a number of people with only a vague sense of belonging together being molded into an identity called Okinawan.

Okinawan leaders, often journalists or educators, were keenly aware of the poor standard of living and lack of formal education of their compatriots. There were free public education activities such as lecture tours and magic-lantern shows at labor camps. There were journals to give vent to their frustrations and voice hope for the future. However, because the villagers' stay in Hawaii was supposed to be only a temporary sojourn until they earned enough money to return home in triumph, there was no permanent organization to represent the entire Okinawan community in Hawaii until after World War II. The villagers kept to themselves and rejected outside interference, just as Okinawans had always dealt with devastating typhoons: Stay home and be patient, because there is no use fighting typhoons.

Overall, life in Hawaii was good to Okinawans. In the words of Toyama Matasuke (one of the first Okinawans to immigrate to Hawaii), "Now I have enought money saved so that I can return home anytime. This is a country best suited for money-making." This was the single, strongest motive for immigration to Hawaii.

Observers from Okinawa in the 1920s were impressed with the immigrants' living conditions in Hawaii, particularly with respect to children's health and education. It was possible to attain a high school and college education—difficult to imagine in Okinawa.

In fact, Okinawans began moving away from plantations in the 1920s to urban areas and into occupations other than agriculture. Buddhist and Christian missionaries started arriving. By the early 1930s, Okinawans began graduating from colleges and universities to enter the urban middle class.

The first association of Okinawans was formed in 1907, and it was followed by several others over the years. However, none lasted for long until the United Okinawan Association of Hawaii was founded in 1951. What united Okinawans in 1951, but not before? The impact of the war in the Pacific, particularly the Battle of Okinawa in 1945, united them. Simply put, the detention of the old leadership eliminated traditionbound factional strife. The wartime prohibition against the public use of the Japanese language and the meetings among enemy aliens effectively transferred community leadership to the English-speaking younger generation, who had American citizenship and a shared public school education. Sharing wartime crises as Japanese either at home or at the front united the entire Japanese community, including Okinawans. The economic disparity between the naichi (non-Okinawan) Japanese and Okinawans markedly diminished as the war boom favored Okinawans, who were heavily into agriculture, animal husbandry, and urban eateries, over naichi Japanese, who tended to be in lower white-collar occupations. Lastly, widely organized relief efforts from all areas of Hawaii for war-devastated Okinawa in 1945 served as an impetus to unite the Okinawan community. The continuing American occupation of Okinawa led the ad hoc relief committees to coalesce into the permanent United Okinawan Association of Hawaii in 1951.

During the twenty-seven years of American occupation of Okinawa (1945–1972), Okinawans in Hawaii made tremendous efforts to help

Okinawa. In Hawaii, unlike on the mainland, only a few hundred Japanese, including Okinawan leaders, were interned during the war. The majority continued to live free and prosper. Thus Okinawans were able to lead the way in the reconstruction of Okinawa, such as inviting Okinawan students to Hawaii. Their assistance to Okinawa had positive outcomes that they did not anticipate. Those born in Okinawa found that their knowledge of language and of Okinawa was still valuable; they and Okinawans born in Hawaii found that they had to cooperate with each other to be fully effective. This brought about a smooth generational transition of community leadership; and frequent contacts with Okinawa inevitably brought about a revived interest in things Okinawan. This revived interest in Okinawan culture

helped make the University of Hawaii's East/West Center an informal center for Okinawan studies in the United States.

In Hawaii, Okinawans faced active prejudice and discrimination from the naichi. The naichi first arrived in Hawaii in 1868, and by the time the Okinawans arrived in 1900, the naichi were well established. Because Okinawa was the poorest and least modernized prefecture in Japan and, more significant, because Okinawa did not share a common history and language with naichi Japan, Okinawans were treated as second-class Japanese. On the other hand, Okinawans defied the majority naichi. The ruling white elite did not favor one over the other. This attitude won the lasting gratitude of the Okinawans. The rivalry was further intensified in 1944. On the eve of the American

Tattoos on the backs of women's hands, as illustrated on the Okinawan woman in the center, were an old custom signifying the reaching of puberty. The woman on the right is a shaman in the Okinawan religion. (Dave Au/United Okinawan Association of Hawaii)

invasion of Okinawa, a prominent Okinawan missionary, Seikan Higa, himself having graduated from a seminary in Tokyo, declared to the American authorities his undying hatred of Japanese and his promise of wholehearted cooperation in driving the Japanese out of Okinawa. Of course, not all Okinawans were anti-Japanese. One Okinawan led the diehard Hawaii Nihon Hissho-kai (Japan Victory Association of Hawaii). The leaders wanted to be accepted as full-fledged Japanese even while hating the naichi for their prejudice and rejection.

In general, Okinawans in Hawaii were pro-American as opposed to pro-Japanese. The majority of Okinawans in Hawaii opposed the reversion of Okinawa to Japan. When Okinawa was finally returned to Japan in 1972, Okinawans in Hawaii acquiesced to the choice made in Okinawa. However, if asked about nationality, an Okinawan in Hawaii would answer, "Japanese, but from Okinawa." In pre–World War II days, the phrase was used derogatively by the naichi, but now it is used with pride by Okinawans. Among the young, particularly, there is no question that they are Okinawan first. Okinawans are the only prefectural group to hold an annual cultural jubilee, have their history and culture taught for credit at the University of Hawaii, and have their own Hawaii Okinawa Center, in spite of the fact that they are also a member organization of the Center for Japanese Culture, three of whose presidents were Okinawan.

Culture organizations such as Okinawan poetic societies and Okinawan dance groups have grown increasingly popular. In the 1920s, efforts were made to discourage propagation of the Okinawan culture because it was believed it would interfere with Japanization. Buddhism in Hawaii has adopted some Christian practices, such as weekly Sunday services. Okinawans have an Okinawan temple with an Okinawan congregation. Major holidays such as Obon, a festival for the spirits of the ancestors, seem to be well accepted by the public. Yet Buddhism seems to be losing its appeal to the young in favor of Christianity. Okinawa's native shamanism survives in modified form. However, the Okinawan language is all but extinct. Among the young, the preferred language is definitely English, and among the old, it is a peculiar localism comprised of Japanese, Okinawan, and English words and locution. Meanwhile, a serious effort is being made to compile the first Okinawan-to-English dictionary.

Okinawan solidarity, however, is being undermined by its own success. Success in life, whether in business or in a profession, necessarily brings dispersal of the community socially, geographically, and in other ways. Decades ago most Okinawans lived in the same plantation village or in the same district in a city, but now they have mostly moved to be closer to their jobs. Their friends and colleagues are more likely to be non-Okinawans. As of 1981, a total of 40 percent of Okinawans in Hawaii outmarried, and 70 percent of this group married naichi Japanese, followed by whites, Chinese, Koreans, and Filipinos. Okinawans no longer marry exclusively within their group.

To survive as a group, the Okinawan community must find a real need to fulfill beyond providing official-sounding titles to its elders.

*See also:*  JAPANESE

## Bibliography

Ethnic Studies Oral History Program, University of Hawaii at Manoa, comp. (1981). *Uchinanchu: A History of Okinawans in Hawaii*. Honolulu: Author.

Kimura, Y. (1988). *Issei: Japanese Immigrants in Hawaii*. Honolulu: University of Hawaii Press.

McDermott, J. F., Jr.; Tseng, W. S.; and Maretzki, T. W., comps. (1980). *People and Cultures of Hawaii*. Honolulu: University of Hawaii Press.

Nakasone, R. Y., ed. (1996). *Reflections on the Okinawan Experience*. Freemont, CA: Dharma Cloud Publishers.

Okinawa Club of America, comp. (1988). *History of the Okinawans in North America*, translated by B. Kobashikawa. Los Angeles: Author.

Sakihara, M. (1983). "Okinawan Immigrants" (in Japanese). *Gengo* 12(4):284–289.

MITSUGU SAKIHARA

# PACIFIC ISLANDERS

*See* GUAMANIANS; PACIFIC ISLANDERS IN HAWAII; SAMOANS; TONGANS

# PACIFIC ISLANDERS IN HAWAII

Scattered across the central and western Pacific are thousands of islands inhabited by several millions of people. The many diverse Pacific island peoples are frequently gathered for analytical purposes into three large groups. While these are Europeans', not Pacific Islanders', distinctions, they are commonly recognized in the region. The first, Polynesia, is a large, triangle-shaped swathe of ocean and islands whose peoples share close linguistic and ancestral ties. It stretches from Hawaii in the north to Aotearoa (New Zealand) in the south, from Easter Island in the east through Tahiti, the Cook Islands, and Samoa to Tonga in the west. Farther west, Melanesia stretches in an arc of mainly large islands, from Fiji through New Caledonia, Vanuatu, and the Solomon Islands to Papua-New Guinea and Irian Jaya. Micronesia, another arc

farther to the north, echoes the shape of Melanesia. Micronesia's tiny islands start in Kiribati in the east and reach through Nauru, the Marshall Islands, Ponape, Guam, Saipan, and Yap to Palau in the west.

Old chants commemorate and recent voyages confirm that Pacific island peoples have traveled by sailing canoe throughout this vast region for many hundreds of years. In modern times, international economic forces, two world wars, Euro-American and Japanese colonialism, and jumbo jets have vastly accelerated the pace and scale of these migrations. These days it is not remarkable for a person to be born in Tonga; raised in New Zealand, Australia, and then back in Tonga; achieve a college education in Hawaii and the U.S. mainland; work in Samoa and California; and then spend her or his declining years alternating residence among Hawaii, Tonga, and the mainland United States.

This swirl of migration around the Pacific has resulted in hundreds of thousands of Pacific Islanders taking up residence in the Western, industrialized countries that border the region (New Zealand, the United States, and Australia). In addition, hundreds of thousands more reside within the Pacific, yet outside their native islands. Hawaii,

A group of Pacific Islander women carry gifts and wear traditional dress to greet the arrival of a sailing canoe. (Dean Wong/Corbis)

both part of the Pacific and part of the United States, has been the avenue of entry into the United States for many Pacific island immigrants. After California, Hawaii has the highest number of Pacific Islander residents among the fifty states.

The total number of Pacific Islanders in Hawaii (excluding Hawaiians, who for the purposes of this publication are considered an ethnic group indigeneous to the United States) is 23,509, or 2 percent of the total state population, according to the 1990 U.S. Census. The largest Pacific Islander groups in Hawaii are Samoans (15,034), Tongans (3,088), and Chamorros or Guamanians (2,102). There are lesser numbers of Tahitians, Palauans, Maoris, Fijians, and others. Most Pacific Islanders in Hawaii reside on Oahu, the mainly urban island that contains Honolulu.

Any count is difficult to make precisely because of the large number of Pacific Islanders who possess mixed ancestry. This mixedness results in flexibility of ethnic definitions among Pacific island peoples, not just in Hawaii but also throughout the Pacific. Individuals frequently function in more than a single ethnic world. Generally speaking, if one has an ancestor who is Samoan, if one can identify the place in Samoa from which one's people come, if one engages with and is known by a network of Samoan relatives, and if one is known to practice Samoan cultural values, then one can claim a Samoan identity; the same may be said for other Pacific Islander identities. Many people throughout the Pacific have ancestries that lead back to more than one island chain, and many maintain more than a single ethnic identity on immigrating to Hawaii.

## Immigration

Immigration of Pacific Islanders to Hawaii is not a new thing: The first Polynesian seafarers came in large, double-hulled canoes two thousand years ago. Such immigrations continued down to at least the thirteenth century C.E., when immigrants from what is now French Polynesia migrated north to Hawaii.

From the late eighteenth century on, sailors from various island groups worked the European ships that plied the Pacific, including Hawaiian waters. The first modern immigration of Pacific Islanders to Hawaii was of workers who were imported to work on sugar plantations in the late nineteenth century. They were followed in the 1920s by Samoans, Tongans, and others who came to Laie on Oahu to help build the Mormon temple there.

The bulk of Pacific Islander immigration to Hawaii, as to the rest of the United States, has come since World War II, however. For five decades the U.S. Navy administered half the Samoan island chain as an American colony and employed many Samoans at the Pago Pago naval base. Residents of American Samoa saw a war-era boom turn bust when the Navy pulled up stakes for Hawaii in 1951. Many Samoans followed the Navy to Hawaii, with the encouragement of the governments of both territories. As U.S. nationals but not citizens, residents of American Samoa had what was for many an attractive career option: service in the U.S. military. Once their service was complete, many stayed in Hawaii, while others went to the mainland. Their American standard of living attracted family members back in Samoa, and a chain of immigration was begun. Relatives from the independent half of the islands, Western Samoa, joined the chain as well, though without the benefits of American nationality at first.

The Organic Act passed by the U.S. Congress in 1950 conferred American citizenship on the inhabitants of another U.S. territory dominated by the military, Guam. The population of Guam is ethnically mixed. The indigenous Chamorros (Micronesians who came to the island from Asia some four thousand years ago) have mixed for several centuries with Filipinos, Spanish, Americans, and others. Much of the expressive culture that once existed on the island has been lost. American citizenship meant that residents of Guam could come and go freely between their homeland and the United States. Taking the option of military service, thousands immigrated to Hawaii in the decades after the Organic Act was passed. Thousands more went to the American mainland, particularly to West Coast cities such as San Diego, San Francisco, Los Angeles, and Seattle that were close to naval shipyards.

Tongan immigration became a factor in Hawaiian history in the 1960s. Declining economic opportunities at home drove islanders out of Tonga in search of work. The rapid growth in Tonga of the Church of Jesus Christ of Latter-Day Saints encouraged many Tongan emigrants to choose the United States as their destination. Some migrated to Hawaii, especially to the community of Laie on the northern shore of Oahu, where the Mormon temple is located. Others went to California and Utah.

Early Tongan immigrants quickly brought their relatives in immigration chains similar to those of Samoans and Chamorros. Once an immigrant had acquired U.S. citizenship, he or she would sponsor other relatives who would come, intent on getting jobs, pursuing education, or obtaining American material possessions.

Pacific island peoples in Hawaii live mainly on the island of Oahu. They live on every part of the island but are especially concentrated in two locations: the working-class section of Honolulu known as Kalihi-Palama, and the villages of Laie and Kahuku on the North Shore.

In much of the analysis to follow, Pacific Islanders in Hawaii are much like the indigenous people of the Hawaiian Islands, who, though they are not immigrants to the United States, are Pacific Islanders nonetheless.

## Social Organization and Community Life

Mainland Samoans, Tongans, and other Pacific island immigrants and their descendants often complain that they are invisible — unnoticed and not understood by their non-Pacific Islander neighbors. The U.S. and local governments, schools, and many other mainland institutions even list Pacific Islanders as a subset of Asian

Americans—which assuredly they are not—on bureaucratic forms. In contrast, Pacific Islanders are fairly prominent in the social life of Hawaii. In 1996 there was a Samoan on the Honolulu City Council and a Tongan quarterback on the Oahu championship high school football team. There are numerous Pacific Islander teachers, police officers, businesspeople, neighborhood community leaders, and religious figures, as well as a small but highly visible cadre of Pacific Islander former Hawaii residents who have gone on to employment in the National Football League. Another point of visibility for Hawaii's Pacific Islanders is in the tourist industry, at places such as the Polynesian Cultural Center and in Waikiki hotels and nightclubs, where they bring the performance culture of the other islands to visitors to Hawaii from North America and Asia.

The central institution of community life in the Pacific islands is the family. Although most island groups have imported the Western idea of the nuclear family (and in some cases the term *famili* as well), kit is the larger, extended kin group that is the atom of island society. Called the *matavuvale* in Fiji, the *kainga* in Tonga, the *aiga* in Samoa, and the *ke utu* in Kiribati, this larger family unit includes at least three generations and a wide circle of collateral kin. Within the extended family there is usually a designated leader, most often a male of the older generation, such as the *matai* in Samoa—the person who carries the title to family land and honors, who convenes family councils, and who bears the largest responsibility for decision making. Living and decision making are largely communal and generation graded. For example, parents, aunts, and uncles all can act in the role of parent to an individual child, up to and including administering physical punishment.

This family system has been sustained into the diaspora, though not without some strains. American family models stress individual achievement and self-actualization, in marked contrast to the communal, cooperative, and self-sacrificing qualities called for in Pacific Islander family models. The American family depends far less than its

Pacific island counterpart on respect for the authority of age over youth, or of males over females. Today, American ideas about child discipline seldom include approval of physical punishment, whereas Pacific Islanders tend to see it as an expression of love and a vehicle for character development. In many Pacific Islander families in Hawaii, one can observe cultural change and conflict between the Pacific Islander extended model and the American nuclear model. There may be hesitation to give automatically and lavishly to relatives back in the home islands; or elements of equality between the sexes; or nuclear family gatherings, including children and parents but not extended kin, to make decisions about marriage, buying a home, or sending a child to college.

Pacific Islanders in Hawaii tend to occupy middle- or working-class economic strata. They are less likely than island Asians or *haoles* (whites) to complete high school or attend college (there is variation among the Pacific island groups in this,

A Pacific Islander harvests dendrobiums at a flower farm in Hawaii. (Richard A. Cooke III/Corbis)

with Tongans, Maoris, and Micronesians approaching the white population, and the other groups lagging). Pacific Islanders are more likely to be found among those who work with their bodies and hands rather than among professionals and office workers. For the immigrant generation, the agricultural and fishing skills that were useful in their home islands are far less useful in the urban context of Honolulu. Yet unemployment is not high, for there is a very strong work ethic among most Pacific island peoples in Hawaii.

The higher American living standard means that many Pacific Islanders are able to send money back to their families in the islands. This, in turn, assures that there is a continuing stream of people coming from the various island groups to join their relatives in Hawaii. Added to the generally crowded housing situation on Oahu, this migration stream often puts ten or fifteen people under a single roof. The family works together to help the newcomers adjust, learn the language, get a job, start an education. Everyone in the household ordinarily works to contribute to the communal welfare. More than a few immigrants use Hawaii as a way station to the United States mainland, where the family network continues.

One of the strongest Pacific Islander community organizations is the church. Most Tongans in Hawaii are members of the Church of Jesus Christ of Latter-Day Saints, although others are Methodists. Most Chamorros are Roman Catholics. The largest Samoan church is the Samoan Congregational Christian Church, an institutional descendant of the London Missionary Society, which took the lead in missionary activity in the Pacific in the nineteenth century. There are also civic and community welfare organizations, sports teams, and youth gangs in working-class neighborhoods that often take on an island-specific ethnic character.

Church, family, and community all play their parts in helping immigrants and their children — there is not much of a third generation yet — build lives in Hawaii that are embedded in America's economy and culture, yet preserve elements of island culture and networks of connection. Samo-

ans call what they seek to preserve *fa'a samoa* ("the Samoan way"); other peoples have similar phrases. They all speak of the attempt to continue to be Pacific island peoples and to be so together with the others from their own island homeland, amid the whirl of people across the Pacific and around the globe.

*See also:* GUAMANIANS; SAMOANS; TONGANS

## Bibliography

Campbell, I. C. (1989). *A History of the Pacific Islands.* Berkeley: University of California Press.

Cowling, W. E. (1990). "Motivations for Contemporary Tongan Migration." In *Tongan Culture and History,* edited by P. Herda, J. Terrell, and N. Gunson. Canberra: Australian National University.

Franco, R. W. (1985). "Samoan Perceptions of Work: Moving Up and Moving Around." Ph.D. diss., University of Hawaii.

Janes, C. R. (1990). *Migration, Social Change, and Health: A Samoan Community.* Stanford, CA: Stanford University Press.

Kluge, P. F. (1991). *The Edge of Paradise: America in Micronesia.* Honolulu: University of Hawaii Press.

Macpherson, C.; Shore, B.; and Franco, R., eds. (1978). *New Neighbors: Islanders in Adaptation.* Santa Cruz: University of California.

Mason, L., and Hereniko, P., eds. (1987). *In Search of a Home.* Suva, Fiji: University of the South Pacific.

Muñoz, F. U. (1979). "An Exploratory Study of Island Migration: Chamorros of Guam." D.S.W. diss., University of California at Los Angeles.

Nevin, D. (1977). *The American Touch in Micronesia.* New York: W. W. Norton.

Spickard, P. R., ed. (1994). *Pacific Island Peoples in Hawaii.* Honolulu: University of Hawaii Press.

Spickard, P. R., et al. (1995). *Pacific Islander Americans: An Annotated Bibliography in the Social Sciences.* Laie, HI: Institute for Polynesian Studies, Brigham Young University, Hawaii.

Spickard, P. R., and Fong, R. (1995). "Pacific Islander Americans and Multiethnicity: A Vision of America's Future?" *Social Forces* 73(4):1365–1383.

Young, N. F., ed. (1977). *Samoans in Hawaii: Selected Readings.* Honolulu: University of Hawaii.

PAUL R. SPICKARD

# PAKISTANIS

The Pakistani community in the United States has grown drastically since the early 1960s and now constitutes an influential segment of both the South Asian and Muslim populations. While some reports estimate the Pakistani population in the United States at 500,000 to 750,000, the 1990 U.S. Census, which is subject to underreporting because of the possible categorization of Pakistanis as South Asians, reported only around 100,000 Pakistanis living in the United States at that time. However, regardless of the actual count, virtually all Pakistani immigrants arrived in the United States after the implementation of the U.S. Immigration Act of 1965.

## Background

Pakistan was formed in 1947 with the partitioning of British-ruled India; the area with a predominantly Hindu population became independent India, and the areas with largely Muslim populations came to constitute Pakistan. Initially, the new country of Pakistan was divided into East Pakistan and West Pakistan, with the two regions separated by more than one thousand miles of Indian territory. Because of this separation, there was virtually no contact between the two wings of the country, and there was no development of a common identity. In 1971, East Pakistan seceded to form the new nation of Bangladesh, and West Pakistan became Pakistan.

Pakistan, which is now bordered by India to the southeast and Iran and Afghanistan to the northwest, consists of four major regions: Sarhad, Punjab, Sindh, and Baluchistan. These regions each possess their own highly developed languages (Pushto, Punjabi, Sindhi, and Baluchi, respectively) and cultures. More than half of the 135 million Pakistanis reside in the Punjab region.

The historical roots of the people of Pakistan lie in Arabia, Iran, and Afghanistan. Consequently, the language, religion, and culture of Pakistan are more akin to those of the people of West Asia, more commonly known as the Middle East. The religious divisions within the Pakistani population reflect this relationship in that a total of 95 percent of Pakistanis are Muslim (12% Shi'a and 83% Sunni). Christians constitute 2 percent of the population, Hindus account for 1.5 percent, and other religious minorities (such as Buddhists, Jains, and Zoroastrians) represent the rest of the population.

These regional and religious characteristics of Pakistan are also representative of the Pakistani population in the United States, where the vast majority of Pakistani immigrants come from the Punjab region and more than 80 percent are Sunni Muslims. As a result, the Islamic code of behavior in dietary habits and personal life is an important aspect of the Pakistani-American community.

## Immigration History

The first major wave of immigration to the United States from Pakistan arrived after the implementation of the Immigration Act of 1965, which initiated changes in U.S. immigration policies. The new law, which abolished the national-origins quota system and allowed for a larger number of non-European immigrants, gave preference to relatives of U.S. citizens, specialists with needed skills, and refugees from political, racial, or religious persecution. Consequently, Pakistanis arriving in the 1960s and early 1970s constituted a highly educated group of engineers, bankers, scientists, and pharmacists.

The educational, professional, and economic background that was required of initial post-1965 Pakistani immigrants enabled them to make the necessary adjustments to U.S. society without losing their religious or cultural identities. They settled primarily in large urban centers such as New York City, Chicago, Los Angeles, and San Francisco. In fact, the three states with the largest Pakistani populations according to the 1990 U.S. Census were New York (19.2%), California (17.7%), and Illinois (11.2%).

The first wave of immigrants began to naturalize as U.S. citizens in the 1970s. Once they had obtained citizenship, they were able to serve as sponsors for the second immigration wave, which consisted of their parents and less-educated kin. Members of this second wave found employment in a wide variety of businesses, such as boutiques, computer stores, restaurants, gas stations, dry cleaners, convenience stores, Halal meat markets, and real-estate agencies.

## Community Characteristics

Very little has actually been written in particular about the Pakistani-American community. Most sources tend to cover Pakistanis within the broad context of South Asians because of the geographical connection. Others tend to include them in the Arab Muslim community because of the religious connection. Therefore, very few sources actually discuss Pakistani-American culture as a distinct entity.

Pakistani immigrants bring with them to the United States the tradition of preserving close family ties; the family always takes precedence over the individual. The average number of children in a Pakistani family is three, and respect and support, especially emotional support, are traditionally granted by these children to their parents and parents-in-law.

There is a well-defined division of labor within Pakistani families; the husbands perform the "outdoor" chores, and the wives perform the "indoor" tasks. Husbands seldom interfere in the running of the family or the decoration of the house. As more and more Pakistani families become two-profession families, the division of labor in the home is often adjusted to accommodate the job commitments of the individual spouses. Still, arranging marriages for the children is considered to be the mothers' responsibility, and the vast majority of

A Pakistani family sits together near a river in Alexandria, Virginia. (Joseph Sohm/ChromoSohm Inc./Corbis)

Pakistani immigrant marriages continue to be arranged marriages (even among the more than 90 percent of the immigrant population who arrived in the United States as students, trainees, or medical interns). The divorce rate for these arranged marriages is extremely low, only 2 to 3 percent. However, the concept of arranged marriages is rapidly changing among Pakistani immigrants, and so is the related divorce rate. While only 3 to 4 percent of Pakistani immigrants have American spouses, the divorce rate among this group is 55 to 60 percent.

Children in Pakistani families traditionally receive a great deal of attention and support from their parents. Baby-sitters are rarely used, and the children invariably accompany their parents to most Pakistani and Islamic functions. This participation enables the children to develop a strong community affinity. Most children speak Urdu (the national language of Pakistan) and the language of their parents: Punjabi, Sindhi, or Baluchi. Arabic is taught as the language of the Koran and of prayers at Sunday schools at the mosques. Education is considered to be an important asset among Pakistanis, and it is estimated that 70 to 75 percent of Pakistani-American children have no financial obligations pending upon the completion of their college education.

These values of strong family ties, the importance of education, and a diligent work ethic pervade the Pakistani-American community. Because of these values, the community has been able to become a dynamic ethnic group despite the fact that its size is relatively small compared to the entire U.S. population.

One community that might be considered typical of the Pakistani population is Rochester, New York. A 1988 study of the eighty-eight Pakistani families living in that city at that time revealed that the average age of the head of a Pakistani family was forty-four years. The families averaged 2.5 cars per household, and the average price of a Pakistani-owned house was more than 2.5 times the average price for a house in that area. The growth of the Pakistani-American population is also reflected in this community, which saw the number of Pakistani families almost double during the decade following the initial study.

On the larger scale, Pakistanis have owned and operated a number of businesses and corporations. At least one such company, AST Research, had a Pakistani chairman and was a Fortune-500 company. Health Net, the largest Health Maintenance Organization in the United States, is largely owned and operated by a Pakistani American, as is Aztesia, one of the largest knitting and dyeing companies in the country. In 1991, Municipal Engineers, a Pakistani-owned engineering consulting firm in Wichita, Kansas, was the recipient of a Presidential Award for small businesses. In 1996, NexGen, a Silicon Valley maker of computer chips, had a Pakistani chief executive officer and was acquired by Advanced Micro Devices for $800 million. Inventions such as the Mobinuddin Umbrella and the Omayya Shunt demonstrate the Pakistani-American contributions to the medical field.

## Political and Religious Contributions

Pakistani Americans have made considerable contributions to American politics since the 1960s, but it was only in the 1990s that the area became a major focus for the community. This involvement was evident in the 1994 Illinois gubernatorial election, with the subsequent appointment of two Pakistanis to state positions. Pakistani influence could also be seen at the national level in the defeats of a New York congressman and a Nebraska senator who were both anti-Pakistani and running for re-election.

Spiritually, Pakistani Americans have played a key role in the development and growth of Muslim communities across the United States. In addition to founding a large number of Islamic centers, Pakistanis have participated in interfaith dialogues and served as active members of Christian-Muslim commissions and on Jewish-Muslim dialogue committees. Some of the leading Muslim organizations in the United States that have been led by Pakistani Americans include the Islamic Society of North America, the Islamic Council of North America,

Pakistani Americans in Chicago gather together to celebrate Pakistan's Independence Day. (Mukul Roy)

the American Muslim Alliance, the American Muslim Council, the Muslim Educational Council of North America, the United Muslims of America, the Association of Muslim Social Scientists of North America, and the Association of Muslim Scientists and Engineers.

## Community Organization

There are many Pakistani cultural and educational organizations operating throughout the United States; every major university has a Pakistan Students Association, and every major city has a Pakistani-American Association. The focal point of these organizations is to provide cultural and educational exposure to the membership's American compatriots.

Among the leading ethnic and professional organizations of Pakistani Americans are the Pakistani American Congress (a national organization representing local Pakistan-American societies),

the Indus Society of Chicago (named after the main river tributary in Pakistan), and the Association of Pakistani Physicians of North America.

In addition to coordinating regular social events, organizations in major U.S. metropolitan areas participate in the annual celebration of two important holidays: Pakistan Day (March 23) and Independence Day (August 14). The 1992 Independence Day parade in New York City was dubbed by *India Abroad* to be among the largest ethnic events in the city.

The cohesiveness of the Pakistani community is also reinforced by the ethnic press, which provides sources for news and views on national and spiritual issues. There are more than twenty-four ethnic weeklies and bi-weeklies in regular publication. *Pakistan Link*, an English-Urdu weekly with a circulation of thirty-five thousand, is the leader among these publications and appears simultaneously in Los Angeles, Chicago, and Toronto.

## Homeland Involvement

Pakistani Americans have, since the mid-1990s, started to focus attention on developments, at both the individual and collective levels, in Pakistan. At the national level, selected Pakistani-American individuals played significant roles in the interim governments created in Pakistan in 1993 and 1996. At the local level, the Association of Pakistani Physicians of North America has played an important role in launching village-level health programs in Pakistan, including the donation of critical health maintenance equipment to hospitals. The health programs emphasize clean water, improved sanitation, and higher immunization rates to control the maternity/infant mortality rate. Other Pakistani organizations are fostering educational and scholarship programs in Pakistan. All of these strategies are simply ways for successful Pakistani Americans to contribute to the betterment of their home country.

*See also:* BANGLADESHIS; PUNJABIS; SINDHIS

## Bibliography

Awan, S. N. A. (1976). *People of Pakistani Origin in Canada: The First Quarter Century*. Ottawa, Canada: Author.

Awan, S. N. A. (1989). *People of the Indus Valley: Pakistani-Canadians*. Ottawa, Canada: Author.

Khan, S. (1981). "A Brief History of Pakistanis in the Western United States." M.A. thesis, California State University, Sacramento.

Malik, I. H. (1979). "A Study of Acculturation of the Pakistanis in South-East Michigan in Reference to Three Variables: Family, Profession, and Ethnicity." Ph.D. thesis, Michigan State University, Ann Arbor.

Malik, I. H. (1989). *Pakistanis in Michigan*. New York: AMS Press.

Malik, S. (1993). "Pakistanis in Rochester, New York: Establishing Islamic Identity in the American Melting Pot." *Islamic Studies* LXIII:461–475.

Williams, R. B. (1988). *Religions of Immigrants from India and Pakistan: New Threads in the American Tapestry*. Cambridge, Eng.: Cambridge University Press.

SALAHUDDIN MALIK

# PALESTINIANS

Palestinians and Palestinian Americans originate from the Middle East in the land bounded by the Mediterranean Sea to the west, the Jordan River to the east, the Red Sea to the south, and Lebanon to the north. Today this area is part of the modern State of Israel and the Israeli-occupied territories. Palestinians believe that they are descended from native peoples who have inhabited the Holy Land for centuries, dating as far back as the ancient Canaanites.

Palestinians see their view of the Arab-Israeli conflict and history as a distinctive part of their identity. Historically their country had been part of the Ottoman Empire (in Palestine from 1516 to 1920), until the British governed Palestine under a League of Nations mandate (1920–1948). The Palestinians had a culture that was primarily agricultural—the first British census, on 1921, found that 80 percent of the predominately Arab indigenous population of Palestine depended on agriculture for their livelihood. By 1948, two-thirds of Palestine's population was still rural.

Jerusalem was the cultural, spiritual, and economic center of Palestinian life. Other major Arab cities such as Acre, Haifa, and Jaffa were centers of trade. The culture of pre-1948 Palestine was overwhelmingly Arab. At the time of the partition in 1948, the Jewish population did not exceed 33 percent (the first modern Jewish settlement in Palestine was established in 1896), and this was only after massive waves of immigration following the end of World War II in 1945. With Jewish landownership not in excess of 5.6 percent of Palestine in 1948, the Palestinians were unable to accept the partition plan suggested by the United Nations, dividing the country into two countries, Israel and Palestine.

With the vote to partition Palestine, war ensued between the Israeli forces and the other Arab front-line countries. The Israelis emerged with control of three-fourths of the land area of Palestine. The inception of the modern State of Israel resulted in the creation of some 700,000 Palestinian refugees. In 1967, approximately 500,000 additional Palestinians were made refugees, carrying their Palestinian identity with them. Of the approximately 5.2 million Palestinians in the world today, some 1.5 million still live in the West Bank and Gaza, and approximately 70,000 inside Israel proper. Millions of Palestinians live in the surrounding Arab countries. Approximately 300,000 Palestinians are believed to have immigrated to the United States, although no accurate count is available of Palestinian Americans.

Today Palestinians have a strong sense of national identity based on their geographic ties to the land of their origin that has been intensified by the conflict over the land with the Israelis. While most Palestinians also identify as Arabs, their keen sense of national Palestinian identity makes them a distinct subgroup of Arabs. They share the Arabic language and the common history of the region with other Arabs. The memory of the loss of their country in 1948, which they call the *Nakba* (Disaster), is firmly rooted in the psyche of most Palestinians, as is the occupation of the West Bank and Gaza in 1967.

Over time, Palestinians developed a strong village-based culture. They still identify today by their villages and cities of origin in Palestine. In the United States this has taken the form of village clubs such as the Ramallah Club. Palestinians developed, over the centuries, local village dialects and distinctive village dress. The major differences in their local dialects of Arabic are between city dwellers (*medani*) and those from villages (*fellaheen*). In general, Palestinian Arabic can be distinguished from other Arabic dialects of the Levant by a distinctive voweling.

Prior to 1948, there were approximately one thousand Palestinian villages, but more than four hundred Palestinian villages have been destroyed in the Arab-Israeli conflict. A Palestinian woman used to be identifiable to village and region by her distinctive embroidered dress (*thob*). Each village had its own separate and unique embroidery pattern, taken from elements of nature or geometric in pattern. For example, the traditional West Bank village dress is usually black with brightly colored embroidery designs, often red and other colors. Wheat, roses, birds, and repetitive geometric designs cover the bodice, sleeves, and hems of these dresses. Palestinian men could be identified by their black and white headdress (*kuffiya*). The younger generations of Palestinians are not wearing the distinctive dress as much and have adopted more Western clothing, but the embroidery, in the form of pillowcases and other items, is still cherished. Even in America, one sometimes still sees an older Palestinian woman wearing her village dress.

Palestinian crafts, such as handcarved olive wood figurines, blown glass, pottery, basketweaving, brassware, jewelry, mother-of-pearl inlaid furniture, and the embroidery and weaving designs, are distinctively unique to the regions of Palestine. The Palestinian flag, although similar to the Jordanian flag, contains the colors red, black, white, and green. The Palestinian flag and other cultural items are very popular with Palestinians and are found in most Palestinian-American households. Many Palestinian refugees kept the keys to their houses confiscated by the Israelis and some display the keys prominately in their homes in America.

Palestinians may also self-identify according to religious affiliations, although they appear much less divided by religion than other Arabs. Some avoid public self-identifying by religion altogether because they see it as divisive. The majority of Palestinians are Sunni Muslims. Palestine also historically contained a large Christian minority (once believed to be as high as 20 percent of the Palestinian population) consisting of Roman Catholics, Eastern Orthodox, some Protestants, and other Christian sects. A disproportionate number of Palestinian Christians have left their homeland, leaving some to wonder about the future of Christianity in the Holy Land. The other religions of the country include some Druze and Baha'i. The Baha'i faith originated in Palestine, in the city of Haifa.

Prior to the peace accords signed in 1992, Palestinians were divided by a multitude of political factions. The Palestine Liberation Organization (PLO), under the leadership of Yasir Arafat, was the umbrella group of these many factions. The factions were divided according to ideologies and among the various personalities leading the factions. Some of the factions were more leftist and militant in their approaches to the Israeli conflict. While some of the factions still existed in the mid-1990s, the major political division among Palestinians is now between the PLO and Hamas (the major Muslim religious/political Palestinian group). Most of the Palestinians who immigrated to the United States tired of these factional differences and no longer identify highly with any political faction.

## Immigration and Settlement

Palestinian immigration to the United States can be characterized according to the major waves of Arab immigration to America. Arab and Palestinian immigration to the United States have been limited by immigration law. Identity problems with ethnic/racial designations in immigration law controlled Arab immigration. The first significant wave of Arab immigrants to the United States arrived between 1878 and 1924. Prior to World War I, Arabs (because of the Turkish Ottoman Empire) were classified as "Turks in Asia." The first wave of Arabs was mostly Arabs from what was then Greater Syria, primarily the Mount Lebanon area. These early Syrian/Lebanese immigrants were predominantly Christian. A small number of Palestinians was among the first wave of Arab immigrants. For example, some Palestinians from the West Bank town of Ramallah came to the United States around 1900 and set up small businesses in midwestern cities.

The first wave of Arab immigration ended abruptly in 1924. Their designation as Asians meant that Arabs were mainly excluded from immigration to the United States. This was accomplished by the Asian Exclusionary Act of 1924 and by the Johnson-Reed Immigration Act of 1924, which set very low immigration quotas for Asians and consequently for Arabs. The McCarran-Walter Act of 1952 relaxed the quota system, allowing for greater Arab immigration. Today quotas still effectively exist, although immigration laws have changed. Arab Americans are now listed by country of origin. Palestinians are usually classified according to the last country they inhabited, not always reflective of their origin or identity as Palestinian.

The majority of the second wave of Arab immigration (1948–1966) to the United States was Palestinian. This second wave of Arab immigrants was 60 percent Muslim, reflecting the majority religious background of Palestinians. The second wave of Arab immigrants was more educated than the first, containing more white-collar workers and professionals. This period of immigration

Three Palestinian refugee boys gather together in the late 1970s. (Owen Franken/Corbis)

to the United States was also considered to be the beginning of the "brain drain" of Arab intellectuals to the United States. Education is highly valued by Palestinians, and many immigrated to the United States for educational and professional opportunities.

Palestinians who immigrated during this period tended to suffer from more ambiguity over permanent settlement in the United States than the earlier wave of Arab immigrants. This reflected their hopes to return to Palestine someday. While Palestinian Americans of this wave became acculturated and some assimilated into American culture, it was with some reluctance. Palestinian pride and feelings of being discriminated against may have contributed to the retention of Palestinian identity.

The third wave of Arab immigration to the United States began in 1967 and is marked by the Arab-Israeli War of 1967. This wave is sometimes considered to have ended with the recent Gulf War, although some scholars consider this wave of immigration to be ongoing. With the occupation of the West Bank and Gaza, another large group of Palestinian refugees was created. This contributed to a surge in Palestinian immigration to the United States. Palestinian students, studying in the United States at the end of the Arab-Israeli War of 1967, found themselves homeless and disenfranchised. The Israelis denied them the right to return. Most of the students were forced to seek American residence and/or citizenship. The overwhelming choice of area of study by young Palestinians of the third wave is engineering (although there is now a trend toward greater diversity in majors with emphasis on business and service careers). Palestinian engineers have settled in many of the suburbs of major industrial cities such as Detroit and Los Angeles. However, Palestinians have settled in various areas of the United States. States such as California, Texas, Michigan, New York, Illinois, and Florida are popular with Palestinians. Detroit, New York (Brooklyn), Chicago, Houston, and Jacksonville, Florida, are some of the cities that host larger Palestinian-American populations.

Palestinian Americans, by virtue of their higher education levels, are thought to have higher socioeconomic status than most Arab Americans and other Americans. Palestinian doctors, lawyers, engineers, and other professionals have generally been quite successful. In addition, Palestinians have one of the highest percentages of doctoral degrees per capita in the world.

## Families and Kinship

The basic family structure for Palestinians, like other Arabs, is the extended family. Although in America there is an increasing trend toward smaller, more nuclear families, larger families are still prevalent among Palestinian Americans. It is not uncommon to have grandparents, aunts, uncles, cousins, or other relatives living in the same household as part of the extended family group.

Palestinians who originated in the villages tend to marry someone from the same village. First-cousin marriage (a daughter marrying her father's brother's son) is common although not necessarily the rule among Palestinian Americans. This strong village identification persists even in America, and children are encouraged to socialize and marry others from the same village. Palestinians from villages tend to be more conservative, preserving more of the village attitudes toward separation of the sexes and modesty in dress and action. There is concern by parents that their children, particularly the girls, do not adopt Western dating practices.

The more educated Palestinian Americans tend to be more liberal in their attitudes. Many Palestinian-American women have succeeded in business and the professions. There are class distinctions among Palestinians, most based on city versus village origin and by education levels. Wealth and socioeconomics also play roles in these divisions. With the development of Palestinian educational institutions and universities on the West Bank since the late 1960s, the traditional class distinctions began to fade as more Palestinians received higher degrees.

Three Palestinian-American women gather together as part of a 1997 luncheon in honor of a visiting delegation of female members of the Palestinian Legislative Council. (Najat Arafat Khelil)

## Palestinian Women in the United States

The most complete discussion of Palestinian women in the United States to date is presented by Louise Cainkar (1990), using examples from her studies in Chicago's Palestinian communities. Cainkar distinguishes between the lives of Palestinian women who were born and/or raised in their homeland and those who were born and raised in the United States. Most Palestinian women immigrate as wives, mothers, or daughters—as distinct from many Palestinian men who often immigrate as single men. Cainkar points out that many of the Palestinian women keenly feel the exile and separation from their extended families back home. In contrast, many of the generation of Palestinian women born in the United States, especially those that are educated, feel an isolation from traditional Palestinian culture. To some extent, their education and lifestyle as professional working women places them at odds with some of the more traditional lifestyles. Whether a woman originated from an urban center or rural village also affects the ease of acculturation and the lifestyle choices available to her. Palestinian women in the United States play important roles in their families and as preservers of Palestinian culture in this new environment.

## Arts and Culture

Palestinians in the United States have relied heavily on contacts with their homeland for their arts. They have imported dance troupes, touring plays, poets, musicians, and cultural displays from their homeland to the United States. This cultural exchange has strengthened ties between Palestinians in the Middle East and those living in the United States.

Palestinians have their own distinct traditional style of line dances (*dabke*), which differ from those of other Arabs. Their dances reflect a long-standing tradition. Palestinian music and poetry tend to express the Palestinian experience and political consciousness.

The younger generations of Palestinian Americans are beginning to lose their Arabic-language skills, making it more difficult for them to understand the poetry and the words of the music. Their parents often express concern over this loss of language ability and cultural loss. In response there has been an emergence of young English-language Palestinian poets and artists. Also, many local Palestinian groups have their own American-born youth *dabke* dance groups to reintroduce the young people to their culture in a fun way.

America has also become a place of refuge and freedom of expression for many performing artists who have chosen residence in the United States. Palestinian Americans have published books, collections of poems, cookbooks, children's books, and other literary works describing their experiences. Palestinian Americans host accomplished Palestinian performers and musicians.

## Health Issues

Many of the health concerns of Palestinian Americans are focused on trying to improve the health and well-being of relatives and Palestinians living in the Middle East. Most of the private Arab hospitals and charities in Jerusalem and the occupied territories have relied heavily on the generosity of Palestinian Americans. In general, Palestinians have sent monies to help support family and relatives left behind in the Middle East. Palestinian Americans have provided ambulances and basic health services for towns and villages in the West Bank, Gaza, and inside Israel proper. Concerns over lack of clean drinking water, basic sanitation, and access to health care for family members in the homeland predominate among Palestinians.

In the United States, there have been few studies of health issues affecting Palestinian Americans and other Arab Americans. Available data from one study of Detroit-area Palestinian/Jordanian Americans indicate that hypertension, diabetes, and high cholesterol may be common health problems for Palestinian Americans (and other Arab Americans). An increased consumption of red meat and other changes in the traditional Palestinian/Arabic diet, with reduced levels of exercise, appear to correlate with hypertension and other diseases.

## Identity, Stereotyping, and Discrimination

Palestinian identity has persisted in the children of the first wave of immigrants and in the subsequent waves. Their national aspiration for self-determination and statehood has kept the idea of return alive. Many of the Palestinians who immigrated since 1967 have retained their residency in their homeland and make periodic trips back to the cities and villages of origin. Another factor contributing to the persistence of Palestinian identity in the United States is the feeling of discrimination and marginalization stemming from the stereotyping of Palestinians.

The media image of Palestinians, especially prevalent in the 1960s and 1970s, as terrorists is particularly resented by most Palestinian Americans; the idea that their entire culture, history, and contributions have been reduced to this one image is particularly disheartening. The acts of violence resulting from the Arab-Israeli conflict were understood by Palestinians in the context of that struggle for freedom, and they resent the characterization of all Palestinian people as inherently violent. They see themselves as having been victims of violence in the Middle East. There is a strong desire by Palestinians to tell others about their experiences as refugees and victims of occupation.

The perception that the American media have been generally biased and anti-Palestinian has led many Palestinians to become informal activists in their communities to attempt to explain their culture to other Americans and counter the biases by speaking out. Palestinian Americans have suffered disproportionately from hate crimes, such as vandalism, destruction of property, and other more violent crimes. As with other Arab Americans, when conflicts break out in the Middle East, the incidents of hate crimes against Arabs in the

United States increase. Complaints about surveillance and harassment of Palestinian Americans have also surfaced. With the 1992 peace accords, there is hope among Palestinians that their side of the story will be heard and their national aspirations achieved. In the meantime, Palestinian identity and culture persist and flourish in America.

## Bibliography

Abraham, S. Y., and Abraham, N., eds. (1981). *The Arab World and Arab Americans: Understanding a Neglected Minority*. Detroit: Center for Urban Studies, Wayne State University.

Ata, I. W. (1986). *The West Bank Palestinian Family*. London: Routledge and Kegan Paul.

Cainkar, L. (1990). "Palestinian Women in the U.S.: Who Are They and What Kind of Lives Do They Lead?" In *Images and Reality: Palestinian Women Under Occupation and in the Diaspora*. Washington, DC: Institute for Arab Women's Studies.

Christison, K. (1989). "The American Experience: Palestinians in the U.S." *Journal of Palestine Studies* 17(4):18–36.

Giacamen, R. (1988). *Life and Health in Three Palestinian Villages*. London: Ithaca Press.

Hassoun, R. J. (1995). "A Bioanthropological Perspective of Hypertension in Arab Americans in the Metropolitan Detroit Area." Ph.D. diss., University of Florida, Gainesville.

Hill, A. G. (1983). "The Palestinian Population of the Middle East." *Populations Development Review* 9:85–103.

Hilterman, J. (1993). "Abu Jamal: A Palestinian Urban Villager." In *The Modern Middle East*, edited by E. Burke. Berkeley: University of California Press.

Khalidi, W. (1984). *Before Their Diaspora*. Washington, DC: Institute for Palestine Studies.

Naff, A. (1985). *Becoming American: The Early Arab Immigrants' Experience*. Carbondale: Southern Illinois University Press.

Nigem, E. T. (1986). "Arab Americans: Migration, Socioeconomic and Demographic Characteristics." *International Migration Review* 20:629–649.

Orfalea, G. (1988). *Before the Flames: A Quest for the History of Arab Americans*. Austin: University of Texas Press.

Rish, S. A. (1989). *Children of Bethany: The Story of a Palestinian Family*. Bloomington: Indiana University Press.

Rose, J.; Milton, C.; and Lilenfield, L. S. (1986). "UNRWA and the Health of Palestinian Refugees." *New England Journal of Medicine* 315:596–600.

Shaheen, J. (1984). *The TV Arab: Our Popular Press*. Bowling Green, OH: Bowling Green University Popular Press.

Shaheen, J. (1990). "Our Cultural Demon: The Ugly Arab." *Washington Post*, August 19.

Zaghul, A. S., and Ahlawat, S. (1989). "Nuclear and Extended Family Attributes of Jordanian Arabs." *Marriage and Family Review* 14:251–273.

Zogby, J. (1990). *Arab-America Today: A Demographic Profile of Arab Americans*. Washington, DC: Arab-American Institute.

ROSINA HASSOUN

# PANAMANIANS

The term "Panamanian" refers to citizens of the Republic of Panama. Under the present constitution of Panama, Panamanian citizenship is irrevocable and therefore extends to persons of Panamanian birth or registration who are now residing in the United States, notwithstanding their legal status in the United States. For purposes of this entry, the definition will be extended to include U.S. citizens or U.S. residents who were not born in Panama but identify themselves with Panama through ancestry.

## Background

The Republic of Panama, which occupies the Isthmus of Panama (a tropical landform comprising the narrowest and southernmost segment of Central America) is located approximately nine degrees north of the equator. Panama is bordered on the west by the Republic of Costa Rica, on the east by the Republic of Colombia, on the north by the Caribbean Sea, and on the south by the Pacific Ocean.

The four largest ethnic groups in Panama are the mestizos (65%), the blacks and mulattos (14%), the whites (10%), and the Amerindians (8%). Although Spanish is the official and predominant language of the nation, many people commonly use English (which is taught as a second language of instruction in bilingual education in many parts of the country) in the workplace and for business and personal transactions. It even serves as a first or rivalling language of communication for some households and in some private situations. Roman Catholicism is the dominant religious affiliation, but other faiths such as Protestantism, Judaism, Islam, Buddhism, and Baha'i are represented among the population.

## Immigration History

The first serious immigration to the United States from Panama may have begun in the mid-nineteenth century in connection with the building of the Panama Railroad. The railway was constructed by an American company to facilitate the travels of East Coast speculators who wanted to avoid crossing the continental United States on their way to the California Gold Rush. In addition, however, the railway undoubtedly served as a baseline for the immigration of Panamanians, including former railroad workers, to the United States.

Subsequent American projects in Central America contributed to other more pronounced Panamanian immigration to the United States. One such endeavor was the building of the Panama Canal. The man-made waterway, which was opened in 1914 after ten years of construction, was governed solely by U.S. administration until changes were authorized by the Carter-Torrijos Treaty of 1977. This treaty, which stipulated the complete turning over of control of the canal to Panama by the year 1999, was followed by the Panama Canal Act of 1979, which guaranteed certain longtime employees in the operation of the canal entry to the United States as residents.

Another strong American influence in Panama during the early part of the twentieth century was the United Fruit Company, which operated banana plantations, railroads, and wharves, as well as a fleet of more than one hundred ships to carry their product from Central America to the processing, packing, and redistribution plants in the United States. In addition to providing jobs for those individuals no longer employed in the building of the Panama Canal, this company (in the form of its shipping fleet) provided one of the most practical means for English-speaking residents and citizens of Panama to immigrate to the United States. Similar benefits were gained by individuals working for other American companies operating in Central America and the Caribbean.

After the Panama Canal was opened in 1914 (the same year that World War I began), the workers who labored to build the canal were dispersed. While many remained on their own in Panama, thousands of former canal workers (sometimes with their Panamanian-born relatives) returned to the West Indies, went on to other American projects and plantations in Central America or the Spanish-speaking islands of the Caribbean, or immigrated directly to the United States. In the latter case, they, together with migrants from the southern United States and other immigrants from the Caribbean, were responding to labor needs that had been created (by World War I) in the industrial and coastal states of the United States. These labor shortages resulted from the fact that the war industries were expanding at the same time that American males were enlisting in the armed services and the customary waves of European immigrants were being disrupted.

The Great Depression of the 1930s represented a period of low immigration for Panamanians, as there was no longer an expansive war machine in the United States demanding manpower and unemployment was high, even among the native-born population of the United States. World War II, which saw a revival of general immigration to the United States, also saw Panama emerge as a target (rather than a source) of similar immigration. These new immigrants to Panama were recruited and employed by contract to assist in overhauling the Panama Canal and to help meet the labor needs resulting from increases in the number of U.S. military personnel installed in Panama for defense of the waterway.

After World War II, however, a streamlining of canal operations and support facilities, as well as a reduction of residential communities and military bases, began to occur. This in turn led to a massive reduction in canal laborers and the repatriation to their homelands of many who had come from other parts of the region to work on contract. These events had a negative effect on the overall economy of Panama. In view of this economic decline, immigration to the United States was an attractive, though sometimes desperate, alternative.

Even when the Korean War in the 1950s resulted in increased trafficking through the canal to the Pacific Ocean, augmenting the presence of the U.S. military (an act that would have created jobs and business in earlier periods) in the region, Panamanian immigration to the United States continued at a noticeable rate. In fact, the period witnessed the beginning of a trend by Panamanians to enlist in the U.S. armed forces. Some, to whom direct enlistment was not available in Panama, immigrated to the United States (whether legally or illegally) in order to enlist in the U.S. armed forces.

Most of the Panamanian immigrants prior to the 1970s tended to be people of color from working- or middle-class backgrounds who immigrated to the United States in search of work and other opportunities. In the early 1970s, however, there was a brief and unusually pronounced influx of business-class individuals and members of Panama's white elite who arrived in the United States (Miami in particular) as political exiles. Many of these exiles later returned to Panama, but there were some who chose to remain in the United States.

Intense political antagonisms, both within Panama itself and between Panama and the United States, began to occur during the early 1980s. The international conflict culminated in U.S. sanctions against the Noriega regime. Many Panamanians began to lose their sense of personal security, as well as their confidence in legitimate business growth and the ability of the government to pay its bills or its employees. As a result, increased emigration from Panama began to occur. The subsequent reinstallation of a democratic government and peaceful relations with the United States have not seemed to cause any serious changes, quantitatively or qualitatively, in Panamanian immigration to the United States.

## Settlement Patterns

In the past, the population clusters of Panamanians in the United States were centered near port cities that had shipping or airline connections with Panama, such as New Orleans and Boston, or sites with schools of higher education, such as New York and Washington, D.C., where Panamanians may have studied and remained to pursue their professions. This trend is consistent with the fact that the majority of newly arriving Panamanians settle first in the urban centers where previous family networks exist, along with employment, educational, and housing opportunities.

Although new clusters of Panamanians are being reported in cities in Colorado, Texas, the Carolinas, and Washington State, the Panamanian population continues to be concentrated mainly in the larger coastal or industrial cities. The New York City metropolitan area is the principal location for resettlement of Panamanians, but additional Panamanian populations of significant size exist in Miami, Chicago, Los Angeles, Boston, Atlanta, and Washington, D.C. Indications of smaller and more selective settlements of Panamanian immigrants are being noted among outlying suburban areas.

## Demographics

According to the 1990 U.S. Census, there are approximately eighty-six thousand persons of Panamanian birth in the United States. However, this statistic probably involves some undercounting of the population. For example, many Panamanian immigrants may be identifying themselves with other Caribbean ethnic groups, some may simply identify themselves as Americans, and others may fail to disclose their Panamanian identity because of a fear of reprisal related to ambiguity of their legal status as immigrants. Furthermore, thousands of persons who are of whole or partial Panamanian ancestry are instead counted among the general Hispanic-origin, native-born, and foreign-born categories.

The U.S. Immigration and Naturalization Service (INS) reports that the annual flow of the legal admission of persons of Panamanian birth into the United States rose from approximately 2,200 in 1984 to about 4,204 in 1991 and then fell back to 2,247 by 1995. In addition, the INS reports that several thousands of Panamanians entered the United States in 1994 as legal non-immigrants. Even though their stay and privileges are limited, persons in such categories may have some effect on the image and influence of the community. From all indications, however, Panama contributes in rather small numbers (or proportions) to the statistics for undocumented immigrants in the United States.

The Panama-born population in the United States is characterized by a median age of 37.3 years, with a sex ratio of five males to three females and a marital ratio of three married individuals to every five unmarried individuals. Women between the ages of thirty-five and forty-four have an average of two children each; the average is lower for younger women. According to the group's educational profile for those individuals over twenty-five years of age, 28 percent hold high school diplomas or the equivalent, another 28 percent hold some pre-baccalaureate college education, and 17 percent hold a bachelor's degree or higher. At the same time, 31 percent of the population reported not speaking English very well, with 9 percent reporting living in a linguistically isolated (presumably Spanish-speaking) home.

Panamanians in the United States who are employed largely occupy managerial, professional, technical, service, and administrative support occupations with overwhelming concentration in professional and related (both medical and educa-tional) services, followed by manufacturing, wholesale and retail trade, and high representation as private wage and salary workers. Most families among this population involve at least two working persons, and the median and mean incomes for families are $28,000 and $34,000, respectively.

A little more than half of all individuals who were born in Panama and now live in the United States have acquired U.S. citizenship by naturalization.

## Values and Norms

The Panamanian immigrant community is quite multicultural in its makeup, with an increasing tendency for the younger and more recent immigrants to be bilingual (rather than either Spanish- or English-dominant). There is also a tendency for the more recent immigrants to be more Hispanic oriented in their cultural and educational background than those who preceded them. On the one hand, this bilingual, multiethnic composition gives Panamanians access to a wider range of contacts than those generally available to immigrant groups, allowing Panamanians to serve as liaisons between ethnic groups that are normally divided. On the other hand, Panamanians (because they are not readily included in larger, less ambiguous ethnic minorities) experience on occasion some degree of difficulty or underrepresentation in the sharing of power and opportunities for public gain.

Panamanian immigrants generally have an urban background and substantial previous exposure to or acquaintance with American culture (due to the presence of American operations in Panama since the second half of the nineteenth century). These aspects of American culture include education, media, linguistic styles, currency, business practices, work demands and conditions, sports, and religion. Because of this general knowledge of American culture, the Panamanian immigrants arrive in the United States already armed with the "American Dream." These immigrants are therefore equipped with a sense of familiarity, cultural readiness, and a rich repertoire of references and responses for adapting to the wide range of styles and standards that are necessary for settlement and success in the United States.

Combined with this knowledge of American culture are the principal values and norms—thriftiness, sacrifice, respectability, ambition, educational attainment, career development, family responsibility, homeownership, self-confidence, and, for some, a good degree of religious faith—that Panamanians have traditionally tried to instill in their offspring. These are all traits believed to be crucial to mobility and success in the United States.

## Cultural and Social Activities

Cultural affairs among the Panamanian immigrant population in the United States cover a wide array of activities, some of which are commonplace and occur in different parts of the country at the same time. These nationwide activities generally involve the celebration of Panamanian national holidays, where patriotic speeches, artistic renditions, and ecumenical services are prominent. Traditional food, music, dance, dress, and visual arts decorations are combined with announcements, awards, and nostalgic exchanges to give added meaning to these observances. Attendance usually involves all socioeconomic and ethnic groups as well as officials of the host city, which in turn often declare a special day in honor of the community or the home country. Official participation by representatives of the Panamanian government is customary. Sometimes the involvement reaches the level of co-sponsoring the activity, but at other times involvement of the Panamanian government is limited to underwriting of their representatives from Panama who deliver formal speeches or cultural performances for the overseas community. These events, especially in the urban centers, often are followed by programs or parties in Panamanian clubs or in private homes.

Many nationwide attempts at the coordination of sustained activities have foundered or ended at best in splintered remnants of the original idea. Currently in vogue is the sponsorship each year of a Panamanian Family Reunion. These "reunions" occur in a different city each year and have an attendance usually numbering in excess of five thousand, including individuals from all over the United States and Panama who are organized as extended families or as specific social groups. In addition, many non-Panamanian participants attend merely as friends or as curious first-timers.

Aside from the national holidays and the annual Panamanian Family Reunion, the cultural family activities among Panamanian immigrants involve the standard birthdays, graduations, weddings, anniversaries, funerals, and ecumenical or commemorative services. Social activities outside the family include concerts, banquets, and dances held by social clubs. Community activities include class and school alumni reunions, athletic contests, junior leagues, art shows or plays, conferences or workshops (generally about health, immigration, and community affairs), bilingual consultation and social services for recently arrived immigrants, and excursions or business trips to Panama. Of worthwhile note among the practices observed by the leading social organizations of the Panamanian community have been the raising of substantial scholarship funds for assisting Panamanians who wish to pursue undergraduate studies in the United States and the providing of toys (and, when necessary, emergency funds and other usable items) to unfortunate sectors of the population still living in Panama. Occasionally, members of the community in the United States are invited to serve as artists, consultants, researchers, conference participants, or faculty members by private or public institutions in Panama, and some individuals have even been selected by the Panamanian government to hold consular or diplomatic posts.

Consistent with its motives for having immigrated, the U.S.-based community tends to circulate and celebrate known cases of achievement or success of this type from within its ranks and among its offspring or relatives. Persons who return to positions of prominence in Panama are also celebrated. Compared to other immigrant groups in the United States from Central America, the Panamanian community shows less success in the formation of corporate enterprises or communal agencies among its members. Rather, it is characterized by an impressive array of persons who have gained individual prominence or achieved leadership in their respective fields of interest (e.g., business, sports, arts, academics, politics, professions, and public service).

## Political Organization

Panamanian immigrants, including many who are now naturalized American citizens, are keenly interested in the implications of any U.S. political actions, whether domestic or international, that affect Panama. Since a significant proportion of the U.S.-based Panamanian community has had historical connections with the Panama Canal and its terminal cities, a great deal of excitement has been generated about the future use of the canal and potential opportunities related to the reverting of the canal land and facilities to Panama at the end of the twentieth century. However, overseas absentee voting is not allowed by Panamanian law, and there are no large-scale formal branches of political parties, whether American or Panamanian, operating within the immigrant community. Nor are there any fraternal orders or pressure groups made up exclusively or even predominantly by Panamanians. The majority of political activities for Panamanian immigrants, therefore, involve periodic debates at public assemblies (or through local media when in operation) to discuss timely issues of concern to the community.

The supply of information for these political and social debates was greatly decreased when the English-language *Panama Tribune*, which was produced in Panama and served readers in both the United States and Panama, ceased publication in the 1970s. Over the years, the American-based Panamanian community has been forced to rely on a series of local publications that have often been small and short-lived and on clippings from newspapers printed in Panama (a few of which are printed in English, but most of which are printed in Spanish). To compensate for this lack of a reliable, single news source, some immigrants in the United States maintain contact (by correspondence, telephone, cassettes, and telecommunication) with relatives or friends in Panama. These contacts provide information on political and business developments in Panama, as well as personal family affairs, the weekly results of the national lottery, sports, politics, and news of former social or residential communities. A supplementary source of news of public importance is, of course, those national and international television networks that give attention to Latin American and Caribbean events.

In view of the absence of large-scale Panamanian organizations and the lack of a significant ethnic press, most interested individuals have joined larger, more established ethnic or political interest groups that have broader bases. In fact, the young members of the Panamanian immigrant community show greater inclination toward expanding their identities as gained through their peer associations, outside activities, and general references with these multiethnic organizations. While many older members of the Panamanian immigrant middle class remain isolated, selective, and parochial in their involvements, others (even some who have become naturalized U.S. citizens or have U.S.-born dependents) return to Panama for longer, more frequent visits or even purchase a home and return permanently to their homeland.

## Conclusion

Many Panamanian immigrants believe upon arriving in the United States that they have finally reached the great land they have been taught so much about: a land of promise, high standards, and modern advancement with open and equal opportunities for improvement of both themselves and their families. In practice, however, many immigrants find it more difficult (if not impossible) to accomplish their goals as quickly or as easily as they may have been led to believe was possible before immigrating to the United States. Still, whether they plan to remain in the United States or return to Panama, most Panamanian immigrants are strongly committed to pursuing their goals, being successful, retaining links with Panama, and opening paths of mobility for their offspring and for other relatives who might want to move to the United States from Panama or to Panama from the United States.

## Bibliography

Alcoff, L. (1995). "Mestizo Identity." In *American Mixed Race: The Culture of Microdiversity*, edited by N. Zack. Lanham, MD: Rowan & Littlefield.

Bayne-Smith, M., and Bryce-Laporte, R. S. (1995). "Panamanians in New York." In *Encyclopedia of New York City*, edited by K. T. Jackson. New York: New York Historical Society.

Bryce-Laporte, R. S. (1972). "Black Immigrants: The Experience of Invisibility and Inequality." *Journal of Black Studies* 3(1):29–51.

Bryce-Laporte, R. S. (1993). "Que Vision Tiene el Panameno del Canal? Vision de un Sociologo Desde el Exterior." In *El Futuro del Canal de Panama en el Ano 2000*. Panama City: Fundacion Istmena de Estudios Economicos y Sociales.

Conniff, M. (1985). *Black Labor on a White Canal: Panama, 1904–1981*. Pittsburgh: University of Pittsburgh Press.

Downer-Marcel, J. (1996). "Urbanizacion y Autonomia Politica de la Provincia de Colon." *Revista Cultural Loteria Numero* 425:7–19.

Lindsay, A. (1996). *Santeria Aesthetics in Contemporary Latin American Art*. Washington, DC: Smithsonian Institution Press.

Miller, E. E. (1994). *First Light* ("Panama"). Baltimore, MD: Black Classic Press.

Priestly, G. (1990). "Ethnicity, Class, and National Questions in Panama: The Emerging Literature." In *Emerging Perspectives on the Black Diaspora*, edited by A. W. Bonnett and G. L. Watson. Lanham, MD: University Press of America.

Thomas, L. (1981). *The Bathers* ("Negritude"). New York: Reed and Cannon.

Thomas Brereton, L. (1993). *Dictionary of Panamanian English*. New York: Graphicart.

U.S. Bureau of the Census. (1990a). *1990 Census of the Population: General Population Characteristics (United States)*. Washington, DC: U.S. Government Printing Office.

U.S. Bureau of the Census. (1990b). *1990 Census of the Population: Social and Economic Characteristics (United States)*. Washington, DC: U.S. Government Printing Office.

U.S. Bureau of the Census. (1990c). *Population of Housing: General Housing Characteristics*. Washington, DC: U.S. Government Printing Office.

U.S. Immigration and Naturalization Service. (1997). *Statistical Yearbook of the Immigration and Naturalization Service, 1995*. Washington, DC: U.S. Government Printing Office.

Westerman, G. (1980). *Los Immigrantes Antillanos en Panama*. Panama: Instituto Nacional de Cultura.

ROY S. BRYCE-LAPORTE

# PERUVIANS

Peruvians are one of the United States' most recent immigrant groups. The overwhelming majority of Peruvian immigrants have arrived in the United States since 1980; the recency of their immigration and their relatively small numbers (175,000 people who identified themselves as Peruvian were enumerated in the 1990 U.S. Census) appear to be the principal factors in the scant literature about them.

As most Peruvians in the United States are first-generation immigrants, their identity is still very much rooted in their country of origin. Peruvian immigrants and their descendants trace their roots to the South American country of Peru, located on the Pacific coast of South America between Ecuador and Colombia to the north, Chile to the south, and Brazil and Bolivia to the east. Peru was the home of the great Incan Empire during the fifteenth and sixteenth centuries until 1532, when they were defeated by the Spaniards and Peru became a Spanish colony. In 1821, Peru won its independence from Spain, but it remains a country highly polarized between the large Indian population and the smaller groups of direct descendants of the Spaniards and mestizos, or people of mixed ancestry. Peru imported Africans late in the colonial era as laborers and slaves on coastal plantations and in highland ranches; in the late nineteenth and early twentieth centuries thousands of Chinese and Japanese laborers were brought to Peru as well.

These racial and ethnic groups have become ranked in a class hierarchy, a phenomenon sometimes termed a "pigmentocracy" by social scientists and one brought with Peruvians to the United States. Those individuals of lighter skin and more

European physical features, dress, and customs occupy the higher social strata, while people of darker Indian or African features and those who wear indigenous dress styles and practice traditional customs occupy the lower social strata. Even the Asian population, who over generations have risen from laborers to entrepreneurs and who can boast a national president (Alberto Fujimori, elected to the presidency in the 1990) still encounter barriers to social acceptance.

Another factor affecting Peruvian immigrants' identity is the geographic zone of the country that they, or their ancestors, are from. For example, Costeños are people from coastal Peru, Sharapas signifies those from the jungle regions of the country, Serranos indicates those from the highlands (and Cholos are indigenous highlanders), and Mazamorreros are Peruvians from the capital city of Lima.

The dominant language spoken by Peruvians is Spanish. Quechua, the native tongue of Indian populations in the highlands, is spoken by few immigrants to the United States, owing to the very limited immigration of indigenous Peruvians. English is spoken widely by Peruvians born in the United States, while nearly 60 percent of foreign-born Peruvians do not speak English well, according to the 1990 U.S. Census. Spanish is the language most often spoken at home among first-generation immigrants; their children generally learn Spanish at home and English once they enter school.

## Immigration History

The earliest recorded immigration of Peruvians to the United States dates back to the California Gold Rush in the mid-nineteenth century. Adventurers from many parts of Latin America, including a number of Peruvians, sought their fortunes in the mountains of California—at least until a tax on foreign miners was imposed and other discriminatory practices discouraged their efforts. From the 1850s until World War II, there is no record of significant Peruvian immigration to the United States. An unfortunate chapter in Peruvian-American history began during World War II. At that time the U.S. government took advantage of wartime conditions and forced eighteen hundred Peruvians of Japanese descent to enter the United States, where they were placed in internment camps in Texas, much as were Japanese Americans. Some of the Peruvians were traded to Japan in exchange for U.S. prisoners-of-war. This was done ostensibly to skirt legal and constitutional questions that would have arisen if U.S.-born citizens of Japanese heritage were involved in prisoner-of-war exchanges. After the war ended, many of the remaining interned Japanese Peruvians were deported to Japan—Peru would not accept them back—while several hundred fought deportation for many years and ultimately remained in the United States. Decades later, in 1990, the United States finally sent letters of apology and partial compensation to the detainees and their descendants.

Peruvian immigration to the United States was a mere trickle, including a number of shepherds recruited to work on large ranches in the West, until economic and political crises in Peru beginning in the 1970s caused deterioration in living conditions, spurring the country's professional and middle classes to flee. For centuries Peru's elite have immigrated to Europe, especially Spain, for educational and occupational opportunities. The United States became a targeted destination after the 1960s, when the United States increased its visibility in Peru through activities organized by the Peace Corps and the Alliance for Progress. During this time wealthier, urban Peruvians were exposed to American television shows and movies that also brought the two countries closer culturally. These links to the United States became increasingly important during the 1970s, when Peru was ruled by a repressive military government. Late in that decade inflation soared and the value of Peruvian workers' wages began to fall dramatically. This spurred Peruvians with the economic means to leave the country; many chose the United States.

In 1980, Shining Path (in Spanish, Sendero Luminoso), a leftist guerrilla organization that became active in the highlands during the 1970s, declared its existence publicly and began a civil war against the Peruvian military forces. During the 1980s and until 1992, when the leader of Shining Path, Abimael Guzmán, was captured and incarcerated, bombings, assassinations, kidnappings, and military repression characterized life in Peru. Much of the nation's infrastructure was destroyed, its economy was devastated, and inflation skyrocketed in the mid-1980s. The worst violence took place in the highlands, displacing millions of peasants and indigenous Peruvians, who fled to the coast. By 1990, one-third of Peru's population was concentrated in the capital of Lima. While the poorest social classes migrated from rural communities to urban centers, the middle strata who had the economic means fled abroad. Some had been persecuted by the guerrillas or the military; most feared for their safety and found that living conditions had deteriorated so dramatically that they could no longer support their families by working in Peru. The wealthiest and most powerful families were able to obtain legal tourist visas for their members to enter the United States and other countries legally; the less fortunate, who lacked substantial bank accounts and properties in Peru, generally purchased counterfeit visas. Other Peruvians paid for passage into Central America or Mexico and then tried to enter the United States by crossing the U.S.-Mexico border illegally. In the early 1990s, the cost of such a trip (with the destination of New York City) was $5,000 to $7,000 per person. This expense prohibits poorer Peruvians from immigrating, creating a populace in the United States that underrepresents the Peruvian peasant, urban poor, and Indian populations. The high cost of immigration also fosters "chain" migration, which occurs when immigrants save money to sponsor the immigration of family members or neighbors who, upon arrival in the United States, tend to settle in the same household or vicinity as their sponsors.

## The Peruvian-American Community

The 175,000 Peruvians enumerated in the 1990 U.S. Census are almost equally divided be-

tween males and females. Their median age is 35.1 years for females and 34.5 years for males, making them slightly older than the overall U.S. population. Of the total, 83,000 Peruvians immigrated to the United States between 1980 and 1990, 51,000 entered before 1980, and 40,500 (23%) are native-born.

The largest concentration of Peruvians is in the New York metropolitan area, where some 54,000 live. Ethnic neighborhoods marked by Peruvian storefronts and restaurants are most notable in Queens, New York, and Paterson and Passaic, New Jersey. The next largest settlement is in Los Angeles, where 27,000 live, followed by Miami with 16,000, Washington, D.C., with 11,000, and San Francisco with 9,000.

The immigration status of foreign-born Peruvians in the United States is mixed; some are undocumented (by entering the United States illegally or by entering with valid visas but overstaying their authorized visits), but most are legal permanent residents (often referred to as "green card" holders), and about one-fourth have become citizens. Records kept by the U.S. Immigration and Naturalization Service (INS) for the 1980s indicate that 64,000 Peruvians obtained legal residency. Around 20,000 of these people were undocumented Peruvians who applied for legal status under a special law passed by Congress in 1986 (the Immigration Reform and Control Act).

On average, Peruvians are more educated than many other immigrant groups from Latin America, and they are slightly more educated than the overall U.S. population. A total of 21 percent of foreign-born adults over age twenty-five and 33 percent of the native-born adults have a four-year college degree or higher, while 22 percent of the foreign-born adults and 13 percent of the native-born adults have not completed high school.

More than 75 percent of Peruvian adults are in the work force, a figure higher than the U.S. average, and 65 percent of Peruvian women work, compared to only 57 percent nationally. Despite their educational achievement, Peruvians are concentrated in poorer-paying sectors of the economy. More than 50 percent are employed in sales,

A Peruvian-American shepherd and his two dogs watch a large herd of grazing sheep about five miles north of Bridgeport, California. (Phil Schermeister/Corbis)

administrative support, and service jobs, such as in restaurants; another 30 percent are employed as blue-collar workers, while only 20 percent find jobs as managers or professionals. Perhaps due to their high participation in the labor force, Peruvians' income, unemployment, and poverty levels are comparable to those of the overall U.S. population.

## Social Organization

*Kinship and Family.* Among Peruvians, the nuclear family characterized by mother, father, and children is the most common residential unit. Three-quarters of all Peruvian families are headed by married couples; only one in six is female-headed. The extended family is also very important, and siblings often will reside with their fam-

ilies in the same or neighboring communities and socialize on weekends and holidays. Families may reside together to lower the costs of housing in expensive areas such as New York, and it is not uncommon for newly arrived family members and friends to stay for limited periods of time within others' households. The preferred pattern, however, is for couples with children to set up independent households.

Groups of kinswomen spend Sundays preparing favorite foods for large family get-togethers and on holidays. Among the most popular dishes are *ceviche* (raw fish seasoned with lemons, onions, tomatoes, cilantro, potatoes, and sweet potatoes), *mondonguito* (tripe stewed with potatoes, cilantro, and vegetables) and *papa a la Huancaina* (boiled potatoes sliced and covered with layers of creamy cheese, sliced boiled eggs, cilantro, and mild peppers). Peruvians have also adopted the American tradition of summer barbecues, particularly on July 28, Peruvian Independence Day. Kin bonds are strongest, but Peruvians form fictive kin relationships with friends through the rituals of marriage and baptism. This practice is called *compadrazgo*. Parents will ask one male and one female friend (often a couple) to serve as *padrinos*, close attendants at their wedding and later godparents to their first child. In Peru the godparents are theoretically responsible for the child if anything happens to the parents, and the godparents may provide financial assistance for schooling or birthday parties to their godchild. Compadrazgo, moreover, links the two sets of adults into tighter bonds of mutual assistance. In the United States these functions of compadrazgo have weakened, though the practice maintains a ceremonial importance. Finally, Peruvians celebrate a major rite of passage for their daughters when they turn fifteen. The girl is given a *quinceañera* party by relatives and friends. The quinceañera is similar to the American custom of a "sweet sixteen" party or of a debutante or "coming out" ball that announces a girl's entrance into adulthood and approaching readiness for marriage.

*Gender and Generational Roles.* Most first-generation Peruvian immigrants believe in traditional male-female gender roles. Women are expected to handle domestic chores and childrearing, while men are viewed as breadwinners and are freer to move in the public domain. These rigid roles are changing in the United States, owing to the high participation of women in the work force and to the growing numbers of second-generation Peruvians reared in the United States. Conflicts arise between immigrant parents and their children born in the United States, particularly daughters, over the younger generation's desire to socialize unsupervised with friends outside the home and to live independently as young, unmarried adults. Traditionally, grown children are expected to live with their parents until they marry, and this conflicts with American expectations that children leave home after finishing high school.

*Religion.* The overwhelming majority of Peruvians are Roman Catholic, although not all regularly attend church services. Work schedules and family demands may impede devotion to religious activities. Peruvians celebrate several important ethnic religious festivals devoted to important saints during the year. October 18 is the most important festival, El Señor de los Milagros, as well as November 3, St. Martin of Porras, and August 30, St. Rose of Lima. On these days groups of religious devotees carry an effigy of Christ or a saint through local streets and churches, and special Masses are celebrated. Leaders appeal to congregants for expressions of ethnic solidarity and identification as well.

*Social and Political Organizations.* The church is the most important institution among Peruvian immigrants, but Peruvian restaurants serving typical foods are among other popular gathering places. Restaurants hire well-known musical groups to play popular regional music and dances such as *el vals*, *bolero*, and *música andina*. Among men, soccer is a passion. Local businesses and organizations sponsor teams in leagues represented by different countries. Peruvian teams tend to be named "the Inkas" or after the members' hometown or region. Elite men also congregate and network through exclusive clubs such as Club Peru of New York and the Peruvian-American Country Club, as well as clubs based on elite and military schools in Peru. Clubs and fraternal orders prepare Peruvian Independence Day celebrations; in towns with large Peruvian communities these celebrations usually include a parade. Social organizations also assist ethnic and class cohesion in the United States; in contrast, most political activities are focused on Peruvians' homeland. Political organizations and affiliations tied to parties in Peru appear before major elections in Peru but not in the United States. Newspapers edited by Peruvians and aimed at an ethnic audience publicize community events while providing coverage of events and politics in Peru that rarely appear in mainstream newspapers.

*Transnational Organizations.* Peruvians have organized and maintained several types of organizations that link their communities in the United States with people back home. There are two principal types: beneficial aid societies and hometown associations. The societies, such as Solidaridad Peruana and Peruvian-American Association for Cultural Promotion, organize fund-raisers, and the monies raised are donated for humanitarian projects in Peru. The hometown associations often raise funds for similar purposes, but they are run by people from the same Peruvian community, and the support they provide is targeted specifically for that hometown. Finally, since 1984, an annual national convention of Peruvian organizations has been organized. Each year the themes and projects addressed vary, but the object of the conventions is to coordinate group efforts to support the needs of Peruvians in the United States and in their homeland.

## Bibliography

Altamirano, T. (1990). *Los que se Fueron: Peruanos en los Estados Unidos.* Lima, Peru: Fondo Editorial de la Pontificia Universidad Católica de Perú.

Altamirano, T. (1992). *Exodo: Peruanos en el Exterior.* Lima, Peru: Fondo Editorial de la Pontificia Universidad Católica del Perú.

Gelles, P. H., and Martinez, W., dirs. (1993). "Transnational Fiesta: 1992." Berkeley, CA: Center for Media and Independent Learning.

Mahler, S. J. (1995). *American Dreaming: Immigrant Life on the Margins.* Princeton, NJ: Princeton University Press.

McKee, D. L. (1983). "Some Specifics on the Brain Drain from the Andean Region." *International Migration* 21(4):488–499.

Ota, J. (1993). "Justice for All or for Some? Japanese Peruvian Is Tired of Runaround." *Asian Week* 14(47):32.

U.S. Bureau of the Census. (1990). *1990 Census of Population: Persons of Hispanic Origin in the United States.* Washington, DC: U.S. Government Printing Office.

SARAH J. MAHLER
ALEJANDRO F. LOARTE

# POLES

Upon their arrival in North America, the people identified as Poles spoke Polish and belonged to the Catholic Church. They traced their heritage to historic Poland, a country that did not exist as a political and independent unit from 1795 to 1918.

## Immigration History

Although there are unsubstantiated claims of Poles in North America earlier, the first known Poles arrived in Jamestown, Virginia, in 1608. Subsequent Polish immigration history can be divided into five periods. The first period extends to approximately 1800, when relatively few Poles arrived as individuals seeking fortune, freedom, or adventure. The second period, 1800 to 1860, saw an increase in numbers, with some arriving in groups of several hundred political exiles or peasants seeking land. Many settled where land was cheap (e.g., Panna Maria, Texas, founded in 1854 by a contingent of Silesian Polish peasants).

During the third period, 1860 to 1914, Polish immigration to the United States became a major wave of some two million people, with primarily economic and religious motivations for leaving Europe. This immigration reached a peak in 1912–1913, when 174,365 ethnic Poles immigrated, with men outnumbering women two to one.

The annual numbers of immigrants were relatively small during the fourth period, 1914 to 1988, because of the two world wars and the fact that under the U.S. Immigration Act of 1924 Poland's quota was 5,982 immigrants per year. However, there were 151,978 individuals admitted between 1945 and 1953 under various refugee legislative acts and presidential directives, and approximately 40,000 Polish ex-servicemen and underground insurgents were admitted between the end of World War II and 1968.

Combining various sources and best estimates, it appears that a total of 1,780,151 Poles immigrated to the United States between 1885 and 1972.

Another 297,590 arrived and later returned to Poland, and 669,392 were nonimmigrant, temporary visitors to the United States.

The fifth period of Polish immigration consists of that since 1988. The number of legal immigrants has increased and is augmented by people staying in the United States after their visas have expired (the *wakacjusze*). The change in numbers of legal immigrants has been dramatic, from a total of 52,000 in the five years between 1982 and 1987, to 15,101 in 1989; 20,537 in 1990; 19,199 in 1991; and 25,504 in 1992.

These numbers of Polish arrivals and returnees are estimates at best; it is impossible to be accurate. The problem is that even when records are available they list an individual's country of origin and not ethnic affiliation. Before World War I, Poles would be included among immigrants originating in Austria, Germany or Prussia, and Russia. After World War I, minority groups living in Poland were included in Polish numbers.

The Polish immigration shows the characteristics of any large-scale immigration. Before the steamship and later the airplane became common means of transportation, few who crossed the Atlantic returned to Europe. However, beginning with the last part of the nineteenth century, a differentiation exists between the life histories of the political and the economic immigrants.

The refugees and émigrés arrived intent on carrying on the struggle for their political goals from abroad and returning when conditions in their homeland improved. In fact, they seldom returned. Economic immigrants frequently followed a chain migration, joining friends, relatives, or fellow villagers who had preceded them and established residence in the new country. In 1908, virtually all Poles arriving in the United States claimed they were joining relatives or friends. Frequently the immigrants planned to stay in the United States only long enough to save sufficient money for a specified end, such as to buy some livestock or a piece of land or to build a new house on the family farm in Poland. Between 1906 and 1914, about 30 percent of Polish immigrants returned home to Europe. At times, upon returning home new needs arose and the individual left for America again, becoming a "pendulum immigrant." Eventually a portion of the sojourners became settlers. Officials did not track such individuals and recorded only the total number of arrivals and departures. This practice adds another element of uncertainty to the immigration statistics.

Since a portion of the Polish immigration was due to political causes, there was the expectation that when Poland regained independence a large number would return. This massive return did not happen. In 1920–1921, a total of 42,207 returned; in 1921–1922, a total of 31,004 returned.

There is wide disagreement regarding how many individuals residing in the United States should even be considered Poles. The 1990 U.S. Census reported 723,000 individuals who spoke Polish at home. Estimates, by even apparently trustworthy sources, vary widely. In 1969, the federal government estimated that there were 4,021,000 Poles, but the 1990 U.S. Census categorized 9,366,000 as being Polish.

A young Polish immigrant carries a trunk aboard the President Grant at Ellis Island in 1907. (Library of Congress/Corbis)

The difficulty with numbers stems from the fact that official census data are not based on unchanging definitions; the criteria for including or excluding an individual in any given group vary over time. Similarly, categories are added as they become politically important, and discontinued as they become politically less relevant.

## Settlement Patterns

Polish settlements in the United States reflect the economic conditions existing at the time of arrival. Since most of the Poles arriving after the Civil War were peasants and immigrated to the United States *za chlebem* (for bread), they were attracted to areas of the country where jobs for unskilled laborers were plentiful.

In 1911, 10 percent of foreign-born Poles were engaged in agriculture. Some took up farming, settling in places where they were "abandoned" by employers. An example of this is the Polish settlement in the Connecticut River Valley, where some Polish railroad construction workers were laid off in 1887 due to a depression.

Others settled where land was cheap—northern Michigan, Minnesota, Wisconsin, and Nebraska. For example, Sherman County in Nebraska has a high percentage of residents of Polish ancestry, enabling Loup City, the county seat, to dub itself the Polish capital of America based on the percentage rather than the numbers. As generations and economic conditions changed, agricultural employment decreased. While 11 percent of second-generation Poles were engaged in agriculture, only 1 percent of their children were.

Many Poles worked in the meatpacking industry. Since Chicago; Kansas City, Kansas; and South Omaha, Nebraska, were important meatpacking centers, they developed sizable Polish settlements. However, the majority of Poles in the United States obtained work in industry and mining and settled in the industrial "rust belt" north of the Mason-Dixon Line and the Ohio River valley, south of the Great Lakes, and east of the Missouri River. The major settlements were and continue to be Chicago, New York, Pittsburgh, Buffalo, Milwaukee, Detroit, Cleveland, and Philadelphia. According to the 1990 U.S. Census, 37 percent of Poles lived in the Northeast and the same percentage in the Midwest, while 15 percent lived in the South and 11 percent in the West.

During the period of greatest immigration—between the Civil War and World War I—Polish society in the United States was essentially a working-class Roman Catholic society. The individuals who immigrated were not typical peasants or a cross section of Polish urban populations. They were predominantly young, unmarried males. They were not members of organized communities immigrating as a group. The values and needs of the community they created in various locations in the United States were essentially the same across settings, and it was not until after World War II that members of the group began to differentiate according to education and occupation. This was due, in part, to the fact that the new arrivals were middle-class and primarily politically rather than economically motivated immigrants and, in part, because some members of the group already established in the United States were second- or third-generation, continuing their education and beginning to move into professional and white-collar jobs and, thus, into the middle class. The results of this move into the middle class were employment and residence in places where few were of Polish background, leading to aspirations and behavior patterns similar to those of the wider society. In short, increasing numbers were becoming acculturated and socially assimilated to American society.

This assimilation into the structure of the larger society and acculturation to its culture is evidenced by various indicators. Starting in 1929, the Polish ethnic press has continued to decline. In 1977, there were one hundred Polish periodicals; in 1987, ninety-five; but in 1995, only forty.

By 1969, educational, occupational, and social differentiation could be seen in the Polish-American society. Some 16 percent had attended college and 45 percent of the males had white-collar jobs. About 25 percent were skilled workers, and 30 percent were semiskilled or unskilled laborers. Their incomes approximated the national average of the time. By 1980, a total of 23.9 percent had

A woman grinds sausage at a butcher shop in the Polish district of Chicago. (Sandy Felsenthal/Corbis)

four or more years of college. This is significantly above the average for the United States, where in 1980, 16.2 percent of the total population and 17.1 percent of whites had achieved this level of education. In employment, 23.5 percent of Poles in the United States were in the managerial or professional categories and 31.8 percent in technical or administrative positions, while only 18 percent were operators, fabricators, or laborers.

## Polish-American Identity and Culture

It is becoming increasingly difficult to decide who Poles—or more accurately Polish Americans—are. Is it decided by ethnic descent in a "blood" type of relationship, meaning individuals who either consider themselves Poles or whose ancestors considered themselves Poles? In that case, Polish Americans are a varied lot, and many of them have little in common except shared descent. In such an "ancestrally derived" group there would be individuals who themselves immigrated, but come from a variety of backgrounds and classes, and who in Poland would have little to do with one another. There are also individuals whose ancestors have lived in the United States for two, three, four, or more generations or who come from ethnically mixed marriages where the only Polish ancestor may be a grandparent or even a great-grandparent. Where should the line be drawn?

The operative answer would be that each individual decides. When someone feels that he or she is Polish, then they are. If they do not, then they are not—regardless of antecedents.

Another way of viewing the issue is to look at the group's culture and the individuals who participate in it. Which groups participate? To what degree? With what frequency? Does the main interest lie in the rapidly disappearing group of first-generation immigrants (predominantly old men)? In 1990, a total of 39.4 percent of first-generation Polish immigrants were sixty-five or older. In this group, Polish culture probably predominates. Are individuals who did not move to the suburbs but who reside in ethnic neighborhoods in large cities the main interest? These people live in Polish-American neighborhoods, interact primarily with other Polish Americans, and continue to observe the customs, festivals, and interaction patterns they always have followed. This is a rapidly dwindling population. Is there concern about the population that has moved to the suburbs, where both husband and wife work and there are two or three children? In other words, should the focus be on people who are living as most Americans live?

In 1914, everyone knew who the Poles in the United States were. The vast majority had immigrated from Poland and resided in large industrial cities. Their neighborhoods formed communities around their own churches. The men supported families through their blue-collar jobs. Wives did not work outside the home after their first child. They lived in houses where, besides the owner and his family, there were often one or more boarders or roomers. The families were large, with about five children. On the whole, education was not particularly valued, and people preferred to send children to work rather than school. Their attitudes, customs, and worldview were shared with rural inhabitants in the areas of eastern Europe from whence they came.

In the Polish residential areas of Buffalo, Chicago, or Milwaukee just prior to World War I, there was an essentially Polish community. Polish was the language spoken in the streets, churches, other public gatherings, businesses, and homes. Polish food was produced, sold, and served at public gatherings and in homes. Religious holiday traditions such as Wigilia (Christmas Eve supper), with the essential *opłatek* wafer, Święconka (Easter food blessing), or *kolendy* (group Christmas caroling), or customs associated with farming, such as

Dożynki (harvest festival) and Wianki (wreath tossing), were observed with pageantry and ritual very similar, if not identical, to such occasions in Poland. In short, the culture of Polish communities in the United States was a modified version of that of the Polish village or Polish city.

These traditions and customs are still observed, though perhaps not as frequently and ubiquitously as earlier. The difference is that they no longer are automatic actions but rather are matters of choice and of expression of ethnicity and a common bond in the community and among the individuals participating.

However, even in the early 1900s, these communities were neither miniature transplanted Warsaws or Krakows, nor were they replications of Polish villages or the localized cultures of the areas inhabited by Poles at that time. The Polish-American culture was unique, created by the integration of rural Polish cultures with the surrounding American culture. Therefore, one must not think of Polish-American culture as an attenuated or corrupted form of the "real" or "genuine" Polish culture, nor is it a modified version of the "real" American culture of its time. It was and is a unique creation.

One indicator of the magnitude of differences between the cultures found in Poland and in the United States is that whenever sizable numbers of individuals returned to Poland, the majority reimmigrated to the United States. For instance, of the 24,000 or 30,000 (authorities differ) Polish men recruited in the United States to fight in Poland at the end of World War I, some 19,000 returned to the United States. During Word War II there were only 772 Polish volunteers for a similar unit. Second, there is some evidence that when Poles did return to Poland, they returned more as American missionaries intent on reproducing American economic and political systems rather than as native sons reintegrating into their society and continuing where they had left off before immigrating to the United States.

Today, there is a question whether a uniquely Polish culture exists in the United States. Some scholars feel that Polish-American culture is a U.S.

ethnic subculture—a version of the general American culture. Others see it as distinct unit. It is clear that there are few if any areas in the United States where one could live one's entire life among fellow Poles without having to learn more than a smattering of English or to be exposed to the internal culture of the larger society. Among Polish subgroups, Górali, Kashubians, and Mazurians have retained the strongest and most distinctive identity, while immigrants from Galicia and Silesia have retained a less strong identity.

Can a recognizable Polish-American culture be identified? If the answer is yes, what are its characteristics? How widespread is it? How numerous are the people who have it? There are no clear answers to these questions. It is not eating *czarnina* or *szczawiowa zupa*, or speaking Polish

A stained glass artist designs windows for a Polish church in Buffalo, New York. (Hulton Deutsch Collection/Corbis)

the way an individual in Warsaw would, and wishing *smacznego* when serving food or entering a room where people are eating, or men kissing married women's hands. Rather, it consists of three elements.

One of the elements of Polish-American culture is participating in the community's life by attending church services, being a member of and actively participating in various organizations, and being involved in the social life of the group. Are the individual's friends Polish Americans? Has or is it likely that the individual will marry a fellow Polish American? Do the individuals or their children attend (or are they attending if of proper age) one of the 310 parochial schools associated with Polish-American parishes or the *szkoły doksztalcające* (supplementary schools for children attending regular schools where Polish is not a major subject) sponsored either by *rady oświatowe* (educational councils) or some fraternal organizations? Similarly, does the individual attend or participate in *obch* (celebrations consisting of parades, addresses, performances by choral societies and dance groups in national costumes)? Usually these are held to commemorate some important event in Polish history, such as the adoption of the Polish Constitution of 1791 (May 3) or the restoration of Poland's independence in 1918 (November 11); or to mark Pulaski Day (October 11); or to honor a visiting personage.

Is the individual one of the two million persons who are members of the five hundred Polish-American parishes in the Catholic Church or the Polish National Catholic Church and attend their services? Similarly, is the individual one of the 755,000 persons belonging to Polish-American fraternal organizations? These organizations sponsor Polish-language schools, celebrations, and other social activities aiding preservation of the ethnic culture and cultural creativity, and are the financial base of the Polish American Congress. The most important of these are the Polish National Alliance, the Polish Roman Catholic Union, and the Polish Women's Alliance. In 1993, there were some thirty-six Polish fraternal and nonfraternal organizations, with 650,000 members organized in 3,250 groups across the United States.

The second element of Polish-American culture is the attitudes one has toward Poland, the United States, and the Polish-American community. What group serves as the basis for one's identity? Is the identity that of a Pole who happens to be living abroad? Does one see herself or himself as an American whose ancestors happened to be Polish, in part or completely? In the United States there are a great many individuals who will mention that their ancestors were of various nationalities, but this has little or no bearing on their life except as an amusing element of their background. Or does the individual see herself or himself as a member of a distinct group stemming from Poland but living in the United States, fully integrated into the local society, similar to other groups, but with their own shared, specific, and unique ancestry and culture?

Internal culture is the third element. There is a belief in a Polish national character that is transmitted over generations. By all available data, individuals seeing themselves as Poles are more family-oriented than is the norm for the general population in the United States. They see themselves as highly individualistic and uncooperative. Human nature is considered to be prone to sin and evil, requiring strong external controls, and shame is seen as an effective way of socializing people. There is a feeling that people in Poland belong to two different classes, peasants and gentry, with an unbridgeable gap between them. But there is also an insistence on the equality of individuals within a class.

There are some other unusual elements in Polish cultural in the United States. One of them is that since initially the vast majority saw themselves as sojourners rather than settlers, their orientation was toward the society in Poland and later Polish-American community, rather than American society. This made the Poles one of the less readily assimilating ethnic groups in the United States. They derived their sense of identity and status from fellow members of the Polish-American community rather than from members of

the larger society. They were not all that concerned with their image in American eyes. For instance, it was not until the late 1960s and early 1970s that the Polish-American community took active steps to improve its image in the larger society and organized a press campaign against "Polish jokes."

Another such element was their attitude to Poland and its fate. One important factor was the fact that Poland was divided among three countries, and the struggle for regaining independence was cultural as well as political. Consequently the Poles arriving in the United States were already more self-consciously Polish than those immigrant groups where most of them discovered their ethnicity in America only after coming in direct contact with people of other backgrounds. Also, since Poland was not free, the Polish-American community was seen as a fourth province, with the duty to speak for the country, which could not. Paradoxically, this meant that Poles in the United States had less of an identity problem and an easier time in their relationship with Poland when the country was not free than they do now that the country is free and "can speak for itself."

When Poland was not free, then clearly one of the purposes for the existence of the Polish-American community was to support Poland's struggle for freedom. This needed support was used to unify and mobilize Polish Americans. But now that Poland is free, what common goal is there? A goal that is considered moral, worthy, and supported by almost all. Should the Polish-American community become but another ethnic group in the United States, with the certainty of ultimate absorption into the larger society? What should be the attitude and interaction of the average Polish-American individual toward other ethnic groups in America? And how should the individual interact with the people and society in Poland?

This factor also complicates the relationship of the Polish-American community and its leaders with the leaders of independent Poland. How do they establish a common set of goals and ensure that they do not act at cross purposes? Who should lead? Who must follow? The relationship at times has been rather strained. In 1924, the largest Polish-American fraternal association refused full membership to citizens of Poland.

The question of who should lead also has a bearing on the internal social structure of the Polish-American community. When political refugees and educated Poles arrived in the United States, they expected to take over leadership among Polish Americans. They also expected help in adjusting to the new conditions. Most of them were disappointed on both counts. The individuals who already were leaders in the United States did not surrender their positions, feeling that they knew the local situation and had established contacts with leaders of the larger society. Also, material help was relatively sparse. The Poles already established in the United States felt that they had had to struggle, and there was no reason to spare the newcomers the same experience.

## The Future

Will there be a Polish-American community in the United States in the year 2000, 2100, or 2200? The answer is that it depends. Does the question mean, Will there be individuals in the United States who identify themselves as Poles? Certainly there will be in 2000; after that the question becomes much more difficult to answer, and the answer hinges on several factors. Will the descendants of the people in the United States who today are considered and consider themselves Poles continue this identity? If the past is any guide, the answer is that few will so identify themselves. Despite the unfavorable image that the American has of "Polaks" and the popularity of Polish jokes, there is not much prejudice against Poles as such, certainly nothing comparable to the prejudice exhibited toward some other ethnic groups. This means that as the cultural and social distances between the Polish community and "mainstream America" lessens, the Poles will ultimately assimilate. All indicators show that the process to date has not been smooth and uniform, but it is there. With each generation there is more intermarriage

with other ethnic groups and a lessening of the cultural differences.

A second factor is whether Poles will continue to immigrate to the United States in sizable numbers. The larger the future immigration, the more certainty of the persistence of the Polish-American community. The assimilation of future generations of the majority of individuals stemming from the present community is almost inevitable. Thus its persistence will be contingent on "fresh blood." If in the future sizable numbers of Poles continue to arrive, they will provide a critical mass of members for organizations to function and thus provide a way for those who were born in the United States to express their ethnic affiliation.

Another element in the equation is the activities of the government in Poland. If the government fosters personal, artistic, and cultural contacts between Polish Americans and Poland, then Polish-American community may persist for a long time. Again, the important element will be the maintenance of an organizational and activities framework so that individuals can participate if they so wish.

A final element in the equation is the United States and the attitudes and actions of its government and people. If Americans become xenophobic and there is strong condemnation or legal prohibition of the use of non-English languages and of ethnic organizations, then Polish culture in the United States will rapidly disappear.

*See also:*   KASHUBIANS

## Bibliography

Bukowczyk, J. J. (1987). *And My Children Did Not Know Me: A History of the Polish-Americans.* Bloomington: Indiana University Press.

Duscak, T. (1994). "The Polish Presence in North America." *Choice* 32(3):399–419.

Gladsky, T. S. (1992). *Princes, Peasants, and Other Polish Selves: Ethnicity in American Literature.* Amherst: University of Massachusetts Press.

Gory, D. E. (1995). "Polish Immigration to America: Before and After the Fall of the Berlin Wall." *The Polish Review* 40(1):73–79.

Obidinski, E. E., and Zand, H. S., eds. (1987). *Polish Folkways in America: Community and Family*. Polish Studies Series, Vol. I. Lanham, MD: University Press of America.

Poitrowski, T. (1995). *Vengeance of the Swallows: Memoir of a Polish Family's Ordeal Under Soviet Aggression, Ukrainian Ethnic Cleansing and Nazi Enslavement, and their Emigration to America*. Jefferson, NC: McFarland.

Pula, J. S. (1995). *Polish Americans: An Ethnic Community*. New York: Twayne.

Renkiewicz, F. (1973). *The Poles in America, 1608–1972: A Chronology & Fact Book*. Dobbs Ferry, NY: Oceana.

Renkiewicz, F., ed. (1982). *The Polish Presence in Canada and America*. Toronto: Multicultural History Society of Ontario.

Sanders, I. T., and Morowska, E. (1975). *Polish-American Community Life: A Survey of Research*. New York: Polish Institute of Arts and Sciences in America.

Thomas, W. I., and Znaniecki, F. (1984). *The Polish Peasant in Europe and America*, edited and abridged by E. Zaretsky. Urbana: University of Illinois Press.

Wytrwal, J. (1977). *Behold! The Polish Americans*. Detroit, MI: Endurance Press.

Znaniecka-Lopata, H. (1994). *Polish Americans*, 2nd, revised edition. New Brunswick, NJ: Transaction.

Zubrzycki, J. (1988). *Soldiers and Peasants: The Sociology of Polish Immigration*. London: Orbis.

ANDRIS SKREIJA

# POLYNESIANS

*See* PACIFIC ISLANDERS IN HAWAII; SAMOANS; TONGANS

# PORTUGUESE

The Portuguese constitute a diverse population whose presence in the United States dates back to at least the seventeenth century. While some immigrants went as far west as Hawaii, most settled in the small towns and cities of California and southeastern Massachusetts. East Coast settlements of Portuguese also exist in Rhode Island, Connecticut, New Jersey, and New York.

## Colonial History

Portugal is located, together with Spain, on the Iberian Peninsula in southwestern Europe. During the age of the great maritime discoveries of the fifteenth and sixteenth centuries, the Portuguese distinguished themselves as navigators, explorers, and colonizers. As part of a series of fifteenth-century maritime explorations launched by Prince Henry the Navigator, the Portuguese discovered and peopled the previously uninhabited North Atlantic archipelagos of the Azores and Madeira, as well as the archipelago of Cape Verde off the western coast of Africa. The Azores and Madeira have remained regions of Portugal since that time, but they both obtained regional autonomy in 1975. Cape Verde also became part of the Portuguese overseas domains, but it finally gained political emancipation in 1975. These changes in political status for the Azores, Madeira, and Cape Verde were part of the process of decolonization that followed the 1974 Revolution of the Carnations, which overthrew a fifty-year-long fascist dictatorship and restored democracy in Portugal.

Just a few decades after playing a major role in the discovery of the New World, Portugal was faced with continuous economic and political decline. At the time of the decolonization, Portugal was the oldest and poorest colonial power in the world. While remaining the center of vast overseas dominions, Portugal became peripheral to the European center of economic and political power. In the sixteenth century, unable to confront increasing competition from broadening global commercial ventures, Portugal engaged in the "Atlantic Project," which was at first directed toward colonizing and exploring Brazil (1640–1822) and later turned attention to the overseas possessions in Africa. In the nineteenth century, the increasingly impoverished colonial nation began to experience massive emigrations of individuals seeking better living and working conditions. Between 1880 and 1990, more than 2.5 million legal emigrants left Portugal, with about 20 percent of them immigrating to the United States.

## Identification

The definition of "Portuguese" is closely linked to Portugal's colonial and postcolonial histories and remains somewhat fluid. When Portugal's almost five centuries of colonialism came to an end in the mid-1970s, the Portuguese included persons born in continental Portugal, the Azores, and Madeira, as well as their descendants (regardless of their place of birth). During Portugal's colonial era, however, immigrants from Cape Verde were also included among the Portuguese. Speaking the same language and subjected to Portugal's colonial rule, they were identified and tended to identify themselves as Portuguese. Since most Cape Verdeans are of mixed African and Portuguese descent, earlier Portuguese contingents earned the derogatory label of "Black Portugee" and were subjected to racial discrimination. With Cape Verde's political emancipation in 1975, Cape Verdeans mobilized themselves as a distinct ethnic group in the United States. However, ethnic boundaries between the two groups remain blurred in as much as there are still some Cape Verdean immigrants who continue to self-identify as Portuguese. The influence of Portuguese colonialism also impinged on the self-identities of a small group of Californian settlers known as Luso-Sino-Americans or "Portuguese from the Orient," who were originally from Macao, a Chinese territory that was under Portugal's administration from 1557 to 1967. While most of the four thousand persons who immigrated to the United States from Hong Kong and Shanghai after World War II probably entered the United States as "Chinese" immigrants, many of them continued to identify themselves as Macao Portuguese and to form their own Macao-Portuguese associations.

Depending upon the context, the terms "Portuguese Americans" and "Luso-Americans" are used interchangeably to identify and self-identify entire Portuguese communities (which include Azoreans, Madeirans, continental Portuguese, and all of their descendants) in the United States. The terms can also be used solely to express the self-identities of the American-born descendants of persons from the Azores, Madeira, and continental Portugal. Among the Portuguese themselves, the term "Luso-American" serves to self-identify and differentiate the American-born descendants of the pre-1950 immigrants from the post-1950 immigrants. Strong regional and local identifications also distinguish the Azoreans and Madeirans as distinct Portuguese communities that mobilize themselves along regional lines and even according to villages of origin.

Depending upon the situation, the term "community" is often used to identify and self-identify the Portuguese as members of a distinct Portuguese or Portuguese-American collectivity, as well as to designate the diverse Portuguese settlements within the United States according to regions and towns (e.g., the Portuguese of New England or the Portuguese of New Bedford, Massachusetts). Azoreans and Madeirans employ the term in the same ways to further mark their own regional collectivities. In Portugal's postcolonial era, government officials started to invoke the expressions "Portuguese communities spread across the world" and "Portuguese abroad" to refer to the Portuguese living in other countries. The governments of the autonomous regions of the Azores and Madeira use the same type of designations and often emphasize the Azoreans' and Madeirans' "special ways of being Portuguese." In 1981, after Portugal joined the European Union, immigrants from the Azores, Madeira, and continental Portugal who had retained their Portuguese nationality became entitled to request dual citizenship rights and to transmit their Portuguese nationality to offspring and spouses.

## Immigration and Settlement

The movement of Portuguese transnational migration has followed the rhythms and demands of the global economy and local circumstance. Prior to the 1950s, Portuguese labor migrants went primarily to the New World, with the majority of them settling in Brazil (which was Portugal's major overseas possession before it gained independence in 1822). Of the approximately 1.5 million legal emigrants who left Portugal between the 1880s and the 1950s, only 4 percent immigrated to the United States.

Although some published accounts suggest that Portuguese navigators reached North America before Christopher Columbus and even that Columbus was Portuguese, the first Portuguese persons in the United States to attract the attention of historians were Sephardic Jews. Expelled from Portugal during the Inquisition, these individuals originally went to Holland and then Brazil before arriving in the Dutch colony of New Amsterdam (now New York) in 1654. Some of them later moved to Newport, Rhode Island. Other groups of Sephardic Jews arriving from Portugal and Brazil in the 1750s also settled in Newport, where they became involved in the whaling industry, slave trade, and commerce with the West Indies involving rum and sugar.

The earliest period of substantial Portuguese immigration to the United States, however, lasted from 1820 to 1860, during which the U.S. Immigration and Naturalization Service recorded the entry of 5,275 Portuguese individuals. Almost all

Portuguese dory fishermen sit and talk in front of the fishing shack where they store their gear in Provincetown, Massachusetts, in 1942. (Library of Congress/Corbis)

of these immigrants were single men from the Azores who were trying to escape poverty and military service at home. They had initially been recruited as crew members on whaling expeditions that had originated in the United States, and many decided to stay in America once the expeditions had returned to the United States. Most of these men chose to settle in or near their ports of entry: New Bedford and Edgartown, Massachusetts; Sag Harbor and Cold Spring Harbor, New York; Stonington, Connecticut; and San Francisco, Monterey, and San Diego, California.

Substantial immigration to the United States by Azorean *families* started only in the 1870s. The growth at this time of direct shipping between Boston and the port of Horta on the Azorean island of Fayal provided the consistent transportation link between the United States and the Azores that was necessary for the propagation of chain migration, a process whereby immigrants facilitate the subsequent immigration of their family members. Other factors contributing to the growth of Portuguese emigration include years of drought and a widespread system of conscription that had been instituted by the Portuguese government (even though many island people were loath to fight the battles of a remote mainland Portuguese government that lay thousands of miles away across the ocean). Because of the nature of chain migration, new immigrants tended to settle where their relatives had settled previously, which was primarily in the farming and fishing centers of California and, to a lesser extent, New England. In the 1890s, with the rising influence of Ponta Delgada in São Miguel (St. Michael), the largest of the Azorean islands, an American consulate was established in the city, and individuals from that island and nearby Santa Maria started to arrive in New England in large numbers. The nineteenth-century patterns of regional distribution of the Azoreans in the United States continued in the twentieth century: Azoreans from Pico, Fayal, São Jorge (St. George), Flores, and Terceira increasingly settled in the farming and fishing centers of California, while immigrants from St. Michael settled mainly in Massachusetts. To a large extent, these immi-

grants were able to reconstruct their Old World ways of life in these areas because they were arriving as complete families with fully formed and functioning personal social networks.

Many Portuguese also immigrated to Hawaii, and their history took a different course from the one found on the mainland. This immigration started in 1876, when Hawaii was still an independent kingdom, and continued after it became an American territory in 1898. Hawaii lay half a world away from Europe and was beyond the reach of immigrants. All of the Portuguese who reached Hawaii were brought by the Hawaii Sugar Planter's Association to work as contract laborers on the territory's sugar plantations. The planters saw this as one solution to their persistent labor shortage, as well as a means for offsetting the large number of Asians who had already been brought to Hawaii as plantation laborers. An estimated eighteen thousand Portuguese arrived between 1878 and 1913, and the Portuguese population grew during that period from less than 1 percent of the Hawaiian kingdom's population to more than 15 percent. In 1878, just before the organized importation of Portuguese labor began, there were only 486 Portuguese living in Hawaii, a population made up largely of single men who had arrived as sailors on whaling vessels. In 1884, just six years later, this number had been enlarged by the arrival of 10,700 additional Portuguese. In 1920, they still made up more than 10 percent of the Hawaiian territorial population. This influx of Portuguese had wide-ranging effects on Hawaii. One salient example is that the Portuguese are given credit for developing the "Hawaiian" ukulele. By the standards of the time, the Hawaiian labor contracts offered to the Portuguese were very generous. These contracts were for a term of three years and guaranteed the workers their food, lodging, and medical care, as well as a garden plot and a wage of ten dollars per month to be paid in cash. The sugar planters encouraged immigration of entire families by paying the full cost of passage for each man and child and one-half the cost of passage for each woman. (One ship, the Monarch, arrived in 1882 with 202 men, 197 women, and 458 children.) Between

1880 and 1893, the Portuguese children in public schools increased from less than 1 percent of all students to more than 25 percent.

Although there was some emigration from Madeira to the U.S. mainland as a result of the 1852 plague that wiped out Madeira's viticulture (a plight from which the vineyards did not fully recover for almost fifty years), immigrants from Madeira and continental Portugal began arriving in expressive numbers only after the turn of the twentieth century and reached a peak before 1920. This growing Portuguese immigration rate was a result of Portugal's increasing economic crises and ongoing political turmoil that culminated in the end of the monarchy and the establishment of the First Republic in 1910. In fact, while 63,840 Portuguese immigrants had entered the United States between 1870 and 1900, 158,881 individuals entered between 1900 and 1920.

The immigrants that arrived on the U.S. mainland in the early twentieth century continued to settle mainly in California and New England. On the West Coast, newcomers were mostly composed of Azoreans, linked by kinship ties to earlier settlers, who continued to rely on their rural background and engaged in farming, dairy, and fishing activities, either as entrepreneurs or employees. On the East Coast, immigrants from Madeira and continental Portugal (mainly from northern Portugal) joined the uninterrupted arrival of Azoreans (predominantly from St. Michael). Together with other southern and eastern European immigrants, the Portuguese men and women entered the industrial workforce as unskilled laborers in the New England textile mills of such towns as New Bedford, Fall River, and Taunton in Massachusetts and Pawtucket and Providence in Rhode Island. In fact, they already represented 40 percent of the labor force of the mills in New Bedford and Fall River by 1910. Estimates further suggest that 80 percent of the Portuguese settled in New Bedford by 1930 were cotton mill workers; 15 percent were professionals and business people. This workforce concentration resulted in densely populated ethnic neighborhoods in the mill towns. Because of the influence of chain migration, these neighborhoods often reflected particular villages or regions of origins. For example, Fall River's Portuguese neighborhood primarily reflects the absorption of immigrants from St. Michael. Even in New Bedford (considered to be the "Capital of the Portuguese in the United States"), which attracted a more diversified immigrant population from the nine Azorean islands, Madeira, and continental Portugal, two major neighborhoods were formed with one composed predominantly of Madeiran immigrants and the other composed predominantly of Azorean immigrants with some sections of continental Portuguese.

In Hawaii, the Portuguese were settled on the plantations in ethnically homogenous villages, and they very quickly formed a strong and cohesive social group. They often left the plantations after their labor contracts expired. Since the legal structure of Hawaiian land ownership made buying, or even renting, a small farm very difficult, most Portuguese workers abandoned their rural lives and moved into the towns. Many moved to the cities of Hilo, on the island of Hawaii, and Honolulu, on the island of Oahu. The Portuguese neighborhood of Punchbowl in Honolulu, for example, seemed much like the places the immigrants had left in their homeland. It had many outside stone bread ovens, shops that sold Portuguese food, a Portuguese language newspaper, and streets with names like Concordia and Lusitana. The houses, which looked much as they had in Madeira and St. Michael, were painted white, were scrupulously clean, and were surrounded by flowerbeds. On any day of the week, older retired Portuguese men could be seen chatting in the shade outside the Portuguese chapels. Although the number of Portuguese relocations to the cities had increased steadily from 1880, the peak years for this relocation occurred between 1900 and 1930. In fact, by 1930, 45 percent of all the Portuguese in the territory of Hawaii were living in Honolulu. Once settled in the cities, the Portuguese began to gain skills, buy houses, and start businesses. However, they continued to be viewed primarily as laborers even though only 30 percent of the population still held this type of job and the remaining 70 percent could be found in a wide variety of jobs and social settings. This persistent characterization resulted from the continuing rigid social division in Hawaii between the small, privileged "Haole" elite (made up primarily of the descendants of Protestant missionaries from the U.S. mainland) who owned and managed the plantations and the very much larger group of "Local" laborers (made up of people whose ancestors had worked on the plantations under labor contracts). Economic and social concerns superseded racial ones in this hierarchy, so their laborer origins meant the Portuguese were included in a category formed mainly of Asians and Pacific Islanders.

The flood of Portuguese immigration to Hawaii ended abruptly in 1914 with the arrival of the last plantation labor boat from Europe. For various reasons, the sugar planters attention had turned to other parts of the world as a source of labor. There was almost no contact between the Portuguese of Hawaii and those of Europe after 1914. Between 1914 and 1930, there were only thirty immigrant Portuguese admitted to the United States who gave Hawaii as a final destination, and by 1930, the total Hawaiian Portuguese population of 27,588 contained only 12 percent foreign-born individuals. By 1970, there were only 411 foreign-born Portuguese individuals in the state.

The first deterrent to the flow of Portuguese immigration to the U.S. mainland came in the form of a literacy test. Instituted in 1917, the test, which required that persons over sixteen years of age had to be able to read and write some language in order to be admitted into the United States, prevented the admission of illiterate Portuguese immigrants. Between the 1920s and the 1950s, additional restrictive U.S. immigration policies drastically limited the number of new Portuguese immigrants allowed into the United States. The Johnson Act of 1921, along with ensuing revisions, limited the number of immigrants based on the country of origin. The series of revisions to the act ultimately resulted in the Immigration Act of 1924, whereby a quota system was establishment that allowed only 503 Portuguese immigrants per year (al-

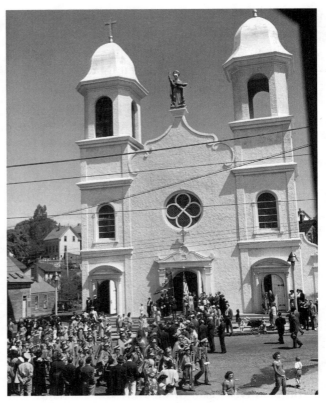

People enter the Portuguese Church of Our Lady of Good Voyage in Gloucester, Massachusetts in 1943. (Library of Congress/Corbis)

though lowered to 440 after 1929) into the United States. With these restrictions in place, the number of arriving Portuguese immigrants dropped from 89,732 in the 1910s to 29,994 in the 1920s. Further decreases in the overall number of Portuguese immigrants are evident in that only 10,752 Portuguese immigrants entered the United States for the entire period from 1931 to 1950.

Portuguese mass immigration to the United States resumed in 1958 as a result of the Azorean Refugee Act. The U.S. government passed the act, which enabled the arrival of forty-eight hundred Azorean immigrants, because of volcanic eruptions and subsequent earthquakes on the island of Fayal. The later U.S. Immigration Act of 1965, which abolished the quota system and fostered the chain migration of individuals related to persons already in the United States, also favored the renewal of Portuguese mass immigration. As a result of these changes to immigration law, 180,565 Portuguese immigrants arrived in the United States between 1961 and 1980, and 40,000 more arrived during the 1980s. These immigrants have renewed and expanded the earlier settlements in California and New England, and they have established a growing nucleus (mostly continental Portuguese) in Newark, New Jersey. Whereas the early Portuguese immigrant population had consisted mainly of impoverished small landholders, landless agricultural laborers, fishermen, and artisans, the more recent immigrant population includes a considerable number of middle-class families. In California, even though the farming, dairy, and fishing industries continue to be the main source of occupations for Portuguese, recent immigrants have found employment in industrial and service jobs. In the New England towns that attracted Portuguese immigrants for so long, such as New Bedford, Fall River, and Taunton, most of the new arrivals began working as "piece workers" in the labor-intensive factories that had replaced the region's diminished textile industry. Those immigrants who learned English, studied a skill, pursued additional education, or accumulated some capital (sometimes by working two factory shifts) were often able to make the transition to other occupations. Others continued to find employment in the fishing and construction industries.

## Return Migration Patterns

Between 1900 and 1920, 25 percent of the Azorean immigrants to the U.S. mainland returned to their homeland. Although many of these individuals would later return to the United States, 94 percent of those who did so left again in less than ten years. The huge distance that separated the Hawaiian Portuguese from Europe meant that contact with their homeland was often minimal and almost none of them returned. If they chose to leave Hawaii, it was most often to resettle in California. The trend of return migration for the mainland Portuguese continued in the 1930s when the Great Depression made it difficult to find work in America. Many Azorean immigrants returned to

their homeland during this period with their entire families, which in many cases included American-born children. During the period of restricted immigration quotas, these American-born individuals could travel freely between their parents' homeland and the United States, and their spouses, whether Portuguese-born or American-born, were allowed to do the same. Because of this freedom to move outside of the quota system, American citizenship and access through kinship and marriage to "American papers" became valuable assets for the Portuguese, especially after the enactment of the Immigration Act of 1965, which, as has been stated, favored family chain migration.

Since post-1965 immigrants were entitled to social security and medicare benefits in the United States, there was a shift in migration strategies. Whereas the earlier immigrants had often intended to remain in the United States only long enough to amass the capital necessary to buy a plot of land in the homeland, the more recent immigrants tended to look forward to the attainment of retirement in the United States, with all the related social benefits. This shift in goals therefore affected the patterns of return migration as more individuals began to settle in the United States permanently. At the same time, because of the still prevalent ideal of return migration, many Portuguese immigrants retained houses, land, and cars in the homeland while working toward purchasing those same items in the United States.

The patterns of return migration changed yet again when dual citizenship became possible in 1981. Many immigrants who were now eligible for both American and Portuguese citizenship took advantage of the opportunity to travel freely between Portugal and the United States, accumulating property in both countries. Some of the retired immigrants who obtained dual citizenship chose to return to their homeland for their retirement, taking with them their American social benefits. Individuals with dual citizenship have also taken advantage of the opportunity to obtain entitlements granted by the homeland. They have made investments and established businesses in their regions of origin in partnership with relatives who had either never immigrated to the United States or who had likewise obtained dual citizenship. The potential for this type of business development, in which decisions involved individuals living in the homeland as well as those living in the United States, served to strengthen the transnational relationships between relatives.

## Language

The immigrants from the Azores, Madeira, and continental Portugal all arrived in America speaking Portuguese, and they continued to speak it at home. While some immigrants on the mainland over the years have made attempts to learn English, there still remain many individuals whose only language is Portuguese. These individuals rely on bilingual relatives (e.g., children, grandchildren, nieces, nephews) for translations of different subjects and in different situations (e.g., hospitals, bureaucracy, work).

The Portuguese in Hawaii experienced a somewhat more diversified language situation because the plantation workers came from many different countries, including China, Japan, Korea, and Hawaii. Therefore, to communicate with their fellow workers, the Portuguese had to learn some Hawaiian, Korean, Japanese, or Chinese. They also had to learn Hawaiian pidgin English because it was the *lingua franca* for all laborers and the language of command used by the plantation bosses. This pidgin, which was a makeshift form of English strongly influenced by Hawaiian grammatical forms and interspersed with Hawaiian words, had started as a simple trade language used between the whalers, early traders, and the native Hawaiians and was then carried on to the plantations. Higher education and most elite social contacts were not available to the Portuguese, so they generally continued to speak pidgin. Since speaking standard American English was the defining characteristic of being Haole, the Portuguese did not readily blend with the Caucasian Haole elite. This bar to higher education is illustrated by the fact that only 15 percent of the Portuguese students in 1900 went beyond the third grade. Even

when a few college preparatory public high schools were opened in 1924, the children of laborers were excluded because the attendance requirements included the ability to speak standard American English. It was not until 1954, under court order, that this two-level education system based on language proficiency was finally abandoned. The fact that the Portuguese spoke only pidgin English was emblematic of their inclusion as part of the Local social group. The implications of this distinction between Haole standard American English and Local pidgin continue in Hawaii to this day. However, the effects of World War II and the end of plantation agriculture dramatically changed the Hawaiian social and economic situation. The Haole elite has increasingly lost control of its social and economic power. Whereas formerly it had always been advantageous to be classified among the Haole elite, there have become an increasing number of situations were it is more advantageous to be a Local. The Portuguese remain the only Caucasian group automatically accepted as Local, which keeps them at the heart of the Hawaiian system of ethnic groups.

## Social Structure

The successive contingents of Portuguese immigrants that settled in the United States are linked among themselves through regional kinship ties. Kin have frequently provided housing for new arrivals, assistance in finding housing and employment, assistance with child care, and support in times of illness or job loss. These expanded kinship networks have constituted the basis of the immigrants' social organization and their primary support in everyday life in the United States.

Examples of Portuguese social organization include the reconstruction in America of the Portuguese tradition of the *serões* (storytelling and musical gatherings reminiscent of a strong oral tradition). Memories of the homeland have been ritualized in many regional folk-religious festivals, and some Portuguese immigrants, particularly the Azoreans, still practice the traditional *matança do porco* (killing of the pig). In addition, stories from the ethnic media (newspapers, radio, and since the 1970s, television) serve as a basis for discussions that bring news of the homeland into the everyday lives of family members, neighbors, and coworkers.

The domestic economy of Portuguese immigrant households is often based on the mutual support of parents, working-age children, and other family members (e.g., grandparents, aunts, uncles, married children) who sometimes live under the same roof. While the entrance of women into the labor market has diminished the traditional male authority, there is a tendency in many households to disguise changing gender roles.

In spite of a prevailing strong family support system that cuts across generations, these households have been affected by conflicts between parents and children. While immigrant parents tend to recreate their homeland's traditions as a way of confronting the dramatic changes associated with immigration, their children have been directly exposed to divergent American and Portuguese cultural values. Ethnic cloistering, a hard work ethic, differing constructions of gender, and paternal authoritarianism have often given way to dramatic generation gaps as children become more receptive to American cultural patterns. Different generations of women and men frequently recall their dramatic experiences of growing up in the middle of a "shock of cultures." Because of the tendency to maintain traditional gender roles, many immigrant women who grew up in the United States, along with American-born Portuguese females, have often experienced resentment at the continuation of the males' ascribed privileges and the repression of females. Many reject their families' preferential system of "arranged marriages" and defy their parents and other relatives in order to pursue an education. While there have been young immigrants and descendants who have conformed with the traditional Portuguese ways of life, many have opted to live their lives as members of the American society. Others have tried to juxtapose their bicultural experiences in the construction of a Luso-American identity.

The individual generations of Portuguese families in the United States have been marked by differing experiences. Earlier immigrants and descendants suffered the experience of living in the United States during the Great Depression of the 1930s. Many faced severe hardships, and their children sometimes had to quit school in order to help support the household. At a time when the U.S. government's policies and ideologies sought to incorporate immigrants through "Americanization" and assimilation, foreignness and racial differences were stigmatized. The presence of Cape Verdeans within the Portuguese population caused the Portuguese to be seen as dark-skinned foreigners, increasing racial prejudice. While the majority of Portuguese immigrants continued to hold on to their traditions, their children tended to disguise their Portuguese ancestry and to anglicize their names as a way of avoiding discrimination and attaining social mobility. Some became proponents of the ongoing Americanization and naturalization campaigns that used the slogan "If you want to be a good Portuguese, become American." Many married into other ethnic groups (e.g., Irish, Italian, English, French Canadian), and their lives became restricted to the United States.

The contingents of Portuguese immigrant families that arrived in the United States after the mid-1960s encountered a different American environment. With cultural pluralism emphasizing the channeling of resources to ethnic groups and minorities, they encountered the support of immigrants' assistance services as well as bilingual schools for their children. While youths still worked to help their families meet the household budgets, they were provided with better opportunities to pursue their studies and obtain college degrees. Bicultural and bilingual immigrants (as well as descendants of immigrants) who became teachers, librarians, nurses, and social workers were able to perform mediation between immigrants and American institutions. While the race issue had faded, Portuguese immigrants still confronted discrimination and stigmatization. Biculturalism and bilingualism began to prevail among younger immigrants and descendants of immigrants, and the postcolonial Portuguese government officials have tried systematically to reinforce the transnationality of these bilingual and bicultural Portuguese. In many cases, these immigrants have been able to act as cultural intermediaries between Portugal and the United States.

As public acceptance has been given to celebrations of ethnic communities as building blocks of the American social fabric, successful Luso-Americans, descendants of the older immigrant families, have re-emphasized their Portuguese ancestry. Although distant from the newer immigrant contingents, prominent Luso-Americans, together with the upwardly mobile immigrants, have reconstructed the legendary Portuguese past as part of their attempts to represent the Portuguese ethnic group as a majority—not a minority—in the U.S. pluralistic society.

## Community Events

The Portuguese are mainly Roman Catholic, although many are anticlerical. They frequent ethnic Portuguese churches that function as centers of Portuguese community life and where Sunday Masses are given alternately in English and Portuguese. Most of these parishes were founded during the early twentieth century, but the oldest, St. John the Baptist (located in New Bedford), dates back to 1869.

Immigrants of rural background express their collective regional identity through the celebration of folk-religious festivals. In New England and California, the Azoreans celebrate the Festival of the Holy Ghost between Easter and the end of July. In the homeland, each island had sponsored a different version of the feast, which included the symbolic transmission of the royal crown to the most indigent. In the postcolonial era, Azorean government officials have turned this feast into a symbol of the archipelago's identity, and some Azorean immigrants in the United States return to their homeland to attend the feast there. Other Azorean feasts celebrated in the United States include the Senhor da Pedra in New Bedford and the Santo Cristo in Fall River. The Festival of the Holy Ghost was also an important religious event for the Portuguese living in Hawaii. Holy Ghost chapels, the focus of this festival, were established in every Honolulu neighborhood and on every island in Hawaii. Each chapel was associated with a large club that maintained the chapel and organized the community's religious and social functions. The Portuguese in Hawaii also created, in 1901 on the island of Oahu, an organization (Irmandade de Nossa Senhora do Monte) based on the most famous religious site in Madeira: the shrine of Our Lady of the Mount. The annual festival sponsored by this organization was held in the mountains behind Honolulu, and thousands of people came from every island to attend. The Madeiran Feast of the Blessed Sacrament, which takes place in New Bedford during the first weekend of August and was established as a local event in 1915 by four Madeiran men in thanks for surviving a shipwreck on their way to the United States, is considered to be the largest Portuguese-American festival in the United States, attracting more than 150,000 visitors annually.

Immigrant community leaders, in conjunction with Portuguese consulates, also organize celebrations of the Day of Portugal, Camões, and the Portuguese Communities, which take place annually during the week of June 10 in Portuguese settlements throughout the world. This day, honoring Luís de Camões (the author of the *Lusiadas*, the epic poem of the Portuguese discoveries), has become associated with the mythical embodiment of the nation. During Portuguese colonialism, when the prevailing ideologies stressed the supremacy of the Luzitan race, this celebration was known as the Day of Portugal, Camões, and the Luzitan Race. After the revolution in 1974, however, the leaders of the Provisional Revolutionary Government transformed the day into a celebration of the "immigrant communities," or the "Portuguese communities abroad." The series of events connected with this national day tend to attract a smaller group of people, composed mostly of professionals (e.g., teachers, librarians, social workers) who bring along their families and

A nun teaches geography in a Roman Catholic Portuguese school in New Bedford, Massachusetts, in 1942. (Library of Congress/Corbis)

friends and place greater emphasis on Portuguese national culture rather than folk-religious events.

## Conclusion

In spite of their enduring presence in the United States, the Portuguese were viewed up to the 1970s as an "invisible minority" and a case of disappearing ethnics. Confronted with discrimination and U.S. Americanization policies that stressed the superiority of American society and the American way of life, descendants of the earlier contingents of immigrants tended to disguise their Portuguese ancestry. With Portugal's entrance into the European Union and the construction of a Portuguese nation "based on population rather than territory" in a historical period marked by American multicultural policies, Portuguese ethnic identity in the mainland United States was renewed.

In Hawaii, the Portuguese have tended to disappear as an autonomous social group since the 1950s. The territorial census always enumerated them separately in the category "Other Caucasians," but the U.S. Bureau of the Census does not view them as a distinct category. This vague statistical profile is compounded by the increasingly cosmopolitan nature of the Hawaiian population. Hawaiian ethnic groups in general have a high rate of outmarriage, but the Portuguese rate is high even within this context. Between 1912 and 1934, 40 percent of the Portuguese in Hawaii married non-Portuguese individuals, and this rate has increased over the years. As a result, there are fewer and fewer individuals of pure Portuguese ancestry. Since they continue, however, to be the only Caucasian group accepted as Local, the ideas of Portuguese and Portugueseness have remained strong.

*See also:* BRAZILIANS; CAPE VERDEANS

## Bibliography

Adams, R.; Livesay, T. M.; and Van Winkle, E. H. (1925). *The Peoples of Hawaii: A Statistical Study.* Honolulu: Institute of Pacific Relations.

Cabral, S. L. (1989). *Tradition and Transformation: Portuguese Feasting in New Bedford.* New York: AMS Press.

Correa, G., and Knowlton, E., Jr. (1982). "The Portuguese in Hawaii." *Social Process in Hawaii* 29:70–78.

Feldman-Bianco, B. (1992). "Multiple Layers of Time and Space: The Construction of Class, Race, Ethnicity, and Nationalism Among Portuguese Immigrants." In *Towards a Transnational Perspective on Migration: Race, Class, Ethnicity, and Nationalism Reconsidered,* edited by N. Glick Schiller, L. Basch, and C. Blanc-Szanton. New York: New York Academy of Sciences.

Felix, J. H., and Senecal, P. F. (1978). The *Portuguese in Hawaii.* Honolulu: Authors.

Hormann, B. L. (1950). "The Caucasian Minority." *Social Process in Hawaii,* no. 14.

Kinloch, G. (1973). "Race, Socio-Economic Status, and Social Distance in Hawaii." *Sociology and Social Research* 57(2):156–167.

Kuykendall, R. S. ([1938] 1967). *The Hawaiian Kingdom.* Honolulu: University of Hawaii Press.

Lamphere, L.; Silva, F. M.; and Sousa, J. P. (1980). "Kin Networks and Strategies of Working-Class Portuguese Families in a New England Town." In *The Versatility of Kinship,* edited by L. Cordell and S. Beckerman. New York: Academy Press.

Lang, H. R. (1892). "The Portuguese Element in New England." *Journal of American Folklore,* January, pp. 9–18.

Lind, A. W., ed. (1967). *Modern Hawaii: Perspectives on the Hawaiian Community.* Honolulu: Labor-Management Education Program, University of Hawaii.

Macedo, D. P., ed. (1980). *Issues in Portuguese Bilingual Education.* Cambridge, MA: Center for Bilingual/Bicultural Education.

Mayone Dias, E. (1984). "Portuguese Immigration to the East Coast of the United States and California: Contrasting Patterns." In *Portugal in Development: Emigration, Industrialization, the European Community,* edited by T. C. Bruneau, V. M. P. Da Rosa, and A. Macleod. Ottawa, Canada: University of Ottawa Press.

Mazzatenta, O. L. (1975). "New England's Little Portugal." *National Geographic* 147 (January): 90–109.

McDermott, J.; Tseng, W.-S.; and Maretski, T., eds. (1976). *Peoples and Cultures of Hawaii.* Honolulu: Department of Psychiatry, University of Hawaii School of Medicine.

Pap, L. (1976). *The Portuguese in the United States: A Bibliography.* New York: Center for Migration Studies.

Pap, L. (1981). *The Portuguese-Americans.* New York: Twayne.

Reinecke, J. (1936). "The Competition of Languages in Hawaii." *Social Process in Hawaii,* no. 2.

Rogers, F. (1974). *Americans of Portuguese Descent: A Lesson in Differentiation.* Beverly Hills, CA: Sage Publications.

Rogers, F. (1976). "The Portuguese Experience in the United States: Double Melt or the Minority Group?" *Journal of the American Portuguese Society,* Spring, pp. 1–15.

Schmitt, R. C. (1977). *Historical Statistics of Hawaii.* Honolulu: University Press of Hawaii.

Smith, E. M. (1974). "Portuguese Enclaves: The Invisible Minority." In *Social and Cultural Identity: Problems of Persistence and Change,* edited by T. K. Fitzgerald. Athens: University of Georgia Press.

Smith, E. M. (1975). "A Tale of Two Cities: Reality of Historical Differences." *Urban Anthropology* IV(1):61–72.

Williams, J. (1982). *And Yet They Come: Portuguese Immigration from the Azores to the United States.* New York: Center for Migration Studies.

Wolforth, S. (1978). *The Portuguese in America.* San Francisco: R & E Research Associates.

BELA FELDMAN-BIANCO
JAMES MACDONALD

# PUERTO RICANS

Puerto Ricans are descendants of people from the island of Puerto Rico, located in the Spanish-speaking Caribbean. They are a people whose homeland was acquired by the United States in 1898 as a result of the Spanish-American War. Puerto Rico is a territory of the United States with limited sovereignty as a commonwealth. Puerto Ricans differ as an ethnic group from other immigrants of Latin American and Caribbean descent because they are American citizens. Citizenship was conferred on the Puerto Rican people in 1917 by the Jones Act. The U.S. Bureau of the Census defines Puerto Ricans as part of a larger population of ethnic minorities designated as Hispanic. The term "Hispanic" is used to define anyone in the United States who has a Spanish surname or comes from a Spanish-speaking background. Many people of Latin American and Caribbean descent, including Puerto Ricans, do not readily identify with the term "Hispanic" and refer to themselves as Latinos or more specifically as part of the ethnic subgroup that reflects their historical experiences. Thus Puerto Ricans will often interchangeably use terms that reflect their relationship to the island, its history, and its traditions as well as the relationship between Puerto Rico and the United States. Many Puerto Ricans identify themselves using the Spanish term *Puertorriqueños*. This is a literal translation of the term "Puerto Rican" and serves as a marker of linguistic and cultural affiliation. Similarly, the Spanish term "Boricua" refers to the descendants of Boriquén, the name given to Puerto Rico by the Amerindians who once lived there. By defining themselves as Boricuas, Puerto Ricans make the historical past an integral part of the present. Puerto Ricans who migrated from the island and settled in New York often define themselves and are defined by others as Nyuoricans. They constitute several generations of Puerto Ricans who are bilingual and bicultural and are conscious of the extent to which they have been oppressed and marginalized members of American society. Contrary to the negative stereotypes attributed to Nuyoricans, they are people who struggle to improve the quality of their lives as they celebrate their multiple identities and experiences.

## Migration

The migration and settlement history of Puerto Ricans in the continental United States forms part of a complex set of economic and social processes. The Puerto Rican people began to migrate in earnest after 1898, when Spain ceded Puerto Rico and other territories to the United States at the end of the Spanish-American War. Thousands of Puerto Rican workers migrated to Hawaii to work in the sugar industry between 1899 and 1901. These migrants were contract laborers who previously worked in the coffee industry in Puerto Rico and became unemployed due to an economic crisis that resulted in the decline of coffee production there. Others traveled in smaller numbers to Cuba, the Dominican Republic, and the U.S. Southwest.

Migration to the continental United States increased during World War I. As of 1910, approximately 1,500 Puerto Ricans were living in the United States. However, the Puerto Rican population living there had increased to 52,774 by 1930. These early migrants worked as contract laborers to produce goods such as ships and ammunition needed for the war. Among these early migrants there were also tailors, cigar makers, carpenters, and skilled artisans who contributed to the growing American economy. The majority of these migrants settled initially in New York City and formed communities where they shared their daily life experiences with other Latin Americans and with black Americans who resided there.

The migration of Puerto Ricans to the U.S. mainland following World War II has been referred to as "the first great airborne migration." As compared to other groups, Puerto Ricans do not need permissions, passports, or visas to travel to the United States. Air transportation is easily accessible and moderately priced; therefore, individuals who have the means to move to the host country can do so. By comparing the number of Puerto Ricans who moved prior to World War II and after it, the magnitude of this migration is best understood. As of 1940, there were 70,000 Puerto Ricans living in the continental United States. Between 1941 and 1945, approximately 4,600 Puerto Ricans migrated annually to the U.S. mainland. From 1946 to 1950, approximately 31,000 Puerto Ricans annually left their homeland. Throughout the 1950s, the number of migrants increased. Nearly 45,000 Puerto Ricans migrated to the U.S. mainland annually. This represented the largest exodus of Puerto Ricans from their homeland in history. The number of Puerto Ricans living in the continental United States approached 900,000 by 1960. By 1970, Puerto Rican–born residents and their descendants living on the mainland totaled almost 1.5 million people. Throughout the 1970s, there was a decline in the number of Puerto Ricans leaving the island — less than 16,500 people migrated annually to the mainland. This decline was in part due to the growth in employment opportunities available in Puerto Rico. In addition, approximately 333,000 Puerto Ricans returned to the island. This downward trend was short-lived. By 1980, more than 2 million Puerto Ricans were living in the United States. The U.S. Bureau of the Census reported that in 1990 more than 2.7 million Puerto Ricans resided on the U.S. mainland and 3.5 million lived on the island.

## Historical Overview

Many socioeconomic factors contributed to the mass exodus of Puerto Ricans to the U.S. mainland. Economic reasons, however, tended to be the principal ones. Throughout the initial stages of migration, Puerto Rican laborers left their homeland in search of employment opportunities. In the 1940s and 1950s, there was a rapid decline in the availability of agricultural labor, and the growing industrial sector was not able to meet the needs of all the displaced agricultural workers. In search of new employment opportunities, many laborers moved from rural sectors of the island to urban centers, where an infrastructure was rapidly developing to meet the social and economic needs of the people. Also, due to improvements in social ser-

vices and in health conditions in particular, the Puerto Rican population rapidly increased.

In the 1940s, the Puerto Rican government engaged in economic and social reforms to create an infrastructure and a labor force that would lead to the industrialization and modernization of Puerto Rico. A program designated as Compañia de Fomento de Puerto Rico (Fomento) was established. Factories were created and operated by the Puerto Rican government to promote internal economic growth. They took advantage of the primary resources available on the island to produce needed consumer goods. However, the initial objectives of the program changed as efforts were made to attract foreign investors, particularly North Americans, to develop factories that many believed would further stimulate economic growth and development on the island via production of goods for export. By 1947, Fomento had laid the groundwork for another industrialization program, known as Manos a la Obra (Operation Bootstrap). Fomento offered North American investors a cheap, disciplined, and abundant labor force in a politically stable environment and with economic incentives to guarantee their success. Throughout this period Puerto Ricans were aggressively encouraged to migrate in greater numbers to the continental United States. The view held by development and modernization experts was that a manageable population size would enhance future prospects toward the modernization of Puerto Rico. In fact, World War II constituted one of the first modernizing experiences in Puerto Rican history and culture. Approximately seventy-six thousand Puerto Ricans served in the U.S. military during that war. Many of these young veterans acquired skills that permitted them to enter the U.S. labor force.

As employment opportunities in the United States became available in the industrial Northeast and Midwest, Puerto Rican men and women joined the U.S. agricultural, manufacturing, and service industries as unskilled and semiskilled laborers. For example, women who migrated occupied low-paying semiskilled jobs in New York's garment district. However, as manufacturing industries left the Northeast and Midwest in search of cheaper sources of labor abroad, many women joined the ranks of the unemployed or became an integral part of the U.S. service industry as clerical workers and receptionists.

The period between 1960 and 1980 is referred to as "the revolving door migration," due to the constant flow of Puerto Ricans traveling to and from the island and the U.S. mainland to improve their socioeconomic well-being. The successes and failures of Operation Bootstrap prompted the out-migration of Puerto Ricans with limited skills from the island. Changes in the U.S. economy, civil unrest, and the Vietnam War contributed to the return migration of Puerto Ricans living on the mainland.

Between 1980 and 1990, migration from Puerto Rico to the U.S. mainland increased as compared to the 1970s. Approximately 301,000 persons migrated from the island in the 1980s, as compared to 165,000 in the previous decade. The growth of the overall Puerto Rican population in the 1980s was partly a reflection of this migration and of a natural increase.

## Return Migration

Many Puerto Ricans have participated in circulatory and return migration. These migratory patterns reflect changes in the Puerto Rican and U.S. economies as well as personal circumstances. The demise of employment opportunities in the northeastern United States and the promise of employment opportunities in Puerto Rico prompted some Puerto Ricans to return to the island in the 1960s. However, some Puerto Ricans returned because the capital and skills they acquired on the U.S. mainland permitted them to purchase land, build homes, develop small businesses, or take advantage of expanding employment opportunities for semiskilled workers, thereby increasing their overall status upon their return. Others found themselves unemployed and opted to return to the island in search of community and familial support. Still others, with varying degrees of available resources, returned to the island due to the preju-

dices they experienced in the United States as members of a minority group that spoke a different language and could not be easily defined along the black and white racial lines that deeply divide Americans. Many Puerto Ricans also decided to retire to the island. Among these return migrants are many who hold steadfast to their memories of Puerto Rico and who must deal with the transformations in Puerto Rican society and culture since their initial departure. Furthermore, return migrants must confront the ways in which negative perceptions Puerto Ricans living on the island have of *Nuyoricans* and returnees affect their well-being. In some cases, return migrants who intended to remain on the island have opted to leave Puerto Rico once again because they no longer feel that they are integral members of the island's society and culture. The sentiment echoed by these migrants is summarized with the statement "*No somos ni de aqui, ni de allá.*" (We don't belong here, and we don't belong there either.) To date there are few sociological studies that address the impact of return and circulatory migration patterns among Puerto Ricans.

## Settlement and Resettlement Patterns

Historically, Puerto Ricans who migrated in search of employment opportunities settled in major cities in the Northeast and Midwest. The largest proportion of Puerto Ricans settled in New York, particularly in neighborhoods where their kin or people from their hometown were located. Family and friends provided important links that helped newly arrived migrants find work, gain access to social services, and become integral members of their new communities. As of 1980, 73.3 percent of the Puerto Rican mainland population resided in the Northeast. The states with the largest concentration of Puerto Ricans in 1980 included New York, New Jersey, and Illinois. However, Florida, Massachusetts, Texas, and Connecticut experienced the greatest growth in the Puerto Rican population in the 1990s. A number of factors have influenced the settlement and dispersion of Puerto Ricans in the 1980s and 1990s. Many Puerto

Ricans have moved to smaller cities due to deteriorating socioeconomic conditions in urban enclaves with widespread crime and scarce employment opportunities. Puerto Ricans who currently migrate from the island continue to settle in New York City, but many are now settling in small cities as well. An extensive network of family members and friends has informed prospective migrants that opportunities in traditional areas of settlement are limited. In the 1990s, cities such as Hartford, Connecticut, and Springfield, Massachusetts, in the Northeast have been experiencing a rapid growth in Puerto Rican population. Another important shift is the movement and settlement of Puerto Ricans to cities in the southern United States, particularly in Florida, Texas, and California. An older population of Puerto Ricans who previously resided in the Northeast and Midwest is migrating from these major urban centers and resettling in southern states. A highly educated population of Puerto Ricans, both from the U.S. mainland as well as from the island, is also settling in these states, where employment opportunities for professionals are more readily available.

## Socioeconomic Characteristics

Clearly, social and economic changes in major cities in the Northeast and Midwest have had an effect on patterns of migration, settlement, and resettlement among Puerto Ricans. These changes have also affected the well-being of the members of these communities. For example, while Puerto Ricans continue to migrate to New York City, these recent migrants join other Puerto Ricans living in New York who are not equipped to deal with a changing employment market where skilled workers and professionals are in greater demand. Studies show that a majority of the recent migrants who initially settled in New York from the island have relatively low educational attainment levels and limited skills in an increasingly technological workplace. Migrants who are unable to find sustainable employment on the island or on the U.S. mainland often need social services to meet some of their basic socioeconomic needs. As impoverished, unemployed, and underemployed individuals

they must contend with limited housing, health care, and other social services that further limit opportunities for educational, social, and economic advancement. The young and the old are at highest risk. According to the U.S. Department of Commerce, the poverty rate for Puerto Ricans on the U.S. mainland in 1990 was 30.3 percent. Although this represents a decline of 6.1 percent over the previous decade, these figures are alarming. Compared to the overall poverty rate in the nation of 13.2 percent, Puerto Ricans have one of the highest poverty rates among all ethnic and racial groups. Poverty rates among women are even greater. The rate of poverty among Puerto Rican female heads of households in 1990 was 31.9 percent, compared to 30.0 percent in 1980. This is representative of an overall increase in the poverty rate among female-headed households nationwide. The adverse effects on children living in these impoverished households and neighborhoods with inadequate social services must be considered. Many of the elderly who migrated in the 1940s and 1950s and worked in the manufacturing industries must now rely solely on Social Security income or small pensions to meet their socioeconomic needs. They often find themselves trapped in an urban milieu and in a society that has failed to ensure their well-being.

The social, economic, and political factors that contribute to these conditions are varied and extremely complex. First, many large urban centers are segregated due to the flight of European Americans to smaller cities and suburbs. Puerto Ricans and members of other racial and ethnic groups with limited resources remain in the urban centers and have to combat many of the social ills of the inner city. Second, Puerto Ricans continually have to adjust to a social setting where other groups — for example, from Latin America and the Caribbean — are also competing for scarce resources, particularly employment opportunities for the unskilled and semiskilled. Finally, the political status of Puerto Rico continues to influence the well-being of Puerto Ricans on the island and on the U.S. mainland. Due to the development of a myriad of social and economic policies and practices on the U.S. mainland and in Puerto

Rico, the Puerto Rican people are often affected in ways that influence their migratory practices and quality of life.

Despite many of the social and economic constraints Puerto Ricans must contend with as an ethnic group, they constitute a very diverse group. Although there are highly educated professionals who are members of America's middle class, most Puerto Ricans are among the working class in America who struggle to ensure that the basic needs of their family are met. Others, as previously mentioned, are the working poor and the very poor. These individuals and families must rely on diminishing social welfare programs to help them meet their subsistence needs.

## Housing, Health Care, and Education

There are several social indicators that reflect the socioeconomic diversity in the Puerto Rican population and the overall well-being of this ethnic group. These indicators include housing, health care, and education.

Due to limited financial resources and opportunities, many Puerto Rican families are not able to secure the funds needed to purchase a home. Puerto Ricans have the lowest rate of home ownership on the U.S. mainland when compared to whites, blacks, and Asians. Access to health care and information is particularly problematic among working poor and poor Puerto Ricans. The lack of health-care practitioners in neighborhoods where Puerto Ricans are located negatively affects the well-being of the population. The Hispanic Health and Nutrition Examination Survey (HANES) reported that Puerto Ricans are more likely than any other Hispanic group to suffer from diabetes, heart problems, and chronic bronchitis. The AIDS epidemic has disproportionately affected the Puerto Rican population as well.

Access to a quality and advanced education is a critical indicator of an ethnic group's well-being and future prospects. In 1990, the Hispanic population had the lowest average level of education in the United States. Among Puerto Ricans age twenty-five or older, 46.5 percent had less than a high school education. Only 9.2 percent of the population in the aforementioned age group had a college education. These figures raise serious concerns regarding the well-being of Puerto Ricans, who are already adversely affected by a labor market that requires skilled and educated workers. There are policymakers, educators, and community activists who are trying to revitalize many of the segregated schools Puerto Rican children attend. These schools often have inadequate resources where children are not provided with the basic skills needed to obtain an advanced education to compete in the American workplace.

## Cultural Persistence and Assimilation

For some Puerto Ricans, the process of assimilation and transculturation is difficult, and many suffer social dislocation as they struggle with discrimination, racism, and sexism in various social contexts. Others are able to navigate the treacherous waters of assimilation in the continental United States and make transitions that permit them to negotiate their identities as bicultural and bilingual members of American society. And yet others opt to become totally assimilated and identify themselves as Hispanics or Americans, not Puerto Ricans. Family links, interpersonal relationships, and the celebration of cultural values and traditions influence processes of assimilation and transculturation.

## Family and Kinship

Puerto Ricans place great value on the family. Extended kin networks are particularly important. Value is placed on the interaction between members of the extended family. Due to the high rates of marital separation and divorce, Puerto Rican families, particularly female-headed ones, are well aware that they must often rely on the support and assistance of extended family members to ensure their well-being.

Legal marriage is considered an ideal among Puerto Ricans; however, consensual unions also occur. Puerto Ricans validate these consensual unions by according the couple rights and responsibilities as legally married persons. Among Puerto

A group of Puerto Rican women and children hold Puerto Rican flags during a parade in Wilmington, Delaware, in 1993. (Joseph Sohm/ChromoSohm Inc./Corbis)

Ricans each individual is allowed to seek his or her own mate. However, family members will often intercede to ensure that the match is an appropriate one based on factors such as family lineage, class, and status.

A serious problem among poor Puerto Rican youths, particularly in large urban centers, is early pregnancy. This is due in part to limited access to birth control information and other socioeconomic variables that place these individuals at high risk. Teenage pregnancy not only affects the well-being of the individuals involved but the larger society as well.

The elderly also form part of these extended-family networks because they rely on their adult children for assistance and support. As grandparents they are also relied on to assist in child rearing. As a result of these factors, several generations of Puerto Ricans may reside in one household.

Puerto Ricans also incorporate individuals who are not related to them by blood or marriage into their extended-kin network. For example, *compadres* (coparents) are fictive kin who become a child's godparents through the ritual of baptism. They are also accorded rights and responsibilities as extended-family members.

## Interpersonal Relationships

There is variation in behavior between Puerto Ricans of different social classes. Among Puerto Ricans in general, extended-kin and other relationships are based on mutual respect. The elderly, for example, are accorded respect and honored. Male-female relations are part of a patriarchal complex where men are respected as providers for their families. Women are valued as wives and mothers who secure the well-being of their family. These ideals are reflected in daily practices where both men and women seek employment opportunities and resources for their kin. However, as previously discussed, many of the social and economic constraints Puerto Ricans encounter on a daily basis create tensions that negatively affect interpersonal relationships.

## Transnational Relationships

Interpersonal relations between Puerto Ricans are strengthened as individuals travel to and from the island. Important cultural ideas, traditions, and practices are also reinforced. Puerto Ricans residing on the U.S. mainland will often ask their kin traveling to and from the island to visit their relations there. Throughout these visits, information about births, marriages, illnesses, and deaths is exchanged. Social, political, and economic events that affect the well-being of Puerto Ricans are also discussed. Within this context, prospective migrants on the island learn about possible employment opportunities and about new areas of settlement. Many are prompted by their kin to migrate.

Puerto Ricans residing on the U.S. mainland often return to Puerto Rico for the holidays, or to participate in family rituals and community festivals. They often arrive bearing gifts for their kin. These gifts are often goods needed or desired by family members and are markers of an elevated social status because they reinforce the idea that the Puerto Rican migrant has achieved some measure of success in the continental United States. Gifts are also given out of respect and appreciation for the families who serve as hosts throughout the return migrants' visit. While many Puerto Ricans engage in these practices, this is tempered by the experiences of return migrants who have not experienced socioeconomic success.

## Cultural Resilience

Several generations of contact between Puerto Ricans living on the U.S. mainland and those living on the island have affected Puerto Rican cultural traditions and practices. They are imbued with dynamic qualities. This cultural resilience is reflected in their religious beliefs and practices, their literary and artistic works, and their sociopolitical institutions and organizations.

*Religious Beliefs and Practices.* As part of the Spanish Conquest, the people of Latin America and the Spanish-speaking Caribbean were introduced and forced to convert to Roman Catholicism. This legacy exists to the present. The majority of people of Puerto Rican descent are Catholic and generally adhere to the teachings and practices of the Catholic Church. Within recent decades, other religions have come to play a prominent role. Evangelical Protestantism, for example, has increased, particularly among the working poor and socioeconomically disadvantaged. For generations, Puerto Ricans also have engaged in religious practices that incorporate Santeria and Espiritismo. Practioners of Santeria integrate aspects of Catholicism and West African religions. Santeria, a syncretic and highly dynamic religion, is rooted in the beliefs and practices of Africans brought to the Americas as slaves during the Spanish Conquest. Espiritismo is rooted in Catholicism and the religious teachings of Alan Kardec. Practioners of Espiritismo believe that spirits are able to intervene in the world of the living and can impart good and evil with the assistance of mediums. These religious practitioners engage in rituals where they call on the spirit world to help them cure illnesses and secure the well-being of an individual with the use of herbs and physical remedies. They can also cause harm by engaging in similar kinds of rituals.

*Artistic Representations.* Puerto Rican artists, artisans, dramatists, and writers have creatively struggled against the injustices they have experienced as an ethnic group throughout the history of Puerto Rican-U.S. relations. They have also sought avenues to celebrate the richness of their cultural heritage and their experiences on the U.S. mainland as generations of Puerto Ricans have become part of the American cultural landscape. For example, Puerto Ricans in New York established the Puerto Rican Traveling Theater and the Museo del Barrio, where many gifted and talented Puerto Ricans honed their skills and went on to become nationally and internationally known figures in the arts. These community-based artistic centers also served to inform and educate the Puerto Rican community and the society at large regarding the richness and diversity in Puerto Rican culture. Poets, short-story writers, and novelists who are sons and daughters of post–World War II migrants constitute a critical generation of writers. They have eloquently expressed the feelings and sentiments, the rage of many Puerto Ricans who migrated from the island and experienced abject poverty in a society that discriminated against them and defined them as members of a minority, as second-class citizens. These writers are political activists whose work challenges Americans and others to think critically about and engage in activities to combat racism, sexism, and socioeconomic inequalities. Subsequent generations of Puerto Rican writers continue this legacy and write about the contemporary experiences of Puerto Ricans in an urban setting. Others write of the migration, settlement, and return migration of their kin by weaving together life histories and stories that elucidate the wide range of experiences among Puerto Ricans on the continental United States and on the island. By doing so they reveal the rich texture of Puerto Rican culture. Similarly, a cadre of internally known musicians has infused the musical landscape with Afro-Latin rhythms (Latin jazz, *salsa*, Latin rap), key components of musical performances throughout the world. The American visual landscape has also been transformed by generations of young Puerto Ricans who express themselves by appropriating empty spaces in an urban environment. They spread graffiti and produce art as they creatively engage and transform the outer walls of dilapidated buildings and other structures to make their presence felt. Others are appropriating the geographical landscape and transforming it by creating little houses, *casitas*, constructed in the form of traditional Puerto Rican wooden structures. In New York these houses are emblematic of the experiences of many Puerto Ricans throughout the history of their migration to and settlement and resettlement on the U.S. mainland in the face of changing social and economic conditions. They are works of art and markers of the cultural resilience and tenuous position of Puerto Rican people in the continental United States.

*Sociopolitical Institutions and Organizations.* A host of national, state, and local organizations and nonprofit agencies has been created by Puerto Ricans to serve the needs of their compatriots in communities throughout the United States. Some of these are advocacy groups that address public policy issues that affect the well-being of Puerto Ricans on the island and on the U.S. mainland. Other organizations not only address the ways in which public policies and practices affect Puerto Ricans but also try to implement solutions to problems by seeking the support of the community at the local level. They are public policy and advocacy groups that seek to inform and empower Puerto Ricans. Some of the national organizations include the National Congress for Puerto Rican Rights; the National Puerto Rican Coalition; the National Puerto Rican Forum; and the Institute for Puerto Rican Policy. Institutions committed to education and the development of the leadership potential in Puerto Rican and other Latino youths have played a critical role. The ASPIRA Association, established in 1961, encourages Puerto Rican youths to complete their education and develop their intellectual potential. The Centro de Estudios Puertorriqueños (the Center for Puerto Rican Studies), established in 1973 at Hunter College of the City University of New York, encourages analysis of the Puerto Rican experience on the island and in the continental United States. Scholars and community advocates associated with the Center for Puerto Rican Studies are particularly interested in the development of new theories and practices that are indicative of the rapidly changing reality for Puerto Ricans. Other national organizations have established critical links with community groups and individuals at the local level. For example, the Puerto Rican Legal Defense and Education Fund works to protect the civil rights of Puerto Ricans and other Latinos by working to ensure their equal protection under the law in education, employment, housing, health, and welfare. The development throughout history of state and local organizations committed to the well-being of Puerto Ricans are far too numerous to mention. However, they all have a common thread: These organizations emerged as a result of the collective struggle of individuals to combat injustice and maintain dignity.

## Bibliography

Alers-Montalvo, M. (1985). *The Puerto Rican Migrants of New York City: A Study of Anomie.* New York: AMS Press.

Benmayor, R.; Juarbe, A.; Alvarez, C.; and Vázquez, B. (1987). *Stories to Live By: Continuity and Change in Three Generations of Puerto Rican Women.* New York: Centro de Estudios Puertorriqueños, Hunter College of the City of New York.

Benmayor, R.; Torruellas, R. M.; and Juarbe, A. L. (1992). *Responses to Poverty Among Puerto Rican Women: Identity, Community, and Cultural Citizenship.* New York: Centro de Estudios Puertorriqueños, Hunter College of the City University of New York.

Bonilla, F., and Campos, R. (1986). *Industry and Idleness.* New York: History and Migration Task Force, Centro de Estudios Puertorriqueños, Hunter College of the City University of New York.

Campos, R., and Flores, J. (1978). *National Culture and Migration: Perspectives from the Puerto Rican Working Class.* New York: Centro de Estudios Puertorriqueños, Hunter College of the City University of New York.

Falcón, L. M., and Gurak, D. T. (1990). *Features of the Hispanic Underclass: Puerto Ricans and Dominicans in New York City.* Ithaca, NY: Cornell University Working Paper Series 2.09.

Fitzpatrick, J. P. (1995). "Puerto Rican New Yorkers 1990." *Migration World Magazine* XXIII(1–2):16–19.

Freidenberg, J. N. (1995). "Growing Old in Spanish Harlem: A Multimedia, Bilingual Exhibition." *Migration World Magazine* XXIII(1–2):34–38.

Freidenberg, J. N., ed. (1995). *The Anthropology of Lower Income Urban Enclaves: The Case of East Harlem.* New York: New York Academy of Sciences.

Levine, B. B. (1987). "The Puerto Rican Exodus: Development of the Puerto Rican Circuit." In *The Caribbean Exodus,* edited by B. B. Levine. New York: Praeger.

Melendez, E. (1993). *Los que se van, los que regresan: Puerto Rican Migration to and From the United States, 1982–1988.* New York: Centro de Estudios Puertorriqueños, Hunter College of the City University of New York.

Morales Carrión, A. (1983). *Puerto Rico: A Political and Cultural History.* New York: W. W. Norton.

Padilla, F. M. (1987). *Puerto Rican Chicago.* Notre Dame, IN: University of Notre Dame Press.

Rivera-Batiz, F., and Santiago, C. (1995). *Puerto Ricans in the United States: A Changing Reality.* Washington, DC: National Puerto Rican Coalition.

Rodriguez, C. E. (1989). *Puerto Ricans: Born in the U.S.A.* Boston: Unwin Hyman.

Sanchez-Korrol, V. (1983). *From Colonia to Community: The History of Puerto Ricans in New York City, 1917–1948.* Wesport, CT: Greenwood Press.

Scarano, F. A. (1993). *Puerto Rico: Cinco Siglos de Historia.* Mexico City: McGraw-Hill Interamericana.

Torre, C. A.; Rodriguez Vecchini, H.; and Burgos, W. (1994). *The Commuter Nation: Perspectives on Puerto Rican Migration.* Rio Piedras, PR: Editorial de la Universidad de Puerto Rico.

Wagenheim, K. (1975). *A Survey of Puerto Ricans on the U.S. Mainland in the 1970s.* New York: Praeger.

ARLENE TORRES

# PUNJABI MEXICANS

The biethnic group of Punjabi Mexicans was founded by immigrant men from India's northwestern Punjabi-speaking area and women of Mexican and Mexican-American ancestry. The marriages between these men and women in the early twentieth century produced a relatively small but conspicuous group clustered in the agricultural valleys of California, Arizona, and parts of Texas. The name for the group used in earlier decades, not only by outsiders but also by the couples themselves and their children, was "Hindus" or "Mexican Hindus." In the late twentieth century, "Hindu" designates a follower of the Hindu religion, but at the start of the twentieth century it was widely used to designate a person from

Wedding photo of a Punjabi-Mexican couple in Imperial Valley, California, in 1917. (Wilma Chand)

India or Hindustan (the name for India in Sanskrit and Persian). Thus these pioneers and their descendants accepted and used a name later deemed inappropriate by South Asians, including post-1965 South Asian immigrants to the United States. The name "Punjabi Mexicans" more accurately indicates the places of origin of the founders.

Within this group of some four or five hundred predominantly farming families in the American West, there were differences of religion, caste, regional origin, and class. The men were almost all speakers of Punjabi (one of India's sixteen or so major vernaculars) and from contiguous districts in the British Indian province of the Punjab, but they represented three different religions: Sikhism, Islam, and Hinduism. Some 85 percent of the men were Sikhs, followers of a religion developed in Punjab from the fifteenth century that took elements from both Islam and Hinduism to form its own distinctive texts, beliefs, and practices. Another 10 to 12 percent were Muslims, and only a small minority were actually Hindus. Almost all of

the women whom they married were Spanish-speaking Catholics, about half of them from Mexico, immigrants themselves, and half Americans of Mexican ancestry.

Despite their differences of religion, language, and national origin, these men and women formed families, and it was primarily the discriminatory laws of the time that brought them together. Shortly after 1900, Punjabi men from Hong Kong, Shanghai, India, and other parts of the British Empire began immigrating to the United States to work in California, pushed by an expanding agricultural economy coupled with pressure on the land in Punjab and pulled by better salaries abroad. But U.S. immigration policies were moving against Asians, and by 1913, Indians experienced discrimination as they tried to enter the United States. In 1917, the "Barred Zone" Act ended practically all legal immigration from Asia. Thus the Punjabi men, many of them already married, were not able to bring their wives from India to the United States. Those who wanted to settle down in the United States looked for local spouses, but in California, as in many other states, laws prohibited marriage between members of different races (until 1948 in California and until a Federal Supreme Court decision in 1967 ended all such state laws). The men from India were technically Caucasian, but they had difficulty securing licenses from county clerks to marry "white" brides. However, marriages between the Indian immigrants and women of Mexican ancestry were not opposed by the dominant Anglo or white society, and the first recorded marriage in 1916 was followed by many more.

Another external impetus behind these Punjabi-Mexican marriages was the Mexican Civil War, sending refugee women and children across the border from 1910. The Indian immigrants were among the pioneer cotton farmers in the California, Arizona, and Texas valleys along the Mexican border at that time, and they employed Mexican women and children in their cotton fields. Both attraction and economic need brought them together, and once a few women had married the "foreigners" and found them hardworking and ambitious, they arranged marriages for other Punjabi men with their sisters and nieces. Typically, Punjabi partners in farming, men in their thirties and forties, married sets of sisters, women in their teens and twenties.

## Community Structure

Internally, the community was structured in several ways. Since Punjabi families in India usually sent out only one or two among several sons to work overseas, the men were more likely to be friends or partners in farming than relatives, while many of the women were sets of sisters or otherwise related to each other. The men were also divided by religious, regional, and caste differences, which back in Punjab limited intermarriages and social intercourse; such divisiveness was lessened by their minority position in U.S. society, but it surfaced occasionally. Punjabi competitive spirit, particularly centered on the acquisition of land, produced disputes that could and often did break up the men's partnerships. In contrast, the women's kinship links remained strong. Also, the Catholic system of *compadrazgo* (godparenthood) made men and women godparents to each other's children. The compadrazgo system operated among these families despite the fact that the men did not convert to Catholicism; they retained their own religions but allowed their wives to bring up the children as Christians. Mostly illiterate and with few or no religious specialists or texts among them, the men worked long, hard days in the fields. They left the childrearing, including the teaching of religion, to the women.

Yet Sikhism, the religion of most of the men, also provided an important basis for community life among the Punjabi-Mexican families, since a Sikh temple was founded in 1912 in Stockton, California, which became a very popular center for all the Punjabis and their families. The Stockton temple, in the San Joaquin Valley on the migratory labor route from southern to northern California, hosted social and political events perhaps as frequently as religious ones well into the 1950s. Along with picnics and family reunions where

agricultural workers from Arizona, Utah, and California met on the way to seasonal jobs with "Hindu bosses" (labor contractors), gatherings to support social reforms such as female education in India or to achieve political goals were often held at the Stockton Sikh temple.

The Punjabi men fought for political rights in both India and the United States. They contributed time and money to campaigns for India's independence from British colonial rule, most notably by forming the Ghadar party in California in 1913 and sponsoring militant activities in India. They also organized and fought for citizenship rights in the United States. Some fifty-nine men had become U.S. citizens, but then access to citizenship was taken away by the U.S. Supreme Court's *Thind* decision of 1923, which stated that although Indians were Caucasian or Aryan, they were not "white" in the popular view. (U.S. citizenship was based on race; one had to be white or of African ancestry until the 1940s). This decision that the Punjabis were, like other Asians, "aliens ineligible to citizenship" had the immediate effect of denying them the right to lease or own agricultural land in California, where "alien land laws" had been passed from 1913 on to block the spectacular success of Japanese immigrant farmers. These and other discriminatory decisions and laws in the United States threatened the men's livelihoods and increased their political activism.

## Demographics

The Punjabi Mexicans were not large in number, but they had a high profile in their rural localities and in the Indian immigrant community in the United States. There were only 815 to 1,948 Indian immigrants in California at any decadal census from 1910 through 1950 (almost all immigrants to the United States from South Asia until then were Punjabis settled in California). Given this small total, the three to four hundred Punjabi Mexican families formed the core of family life in the Indian community.

County and state records show some 378 couples (and there were undoubtedly more), most of them biethnic Punjabi Mexican couples settled in California's southern Imperial County, where the earliest recorded such marriage had taken place. When the couples stayed together (the incidence of divorce and/or desertion was higher than might be expected for rural migrants from religions discouraging such actions), they had many children. The average number of children ever born to those women whose childbearing histories could be traced was 6.4 (but only 5.5 children were living at the time of the last births).

The majority of the Punjabi-Mexican couples continued to reside in the Imperial Valley, although some moved north to the valleys centered in Fresno, Stockton, Sacramento, and Yuba City—Marysville and over to Arizona, Texas, or elsewhere. In northern California the Punjabi men tended to remain bachelors and live in "Hindu camps," at least partly because Mexican migrants were slow to move up the state, making women to marry less available in the north.

## Biethnic Identity

Wherever they went, the men aggressively pursued farming opportunities, working with local Anglo or white farmers, bankers, and lawyers, and they were noticed. Most were big men from India's northwestern frontier area, members of the so-called martial and farming castes, and many had worked previously in British military or police service. The distinctive biethnic nature of the community also occasioned notice. By marrying "Hindus," most of the women had moved out of the developing Mexican-American communities in California, and there was some prejudice against the biethnic families from Mexican Americans and others (some called them "half and halves" or "Mexidus").

The children's names—Maria Jesusita Singh, José Akbar Khan, Emilio Chand—signaled their biethnic heritage. They attended the segregated "foreign section" schools, with predominantly Mexican, Asian, and black children, in the agricultural towns. Although perceived as "Hindus," their

languages were English and Spanish, and few learned Punjabi. The men knew some English from their days in colonial India under the British, and they learned Spanish to speak to Mexican agricultural workers and to their wives; English and Spanish were the usual home languages for the Punjabi Mexicans. The women rarely learned Punjabi or much about Punjabi culture. In fact, the men thought it would be impossible to reestablish contact with India, considered themselves and their families American, and raised the children accordingly. The strongest Punjabi influence in these homes was in the kitchens, where the wives learned to cook chicken curry, *roti* (Indian bread), and various Punjabi vegetables and pickles, and talked of "becoming Hindu," keeping a Hindu household.

The Punjabi-Mexican children were aware of themselves as distinctive from their early years, yet both parental groups were in some ways negative reference groups for them. As Mexicans continued

A Punjabi-Mexican funeral in Yuba City, California, in the mid-1940s. (Isabel Singh Garcia)

to enter the United States and became the largest group of agricultural laborers in the farming valleys, the Punjabi-Mexican children emphasized their "Hindu" identity. Yet the stern authority exercised by the Punjabi fathers, and their disapproval of many aspects of American teenage culture as the children grew up, sometimes led to rebellion and distancing by the children. This was particularly true for some sons, for the boys were expected to work hard for their fathers but would inherit only after their death. As the young people approached marriage age, many fathers forgot they had themselves married without regard for region, religion, or caste, and they tried to arrange marriages for their children. Just as these generational tensions were increasing within the families, external political events changed the contexts in both the United States and South Asia in which these families functioned.

## The Changing Community

South Asians became eligible for U.S. citizenship in 1946 (when the Luce-Celler Bill passed), and when British colonial rule in South Asia ended in 1947, two new nations, India and Pakistan, were born. Suddenly the South Asian men could become U.S. citizens, own their own land, and visit their homelands. Pride grew in the "Hindu" heritage, and wives and children made efforts to learn about and claim their South Asian connections. Descendants of Muslim pioneers from the new Pakistan began using a new name for themselves, "Spanish Pakistanis." A small quota was set for immigration that allowed people to bring relatives from South Asia, and the trickle of new immigrants that began in 1946 was welcomed. However, the number of newcomers increased dramatically after the Immigration Act of 1965, which redressed the discriminatory patterns of the past and welcomed large numbers of Asians, and there are many differences between the old and the new immigrants. The Punjabi-Mexican descendants have become somewhat ambivalent about their Hindu identity. Ultimately the second generation has become a

transitional one, its members mostly marrying either Anglos or Mexican Americans rather than each other or new immigrants from South Asia.

Massive new emigration from South Asia has helped push the Punjabi-Mexican descendants into the American mainstream, as the newcomers do not easily acknowledge these descendants as "Hindus" or South Asians. The new immigrants from India and Pakistan are mostly urban people from all over South Asia, representing its many linguistic regions, castes, and religions and equipped with high educational and professional qualifications. They usually arrive as family units, and they are entering a society that no longer throws up legal barriers against them but often places them very well. They cannot conceive of the conditions the Punjabi pioneer farmers encountered in early twentieth-century America, and they fail to understand the choices the pioneers made. To the newcomers, the biethnic community's "cultural loss" is a shock, one that threatens their ideas about successfully transmitting South Asian culture to their own children.

Further, with incomprehension and rejection from the newcomers, the Punjabi-Mexican descendants respond by emphasizing the values of assimilation. Indeed, unable to speak Punjabi or talk knowledgeably about South Asian religions or cultures, often unable to locate or spell correctly their ancestral places of origin, the descendants are at a considerable disadvantage when they try to place themselves on the map. They talk instead about their own American, not South Asian, identity, and about the necessity of rapid acculturation.

Descendants of the Punjabi-Mexican couples are "ethnic" in the way so many Americans are ethnic, making ethnic claims when the context makes it relevant or advantageous but knowing little about Punjabi (or Mexican) culture back in the homeland. Yet the Punjabi-Mexican descendants take tremendous pride in the political battles waged by their fathers and grandfathers, place great importance on land ownership, hard work, and honoring one's word, and serve delicious chicken curry, roti, and other special Punjabi and

Mexican preparations at festive family dinners. The Punjabi and Mexican heritages persist in these and other meaningful ways and are occasionally displayed at events such as the Yuba City Mexican Hindu Christmas Dance and the Phoenix Spanish Pakistani Reunions, events combining food and music from Mexico, Punjab, and America. Thus the group well illustrates the flexibility of culture and ethnic identity, their relational nature, and the importance of context in shaping them.

*See also:*  PAKISTANIS; PUNJABIS

## Bibliography

Hess, G. R. (1982). "The Asian Indian Immigrants in the United States, 1900–1965." *Population Review* 25:29–34.

Jacoby, H. S. (1979). "Some Demographic and Social Aspects of Early East Indian Life in the United States." In *Sikh Studies,* edited by N. G. Barrier and M. Juergensmeyer. Berkeley, CA: Graduate Theological Union.

Jensen, J. M. (1988). *Passage from India: Asian Indian Immigrants in North America.* New Haven, CT: Yale University Press.

La Brack, B. (1988). *The Sikhs of Northern California, 1904–1975: A Sociohistorical Study.* New York: AMS Press.

Leonard, K. (1992). *Making Ethnic Choices: California's Punjabi-Mexican Americans.* Philadelphia: Temple University Press.

McWilliams, C. (1978). *Factories in the Field: The Story of Migratory Labor in California.* Salt Lake City: Peregrine Smith.

Mears, E. G. (1978). *Resident Orientals on the American Pacific Coast,* 2nd edition. New York: Arno Press.

Puri, H. K. (1983). *Ghadar Movement.* Amritsar, India: Guru Nanak Dev University Press.

Saund, D. S. (1960). *Congressman from India.* New York: E. P. Dutton.

Singh, J., ed. (1988). *South Asians in North American: An Annotated and Selected Bibliography.* Berkeley, CA: Center for South and Southeast Asia Studies.

Taylor, P. S., and Vasey, T. (1936). "Historical Background of California Farm Labor." *Rural Sociology* I:281–295.

KAREN ISAKSEN LEONARD

# PUNJABIS

Punjabis (also spelled "Panjabi") have been and continue to be a dominant South Asian community in the United States. Yet recognition has alluded them because a subcommunity, such as the Sikhs, or a nationality, such as Pakistani or Indian, has received the notoriety or been the primary community of identification. As a result, Punjabis have been a "hidden community."

A Punjabi is one who claims the geographical region of Punjab as his or her ancestral homeland and the Punjabi language as the tongue of identification, whether the individual actually speaks it or not. Punjab is located in the extreme northwestern corner of South Asia and bridges both India and Pakistan. It is bounded by Jammu and Kashmir and Northwest Frontier Province to the north, Afghanistan and Baluchistan to the west, Sind and Rajasthan to the south, and Uttar Pradesh to the east.

Since 1947, Punjab has been divided politically between India and Pakistan, and within India, the states of Haryana and Himachal Pradesh have been created. Since the mid-1980s, the people of Haryana have emphasized their distinctiveness because they are Hindus and do not want to be subordinated to the Sikhs, who claim Punjab as their homeland. The people of Himachel Pradesh are also located in Punjab but are Pahari and, like other people of the mountains, claim Mongolian ancestry, while Punjabis claim descendent from the Aryans.

There is a great deal of diversity among Punjabis. A Punjabi may be a Pakistani or an Indian, a Hindu, Sikh, Christian, or Muslim, and a member of any caste. In spite of this diversity, Punjabis share a common language (Punjabi), dress (*salwarkameez,* a long tunic top over baggy drawstring trousers, with men wearing a turban and the women a *dupata,* a two-meter length of cloth draped over the head and shoulders), history, tradition, kinship pattern, village political structure (especially the *panchayat,* a ruling council of five members), arts, literature, ritual, and cultural concepts.

## Immigration and Settlement History

The immigration of Punjabis to North America began around 1904, when Sikhs of the Punjab immigrated to western Canada. They originated from the Doaba and Malwa regions. Drifting down from Vancouver to Bellingham, Washington, where they worked in the lumber trade, Punjabis were resented by local workers and forced south to seek employment in the rich farming areas of the Sacramento, San Joaquin, and Imperial valleys. Their recorded history centers on the Punjabi community in California. They suffered not only because of discrimination but also because they supported India's struggle for independence — British agents actively worked to have them prosecuted for not maintaining neutrality, especially during the periods surrounding the two world wars.

Their numbers were small. Of the seven thousand people of India entering the United States

A Punjabi Sikh wears the traditional turban. (Mukul Roy)

between 1904 and 1923, probably forty-five hundred were Punjabis. Due to racist laws, there were periods when they, like other Asians, could not become citizens or had their citizenship revoked. In California there were times when they could not own land because they were not citizens. And due to restrictive immigrations laws, especially the Immigration Act of 1917 (also termed the Indian Exclusion Act), they could not return to India or they would not be able to reenter the United States. Thus they could not bring or acquire spouses from India. As a result, some remained in the United States while continuing to send money back to Punjab to support kinsmen. Others married Mexican women, which gave rise to the Punjabi-Mexican community.

During this time, a few students and businessmen entered but were scattered residentially. Some, such as J. J. Singh, gained notoriety as they attempted to persuade America to side with the revolutionary movement in India. Others, such as Bhagat Singh Thind, used the legal system to fight for people from India to have equal rights in the United States.

After World War II, scholarships, primarily under Fulbright-Hays legislation, and exchange programs stimulated Punjabi and other South Asians and foreign students to pursue higher education in the United States; many of them are now respected professors in South Asian colleges and universities. However, the current wave of Punjabi immigration parallels that of the Asian influx into the United States that resulted from passage of the Immigration and Nationality Act of 1965. By eliminating national quotas and implementing a preference system based on family reunification and qualifications, the United States gained a large number of highly educated, professional, and superbly technically qualified Punjabis, as it did from other Asian countries. Also, Punjabis stress education, and when being educated resulted in preference to enter the United States, a host of qualified individuals were ready to take advantage of the opportunity. Also, the Punjabi education system was based on the British format and later was influenced by American practices. Thus those who entered the United States after 1968 generally knew English, were acquainted with American and Western culture, and were highly educated, enabling them to enter the upper economic levels of American society immediately.

Return migration has also increased, starting in the 1990s. Since India, especially the Hyderabad area, has become a place for international companies to set up high-tech and manufacturing operations, Punjabis with managerial skills and professional experience are returning to India to establish a business or to take a management position for a multinational company operating or starting operations in India.

## Demographics

Before the Immigration and Nationality Act of 1965, about 60 percent of South Asians entering the United States were Punjabi. After 1968, when the act went into effect, about 25 percent were Punjabi, so that by the mid-1990s, numbers in the United States were around 300,000, with the vast majority arriving after 1970. Up to 1980, the vast majority were highly trained professional, managerial, and business individuals.

With the family reunification clause of the 1965 legislation, which allowed citizens to sponsor relatives, sponsoring kinsmen accounted for a significant amount of the influx after 1980. Thus, before 1970, most Punjabi immigrants entered via California to work in agriculture or at manual labor, or they were students. Between 1968 and 1980, the vast majority were young, well educated (primarily in medicine, engineering, or other sciences), brought their spouses and children, and were quickly able to obtain good employment in their chosen field.

After 1980, those who became citizens generally sponsored family members. As a result, the average educational and occupational quality of entrants lowered. An hourglass-shaped society began developing, with one group occupying the upper economic stratum, another in the lower economic sphere, and few in the middle. The overall financial and educational average is still very high, so they can claim to be a community with one of the highest family income and education levels in the United States.

## Language

The early settlers who worked in California's agricultural industry spoke Punjabi only. The educated professional Punjabi immigrants, who were very few before 1968 but dominated thereafter, were trilingual, speaking Hindi, Punjabi, and English.

A Punjabi press did not develop, but *Ghadar*, a periodic newspaper published in 1913 that advocated revolution in India, was published in Gurmukhi, a script developed by the second Sikh guru, Guru Angad, in the mid-sixteenth century. Gurmukhi was a modification of the Landa script, the same script used to write Punjabi. Thus Gurmukhi is considered a Punjabi or modified Punjabi script. Gurmukhi is also the script used in the *World Sikh News* and other Sikh publications. But a Punjabi press for Punjabis has not developed.

Today, where language maintenance is concerned, one often hears of classes in Hindi or Gurmukhi but very seldom classes in Punjabi; thus second-generation Punjabis generally do not know their ethnic language.

## Cultural Characteristics

Economically affluent Punjabis are dispersed in the United States. They like privacy but want the availability of kinsmen and friends for socialization and support in times of need. The good road and communication systems of the United States enable social networks to be maintained despite residential scattering. Punjabis can live away from the close scrutiny of other Punjabis yet be with friends and relatives in minutes or hours.

The worldview of the Punjabi is one of self-confidence and superiority. Punjab, located on the invasion route into India, has been a breeding ground for the indigenous population to learn

Punjabi Americans participate in a traditional dance performance. (Mukul Roy)

survival in spite of adversity. Thus Punjabis are self-assured, aggressive, and innovative.

Marriage to another Punjabi of the same caste is preferred. Also, factors such as the *izzat* (honor of the family) as well as the compatibility of the mate are considered. These factors are expecially important to those of rural origin, who often turn to a village of their home region for a spouse. As Punjabis become part of the professions and become more economically affluent and educated, a marriage partner with at least a bachelor of arts degree and raised in the West, but still a Punjabi, becomes more of a priority. Also, the wishes of the individuals involved are particularly important to upper-class urbanized professionals residing in the West.

As marriage partners are closely linked with the land of origin, so are social relationships. Punjabis might invite others to their social functions, but their closest relationships are with kinsmen first, followed by others of the same region, caste, and sociocultural orientation. Although to observe their behavior in their profession, they appear thoroughly Westernized, a close look at home and social networks reveals otherwise. Traditional norms play a very strong role in many areas of life, including beliefs, social relationships, normative and acceptable behavior, marriage, dress, and food.

Punjabi art forms do not have the intricate work of art forms in many other cultures. In music, dance, and pictures they depict a robust and self-confident peasantry who can overcome adversity by hard work, manual dexterity, and quick thinking. However, a distinct school of writing is developing among the emigrant community. Themes abound of nostalgia for the homeland, the captivity of being in the industrialized West, and conflicts resulting from having left the homeland. In practice Punjabis in the United States seem to be as healthy and robust as their arts and worldview indicate.

It is in the area of political, community, and social organization that Punjabis have not been noticeable. Generally, religious or national concerns have taken precedence over those of Punjab. It was only in the later part of the 1980s that Punjabi associations started developing. These associations are for the most part concerned with social and cultural activities. They generally plan events such as performances of musicians and dancers and have social events such as dinners or picnics. When Punjabis immigrate, they usually form an Indian and/or Pakistani association. As their numbers increase, the communities begin to factionalize according to regional or religious affiliation. A Punjabi association would be formed at this time. But since there are few issues concerning Punjabis in general that take precedence over national or religious concerns, the need to establish associations based on being a Punjabi has not been a high priority.

One exception to the above is in academia, where the study of Punjab has been strong because of the success in food production and economic growth in that region. Also, academic study of Punjab has been promoted by the Research Committee on Punjab, a group of scholars who have made the region their focus of study.

## Assimilation and Cultural Persistence

The perception of discrimination among Punjabis varies. A number have made it to the top in their endeavors. Others, both affluent and not so affluent, feel discrimination. Some feel that there is a glass ceiling where, because they are not white, they are not promoted above a certain level. Others feel uncomfortable because when they are seen as not white, they are perceived as different and inferior. Still others resent the fact that their credentials and education may not be given the same recognition as those of a person who has been educated in or had work experience in the United States.

Punjabis, like other South Asians, are working to be part of the pan-Asian movement. Like other Asians, they realize that they alone are not sufficiently strong to have a substantial voice in the judicial and political processes of the United States.

With increased efficiency in international transportation and communication, transnational ties have been maintained, so that Punjabis can live in the United States and yet actively participate in the affairs of their place of origin in Punjab. For most, involvement takes the form of investing, sending money to their family in Punjab, or having land there. Telephone calls are almost weekly and visits to Punjab average once every other year, so transnational personal ties are very strong.

*See also:*   PAKISTANIS; PUNJABI MEXICANS

## Bibliography

Barrier, N. G. (1991). "The Evolution of Punjab Studies, 1972–1978." In *Punjab in Perspective: Proceedings of the Research Committee on Punjab Conference, 1987,* edited by S. Dulai and A. Helweg. East Lansing: Asian Studies Center, Michigan State University.

Bedi, S. S. (1971). *Folklore of Punjab.* New Delhi: National Book Trust.

Dulai, S. S. (1991). "The Severed Kite: Punjabi Writing in Great Britain and North America." In *Punjab in Perspective: Proceedings of the Research Committee on Punjab Conference, 1987,* edited by S. Dulai and A. Helweg. East Lansing: Asian Studies Center, Michigan State University.

Fenton, J. Y. (1988). *Transplanting Religious Traditions: Asian Indians in America.* New York: Praeger.

Gibson, M. A. (1988). *Accomodation Without Assimilation: Sikh Immigrants in an America High School.* Ithaca, NY: Cornell University Press.

Helweg, A. (1991). "Punjabi Immigrants in America: Focus on the Family." In *Punjab in Perspective: Proceedings of the Research Committee on Punjab Conference, 1987,* edited by S. Dulai and A. Helweg. East Lansing: Asian Studies Center, Michigan State University.

Judge, P. (1993). *Punjabis in Canada: A Study of Formation of an Ethnic Community.* Delhi: Chanakaya Books.

Kessinger, T. G. (1974). *Vilyatpur, 1848–1968: Social and Economic Change in a North Indian Village.* Berkeley: University of California Press.

La Brack, B. (1988). *The Sikhs of Northern California, 1904–1975.* New York: AMS Press.

Leaf, M. J. (1984). *Song of Hope: The Green Revolution in a Punjab Village.* New Brunswick, NJ: Rutgers University Press.

Leonard, K. I. (1992). *Making Ethnic Choices: Cali-

*fornia's Punjabi Mexican Americans.* Philadelphia: Temple University Press.

Mehta, V. (1984). *The Ledge Between the Streams.* New York: W. W. Norton.

Saberwal, S. (1990). *Mobile Men.* New Delhi: Manohar.

Tandon, P. (1961). *Punjabi Century, 1857–1947.* Berkeley: University of California Press.

Tandon, P. (1971). *Beyond Punjab.* Delhi: Thomson Press.

Tandon, P. (1980). *Return to Punjab.* New Delhi: Vikas.

Tewari, V. N. (1984). *Punjab: A Cultural Profile.* New Delhi: Vikas.

ARTHUR W. HELWEG

# QUÉBECOIS

*See* FRENCH CANADIANS

# ROMANIANS

Romanians (also known as Rumanians or Roumanians) first immigrated to the United States in significant numbers between 1895 and 1920. During that time there were many complications in determining exactly who was Romanian. Some scholars and Romanian nationalists firmly equate Romanianess with membership in the Romanian Orthodox Church, but the issue is not that simple. By 1920, about 9 percent of Romanian immigrants in the United States had come from the Old Kingdom of Romania; 85 percent from Transylvania, Bukovina, and the Banat; and the remainder from Bulgaria, Serbia, Macedonia, Thrace, and Greece. Thus a majority of Romanian immigrants before 1918, when the Romanian Kingdom (Greater Romania) was established, came from parts of the Balkans that did not belong to Romania, and were often counted as Russians, Austrians, Hungarians, or some other nationality, even though they were ethnic Romanians and spoke Romanian. Furthermore, some immigrants, such as Hungarians coming from Romanian Transylvania after 1918, were erroneously counted as Romanian. In addition, there was the question of how to count Romanian-speaking Jews from the region. Early census figures were therefore often misleading and inaccurate. Generally scholars of Romanian immigration treat as Romanian all who call themselves Romanian, even if they are not members of the Romanian Orthodox Church. Thus Jews, Protestants, Catholics, and Uniates (Byzantine-rite Greek Catholics) are included, while Hungarians from Romania are not.

## Group Definition

While Romanians were usually identified by their membership in the Orthodox Church, criteria for group identity can also include marriage within the group and retention of language. Thus while the establishment of Romanian Orthodox churches and residential neighborhoods in communities across America offered visible ethnic identity, the perpetuation of this ethnicity depended on keeping the culture through marrying within the group and speaking the language. In addition, variations within the Romanian communities included the previously cited non-Orthodox Christian groups from Romania. From the past to the present, Romanians Jews have also constituted a subgroup within the Romanian immigrant community. In the early period of immigration, Romanian Baptists

Three Romanian immigrants, upon their arrival in New York City in 1949, drink a toast to each other before going their separate ways to join family members who had previously immigrated to the United States. (UPI/Corbis-Bettmann)

founded churches in the United States in several cities, and since the 1970s, noticeable pockets of Romanian Pentecostal groups have arrived. Small numbers of Roman Catholics and Uniates of Romanian ethnicity also came during the early period.

## Immigration and Settlement History

Most of the early Romanian immigrants arriving between 1895 and 1920 were men aged eighteen to forty-five. Many were married, with children; the dependents were sent for after the men became established, usually within five years. Lack of equitable land distribution and a high birthrate forced many peasant families from the land in Romania, and labor opportunities in North America beckoned. The largest numbers came from Bukovina and Transylvania.

Many early immigrants intended to make money in the United States and return. The phrase *mia și drumul* expressed this: $1,000 and home again. In fact, there was considerable return migration, with perhaps 20 percent moving back to Romania from 1906 to 1920.

The initial emigration from Romania was hard. They left from Bremen, Hanover, and Trieste after a long overland journey in Europe. The sea voyage in steerage was difficult; each year, scores died en route. Many feared being turned back in New York, and about 2 percent were.

Most of the Romanian immigrants got jobs as laborers in the iron and steel industry, and in coal mining, automobile manufacturing, and in the rubber and meat packing industries. This took them to such cities as Pittsburgh, Erie, Cleveland, Detroit, Gary, Indiana Harbor, and Chicago. There were smaller communities in Minneapolis, St.

Paul, South St. Paul, St. Louis, Los Angeles, and San Francisco. Until the 1970s, Cleveland and Detroit had the largest Romanian communities. While most of the early immigrants had been peasant farmers, more than 90 percent worked as urban laborers in the United States. (This is very different from the early Romanian immigrants to Canada, most of whom became homesteading farmers in the praire provinces of Saksatchewan and Alberta.)

Three groups have arrived since the end of World War II: the Forty-eighters, the *noi veniţi* (newly arrived), and the postcommunism immigrants. Members of the first group were victims of the war and arrived from refugee camps in Europe in the 1940s and 1950s. The *noi veniţi* escaped from Communist Romania from the 1960s until the fall of the regime in 1989. Soon after 1989, restrictive immigration policies limited the number of Romanians allowed into the United States, as their refugee status was removed.

The traditional Romanian immigrant centers of Cleveland, Detroit, and Chicago began to decrease in importance in the 1970s. Retirees from the old communities moved to Florida, Arizona, and Southern California.

Most of the early immigrants were uneducated peasants. The post–World War II immigrants were better educated. Many who escaped the Communist regime were professional people and found employment opportunities in the New York area and in Los Angeles, the two cities with the fastest-growing Romania population during the 1990s. A number of these most recent Romanian immigrants, due to their higher educational levels and relief at being able to leave Romania, do not need the comfort of an ethnic Romanian community and have settled apart from other Romanians in numerous towns and cities across the country.

## Demographics

There was a trickle of Romanian immigration in the nineteenth century; the largest numbers came from 1900 to 1910, by which time 82,000 had arrived; by 1920, there were about 100,000

Romanians in the United States. Restrictive immigration policies kept the number stable between World War I and World War II. Since that time, however, and especially since the revolution of 1989, the number of Romanians in the United States had increased to 235,774 of first ancestry and 129,770 of second ancestry by 1990. Descendants of the immigrants to the early communities of Cleveland and Detroit have now reached the third and fourth generation and are largely assimilated. With the passing of the Forty-eighters and the *noi veniţi* aging, the demographics of the postcommunism group mimes that of the early immigrants: They are young. It differs from the first group, however, in that there are as many new female immigrants as male.

## Language

The early immigrants were not well educated and spoke only Romanian upon arrival, though they gradually learned English. The better-educated immigrants after World War II often spoke Romanian and French — the second language of educated Romanians in the past — and many knew some English. The fall of communism has seen a significant shift to English as the primary foreign language offered in Romanian schools, and most arrivals since 1989 have some knowledge of English.

The postwar immigrants not only often brought a knowledge of more than one language, they also wanted to shed the cultural baggage associated with a totalitarian political system, so their motivation to learn English and assimilate was strong. This has resulted in a more rapid loss of the language among Romanians in America than among some other immigrant groups. Except in the early period, few Romanian-language schools were associated with the churches; the churches themselves have had to switch their liturgical language from Romanian to English with increasing frequency in response to the loss of the Romanian language within the community.

A Romanian-language press developed early: the first newspaper was *Romanul* (The Romanian), founded in Cleveland in 1905. Following that came *America* in 1906 and *Lumina* (Light) in 1922. Most of the early papers represented religious factions, often virulent; in reaction to them an anticlerical paper called *Crocodilul Roman* (The Romanian Crocodile) was founded. These papers met the needs of the first- and second-generation immigrants but became less relevant to subsequent generations. Among the later arrivals the papers represented antiquated factions of Balkan immigrant feuding with which they wanted no part. The papers began to close in the 1970s.

A revitalization of the Romanian-language press began with the arrival of political refugees in the 1970s and 1980s. Almost overnight *Lumea Libera Romaneasca* (Free Romanian World), *Micro Magazin* (Little Newspaper), and *Miorita Noastra* (Our Legend) were founded in New York, *Lupta* (Struggle) in Providence, and *Universul* (The Universe) in Los Angeles. *Universul* is also printed and distributed in Bucharest and in Chișinau (Kișinev), Moldova.

Although there were once generational differences regarding fluency in English, this has decreased with a younger immigrant population with better schooling, including training in English.

## Cultural Characteristics

Homeland Romanian cultural patterns have generally prepared the immigrants to be successful middle-class Americans. There is a strong work ethic and emphasis on education that has resulted in gradual upward social mobility: The early immigrants were laborers; their children and grandchildren are middle-class business and professional people. The more recent immigrants, a high percentage of whom had professional educations and careers in Romania, have generally been able to regain that status in the United States after some professional relicensing.

Housing patterns for Romanian immigrants have evolved from working-class ethnic neighborhoods near the centers of the early cities of residence, to middle-class suburban living.

More than 90 percent of Romanians in the United States belong to the Romanian Orthodox Church, and to an extent, the church has played a role in perpetuating national cultural values and language, though this role has decreased markedly. Internecine feuding was common in the history of the North American church: A schism occurred in 1952 when the Romanian Orthodox Episcopate of America split from the Romanian Orthodox Missionary Epsicopate in America. The schism is still not healed, though with time the split has become less relevant to the younger generations.

The Romanian worldview in the United States is religious and relatively traditional without being particularly zealous or ethnocentric, though secular and rational views mesh the group with dominant mainstream American thought as education and assimilation increase.

Marriage has tended to be lasting and stable, and family and kinship are important. Extended family networks dominated in the early communities, but assimilation in the United States and the trend toward the nuclear family in the homeland after World War II have weakened this pattern. Romanians practice interpersonal relations in ways consistent with that of mainstream America. Romanian drama, dance, and music have flourished through ethnic artistic groups in the United States. Romanians stress preventive medicine and nutrition; analysis of the Romanian-language press in the United States, with articles and advertisements about such issues, verifies this. Romanians have ethnic-based social and political groups, and a few have moved into positions in local and state government and politics. In short, Romanians are becoming integrated middle-class Americans, indistinguishable from the dominant culture except in terms of religion, language, and cuisine.

## Assimilation and Cultural Persistence

Romanian ethnicity in the United States tends not to be nonrational, primordial, and coercive. Rather it is voluntary, pragmatic, functional, and situational. Many Romanian Americans wear their ethnic hats when it suits them and act like mainstream, assimilated Americans the rest of the time. Much of Romanian ethnicity in America is symbolic, with some of the rites of passage, folk dancing, holiday celebrations, and homeland food consumption a re-created tradition, especially among the third and fourth generations.

Assimilation among Romanians in North America has been measured using two primary criteria: marriage outside the group and loss of language. Using these measures, some 80 to 90 percent of the descendants of the early immigrants have become assimilated, while the new arrivals in New York and Los Angeles, even after five to ten years, have rates of marriage outside the group and loss of language of about 50 percent.

Among those Romanians in the United States who are keeping the culture, that culture is somewhat altered from homeland patterns. The inevitable religious, linguistic, ceremonial, and culinary adaptations of Romanian immigrants constitute what could be termed the third culture, neither fully Romanian nor fully American.

That homeland cultural patterns are embraced by fewer and fewer Romanians in America does not mean that the culture is being lost in the new setting, for as new generations assimilate, new arrivals infuse the ethnic communities with the homeland culture, which is readapted to fit the American situation. Examples of this can be found in food, language, and church liturgy, all of which are constantly being revised and partially Americanized.

Little discrimination has been experienced by Romanians in America, and relations with other groups are generally good, though there is some mistrust between Romanians and Hungarians, and between Romanian Orthodox Christians and members of the Romanian Jewish community.

The fall of communism and the subsequent freedom to travel to and from Romania have increased the transnational characteristics of some Romanian immigrants. Small numbers have returned from the United States to Romania to live and work, but some of these have become disillusioned and reimmigrated to the United States. Judging by the increase in travel agency use and

flights between the United States and Romania, there is a greater interchange between the two countries than ever before, suggesting an increasing transnational adaptation by some recent immigrants, who, while better able than their predecessors to assimilate behaviorally, are also able to retain their biculturality due to favorable political relations and easy communication and movement between the two countries.

Nevertheless, even among the immigrants of the 1990s, more are assimilating than keeping strong homeland ties. Most Romanians in America are proud Americans, relieved and glad to be in the country, and have little interest in returning to the poor, unstable country they or their ancestors left. The Romanians in the United States do not reject their Romanian heritage and proudly celebrate it when it meets their needs to do so, but they do not consider it essential to perpetuate in America a homeland culture which has been less sustaining and gratifying to them than the homeland culture of many other immigrants. They are assimilating.

*See also:* AUSTRIANS; BULGARIANS; GREEKS; HUNGARIANS; MACEDONIANS; SERBS

## Bibliography

Barton, J. (1976). *Peasants and Strangers: Italians, Rumanians, and Slovaks in an American City, 1890–1950.* Cambridge, MA: Harvard University Press.

Bobango, G. J. (1979). *The Romanian Orthodox Episcopate of America: The First Half Century, 1929–1979.* Jackson, MI: Romanian-American Heritage Center.

Galitzi, C. ([1929] 1968). *A Study of Assimilation Among the Roumanians in the United States.* New York: AMS Press.

Patterson, G. J. (1977). *The Romanians of Saskatchewan: Four Generations of Adaptation.* Ottawa: National Museum of Man.

Patterson, G. J. (1986). "The Persistence of White Ethnicity in Canada: The Case of the Romanians." *East European Quarterly* 19:493–500.

Patterson, G. J. (1991). "Greek and Romanian Immigrants as Hyphenated Americans: Towards a Theory of White Ethnicity." In *New Directions in Greek*

*American Studies,* edited by D. Georgakas and C. C. Moskos. New York: Pella.

Patterson, G. J., and Petrescu, P. (1992). "The Romanian Language Press in America." *East European Quarterly* 27:261–270.

G. JAMES PATTERSON

# RUSSIAN MOLOKANS

Today's Molokans are descendants of Russians who broke away from the official Orthodox Church in the late eighteenth century, suffering various degrees of persecution for their contrary beliefs. There are three main groups: the Steadfast (Postoyannie), the more charismatic Holy Jumpers (Dukhovnie Priguny), and the followers of the more extreme Maxim Rudometkin, the Maximisty. A vast number of these accepted the czarist government's offer of exile in the Caucasus Mountains between southern Russia and Georgia. Later, many took advantage of social liberalization following Russia's 1905 war with Japan and immigrated to California.

The area of Los Angeles where the Molokans settled acquired the name "Russian Town." By the 1930s, the community was suffering its first signs of acculturation as many Molokans gradually abandoned their traditional Russian ways. The more staunch believers felt the inspiration for a *Pokhod* (exodus) and set up communities in other parts of California and Arizona and in South America.

In 1949, members of another large Molokan community that had remained in the Caucasus and later fled from Soviet collectivization across the border to Iran immigrated to America. They flew directly from Iran to settle with their brethren in Los Angeles. However, city life did not agree with them, and in the early 1950s, most migrated to the rural Willamette Valley in Oregon upon hearing tales from religiously affiliated Russian Doukhobors in Canada who had once worked in Oregon. The Oregon community of Molokans now numbers approximately nine hundred. As a recent immigration, the Oregon community preserves the Molokan way of life in a fairly authentic, traditional manner.

There are more than twenty congregations, with an estimated thirty thousand members in North America. There are no statistics on the local communities with regard to population size, family size, and gender ratios. However, the impression derived from the Oregon community is that Molokan families normally consist of four to five children. Second- and third-generation Molokan families appear to have fewer children, probably due to economic factors.

The lack of emphasis among the Molokans on higher education is the reason for the predominance in their ranks of skilled laborers. In former times there was little opportunity for education in the isolated villages and in the remote areas of exile to which the Molokans were sent.

The name "Molokan" derives from the Russian word for milk (*moloko*). They are sometimes referred to as "milk drinkers," since they do not refrain from milk and other foods prohibited during Orthodox fasts. Another explanation refers to the formation of one of the early groups on the Milk River in Russia. Many current-day Molokans account for the name by reference to the Apostle Peter, who remarked that the study of Christ is the milk of spiritual expression.

The Molokan year follows the Jewish calendar "give or take a day or so," as the Molokans say. The names of the holidays on the Molokan calendar, however, refer to Christian events, in contrast to events on the Jewish calendar. For this reason Molokans are sometimes referred to as "Jewish Christians."

The division between the older generation who speak and understand Russian and the influx of second-generation Molokans in California who have all but lost the language eventually resulted in forming other Molokan congregations.

## Meetings

For many dedicated Molokans, services at the *sobraniye* (meetings) are not only the most important events in life but also are the only events that carry significance. All the rest is time, toil, and trouble. One of the older Molokans expressed it clearly by saying, "We just work to survive; get through the week for Sunday; and on Sunday we go to the meeting. And there we sing and worship and feel the Holy Spirit among us."

The meeting hall where services are held is not officially blessed as a church, and only rarely and analogously referred to with outsiders as the "church." Instead the Molokans refer to it as the sobraniye, understood as the place as well as the activity of meeting. For Molokans, congregating at a prayer meeting to stand and sing, and kneel and pray together, creates a holy atmosphere.

The main hall is plain; a rectangular room devoid of any permanent furniture or fixtures, consistent with the Molokans' rejection of what they consider religious idols and artifacts such as crosses, icons, and other religious symbols. At prayer services a table is placed in the eastern corner of the hall. The holy books, bread and salt, and offerings are placed on this makeshift altar.

During prayer services an area is left open beside the table-altar by the worshipers. This area becomes the Krug (Circle). It is the equivalent of the Holy of Holies in a tabernacle, but the Circle exists only during the services. When Molokans gather, pray, and sing, the Holy Spirit is believed to descend to touch those in the Circle with a blessing. Young children are christened in the Circle; young couples are blessed in marriage there; others enter the Circle to make a request and give thanks. At a funeral, the casket is brought into the Circle, and all gather around for the funeral farewell. During times other than prayer, the Circle becomes just another part of the hall. At special events, when there is a dinner, benches and tables can be set up to turn the entire room into a dining hall.

## Nash/Nye Nash

Young people are taught during their formative years to differentiate between those who are Molokans, *nash* (ours), and those who are not, *nye nash* (not our own). Children and young people are consistently steered toward activities within the Molokan community. Contact with outsiders is discouraged.

Though Molokan children attend public school and have friends there, they are encouraged not to bring these friends into the Molokan community. After school, children are encouraged to take part in community activities with other Molokans. Molokans place great emphasis on the importance of marrying within the faith. Those who marry outsiders are restricted from full participation in the Molokan community.

The selection of officials, or any collective act, is accomplished in the Molokan Church through inspiration and confirmation by the Holy Spirit, working through the members to indicate a harmonious, consensual agreement.

## Singing

The Molokans love to sing. They sing at services, during their dinners, and when they have other gatherings. The "Word," as spoken or sung, establishes their direct relationship with God, eliminating the need for an ordained priest.

They occasionally break into harmony while singing hymns with a strong cadence. Both psalms and hymns form an extremely important part of the service and are sung in Russian.

## Appearance and Language

Molokans usually wear traditional clothing, reminiscent of South Russian Cossack dress, for their religious services. A man wears a *rubashka* (shirt) and a *poyas* (cord belt) with tasseled ends tied around the waist. There is a decided preference for beards. A woman wears a long-sleeved jacket-style bodice with a matching full skirt that extends below the ankles and an apron. A married woman wears a *kosinka* (special scarf). Regular Western clothing is worn at times other than religious worship services. It would be difficult to tell a Molokan by appearance during weekdays.

Where there are a number of older members not conversant in English, religious services are conducted for the most part in the Russian language. The young, on the other hand, and older second-generation Americans, have lost conversational Russian. However, they have been exposed to the principal phrases used within the religious services and voice them when speaking. Molokan Sunday schools teach Russian and Scripture with mixed success in many congregations.

Since the breakup of the Soviet Union, contact with Molokans in Russia is revitalizing many of the traditions, and exchanges have renewed an interest in the Russian language for American Molokans.

## Authority Patterns

Molokan authority is not characteristically stringent. The concept of Molokan harmony is based on the communal aspects of their communities, with a lay pastor for their religious services. Men, certainly, take leading roles. It is the men who lead the way into the Sobraniye, walking the women in and saying a prayer for the family group. It is the men who give the *besedi* (testimonies), say the common prayers, start the singing, and take responsibility for conduct in the family. Molokans are historically conscientious objectors and do not believe in carrying weapons. Their prohibition against war and killing is connected to the concept that every person is a brother or sister, inasmuch as all people are made in God's image.

## Food and Drink

Molokans subscribe to Mosaic laws in connection with food and its preparation. Permitted are the meat of animals with cloven hoof, fowl, and scaly fish. Pork, pawed animals, and shellfish are excluded. Moreover, the food should be prepared in a ritually clean manner by one's own people.

The older Molokans raise much of their own food in a garden and keep their own animals. They avoid eating in restaurants when making long road trips to join other Molokan festivities. However, younger Molokans have fewer inhibitions about buying food in markets or eating in restaurants.

Molokans enjoy tea and serve it as a mark of hospitality. Also, tea is used to seal agreements on engagements, weddings, or other important occasions. To be invited for "tea" means that something special will take place. Alcoholic beverages are strictly forbidden.

## Conclusion

With regard to social integration, Molokans tend to keep to themselves and tend not to participate in outside community functions. In times of hardships or adversity, they turn to their Sobraniye, tolerating the event until the danger has passed.

The elder Molokans are the most content. Their involvement and participation in religious services reach far beyond the mere activities and includes their frame of reference. Having been born and raised in troubled times and difficult places, Molokans revere their Sobraniye as a place of solace, salvation, and sanctity. These more abstract boundaries have remained invulnerable to threats, persecutions, and outright abuse. It is for these boundaries that the Molokans express thanks by saying in their own particular way, *Spasy Gospod* (God save).

*See also:*   RUSSIAN OLD BELIEVERS; RUSSIANS

## Bibliography

Dunn, E., and Dunn, S. P. (1977a). "Molokans in America." *Dialectic Anthropology* 2:4.

Dunn, E., and Dunn, S. P. (1977b). "Religion and Ethnicity: The Case of the American Molokans." *Ethnicity* 4:370–379.

Dunn, S., and Dunn, E. (1964). "Religion as an Instrument of Culture Change: The Problem of the Sects in the Soviet Union." *Slavic Review* 23:459–478.

Dunn, S., and Dunn, E. (1967). *The Peasants of Central Russia.* New York: Holt, Rinehart and Winston.

Hardwick, S. (1993). *Russian Refuge: Religion, Migration, and Settlement on the North American Pacific Rim.* Chicago: University of Chicago Press.

Moore, W. B. (1973). *Molokan Oral Tradition: Legends and Memorates of an Ethnic Sect.* Berkeley: University of California Press.

Moore, W. B. (1976). "Communal Experiments as Resolution of Sectarian Identity Crises." *International Review of Modern Sociology* 6:92–112.

Morris, R. A. (1991). *Old Russian Ways: Cultural Variations Among Three Russian Groups in Oregon.* New York: AMS Press.

Young, P. V. (1932). *Pilgrims of Russian-Town: The Community of Spiritual Christian Jumpers in America.* New York: Russell & Russell.

RICHARD A. MORRIS
SERAFIMA E. NIKITINA

# RUSSIAN OLD BELIEVERS

Descendants of Orthodox Russians whose ancestors refused to accept the church reforms to the ritual of the mid-seventeenth century are known as Old Ritualists, or Old Believers. Reformists of the day referred to them as *raskol'niki* (those who have split away). Old Believers, however, insist that they continue on the true path of Russian Orthodoxy and that the reformists have broken with the faith.

In America, there are two main communities of Old Believers. The community that settled in the area of Erie, Pennsylvania, around 1905 has largely integrated into the host society. Few speak Russian, and their observances of Old Ritualism are largely restricted to religious services conducted in English. The Erie Old Believers number roughly seven hundred in all, but they have splintered into various subgroups.

The other—the Old Believer community in Oregon—began arriving in the United States in the early 1960s, and now boasts more than six thousand members. The Oregon community continues to preserve traditional Russian religious and cultural ways, does not recognize the validity of the Erie community, and has its own distinct history. Associated Old Believer groups have since migrated from Oregon to Alaska (approximately one thousand) and Canada (approximately five hundred).

## Historical Background

Since the christening of Rus in 988 by declaration of Grand Prince Vladimir, and the later transformations of Rus into Russia and other eastern Slavic countries, Christian Orthodoxy has been the chief religion of Russia, and at times its state religion. This offshoot of Eastern Orthodox Christianity originated in Byzantium and Greece. Its rituals and doctrines were introduced into converted countries through vernacular languages, with a consequent cultural-laden "drift" from the original. Thus developed Russian Pravoslavia, a particular version of Eastern Orthodoxy imbued with elements of Russian culture.

In the mid-seventeenth century, the newly appointed patriarch of the Russian Orthodox Church, Nikon, undertook church reforms. He revised not only the church books but also elements of the service ritual itself. These changes were interpreted as sacrilegious by vast numbers of the Russian populace, and they refused to conform. When Czar Alexei Mikhailovich Romanov approved these reforms, large segments of the faithful considered themselves alienated from their church and from their czar. The period of these events became known as the Great Church Schism, or Raskol, in Russian history. Among the numerous reforms, one issue became a symbol for the antireformists: making the sign of the cross with two fingers, rather than with three, as the reforms now demanded. Making the sign of the cross held special significance, as it was an action believers performed many times each day.

## Persecution and Immigration

In Russia, Old Believers were periodically persecuted for their refusal to accept the church reforms and for their subsequent dedication to the Old Rite. Many were forced into rejoining the dominant church. Others moved to remote areas of Russia or beyond. Often Old Believers have accommodated their religious services when circumstances did not permit the fullness of the Old Rite (e.g., the absence of priests in some cases). Despite these and other adversities, however, they have faithfully preserved much of their religiocultural way of life for three and one-half centuries. Over the course of the centuries, doctrinal divisions have divided Old Believers into a number of exclusive "agreements," each subgroup insisting on its own correctness and condemning the others as deviant or heretical.

In 1905, Russian authorities eased social restrictions that led a group of Old Believers to immigrate to the Erie, Pennsylvania, area. Over the years these Old Believers formed splinter groups. Their young have largely integrated and acculturated into American social life.

During the early years of Soviet rule, and especially during the period of collectivization (c. 1929–1933), individuals, families, and groups of Old Believers and other religious groups in the USSR were subjected to increased persecution. Groups of Old Believers made their way out of the country and settled in China. In rural Sinkiang and Manchuria provinces, numerous groups of Old Believers created small communities, where they preserved the Old Rite. After the Communist revolution in China (1949), some Old Believers managed to immigrate to Hong Kong. There they received invitations from Australia and countries of South America, chiefly Brazil. In Brazil, Old Believers remained for four years before beginning their immigration to the United States (c. 1964). Others remained in South America and Australia yet maintain contact with their kinfolk in other lands.

## Old Believer Communities in North America

The Old Believer communities of North America have roots in western Russia, Siberia, the Far East, and Turkey. However, few community elders were born in Russia. The majority, though they represent authentic Russian Old Orthodoxy, have never been in Russia.

In Old Believer communities of Oregon, Alaska, and Canada, members tend to speak Russian and to pursue a traditional Russian way of life. Many older members of the community speak only Russian. Naturally, the elders strive to instill their way of life in younger generations. This effort competes with the American culture and values that the young meet daily. Public schooling, often the purveyor of common values in a society, contrasts considerably with the values promoted in the Old Believer family. This clash of cultures often creates in the younger members a composite culture that combines elements of both the Russian traditional and the American cultures. At the same time, when required, the younger generation of Old Believers can behave as normal members of either community.

Without a doubt, contact with the host community and competing cultural norms results in a definite cultural drift from their traditional ways among Old Believers in North America. Nonetheless, most Old Believers succeed in preserving the religious precepts of the Old Rite. The young are urged to marry within the faith and threatened with excommunication for failure to do so; once married, the young tend to become more conservative and perpetuate their unique identity.

## Clothing and Appearance

The uniqueness of Old Believers presents many contrasts to contemporary American life. Old Believers wear clothing reminiscent of the eighteenth and nineteenth centuries. In keeping with the Old Rite, three elements given at baptism—the shirt, belt, and cross—must be worn at all times by the faithful. Hence men and boys are seen in the long Russian shirt, or *rubashka*, girded with a belt. Women and girls lengthen the shirt to form a blouse/slip combination and wear over it a jumper, or *sarafan*; sometimes with a peasant apron. Holiday clothing is more fanciful and colorful but of the same style.

Their holy books also dictate the hairstyles of the Old Believers. Men wear their hair closely

Russian Old Believers in traditional clothing gather for a wedding celebration. The men with belts across their chests are members of the extended family who are helping with the celebration by pouring *braga* (a homemade wine drink) for the guests. (Richard A. Morris)

cropped, but their beards are left untrimmed. Women must not cut their hair. Unmarried women plait their hair in a single braid and after marriage keep it bound with two braids under a cap, or *shashmura*, covered with a kerchief.

## Religious Practices

Members of one "agreement" of Old Believers in Oregon and Canada have accepted priests from an Old Believer hierarchy in Romania (formerly Austro-Hungary). Members of the other "agreement" have no priests. They are led instead by a spiritual *nastavnik* (lay pastor).

The Old Believers adhere strictly to the ritual and church writings as constituted in the mid-seventeenth century. At that time, ascetic Greek monks taught their interpretation of proper religious conduct to the Russians. Their ritual emphasized self-deprivation: long, strict fasting periods and prolonged worship services akin to all-night

vigils. Much of this ritual remains with the Old Believers of today. Essentially, theirs is a monastic rite. The religious service begins at 2:00 A.M. on Sundays, and on frequent holidays, and lasts some five to six hours. Worshippers stand throughout most of the service. The Easter service can last up to fifteen hours. During the week following Easter, Old Believers celebrate by going from house to house to sing their praise of Christ, or Slavit Krista, and enjoy the abundant delicacies of food and *braga* (a homemade wine brewed from berries) from which they abstained during the long Great (Lenten) Fast.

Fasting requirements for Old Believers total more than two hundred days per year. Wednesdays and Fridays are regular fast days, in addition to four prolonged fasting periods throughout the year. During these periods Old Believers must refrain from all animal products, including milk and egg products.

Discipline within the family, and within the consensus of the Sobor (church group), is strict.

Obedience is a virtue and is still measured by the seventeenth-century Orthodox Russian standard.

With regard to outsiders, Old Believers carefully maintain rules of sacred cleanliness. They do not allow outsiders or those not "in union" to eat with them in their homes. Nonbeliever guests are treated very hospitably, but they are fed apart from the hosts in dishes that are stored and washed separately, often under an outdoor faucet. Similarly, Old Believers do not accept food from outsiders, either in homes or in restaurants. They traditionally avoid alcoholic beverages, save for their own homemade braga.

## Social Events

Community events are restricted chiefly to religious holy days and special events such as christenings, name days, and weddings, all of which are celebrated within the community or subcommunities. Ritual cleanliness within the religion militates against including outsiders in these events, though persons well known to the Old Believers may participate as marginal observers.

Weddings are traditional peasant village affairs reminiscent of prerevolutionary Russia. Engagement negotiations, called the *obruchanoe* or *tri poklona*, take place between the parents of the betrothed prior to the wedding, and the engagement agreement is marked with an exchange of presents and drink. Also common to wedding festivities are the *devichniki*, prewedding sewing gatherings between the bride and her girlfriends, and evening parties when the groom and his friends come to call. The songs sung at these events are traditional lamentations for the bride. There is also a lighthearted "buying of the bride," when the groom comes to take the bride away to her new family, followed by the serious *proshchanoe* (ritual of farewell between the bride and her parents).

The *venchanoe* (crowning ceremony) takes place after regular Sunday service, and the *svad'ba* (wedding) is celebrated for up to three days at the home of the groom's father. The bride's kinsmen deliver her *yaschchik* (trunk) and "sell" it to the groom's family. Later, after a sumptuous meal, the young couple stands for the *poklony* (bowing ceremony)—an opportunity for friends and relatives to offer advice and gifts. On the final day of the wedding, the newlyweds must "pay" for their wedding gifts from the best man and matrons of honor with kisses, bows, and witticisms.

## Language

Russian is spoken in the home and in most work activities. Given the size of the Russian community in Oregon, there is ample opportunity for men to form groups for contract work or to work together in factories. There is little need for members, especially women, to speak English. Consequently, Old Believers over age thirty who have not attended school and have had limited exposure to English generally prefer to speak Russian. Their Russian is grammatically correct but is sprinkled with traditional peasant expressions of centuries past. Old Believers who immigrated to the United States via Turkey speak a slightly different dialect of Russian that includes words imported from the Ukrainian and Turkish languages. Church Slavonic, a distinct early form of contemporary Russian, is used for religious services in all Old Believer communities of the western United States and Canada.

## Schooling and Occupational Habits

U.S. law requires that Old Believer children receive a certain level of formal schooling. Initially, however, Russian parents were somewhat lax about enforcing regular school attendance. Frequent family and religious obligations kept Old Believer children out of school. In recent years young members of the community have expressed an interest in acquiring a higher education. A number have completed college and university degrees, usually in practical fields such as business, accounting, nursing, and computer sciences.

In Oregon they have established an economic base in agriculture, acquiring land to raise berries and fruit, as well as grain for cattle. At the same time, they work in factories: Men employ their carpentry skills, and women, their sewing skills. Others engage in forestry work. In Alaska, Old Believers are successful commercial fishermen and builders of commercial fishing boats.

Old Believers are quick to adapt modern methods and technology as long as it does not violate religiocultural precepts of the Old Rite. Yet they still tend their farms and gardens in their spare time, though never on Sundays or on other church holidays.

Old Orthodox Old Believers have incorporated a "Protestant" ethic into their work style, having disassociated themselves from the dominant Orthodox Church hierarchy and much of the social milieu. In many cases, left without priests, they became, like the early Protestants, directly responsible before God for their own well-being. Old Believers value hard work, thrift, and self-sufficiency as proper behaviors. They see wordly success as a blessing from God. Material rewards are for personal gain, but also must be saved and shared in the community.

Many Old Believers in the United States have become American citizens and participate in local and national elections. They understand their rights and observe their civic obligations. A number have served and are serving in the U.S. armed forces.

## Intergroup Contact

There is continued contact between the "village" settlements of Old Believers in Oregon and Alaska and other settlements in Canada, Australia, and South America. These settlements are integrated into an exchange network of kin and resources, with certain advantages for all. For instance, Alaskan kin bring down salmon and other fish to Oregon and take back berries, fruit, nuts, and preserves. Oregon families travel to Alaska during the fishing season to assist relatives with the catch. Alaskans and Canadians travel to Oregon in the winter to work in the woods. Young men who journey to other Old Believer settlements use these occasions to seek eligible marriage partners.

## Conclusion

Russian Old Believers possess an eminently traditional culture whose ways are referenced to a seventeenth-century ethic. They feel a strong sense of obligation to preserve the religious ritual of the prereform Orthodox Church. This insistence has often resulted in persecution and dislocation.

In the United States, Old Believers have found religious freedom and economic stability. Yet close contact with American society has introduced them to the temptations of a modern, secular world. The consequence of such contact is an erosion of traditional religious and cultural discipline among their young. In response, some Old Believer families have moved on to more remote locations. Old Believers feel that the retention of close community ties will allow them to control the future direction of their lives. If the experience of middle-aged Old Believers in North America can be used to judge, that direction points toward the capability to interact with the host society while maintaining the core values of their religion and cultural ways.

*See also:* RUSSIAN MOLOKANS; RUSSIANS

## Bibliography

Billington, J. H. (1966). *The Icon and the Axe: An Interpretive History of Russian Culture.* New York: Knopf.

Conybeare, F. C. (1962). *Russian Dissenters.* New York: Russell & Russell.

Crummey, R. O. (1970). *The Old Believers and the World of Anti-Christ: The Vyg Community and the Russian State, 1694–1855.* Madison: University of Wisconsin Press.

Fedotov, G. P. (1966). *The Russian Religious Mind*, Vol. II: *The Middle Ages: 13th to 15th Centuries.* Cambridge, MA: Harvard University Press.

Hall, R. (1969). *Marion County History*, Vol. 10: *The Russian Old Believers of Marion County, Oregon.* Salem, OR: Marion County Historical Society.

Hardwick, S. (1993). *Russian Refuge: Religion, Migration, and Settlement on the North American Pacific Rim.* Chicago: University of Chicago Press.

Heard, A. F. ([1887] 1971). *The Russian Church and*

*Russian Dissent Comprising Orthodoxy, Dissent, and Erratic Sects.* New York: AMS Press.

Miliukov, P. (1943). *Outlines of Russian Culture,* Part I: *Religion and the Church.* Philadelphia: University of Pennsylvania Press.

Morris, R. A. (1991). *Old Russian Ways: Cultural Variations Among Three Russian Groups in Oregon.* New York: AMS Press.

RICHARD A. MORRIS

# RUSSIANS

The name "Russian" is and was adopted by people irrespective of their ethnic background who were citizens of the Russian Empire or of the Soviet Union (USSR). The Cossacks are mainly ethnic Russians, though many of them are of mixed ancestry. Carpatho-Rusyns from pre–World War I Austria-Hungary identified themselves with Russians. Like the United States, Russia was and continues to be a melting pot. People of many nationalities, ethnic backgrounds, and religious affiliations speak Russian at home, are immersed in Russian culture, and call themselves Russians or Russian-speakers.

## Orientation

*Identification.* Russians belong to the Eastern Slavs, a group that also includes Belarusans and Ukrainians. The name "Russian" originates from the name Rus, or Kievan (after the city of Kiev) Rus, the ancient group of principalities that spread across present-day European Russia, Belarus, and Ukraine.

*Location.* Of the persons who claimed Russian ancestry in the 1990 U.S. Census, 44 percent resided in the Northeast, 16 percent in the Midwest, 18 percent in the South, and 22 percent in the West. Areas where Russians are clustered are indicated by the locations of churches listed in telephone books as Eastern Orthodox or Russian.

*Demography.* U.S. Census figures (which had 2.95 million Americans claiming Russian ancestry

in 1990) are insufficient to provide data on the number of *ethnic* Russians in the United States. The estimated total population for ethnic Russians in the United States ranges from 750,000 to 2,000,000. A poll conducted in 1996 among 1,110 Russian Americans shows that 26 percent of them are younger than twenty years, 40 percent are twenty-one to sixty-five years old, and 34 percent are more than sixty-six years old; 39 percent were born in the United States, 53 percent in Russia or the USSR, and 8 percent in other countries; 28 percent have a college education. There are 10 percent more females than males. Between 1991 and 1996, there was only 1 birth per 1.6 deaths, which shows a demographic decline within the ethnic group.

*Linguistic Affiliation.* Russian is the official language in an area that stretches from the Baltic Sea to the Pacific Ocean and from the Arctic Sea to the Black Sea. In the Russian Federation, 150,000,000 people speak Russian. More than 25,000,000 ethnic Russians live in other republics of the former Soviet Union. A total of 284,000,000 people worldwide speak Russian. However, in the United States only 242,000 people have command of Russian. This indicates the degree to which assimilation has progressed, which usually takes its toll in the third generation and is enhanced by mixed marriages.

During the period of Russian rule, education in primary schools in Alaska was in Russian and in one of the native languages. As a result of these cultural contacts, the modern Aleut language contains 700 Russian words, the Aleutiik 600, the Tanaina 500, the Yup'ik 200, and the Eskimo 150. Many places in Alaska have Russian names.

In the United States, Russian is still studied in a number of Sunday schools affiliated with the Russian Orthodox Church Outside Russia.

## History and Cultural Relations

*Russian America.* The first Russian trappers, traders, and missionaries reached America from Siberia. They immigrated east, like the Americans, who were moving west. In 1741, two Russian ships under the command of Vitus Bering and Alexei

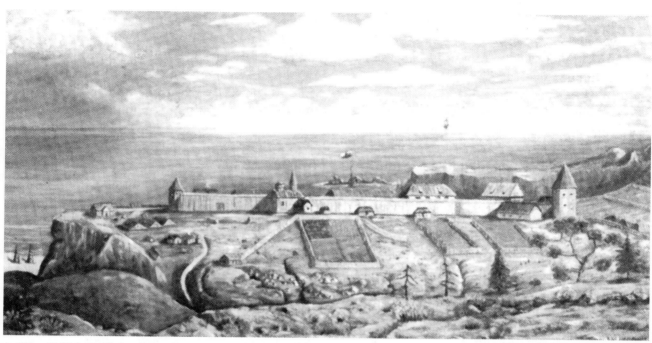

A Wassili Ushanoff painting depicts Fort Ross, California, in 1828. (Eugene A. Alexandrov/Congress of Russian-Americans)

Chirikov reached the coast of the North American continent. The first permanent Russian settlement in America was founded without official government approval on Kodiak Island in 1784 by Gregory Shelikhov, a fur trader. His enterprise developed into the Russian-American Company, which received a charter from the imperial government in 1799. Russian America appeared on maps next to British America (Canada) and the United States. Eight missionaries from Valaam Monastery arrived in Alaska in 1794. They built churches and started schools, studied the indigenous languages, converted the Aleuts and Indians to Orthodox Christianity, and interceded on their behalf before the Russian administration in cases of unjust treatment. Russians of all ranks married local women without prejudice. In addition to primary schools, there was a theological seminary and a junior college. Medical service was provided, farming was introduced, and shipbuilding started in 1807. Some ships traveling from Europe to Alaska made the long journey around South America and even Africa.

By order of the governor of Russian America, Alexander Baranov, Fort Ross was founded in 1812 in northern California to trade with the Spaniards and to provide agricultural products for Alaska. However, the fort was sold in 1848 to John Sutter and is now a state historical park. From 1815 to 1817, there was an unsuccessful attempt to colonize Hawaii by building Fort Elizabeth (Yelisaveta), now also a state park, on the island of Kauai.

The Russian possessions in Alaska were sold to the United States in 1867 for $7,200,000. The Russian government considered Alaska unprofitable because of a decline in the fur animal population and the potential risk of a territorial conflict with Britain. Most of the Russians returned to Russia, but some of them resettled in California and Canada. A total of 12,000 Orthodox Christian Alaskans, including many descendants of mixed marriages with Russian surnames, came under American jurisdiction.

*Early Immigration.* Fedor Karzhavin crossed the Atlantic in 1776 and outfitted three ships with supplies for the Revolutionary Army at his own expense in French Caribbean possessions. In 1792, Prince Demetrius Galitzin arrived in America, where he became a Roman Catholic missionary and helped to settle frontier lands in Pennsylvania.

During the nineteenth century small groups of Russian immigrants started congregating in New York and San Francisco. Most of them were educated and had command of at least one European language. This made it easier for them to adopt to the new country. A few arrived with some knowledge of English. They also experimented with communal farming. During the American Civil War, Russia sided with the North and sent squadrons of warships to New York and to San Francisco. John Basil Turchin (Turchaninov), a former Russian colonel, arrived in 1861 and fought in the Union army, retiring as a brigadier general. Turchin is also known as the founder of the city of Radom, Illinois, where the first settlers were Polish. Peter A. Dementieff (Demens), also a former Russian officer, started as a laborer, then became a businessman and railroad builder, and founded St. Petersburg, Florida, in 1888.

*Mass Immigration.* During the second half of the nineteenth century, immigrants from Russia started arriving in America. Of these, 60 percent were Jews escaping the Pale (a region, established in 1786 after the partition of Poland, in which the Jews were compelled to live); the rest were Poles, ethnic Russians, Ukrainians, Belarusans, Lithuanians, and German Mennonites. As soon as all these immigrants landed on American shores, they joined their respective ethnic and religious groups, which assisted them in integrating into the American way of life. There were 100,000 Russian-speaking people in the United States in 1914.

From 1898 to 1899, a total of 50,000 pacifist Dukhobors, who were in conflict with the Orthodox Church and the Russian government, left Russia with the help of Leo Tolstoy and started farming in Canada. A small number of them moved to the United States. Russian Molokans, another pacifist sect, arrived between 1905 and 1907; 17,000 of them settled in Los Angeles and 3,000 in San Francisco and in Oregon. A group of Molokans moved to Mexico, where they founded the Guadelupe Colony. There are also 8,000 Old Believers, dissenters from the official church in

Russia since the seventeenth century. Some immigrated to the United States before World War I. Others arrived after escaping from the Communists in Russia and China. One group arrived from Turkey, where they had lived for more than two hundred years while preserving the Russian language and their religion. The Old Believers settled in Pennsylvania, New Jersey, Oregon, and Alaska (where in 1967 they founded the village of Nikolaevsk on the Kenai Peninsula).

In the 1920s, 20,000 Russian anti-Communist refugees arrived in America, forming the second wave of immigrants. These people were military men, engineers, scientists, actors, intellectuals, and representatives of the Russian nobility. After the end of World War II, 30,000 ethnic Russians formed the third wave of immigrants to the United States. Many of these Russians were already expatriates living outside Russia, and many were born in foreign countries. According to the 1945 Yalta agreement, "displaced persons" (prisoners of war, laborers, and refugees) from the Soviet Union who wound up in the territories occupied by the Allies had to be returned to the USSR regardless of their desires. This resulted in forced repatriations, with violations of human rights and suicides. Displaced persons of other nationalities had the option to return to their native lands or to resettle to other countries. Eleanore Roosevelt interceded at the United Nations on behalf of displaced persons from the USSR. As a result, they were granted safety and freedom in the United States.

Russians from Manchuria and the rest of China became refugees in 1949–1950 due to the Communist takeover and immigrated in great numbers to the United States and Canada. Since the establishment of the Communist regime in Russia, and during the period of the Cold War, there was no legal way for Soviet citizens to emigrate. The enactment of the Jackson-Vanik amendment to the 1974 Trade Act was aimed at Soviet restrictions on the emigration of Jews. As a result, the Soviet government yielded and started issuing exit visas. This did not apply to ethnic Russians unless they could prove that they were subject to discrimination. A new wave of immigrants started arriving in the 1970s and formed communities in major cities of America, with many intellectuals, scientists, writers and poets, businesspeople, and artists.

*War Veterans.* A large number of Russians served in the U.S. Army during World War I, World War II, the Korean War, and the Vietnam War. Memorials to American veterans contain names of fallen Russian immigrants and of their descendants. Russian veterans of foreign wars (World War I and the Russian Civil War) also had organizations that faded away with time.

## Religion and Expressive Culture

*Religion.* When Alaska was sold to the United States in 1867, Russian Orthodox priests remained to continue their duties and to start spreading their activities over the entire country. The services in Alaska were originally in Church Slavonic and native languages. Gradually English was introduced. This created a cross-ethnic spiritual and cultural liaison. All Orthodox churches in America are of traditional architecture and are adorned with icons and frescoes on the inside walls.

In the United States the Orthodox Church is represented by dioceses that belong to three jurisdictions—the Orthodox Church in America, which has three theological seminaries; the conservative Russian Orthodox Church Outside Russia, with one seminary; and the Russian Orthodox Church, under the jurisdiction of the patriarch of Moscow. The churches are the principal centers of religious, social, and cultural life of Russian Americans. Because of religious differences, groups of Old Believers, Molokans, Dukhobors, and Baptists live separate from the Russian-American communities.

*Traditions.* Ethnic and religious customs are preserved in families and communities. The annual cycle includes the twelve most important religious holidays, especially Easter, as well as birthdays, name days, and wedding anniversaries. The holidays, preceded by periods of fasting, feature lavish dishes prepared according to recipes brought from the old country. The preparation of food is seen as

A delegation of Russian Americans presents a commemorative medal dedicated to the Millennium of Christianity in Russia to President Ronald Regan on December 18, 1988. (Eugene A. Alexandrov/White House)

an art to be passed on with love from one generation to another. Some women and girls wear national dress during festivals. The Old Believers and Molokans wear Russian peasant costumes, and the men have beards.

*Science and Engineering.* Russian professors teach in many American universities. Russian studies and research are conducted in two hundred American universities and colleges. Outstanding contributions to American technology and culture were made by Vladimir V. Zvorykin (the "Father of Television"), Igor I. Sikorsky (designer of airplanes and helicopters), Vladmimir N. Ipatieff (author of seventy American patents for petroleum refining, which helped America and the Allies win World War II), Wassili Leontief (Nobel Price laureate in economics), George Kistiakovski (creator of the explosive device for the atomic bomb), Stepan P. Timoshenko (researcher in strength of materials), and many others. Nina Fedoroff, a geneticist, was elected in 1990 to the National Academy of Sciences.

*Arts.* Art in America has been greatly enriched by the works of Russian immigrants. Nine museums in the United States are dedicated to the Russian historical and military heritage and to the arts, including five museums founded by immigrants. Eight state parks and one national park commemorate Russian-American heritage and history. Several museums and galleries, especially the National Gallery of Art and the Hillwood Museum of Russian Art in Washington, D.C., exhibit paintings and precious objects from Russian museums and churches that were sold abroad by the Soviets.

## Marriage and Kinship

Traditional marriages do not differ much from American customs, except for the religious rites, which are followed by sumptuous receptions. The stability of Russian-American families is reflected in the comparatively low ratio of divorces. According to a poll conducted among parishes in 1996, there was only one divorce in ten marriages. Inter-

marriage with individuals from other ethnic backgrounds is on the rise.

Kinship was important among immigrants before World War I. It served as a form of support for the new arrivals. Wars and Communist repressions in the USSR decimated many families. Survivors who managed to escape abroad tried to restore families and searched for missing members in the former USSR. New kinships developed among young generations through interethnic marriages.

## Economy

Russians, including those Belarusans and Ukrainians who arrived before World War I, usually identified themselves as Russians. They were young peasants who wanted to stay and to work in factories or mines and on farms. After they established themselves in the new country, they were joined by family members and relatives. However, some of them were circular immigrants. They lived in the United States only for limited periods of time sufficient to earn enough funds to improve their economic standards in the old country. In the 1930s, most of these returnees were deprived of their property and sent by the Soviets to forced labor camps. Those who stayed in the United States became American citizens. They adapted fully to the American way of life while preserving some of their ethnic traditions. Their descendants are engaged in various fields, as engineers, educators, government employees, and workers. Some blue-collar workers live in the same neighborhoods where their parents settled. There are almost no farmers among Russian Americans. Those who escaped Communist persecution in the 1920s took jobs as factory workers, with some later returning to prominence in industry, science, and society. Immigrants of the 1950s were engineers, teachers, and white-collar workers, with a minority of blue-collar workers. Almost all preferred to live in one-family houses. The average income of a Russian-American household today corresponds to that of the American middle class. Less than 1 percent of ethnic Russians are on welfare.

## Sociopolitical Organization

*Social Organizations.* Russian organizations started appearing in the United States in 1872. The Russian Orthodox Society of Mutual Aid was founded in 1895, the Russian Brotherhood Society in 1900, the Society to Help Russian Children in 1926, and the Tolstoy Foundation in 1939. Others include the Orthodox Theological Fund in New York, the Ivan Koulaeff Foundation in San Francisco, and the Association of Russian-American Scholars. There are also organizations of alumni from Russian schools that existed outside the Soviet Union until World War II. A number of social and cultural clubs operate in areas with major concentrations of Russians. Since 1972 the Congress of Russian Americans has represented the interests of American citizens of Russian descent. There are three organizations of Russian Scouts.

*Political Organizations.* A broad spectrum of Russian political organizations ranged from social-democratic to conservative and monarchist; many strove to expose the dangers of communism in memorandums, lectures, books, and periodicals. The Democratic party is popular among the descendants of blue-collar workers who arrived before World War I. Those who arrived after World War II and their children prefer the Republican party. November 7, the day when the Bolsheviks abolished democracy and seized power in Russia in 1917, is designated by the Congress of Russian Americans and other Russian organizations as the "Memorial Day for Victims of Communism."

*Discrimination.* Before World War I, immigrants from Russia were met with prejudice and characterized as being backward and having a low IQ. After the Bolshevik Revolution, Russians in the United States were treated with suspicion as potential Bolshevik sympathizers. Many who were active in labor unions or had socialist leanings were rounded up and deported without proper hearings.

Russian Americans picket outside the Soviet mission to the United Nations in 1954. (Eugene A. Alexandrov/ N. Teliatnikow)

Public Law 86-90, known since 1956 as the Captive Nations Law, listed nations under Communist rule as victims of "Russian communism." The Russian nation, the first victim of communism, was not included in the text of the law. News media routinely equated the names "Russian" and "Soviet" or even "Communist." The image of ethnic Russians, especially that of women, in the press and even in commercial advertisements was presented as an ugly caricature with racist overtones.

*Russian Press in the United States.* The first bilingual newspaper, the *Alaskan Herald*, was published in San Francisco by a priest, Agapius Goncharenko, on March 1, 1868, to introduce Russians to the U.S. Constitution. About two hundred Russian newspapers, bulletins, and journals existed in the United States for various periods. They served as liaison among various groups of immigrants and represented a broad spectrum of trends, ranging from liberal and socialist to moderate and conservative-monarchist. Many publications have also been dedicated to the military history of the twentieth century and to religious life. A daily newspaper published in Russian since 1910 is *Novoye Russkoye Slovo* (The New Russian Word) in New York; another is *Russkaya Zhizn* (Russian Life), founded in San Francisco in 1920. Hundreds of books in Russian were published in the United States during the twentieth century, thus enriching the multiethnic culture of the country.

*See also:* CARPATHO-RUSYNS; GERMANS FROM RUSSIA; RUSSIAN MOLOKANS; RUSSIAN OLD BELIEVERS

## Bibliography

Chevigny, H. (1965). *Russian America: The Great Alaskan Venture, 1741–1867*. New York: Viking Press.

Eubank, N. (1973). *The Russians in America*. Minneapolis, MN: Lerner.

Gibson, J. R. (1978). "Old Russia in the New World: Adversaries and Adversities in Russian America." In *European Settlement and Development in North America*, edited by J. R. Gibson. Toronto: University of Toronto Press.

Jeletzky, T. F., ed. (1983). *Russian Canadians: Their Past and Present*. Ottawa: Borealis Press.

Klimenko, G. (1977). "Russians in New Jersey." In *The New Jersey Ethnic Experience*, edited by B. Cunningham. Union City, NJ: Wm. H. Wise.

Magocsi, P. R. (1987). *The Russian Americans*. New York: Chelsea House.

Mohoff, G. W. (1993). *The Russian Colony of Guadelupe Molokans in Mexico*. Montebello, CA: George Mohoff.

Reardon, J. (1972). "Nikolaevsk. A Bit of Old Russia Takes Root in Alaska." *National Geographic* 142(3):400–425.

Smith, B. S., and Barnett, B. J., eds. (1990). *Russian America: The Forgotten Frontier*. Tacoma: Washington State Historical Society.

Starr, S. F., ed. (1987). *Russia's American Colony*. Durham, NC: Duke University Press.

Tarasar, C., gen. ed. (1975). *Orthodox America, 1794–1976*. Syosset, NY: Orthodox Church of America.

Tolstoy, N. (1977). *The Secret Betrayal, 1944–1947*. New York: Scribner.

Westerman, V. (1977). *The Russians in America: A Chronology & Fact Book*. Dobbs Ferry, NY: Oceana.

Williams, R. C. (1980). *Russian Art and American Money, 1900–1940*. Cambridge, MA: Harvard University Press.

EUGENE A. ALEXANDROV

## SALVADORANS

An estimated 500,000 to one million Salvadorans (El Salvadorans, El Salvadoreans, Salvadorians, Salvadoreans, Guanacos, Salvadoreños) live in the United States, the vast majority of whom arrived during the Salvadoran civil war from 1979 to 1992. During that period the influx of Salvadorans was so dramatic that what was a tiny ethnic group grew into the fourth-largest Latino population in the United States. Salvadorans trace their roots to the Central American country of El Salvador, located along the Pacific Coast and bordered by Guatemala and Honduras. As most Salvadorans are recent immigrants to the United States, their identity is still very much rooted in their homeland. They are the descendants of the Spanish who colonized Central America and of the indigenous peoples who originally inhabited the country. Salvadorans do not think of themselves as Indian, however, which can be traced to 1932, when the Salvadoran military massacred thirty thousand peasants—including most remaining Indians—who protested poor working conditions. For centuries El Salvador has been a country characterized by extremes of rich and poor. A few elite own most of the land and industries; the vast majority of the population consists of peasants with little or no land and urban shantytown dwellers. A visible middle class emerged in the 1960s as the country moved toward industrialization, but it is largely limited to the country's three major cities. Given El Salvador's history, it should not be surprising that most Salvadoran immigrants arrive in the United States with low levels of both formal education and marketable skills.

The 1990 U.S. Census enumerated 565,000 Salvadorans, a figure considered very low by scholars, who usually cite a figure of one million. At least one report confirms an undercount of Salvadorans, suggesting that unusual housing conditions, low levels of literacy, and illegal immigration status were the principal causes. There are no large-scale national studies of Salvadorans to date, hence census records provide the best available data. According to the census, four out of every five Salvadorans in the United States are foreign-born. They are equally divided between males and females and their median age is twenty-six, seven years younger than the overall U.S. population. Two-thirds of Salvadorans over age twenty-five have not completed high school, and only 5 percent are college graduates. Most Salvadorans arrived illegally in the United States after fleeing the civil war and have lived all or part of their lives in the United States as undocumented immigrants. This status does not permit them to work legally, impeding Salvadorans from obtaining good jobs. Workers are concentrated in manufacturing and service sectors of the economy; only 6 percent are in managerial or professional occupations. Despite the fact that more Salvadoran men and women are in the work force than the U.S. average, 22 percent of Salvadoran families live below the poverty line, and per capita income is $7,200 (compared to $14,420 for the United States overall). In short, Salvadorans are a working poor population.

Salvadorans are residentially concentrated in several metropolitan areas. Nearly 50 percent live in Los Angeles and its suburbs, 11 percent in New York, 9 percent in Washington, D.C., 8 percent in San Francisco, and 7 percent in Houston. Ethnic neighborhoods marked by Salvadoran storefronts such as *pupuserías* (restaurants) are notable in these cities—for example, the Pico Union district of downtown Los Angeles, Hempstead, Long Island (a suburb of New York City), and the Columbia Road neighborhood of Washington. In contrast to the vast Los Angeles population, which is quite representative of El Salvador's social classes and different regions, other Salvadoran communities are products of narrower immigration patterns. A case in point is Washington, where Salvadorans tend to be from the same small town in southeastern El Salvador, Intipucá. Similarly, Salvadorans living on Long Island are overwhelmingly from peasant backgrounds and hail almost exclusively from towns in northeastern El Salvador.

Spanish is the language spoken by the overwhelming majority of Salvadorans. Linguistic characteristics such as the substitution of *vos* for *tú* (the informal form of "you") and the use of *va* in spoken pauses (similar to "ya know" in English) help identify Salvadorans from other Spanish-speakers. Salvadoran children born in the United States are caught between Spanish and English. They learn English in school and through television, have a stronger command of it than their parents, and often prefer to respond to their par-

ents in English. Bilingual children become interpreters for their parents, inverting the normal dominant parent-child role. This inversion is also exacerbated when parents are illiterate. Education was disrupted during the civil war in El Salvador, and older Salvadorans of peasant backgrounds tend to have little or no education. This illiteracy in their native language makes handling life in the United States, including learning English, ever more difficult while it exacerbates parents' dependency on their children's language skills.

## Immigration History

According to records kept by the U.S. Immigration and Naturalization Service (INS), fewer than 30,000 Salvadorans immigrated to the United States prior to 1970. This small group included diplomats and students as well as some people who were recruited to work in U.S. factories. During the 1970s, political and economic unrest in El Salvador and severe government repression led thousands of Salvadorans to flee their homeland, most to the United States. By 1980, the population of Salvadorans in the United States had swollen to at least 100,000. But the great exodus occurred during the years of the Salvadoran civil war (1979–1992), when more than 500,000 sought refuge in the United States. The two sides fighting the war were the Salvadoran armed forces and the FMLN (Farabundo Martí Front for National Liberation) guerrillas. This war was notorious for brutalities against civilians; an estimated 75,000 people died, most at the hands of the Salvadoran military. (The war left Salvadorans with a deep-seated fear of all uniformed officials, a fear carried into the United States.)

Despite documentation in the U.S. press of the atrocities during the early 1980s, then president Ronald Reagan declared that the Salvadorans were entering the United States for economic reasons, and his government refused to treat them as refugees. This policy stood throughout the 1980s; applications Salvadorans submitted for political asylum were systematically denied. In 1991, the U.S. government finally acknowledged the plight

Salvadoran refugees attend a meeting in Los Angeles to discuss community issues. (Nik Wheeler/Corbis)

of the Salvadorans, permitting them to apply for temporary legal status and to have their asylum applications reconsidered. Nearly 200,000 obtained work permits through this program but not permission to visit loved ones in their homeland. In 1994, citing the end of the civil war in 1992, President Bill Clinton terminated Salvadorans' temporary legal status. Despite the cessation of warfare, Salvadorans continue to emigrate. They cite El Salvador's devastated economy and infrastructure, a postwar crime wave, and families' dependence on monies remitted from the United States as reasons. Additionally, transnational trends have emerged linking Salvadorans to both the United States and El Salvador. Older Salvadorans return home and send their children to take their place, creating a trend toward intergenerational migration. When possible, Salvadorans who enjoy legal immigration status return home to visit family and participate in local festivals and events, returning to the United States soon after. A corps of these individuals have become couriers, people who fly back and forth between the United States and El Salvador, picking up and delivering mail, remittances, and packages of goods.

## Family and Social Relations

In less than a generation, El Salvador was transformed into a culture of international migration. In this process, traditional patterns of kinship and social relations have been transformed. The Salvadoran countryside is characterized by tightly knit peasant hamlets called *caserios*, consisting of extended families and fictive kin or *compadres*. *Compadrazgo*, found throughout Latin America and a custom sustained by some Salvadorans in the

United States, is established when a couple asks close friends to be godparents to their children or to serve as best man or maid or matron of honor at their marriage. In the caserios and also to a large extent in the urban neighborhoods of El Salvador's cities, most inhabitants are linked together by either kinship or compadrazgo. This creates an extensive group of people who are available in times of need.

The close, intense social ties characteristic of El Salvador are very difficult for Salvadorans in the United States to sustain. There are many reasons for this. Principal among them is their uncertain and often complex immigration status. Families frequently are divided by legal status. Consider a couple who fled El Salvador and entered the United State illegally, leaving behind their children in care of relatives, and later had children born in the United States. This family cannot be reunited, nor can they visit, because the parents cannot go back to their homeland and return to the United States legally. The couple's children in El Salvador cannot visit the United States because they are probably too poor to qualify for tourist visas. Such predicaments are common and cause families high levels of stress and emotional torment. Salvadorans are also known to suffer from stress-related psychological health problems owing, in large part, to the atrocities they witnessed during the civil war in their homeland. The jobs they hold generally do not offer medical insurance, and low-cost clinics are only sporadically available; consequently Salvadorans seek support from each other, suffer in silence, or turn to alcohol and other substance abuse outlets.

Economic pressures also affect social relations. Salvadorans tend to earn low salaries, too low to cover their expenses and remittances to their homeland. To compensate, they work at two jobs or on extra shifts. Two-thirds of Salvadoran women have also entered the work force, a figure above the U.S. average. This contrasts to El Salvador, where women, particularly in rural areas, are expected to stay at home. Salvadorans express dismay at how little time they have to socialize in the United States, even with close kin. Whereas in El Salvador there was ample time each day to fraternize, in the United States Sundays are usually the only days available, and time to socialize is limited by other activities, such as shopping, doing the laundry, and cleaning the home. In their free time, groups of Salvadoran women can be seen congregating in kitchens, cooking large potsfull of *sancocho* (thick meat and vegetable soup), and making rice and *tamales* (cornmeal patties stuffed with meat, chickpeas, olives, and spices). The men occupy the living room, gather outside in groups fixing their cars, or meet at playing fields to watch or participate in games of soccer known as *futbol*. During these few hours, conversations flow and information is exchanged about everything, from where to find bargains and jobs to the latest news from hometowns in El Salvador.

## Marriage and Religion

In El Salvador, despite the country's Catholic legacy (its name means "the savior"), most couples do not marry formally in a civil or religious service. Common-law unions are prevalent, and this custom has carried over into the United States. Salvadorans distinguish between married couples (*casados*) and those in a common-law relationship (*acompañados*). This distinction is derived from Roman law and was brought to Latin America by the Spaniards. Common-law unions are not considered illegitimate, nor are children born to the union as long as they are recognized by the father on the child's birth certificate. Many Salvadoran women have expressed a preference for common-law marriage over a church wedding because divorce is banned by Catholic tradition.

Salvadorans' preference for common-law unions becomes problematic in the United States because immigration laws recognize only civil or church marriages. Consequently, people who have lived as acompañados for many years may marry so a spouse can obtain an immigration benefit.

Two groups of Salvadorans prefer formal, religious marriages: persons of higher social class, and members of Protestant evangelical churches. In El Salvador and in the United States the most well-known denominations of evangelicals are the Pentecostal Church and the Apostles and Prophets Church. The evangelical churches are very strict regarding relationships between the sexes; they also ban alcohol consumption and other activities deemed amoral. Until the 1980s, nearly all Salvadorans were Catholic, but Protestantism gained popularity during the civil war. In Salvadoran communities, both in the United States and in their homeland, white lace scarves worn by evangelical women are visible indicators of this transformation.

## Social Organizations

Several institutions form the backbone of Salvadoran communities in the United States. Churches are key. Salvadorans seek spiritual and material assistance from churches. The Catholic Church provides an extensive array of social services as well as Masses in Spanish. Catholic Charities has served as an important resource to Salvadorans who have been excluded from welfare and other social programs owing to their undocumented status. The churches' outreach centers provide food, housing, employment, and immigration assistance to a degree unmet by other organizations.

Central American Refugee Centers (CARE-CEN) and similar offices have championed Salvadorans' legal rights while providing information and other support. As an extremely new immigrant group and one with strained financial resources, Salvadorans have not established a wide net of mutual aid societies, organizations associated with earlier generations of immigrants. But they are emerging.

Key institutions include soccer clubs and federations. Although ostensibly organized around the game, the teams link players from the same hometown or region and thereby provide social contacts useful to players and their families off the field. After games, players socialize in pupuserías, eating Salvadoran food and conversing.

In areas with significant Salvadoran populations, Independence Day parades are common. Organizing for these events starts months before the designated date (usually the Saturday nearest to September 15, Central American Independence Day). Leaders enlist the help of local Salvadoran merchants and personalities such as local television and radio broadcasters. On the day of the parade, festive floats sponsored by businesses, churches, soccer clubs, and other organizations travel down streets awash in a sea of blue and white Salvadoran flags waved by exuberant onlookers.

Another area of social cohesion is hometown associations. People who grew up in the same community in El Salvador form solidarity relationships with those towns, raising funds for civic projects there such as building roads and parks or repairing churches. This has been one of the

A young girl wears a traditional dress of El Salvador in a Central American ethnic pride parade in Chicago in 1995. (Sandy Felsenthal/Corbis)

positive contributions of Salvadorans' migration; a much less beneficial phenomenon has been the deportation of hundreds of Salvadoran youths who have been gang members in Los Angeles and other U.S. cities. Upon arrival, many have reconstituted gangs in El Salvador. Gang graffiti and gang-related violence are rampant, leaving many Salvadorans feeling ambivalent about their brisk transformation into a culture of migration.

## Bibliography

Armstrong, R., and Shenk, J. (1982). *El Salvador: The Face of Revolution.* Boston: South End Press.

Chavez, L. R. (1994). "The Power of the Imagined Community: The Settlement of Undocumented Mexicans and Central Americans in the United States." *American Anthropologist* 96(1):52–73.

Chinchilla, N.; Hamilton, N.; and Loucky, J. (1993). "Central Americans in Los Angeles: An Immigrant Community in Transition." In *In the Barrios: Latinos and the Underclass Debate,* edited by J. Moore and R. Pinderhughes. New York: Russell Sage Foundation.

Hamilton, N., and Chinchilla, N. (1991). "Central American Migration: A Framework for Analysis." *Latin American Research Review* 26(1):75–110.

Jenkins, J. H. (1991). "The State Construction of Affect: Political Ethos and Mental Health Among Salvadoran Refugees." *Culture, Medicine and Psychiatry* 15:139–165.

Mahler, S. J. (1993). "Alternative Enumeration of Undocumented Salvadorans on Long Island." Final Report for Joint Statistical Agreement 89-46, U.S. Bureau of the Census.

Mahler, S. J. (1995). *American Dreaming: Immigrant Life on the Margins.* Princeton, NJ: Princeton University Press.

Mahler, S. J. (1996). *Salvadorans in Suburbia: Symbiosis and Conflict.* Needham Heights, MA: Allyn & Bacon.

Montes Mozo, S., and Garcia Vasquez, J. J. (1988). *Salvadoran Migration to the United States: An Exploratory Study.* Washington, DC: Hemispheric Migration Project, Center for Immigration Policy and Refugee Assistance, Georgetown University.

Repak, T. A. (1995). *Waiting on Washington: Central American Workers in the Nation's Capital.* Philadelphia: Temple University Press.

Siems, L. (1994). *Between the Lines: Letters Between Undocumented Mexican and Central American Immigrants.* Hopewell, NJ: Ecco Press.

Stanley, W. D. (1987). "Economic Migrants or Refugees from Violence? A Time-Series Analysis of Salvadoran Migration to the United States." *Latin American Research Review* 22(1):132–154.

Suarez-Orozco, M. M. (1989). *Central American Refugees and U.S. High Schools: A Psychological Study of Motivation and Achievement.* Stanford, CA: Stanford University Press.

U.S. Bureau of the Census. (1990). *1990 Census of Population: Persons of Hispanic Origin in the United States,* Series CP-3-3. Washington, DC: U.S. Government Printing Office.

SARAH J. MAHLER

# SAMOANS

Samoans in the United States trace their ancestry to the Samoan archipelago, located at 169–174 degrees west longitude and 10–15 degrees south latitude. Defining the Samoan community in the United States requires a general consideration of the political division of Samoa, which produces "American Samoans" and "Western Samoans."

In the late nineteenth century, the Samoan Islands were the center of political competition among the United States, Great Britain, and Germany. Representatives of these three governments allied themselves with different ruling families in Samoa and became enmeshed in the subtleties of traditional chiefly rivalry, nearly going to war in 1889. Ten years later, after continuing skirmishes on the island of Upolu, the three powers signed the Treaty of Berlin, which imposed a political boundary between Eastern Samoa (primarily the islands of Tutuila and the Manua group) and Western Samoa (primarily the islands of Upolu, Savaii, Manono, and Apolima). Separate deeds of cession for Tutuila in 1900 and Manua in 1904 established American Samoa as an "unincorporated and unorganized" territory. Western Samoa became a

German territory from 1900 to 1914, when it relinquished control to New Zealand, which administered the islands until the end of 1961. On January 1, 1962, Western Samoa became the first Pacific island polity to achieve independence from Western colonial control.

## Migration and Immigration

Samoans first entered Hawaii (not a state until 1959) and the mainland United States after World War I. This initial migration was motivated by military and religious commitments and affiliations. The completion of the Mormon Temple in Laie, Hawaii, in 1919 attracted the first group of Mormon Samoans to Oahu's northern shore. This religion-focused migration continues today and extends to the Mormon center in Provo, Utah.

Large-scale movements of American Samoans to Hawaii and the continental United States, and of Western Samoans to New Zealand, began in the early 1950s. During World War II, American and Western Samoans developed transportation, communication, and supply skills at the Tutuila Naval Station at Pago Pago, and at the end of the war many of those skilled workers were eager to succeed in overseas labor markets. In addition, hundreds of American Samoans who joined the U.S. armed forces during the war were brought to Hawaii when the naval station was closed in 1951. The first major movements of American Samoans to Hawaii were thus partly voluntary and economic and partly the result of military relocation. Since 1951, movement from American Samoa has been stimulated by economics and military enlistment. In addition, the Samoan perception of better educational opportunities in the United States proper has motivated migration. American Samoans are American nationals, and their movement to the United States proper is unencumbered by immigration restrictions. For this reason they often visit American Samoa while maintaining employment and schooling in the United States proper (the fifty states).

There are two important differences between American and Western Samoans. The first is that Western Samoans must go through the extensive immigration clearance process, like all foreign immigrants. Western Samoans may enter American Samoa on work visas, and as long as they maintain viable employment, usually at the tuna cannery complex where they comprise a majority of the labor force, or in the private sector, their visas are renewed annually. Many Western Samoans move first to American Samoa, where they can earn as much in a month as they can earn in a year at home, and await their immigration clearance to enter the United States proper.

A second important difference results from nearly a century of American cultural influence in American Samoa. From 1900 to 1942, the U.S. presence in American Samoa was centered in the Pago Pago Harbor area, which the U.S. Navy viewed as affording perfect protection and stronger for defense than Gibraltar. In 1900, the population of the territory was approximately 5,000, and it had grown to 12,000 by 1940. From December 7, 1941, and the bombing of Pearl Harbor to March 1944, American Samoa served as the advance base for the U.S. military campaigns in the Pacific. During this period, often referred to as the "Marine Era," more than 15,000 American servicemen passed through American Samoa. In 1950, the population of the territory was nearly 19,000. Thus, in the 1940s, the population of the territory grew by as much as it had in the first forty years of the twentieth century. The period from 1950 to 1990 saw the development of a multimillion-dollar tuna complex and government infrastructure and the introduction of American television, initially for educational purposes and largely unsuccessful but now a constant connection to American society and its values. Western Samoa, on the other hand, has maintained a rural agricultural economy and a generally more conservative stance toward cultural change. Western Samoans residing at home are able to use substantial remittances from kinsmen abroad to supplement their locally derived income.

Although these two differences—freedom of movement and extent of American cultural influence—are important, they are sometimes overemphasized. Samoans often view the political boundary established by the Treaty of Berlin as artificial and invisible. Kinship connections reckoned through complex, deep, and well-remembered genealogies precede the nation-territory formation of the twentieth century by more than three thousand years. Marriage and family formations between residents of Western Samoa and American Samoa frequently blur the distinction between "Western Samoan" and "American Samoan."

## Demography

In 1980, for the first time, Samoans were enumerated on censuses in both American Samoa and the fifty states. The 1980 U.S. Census provided detailed data by state, whereas the available 1990 U.S. Census data are at the national level only. The Samoan stateside population in 1980 was 41,948. More than four Samoans in five lived in Hawaii or California, with population clusters in Washington State, Utah, Missouri, and around U.S. military bases. Nearly half (20,089, or 47.9%) of the Samoan population was residing in California, while more than one-third (14,073, or 33.4%) was in Hawaii. The Samoan population in the United States proper in 1980 was greater than the population in American Samoa (32,297) by approximately 10,000 but was only one-fourth the size of the Western Samoan population (153,130).

Samoan movement to the United States proper is largely a rural-island-to-urban migration. In 1980, approximately 96 percent of the Samoans living within the fifty states resided in urban areas, with the largest concentrations being in Honolulu (13,811), Los Angeles–Long Beach (8,049), and San Francisco–Oakland (4,329).

There were more Western Samoa–born individuals (13,238) than American Samoa–born individuals (9,361) residing in the United States proper in 1980. Approximately 57 percent of Western Samoans immigrated between 1970 and 1980, 20 percent between 1970 and 1974, and 37 percent between 1975 and 1980. Because of American Samoans' freedom of movement, it is more difficult to determine their year of first migration. As of 1980, Samoa-born individuals living in the United States (22,599) outnumbered Samoans born in the United States.

In 1980, Samoan households in Hawaii contained an average of 5.0 persons, compared with an average of 2.7 persons for all Hawaii households. Fewer than seven out of ten Samoan families in Hawaii contained both husband and wife, whereas more than eight out of ten families did throughout Hawaii. Furthermore, the 26.8 percent of Hawaii Samoan families headed by a woman with no husband present was more than twice the Hawaii state figure of 12.5 percent. The Samoan community in California had a higher percentage of families with both spouses present (81.8%) and a lower percentage of families headed by females with no husband present (14.7%) than the Hawaii Samoan community.

In Hawaii between 1975 and 1984, a total of 60.5 percent of Samoan women and 58.8 percent of Samoan men married a Samoan spouse. Samoan women who outmarried tended to marry, in proportional order, European Americans, African Americans, or Hawaiians/part-Hawaiians. Samoan men who outmarried tended to marry, in proportional order, Hawaiians/part-Hawaiians or European Americans. There was little intermarriage between Samoans and the various Asian-American groups in Hawaii. Comparable data for Samoans in California are not available.

Using the number of children ever born per one thousand females as an indicator, it is clear that Samoan females had higher fertility in 1980 than Hawaii females in general and that their fertility was very similar to that of California Samoan females. For Samoan females in Hawaii and California, the number of children ever born per one thousand females for the age groups 15–24, 25–34, and 35–44 averaged 470, 2,597, and 4,291, respectively.

In 1980, Samoans in California had higher levels of educational and economic achievement than Samoans in Hawaii. In California, 73.0 percent of Samoan men and 51.5 percent of Samoan women were in the labor force, compared to 68.1 percent of Samoan men and only 37.7 percent of

Samoan women in Hawaii. Educationally, in California 65.5 percent of Samoan men and 61.2 percent of Samoan women had completed high school, compared to 58.4 percent of Samoan men and 44.3 percent of Samoan women in Hawaii. Both personal and household income levels were higher for Samoans in California, and Samoans in California were more likely to be in skilled occupations than Samoans in Hawaii.

The 1990 U.S. Census enumerated 62,964 Samoans, representing a 50 percent increase in the Samoan population in the United States proper. The Samoan population in California grew by 55.3 percent, to 31,197, while the Samoan population in Hawaii grew by only 6.8 percent, to 15,034. More than one Samoan in five (22.7%) was foreign-born; 40.1 percent of this population arrived in the United States in the 1980s, 21.8 percent between 1975 and 1979, and 31.4 percent before 1975. More than half (52.4%) had become naturalized citizens. Data on the number of "American nationals" (American Samoans) were not available.

The 1990 U.S. Census provides national-level data on Samoan socioeconomic characteristics, so comparisons will be made with the total U.S. population. The age structure of the Samoan population remains very young, with 42.3 percent under eighteen years of age, compared with only 25.6 percent of the overall U.S. population. The median age for the Samoan population was 21.5 years, compared with 32.9 years in the total U.S. population. Nearly one Samoan family in five (19.6%) had a female household head with no husband present, compared with nearly one family in six (16.5%) in the total U.S. population. Two-thirds of the Samoan population five years or older (66.4%) speak a language other than English in the household, compared with only 13.8 percent of the total U.S. population.

In 1990, Samoan educational levels were generally lower than those of the total American population. Nearly four of five Samoans (79.5%) had completed high school, but fewer than one in eight (11.9%) had a bachelor's degree. These completion rates compare with total U.S. population figures of 75.2 percent and 20.3 percent, respectively. Only one Samoan woman in ten (10.7%) had a bachelor's degree, compared with one woman in six (17.8%) in the total U.S. population.

Data concerning Samoan employment and income also present a less favorable picture than that for the U.S. population as a whole. The Samoan unemployment rate was 8.9 percent, compared with the overall rate of 8.3 percent. For Samoan women the unemployment rate was 10.7 percent, compared with total U.S. female rate of 8.2 percent. Median income for Samoan households was $27,511, compared with the total U.S. household median income of $30,056. Samoan per capita income was only $7,690, compared to an overall per capita income of $14,149. One Samoan family in four (24.9%) was living below the poverty level, compared to one family in ten (10.0%) in the total U.S. population.

## Community Characteristics

By 1995, after nearly half a century of international migration, immigration, and circulation, the *fa'a Samoa* (Samoan way of life) connected families in Western and American Samoa to well-established overseas communities in Australia, New Zealand, Hawaii, and the continental United States. At least 325,000 Samoans reside in these locales, with about half of this population in Western Samoa.

The character of each Samoan community differs. Western Samoa is the traditional and contemporary cultural and political center. American Samoa is also a cultural center as well as the economic center of the overall network. The most established and visible overseas Samoan community is in New Zealand. The Samoan community in Hawaii is in its third generation of hosting eastbound and westbound visiting kin and church groups (*malaga*). The California Samoan community is growing rapidly and is politically mobilized. Most Samoans in Australia spent some time in New Zealand first.

This transpacific movement system, although attenuated, is held together by frequent visiting of kin, church, and sports malaga and by resilient cultural values such as mutual support in times of need (fa'alavelave), helping out to meet temporary financial shortfalls (fesoasoani), and service (tautua) to the family and chiefs (matai). These cultural connections keep Samoans strongly committed to the Samoan way of life, their language, spirituality, music, dance, and the arts.

Samoans in the United States continue to be devout Christians, most attending Congregationalist churches to some degree connected to the London Missionary Society (Lamosa) administrative structure in Samoa. Ministers (faifeau) provide both spiritual and secular guidance, and churches are crucial centers of social solidarity for Samoans wherever they reside. Within the churches women incorporate elements of traditional dance in their worship and play an active role in church fund-raising activities. Samoan men and women join in choral singing that has received international recognition. After the Sunday morning service, ministers meet with titled chiefs, who are often deacons within the church, and other community leaders to share a large meal (to'onai) and discuss church and community development issues. Many Samoans return on Sunday evening for a second church service.

In California, the National Office of Samoan Affairs (NOSA) attempts to coordinate community development efforts with well-established offices in San Francisco, Los Angeles, and San Diego. The NOSA board is comprised of ministers, chiefs, and younger, well-educated Samoan leaders. This provides a unique decision-making system integrating Christian, traditional chiefly, and contemporary, urban perspectives. NOSA has been successful in providing job training, delivering nutrition and other programs to Samoan elderly, documenting health needs, particularly relating to cardiovascular diseases, diabetes, and cancer, and generally providing political visibility for a relatively small population in a huge state.

In Hawaii, the Samoan Roundtable attempts to provide overall coordination of Samoan community developments. The roundtable also attempts to integrate the perspectives of ministers, titled chiefs and young, well-educated Samoan leaders. The Samoan Service Providers Association has been successful in working with NOSA and in providing job training opportunites. The Fetu Ao organization has the longest history as a Samoan organization in Hawaii and has focused its efforts on developing summer programs for Samoan youths in public housing, and more recently on HIV/AIDS prevention education and cancer control. The HIV/AIDS education program was developed in Hawaii because of its central location for highly mobile Samoans. There have been very few reported cases of HIV/AIDS in the Samoan population, and the program is hoping to play a significant role in prevention.

Most Samoans in the United States proper maintain their cultural heritage to some degree, and the overall pattern has been one of strong adherence to tradition and a slow rate of assimilation. Their mobility, connectedness to home, and commitment to a Samoan way of life that effectively withstood Western colonizing influences contribute to their cultural resilience in the United States. Samoans are justifiably proud of their culture and their history of conservative resistance to Western influence. However, the Samoan resistance to assimilation within a dominant American culture is problematic in many ways.

Samoan commitment to kin residing elsewhere diverts resources that might be invested in improved housing, education, and health care. Traveling home and visiting kin can affect employment and career mobility. Commitment to the Samoan language can affect educational opportunities. Church participation and donations, a source of tremendous self-worth for many Samoans, can also negatively affect improvements in standard of living. Most Samoans feel that they are rich in family and blessed by an abundance of familial and Christian love, and many trust in the day when they can return to their beloved Samoa.

Samoans clearly perceive their own cultural identity and clearly feel the sharp sting of discrimination. They are overrepresented in the prison systems of Hawaii and California, and many community leaders feel the news media have played a powerful role in promoting negative stereotypes. Samoan community leaders are deeply concerned that a new generation of Samoans and part-Samoans born in the United States proper will not benefit from Samoan cultural values but only suffer from existing educational and economic conditions and the negative stereotypes they confront. Most feel that there is an urgency to helping Samoans in the United States become bilingual and multicultural, but with a solid commitment to the Samoan way of life.

See also:   PACIFIC ISLANDERS IN HAWAII

## Bibliography

Davidson, J. W. (1967). *Samoa mo Samoa.* Melbourne: Oxford University Press.

Franco, R. (1987). *Samoans in Hawaii: A Demographic Profile.* Honolulu: Population Institute, East-West Center.

Franco, R. (1989). "Samoan Representations of World War II and Military Work: The Emergence of International Movement Networks." In *The Pacific Theater: Island Representations of World War II,* edited by G. White and L. Lindstrom. Honolulu: University of Hawaii Press.

Franco, R. (1991). *Samoan Perceptions of Work: Moving Up and Moving Around.* New York: AMS Press.

Franco, R. (1992). "Western Schooling and Transformations in Samoan Social Status in Hawaii." In *Social Change in the Pacific,* edited by B. Robillard. London: Kegan Paul.

Franco, R. (1993a). "International Movement and Samoan Marriage in Hawaii." In *The Business of Marriage in the Contemporary Pacific,* edited by R. Marksbury. Pittsburgh: University of Pittsburgh Press.

Franco, R. (1993b). "Samoan and Micronesian Migration: 'Relative Economies.'" In *A World Perspectives on Pacific Islander Migration,* edited by G. McCall and J. Connell. Sydney: Center for South Pacific Studies, University of New South Wales.

Lewthwaite, G.; Mainzer, C.; and Holland, P. J. (1973). "From Polynesia to California: Samoan Migration and Its Sequel." *Journal of Pacific History* 8:133–157.

Macpherson, C.; Shore, B.; and Franco, R. (1978). *New Neighbors: Islanders in Adaptation.* Santa Cruz, CA: Center for South Pacific Studies.

Pirie, P. D. (1970). "Samoa: Two Approaches to Population and Resource Problems." In *Geography in a Crowding World: A Symposium on Population Pressures Upon Physical and Social Resources in the Developing Lands,* edited by W. Zelinsky, L. A. Kosinsky, and R. M. Prothero. New York: Oxford University Press.

U.S. Department of Commerce. (1993). *We the American Pacific Islanders.* Washington, DC: Economic and Statistics Administration, Bureau of the Census.

ROBERT W. FRANCO

# SARDINIANS

Sardinians inhabit the island of Sardinia, an autonomous region of Italy. Italian by nationality, Sardinians see themselves as a distinct ethnic group. Most Sardinians speak Italian, but some still speak their local Sardinian language, a dialect derived from the ancient Latin of the Romans. In addition, there are small pockets of populations that speak other colonial languages, such as Catalonian Spanish.

## Geography and History

The island of Sardinia lies in the central Mediterranean Sea, 115 miles north of the African coast, 130 miles southwest of the Italian port city of Civitavecchia, and separated from Corsica to the north by the Strait of Bonifacio. After Sicily, Sardinia is the second-largest Mediterranean island.

Sardinia has roughly 1.6 million inhabitants and is the least densely populated region of Italy. The two main urban centers are Cagliari, the provincial capital of the South, and Sassari, provincial capital of the North.

Sardinia has been inhabited since prehistoric times, though little is known about the original inhabitants of the island. The Phoenicians established contact with the Sardinians around 1000 B.C.E. for the purpose of trade. Both the Carthaginians and the Romans conquered the island, imposed military and political domination, and exploited the people and the land. The indigenous peoples were either subjugated or sought refuge in the highlands, and Sardinia became divided into two socioeconomic subregions: the foreign-dominated agricultural lowlands and the independent but impoverished highlands. This separation has characterized Sardinia up to modern times. The island was again conquered by the Vandals and later by Byzantium. By the eighth century, foreign rule began to withdraw from Sardinia, ushering in a period of autonomous government. The absence of a strong military power on the island, however, lent itself to further invasion, and from 1323 to 1478, Aragon won control of Sardinia, initiating four centuries of Spanish domination. Finally, in 1861, Sardinia was incorporated into the newly unified Italian state.

Until recently, the Sardinian economy had been primarily subsistence, with very limited commerce and handicrafts making up the only industries. Today, the service sector, including government employment and small business, employs more Sardinians than any other. A small-crafts industry produces items for the tourist trade and for export. The two major industries are petrochemical processing and mining; the latter is in decline.

## Immigration

The economic conditions of Sardinians at the time of emigration were extremely low. Most of the land is unsuitable for agriculture with the exception of the Campidano Plain, a corridor of fertile lowlands in the southwest. Two-thirds of the island, however, is suitable for pastoralism. The Sardinian emigrants were in general poor farmers at low levels of specialization in agriculture, or *servi pastori* (servant shepherds) who worked as shepherds but did not own the sheep themselves.

Seeking better economic opportunities elsewhere, Sardinians began to emigrate at the end of the nineteenth century. From 1876 to 1913, a total of 23,336 Sardinians left their homeland for South America and the United States. The majority of these Sardinians immigrated to South America (particularly Argentina and Brazil) rather than to the United States. In 1882, for example, emigrants from Villacidro, a village in southern Sardinia, embarked for South America to work on the plantations and in the construction of railways. In fact, Sardinia represents one of the Italian regions that have had the least number of people immigrating to the United States.

As a whole, Sardinians engaged heavily in return migration. Being deeply rooted in the Sardinian soil, many of them never had any intention of remaining in America permanently. A large number of them planned to improve their economic conditions and return to Sardinia. Thus the immigration tended to be predominately male, accompanied by few wives or other female members of the family.

## Life in America

Many Sardinian emigrants came from Carloforte, where they had been sailors; some were even deserters from the Italian Merchant Navy. In America, many of these men worked as longshoremen. Other Sardinians worked in the mining camps of Virginia, in the cotton mills of Massachusetts, in the road constructions of Connecticut, and in the various odd jobs of large cities such as New York, Philadelphia, and Chicago.

Because of their small numbers, Sardinians, unlike other Italians, did not form ethnic neighborhoods. A group larger than four or five Sardinians was difficult to find almost anywhere in the United States. Thus, though Sardinians joined established Roman Catholic churches in America, there are no distinct Sardinian church-related organizations. Also, there are few fraternal activities or ethnic organizations identified with Sardinians in America. The Fraterna Carolina (Caroline Brotherhood) was one known institution organized by Sardinians in New York around 1916. The brotherhood consisted of 380 members, all from Carloforte. It lasted until about 1950, and it provided, among other things, medical assistance to all immigrants from Carloforte and social amusements such as dances.

Sardinians who remained in America and raised children realized upward mobility with the second generation. Often the children of the first immigrants were able to go to college and become professionals. Many other Sardinian Americans acquired wealth through commercial activities.

Today, many Sardinians continue the trek between Sardinia and the United States. There are even those who own property in both countries and live for part of the year in each.

*See also:* ITALIANS

## Bibliography

Foerster, R. (1969). *The Italian Emigration of Our Times.* New York: Arno Press.

Unali, L., and Mulas, F. (1986). "Peculiarities in the Immigration to America of Sardinians from Carloforte, 1900–1930." In *Support and Struggle: Italians and Italian Americans in a Comparative Perspective* (Proceedings of the Seventeenth Annual Conference of the American Italian Historical Association), edited by J. Tropea, J. E. Miller, and C. Bettie-Repetti. New York: American Italian Historical Association.

Unali, L., and Mulas, F. (1987). "Sardinian Immigration to the Americas Since 1900 Projected into the Year 2000." In *The Melting Pot and Beyond: Italian Americans in the Year 2000* (Proceedings of the Eighteenth Annual Conference of the American Italian Historical Association), edited by J. Krase and W. Egelman. New York: American Italian Historical Association.

Unali, L., and Mulas, F. (1989). "Assimilation and Mobility of the Sardinian Immigrants to America: Garments and Solitude." In *Italian Americans: The Search for a Usable Past* (Proceedings of the Nineteenth Annual Conference of the American Italian Historical Association), edited by R. N. Juliani and P. V. Cannistraro. New York: American Italian Historical Association.

DIANE C. VECCHIO

# SCOTCH-IRISH

The Scotch-Irish ethnic group is defined by the two geographical regions of the British Isles in which they once lived: Scotland and Ireland. The group has been also referred to as Scots-Irish, Ulster Scots, Ulstermen, and Northern Irishmen. Since they were originally Lowland Scots, they were somewhat less Scotch than Highland Scotsmen. And having come from Scotland, they were far less Irish than Irishmen. Yet they were nearly as Celtic as other northern and western peoples of the British Isles. Are they Scotch or Scot? The adjective "Scotch" identifies whiskey, or plaid cloth, or candy such as butterscotch. But "Scot" meaning Scotsman could lead to the possible term "Scots-Irish." However, throughout the literature and here as well, "Scotch-Irish" is the proper and widely accepted term. While in Northern Ireland's Ulster Province, they thought of themselves as the "Irish of the North." Upon arrival in America they probably identified themselves as "Irish," as the term "Scotch-Irish" was so rare. It was not until much later that they would become known as the Scotch-Irish people and even then not without controversy. In eighteenth-century America outsiders called the Scotch-Irish people "Ulster Irish," "Northern Irish," "Presbyterian Irish," or simply "Irish" because the ships they came in had embarked from Irish port cities. Twentieth-century American descendants of the Scotch-Irish have been called "mountaineers," "hillbillies," and "rednecks." Derogatory terms such as "poor whites" and "white trash" have been applied to some

Scotch-Irish descendants based on their economic status and, unfortunately, what others think of them.

The history of the term "Scotch-Irish" is clouded in mystery. The first recorded use of the term was on April 14, 1573, when Queen Elizabeth I used "Scotch-Irish" to refer to the intermarrying of Scottish Highlanders with Irish native folk in County Antrim in Ireland. The queen's use of the term did not refer to the genuine Scotch-Irish people, who, beginning in 1610, immigrated as Lowland Scots to Northern Ireland's Ulster Province. The first record of the term in America was in 1695, when Sir Thomas Lawrence, secretary of Maryland, reported of "Scotch-Irish" people there wearing linen and wool clothing and living in Dorchester and Somerset counties, Maryland. This use of the term preceded the major immigrations of the folk to America by twenty-two years! While they were immigrating to America from 1717 to 1775, they were rarely called "Scotch-Irish" but rather were most often referred to as "Irish." Between 1776 and 1850, the term "Scotch-Irish" virtually disappears from the record and is not revived until the mid-nineteenth century, and then only as a term of prejudice. Following the Irish potato famine in Ireland in the 1840s, thousands of Irish immigrants poured into Eastern Seaboard cities. The distinction was then made between the older, more established, quite Americanized Scotch-Irish and the newly arrived, impoverished, foreign Irish. Unlike the Irish of the 1840s, the Scotch-Irish did not linger in eastern ports. Between 1717 and 1775, they quickly migrated westward and southward in an ever-widening dispersal, all the while becoming more and more American as they developed the way of life of the frontier-people in the wilderness interior of colonial America.

## Immigration and Settlement History

The Scotch-Irish originally were groups of Celtic folk of a Scottish nature who came from the Lowlands and the hill areas of southern Scotland, the border country between Scotland and England, and the western Scottish coast and Hebrides Islands. Beginning in 1610, they moved a mere twenty miles across the North Channel in the Irish Sea to Northern Ireland (Ulster), where they were situated on "plantations," colonies of settlements established by King James I (for whom the King James Bible and Jamestown, Virginia, are named). In spite of several generations of successful development in agriculture and the woolen and linen industries, the group came under attack by English trade policies and by rent-racking schemes of local landlords so that many Scotch-Irish immigrated to America during much of the eighteenth century.

From 1717 to 1775, the Scotch-Irish and their descendants began major immigrations to the Americas. Contrary to popular belief, the Scotch-Irish immigration did *not* uniformly land on the Atlantic shores in eastern North America and sweep directly westward but formed two widely separated streams that entered through the ports of Philadelphia and Charleston, South Carolina. Through the ensuing generations, the population streams grew toward each other, creating an arc of Scotch-Irish settlement in colonial America. The larger, more important stream entered through Philadelphia and established a cultural hearth, a gathering place and staging area in the Susquehanna River valley just west of Philadelphia between 1710 and 1730. The subsequent migration went as far as the Allegheny Plateau escarpment, where it took a major course southward, following the Great Valley in the Ridge and Valley Province to southwestern Virgina by 1735. From interior Virginia the routes took several divergent courses. One continued straight down the valley trend toward northeastern Tennessee and later threaded northwestward through the Cumberland Gap to lead settlers deep into Kentucky. A larger route went southeasterly, passed through the Roanoke and New River gaps, and spilled immigrants out onto the Piedmont region of North Carolina. An important hearth of Scotch-Irish settlement formed here between the Yadkin and Catawba River valleys in the 1740s and 1750s.

A secondary stream from the southeastern Pennsylvania hearth pushed directly westward to form another Scotch-Irish hearth, in the Pittsburgh vicinity, between 1768 and 1790. From this Pittsburgh hearth, continuing migrations would lead into the Ohio River Valley in the late eighteenth and well into the nineteenth centuries.

In South Carolina, another migration stream of Scotch-Irish began from the port of Charleston as early as 1732 and pushed seventy-five miles northward, to the Kingstree settlement. As more people arrived, the migration streams pushed inland to the upcountry in the South Carolina Piedmont to form another Scotch-Irish hearth. From this interior South Carolina hearth, smaller streams pushed southwestward to Georgia and northeastward to North Carolina to eventually link up with the North Carolina Piedmont hearth in the Catawba and Yadkin River valleys.

Throughout the region, other migration routes formed, and the settling process continued. From the North Carolina Piedmont hearth, settlers led by Daniel Boone, James Robertson, and John Sevier in 1771–1772 crossed the Blue Ridge Mountains of southern Appalachia and followed the Watauga River directly westward to settle northeastern Tennessee. From these Watauga settlements of early Tennessee, additional westward migration was carried directly overland and via the Tennessee River in 1779–1780 to establish settlement in the Nashville Basin. Meanwhile, many settlers coming down the Great Valley turned northwestward through the Cumberland Gap to dominate the Blue Grass Basin in central Kentucky. Migrations continued down the valley trends toward the areas that were to become Knoxville, Chattanooga, and Birmingham as threats of Indian attacks lessened and lands were opened for permanent settlement. Out of the South Carolina hearth, settlers migrated northward through the Blue Ridge Mountains through the Saluda Gap to forge their way into the Asheville Basin and eventually westward to Tennessee. The southern Appalachian region was the homeland of Cherokee and other Native American groups, so much of the land was closed to European settlement until after the 1790s. Much of the South's interior to the west and south was Chocktaw, Chickasaw, and other Native American–held territory that prevented major European incursions until after 1830. Once in America, the Scotch-Irish quickly made a home for themselves and did not make circular or return migrations to the British Isles.

## Demography

It is unclear how many Scotch-Irish immigrated to America. An estimated 114,000 immigrants arrived in the colonies between 1718 and 1778, but the estimates for the period 1707–1783 range between 102,000 and 125,000. Even in America, Scotch-Irish populations had to be estimated because the census for 1790 did not identify persons of Scotch-Irish ancestry. In 1902, Charles A. Hanna used the 1790 census to proportion the population from 1775 to estimate a total of 335,000 Scotch-Irish *and* Scots for the following states: Pennsylvania, 100,000; Delaware, 10,000; Maryland, 30,000; Virginia, 75,000; North Carolina, 65,000; South Carolina, 45,000; and Georgia, 10,000.

Attempts to determine the populations of early groups from the British Isles continued in disagreement. In 1909, the U.S. Census Bureau estimated the Scotch-Irish population to be 14.3 percent of the 1790 total population of 3,172,444, or 453,659 persons with an apparent Scotch-Irish identity. In 1931, a committee of historians estimated the Scotch-Irish to be 6.7 percent of the 1790 population, thus accounting for about 212,554 persons as Scotch-Irish. Modern historians have attempted to separate the immigrants by Scotch, Irish, and Welsh surnames, while other scholars continue to make percentage estimates. Still, it is unclear. Which Scots came from Ulster? Which Scots were directly from Scotland, and were they Highland or Lowland Scots? Which Irish were exclusively from Ulster? Which immigrants were truly Irish, from southern Ireland, and which were English? There is no clear way of knowing. However, the general pattern after 1790 and until about 1860 shows that about half the population in the American South was composed of Scotch, Irish, and Welsh, and about one-fourth of the population had come from western and northern England.

To simplify, approximately 200,000 Scotch-Irish immigrants arrived in what was to become

the United States during the major years of immigration between 1717 and 1775. By 1790, the
Scotch-Irish population had grown to about
250,000, making it the second-largest group next
to the English in the United States at that time. The
best opportunity to take the pulse of this elusive
group is in the 1990 U.S. Census, in which the U.S.
population expresses its ancestry in the clearest
terms yet. The response is a current population of
5,617,773 Americans who claim Scotch-Irish ancestry. This represents approximately 2.3 percent
of the total population of 248,709,873 for 1990 in
the United States. Urban populations of Scotch-
Irish account for 4,026,024 people, while rural
populations total 1,591,749. One might expect the
rural populations to be larger, but they are not. For
example, only 92,456 people with Scotch-Irish
ancestry live in places with a population of less
than 1,000; and for places with a population of
1,000 to 2,999, the total is 178,739. Those living
in rural areas who are still farmers account for
101,876 people.

The 1990 U.S. Census identifies a smaller
subgroup of native, American-born Scotch-Irish to
be 4,303,899 people, which divides into 2,021,654
males and 2,282,245 females in the native population. The population is composed of three major
age groups. There are 926,316 children and young
people, whose ages range from less than one year
to twenty-one years. Those in the primary working
age group, between twenty-two and sixty-four,
account for 2,421,916. People sixty-five or over
total 955,667 persons.

A valid Scotch-Irish representation in the
population endures in those areas of first effective
settlement. Strong concentrations of contemporary Scotch-Irish can be found in the old areas
of initial settlement in Pennsylvania (270,299
Scotch-Irish descendants), North Carolina
(343,345), and South Carolina (159,534), with
concentrations in some of the adjacent states
such as Ohio (217,478), New York (165,952),
Virginia (195,722), Tennessee (197,942), Missouri
(129,228), Georgia (192,187), Alabama (127,826),
and on to Texas (495,886), to which nineteenth-
century migrations took numerous Scotch-Irish.

Concentrations of Scotch-Irish in parts of Ohio
and especially Michigan (157,483) and Illinois
(173,035) are largely attributed to movements of
Scotch-Irish descendants from southern states to
industrial factories in the North during and after
World War II. The Washington State (154,566)
concentration is tied to two phenomena: (1) the
movement of southern Appalachian Scotch-Irish
descendants who established rural farming communities in Washington State between 1884 and
1937, and (2) a later movement by those attracted
to the logging industry and to aircraft manufacturing in the Pacific Northwest. The huge California
contingent of 546,496 Scotch-Irish descendants is
explained by several migrations of peoples from
the East, the South, and from the Plains states. The
California Gold Rush of 1849 brought many
Scotch-Irish settlers to the West. In the 1930s,
thousands of Scotch-Irish descendants from poor
southern states and from the dust bowl states
during the Great Depression migrated to California
looking for work, much like the fictitious Joad
family in John Steinbeck's *The Grapes of Wrath*.
After World War II many Scotch-Irish descendants
made new homes in California as many returning
servicemen chose to live on the West Coast. From
the 1950s to the 1970s, southern and eastern
Scotch-Irish descendants migrated to California to
seek the perceived good life. Additional migrations
have been made by retirees who reflect a pattern
of settlement, especially in Florida (320,217) and
California.

## Language

The Scotch-Irish on arrival in America spoke a
form of Gaelic and/or English with a distinctive
brogue or accent. Scholars have since discovered
in the southern Appalachians that the folk speech
there is English, too, The word *hit* (as in "*Hit don't
matter*") is the third person singular neuter pro-
noun for *it*, a proper form of Old English. Words
such as yonder and nigh for over there and near,
respectively, are still widely used. His'n, our'n,
your'n, and her'n are possessives much like mine
and thine and were quite proper English in an-

Scotch-Irish settlers adopted folk architecture of the English pen tradition, as shown in this double pen saddlebag house and four crib barn in the Great Smoky Mountains National Park in Sevier County, Tennessee. (John B. Rehder)

other century. Colorful speech with analogies and sayings pervade Scotch-Irish speech: "Hit's blue cold out thar!" "He's quick as double-geared lightnin'." "She's as slow as molasses but near 'bout as sweet."

There are no major or official language maintenance programs for preserving the accents of southern mountain speech. Isolation was and still is the best preserver of dialect. Articles such as "Folk Speech Is English, Too" and booklets on southern mountain English described as "The Queen's English" along with various publications on how to talk like a "redneck" can be found, but most are used for entertainment. Preservation practices of a more serious nature have been instituted since the mid-1930s, but mainly to collect folk songs and folk stories.

## Cultural Characteristics

When the Scotch-Irish immigrated to America, the majority of them were small subsistence farmers, as the Industrial Revolution had not yet taken place. For two centuries thereafter the Scotch-Irish were still largely identified as small, independent farmers and until the 1950s, some were still eking out a living on subsistence farms. Current trends in the total work force of 2,067,143 people above age sixteen show a diversity in occupations: 28 percent in health, education, or other professional services, 15 percent in retail trade, 14.7 percent in manufacturing, and 9.3 percent in construction or transportation. A mere 2.5 percent of the work force continues in agriculture/forestry/fisheries. When divided by sex, the figures are 36.2

percent of all work force females and 34.3 percent of the males are in managerial occupations, 44.3 percent of the females and 24.5 percent of the males are in technical/sales/administrative support occupations, and 14 percent of the males and 4.9 percent of the females are in operator/fabricator/laborer occupations.

Historically, the Scotch-Irish in America were known for their fierce independence by living in isolated log cabins on the backwoods frontier. Folk house types largely followed the pattern of the English pen tradition, for which a pen represents an individual room unit, much like a one-room cabin. In the typology, houses evolved from single-pen houses; to double-pen houses with two rooms and called dogtrot, saddlebag, or Cumberland houses; to I-houses that were two stories tall, two rooms wide, and one room deep; to four-pen houses that had four rooms over four rooms. Construction techniques and materials were either horizontal, rounded, or squared hewn logs with corner notches, or later framed sawn lumber, but rarely brick or stone. Log construction, the primary building method, was introduced early to America by Swedish, Finnish, and German immigrants and was quickly adopted by Scotch-Irish settlers and their descendants. The many types of corner notching included saddle notch, saddle V notch, V notch, half dovetail notch, full dovetail notch, square notch, half notch, diamond notch, and half-log or semilunate crown notch.

Scotch-Irish independence continues to be reflected in their choice of contemporary housing. According to the 1990 U.S. Census, of the 1,994,366 total housing units occupied by native Scotch-Irish descendants, there were 1,345,919 single-unit, freestanding dwellings, representing 67.5 percent. Another 135,319 shelters were mobile homes. There were 1,433,903 owner-occupied housing units and 510,463 renter-occupied units. In the owner-occupied units, 4,925 places lacked complete plumbing facilities. In the renter category there were 2,274 units that lacked complete plumbing facilities.

The religion of the Scotch-Irish originally was Presbyterian in Ulster and remained Presbyterian for generations in America. Over time, numerous Scotch-Irish adopted other denominations, chiefly Baptist, Methodist, and Church of Christ, and founded numerous fundamentalist splinter groups. Their worldview in the past was extremely limited, perhaps restricted to just a hollow, a ridge, or a county, and would have continued in this narrow direction were it not for wars fought in foreign lands, improved transportation, and television and other forms of electronic communication that now reach nearly everyone. In the past, family and kinship ties were very strong for the Scotch-Irish. In rural isolation, clans formed enclaves of kin and kindred folk and stuck by each other, enduring all types of hardships together. Many of the older generations still hold to these values, and marriages remain strong. The 1990 U.S. Census indicates that there were 2,113,946 married Scotch-Irish descendants over age fifteen whose spouse currently lived with them. However, the national trend embracing easy divorce also affects families of Scotch-Irish ancestry. The 1990 U.S. Census shows that 130,903 males and 206,105 females over age fifteen are divorced.

For centuries the Scotch-Irish were not a group known for fine arts of any kind. But their folk art has been distinctive. Of particular note are the rich traditions in storytelling and folklore. Their folk songs have evolved into the broader realms of country and bluegrass music. Other artistic contributions are in folk dancing, especially clogging, and crafts such as quiltmaking and woodworking.

Illness, death, and hardship are main points on the compass of conversation. The Scotch-Irish as well as the Scots have had a tendency to "enjoy poor health," meaning that when asked about their health, they like nothing better than to tell all the details of what is ailing them.

The Scotch-Irish have mostly avoided the national political arena, often choosing instead to deal with political matters using frontier justice. However, some of America's leaders came from Scotch-Irish stock. James Buchanan, fifteenth president of the United States, was from Scotch-Irish ancestry in Pennsylvania. Jimmy Carter,

America's thirty-ninth president, came from Scotch-Irish folk who had migrated early from Virginia to Georgia, where the Carters became peanut farmers. As political parties developed, most Scotch-Irish identified with grassroots politics, following the lines of the Democratic party.

## Extent of Assimilation

The Scotch-Irish are probably the most rapidly and most thoroughly assimilated ethnic group in America. Their identity was clouded and uncertain for more than 140 years until the 1850s, and by then the Scotch-Irish were already probably the most Americanized of ethnic groups. Their identity was never quite clear in the British Isles either, and it was virtually lost in America until the arrival of Irish potato famine survivors in the 1840s. By then, most people of Scotch-Irish ancestry were already American. Today cultural persistence remains in regional dialect, religion, and independence, but to a lesser degree in the material culture. While they are economically and socially stratified, the Scotch-Irish are in an ethnic mist, so clouded by their Americanism and so poorly identified except for the 1990 U.S. Census that they rarely experience direct ethnic discrimination. Their relations with other groups have been wry, but when it comes to dealing with them on a one-to-one basis—in the South, at least—the underlying question still comes down to "Who's yer daddy?"

*See also:* IRISH; SCOTS; TRAVELERS

## Bibliography

Cunningham, R. (1987). *Apples on the Flood: The Southern Mountain Experience.* Knoxville: University of Tennessee Press.

Dial, W. P. (1970). "Folk Speech Is English, Too." *Mountain Life and Work* 46(March):15–17.

Green, E. R. (1992). *Essays in Scotch-Irish History.* Belfast: Ulster Historical Foundation.

Green, S. S. ([1895] 1970). *The Scotch-Irish in America.* San Francisco: R & E Research Associates.

Hanna, C. A. ([1902] 1985). *The Scotch-Irish, or The Scot in North Britain, North Ireland, and North America,* 2 vols. Baltimore, MD: Genealogical Publishing Company.

Jackson, C. (1993). *A Social History of the Scotch-Irish.* Lanham, MD: Madison Books.

Johnson, J. E. (1966). *The Scots and Scotch-Irish in America.* Minneapolis: Lerner.

Jordan, T. G., and Kaups, M. (1989). *The American Backwoods Frontier.* Baltimore, MD: Johns Hopkins University Press.

Kennedy, B. (1995). *The Scots-Irish in East Tennessee.* Londonderry, Ireland: Causeway Press.

Kingsmore, R. K. (1995). *Ulster Scots Speech: A Sociolinguistic Study.* Tuscaloosa: University of Alabama Press.

Lehmann, W. C. (1978). *Scottish and Scotch-Irish Contributions to Early American Life and Culture.* Port Washington, NY: National University Publications.

Leyburn, J. G. (1962). *The Scotch-Irish: A Social History.* Chapel Hill: University of North Carolina Press.

Rehder, J. B. (1992). "The Scotch-Irish and English in Appalachia." In *To Build in a New Land: Ethnic Landscapes in North America*, edited by A. G Noble. Baltimore, MD: Johns Hopkins University Press.

Reid, W. ([1911] 1970). *The Scot in America, and the Ulster Scot.* San Francisco: R & E Research Associates.

Wells, R. A., comp. (1991). *Ulster Migration to America: Letters from Three Irish Families.* New York: P. Lang.

JOHN B. REHDER

# SCOTS

The ethnic group known as Scots in the United States refers directly to those people who over several generations, from the mid-seventeenth century through the late eighteenth century, immigrated directly from Scotland to the Americas. Commonly used names for Scottish immigrants have been either Highland Scots or Highlanders or for those from southern Scotland, Lowland Scots. Although Lowland Scots were certainly part of the immigrations, more attention has been given to Highland Scots, the clans from northern Scotland known symbolically for their tartans, bagpipes, Highland games, and rich, thick Gaelic language and brogue accents. When Scottish people first arrived in America, they were called "Scots," "Scotsmen," even "Scotch." In nineteenth- and twentieth-century America they have been referred to as "blue bloods," as in "blue-blooded Scots," at the perceived upper end of the social scale, but at the lower end of the scale some have been called "rednecks." The Scots are not to be confused with the Scotch-Irish. Scots were from Scotland pure and simple. The people known as Scotch-Irish were an ethnic group that originated as seventeenth-century Presbyterian Scots from Lowland Scotland and immigrated to "plantations" established by King James I in Northern Ireland's Ulster Province after 1610. Additional Scottish immigrants came to Ulster from the area that borders present-day southern Scotland and northern England, while others were from the western coastal Highlands of Scotland and the Hebrides Islands. Collectively these Scottish immigrants to Ulster remained in Ireland for more than one hundred years before immigrating to America from 1717 to 1775. Once in America the Scotch-Irish were difficult to define because the early census did not identify them as Scotch-Irish. Still, the Scotch-Irish have received more attention from historians than the less numerous but potentially more easily identified Scots. There were times when Scottish immigrants were counted along with Scotch-Irish. In 1902, for example, Charles A. Hanna examined the 1790 U.S. Census and adjusted the figures for the year 1775 to estimate a total of 335,000 Scotch-Irish *and* Scots for the following states: Pennsylvania, 100,000; Delaware, 10,000; Maryland, 30,000; Virginia, 75,000; North Carolina, 65,000; South Carolina, 45,000; and Georgia, 10,000. While this combines the two similar ethnic groups, the information can be used to view the immigrant population on a state-by-state basis. Modern historians Forrest and Helen McDonald examined surnames in the 1790 U.S. Census and calculated that 32.9 percent of the South Carolina population were Scots in 1790.

## Immigration History

The Scots who immigrated to what was to become the United States began their travel somewhat slowly. Before 1650, only a few hundred Scots were in America. By the 1770s, there were thousands of Scottish immigrants arriving, and according to some estimates as many as 10,000 arrived each year for several consecutive years. Because of the lack of solid documentary evidence, scholars have been forced to estimate the number of immigrants, especially for those from the British Isles. The simplest, best conservative estimate for numbers of Scottish immigrants to America is approximately 150,000 by 1785. This compares favorably with the conservative estimate of about 200,000 Scotch-Irish immigrants for the same period.

For centuries Scots had been emigrating from Scotland to such locations as Poland, the Netherlands, England, and, of course, Northern Ireland's Ulster Province, but until the late 1600s and 1700s, few had found their way to colonial America. Many of the seventeenth-century Scottish immigrants had no choice, as they were criminals and prisoners. Numerous Scottish prisoners were sent to Virginia, New England, and the West Indies. Other Scots were seeking religious freedom in the 1680s, such as the attempt to settle a Scottish Presbyterian settlement in South Carolina and the movement of Scottish Quakers into New Jersey. Economic trade factors were important motivations for emigration, as English trade restrictions affected Scottish trade. Furthermore, the Scots were becoming aware of the market potential of American raw materials and agricultural products in a European market.

The major Scottish immigrations to America occurred in the 1700s. Among the first groups were Jacobite prisoners who were banished from Scotland to occupy American "plantations" of settlements in 1715 and again in 1745. Waves of Lowland Scots arrived next, as individuals and their families voluntarily sought freedom and economic prosperity in the New World. Beginning in the 1730s, however, Highland Scots, traveling in groups, perhaps clans, immigrated to colonial America.

Scots initially settled in pods or small enclaves in the midst of the English-settled Atlantic coastal regions. Many Lowland Scots were merchants, craftsmen, traders, and others associated with urban occupations and focused their settlements in English colonial coastal cities from New England, down the coast to Georgia; they especially settled in Virginia. Highlander Scots established new frontier settlements on the interior edges of English-held areas in the Carolinas, New York, and Georgia. Although the Highlander Scots may have thought that they were going great distances inland, their migrations were not nearly as deeply penetrating as the movements of the Scotch-Irish into the frontier wilderness. But unlike the ever-moving Scotch-Irish, the Highland Scots stayed put in the places where they initially settled. This sedentary way of life in enclaves on the edge of the wilderness helped to preserve their Scottish traditional culture. A good example is North Carolina, where, in the vicinity of the present-day cities of Fayetteville (Cumberland County), Aberdeen (Moore County), and Laurinburg (Scotland County), the initial Highlanders began to arrive in 1739. This region experienced continual arrivals of additional Scots from Scotland for many years into the nineteenth century. The Scottish presence is still vigorously felt in the area.

Scottish immigration in the second half of the eighteenth century came in many different forms. In 1746, nearly 1,000 men, women, and children were banished from Scotland to be sold as indentured servants in America. During the French and Indian War, between 1754 and 1763, Highland regiments entered the fight, but after the war many Scottish soldiers chose to settle the Mohawk River Valley in upstate New York. In 1782 and 1783, failed crops in the Scottish Highlands drove many Highlanders to seek their fortune in America. In Canada the Maritime Provinces of New Brunswick, Prince Edward Island, and particularly Nova Scotia (New Scotland) were richly populated by Scots beginning in the 1760s and especially up to 1785. Once the Scots had initially settled a region, permanent settlement generally followed, so that patterns of return migration to Scotland were uncommon. This was true among Scotch-Irish immigrants as well. However, contemporary interests in "all things Scottish" have drawn many Scottish Americans and non-Scots to choose Scotland as a travel destination. Genealogical searches also have become major activities for Scottish Americans.

## Demographics

In the first U.S. Census, which was the one taken in 1790, the total population of the United States was 3,172,444 persons. The ethnic composition was as follows: English, 2,605,699; Scotch, 221,562; Germany, 176,407; Dutch, 78,959; Irish, 61,534; French, 17,619; Hebrew, 1,243; all others, 9,421. Controversy surrounds the census because the Scotch-Irish population, which was surely present in the new country, was not specifically identified. So it is not known how many of the "Scotch" and how many of the "Irish" were actually "Scotch-Irish," and more important here, how many Scots were in the "Scotch" category.

In the 1990 U.S. Census, 5,393,581 people claimed Scottish ancestry. In previous years census figures have shown far more Scots than for 1990. For example, it was estimated in 1979 that fourteen million of the U.S. population were of Scottish ancestry, but when the official 1980 U.S. Census was completed, ten million people were identified as having Scottish ancestry. The 1990 U.S. Census figure is much smaller but is possibly more accurate because it clearly separates Scots from Scotch-Irish, and both of these from those of Irish ancestry.

Of the total 5,393,581 people with Scottish ancestry, urban populations account for 4,013,188, while rural populations total 1,380,393. One might expect the rural populations to be larger, but they are not. For example, only 67,617 people with Scottish ancestry live in places with fewer than 1,000 population; and for places with 1,000 to 2,999 population, the total is 154,025. Those living in rural areas who are designated farmers account for 82,329 people.

The 1990 U.S. Census indicates a subgroup of native, American-born Scottish people to be 3,162,610, which divides into 1,688,870 males and

1,473,740 females in the native population. The current Scottish native, American-born population can be divided into three major age groups. There are 730,816 children and young people, whose ages range from less than one year to twenty-one years. Those in the primary working age group, between twenty-two and sixty-four, account for 1,913,449. People sixty-five or over total 518,345 persons.

Some of the Atlantic coastal states show concentrations of Scots owing to the ports of entry during the initial phases of early Scottish settlement. New York with 266,312 people of Scottish ancestry stands out especially for this reason. However, Massachusetts (199,489), Pennsylvania (223,544), Virginia (166,959), North Carolina (177,699), and Georgia (141,833) reflect relatively large numbers of Scottish descendants. North Carolina had the largest Scottish population in America from 1732 to 1776, and the state maintains a population of 177,699 people claiming Scottish descent. The interior states of Ohio (224,351), Michigan (252,104), and Illinois (176,096) reflect both early eighteenth- and nineteenth-century westward migration patterns. More important, they reflect twentieth-century patterns of people seeking employment in northern industrial cities from 1930 to 1960. The large contingent of Scots in Texas (306,854) reflects the nineteenth-century migrations of people from the Atlantic Seaboard states as well as some from interior states such as Tennessee and Kentucky. California has the largest population of Scottish descendants, with 646,674 people, accounting for about 12 percent of the total of 5,393,581 persons claiming Scottish ancestry. Here again, sporadic migrations over time account for the ethnicity in the state. The Gold Rush to California in 1849 would have attracted Scottish folk probably as much as the Great Depression of the 1930s drove many out of the South and Midwest to seek employment in California. Post–World War II migrations would have brought peoples of Scottish descent to California, Washington State, and Florida for employment, amenities, or retirement.

## Language

Upon arrival in America many Scottish immigrants spoke Gaelic. In the initial phases of settlement in eighteenth-century North Carolina, existing groups complained about the newly arrived Scots' unintelligible Gaelic speech. In 1756, Hugh McAden reported that several Scots scarcely knew one word of English. Even as English speech took over, there were survivals of Gaelic in America for more than a century. There are few if any formal language maintenance programs for the preservation of the Scottish dialect or brogue accent. However, some Presbyterian churches have made the effort to secure clergymen directly from Scotland to feature the "Scottish" brogue in church sermons. In the South, characteristic Scottish speech can be heard in words such as whar, that, dar, fahr in place of where, there, dare, and fire, respectively. In the vernacular of the inner coastal plain of North Carolina one might hear "Far engines run on rubber tars, and we fix 'em with bailing war and plars" (Fire engines run on rubber tires, and we fix them with boiling wire and pliers).

## Cultural Characteristics

When the Scots immigrated to America, many of those who settled in places such as North Carolina were men of wealth who had brought a level of prosperity with them from Scotland. Many had the agricultural skills and Scottish thrift that helped them later develop large, prosperous farms. For two and a half centuries thereafter in North Carolina, Scots were still largely identified as independent farmers with large holdings that had passed from generation to generation but clearly kept within the family. For example in Scotland County, North Carolina, the largest farms in cotton, tobacco, and cattle are still held by "blue-blooded Scots" with names such as McNair, McArthur, and McLloyd.

Employment trends in the total work force of 1,673,890 people above age sixteen show a diversity in occupations: 27 percent are in health/education/other professional services, 14.4 percent in retail trade, 15.8 percent in manufacturing, and 9.8 percent work in construction or transportation. Only 2.5 percent of the work force continues in agriculture/forestry/fisheries. When divided by sex, the figures are 38.1 percent of the females in the work force and 37.1 percent of males are in managerial occupations, 42.9 percent of the female work force and 24.3 percent of the males are in technical/sales/administrative support occupations, and 12.5 percent of the males and 4.4 percent of the females in the work force are in operators/fabricators/laborers occupations.

In eighteenth-century America, the initial Scots lived in relatively crudely constructed pine log houses. Very soon thereafter, houses of sawn planks came into vogue as sawmills were built. More important, the English from quite early on emphasized building with sawn lumber, so it was natural for the Scottish immigrants to adopt the construction techniques already established. House types in the Scottish communities began following the pattern of the English Pen tradition, in which a pen represents an individual room unit, much like a one-room cabin. In the typology, houses evolved from single-pen houses to double-pen houses (two rooms) to I-houses that were two stories tall, two rooms wide, and one room deep to four-pen houses that had four rooms over four rooms. Construction techniques and materials were originally horizontal round logs with corner saddle notches, or later framed sawn lumber, but rarely brick or stone.

Scottish independence continues to be shown in their choice of contemporary housing. According to the 1990 U.S. Census, of the 1,456,998 total housing units occupied by American-born Scottish descendants there were 994,055 single-unit, freestanding dwellings, representing 68.2 percent. There were 86,055 mobile homes. Owner-occupied housing units accounted for 1,050,181 places. There were 415,817 renter-occupied units. In the owner-occupied units, 3,445 places lacked complete plumbing facilities. In the renter category there were 1,838 units that lacked complete plumbing facilities.

The religion of the Scottish immigrant groups was predominantly Presbyterian in Scotland, and it remained Presbyterian for generations in America. Over time some Scots adopted other denominations, chiefly Baptist, Methodist, or fundamentalist splinter groups. Historically the Scottish worldview was limited to a community or a county and would have continued to be so were it not for America's participation in foreign wars, improved transportation, and forms of electronic communication via telephone, radio, and television. The Scots in America use illness, death, and hardship as main points of conversation. Scotch-Irish *and* Scots have a tendency to "enjoy poor health," meaning that when asked about their health, they like to tell all the details of what is ailing them.

Family and kinship ties have always been strong for Scots. Much like the clans in Scotland, groups in America formed enclaves of kinfolk who lived in close proximity to each other. Primary families and extended families were often very very close, working together, protecting each other, enduring hardships, and visiting together. Most get-togethers were devoted to visiting kinfolk on Sunday afternoons. Many of the older Scottish generations still hold to these values, and marriages remain strong. The 1990 U.S. Census indicates that there were 1,649,136 married people of Scottish ancestry over age fifteen who were still living with their spouse. However, the national trend for divorce also affects families of Scottish ancestry. The 1990 U.S. Census indicates that 104,893 males and 117,586 females over age fifteen are divorced.

Scottish Highland games and Scottish festivals are among the fastest-growing interest activities among Scottish descendants and non-Scots in North America. There are 194 annual scheduled events in Scottish games and festivals in North America with 168 in the United States and 26 in Canada. In Scotland about 40 events are held annually. Highland games, also called Caledonian games, are athletic events that originated in the

A kilted competitor at the 1987 Scottish Highland Games in Santa Rosa, California, tosses the caber. The object is to toss the caber both the longest distance and hard enough for it to fall on its far end and topple away from the thrower. (DeWitt Jones/Corbis)

Scottish Highlands as part of the traditional gathering of the clans. Competitions are held in footraces; jumping events; hill racing; wrestling; hammer throwing; shot-putting with a heavy stone; and caber tossing, which involves throwing a tree trunk that weights one hundred pounds and is sixteen to nineteen feet long end over end. Kilts are worn, bagpipes are played, and Scottish terriers are shown amid much pageantry and ceremony.

In addition to the growing interest in Highland games are the organized Scottish clans and families that celebrate their Scottish heritage. There are 81 formal Scottish clan organizations in the United States and Canada. Scottish-American clans and families seek kin and kindred interests in all things Scottish. This important step in the preservation of the culture and the search for cultural heritage and ethnicity leads to genealogical research, tourism to

Scotland, and the collection and promotion of "all things Scottish," such as bagpipes, pipe and drum corps, kilts, tartan plaid fabrics, tams, Scotch whiskey, haggis (a delicacy made from various ingredients boiled in the stomach of sheep), Scottish folk songs, Scottish folk stories, Gaelic language, Scottish accents, and Scottish terriers.

The social organization of Scots in America has closely matched but does not mirror exactly the social structure in Scotland. Families and kinships were and remain strong in both Scotland and North America. However, clans remain much stronger in Scotland than in America because of the greater freedom and mobility of American groups. Clannish, yes, but in varying degree are the Scots. Politically, the Scots in America are known to be largely conservative, partly owning to their tradition of thriftiness.

## Extent of Assimilation

The extent of assimilation of the Scots has not been as rapid or as thorough as that of the Scotch-Irish in America. Scottish identity was relatively good and, for some, it has remained so for more than three centuries. Scottish identity has always been quite clear in the British Isles, and while it has been diluted in greater measure in America, still there were enclaves of Scots who made certain that while they were becoming Americanized, they would hold to their ethnic Scottish identity, even if only in memory. The Scottish cultural persistence is still strong in religion, independence, and especially in the resurgence of interest in material culture, Scottish Highland games, and Scottish festivals.

*See also:* SCOTCH-IRISH; TRAVELERS

## Bibliography

Aspinwall, B. (1984). *Portable Utopia: Glasgow and the United States, 1820–1920.* Aberdeen: Aberdeen University Press.

Black, G. F. ([1921] 1972). *Scotland's Mark on America.* San Francisco: R & E Research Associates.

Brownlee, R. (1986). *An American Odyssey: The Autobiography of a 19th Century Scotsman, Robert Brownlee, at the Request of His Children: Napa County, California, October 1892.* Fayetteville: University of Arkansas Press.

Dobson, D. (1984). *Directory of Scottish Settlers in North America, 1625–1825,* 4 vols. Baltimore, MD: Genealogical Publishing Company.

Dobson, D. (1994). *Scottish Emigration to Colonial America, 1607–1785.* Athens: University of Georgia Press.

Erickson, C. (1972). *Invisible Immigrants: The Adaptation of English and Scottish Immigrants in Nineteenth-Century America.* Coral Gables, FL: University of Miami Press.

Graham, I. C. C. (1956). *Colonists from Scotland: Emigration to North America, 1707–1783.* Ithaca, NY: Cornell University Press.

Johnson, J. E. (1966). *The Scots and Scotch-Irish in America.* Minneapolis: Lerner.

Jordan, T. G., and Kaups, M. (1989). *The American Backwoods Frontier.* Baltimore, MD: Johns Hopkins University Press.

Karras, A. L. (1992). *Sojourners in the Sun: Scottish Migrants in Jamaica and the Chesapeake, 1740–1800.* Ithaca, NY: Cornell University Press.

Landsman, N. C. (1985). *Scotland and Its First American Colony, 1683–1765.* Princeton, NJ: Princeton University Press.

Lefler, H. T., and Newsome, A. R. (1963). *North Carolina: The History of a Southern State,* revised edition. Chapel Hill: University of North Carolina Press.

Lehmann, W. C. (1978). *Scottish and Scotch-Irish Contributions to Early American Life and Culture.* Port Washington, NY: National University Publications.

Maclean, J. P. ([1900] 1978). *An Historical Account of Settlements of Scotch Highlanders in America Prior to the Peace of 1783.* Baltimore, MD: Genealogical Publishing Company.

Meyer, D. G. (1961). *The Highland Scots of North Carolina.* Chapel Hill: University of North Carolina Press.

Redmond, G. (1971). *The Caledonian Games in Nineteenth-Century America.* Rutherford, NJ: Fairleigh Dickinson University Press.

Reid, W. ([1911] 1970). *The Scot in America, and the Ulster Scot.* San Francisco: R & E Research Associates.

Scarlett, J. D. (1976). *The Tartans Spotter's Guide.* New York: Van Nostrand Reinhold.

JOHN B. REHDER

# SEA ISLANDERS

Sea Islanders are African Americans living on the numerous Sea Islands off the coasts of South Carolina, Georgia, and the northern tip of Florida. Sea Islanders, their language, and their culture have been labeled Gullah by non-Sea Islander academics and Geechee by non-Sea Island everyday people. Sea Islanders, however, consider both Gullah and Geechee to be derogatory terms.

More than one thousand barrier islands make up the Sea Island chain. The islands are characterized by winding and twisting rivers, tidal marshes, swampy lands, estuaries, rich wetlands, and breathtakingly beautiful hanging Spanish moss. Known as the "low country," the islands are flat, with elevations ranging from near sea level to a little more than one hundred feet. The yearly temperature ranges between forty-five and eighty degrees Fahrenheit. The rainfall averages fifty inches per year.

Most Sea Islands are small and uninhabited. The larger islands, where Sea Islanders live, vary greatly in size. For instance, while Johns Island, the second-largest island in the United States, is about one hundred square miles, St. Helena Island extends only fifteen square miles. Most of the larger Sea Islands are connected to the mainland by causeways or bridges. On inhabited Sea Islands that lack bridges or causeways, residents rely on boats to ferry them back and forth. Many islanders, including high school students, commute daily to and from the mainland by boat. (Many island schools stop at the eighth grade.)

Besides serving as dwelling sites for Sea Islanders, islands function in other ways as well. Parris Island, South Carolina, is the location of a U.S. Marine base. Several Sea Islands attract wealthy non-Sea Islanders to their luxurious resorts and vacation or retirement communities. Other Sea Islands are sites for public parks and wildlife refuges.

The descendants of slaves, Sea Islanders are of great interest to scholars and the general public. Many scholars maintain that the Sea Islanders are the most authentic source of African-American history and culture, as they retain many remnants of both the slave experience and traditions of West Africa. On the Sea Islands, cultural homogeneity was retained as slaves passed from the Old World to the New. Sea Islanders combine American acculturation and traditional West African traits in clearer forms than are evident elsewhere in the United States. Even more significantly, Sea Islanders have created a new, dynamic, and vibrant African-American culture.

In part, Sea Islanders became a depository of African-American life and culture because of their social, physical, linguistic, and cultural isolation. Before the construction of bridges and causeways

A Sea Islander woman winnows corn to remove the chaff. (Patricia Guthrie)

connecting the islands to the mainland in the early 1940s, Sea Islanders were isolated. Also because freed slaves purchased Sea Island land shortly after the end of the Civil War, Sea Islanders are land owners and lack any tradition of tenant farming or renting. It was therefore possible for Sea Islanders, if they so chose, to remain in one area generation after generation. Even if individuals left for seasonal work or military service, they could always return to the land. It is common to find Sea Islanders still living on the same land that was purchased by their predecessors in the late 1800s. Because Sea Islander families remained in the same places for so long, a unique culture and society, with roots in American slavery and West Africa, flourished without significant interruption or intrusion.

## Immigration and Demography

The slave trade started in 1619 when a Dutch captain sold twenty Africans in Jamestown, Virginia. Most slaves came from "Guinea" West Africa. Sea Island slaves are believed to come from the Congo and Angola as well. Plantation owners in the region purchased human chattel at the slave market in Charleston, South Carolina. Until 1680 only a small number of slaves were imported into the United States. However, between 1680 and 1750, the number of slaves in South Carolina increased from 17 percent to 61 percent of the entire population.

Between 1790 and 1860, the number of Sea Island slaves nearly doubled. At the beginning of the nineteenth century, within a fifty-year span, the distribution of slaves in the United States shifted. Before this, the majority of slaves toiled in Virginia and Maryland. After the shift, most slaves labored in the Deep South, which included the Sea Islands. The shift occurred because of the demand for cotton cloth. Cotton was king, and Sea Island long stable cotton brought the highest price on the international market. By 1865, when the Thirteenth Amendment brought an end to slavery in the United States, slaves made up more than 80 percent of the total coastal population.

With the coming of freedom, Sea Islanders started migrating to urban centers. Some islanders who move away ultimately return when they retire or if they encounter difficult times. Population trends on specific islands vary greatly. On James Island the population of Sea Islanders increased from 2,709 to 6,173 between 1940 and 1980. During the same time, the number of Sea Islanders living on Wadmalaw remained constant, at about 1,800.

The most significant demographic change on the Sea Islands relates to the increase in the number of European Americans living there. The increase results from the development of the tourist and resort industry. In 1940, on Johns Island, 80 percent of the residents were Sea Islanders. By 1990, they accounted for only 40 percent of the total population. Elsewhere, even where the tourist industry is not fully developed, significant numbers of non-Sea Islanders have chosen to make the Sea Islands their home.

## Language

Linguistic literature focusing on Sea Islanders contains grammatical analyses and discussions of the history of Sea Island Creole. Historically, linguists have referred to this language as Gullah. The exact derivation of Gullah remains uncertain. It is possibly a corruption of the names of Liberian Gola or Gora tribes, but the term "Gullah" also could have come from Angola.

Since the early 1970s, many prefer to use the term "Sea Island Creole." The language is classified as a creole, one of the types of language that can result when a "new" language is created as groups with different language traditions need to communicate quickly. In this case, slaves, speaking various West African languages, were forced into contact with English-speakers. However, the Sea Islanders developed a mode of communication among themselves that was common to all the slaves in the area.

The vocabulary of Sea Island Creole is based primarily on seventeenth- and eighteenth-century English, but the phonology, morphology, and syntax are in many ways quite different from those of English and are more closely connected to West African languages such as Yoruba, Igbo, Hausa, Mende, Ewe, and Twi. Linguists have identified approximately six thousand African words in Sea Island Creole. Since Sea Island Creole is historically and linguistically related to English, speakers can shift toward English to communicate with outsiders; however, Sea Island Creole is considered a separate language. When Sea Islanders speak with non-Sea Islanders, they communicate with a variety of African-American English dialects. Among themselves, Sea Island Creole is the language of choice. Sea Island children learn Sea Island Creole as their first language. *Gumbo* (okra), *goober* (peanut), *voodoo* (witchcraft), and *juke* (jukebox) are some Sea Island Creole words that have entered the English language.

## Cultural and Social Characteristics

All mentally sound adult Sea Islanders are expected to marry and rear a family. Ideally, when a man marries for the first time, he brings his wife to live in the house where he grew up. As soon as the newlyweds are able, they construct a house in the "yard" of the husband's parents. If a couple cannot build in the husband's parents' yard, they seek to establish a home somewhere in the immediate vicinity. Until the 1960s, many newlyweds remained with the husband's parents for years because of difficulty in saving the funds necessary for construction of a house. After the 1960s, when it became easier to secure funds from lending institutions, many couples were able to build homes at a faster rate. Also, because they are economical and convenient, trailer homes have become popular among Sea Islanders. A house or a trailer becomes a social unit when it contains a stove and a wife to do the cooking. Persons eating from the same pot hold membership in that unit.

The yard constitutes a larger social unit. Sea Islanders situate their homes/trailers in clusters based on ties of kinship.

A yard is likely to contain the home of the parental couple along with the individual houses of their sons, their wives, and their children. ("Children" refers to offspring of the married couples, adopted or foster children, and children born before a woman marries.) It is also common for a "grand" (grandchild) or two to hold membership in the parental couple's household. Extended-family members sharing residence in the same yard greatly support and help one another. If both parents in one household work outside the home, a family member in the yard will look after any minor children. If someone's automobile is broken, a family member in the yard will help out until the car is repaired.

On occasion, a Sea Island yard includes a residence belonging to the married daughter of the parental couple. It is unusual for single Sea Islanders to establish separate households. A daughter living in her parents' yard is there for one of several reasons: She is a widow who returned home when her husband died; her husband remains alive, but the marriage has dissolved; or the wife's parents are in a better position to grant land to the couple than are the husband's parents.

Land on the Sea Islands generally passes from one generation to the next through what is called "heir's property." Sea Islanders inherit land from their parents. Males and females inherit equally. Couples who marry and elect to remain in their parents' yard receive an early inheritance in the form of land for a residence site. The land is freely given; parents want their married children living in their yard. On St. Helena, parents give their married children land for a dwelling on the basis of "love, one dollar, and affection." As is the case throughout the Sea Islands, the one dollar makes the transaction legal.

Scattered on the paved and dirt roads of the islands are individual homes and clusters of houses making up separate and individual yards. Houses belonging to Sea Islanders run the gamut from spacious, modern, brick homes to older, weather-beaten, wooden, two-room shanties. Some Sea Islanders build their homes of cinder blocks, and others use aluminum for roofs and siding. Many Sea Island homes (and churches) have porches, and a number of Sea Islanders paint the ceilings of their porches a sky blue.

Sea Islanders support themselves in a wide variety of mainland and island jobs. Islanders work in hospitals and clinics, schools, and retail outlets, and for the federal and local governments. The resort industry also employs a significant number of Sea Islanders. Though very few Sea Islanders earn a full-time living by farming or fishing, islanders still engage in both activities when time permits. Both men and women use vacation time to sow and harvest a variety of vegetables such as corn, peanuts, potatoes, and okra. Tomatoes and "cukes" (cucumbers) are grown and sold to outsiders. Rice remains a staple of the Sea Island diet, though it is no longer grown by islanders. Men fish and gather shrimp, crabs, and oysters. On all of the Sea Islands, there is lively trade and exchange of home-grown vegetables, fish, and seafood. In addition to the small number of Sea Islanders owning stores and fish markets, some islanders sell their produce, fish, and seafood directly to friends and neighbors.

Some individuals also earn money by making and selling coiled baskets made from sweet grass and pine needles. These are sold to tourists, wholesalers, serious collectors, and museum curators. Folklorists report that the designs and patterns of Sea Island basketry are similar to baskets produced in the West Africa countries of Nigeria, Togo, Ghana, and Benin.

Before beginning a full-time job or career, some Sea Islanders attend college. Sea Islanders have a long tradition of and appreciation for education. For example, the Penn Normal and Industrial and Agricultural School, opened on St. Helena in 1864, was the first school for freed slaves in the United States.

Ideologically, Sea Islanders are linked by a shared worldview and belief system rooted in both Christianity and Sea Island spirituality. Virtually all Sea Islanders are in some way connected to a Baptist or a Methodist church. Churches, by far the most important Sea Island social as well as religious community institutions, serve also to spread political information and resolve local disputes. On St. Helena, for instance, Baptist churches are affiliated with "praise houses," small buildings where a handful of neighbors meet for worship during the week and on Sunday evenings after regular church services have ended. Should a problem or a dispute arise between church members, the grievance is taken to the appropriate "praise house" or to church officials.

Regular "praise house" worship ended in most Sea Island communities in the late 1960s and early 1970s. Nevertheless, Sea Islanders still look to the "praise house" structure and the church to reestablish order in the community whenever problems develop. Church and "praise house" officials desire only a confession from the guilty party; restoration

A Sea Islander praise house located on St. Helena Island, South Carolina. (Patricia Guthrie)

when it is called for; and the "taking of hands" (shaking hands), which symbolizes the return of peace and harmony to the community.

Sea Island spirituality involves belief in "ghosts" and "spirits." One well-known "spirit" is "hag," an older woman who has just died or is very near to dying. If a person gives "hag" any trouble, then "hag" will "ride your chest" (sit on top of you) while sleeping.

*Voodoo* or *hoodoo* is another aspect of Sea Island spirituality. Through the power of "root doctors," some Sea Islanders "conjure" good and evil spirits for many different reasons and occasions. "Root doctors," for example, may be asked to offer predictions, secure a love relationship, thwart an enemy, or cure anything from a common cold to cancer. When they are sick, Sea Islanders also use local herbs or home remedies as well as Western medicine.

## Assimilation and Cultural Persistence

Outsiders have not always treated islanders with respect. Oftentimes they were ridiculed or taunted because of their speech and cultural beliefs. Therefore, islanders tend to be suspicious of strangers and newcomers.

Sea Islanders are exposed to the mass media, tourism, education, literature, and the Worldwide Web. Nevertheless, they continue to practice aspects of traditional Sea Island culture. A project cosponsored by the Sea Island Literacy Project (Sea Island community members) and the Summer Institute of Linguistics focuses on translating the Bible into Sea Island Creole. In some cases, island practices have come back into fashion even though they were once dormant. As a result of the efforts of the Penn Community Center on St. Helena, for instance, there is now revived interest in praise house worship.

During the 1980s, the president of Sierra Leone visited the Sea Islands. In return, a delegation of islanders traveled to Sierra Leone, where they were welcomed like long-lost family members.

*See also:*   AFRICAN AMERICANS

## Bibliography

Carawan, C., and Carawan, G. (1966). *Ain't You Got a Right to the Tree of Life?: The People of John's Island, South Carolina—Their Faces, Their Words, and Their Songs.* New York: Simon & Schuster.

Conway, P. (1972). *The Water Is Wide.* Boston: Houghton Mifflin.

Creel, M. (1988). *A Peculiar People: Slave Religion and Community Culture Among the Gullah.* New York: New York University Press.

Day, K. Y. (1983). "Kinship in a Changing Economy: A View from the Sea Islands." In *Holding on to the Land and the Lord: Kinship, Ritual, Land Tenure, and Social Policy in the Rural South,* edited by R. L. Hall and C. B. Stack. Athens: University of Georgia Press.

Guthrie, P. (1996). *Catching Sense: African-American Communities on a South Carolina Sea Island.* Westport, CT: Bergin & Garvey.

Jackson, J.; Slaughter, S.; and Blake, H. (1974). "New Research in Black Culture: The Sea Islands as a Cultural Resource." *The Black Scholar* 6:32–39.

Johnson, G. B. (1940). *Drums and Shadows.* Athens: University of Georgia Press.

Johnson, G. G. (1969). *A Social History of the Sea Islands.* New York: Negro Universities Press.

Jones-Jackson, P. A. (1987). *When Roots Die: Endangered Traditions on the Sea Islands.* Athens: University of Georgia Press.

Rose, W. L. N. (1964). *Rehearsal for Reconstruction: The Port Royal Experiment.* New York: Vintage Books.

Spears, A. K. (1988). "Black American English." In *Anthropology for the Nineties,* edited by J. B. Cole. New York: Free Press.

Stewart, J., ed. (1983). *Bessie Jones: For the Ancestors.* Urbana: University of Illinois Press.

Turner, L. D. ([1949] 1974). *Africanisms in the Gullah Dialect.* Ann Arbor: University of Michigan Press.

Twining, M. A., and Baird, K. E., eds. (1991). *African Presence in Carolina and Georgia: Sea Island Roots.* Trenton, NJ: African World Press.

Woofter, T. J., Jr. (1930). *Black Yeomanry: Life on St. Helena Island.* New York: Henry Holt.

PATRICIA GUTHRIE

# SERBS

The Serbs are the largest of the ethnic groups living in the former Yugoslavia. In 1994, they comprised about 42 percent of its estimated population of twenty-two million. Like the Croats, Macedonians, South Slav Muslims, Slovenes, and Bulgarians, they are a South Slavic people whose ancestors migrated to the Balkans in the sixth and seventh centuries from an ancestral homeland believed to be somewhere in present-day Belarus or Ukraine. As do the Croats and Slav Muslims, they speak dialects of Serbo-Croatian, one of several closely related South Slavic languages. However, unlike the Roman Catholic Croats and most Slav Muslims who employ the Latin alphabet, the Serbs use Cyrillic letters, as do other Orthodox Slavs.

The Serbs settled in the Balkan Peninsula to the south and east of the Croats and Slovenes. They absorbed and Slavicized much of the indigenous population, most notably the Illyrians, whose descendants are thought to be the contemporary Albanians. The territory occupied by the Serbs was within the sphere of the Eastern Roman Empire and thus under the cultural and political influence of the Byzantine Greeks, from whom they accepted Christianity in the ninth century. As a consequence, the majority of Serbs belong to the Serbian Orthodox Church, the single most salient characteristic distinguishing them from the Croats and Slav Muslims.

During the medieval period, the Serbs built a substantial empire that at its height in the fourteenth century included much of contemporary Serbia, Montenegro, Albania, Macedonia, and parts of northern Greece. However, in 1389, at the Battle of Kosovo, the Serbs were defeated by the Ottoman Turks and subsequently came under Ottoman domination lasting almost five hundred years. Beginning in the late seventeenth century, many Serbs migrated northward into the sparsely populated southern borderlands of the Austro-Hungarian Empire, invited by its Hapsburg rulers to establish themselves as armed settlers along the frontier with Turkey. Other Serbs, seeking freedom from Turkish oppression, moved northwestward into the rugged Dinaric Mountains of Montenegro and Hercegovina. This terrain lent itself to defense and raiding, and the Turks were never able to totally subdue the Montenegrin Serbs, who today take great pride in their centuries-long resistance to Muslim rule. Beginning in 1804, the Serbs rose up in several rebellions, eventually liberating most of Serbia proper from Ottoman occupation. The last vestige of Turkish sovereignty in the Balkans ended following the First Balkan War of 1912. Six years later, after the Allied victory in World War I and the dissolution of the Austro-Hungarian Empire, the kingdoms of Serbia and Montenegro joined with the Croats and Slovenes, who had previously lived under Hapsburg rule, to form Yugoslavia (initially called the Kingdom of the Serbs, Croats, and Slovenes). Thus, Serbs from the former Austro-Hungarian provinces of Croatia, Vojvodina, and Bosnia-Hercegovina were united for the first time with their conationals from Serbia and Montenegro.

## Ethnic Identity

While the majority of Serbs regard themselves as a single nationality, regional loyalties are quite strong. For example, the Montenegrins have a strong sense of identity, and a minority regard themselves as a separate ethnic group, albeit one closely related to the Serbs. To a lesser extent, most Serbs also define themselves in terms of their regions of ancestral origin, as do many Serbian Americans. These differences are reflected culturally, and, for instance, a sharp contrast can be drawn between the customs and dialects of Serbia proper and those of areas long under Austro-Hungarian rule. Similarly, the traditions of the remote mountains of western Yugoslavia are quite distinct from those of the eastern plains of Vojvodina and Slavonia, long under Hapsburg influence. Thus, while the Serbs are united by their Eastern Orthodox faith, a common language, and a sense of shared history and tradition, the spectrum of regional variation is quite broad. This can be attributed to the fact thay they long occupied a volatile frontier between three great civilizations: Roman Catholicism, Byzantine Orthodoxy, and Islam. However, in spite of such diversity, there prevails an overarching sense of common identity as a single people. This unity is embodied in the abstract term *srpstvo* (the Serbian nation), while the unique characteristics of Serbian Orthodoxy, in contrast to those of other Eastern Orthodox churches, are crystallized in the concept of *sveto nsavlje* (the cult of St. Sava, the twelfth-century founder of the Serbian Orthodox Church). Specifically, Serbian Orthodoxy is distinguished by the veneration of particular saints and the observance of unique religious holidays. The most important of the latter is the celebration of the *krsna slava*, a family patron-saint day inherited through the male line and ostensibly commemorating ancestral conversion to Christianity. It is said that "one cannot feel Serbian without a *slava*." Other Serbian religious observances include the celebration of St. Sava's Day on January 27 and St. Vitus's Day (Vidovdan) on June 28. Vidovdan commemorates the Serbian defeat by the Turks at Kosovo in 1389 and has come to symbolize a spiritual victory, assuming an almost sacred, mythological place in Serbian history. Another distinctive feature is the adherence of the Serbian Church to the Julian calendar; thus, Christmas and other major holidays (with the sometimes exception of Easter) are celebrated thirteen days later than among Catholics, Protestants, and some other Orthodox who have adopted the Gregorian calendar.

## Immigration and Settlement

It is difficult to know how many Serbs have immigrated to the United States, since immigration records before World War I either categorized them with other South Slavic groups or identified them in terms of their regions or countries of origin. Thus, during the period of peak immigration around 1900, they were variously recorded as "Bulgars, Serbs, and Montenegrins"; "Dalmatians, Bosnians, and Hercegovinians"; "Croats and Slovenes"; or "Austrians and Hungarians." Compared to many others in the United States, the Serbs comprise a relatively small ethnic group. In 1980, their numbers were estimated at 175,000 to 300,000. However, far fewer were actively involved in the cultural and religious life of the community. This sense of identity has been most effectively preserved in the major centers of Serbian settlement, in such places as Chicago, Pittsburgh, Milwaukee, San Francisco, and Los Angeles.

By the 1830s, a small number of Serbs had settled in New Orleans and along the Gulf Coast. Two decades later, others immigrated to the West during the years immediately following the Gold Rush of 1849. These settlers were drawn principally from regions just east of the southern Adriatic Sea: from Montenegro, the Bay of Kotor, and Hercegovina. Although these immigrants were primarily of peasant origin, few chose to work in agriculture. Rather, they were attracted to mining or established small businesses, especially restaurants, saloons, coffeehouses, and grocery stores. By the second half of the nineteenth century, Serbian colonies had been established in California in San Francisco and in the rural counties of the Sierra Nevada foothills, where gold mining and the timber industry provided work. During this period Serbs were also attracted to the mining towns of Arizona, Nevada, Colorado, and Montana. These early immigrants established the first Serbian institutions and voluntary associations, and consequently their regional traditions deeply influenced the future development of Serbian-American culture in the West.

In 1857, the oldest South Slav association in America, the Slavonic Illyric Mutual Benevolent Society, was formed in San Francisco. In 1880, in the same city, the first purely Serbian organization was established as the Serbian Montenegrin Literary and Benevolent Society. In addition to its function as a burial and insurance association, it founded the first South Slav library in the United States. The society, now known as the First Serbian Benevolent Society, is still active. In 1872, the Serbs of California's Mother Lode region organized the Slavonic Benevolent Society and built a social hall in the little town of Sutter Creek. Fourteen years later, the Serbs of the nearby town of Jackson purchased land for a cemetery and in 1893 built the first Serbian Orthodox church in America.

Toward the end of the nineteenth century, immigrants from the southern Adriatic were drawn to the Gulf Coast, which, like California, reminded them of their native region. Here they entered the fishing and oyster industries or became proprietors of small shops, restaurants, or saloons. In 1896, the second Serbian church in America was dedicated in Galveston, Texas. Another pioneer settlement by Serbs from the southern Adriatic area was established in Chicago.

After 1880, Serbian immigration changed radically. New settlers from the former Austro-Hungarian regions of Croatia, Slavonia, Vojvodina, and Lika, and the Montenegrin interior soon outnumbered earlier immigrants and their descendants. These newcomers were also of peasant origin and, like their predecessors, were not attracted to agriculture. Rather, they sought employment in the steel mills of Pennsylvania and Ohio, the industrial cities of the Great Lakes, and the mines of Minnesota, Utah, Colorado, Nevada, Arizona, and Montana. During this time settlement was largely in ethnically homogeneous communities, where earlier immigrants from the same regions had put down roots. Important colonies were established in the areas of Pittsburgh, Youngstown, Detroit, South Chicago, Gary, Milwaukee, and the iron-ore region of northern Minnesota, as well as in such western towns as Butte, Globe, Bisbee, Los Angeles, Sacramento, and San Francisco. Serbian immigrants came for largely economic reasons stemming from rural overpopulation, the paucity of arable land (especially in the rocky Dinaric Mountains east of the Adriatic), the lack of industry, and a cash-poor economy. Many young men also sought to escape military service in the Austro-Hungarian Empire.

Immigration decreased significantly during the Balkan wars of 1912–1913 and World War I. During this time, thousands of men volunteered to return home to fight for Serbia, and few of those who survived returned to America. Following World War I, agrarian reform and improving eco-

nomic conditions in Yugoslavia eliminated much of the impetus for emigration. Also, the restrictive immigration laws of the 1920s assigned the Yugoslavs very low quotas. Another factor limiting immigration was the Great Depression of the 1930s. Nevertheless, a trickle of Serbs continued to arrive in America until World War II.

Following the war, Serbian immigration assumed a very different character. Under the Displaced Persons Act of 1948 and the Refugee Relief Act of 1953, more than 50,000 Yugoslavs were allowed into the United States, many of them Serbs. Although earlier immigrants had been largely uneducated, many of the new arrivals were political refugees and displaced persons (so-called DPs) who were, on the whole, better educated, more urban, and from geographically diverse regions of Yugoslavia, including Serbia proper. Many were former officers in the Yugoslav Army or members of the proroyalist Chetniks, who had fought against both the Axis occupation forces and Tito's Communist Partisans. Others were refugees who had been brought to Germany as forced laborers during the war. They not only introduced new cultural forms but also injected an element of "old country" politics into Serbian-American life, an activism that sometimes caused conflict with the established community. Nevertheless, most of these newcomers were easily integrated into Serbian-American life, with many of them marrying American-born Serbs. Unlike earlier groups, many were from Serbia proper or had been educated there and spoke the eastern *ekavian* dialect of Serbo-Croatian, in contrast to the western *jekavian* speech typical of the majority of earlier arrivals. The language of the newcomers was more contemporary and less influenced by English, and it soon dominated the Serbian-American media. A significant role in this transformation was played by anti-Communist émigré intellectuals who counteracted earlier socialist trends among Serbian immigrants who had been very active in the union movement.

Throughout the 1960s, 1970s, and 1980s, there was a small but steady flow of Serbian immigrants, for the most part skilled and relatively

A group of Serbian-American men play pool in the recreation room in the Serbian Club in Aliquippa, Pennsylvanian, in 1941. (Library of Congress/Corbis)

well-educated persons, seeking both economic opportunity and escape from the authoritarian Yugoslav Marxist regime. Many of these were secular in orientation, entered into ethnically mixed marriages, and settled outside established Serbian communities. With the outbreak of civil war in 1991 in the former Yugoslavia, there began a modest immigration consisting mostly of professionals and intellectuals escaping the chaos in their native land. As of late 1996, relatively few Serbian refugees from the war zones in Croatia and Bosnia-Hercegovina had arrived in the United States.

## The Serbian Orthodox Church

Among Serbian Americans, the single most important institution and center of community life has always been the Serbian Orthodox Church. Until it was possible to establish their own parishes, early immigrants joined other Orthodox congregations, particularly Russian and Greek. The first Serbian parishes in America were under the administration of the Russian Orthodox Church, but in 1921, the Patriarch of Serbia created the Serbian Orthodox Diocese of the United States and Canada under his jurisdiction. The Monastery of St. Sava at Libertyville, Illinois, became the seat of the diocese in 1931, and since that time a constantly increasing number of priests have been American born and trained. Moreover, in many parishes English has partially replaced the liturgical Old Church Slavonic (the ninth-century spoken language of Macedonia into which the Greek religious texts were first translated—analogous to the former use of Latin in Roman Catholic services).

In 1963, a political schism split the Serbian Church in America when the Holy Synod in Belgrade suspended the American bishop, Dionisije, pending an investigation of charges of misconduct. Supporters of Bishop Dionisije formed the Serbian Church in America, accusing the Belgrade loyalists (members of the so-called Mother Church) of allegiance to a church under the domination of a Communist regime. Although both factions were anti-Communist, the Serbian Church in America rejected any ties to the Serbian Church in Yugoslavia. This caused an angry rift in Serbian communities all over America, and by 1977, of the ninety-one congregations in the United States, thirty-nine had joined the anti-Belgrade faction. A process of reconciliation was initiated in 1991, and an accord was reached allowing joint services and celebrations. The Holy Synod of the Serbian Orthodox Church in Belgrade set a goal of 1998 for the complete administrative reintegration of the two churches.

## Voluntary Associations

A variety of other institutions have also contributed to the maintenance of ethnic identity. During the early periods of immigration, fraternal and mutual-aid societies in the U.S. played a crucial role in aiding newcomers to adapt to new conditions of life. In addition to those previously noted, of particular historical significance was the Serbian Unity of Chicago, founded in 1881. Others soon followed, including the Serbian Benevolent Society "Obilić" in Chicago, United Serbs in New York, and the Serbian Benevolent Society "Dušan the Mighty" in Los Angeles. A number of these organizations eventually joined to form the Serbian Montenegrin Federation, with headquarters in Butte, Montana. However, this society lost most of its fifteen hundred members when they volunteered to fight in the Balkan wars and World War I.

The Serbian National Union was formed in 1901 in McKeesport, Pennsylvania. Based today in Pittsburgh, it grew into the largest Serbian association in America and is now known as the Serbian National Federation (SNF). At the end of the nineteenth and during the first half of the twentieth century, this society fulfilled a great need for its members, who were largely miners and industrial workers. It provided benefits for those in accidents, and burial expenses. Today, with the increased social mobility of Serbian Americans and the availability of Social Security, retirement plans, and medical insurance, the insurance aspects of benevolent societies such as the SNF are of less significance than they had been previously. Nevertheless, the SNF continues to provide a bond between the generations and the American- and foreign-born Serbs. It promotes a spectrum of social, cultural, educational, and athletic organizations whose activities attract participants nationwide.

A notable accomplishment of the SNF is the publication of the largest Serbian newspaper in the United States, *American Srbobran*. It appears weekly, with both Serbo-Croatian and English sections. While it has traditionally held a strong anti-Communist viewpoint, it has not been the organ of any political faction but has strived to instill a sense of pride in the Serbian heritage and immigrant accomplishments. However, with the dissolution of Yugoslavia and the ensuing civil war, *Srbobran* increasingly defended Serbian interests and attempted to combat what it perceived as the anti-Serbian bias of American foreign policy and media. In 1995, there were approximately four thousand regular subscribers. Not all Serbian publications have enjoyed the longevity of *Srbobran*, and more than fifty Serbian newspapers and periodicals are no longer in print. However, a large number are still in circulation, many of them relatively new and local. In 1985, an English-language magazine, *Serb World USA*, began publication. Its well-illustrated articles focus on Serbian and Serbian-American history and culture. Assuming a more academic perspective is the quarterly journal *Serbian Studies*, published by the North American Society for Serbian Studies. In response to the civil war in the former Yugoslavia, two organizations were founded in the early 1990s, the Serbian Unity Congress and Serb Net. They publish news bulletins and raise money as part of lobbying efforts on behalf of the Serbian cause.

Early in the twentieth century, women's clubs, called Circles of Serbian Sisters, were organized in several midwestern cities, and the Federation of Circles of Serbian Sisters came into being as a single organization in 1945. These societies are associated with Serbian Orthodox parishes and are active in raising money for children's camps and various other charitable purposes.

The largest and oldest Serbian patriotic association in the United States is the Serbian National Defense. It takes its name from an organization formed in Serbia in 1908 in response to the crisis engendered by Austro-Hungarian annexation of Bosnia-Hercegovina. During World War I, it recruited thousands of volunteers from America to fight for Serbia and raised more than $500,000 for the Serbian cause. Following the war it became inactive, but it was revived during World War II, supporting the proroyalist guerrillas of Draža Mihailović. Following the war, the Serbian National Defense sent food, clothing, and other aid to the thousands of Serbs in European displaced-persons camps and helped many of these refugees to immigrate to America.

## Cultural Life

As has been the case with other ethnic groups in the United States, many of the descendants of Serbian immigrants have assimilated into mainstream American society. However, many aspects of Serbian culture and values have been maintained over the generations by those who have continued to identify with their ancestral roots.

Among American Serbs, as in their ancestral homeland, there has always been a stress on family and kinship. To understand this strong sense of familism it is necessary to know something of its underlying ideology, an ideology differing significantly from the loosely knit, egalitarian, individualistic worldview held by many Americans. Large numbers of nineteenth-century Serbian immigrants

had grown up in large, rural, patrilocally extended households called *zadruge*, often consisting of a dozen or more coresident members. Thus, these early settlers brought with them the concept of an extended, corporate family with very close intergenerational ties. Of course, such large households were not generally possibly in America, but many of the values associated with them have persisted to the present.

While relatively few American-born Serbs speak Serbo-Croatian fluently, and even fewer can read or write Cyrillic, other aspects of Serbian culture have flourished. For example, music plays a very important role in almost all community events. Since the holy liturgy is chanted and sung, and musical instruments are not part of the Orthodox tradition, almost every Serbian church in America eventually organized a choir, and these were joined in 1931 with the founding of the Serbian Singing Federation. In addition, Serbian parishes frequently support dance and musical folklore groups as well as religious and cultural study classes.

Serbian-American social events, be they religious holidays, picnics, or even golf tournaments, are regarded as incomplete without a *tamburica* ensemble. The tamburica is a South Slav stringed instrument common to both Serbs and Croats (similar to the mandolin or the Greek *bouzouki*) and was brought to the United States by immigrants from areas of the former Austro-Hungarian Empire. It comes in a variety of sizes, shapes, and ranges and is usually played by four or five musicans/singers, although some much larger orchestras perform concertized folk music. The tamburica illustrates the fact that immigrant cultures are never identical to those of their homelands and always involve innovative adaptations by successive waves of immigrants. Not only did the tamburica spread in popularity among immigrants from areas where it was virtually unknown, it also has enjoyed far greater popularity in America than in Yugoslavia. In the period following World War II, new musical forms from Serbia, Bosnia-Hercegovina, and even Macedonia have become increasingly popular. This new genre employs accordions, trumpets, drums, and amplified guitars and is far more heavily influenced by Balkan and Middle Eastern tastes than was the more central European tamburica music. Cuisine, folklore, language, and even ritual have also been enriched in this manner. At the same time, the role of contemporary American culture is reflected in the emergence during the late 1980s of "Serbian rock," a syncretic blend of traditional Balkan styles and contemporary Western pop music.

Many Serbian Americans are now seeking to rediscover ancestral traditions, focusing largely on such enjoyable and highly visible forms as music, dance, folklore, ritual, and cuisine. While in the past it was the family that cultivated Serbian ethnic consciousness, today this task has shifted mainly to the Serbian Orthodox Church and a variety of voluntary associations. Also, the civil war in the former Yugoslavia has generated a new sense of political and national consciousness, as well as a renewed awareness of ties to the ancestral homeland.

*See also:* AUSTRIANS; CROATIANS; HUNGARIANS; MONTENEGRINS; SLOVENES

## Bibliography

Bennett, L. A. (1978). *Personal Choice in Ethnic Identity: Serbs, Croats, and Slovenes in Washington, D.C.* Palo Alto, CA: Ragusan Press.

Čolaković, B. M. (1973). *Yugoslav Migrations to America.* San Francisco: R & E Research Associates.

Gakovich, R. P., and Radovich, M. M. (1992). *Serbs in the United States and Canada: A Comprehensive Bibliography.* St. Paul: Immigration History Research Center, University of Minnesota.

Govorchin, G. G. (1961). *Americans from Yugoslavia.* Gainesville: University of Florida Press.

Halley, L. (1980). "Old Country Survivals in the New: An Essay on Some Aspects of Yugoslav Family Structure and Dynamics." *Journal of Psychological Anthropology* 3:119–141.

Halpern, J. M. (1967). *A Serbian Village.* New York: Harper & Row.

Kisslinger, J. (1990). *The Serbian Americans.* New York: Chelsea House.

Pavlovich, P. (1983). *Serbians: The Story of a People.* Toronto: Heritage Books.

Simić, A. (1982). "The Serbian Family in America: Cultural Continuity, Syncretism, and Assimilation." *Serbian Studies* 1:21–36.

Simić, A. (1989). "The Serbian Slava." *The World & I* 4:680–689.

ANDREI SIMIĆ
JOEL M. HALPERN

# SICILIANS

The five million inhabitants of the island of Sicily are a subgroup of the Italians. The native language of Sicilians is Italian, with a vocabulary that includes many words borrowed from Arabic and from other cultures that influenced Sicily.

Sicily, the largest island in the Mediterranean Sea, derives its name from the Sicels, a people who settled the island in prehistoric times. Located only ninety miles from Tunisia in North Africa, Sicily has historically been a bridge between Africa and Europe. The island is separated from the Italian mainland to the northeast by the Strait of Messina.

Sicily's history, culture, and customs were shaped in large part by the invasions and settlements of Greeks, Carthaginians, Byzantines, and Arabs. During the Middle Ages Normans and Germans invaded Sicily, followed by French and Spanish, who dominated the island until the 1860s, when the *risorgimento* (reunification) created a combined Italian state.

Between 1880 and 1920, nearly four million Italians immigrated to America. The majority were from southern Italy, with Sicilians having the greatest number. Nearly 27.4 percent came from the Naples area, while 16.2 percent were from Abruzzi and Molise; 7.4 percent from Apulia; 5.8 percent from Basilicata; 13 percent from Calabria; and 29.9 percent from Sicily. A combination of factors caused this massive immigration. Peasants faced oppressive conditions in Sicily. The best land was held by powerful absentee landlords. On these large estates, called *latifondi*, a rigid system of *mezzadria* (sharecropping) evolved. The *gabelloti*, a class of ruthless rural entrepreneurs, typically rented extensive acreage from landlords for wheat production worked by the *contadini* (peasants). The gabelloti controlled rents, capital, tools, animals, mills, and markets. According to Donna Gabaccia in *Militants and Migrants* (1988), no individual in Sicily was hated as much as the gabelloto, who hired day laborers in the piazza marketplace, carried a gun as he supervised harvesters' work in the fields, and cheated sharecroppers out of grain each harvest. In addition to this repressive and exploitative system, wages for landless day workers was extremely low.

Sicily experienced a series of agricultural crises in the late nineteenth century that contributed to emigration. Much of the island's economic foundation was based on grain exports. A worldwide glut of wheat depressed Sicilian markets in the late nineteenth century, making Sicilian wheat less competitive and plummeting prices. The economy was further weakened when the United States cut its imports of Italian citrus fruits due to improved production in California and Florida. At the same time, phylloxera, a disease attacking vines, affected almost every important grape-growing region of Sicily. Wine prices dropped further during Italy's trade war with France. The increase in Sicily's population, which rose from 1,000,000 persons in 1800 to 2,408,521 in 1861 and to 3,568,124 in 1909, contributed greatly to pressure on the land and the people.

Not only the peasants were hurt by changing economic circumstances; the artisans were as well. The importation of cheap manufactured goods from industrialized Western Europe eventually displaced local crafts in Sicily and spurred the emigration of large numbers of unemployed artisans. A sample of occupations from the passports of emigrating Sicilians reveals that the largest percentage of those emigrating were peasants. Also to be found were *braccianti* (farm laborers), fishermen, and skilled tradesmen. Many Sicilian men, often labeled "birds of passage" by Americans who looked disapprovingly at this practice, never intended to stay in America but to return with the money they earned to Sicily. Other Sicilian immigrants in America helped sustain the family members they left behind by sending a portion of their paychecks back home regularly.

## Settlement Patterns and Economics

Sicilians, like other Italians, settled in all regions of the United States, both rural and urban. However, several areas of settlement were specifically Sicilian. Western Sicilians found their way to the mining frontier of America, working in the silver, gold, and lead fields of Colorado and Utah. Others trickled into the coal regions of Pennsylvania. As early as 1870, Sicilians were supplying much of San Francisco with fish, as fishermen or fish merchants. Sicilians from the province of Caltanissetta settled in the Birmingham area to work in the steel mines, while emigrants from the provinces of Messina, Siracusa, and Palermo settled in Milwaukee, where many of them supplied fruits and vegetables to the city.

A large number of Sicilians immigrated to Tampa, Florida, where they worked in the cigar factories in Ybor City. Tampa's foreign-born Italians, totaling three thousand by 1920, came from a handful of villages in southwestern Sicily. One community, Santo Stefano Quisquina, supplied more than 60 percent of the total Italian population in Tampa. This is an example of what historians describe as chain migration. Immigrants arrived in America as links in such chains. People, linked socially by family and village, created bonds between the villages of southern Italy and communities in America. Residents of Sambuca, Sicily, immigrated to Chicago and Rockford, Illinois, between 1900 and 1905. Railroad maintenance work brought them to Rockford, where Sicilians from Sambuca made up more than 10 percent of the Italian residents of the town. Italian *padroni* (labor bosses who recruited men in Italy for work in America and were paid a fee) channeled Sicilian immigrants into Chicago, where they worked in excavation, construction, and railroad and street work. Padroni also wrote letters and often acted as bankers and translators for immigrants. While padroni played an important role helping Italian immigrants in their adjustment to America, they were also seen as those who exploited their own people for monetary gain.

One of the most important regions of Sicilian settlement was Louisiana. Thousands of Italians settled in New Orleans—5,644 during the years 1891 and 1892 alone. All but sixty-two of them were Sicilians. During the 1880s and 1890s, Sicilians began to monopolize the fishing industry and the oyster trade. They labored on the docks, controlled the lucrative fruit trade, and operated small shops and stores. The famous French Market became an Italian market, resembling those in the Porta di Castro area of Palermo. By 1920, there were nearly eight thousand Italians in New Orleans; nearly 90 percent were from western Sicily. No other Italian community in the United States had such a homogeneous background.

Sicilians also worked in Louisiana's sugar and cotton plantations. Plantation owners recruited Italians to replace the outmigration of blacks, who had made up the work force in the antebellum South. Sicilians worked for low wages in the sugarcane fields during the sugar season and also put their skills to work on small plots of what was considered useless land, where they produced vegetables and fruits.

Elsewhere, Sicilians lived and worked in New York City and were employed in the garment trade, as laborers digging tunnels and excavating subways, on the docks, and in the building trades. They worked in the skilled trades as tailors, barbers, musicians, shoemakers, bakers, and butchers. Skilled workers in the construction trades were employed as painters, masons, plasterers, and plumbers. Many Sicilians in urban areas were small-business owners, working as peddlers of fruits and vegetables, as grocers, or as dealers in coal, ice, or wood.

On average, Italian immigrants generally received less pay than the native worker, and since they usually had larger families, their standard of living was necessarily lower. Since fathers alone could rarely maintain the family, Italians had to depend on other sources of income. Italian women took in boarders and worked at home in the finishing trades and in factories in the garment trade. In Milwaukee a large number of Sicilian women operated home-based businesses, such as grocery stores, restaurants, or dry-goods stores, where they could combine child-rearing responsibilities with earning a living.

## Family

Centuries of foreign invasion, domination, and exploitation made Sicilians suspicious of outsiders. Thus the most important social unit among Sicilians was the nuclear family, the basis of self-identity and location in the community. The nuclear family provided the individual with status, security, and honor in the eyes of others. Culturally, Sicilians are much more conservative than Italians of the mainland. Limited communication between Sicily and the mainland allowed Sicilians to preserve their traditions through the centuries with little change.

Family values are paramount to Sicilians, and the behavior of each family member is particularly important. A primary value is placed on family honor, with individual honor always reflecting on it. One source of family honor was the virginity and purity of women. The woman was a symbol of sexual purity, which required strict control of her behavior during her childbearing years. Endowed with the proper sentiment of shame, she had to avoid contacts that might endanger her honor. The men of the family had the duty to protect her, for the entire family would suffer if she were to behave shamefully.

Sicilian women have often been characterized as powerless or limited to family roles. Some historians have challenged this view and suggested that women, as wives and mothers, make many decisions acting in their family's interests, drawing attention to the important fact that family roles can be a source of considerable power.

Sicilians believe that a family must try to *fare bella figura* (cut a fine figure) in the eyes of others. What others believe is all-important. While life in

America has challenged many of these traditional values, Sicilians, like other Italians, retain strong family ties. The Sicilian-American family is still viewed as a tightly knit unit, encompassing a wide range of relationships and retaining close ties even after the marriage of the children.

## Religion

Christianity was introduced to the island of Sicily soon after the origin of the religion. Almost all Sicilians are Roman Catholic. However, Sicilians are influenced by a combination of Christian and pre-Christian elements, such as animism, polytheism, and sorcery, along with the sacraments of the church. Sicilians transplanted their religious practices to America. Religious lucky charms in the shape of horns (*corne*) are worn by men and women to ward off evil spirits. The "evil eye" (*il mal occhio*) was greatly feared, for Sicilians believed that certain people had powers to give the "evil eye" to others, resulting in misfortune or ill health. Southern Italians attribute special powers to individual saints. These local saints are believed to be significant personages whose favors are valuable to the peasants. For Sicilians, devotion to the Virgin Mary in her maternal role is particularly strong, and she, as well as saints such as Joseph, Agatha, Anthony, Lucy, and Rosalia (the patron saint of Sicily), are revered as intercessors with Christ.

One of the most significant aspects of religion for Sicilians is the feast day (*festa*) of the madonna or patron saint. Festa Italiana in Milwaukee is only one example of many successful Italian-American feast days celebrated in America today. It is described as the largest and most successful Italian festival in the country; its origins are traced to 1905, when the first festa was celebrated in Milwaukee by Sicilian immigrants from Santo Stefano de Camastra.

## Ethnic Community Development

From the beginning of Italian settlement in America, immigrants settled in ethnic communities called "Little Italys." In New Orleans, the Sicilian population was large enough to warrant the name "Little Palermo." In these ethnic enclaves, immigrants spoke and heard a familiar language, built their own churches, and operated their own stores and restaurants.

An integral part of community development was the creation of mutual aid societies, which Sicilians transplanted from the old country. Early societies committed themselves to aid members in times of sickness, unemployment, or death. Societies also expressed a concern for education and the moral and intellectual advancement of their members. Members of a Rome, New York, society sought to attain proficiency in art, literature, and music. Also important were their social functions. Societies typically held several social gatherings a year, a dance in the winter, or a summer outing in a local park. Utica, New York's, Giuseppe Garibaldi Society emphasized classes in American citizenship to improve the lives of immigrants. Another Utica society, the Italian Empire Athletic Club, provided organized outlets for exercise and sports. Societies could also deal collectively with the broader community and promote their interests. In 1903, Italians in the Progress and Aid Society petitoned Governor George Clinton of New York State to declare October 12 (Columbus Day) a legal holiday.

In New Orleans, Sicilians organized a number of mutual aid societies, including one society that financed a yearly festival in honor of St. Rosalia, the patroness of their hometown. The first Sicilian mutual-aid society in Chicago, organized in 1892, was the Trincria Fratellanza Siciliana. The Liberta Siciliano, Cristoforo Colombo, Santa Croce, and the Society of St. Joseph were just a few of the mutual aid societies that were founded by Sicilians in Milwaukee.

In recent years, Sicilian Americans have worked to preserve their ethnic origin. In Los Angeles in 1977, Americans of Silician heritage organized La Societa Garibaldina di Mutua Beneficenza to establish a center to keep alive the culture and traditions of Italy and to provide charitable programs. The Italian immigrant community of

Milwaukee built a multimillion-dollar Italian community center in the 1980s to facilitate educational, cultural, and social programs for the Italian-American community.

Another important aspect of community building among immigrants was the establishment of an immigrant press. In 1849, the first New York City newspapers printed entirely in Italian were founded: *L'Europeo Americano, L'Esule Italiano*, and *L'Eco d'Italia*. Italian newspapers began to flourish when an expanding Italian population was substantial enough to sustain it. The immigrant press promoted Italian national pride and helped strengthen ties with Italy. At the same time, however, it was instrumental in assisting with the assimilation of immigrants into American society. Today the country's leading Italian newspaper is *Il Progresso Italo-Americano* (first printed in 1880) of New York.

## Discrimination

Perhaps more than other European ethnic groups, Italians faced considerable prejudice in America. They were hired for low wages and, along with other southern Europeans of dark skin, labeled as "swarthy." In Louisiana, whites called Sicilian immigrants who worked in the southern plantations "black dagos." In 1891, Sicilians were the victims of violence when the leading citizens of New Orleans led a lynching party into the prison and systematically slaughtered eleven Sicilian men who had just been found not guilty of a murder charge. During the late nineteenth century, Italians became a target of nativism, espoused by many native-born Americans and characterized by anti-Catholic and anti-immigrant attitudes.

In addition to the antiforeign sentiment that permeated American society in the late nineteenth century, Sicilians in particular were targets for a specific ethnic stereotype: association with organized crime. Although all ethnic groups participated in organized crime to a certain extent, Italians became the dominant ethnic element by the 1930s. The Mafia, with its roots in Sicily, is a criminal organization that has become synonymous with organized crime in America. The very small percentage of Italian Americans who have been involved with organized crime have colored public perceptions of law-abiding Italian Americans, who comprise the vast majority of the group. After a series of demonstrations and protests by Italian Americans in the spring and summer of 1970, the Department of Justice dropped the terms "Mafia" and "Cosa Nostra" as generic for organized crime.

## Contributions to the Immigrant Experience

Sicilian-American writers have poignantly depicted the Sicilian immigrant experience. The life of Sicilian immigrants in Rochester, New York, is artistically rendered by Jerre Mangione in his autobiographical chronicle *Mount Allegro* (1943). Another Sicilian American who has written of life both in Sicily and in America, in three novels, is Ben Morreale. The experience of life in a small Sicilian village, Palazzo Adriana, and in Standing Pine, Mississippi, is the subject of the book *A Highly Ramified Tree* (1976) by poet and novelist Robert Canzoneri. Lucia Chiavola Birnbaum is a Sicilian American who has written numerous articles about Italian-American women. Mario Puzo's novels on Sicilian-American life, *The Godfather* (1969) and *The Sicilian* (1984), were immortalized in screen adaptations.

## Conclusion

In America the Sicilian immigrant found new opportunities for personal mobility and advancement. Those who established permanent residence in the United States could measure their personal advancement in terms of occupational, educational, and social mobility. While Sicilian Americans have become well integrated into American society, they have nonetheless retained traditions of their ethnic heritage. Sicilians remain loyal to the Catholic Church, yet are more likely than members of earlier generations to marry outside the ethnic group. The Sicilian-American family resembles the smaller American middle-class family, with fertility rates among all Italian-American women lower than for other American women. The descendants of Sicilians in America continue to celebrate the traditional foods, the holidays, and the religious feste brought to America by their ancestors.

*See also:* ITALIANS

## Bibliography

Briggs, J. (1978). *An Italian Passage.* New Haven, CT: Yale University Press.

Cinel, D. (1990). "Sicilians in the Deep South: The Ironic Outcome of Isolation." *Studi Emigrazione: Études Migrations* 27:55–56.

Gabaccia, D. (1984). *From Sicily to Elizabeth Street: Housing and Social Change Among Italian Immigrants, 1880–1930.* Albany: State University of New York Press.

Gabaccia, D. (1988). *Militants and Migrants: Rural Sicilians Become American Workers.* New Brunswick, NJ: Rutgers University Press.

Gallo, P. (1981). *Old Bread, New Wine: A Portrait of the Italian Americans.* Chicago: Nelson-Hall.

Gambino, R. (1977). *Vendetta: A True Story of the Worst Lynching in America, the Mass Murder of Italian Americans in New Orleans in 1891, the Vicious Motivations Behind It, and the Repercussions that Linger to This Day.* Garden City, NY: Doubleday.

Lopreato, J. (1970). *Italian Americans.* New York: Random House.

Mormino, G., and Pozzetta, G. (1987). *The Immigrant World of Ybor City.* Urbana: University of Illinois Press.

Scarpaci, J. (1975). "Immigrants in Louisiana's Sugar Parishes, 1880–1910." *Labor History* 16(Spring): 165–183.

DIANE C. VECCHIO

# SIKHS

The United States first entered the Sikh imagination when groups of Sikh soldiers in the British imperial army visited Canada and the West Coast at the turn of the twentieth century. They were returning from Britain, having participated in the celebrations of the diamond jubilee of Queen Victoria in 1897, and later, in 1902, the coronation of Edward VII. The soldiers brought back the stories of the richness and vastness of this new land to the place of their origin, the Punjab, a northwestern province of India. In the following years, a few thousand Sikhs, including some who were already working for the British in places such as Hong Kong or Shanghai, arrived at the West Coast directly, or sometimes via Canada.

The European Americans already settled on the West Coast referred to the Sikh immigrants as "Hindus," a generic term used indiscriminately for any person of South Asian origin, since they were all thought to follow Hinduism. Sikhs believed that this label was a synonym for "Asian Indians" and did not object to its appearing in the local literature. Changes in immigration policy toward Asians implemented in the 1920s brought early Sikh immigration to a standstill, and from the early 1930s to the mid-1940s, direct links with Punjab were completely severed. From 1946 onward, however, further changes in the immigration and citizenship laws of the United States resulted in the growth of a sizable Sikh community. Present estimates about the number of Sikhs in the United States vary from 150,000 to more than 200,000. The Sikh community in the United States is distinguished by its vibrancy and rich internal diversity.

## Who Are the Sikhs?

Sikhism is the youngest and relatively lesser known of the world's monotheistic religious traditions. While in his late twenties, at the end of the fifteenth century, Nanak, the founder of the Sikh community, is said to have had a divine revelation that resulted in his leaving the routine domestic life behind and embarking on extensive travel. After about twenty years he acquired farmland in the lush plains of the central Punjab and founded a town named Kartarpur (City of God). At Kartarpur Nanak became Guru Nanak (Nanak, the preceptor), and the daily routine of the lives of his

Sikhs (followers) was constructed around his ideals of spirituality.

Guru Nanak's theology pivots around the foundational concept of the unity of God, the creator lord (kartar) of the universe who governs by means of the twin principles of justice (nian) and grace (mihar). This all-powerful God is the sole legitimate object of human worship. Being the creation of God, the world and all the human beings in it are assigned a high degree of sanctity. The ultimate goal of life is to achieve liberation, which means becoming one with God (mukati). According to Guru Nanak, liberation can be attained (1) by developing a relationship with God based on love (bhau) and fear (bhai) and cultivation of a constant remembrance (nam simran) of his power, and (2) by living a life of ethical and moral responsibility imbued with the three basic values of hard work (kirat), charity (dan), and service to one's fellow human beings (seva).

Guru Nanak nurtured the early Sikh community at Kartarpur and provided it with an institutional structure. He created the practice of daily prayers, composed hymns that were to form the core of the Sikh sacred text, the Adi Granth, and established the institution of community kitchen (langar), where all Sikhs were to eat in a manner that embodied his belief in human equality. At the time of his death in 1539, Guru Nanak appointed one of his followers, Angad, to be his successor, and by doing so institutionalized the office of guru, which continued until the death of Guru Gobind Singh, the tenth Sikh guru, in 1708.

By the end of the sixteenth century, the Nanak Panth (Community of Nanak) had become powerful enough to be seen as a threat by the Mogul administration in both Lahore (the provincial headquarters) and Delhi. A phase of tension culminated in the execution of Guru Arjan, the fifth Sikh guru, in 1606. The Sikh community, under the leadership of his successor, Guru Hargobind, responded by formally rejecting Mogul authority and declaring the Sikh guru to be its sole spiritual and temporal head. Sikhs were forced to leave the Punjab plains, however, and move to the Himalayan foothills, where they remained throughout the seventeenth century. An attempt to revive the community in the plains during the leadership of Guru Tegh Bahadur, the ninth Sikh guru, ended with his execution in Delhi in 1675.

Given this existing atmosphere of political tyranny, the Sikh belief in God's justice took the form of the institution of the Khalsa (Pure) under the leadership of Guru Gobind Singh. This meant a new ceremony of initiation, with three well-defined dimensions. First, the Sikh drinks the nectar prepared with a double-edged sword (khande da amrit), which symbolizes God's power and justice. Second, having drunk the nectar, the Sikh becomes the Khalsa, with a special relationship to God and the obligation to participate in the divine mission of establishing the khalsa raj (Kingdom of God). Third, the Khalsa Sikh has a strict code of conduct (rahit) to follow. This involves the carrying of five k's: kes (uncut hair), kangha (comb), kirpan (sword), karha (steel bracelet), and kachha (long shorts). All male Khalsa Sikhs were given the last name Singh (Lion) and females Kaur (Princess).

Guru Gobind Singh thus gave the community a strengthened sense of identity and the religio-political vision of establishing khalsa raj. At the time of his death, he is said to have declared that henceforth the scriptural texts would be the guru; hence the honorfic title Guru Granth Sahib (honorable guru in the book form). The early text containing Guru Nanak's hymns had been expanded to include the hymns of his successors and other saints, both Hindu and Muslim, whose philosophies were in complete harmony with the Sikh belief system. The centrality of the authority of the Guru Granth Sahib functioned as the community (guru panth) gathered in its presence and tried to reach a consensus that would be considered mandatory for all Sikhs, whether present or not.

Fired up with their mission to establish the khalsa raj in the Punjab, the Sikhs waged relentless military campaigns in the eighteenth century, and finally, under the leadership of Ranjit Singh, created a powerful kingdom in the region. The Sikhs never had the ambition to convert others to their faith, however, and even at the height of their political ascendancy they remained a small minority in the Punjab.

With the death of Ranjit Singh in 1839 began a period of instability, and the Punjab was ultimately annexed by the British in 1849. After an early phase of painful introspection and reflection on the fall of the *khalsa raj*, the Sikhs went on to work closely with their conquerors. The British declared the Sikhs to be a martial race and recruited them into the army and the police, creating opportunities for worldwide travel. This was the background for the Sikhs' arrival in the United States at the turn of the twentieth century.

## Sikh Immigration

The stories about North America told by Sikh soldiers at the turn of the twentieth century in the Punjab resulted in Sikh immigration to the United States, beginning with a group of Sikh men arriving in California in 1903. All were from small, landowning families and had left their villages to make money to expand their holdings and improve their family status.

The Sikh immigrants found the California valleys similar to the plains of the Punjab, and with their background in farming and a demanding work ethic, adjusted to their new habitat quickly. They moved around the countryside in groups, searching for seasonal labor such as digging potatoes or picking grapes. In the following ten years or so, some of them acquired sufficient capital to buy or lease small farms in the San Joaquin, Sacramento, and Imperial valleys of California.

Unfortunately, however, the Sikh arrival on the West Coast coincided with a growing hostility among European Americans against the Chinese and Japanese, and the Sikhs were also seen as part of the "Yellow Peril." With their long hair covered with turbans they got the name "ragheads," and the newspapers alerted the local people to an imminent "turbaned tide."

Racial discrimination was officially instituted in legal hurdles designed to obstruct the process of settlement of Asian immigrants. In 1913, the California legislature passed the Alien Land Laws, which barred Asians from owning land in California. This made it difficult for Sikhs to buy or even hold on to their existing farms. Their attempts to move to neighboring states were not successful, as similar laws were passed in other states, such as Arizona.

The Immigration Act of 1917, which barred immigration from certain areas of the world, including South Asia, had a double-pronged effect on Sikhs in the United States. First, they were declared to be ineligible for U.S. citizenship and consequently lost any right to own property. Bhagat Singh Thind, a Sikh who had arrived in the United States in 1912, married an American woman, and served in the U.S. Army, contested the

A Sikh woodworker, who is part of a large settlement of American Sikhs in northern New Mexico, works in his shop. (Buddy Mays/Corbis)

loss of his citizenship in the U.S. Supreme Court but lost. Second, the ban on immigration from Asia included the wives of workers already settled in the United States. Sikhs continued to come illegally through Mexico for some years, but this stopped with the Great Depression in the 1930s.

The difficult situation concerning immigration deeply affected the personal lives of those Sikhs settled in the United States. Discriminatory pressures forced them to conform to American standards of dress. Many Sikhs cut their hair and shaved their beards, indivisible signs of their *khalsa* Sikh identity. With no provision for bringing Sikh spouses from the Punjab, about half of these immigrants married Mexican women—a few married European Americans—and the other half remained single. The children from these marriages were normally given Christian names to save them from social ridicule.

Because they came from a nonproselytizing tradition, the Sikhs did not ask their wives to convert to Sikhism, nor did they discourage their children from attending Catholic church services with their mothers. Under constant work pressure they did not have time to teach their wives or children about Sikh religious beliefs. For such families, the Sikh culture remained confined to a knowledge of Sikh food habits and cremation rituals.

The importance of Punjabi, the language spoken by Sikhs, is more than simply cultural. The ability to read Punjabi written in Gurmukhi, the script in which the text of the Guru Granth Sahib is recorded, is considered a religious obligation among Sikhs. The California Sikhs, however, did not have the time, nor perhaps the know-how, to teach Punjabi to their wives and children; instead, they learned English and Spanish to speak with them.

This was a period of extreme personal hardship for the Sikhs in the United States. They attempted to assimilate in the local culture. Those who married had little success transmitting the Sikh heritage to their families. Their numbers in the United States, which in the early 1920s had risen to more than six thousand, dwindled to

approximately one thousand by 1945. However, the Sikhs had worked out ways to keep their properties intact by putting them in the names of their Mexican wives, European-American friends, or by entering into partnerships with U.S. citizens.

The key manifestation of Sikh community life from 1900 to 1945 was the establishment of the Pacific Coast Khalsa Diwan, a Sikh organization in Stockton, in 1912, and its opening of a *gurdwara* (Sikh temple) there in 1913. The activities of the Stockton gurdwara included readings of the Guru Granth Sahib, marriage ceremonies, and funeral rites. The gurdwara remained the sole center of Sikh religious life all through this period, and Sikhs gathered in large numbers on days of religious festivals. Assimilationist tendencies manifested themselves in the performance of rituals in the gurdwara.

In the early years, particularly until 1915, the Sikhs in California were involved in a political movement known as the Ghadar Party, committed to the ousting of the British from India. This political agenda was soon dismantled; their later activities were limited to sending back money to support their families, or to be used for constructing gurdwaras and helping the needy children in their villages.

Sikh immigration from 1946 to 1990 involves three successive phases. The first began with the passage of the Luce-Celler Bill in July 1946; the second began with the Immigration Law of 1965; and the third was related to the political unrest in the Punjab during the 1980s.

The Luce-Celler Bill, resulting in the Indian Immigration and Naturalization Act of 1946, was a landmark in the history of immigration law in the United States. The act entitled Asian Indians, and hence Sikhs living in the United States, to become citizens, and a quota was revived that allowed one hundred Asian Indians to enter the country each year. The act thus initiated a process of easing restrictions on Asian Indian immigration and a beginning of expansion of the Sikh community in the United States.

The permission to acquire citizenship in the United States had far-reaching effects on the Sikhs' way of life. Sikhs could now legally own property, which gave them a degree of self-confidence unknown in previous decades. They now had the freedom to travel to the Punjab and return to the United States without fear of not being permitted to reenter. And they had the legal right to bring spouses from the Punjab who, in some cases, had been waiting for decades to join their husbands.

The limited immigration quota assigned to Asian Indians provided Sikhs with the opportunity to bring close relatives to the United States. In the 1950s and 1960s, the number of dependents coming to join Sikh immigrants could not have been large, but with this new act the psychological profile of the community improved dramatically. A substantial rise in the number of Sikh students gaining admission to Stanford, the University of California at Berkeley, and other colleges helped inspire new confidence in the community, which reached its peak in 1956 with the election of a Sikh, Dalip Singh Saund, as the first South Asian to enter Congress. Saund had originally entered the United States as a student at the University of California at Berkeley.

The Immigration Act of 1965 resulted in further changes, as immigration came to be based on a preferential scale that took into consideration employment demands rather than country of origin. This opened the doors for educated Sikhs with degrees in medicine, engineering, and other professions. Sikh professionals of this period arrived in large cities such as New York and Chicago, where the infrastructure was available to reorient them to American work demands. Having undergone the required training, they spread all over the United States, depending on the availability of jobs in their areas of expertise.

For the first time, Sikh immigrants to the United States included Sikhs who had come from areas other than the Punjab. These were people whose families had left the Punjab at the turn of the twentieth century and settled in East Africa, but were subsequently forced to leave their adopted homes due to political pressure. Another large group left Kabul when war broke out in Afghani-stan. These people usually arrived in the United States with considerable experience in business and were quick to plant roots in large urban centers such as those in the metropolitan New York area.

A third wave of Sikh immigration occurred during the 1980s. The Punjab went through a period of political turmoil when Sikhs attempted to secede from India and establish an independent country called Khalistan (the Land of the Khalsa), a modern-day version of the *khalsa raj*. To control the situation, the Indian government declared martial law in the Punjab, and Sikh youths living in the villages became subject to routine and brutal intimidation. This resulted in their flight to various Western countries, including the United States, in large numbers, through both legal and illegal means, once again adding a new element to the community's composition.

## Sikhism in America

A unique development in Sikh religious history began to unfold in the United States in the 1970s when a group of Americans of European descent converted to Sikhism under the spiritual guidance of Harbhajan Singh Yogi, a Punjabi Sikh who had arrived in the United States in 1968. They were originally based in Los Angeles, but subsequent decades have seen them emerge as a notable religious movement, with 120 centers around the world. The Khalsa identity is undoubtedly at the center of Harbhajan Singh Yogi's understanding of Sikhism. He is acutely aware of the importance of a close relationship between his followers, popularly known as the American Sikhs, and the Sikh community both in the United States and in the Punjab and has taken positive measures to cultivate this relationship.

By the mid-1990s, the heterogeneous mix of the Sikh community was composed of people of varied backgrounds and levels of education. The community has brought forth a tremendous amount of institutional growth. From having just a single gurdwara in Stockton during the first half of the twentieth century, there are now more than

A Sikh woman meditates in privacy; Sikhism has few communal religious ceremonies. (Buddy Mays/Corbis)

sixty gurdwaras all over the country, ready to meet the religious and spiritual needs of the community. In addition, there are American Sikh centers. The activities of these gurdwaras and centers range from daily services to special events such as naming newly born Sikh children, weddings, and funeral rites.

The ethical monotheism of Sikhism meshes well with the Judeo-Christian belief system that is at the heart of American culture. Change in racial attitudes of Americans in the 1960s created a positive environment in which newly arrived Sikhs did not feel the need to compromise their religious beliefs by shaving their hair to conform to "American" standards. They have, in fact, succeeded in containing and reversing the assimilationist tendencies of their predecessors. The Anglicized practices that were incorporated into worship in the Stockton gurdwara in the middle part of the twen-

tieth century were replaced with indigenous Sikh Punjabi ones.

The effort to maintain Sikh religious symbols has, however, created problems that have yet to be resolved. The practice of Sikh males keeping long hair and covering it with a turban has barred them from joining the U.S. Army, and there have been cases of Sikhs being fired from their jobs for not agreeing to remove their turbans and wear hard hats. Sikh children are not permitted to carry their ritual swords in some school districts. Sikhs have sought legal redress for these grievances.

## Community Concerns

Contemporary debate about the concerns of the Sikh community in the United States is centered on three basic issues. First is the community's support of the "struggle" for a Sikh state in the Punjab. The gurdwaras have served as focal points in this debate. The World Sikh Organization, formed in 1984, and its weekly newspaper *World Sikh News*, published in Stockton, and the International Sikh Organization, under the leadership of Gurmit Singh Aulakh, have done important work organizing around this issue. Concerted efforts have also been made to brief human rights organizations about alleged atrocities committed in the Punjab by agencies of the Indian government.

The second issue is the community's need to explain the Sikh heritage to Americans. Sikh leaders have attempted to establish contacts with American politicians and with leaders from other religious traditions to brief them on Sikh issues, here and in the Punjab, and win their support. In places where they have large populations, Sikhs have tended to hold public parades to show others their religious heritage. Since 1988, a Vaisakhi Day parade to commemorate the institution of the Khalsa has become an important event in New York City. More than twenty-five thousand Sikhs from throughout the East Coast gather annually to march down Broadway and distribute literature to interested passersby. Efforts have been made to sponsor programs in Sikh studies at leading universities such as Columbia University, the University of California at Berkeley, and the University of Michigan. It is envisaged that these university programs will help to disseminate information about Sikhism and the Sikh community to American students.

Third, a number of individuals and organizations have focused on how best to transmit the Sikh heritage to the next generations of Sikhs. Their work includes the holding of Sunday classes in local gurdwaras to teach Sikh history and Punjabi written in Gurmukhi script to Sikh children. This type of activity also takes the form of summer camps in several states, where children are given a chance to immerse themselves in the Sikh way of life for a week or two. These camps are helpful to Sikh children, who are able to learn about the belief system of their own religion and make friends with other Sikh children, which they may not be able to do in their normal school environment.

## Conclusion

The Sikh community in the United States is a vibrant one that is in the process of simultaneously defining itself vis-à-vis its internal diversity and its relationship with the parent community in the Punjab. This runs parallel to the Sikh leadership's efforts to define the course of the community's future in the United States and work out ways and means to contribute more effectively to the life of its adopted country.

*See also:*   PUNJABI MEXICANS; PUNJABIS

## Bibliography

Barrier, N. G., and Dusenbery, V. A., eds. (1989). *The Sikh Diaspora: Migration and the Experiences Beyond Punjab.* Columbia, MO: South Asia Books.

Cole, W. O., and Sambhi, P. S. (1995). *The Sikhs: Their Religious Beliefs and Practices.* Brighton, Eng.: Sussex Academic Press.

Gibson, M. A. (1988). *Accommodation Without Assimilation: Sikh Immigrants in an American High School.* Ithaca, NY: Cornell University Press.

Grewal, J. S. (1990). *The Sikhs of the Punjab.* New York: Cambridge University Press.

Hawley, J. S., and Mann, G. S., eds. (1993). *Studying the Sikhs: Issues for North America.* Albany: State University of New York Press.

Helweg, A. W., and Helweg, U. M. (1990). *An Immigrant Success Story.* Philadelphia: University of Pennsylvania Press.

Jensen, J. M. (1988). *Passage from India: Asian Indian Immigrants in North America.* New Haven, CT: Yale University Press.

Khalsa, S. K. (1995). *The History of the Sikh Dharma of the Western Hemisphere.* Espanola, NM: Sikh Dharma Publications.

La Brack, B. (1988). *The Sikhs of Northern California, 1904–1975.* New York: AMS Press.

Leonard, K. I. (1992). *Making Ethnic Choices: California's Punjabi Mexican Americans.* Philadelphia: Temple University Press.

McLeod, W. H. (1989). *The Sikhs: History, Religion, and Society.* New York: Columbia University Press.

Tatla, D. S. (1991). *Sikhs in Amrica: An Annotated Bibliography.* Westport, CT: Greenwood Press.

GURINDER SINGH MANN

# SINDHIS

Among the Sindhis there is a saying, "Three things you will find all over the world: Bata Shoes, Coca Cola, and a Sindhi." Sindhis seem to be everywhere in India and can be found wherever Indian commercial communities exist abroad—Africa, South America, East Asia, Europe, the Caribbean, and the United States.

## The Province of Sind

The Sindhis in the United States came originally from the northwest province of Sind, located in India in the lower Indus River delta. The Sind is ecologically similar to the contemporary Nile and Tigres-Euphrates valleys. When it was the cradle of neolithic civilization, the Sind was lush and fertile, but today it is is a semiarid area that is an extension of India's Thar Desert. Muslim invaders in 644 C.E. wrote that the Sind was bounded on all sides by deserts and mountains, and a Muslim leader at the time wrote, "If a few troops are sent here, they will be slain; if more than a few, they will starve." To supplement their meager farming, the Sindhis were forced to engage in pirating and trade at the mouth of the Indus River to survive. Throughout India's history, the merchant class of the Sind prospered in business with the Persian Gulf countries and China.

Karachi became a port for long distance trade routes. Its commercial importance to the Indian Ocean trade as well as to the overland passway to the north resulted in a strong and resilient trader/merchant Hindu class. As the Arabs expanded Islam through the East, so did the Sindhi traders consolidate their commercial power in these areas. Commercial and political ties between the Persian Gulf and India evolved into integrated trading empires, with the Sind becoming the doorway to trade with India and China. With the expansion of trade to India and China, there was also expansion to Indonesia and the Malay Peninsula. The Sind became a center of trade, attaining great prosperity for the Hindu merchants and traders who managed to live separately from the Muslim majority.

Like other Asian Indians from the north of India, the Sindhi population is Caucasoid. This population probably descended from people who entered the subcontinent from the northwest. Although there was much diversity in the Sind, the people are still identifiable from the people of the south, who are classified as Dravidian, and the people of the east, who are smaller and darker. This difference in physical characteristics, a result of reoccurring invasions by the Aryans through the Kyber Pass and by Mediterranean sailors and merchants, has led to the classification of Sindhis into either the Nordic type or the Mediterranean type. Sindhis are an attractive people, very cosmopolitan in appearance, and blend in wherever they live.

With the partition of India by the British in 1947, the Sind became part of Pakistan, a country separate from the rest of India, and those provinces with a predominantly Muslim population were turned over to East and West Pakistan. This territory included the lower Indus Plain and the southeastern lowlands of Sind. Today those who reside in these regions no longer call themselves Sindhis, but Pakistanis.

Except for a very small population, most Hindus left the Sind when Pakistan was formed. They migrated to cities across India and to the colonies of Great Britain. The Muslims stayed in Pakistan, and several came to be prominent leaders there. A Sindhi, Zulfikar Ali Bhutto of the Pakistan People's Party, became the president of Pakistan in 1971 (with the title changed to prime minister in 1973) and established Islamic socialism there.

The post–World War II period was the era of greatest migration for Sindhis. When Pakistan separated from India, the area to the south of the Sind was kept by India. At that time it was estimated that six million people were uprooted from their homes. Both Hindus and Sikhs left West Pakistan. These Sindhi refugees who fled the province of Sind were merchants and traders who chose the port cities of Bombay, Calcutta, and Madras as their new homes. Many others adventured to Singapore, Hong Kong, Malaysia, and the Carribbean. After the U.S. Immigration Act of 1965, Sindhi immigration from India and the former British colonies to the United States began in earnest.

## Immigration to the United States

The changes in the United States immigration laws in 1965 came at a time when Great Britain was erecting barriers to halt the immigration of Asian Indians; racism with violence was increasing in England and Canada. Political upheavals in countries in Africa and South America acted as an impetus for Indian businessmen to leave Kenya, Uganda, South Africa, and small island countries in the Carribbean. Indian immigration to America became a wave of the Indian elite, with most entering under the classification of "professional/ technical workers" or as spouses and children of professional/technical workers. Once a family member became a legal resident, other family members could join him as business investors. The tendency was to locate in the larger metropolitan areas of New York, Miami, Los Angeles, Detroit, Houston, and Chicago.

The Sindhi population of the United States is estimated to be around fifty thousand. The U.S. Census does not keep records on ethnicity of Indian immigrants, so this number was arrived at by the National Sindhi Association membership rolls. While research in other parts of the world has found that the Sindhi population is usually approximately 1.7 percent of the total immigrant Indian population, research in America has shown that Sindhis make up approximately 5 percent of the total Indian immigrant population. The 1990 U.S. Census showed the total Asian Indian population to be a little more than one million. Their occupational profile shows them to be concentrated mainly in the professional/technical fields (50%), with the next highest occupational category being managerial/sales (20%). Asian Indians are the fourth highest ethnic group in income, and the second highest in academic achievements.

Since no census information is available specifically for the Sindhi population, demographic information must be deduced from the information available on Asian Indian immigrants. But there is a pattern whereby Sindhis do not immigrate directly from India; many live in British commonwealth countries before moving to America. In the early 1990s, a large number of Sindhis immigrated from Hong Kong to the United States after living for some time in Canada. With them they brought capital for investment and entrepreneurial skills.

Sindhis are reluctant to acquire U.S. citizenship, only doing so when pressured by their children. The majority are legal immigrants who have family already residing in the United States, providing support until the newcomers are established in businesses. Those Sindhis who become U.S. citizens often keep their former citizenship when their country of origin allows citizenship.

## Hinduism

Although the majority of the population was Islamic at the time of partition, the Sindhis in the United States are mainly Hindus. The Sind was predominantly Hindu until the significant penetration of Islam into the region in 711 C.E. Hinduism is a vast mix of beliefs ranging from animism to polytheism to monotheism. It has no formal creed, no standardized cult practice, and no controlling ecclesiastical organization, other than the Veda. It is a doctrine of reincarnation determined by one's life works. The precise form of rebirth is determined by the balancing of deeds both good and bad in previous existences and one's present caste position. In most Sindhi homes the elephant-headed god Ganesha (the god of education, wealth, and prosperity) is always present along with the other prominent Hindu gods. Many are followers of Sai Baba and Shivaratri. If a temple is not local, *puja* (worship) is held in the home with family and fictive kin present. Some Sindhis do not practice pure vegetarianism and have been known on occasion to eat fish and meat. The women fast on Mondays and other significant Hindu occasions.

Diwali is the most important holiday celebrated in the United States. It is a time of forgiveness and renewal and is celebrated with new Indian clothing. Wives and children are given new gold jewelry by husbands and fathers. Holi and India's Republic Day are also holidays celebrated as a community. The Sindhis join together with other Indian communities to participate in the Indian ethnic festivals and local garba dances and song fetes. In the larger American cities the Sindhis have their Sindhi Ball, which is notorious for the women's ostentatious displays of wealth. The American holiday of Mother's Day has been recently included in their annual celebrations.

Entertainment is always family oriented and includes the preparation of Indian foods, particularly Sindhi dal curry. Imported Indian movies and the singing of old Hindu ragas and old movie songs are regular occurrences. The men enjoy games of badminton.

## Social Structure

Sindhis are divided into a large number of tribes, occupational and geographical groups that engage in farming, business, and craft production. Those who live in the United States engage in business, are in professions such as medicine and engineering, and invest in the stock market.

The Sindhis who chose to leave the Sind at the time of partition were mainly of the Hindu faith. The social structure of Hinduism is defined by the caste system, which arranges mankind in a hierarchy of groups of different nontransferable worth. It prescribes regulations concerning marriage, eating, and rituals in the various phases of life through restrictions. In theory, each caste has a separate social function or occupation.

The four majors castes are the Brahmans (priests), Kshatriyas (warriors, temporal rulers), Vaisyas (merchants and artisans), and Sudras (servants and laborers). Most Sindhis in America are "twice born" or of the merchant/trader castes. The three sub-castes to which they belong are Amils (educated professionals, such as accountants), Bhaiban (merchant/traders, usually not having college degrees), and the Chikarpuri (employees).

## The Family

The Sindh family in the United States is still male oriented, although the women are left alone for long periods to care for the children while the men travel on business. A couple usually has two children, unless the first children are girls, in which case the couple will continue to have children with the hope of producing a boy.

The extended family, which was the rule in towns and villages of India, is not the norm in the United States, though relatives try to settle near one another. The effort that goes into maintaining long-distance kin ties can be considered as a form of work in that it contributes in the long run to the welfare or survival of the household. This networking is maintained largely, although not ex-

An arranged Sindhi marriage in Boca Raton, Florida. The bride wears a traditional red dress embroidered with gold threads, and her hands and feet are covered with *mendhi* (red henna), giving the appearance of red lace. The groom is tied to the end of the bride's dress, and he carries a coconut in a golden pouch for good luck and a ritual knife symbolic of his role as family protector. The crown on the groom's head is symbolic of his new position as head of a family. (Carol Kohn Sheikh)

clusively, by the women in the family. The Sindhi family is transnational in that it stays in constant contact with members in other countries by telephone, fax, and electronic mail. Many also make yearly visits abroad to see their relatives.

Social life is built around kin and fictive kin relationships. Marriages are still arranged (traditionally to relatives), but the young people are allowed to meet with each other before the engagement with the hope that they will fall in love. Marriages are celebrated elaborately, and dowry and gift exchanges are still the tradition. Marriages between cousins are seen as the best, but there is also a practice of having at least one family member marry a member of the indigenous community in the host country. This practice ensures that at least one child in the extended family is a native-born citizen of the country of residence. As a result, the greater extended family has native-born citizens for all the countries to which they have immigrated.

The 1990 U.S. Census indicated that the Asian Indian family is remarkably stable. Ninety-three percent of Indian children live in homes with both parents. Although a college education is not as valuable to the Sandhi businessman as work experience, most have had some college education. Sindhi women tend to be less educated than their spouses. The second generation, including the girls, is beginning to attend college, usually close to home so that the student can still live with his or her family. In this way there is acculturation without complete assimilation. It is not uncommon to hear of children being removed from universities because the family felt they were becoming too Americanized.

## Language

An Indo-Aryan language, Sindhi is spoken in the homes of Sindhis and wherever Sindhis gather together. It is called "the mother tongue," which expresses the warmth of sentiment felt by Sindhis for their language. All Sindhis read, write, and speak English because it is the language of world business. Wherever they live, they also learn the local language. It is not unusual for a Sindhi to be fluent in as many as five or six languages.

## Politics

The upper- and middle-class Sindhis in America, like other immigrant Asian Indians, are conservative and usually ally with the Republican party. They are joiners and belong to many Asian Indian as well as Sindhi associations. They do not participate directly in local or national politics unless they feel an economic need for it. They prefer to be involved behind the scenes and do not run for political offices. They will give large donations to both parties at election time, hoping to gain some influence with the winner.

*See also:* PAKISTANIS

## Bibliography

Barkan, E. R. (1992). *Asian and Pacific Islander Migration to the United States: A Model of New Global Patterns.* Westport, CT: Greenwood.

Barringer, H.; Gardner, R. W.; and Levin, M. J. (1993). *Asians and Pacific Islanders in the United States.* New York: Russell Sage Foundation.

Helweg, A. W., and Helweg, U. M. (1990). *An Immigrant Success Story: East Indians in America.* Philadelphia: University of Pennsylvania.

Kitano, H. H. L., and Daniels, R. (1995). *Asian Americans: Emerging Minorities,* 2nd edition. Englewood Cliffs, NJ: Prentice Hall.

Leonard, K. I. (1992). *Making Ethnic Choices: California's Punjabi Mexican Americans.* Phidadelphia: Temple University Press.

Mearns, D. J. (1995). *Shiva's Other Children: Religion and Social Identity Amongst Overseas Indians.* New Delhi: Sage Publications India.

Min, P. G. (1995). *Asian Americans: Contemporary Trends and Issues.* Thousand Oaks, CA: Sage Publications.

Moreland, W. H., and Chatterjee, A. C. (1962). *A Short History of India,* 4th edition. New York: David McKay.

Portes, A., and Rumbaut, R. G. (1990). *Immigrant America: A Portrait.* Berkeley: University of California Press.

Sharma, U. (1989). *Women's Work, Class, and the Urban Household.* London: Tavistock.

Spear, P. (1958). *India, Pakistan, and the West,* 3rd edition. London: Oxford University Press.

Takaki, R. (1989). *Strangers from a Different Shore: A History of Asian Americans.* New York: Penguin.

Uberoi, P. (1993). *Family, Kinship, and Marriage in India.* Delhi: Oxford University Press.

Wink, A. (1990). *Al-Hind: The Making of the Indo-Islamic World.* Leiden, Netherlands: E. J. Brill.

Wolpert, S. (1982). *A New History of India,* 2nd edition. New York: Oxford University Press.

CAROL KOHN SHEIKH

# SINHALESE

The Sinhalese originate from Sri Lanka (formerly known as Ceylon), an island of twenty-five thousand square miles (about the size of West Virginia) situated off the southeastern tip of India. Their language, known as Sinhala, belongs to the Indo-European family spoken in North India. The term "Sinhalese" is an anglicized form of "Sinhala," the indigenous name of the community. Sinhala means "of the bosom of the lion" and refers to the myth of origin of the group according to which they are descended from the incestuous union of brother and sister, who in turn were the offspring of the union of a princess and a lion.

The Sinhalese in Sri Lanka consist of two broad divisions, those who inhabit the central hill region of the island and those who occupy the southern and southwestern lowlands and seaboard. The former are known in English as Kandyans (referring to Kandy, the capital of the region) or up-country Sinhalese, and the latter are known as the low-country Sinhalese. The Sinhalese have a system of castes, though not one as rigid as that of India. The geographical Kandyan/low-country division has diminished much in importance, as has caste. However, these divisions still prevail in subtle forms and are important in certain social situations, particularly marriage.

## Demographic Facts and Settlement History

In the absence of statistics, there can be no definitive statement about the demography of the immigrant Sinhalese community. However, a reasonable estimate of the population is 50,000. The majority are concentrated in a few locations: California, 20,000; New York City, 12,000; Washington, D.C., 5,000; Chicago, 3,000; Texas, 3,000; and Florida, 2,000. The remaining 5,000 individuals are scattered elsewhere in the United States. The Sinhalese are mainly concentrated in large cities, and they have mostly taken up residence in regions that are sunny and warm, clearly reminiscent of their tropical homeland.

Very little is known about the immigration history of the Sinhalese. There are no published accounts of the early period, creating a dependence on statements of knowledgeable senior members of the immigrant community. These individuals mention an elephant trainer who arrived in America with a circus company in the 1930s and a touring dancer, named Kira, who settled down in New York in the 1940s. Kira started a restaurant, the Ceylon-India Inn, on 47th Street in New York. According to the folklore of the group, there were also a handful of Sinhalese in New York at that time who had jumped ship to remain in America. The accuracy of these bits of information are virtually impossible to verify, but they illustrate the fact that there was no significant Sri Lankan immigration in the first half of the twentieth century. Not until the 1950s does a steady and significant stream of Sri Lankan immigrants begin.

Immigration from Sri Lanka has been closely related to education and professionalism, especially between the 1950s and the 1970s. From the 1950s on, there is clear evidence that students arrived in America through scholarship programs set up by either the U.S. government or individual schools and universities. Significant numbers of these students decided to stay on. The most important in the category of professionals are doctors. Sri Lanka was one of the centers in South Asia where the U.S. government held its examinations to enlist recruits to medical colleges, and many young Sri Lankan medical school graduates made use of this opportunity, especially in the late 1960s and the 1970s. The large majority of these medical students eventually settled in America and have distinguished themselves in their careers. Sizable contingents of Sinhalese doctors live and work in every state, although they are especially concentrated in the major metropolitan centers of New York, Florida, and California. A significant number of Sinhalese women in America are involved in the teaching profession, employing the Montessori method. This method for teaching preschoolers was developed by the Italian educationist Maria Montessori, who lived and worked for a time in Sri Lanka and trained Sinhalese women in the method. Families of bureaucrats who work in the United States for international organizations such as the United Nations, the World Bank, and the International Monetary Fund have contributed to the Sri Lankan immigrant population, especially of New York and Washington, D.C.

In examining the composition of the Sinhalese immigrant community, two clear patterns are discernible. First, the large majority of the Sinhalese immigrants arrived in the United States not as families but as individuals. In addition, many individuals were not planning to settle permanently in the United States; the decision to remain was usually made only after some years of training and working. The second pattern is a lowering of the professional content in the employment of the immigrant population. As noted above, the early immigrant community, the bulk of which took shape in the 1950s, 1960s, and 1970s, were largely "high professionals" (i.e., doctors, lawyers, engineers, academics, and high bureaucrats). From the late 1970s on, both as a result of some of the offspring of these high-profession families going into low-profession occupations and the later influx of low-profession contingents, the low-profession ratio has risen significantly. However, it is clear that, in the broad sense of being employed in salaried jobs (as opposed to casual or menial labor), the overwhelming majority of Sinhalese immigrants are still professional.

## Language

Sri Lanka was a British colony between 1815 and 1948, which led to the growth of an indigenous elite that was highly proficient in English. Until the late 1950s, the medium of higher education was English, and many elite households used English as their home language. Thus, up to the 1970s, immigrants had excellent proficiency in English. Due to changes in language policy in Sri Lanka, the post-1970s immigrants in general are less proficient in English, though they still possess good knowledge. This generational difference has affected bilingualism. Among the pre-1970s immigrants, the language is nearly exclusively English, though Sinhalese may be spoken sparingly, especially if the families spoke some Sinhalese prior to immigration. Post-1970s immigrants, on the other hand, are likely to be more bilingual. In all cases, however, the younger generations, those who arrived very young or were born in the United States, are not often proficient in Sinhalese. This does not indicate a dying out of the language. In the cities, where there are large concentrations, including Sri Lankan residents on temporary assignments in the United States, the language has a chance to survive. Social occasions and interaction, which are frequent, and conscious attempts to teach the language to the young through organized means contribute to a degree of proficiency in the language even for some of the young members of the community. Where population concentrations and other mechanisms for handing down the language are not available, such as in the smaller towns and cities across the country, keeping the young conversant in the language is an uphill struggle that is often unlikely to succeed.

## Kinship, Marriage, Family, and Household

In Sri Lanka, as in most traditional societies, ties of kinship and marriage are strong. The unit of society is not the individual but the group, usually the family. The Sinhalese are bilateral; they recognize kinship on both the maternal and paternal sides more or less on an equal basis. The preferred form of marriage is putative cross-cousin marriage, and actual cross-cousin marriages are considered to be the best. Marriage is a concern of the group, which means marriages are "arranged" by the families involved rather than left to the whims of the two principals. In arranging a marriage, matters of caste, wealth, status, and astrologically determined suitability as expressed in the compatibility of the two horoscopes are all considered. This general patterns applies for all except a tiny minority of sceptics.

The Sinhalese community in the United States generally accepts this framework of marriage, though some variations are unavoidable due to practical as well as cognitive reasons. Instances of two young people meeting and finding each other attractive as marriage partners is not uncommon. Often such instances concern a young person's choice of a non-Sinhalese mate, typically a white American, and such couples may still be refused parental consent. The more frequent pattern is for parents to arrange a marriage for their son or daughter. This may involve any or all of the considerations listed above, and the astrological state of the two people would by no means be the least important. A marriage is arranged through friends, kin, or more formal emissaries, and the partner sought may not necessarily be resident in the United States. Some parents resort to inserting matrimonial advertisements, either in a U.S.-based ethnic publication or, more likely, in newspapers in Sri Lanka. A marriage "proposal" and negotiations would then be conducted across the seas, with the partner then being brought to the United States from Sri Lanka. In such instances, it is most often a bride rather than a bridegroom who is being transported.

The Sinhalese professionals of the top ranks, like other such professionals, are an affluent group. Most other Sinhalese immigrants are comfortable, and destitution or living below the poverty line is rare. In consumption patterns, the Sinhalese show no distinctive feature except for their continued interest in ethnic cuisine, necessitating their patronage of ethnic stores that carry spices and other special items. Except for very rare items that are peculiar to the Sinhalese cuisine, most other items needed are available in ethnic stores that specialize in Indian and Far Eastern culinary fare, usually operated by immigrants from those countries. In view of the small size of the Sinhalese community, it is not surprising that Sinhalese ethnic food stores are uncommon. Any that do exist are likely to be located in the two high-concentration areas, near and around New York City and the major cities of California.

## Religious and Cultural Life

The Sinhalese in the United States, like those in their homeland, are predominantly followers of the orthodox tradition of Buddhism known as Theravada. Religious activity is centered on the idea of "making merit" (i.e., accruing spiritual good either for oneself or to be transferred to the dead by the ritual means of worshipping Buddha, observing the eight moral precepts on full moon days, and supporting the monks who are renouncers). The most sacred day is the full moon of May, known as Vesak, popularly believed to be the day of the birth, enlightenment, and death of Buddha. On this day, merit-making activities are intensified and performed with particular devotion. The temple in traditional Sri Lanka, in addition to being a center of religion, was also a center of learning and social activity.

The Sinhalese immigrants in America adhere to these customs and beliefs. Individual families often make private food offerings to monks for the purpose of transferring merit to dead kin in Sri Lanka. Some at least try to have their children educated in Buddhism, national customs, and the Sinhalese language by sending them to classes organized by the temples. This kind of temple-centered activity is available for only those immigrants who live in areas with access to temples. In the entire nation, however, there were only eight temples in 1996, one in New York City, two in Washington, D.C., and five in Los Angeles.

Perhaps the greatest function of the temple is social. Even when the specific reason for gathering at the temple is religious, which often it is, the occasion is of significance at least as much for the sense of social pleasure it provides, with underlying meanings of cultural identity. Social activity, however, is not confined to the temple. For example, in Washington, D.C., as part of the annual Vesak celebrations, a kite-flying contest is held, this sport being associated with Vesak in Sri Lanka. The temple, though a focal point of the group's unity and identity, also illustrates its factional tensions, which are sometimes carryovers of political tensions in Sri Lanka. Both in Washington, D.C., and in Los Angeles, factional split has been one underlying reason for the emergence of new temples. There are numerous Sri Lankan associations scattered in different parts of the country. The Sri Lankan embassy in Washington, D.C., lists twenty-seven such associations. Organized for social and cultural purposes, these associations serve to maintain the group's identity, although a plurality of these in a given area, such as Los Angeles, also illustrates divergent alliances.

There are two areas of specifically social activity within the Sinhalese immigrant community: entertainment and sport. In the regions with high concentrations of the Sinhalese community, there are arts societies that periodically enact Sinhalese plays. Sometimes, well-known artists from Sri Lanka are invited to do performing tours, which call for coordination among the sponsoring groups in different parts of the United States. In sports, the game, a gift of British colonialism, is cricket, which is avidly pursued in Sri Lanka as a national sport. Cricket games mark the most important national holiday, the Sinhalese New Year, which is celebrated in April. Dinners and fund-raising activities, as well as cricket matches, are often sponsored by social groups organized along ties to old elite schools in Sri Lanka (e.g., the Royal, St. Thomas, Nalanda, Ananda, and Trinity colleges). In addition to all of these social activities, *The Sri Lanka Express*, a Los Angeles–based publication, contributes to a sense of ethnic and cultural identity.

The Sinhalese immigrants in the United States are also very much involved with the culture and way of life in Sri Lanka. However, this should not be taken as an indication of any failure to integrate into the larger society of America. Instead, the involvement of the group with Sri Lankan culture should be interpreted as a genuine biculturality that is enriching the tapestry of American cultural diversity. The Sinhalese immigrants have adapted excellently to their new home, while engaging in Sri Lankan cultural practices that are meaningful and satisfying to them. There is no evidence that the group is subject to any discrimination based purely on the grounds of their ethnic and cultural identity.

*See also:* SRI LANKANS

## Bibliography

Bond, G. (1988). *The Buddhist Revival in Sri Lanka: Religious Tradition, Reinterpretation, and Response.* Columbia: South Carolina University Press.

De Silva, K. M. (1977). *Sri Lanka: A Survey.* Honolulu: University of Hawaii Press.

De Silva, K. M. (1981). *A History of Sri Lanka.* Delhi: Oxford University Press.

De Silva, K. M. (1986). *Managing Ethnic Tensions in Multi-Ethnic Societies: Sri Lanka, 1880–1985.* Lanham, MD: University Press of America.

Dharmadasa, K. N. O. (1992). *Language, Religion, and Ethnic Assertiveness: The Growth of Sinhalese Nationalism in Sri Lanka.* Ann Arbor: University of Michigan Press.

Ludowyk, E. F. C. (1966). *The Modern History of Ceylon.* London: Weidenfeld and Nicolson.

Ludowyk, E. F. C. (1967). *A Short History of Ceylon.* New York: Praeger.

Nicholas, C. W., and Paranavitana, S. (1961). *A Concise History of Ceylon.* Colombo: Ceylon University Press.

Paranavitana, S. (1967). *Sinhalayo.* Colombo: Lake House.

Spencer, J., ed. (1990). *Sri Lanka: History and Roots of Conflict.* London: Routledge.

H. L. SENEVIRATNE

# SLOVAKS

When interacting with each other, the Slovaks have called themselves by this name since the eleventh century. It is derived from *slovo* (word). Hence the Slovaks are people of "the word"—that is, they can understand each other. By contrast, they called the neighboring Germans Nemci (dumb ones) because the Slovaks could not understand their language. The Germans, on the other hand, initially called all Slavs (including the Slovaks) Wenden ("strange ones"). In Latin documents from the Middle Ages, Slovaks were called Sclavi (Slavs). Their Magyar compatriots, who shared the kingdom of Hungary with the Slovaks from the eleventh century to 1918, called them Tóth, which initially meant Slovak, but by the nineteenth century, when relations between the two groups deteriorated due to Magyar attempts to assimilate the Slovaks, it took on a pejorative connotation. Eastern Slovaks called themselves Slovjaks in their own dialect. Still others, who were not nationally conscious, called themselves Austrians or Hungarians to outsiders, because until 1918, the Slovaks lived in the kingdom of Hungary, which was a part of the dual monarchy of Austria-Hungary. In the United States, the Slovaks were (and sometimes still are) called Slavic, Slavish, or Slavonians, because, until they became secure in their true identity in America, some of their leaders, who were pan-Slavs, used these names in trying to link them to their larger Slavic neighbors. After 1918, some Slovaks adopted the designation Czechoslovak to stress their loyalty to the new republic of this name (which existed until 1993). Most, however, remained true to their ancestral name: Slovak.

## Immigration Patterns

The Roman Catholic priest Ján Baltazár Magin defined the Slovak ethnic group in 1728 on the following basis: Slovaks spoke a common language, inhabited a compact territory (they called it Slovensko [Slovakland], while the Magyars called it Upper Hungary), and felt a kinship with each other. This definition has been accepted by subsequent intellectuals, and it forms the basis of Slovak identity today.

Slovaks began immigrating to the United States in large numbers in the 1870s. The first and largest wave arrived between 1870 and 1914. It consisted of about 500,000 agriculturalists in search of work because their own landholdings were too small (or nonexistent) to support themselves or their families. The next wave, between 1919 and 1924, comprised about 30,000 women who immigrated to the United States to be reunited with their husbands, who had arrived in America alone before 1914 and who had been cut off from their families because of World War I. Between 1924 and 1945, very few Slovaks could get into the United States because the U.S. Congress passed a series of discriminatory immigration restriction acts in the 1920s. After World War II, a few

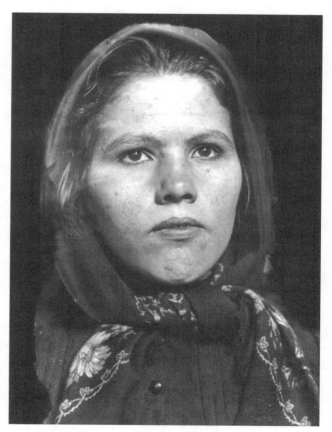

A Slovak immigrant awaits processing at Ellis Island during the early twentieth century. (Corbis-Bettmann)

thousand political émigrés from Slovakia were allowed entry into the United States as refugees fleeing communism (Czechoslovakia became Communist in 1948). Another wave of refugees arrived after the Soviet-led invasion of Czechoslovakia in 1968. Since the termination of Communist rule in Czechoslovakia, there has been a trickle of economic immigrants to the United States.

The four waves of Slovak immigrants to America had different characteristics. The first, and largest, group consisted of poorly educated agriculturalists or day laborers. Most had come from eastern Slovakia; they headed for the coal mines, steel mills, or oil refineries of the industrial Northeast, where they could find the highest-paid unskilled work. Half settled in Pennsylvania and the rest in neighboring New York, New Jersey, Ohio, Michigan, Indiana, and Illinois. Most worked as manual laborers until retirement. In this wave single or newly married men initially arrived alone. They worked in America for about five years, lived in boardinghouses run by enterprising Slovak mothers, and saved their money, planning to return home with their accumulated savings, buy some land, and settle down as prosperous farmers. Approximately 20 percent eventually did just that. The vast majority, however, found that once they had tasted the economic prosperity and political freedom of America, they could no longer live in the old country. Therefore they either sent for or brought with them their wives or girlfriends and settled in America for good.

The two waves of Slovak refugees who arrived in the United States after 1945, however, differed significantly from their predecessors. They were highly educated professionals (lawyers, teachers, writers, engineers, etc.) who came largely from central and western Slovakia. Although many initially had a hard time adjusting to the United States, most eventually did so and became professionals once more. Since they were fleeing from communism, there was no question of their returning home. Most remained aloof from the earlier immigrants or their children because of the class

and educational differences that divided them. Only those postwar immigrants who were fervent nationalists and who wished to join Slovak-American nationalists in calling for the independence of Slovakia buried their differences and cooperated in supporting such political organizations as the Slovak League of America (founded in Cleveland in 1907), which has championed self-determination or independence for the Slovaks from its founding to the present.

According to the 1990 U.S. Census, 1,882,897 people claimed Slovak ancestry. Of these, 1,210,652 individuals recorded Slovak as their primary ancestry, and 672,245 more listed it as their secondary ancestry. Not surprisingly, the largest number lived in Pennsylvania (447,384), followed by Ohio (273,380), Illinois (120,400), New York (118,045), and New Jersey (117,562). Smaller numbers lived in every other state, with particularly large concentrations in California (101,328) and Florida (74,335). The latter states attracted secondary migrants seeking employment and warmer weather, particularly retirees, who moved to Florida.

## Language

All Slovak arrivals initially spoke one of the many dialects of the homeland. These dialects usually reflected the sixteen counties of northern Hungary that the Slovaks inhabited. Linguists have classified the Slovak dialects into three main groups: eastern, central, and western. In the mid-nineteenth century, Slovak intellectuals codified the central Slovak dialects into a literary standard and began to create a literature in this codification. The majority of the first two waves of Slovak immigrants to the United States, however, spoke one of the eastern Slovak dialects. The third and fourth waves, who were better educated, tended to be proficient in the literary language. These dialectical differences also served to divide the first two waves from the later ones. In addition, the earliest arrivals established newspapers in the eastern Slovak dialects. However, a small group of intellectuals, who came largely from central and western Slovakia, saw to it that the Slovak-American press used only the literary standard by 1914. Furthermore, the parochial schools that Slovaks established at half of their Roman Catholic (and a few of their Lutheran) parishes taught the second generation (born in America) only the literary language. Generally speaking, only the first two generations of Slovak Americans were bilingual in Slovak and English. First-generation men were fluent in one of the Slovak dialects and spoke heavily accented English. Their wives usually spoke the same dialect, but often had a weaker command of English because most had to stay home to raise their families and often to take care of Slovak boarders. Members of the second generation, on the other hand, whether male or female, were fluent in English but spoke only haltingly in Slovak. By and large, the third and fourth generations do not speak Slovak at all.

The main reason why Slovaks have not maintained their language in America beyond two generations is that they stopped teaching it in their parochial schools after World War II. The forces of assimilation in the 1950s were so strong that the American-born parents lost interest in maintaining the language of their ancestors. Furthermore, these American-born parents themselves had only a rudimentary knowledge of Slovak, often in one of the nonliterary dialects, and they saw no advantage in passing on these dialects to the third generation. Only after the ethnic revival of the 1960s and 1970s did it become respectable to try to learn the language of one's ancestors again. Thus a few parishes started to sponsor Slovak-language classes to interested individuals in the evening or on Saturdays, if they could find a language teacher (usually a recently arrived immigrant who was educated in Slovakia). Also, in the late 1980s a group of Slovak-American fraternal-benefit societies decided to establish a chair in Slovak language and literature at the University of Pittsburgh. The chair is now functioning and teaches the Slovak language at various levels to several dozen students each year.

## Publications

Meanwhile, between 1885 and the present, Slovak Americans established more than two hundred newspapers, consisting of dailies, weeklies, and monthlies and covering the entire political spectrum from extreme left to extreme right. Furthermore, they were published for both men and women as well as for children and specialized in such topics as politics, religion, humor, labor, the household, literature, and poetry. Major centers of Slovak publishing have appeared in Pittsburgh; Cleveland; New York City; Chicago; Passaic, New Jersey; and Middletown, Pennsylvania. While the Slovak-American press initially functioned entirely in Slovak, bilingual newspapers began to appear in the 1960s to cater to the growing third and fourth generations. Today, of the twenty-odd Slovak-American newspapers still published, only one—*Slovák v Amerike* (the Slovak in America), founded in 1889—is still published exclusively in the Slovak language. Furthermore, while this newspaper was initially published weekly and later became a daily, with up to forty thousand subscribers, today it appears only monthly to a dwindling readership of about one thousand. Meanwhile, the bilingual weekly *Slovak Catholic Falcon*, official organ of the Slovak Catholic Sokol, headquartered in Passaic, and the semimonthly *Jednota* (Union), official organ of the First Catholic Slovak Union of the United States and Canada, headquartered in Independence, Ohio, reach audiences of up to forty thousand because they are mailed as one of the benefits of belonging to these fraternal-benefit societies.

## Religion

Slovaks in the Old World and in the New World were divided not only by the dialects they spoke but also by religion. As a result of the Reformation of the sixteenth century and the Counter-Reformation of the seventeenth, about 80 percent of Slovaks by 1900 were Roman Catholics, 15 percent were Lutherans, and the rest were

Greek Catholics or Calvinists. The immigrants brought their religious traditions with them and in the United States built 241 Roman Catholic, 48 Lutheran, and 9 Calvinist parishes by 1930. The Greek Catholics, whose parishes were multi-ethnic and encompassed Rusyns, Slovaks, Magyars, Croats, and Romanians, built 155 churches. Until the Second Vatican Council of the 1960s permitted the use of the vernacular, Roman Catholic Slovaks heard the official Mass in Latin, but Gospel readings and the sermon were in Slovak. So was the singing of a wide variety of hymns. Greek Catholics, on the other hand, heard the Mass in old Church Slavonic, while Lutherans heard it in old Czech and Calvinists heard it in the Zemplin (eastern Slovakia) dialect. By the 1960s, however, as the churches strove to cater to the third and fourth generations, they began to increase the use of English (some had started to offer English services in the 1940s), and today Slovak churches usually have only one service in Slovak for the "old-timers" and the rest in English.

Even though the Slovaks were divided by religion, they shared a reverence for their parishes. Their churches functioned not only as religious but also as cultural and neighborhood centers. People gathered outside their churches after services on Sunday to greet each other and catch up on gossip, and the church basements often were used for lodge meetings, dances and parties, dramatic or musical performances, and wedding receptions. Indeed, the major rites of passage that Slovaks celebrated—christenings, first communions, weddings, and funerals—all took place in church. The entire religious community participated in these celebrations, with women generally donating baked goods for the festivities and men providing the beverages.

Godparents played a major role in the lives of the first two generations. They were carefully selected by the parents of the newborn for their standing in the community and for their ability to raise the godchildren in case the parents died. Godparents often served as baby-sitters when needed and could discipline their godchildren when necessary.

## Fraternal-Benefit Societies

In addition to establishing parishes and newspapers, Slovak Americans also created a large network of fraternal-benefit societies. The earliest arrivals quickly perceived that America lacked any system of social support in the 1870s. Thus, if a Slovak immigrant fell ill, was the victim of an accident, or died, his family would receive no compensation or support from his employer or any government agency. Therefore, in the 1880s, Slovak Americans created fifty self-help or fraternal-benefit societies in their communities throughout the Northeast. Some were craft-oriented and secular, but the majority were based on religion and named for a patron saint. These lodges collected dues of about fifty cents a month and paid compensation to their members or their families if some tragedy befell them. In addition, they enforced strict codes of conduct based on their various religious denominations and in so doing helped make themselves more acceptable in the eyes of their American neighbors.

In 1890, Slovak-American fraternals started to federate to create nationwide institutions. The first to do so were several secular lodges, which formed the National Slovak Society in Pittsburgh on February 15, 1890. In September of that year, a number of Catholic lodges organized themselves into the First Catholic Slovak Union in Cleveland, Ohio. Since men had founded these fraternals and initially excluded women from membership, their wives established their own organizations. Thus, in 1891, a group of secular Slovak women founded the Živena (Giver of Life) Beneficial Society in New York City, and in 1892, Catholic Slovak women set up the First Catholic Slovak Ladies' Association in Cleveland, Ohio. Similarly, Lutheran Slovak males established the Slovak Evangelical Union in Freeland, Pennsylvania, in 1893, and their wives set up the Slovak Evangelical Ladies' Union a little later. Meanwhile, secular and militantly nationalist Slovaks established the Slovak Gymnastic Union Sokol (Falcon) in Perth Amboy, New Jersey, in 1896, while their more devout brethren broke away and set up the Slovak

Catholic Sokol in Passaic in 1905. In this way, Slovak Americans created about a dozen large nationwide fraternal-benefit societies by 1914. They enrolled about a third of the total Slovak adult population by 1918. Today, about 350,000 Slovaks are still members of fraternal-benefit societies, with the women's organizations leading the way. The First Catholic Slovak Ladies' Association is the largest with 105,000 members. Both the women's and men's organizations began to recruit members of the opposite sex after World War I, and the women's organizations have been more successful in these membership drives.

While the primary function of fraternal-benefit societies was to provide accident, illness, or burial insurance, they also filled some very important community roles. Most Slovak parishes in America were founded and supported by fraternal-benefit societies. Indeed, once the church had been constructed, many fraternals held their monthly meetings in the basement. Some of the men's fraternals that grew and prospered built their own Slovak halls. These secular buildings usually contained a bar, a gymnasium, and a bowling alley. Thus, they increasingly took on the role of community centers and often sponsored sporting events, dancing, and other forms of entertainment. In the early years the fraternals even had their own uniforms and often marched in processions, led by a band, to weddings and funerals of their members. The women's fraternals were less ostentatious (although some also had uniforms), preferring to meet in the church basement and concerning themselves with the decoration of the church. They also generally did the cooking for the many social events held at the church.

With the appearance of television and cheap life insurance in the 1950s, fraternal-benefit societies began a slow decline in the United States. They could not compete with the giant nationwide insurance companies, nor could they overcome the lure of television and other forms of mass entertainment. Thus, Slovak fraternal-benefit societies today are faced with a bleak future. The third and fourth generations consider them to be increasingly irrelevant, while the second generation, which still controls the organizations, is trying to find a way to make them relevant.

## Residential Patterns

As Slovaks and their descendants in the United States slowly moved from unskilled to skilled and then to white-collar and professional occupations over three generations, they also changed their place of residence. The first generation initially lived in cheap and overcrowded company housing (usually shanties) near the mine, mill, or refinery in which they worked. Once they had saved a decent nest egg, they moved some distance away from their place of employment, to a quieter or cleaner neighborhood. Here they invariably planted and cultivated a vegetable garden. Some even kept a few chickens, geese, or pigs until municipal regulations banned the raising of livestock within city limits. The second generation usually lived in the same neighborhood as their parents, often next door. Newlyweds often lived with their parents until they could afford a place of their own. Conversely, once the parents reached retirement age and needed help, their children usually took them in and cared for them until their death. The third generation, meanwhile, abandoned the old neighborhood and moved to the suburbs, as was the nationwide trend after World War II. Thus, the old "Slovak neighborhoods" of America's central cities are rapidly disappearing. Only the parish churches and a few Slovak halls remain to remind a visitor that Slovaks once lived there.

At first glance, Slovak Americans are virtually assimilated into mainstream society. They generally live in the suburbs, dress as do other middle-class Americans, and strive to become a part of the "American dream" with their own homes, cars, and financial independence. However, it took them three generations of struggle to achieve this goal. The first generation, although welcomed by America's capitalists as a source of cheap labor, was shunned and reviled by earlier arrivals, especially the Irish. The latter regarded the Slovaks and other southern and eastern Europeans as competitors for their jobs. Before Slovaks built their own churches, they often tried to worship in Irish churches but found a hostile reception. Slovaks were made to stand at the back of the church and had to hurry home after the services ended, lest some hotheads throw rocks in their direction. Once the Irish perceived the Slovaks as potential allies and voters for the Democratic "machines" the Irish controlled, the tensions between them abated somewhat, but the old suspicions died hard. The arrival of blacks and Puerto Ricans into Slovak neighborhoods after World War II hastened the Slovak flight to the suburbs. Some Slovaks perceived the arrival of the blacks and Puerto Ricans as being the cause for the decline of their neighborhoods and came to resent them, much as the Irish had resented the arrival of the Slovaks a hundred years earlier.

## Customs and Traditions

In spite of their almost total assimilation into the American mainstream, Slovak Americans have preserved a few of their customs and traditions. Most still celebrate Christmas Eve the old way. On this holiday, which eastern Slovaks call Vilija (Vigil) and central and western Slovaks call Štedrý večer (Bounteous Supper), the entire extended family gathers in the home of the parents or grandparents and at dusk begins to consume a twelve-course meal starting with unconsecrated communion wafers and sauerkraut soup, progressing through various fish courses and pastries, and ending with fruit and nuts. The presents used to be opened after this meal, with the children being told that "little Jesus" had brought them. Nowadays presents are opened on Christmas morning, and the person responsible for their appearance is Santa Claus.

At Easter many Slovak families still prepare elaborate Easter baskets. These consist of hand-painted Easter eggs, hams, cheeses, candies, and other goodies, which are blessed in a special ceremony on Easter Saturday and consumed after Mass on Easter Sunday. The ancient practice of dousing teenage girls and married women with water on Easter Monday by their boyfriends or husbands has all but died out in America. This ritualized "battle of the sexes" has no place in the modern "politically correct" world.

Other Slovak customs that have been transformed in America are the three major rites of passage. Baptisms used to be community affairs, with everyone in the neighborhood invited to Mass and to a long and lavish dinner afterward. Nowadays only the godparents, members of the family, and closest friends are invited, and the dinners are becoming less lavish and shorter.

Weddings, which also used to involve the whole community, lasted two or three days in the early years of the Slovak community in America. The parents would save for years to be able to put on a "good spread" for their daughters. Gypsy music, dancing through the night, and endless food and drink were de rigueur. So was an elaborate pre-Mass ceremony that featured the arrival of the groom at the bride's home and the formal request for her hand and the parents' blessing. The highlight of the evening was the bridal dance, when the groom was banished from the room and anyone who paid the bride a dollar would get to dance with her. This was a good way to raise a dowry in America. At the end of this ritual the members of the bride's immediate family danced with her (by then she had shed her white American gown and had changed into a folk costume), her mother tied a kerchief on the bride's head as a sign of marriage, and then the groom reappeared and whisked her away to the bridal chamber. Nowadays Slovak weddings last only one day and are more subdued, although some brides still insist on performing the bridal dance as a ritual of good-bye from their families. The food served is a blend of Slovak (sausages, stuffed cabbage, sauerkraut, and Slovak pastries) and American (chicken, beef, salads, and cookies). Alcohol still flows freely, although very few of the participants drink hard liquor unmixed or undiluted, as the old-timers did. Wine and beer are the beverages of choice today.

Funerals, meanwhile, have become totally Americanized. In the early years funerals were elaborate affairs, with the deceased dressed in his Sunday best and exposed for a day in his coffin for all to see in the parlor of his home, followed by an elaborate funeral Mass, then a procession led by uniform-clad lodge brothers to the Slovak cemetery, and final ceremonies involving the priest and the lodges at the graveyard. Nowadays deceased Slovaks are viewed in funeral homes, transported to cemeteries in limousines, and buried with the appropriate religious ceremonies. Although a few members of the deceased's lodge may still attend, they never come in uniforms, and they seldom participate in the final ceremonies.

Thus, Slovak Americans have come a long way since the late nineteenth century. They have been transformed from agriculturalists into well-educated suburbanites who have joined the American mainstream. Their culture has blended some of the old with lots of the new, and the result is an amalgam that is now called Slovak American.

See also: AUSTRIANS; CZECHS; HUNGARIANS

## Bibliography

Alexander, J. G. (1987). *The Immigrant Church and Community: Pittsburgh's Slovak Catholics and Lutherans, 1880–1915.* Pittsburgh: University of Pittsburgh Press.

Balch, E. G. (1910). *Our Slavic Fellow Citizens.* New York: Charities Publication Committee.

Bell, T. (1941). *Out of This Furnace.* Boston: Little, Brown.

Kirschbaum, S. J. (1995). *A History of Slovakia: The Struggle for Survival.* New York: St. Martin's Press.

Novak, M. (1978). *The Guns of Lattimer: The True Story of a Massacre and a Trial, August 1897–March 1898.* New York: Basic Books.

Stolarik, M. M. (1980). "A Place for Everyone: Slovak Fraternal-Benefit Societies." In *Self-Help in America: Patterns of Minority Economic Development,* edited by S. Cummings. Port Washington, NY: Kennikat Press.

Stolarik, M. M. (1985). *Growing Up on the South Side: Three Generations of Slovaks in Bethlehem, Pennsylvania, 1880–1976.* Lewisburg, PA: Bucknell University Press.

Stolarik, M. M. (1987). "The Slovak-American Press." In *The Ethnic Press in the United States: A Historical Analysis and Handbook,* edited by S. M. Miller. Westport, CT: Greenwood Press.

Stolarik, M. M. (1988). *The Slovak Americans.* New York: Chelsea House.

Stolarik, M. M. (1990). "Slovak Easter Customs in the United States." *The World & I* 5:690–695.

Stolarik, M. M. (1993). "The Slovak Search for Identity in the United States, 1880–1918." *Canadian Review of Studies in Nationalism* 20:45–56.

M. MARK STOLARIK

# SLOVENES

While English-speaking people use the terms "Slovene" and "Slovenian" and Germanic-speakers use the terms "Wendischer," "Windischer," and "Krainer," the self-name for this group is Slovenec (pl., Slovenci). *Grinder* or *griner,* corruptions of the name of the Austrian province of Krain (Carniola) from where many Slovenes emigrated, were pejorative terms for Slovenes in Cleveland and elsewhere in the United States.

Slovenia, formerly part of Yugoslavia and now an independent nation, occupies an area of 20,251 square kilometers. Its population in 1971 was well over 1.7 million. The largest part of Slovenia is mountainous, and much of the land is karstic, rugged, and stony. Only a small eastern section lies within the Pannonian plain. The majority of Slovenes were traditionally peasants, and population pressure on scarce land caused many to leave, beginning in the latter part of the nineteenth century. The main Slovene ethnic community is located in Cleveland.

The Slovenes are distinct from all other peoples of the former Yugoslavia by virtue of their language, Slovenian, a Slavic language very different from the other South Slavic languages spoken in that former federation. They are also differentiated by the Roman Catholic religion they share with the Croatians, whereas the rest of the members of the former federation are either Orthodox or Muslim.

## Immigration and Settlement History

Due to the depressions in the 1890s and 1930s and the early adoption of the rule of primogeniture (which limits inheritance of land to only one son, preferably the eldest), temporary migration, which often became permanent, was the most common solution to poverty in Slovenia. The earliest migration was to Croatia, for temporary work in the forests. By the 1850s, a small number of villagers began to immigrate to the United States, and this continued on an increasingly large scale until 1914 and briefly after World War I (1919–1923). When it became more difficult to immigrate to the United States due to restrictive quotas, Slovene peasants looked for temporary work in western Europe and combined farming in the home village with work in nearby factories, particularly furniture factories, to which the peasants sold lumber.

The last significant wave of Slovene immigration to the United States was from 1949 to 1956. Although the immigrants who arrived before World War I did so for primarily economic reasons, those who arrived after World War II were essentially motivated by political reasons. Census data, which are not entirely reliable, list for Cleveland 14,332 Slovenes in 1910, 30,000 to 40,000 by the 1920s, and 46,000 by 1970. Sometime during the early 1900s, Cleveland became the largest Slovene settlement outside of Slovenia, although a significant number of Slovenes also settled in northeastern Ohio, Wisconsin, Michigan, Minnesota, Pennsylvania, Illinois, and other areas. The estimated total number of Slovene immigrants and their American-born descendants in the United States was 250,000 to 350,000 by 1980. Since the chosen and central location for settlement was Cleveland, the remainder of this entry will refer primarily to that community.

Most Slovenes who immigrated to Cleveland during the period before World War II came from the Slovene area of Carniola, and the regions of Dolenjsko to the southeast and Notranjsko to the northwest. Typically, family heads—bachelors or married men—might travel two, three, or even four times from the home village to the United States to work temporarily in the forests and coal mines of Pennsylvania, or in the iron and copper mines of Michigan and Minnesota. The remittances they sent home made it possible for the villages to survive. The immigrants lived in dormitories and worked as many hours as possible. After 1900, unmarried women began to immigrate, joining their families. They frequently worked in taverns for a period to pay off their fare, which had often been advanced by the tavern owners. When young men who were married were able, and if they were contemplating a fairly long or permanent stay, they sent for their wives and children in Slovenia. After conquering early economic hardships it was not unusual for an enterprising Slovene couple to run a boardinghouse.

Immigrants who found their way to Cleveland settled in the Newburgh area and increasingly along St. Clair Avenue, across from the steel mills. From 1899 on, another area of settlement was the Collinwood area, where the Slovenes found employment in the railroad yards. Those from certain Slovene areas held together, making up local neighborhoods. Thus in the early years of the Cleveland Slovene settlements off St. Clair Avenue, there were separate localities based on areas of origin. For example, immigrants from the Slovene regions of Žužemberk or Ribnica resided in their own neighborhoods.

## Language

The Slovene language is one of the most archaic of the Slavic languages and includes thirty-six dialects and twenty-nine subdialects. In the United States the language culture of the Slovenes was characterized by a tenuous clinging to the mother tongue strengthened by Slovene cultural activities. These activities included instruction in the Slovene language in the Slovene Catholic churches, Slovene singing societies, and dramatic groups using the Slovene language. The pressure to adopt the English language was felt at first only through contact with the authorities but later through interaction with non-Slovene neighbors and exposure to the media. The basic characteristic of American Slovene linguistic culture is its bilinguality, the mixing of Slovene and English in the same speech act, called code switching by linguists. The Slovene part is usually spoken in the local dialect of the immigrant, and in some cases the internal structure of the Slovene language is altered under the influence of English. Thus Slovene may be incorrectly spoken under the influence of English. Not only phonology and the lexicon are transformed, but pragmatics also are affected; for example, while in Slovenia there are two forms of address—the familiar *ti* and its corresponding verbal form, and the polite *vi* and its corresponding verbal form—ethnic Slovenes have dropped the polite form.

By the 1990s, Slovene was rarely spoken by the youths of the third and later generations. In general, from the point of view of language, one can distinguish at least three waves encompassing the early immigrants and the next generations. The first group to arrive in the United States were hardworking pioneers, and when family and children joined them, all felt strong solidarity with the Slovene culture and language. The second generation began to handle both American and Slovene culture, maintained the Slovene language, and felt themselves closely connected to the culture of the homeland. However, members of the third and later generations became embarrassed by the Slovene spoken by their grandparents. But since the late 1960s, there has been an ethnic revival, including a revalorization of the Slovene language. And many who have only the barest command of the language now increasingly participate in Slovene cultural activities and are turning toward a renewed interest in everything Slovene, including visits to Slovenia.

## Economic, Social, and Religious Institutions

Lacking any kind of economic security or supporting social institutions, the early Slovene migrants began to develop cooperative associations, primarily mutual insurance societies. The tradition of cooperatives and mutual aid societies was established under the Austrians, who ruled the Slovenes until Yugoslavia was formed after World War I. Such societies, however, did not exist in Communist Slovenia.

By the 1890s, nationally based organizations began to appear in the United States. The two largest fraternal insurance agencies were the Carniolian Slovenian Catholic Society (Kranjsko-Slovenska Katoliška Jednota [KSKJ]), formed in 1884, which was Catholic oriented (its name was changed in 1996 to the American Slovene Catholic Union [Ameriška Slovenska Katolicka Jednota]), and the anticlerical Slovene National Benefit Society (Slovenska Narodna Podporna Jednota [SNPJ]), founded in 1904. On the local level, society members were grouped into separate lodges; the two main societies each had several lodges in Cleveland. Beginning in the 1920s, such organizations added to their life insurance and death benefit programs the promotion of educational and cultural activities, and each sponsored its own newspaper and other publications. By the mid-1970s, Slovene fraternal organizations in the United States, including the Slovene Women's Organization, had an enrollment of 185,000.

The three most important institutions of the early 1920s were the Catholic Church, the mutual insurance societies, and the taverns (*gostilna*). The Slovene Catholic churches were built from contributions of the Slovene population. The first Slovene national parish was built in 1891 in Chicago and was staffed with a Slovene priest. The second, St. Vitus Parish in Cleveland, was founded in 1893 and also was staffed by a Slovene priest. A few years later, St. Lawrence Church was established in the Newburgh area. Others followed.

As Slovenes in Cleveland advanced from low-paid unskilled labor, earning perhaps two dollars for a ten-hour working day, they began to establish businesses of their own. The tavern was important both economically and socially. On Saturday nights men might go from saloon to saloon. Each saloon had an accordionist who played Slovene

Slovene Americans participate on a float in Cleveland as part of the Fourth of July celebrations. (Irene Portis-Winner)

songs. It was not hard to start a saloon because the potential owner made an agreement with a brewery to sell only its product. Some tavernowners assumed the role of banker and received interest on their loans, as there was an increasingly successful movement toward home ownership. By 1910, the Slovene business community included seventy Slovene-owned establishments: clothing stores, furniture stores, funeral parlors, grocery stores specializing in Slovene food, stores selling Slovene merchandise and Slovene-language publications from Slovenia and the United States, restaurants, and saloons. By the second decade of the twentieth century, the size of the Slovene business community exploded, and there were more than four hundred Slovene enterprises in Cleveland. The early immigrants gradually worked their way up, many leaving the St. Clair Avenue neighborhoods for the Cleveland suburbs, particularly Euclid and Collinwood, which now have large Slovene populations from both waves of immigration.

## Growth of Cultural Institutions, Publications, and the Arts

In Cleveland, Slovene arts, music, literature, drama, song, and dance began to flourish by the turn of the twentieth century. In 1920, the first Slovene singing society, Zora (Dawn), was formed. Later that year, renamed Slovenski Sokol (Slovene Falcon), it expanded its focus to include drama and gymnastics, but it was finally dissolved in 1941. In 1906, the Slovene National Reading Room (Slovenska Narodna Čitalnica) was established. In the early twentieth century it was located in the Slovene National Home (Slovenski Narodni Dom), established in 1924 on St. Clair Avenue. The origins of the national homes can be traced to the early immigrants' taverns. By 1914, there were in Cleveland nine national homes, with many uses, including meetings and dramatic performances. The Triglav Singing and Dramatic Society named after Triglav Mountain, the national symbol of Slovenia, was founded in 1903. The Sokol (Falcon) Society was established in the Collinwood suburb in 1917 and gave thirty concerts in fifteen years. The most ambitious society was the Ivan Cankar Dramatic Society, organized in 1919. Its first performance was the play *Deseti Brat* (The Tenth Brother); the society produced forty-eight plays in five years. In 1924, the play *Brat Martin* (Brother Martin) was staged before two thousand people in the Slovene National Home on St. Clair Avenue.

A Slovene farmland (Slovenska Pristava) was established in 1961 as a recreational center outside Cleveland. It has become a retreat for all kinds of celebrations and feasts and music. It is owned by the Slovene National Benefit Society. A second retreat, organized by a post–World War II group, is called Zastava (Flag).

From 1891 to the 1990s, more than one hundred Slovene-language newspapers and journals were established throughout the United States, but only a few lasted longer than four or five years. One of the first Slovene-language newspapers in the United States was *Ameriški Slovenec* (The American Slovene), which was published first in Chicago and later in Cleveland. It was founded by

Joseph Buh, who was a missionary priest among the Indians of Minnesota and the Dakotas. The newspaper first appeared around 1891 and was published in Slovene and two versions of English, one in standard and one in phonetic spelling. It urged ethnic identity but also understanding of the United States. *Narodna Beseda* (The National Word), the first Slovene newspaper in Cleveland, appeared in 1899. Its name was later changed from *Narodna Beseda* to *Nova Domovina* (The New Homeland) to *Amerika* to *Clevelandska Amerika* (Cleveland America) and finally, in 1914, to *Ameriška Domovina* (American Homeland). *Glas Naroda* (The Voice of the People), founded in 1893 in New York, also became available in Cleveland in 1899.

The Slovenes were hardworking, industrious, and inventive, and they maintained as far as possible a commitment to Slovene culture. For example, Cleveland Slovene parents supported parochial schools and national parishes. The St. Vitus and St. Lawrence parishes each had their own parochial schools, and they could not accept the many who applied. In 1910, St. Vitus had 450 students but only six teachers; thus a new school was established. By 1930, English had become the language of instruction in the parochial schools, with Slovene relegated to special classes.

By the first decade of the twentieth century, a second generation appeared. The community became more diverse, and many more organizations were formed. By 1914, *Clevelandska Amerika* listed fifty-three Cleveland area lodges affiliated with various national organizations with a total membership of seventy-five hundred. By then there were twenty independent insurance agencies and nine educational, singing, dramatic, and economic societies, adding another three thousand members.

Although during the Communist period interest in the rich Slovene folk arts, performances, celebrations, and rituals of all kinds (e.g., a protracted wedding celebration, and gaiety at open markets where clowns performed) dwindled and indeed became almost extinct in Slovenia (a reflection of the grim attitude of the peasants there), ethnic Slovene communities in the United States preserved these activities and even expanded on them. Thus Slovene arts and cultural activities flourished in Cleveland and other areas in America.

## Transnational Society

The Slovene community retained close family relations with kin back home. Since 1950, thousands of immigrants and American Slovenes have visited Slovenia, and villagers from the homeland also have visited Cleveland. The many social support organizations have been an important aspect of the success story of the amalgamation of Slovene and American traditions without losing Slovene ethnic identity, thus disproving the theory of America as a cultural melting pot. There were to some extent chauvinistic attitudes toward other ethnic groups, such as Croatians, Czechs, Italians, and African Americans. Gradually, as inner city ills invaded the traditional Slovene community of St. Clair Avenue, the neighborhood's Slovene nature began to be diluted as more families moved to the suburbs, particularly Euclid and Collinwood.

The term "transnational" can be applied to the Slovene-American community, since ties to the home villages and to Slovene traditions such as Slovene food, music, feasts, dances, hospitality, and, for a large sector, religion, were maintained, and correspondence with Slovenia was frequent; similarly, Slovene villagers maintained strong ties to Cleveland. But there were important internal differences. First, there was a pre–World War I split between the Catholics and the anticlerical group. Thus there were two parallel sets of economic and cultural organizations reflecting the positions of the pro-Catholic group and the secular group, but this has not lessened the strong sense of ethnic identity within either group. Second, there was a split between the immigrants who arrived after World War II and the earlier groups. Finally, there were definite economic differences among members of the earlier group as they developed, although in general the degree of economic success, though gradual, was quite striking.

## Worldview

The Slovene-American worldview is characterized by certain outlooks that are not typically American. For example, Slovenes have a strong sense of obligation to their relatives in the home villages and have not shared in the permissive attitudes toward children's behavior and demands typical of Americans. Typically a Slovene child is not praised for being good, since it is expected, but is chastised for wrong doings. Mary Molek's *Immigrant Woman* describes her childhood in the United States beginning in the 1940s on a farm in Kansas. Molek's work provides striking illustrations of typical Slovene peasant virtues, all of which reinforce the kinds of impression one gathers over and over when listening to Slovene members of the Cleveland society; thus ethnic Slovenes may be described as hardworking, industrious, enterprising, stubborn, frugal, abjuring debts if possible, stoic, proud of the Slovene heritage, not only loyal to family and relatives but also generous in assisting other Slovene immigrants, and finally notable for ritualized hospitality that always includes coffee and sweets and traditionally *slivovka* (plum brandy). All these qualities sustained in the New World have helped to explain the success story of the Slovene immigrants who began under severe hardships. And such values apply equally to the Slovene peasants in Europe who, in spite of all obstacles, maintained their economy.

Even a large number of youths who earlier had resisted Slovene influence in their desire not to be different, have changed their priorities in the 1990s, expressing the general wish to understand their ethnic identity. All ethnic Slovenes now take great pride in the essentially peaceful attainment of independence by Slovenia.

As the Slovenes have become successful and Americanized they have begun to adopt the American spirit of orientation toward the future. For the older generation, memory and nostalgia have not disappeared, while for the young it is a wish to know about their cultural heritage. The future orientation of Slovene Americans, though often somewhat restrained depending on the degree of economic success of the individual, is quite different from that of typical Slovene peasants in Europe, who traditionally have adopted a fatalistic attitude, since they could not significantly improve their lot and believed themselves to be the lowest on the social ladder, exploited by all above them. However, they recall pre-Communist Yugoslavia, and even the Austrian rule before that, with considerable affection and nostalgia. But in the 1990s, those villagers who are obtaining help from the government to modernize their houses and change their way of life welcome the present regime, while the older peasants feel somewhat lost and out of the system. The industriousness and ingenuity of the Slovenes in the home villages is clearly shared by their relatives in the United States who have found ways to fulfill their abilities and remain ethnically Slovene Americans.

*See also:*  AUSTRIANS; CROATIANS; HUNGARIANS; SERBS

## Bibliography

Lenček, R., ed. (1975). *Papers in Slovene Studies*. New York: Society for Slovene Studies.

Lenček, R., ed. (1995). *Twenty Years of Scholarship*. New York: Society for Slovene Studies.

Molek, I. (1978). *Two Worlds*, translated by M. Molek. Dover, DE: M. Molek.

Molek, M. (1976). *Immigrant Woman*. Dover, DE: M. Molek.

Portis-Winner, I. (1978). "Ethnicity Among Urban Slovene Villagers in Cleveland, Ohio." In *Papers in Slovene Studies*, edited by R. Susel. New York: Society for Slovene Studies.

Portis-Winner, I. (1978). "The Question of Cultural Point of View in Determining Boundaries of Ethnic Units: Slovene Villagers in Cleveland." In *Papers in Slovene Studies*, edited by T. M. S. Prietly. New York: Society for Slovene Studies.

Portis-Winner, I. (1993). "Transnationals and the Human Sign." In *Signs of Humanity: L'homme et ses signes*, edited by M. Balat and J. Deledalle-Rhodes. Berlin: Mouton-de Gruyter.

Prisland, M. (1968). *From Slovenia to America*. Chicago: Slovenian Women's Union of America.

Šabec, N. (1995). *Half Pa Pu (Half and Half): The Language of the Slovene-Americans*. Ljubljana: Studia Humanitatis, APES.

Susel, R. (1983). "The Perpetuation and Transformation of Ethnic Identity Among Slovene Immigrants in America and the American-Born Generations: Continuity and Change." In *The Dynamics of East European Ethnicity Outside of Eastern Europe with Special Emphasis on the American Case*, edited by I. PortisWinner and R. Susel. Cambridge, MA: Schenkman.

Van Tassel, D. D., and Grabowski, J. J. (1996). *The Encyclopedia of Slovene History*. Bloomington: Indiana University Press.

Velikonja, J., and Lenček, R. L., eds. (1995). *Who's Who of Slovene Descent in the United States*. New York: Society for Slovene Studies, Reserch and Documentation Center, Institute on East Central Europe, Columbia University Press.

Works Project Administration. (1937). *Annals of Cleveland: Cleveland Foreign-Language Newspaper Digest*, Vol. 7: *Slovenians*. Cleveland: Author.

IRENE PORTIS-WINNER

# SORBS

The Sorbs, also known as Lusatians, Serbo-Lusatians, and Wends, are the smallest of the Slavonic groups and are the least recognized. This problem of name recognition is compounded by several factors. First, the Sorbs never realized the creation of their own nation but remained a minority in Germany. Further contributing to this anonymity and even creating confusion in some instances is the lack of a single, simple, descriptive name. One option is to label them with the name of the region in southeastern Germany in which they reside: Lusatia. R. G. A. de Bray, author of the *Guide to Slavonic Languages* (1951), preferred this term and devoted the last chapter of his book to the language of the people of Lusatia. The term, however, is not ideal because Lusatia is also the home for many German people. The name these people call themselves is "Serbja," but that does not help because the English derivative would be "Serb," the name for a larger ethnic group and a nation in the Balkans. A combination of the two terms Serbo-Lusatian is precise, but possibly too long and exotic. The Germans called these people "Venden" or "Wends," but the term was slightly pejorative and was also used as a generic term for Slavs; for example, the Wends of the Balkans are Slovenes. Another name used on occasion by the Germans was "Sorbs," and that term has become the preferred term in Europe since 1945 and in some academic circles. Among the immigrants in the United States and their descendants, however, the term of choice is "Wend." That was the word used in the nineteenth century, and since that time it has lost its pejorative connotation.

## Location and Early History

The homeland for the Sorbs or Wends is the region in southeastern Germany called Lausitz in German, Lužica in Sorbic, and Lusatia in English. It is a small area approximately fifty miles north and south and twenty-five miles east and west, located between Dresden and the borders of the Czech Republic and Poland. The southern portion, closest to the Czech Republic, is called Upper Lusatia because of its higher altitude; the northern part is called Lower Lusatia. The Spree (Sorbic: Sprjewa) River, which flows through Berlin, first flows through Bautzen (Budyšin), the main city in Upper Lusatia and then Cottbus (Chośebuz), the chief city in Lower Lusatia.

The Sorbs have lived in this region since the tribal migrations of the sixth century, when they and other Slavic groups occupied the region west of the Oder River. The German tribes began their eastward migration shortly thereafter, and in the conflict between German and Slav, the Slavs west of the Oder were either killed, expelled, or assimilated—except the Milceni and Luzici, the ancestors of the Sorbs. They continued to live in Lusatia and perpetuated their language and culture. They lost their political independence, however, by the year 963, when the German forces under Otto the Great completed the conquest. The Germans could not consolidate their control, and for some time that region was also ruled intermittently by the Bohemian, Polish, and Hungarian crowns. The German province of Brandenburg eventually gained control of Lower Lusatia in 1462, and Saxony added Upper Lusatia in 1635.

The geographic area and the number of people associated with the Sorbian culture steadily declined not only under the pressures of German rule but even during the time of Bohemian, Hungarian, and Polish control. Germans excluded Sorbs from guilds and economic activities and discriminated against them in other ways. Many Sorbs saw the advantage of being German and became part of German society. Germanization was more pronounced in Lower Lusatia because Brandenberg fell under Prussian administration while Upper Lusatia remained under Saxony.

## Demography

Using Sorbian statistics, which are higher than the German, there were 164,000 persons in 1840 on the eve of the large emigration who spoke primarily Sorbic and preserved some of the folklore and customs. In 1937, shortly before World War II, there were 111,000; in 1987, there were 50,000. Although the Sorbs adhered to a Slavic culture, they were German citizens, served in the German military, and interacted with German society.

The number who immigrated to the United States prior to the American Civil War was approximately 600 with most being part of a single group that immigrated in 1854. The number of immigrants after the American Civil War was larger, more than 800, but these immigrated in smaller groups or as individuals.

## Linguistic and Religious Affiliations

The language spoken by the Sorbs is a Slavic language that in turn is divided into two dialects. Upper Lusatian, using de Bray's term, or Upper

Sorbic, is based on the Bautzen dialect and is more closely related to the Czech language, while the dialect for Cottbus, or Lower Sorbian, is more akin to Polish. Conversation in the two dialects is difficult but not impossible.

Conversion to Christianity began prior to the German conquest, but the Germans aggressively promoted Christianity, and the Sorbs reluctantly but gradually gave up their pagan ways. For almost five hundred years they remained loyal to the Church of Rome, but in 1530, following the Council of Augsburg, most became Lutheran. The remaining Catholics, centered around the cloister of Marienstern, northwest of Bautzen, trained their priests at the Catholic Lusatian seminary of Saints Peter and Paul at Prague, while the Protestant clergy studied at the University of Leipzig. Sorbic became a written language during the Reformation with Martin Luther's focus on the vernacular, and the first written works were Sorbic translations of the Bible and the catechism. The Lutherans adopted the *Frakturschrift* of the Germans, not ideally suited to a Slavic language, while the Catholics retained the Latin script.

## Contributing Factors for Emigration

The flow of Sorbian history divided in the mid-nineteenth century, when Sorbs became part of the European emigration. The same conditions that influenced Germans to pull up roots also influenced the Sorbs. The first factor was the end of the feudal system. Even though the system ended at different times in the various German provinces, serfdom ceased by the first half of the nineteenth century. Dislocation, unemployment, poverty, and movement of people followed.

Another element that coincided with the end of feudalism was population growth. The increased birthrate and the decrease in infant mortality placed greater demand for the remaining acres of agricultural land for ownership and food production. But in the 1840s, there were also crop failures of both potatoes and flax.

In some cases, for both German and Sorb, there was religious discontent. The strongest con-

Children from the parish school for the St. Paul Lutheran Church (constructed in 1871) in Serbin, Texas, walk to waiting automobiles and buses. (George R. Nielsen)

flict was between the Lutherans who were determined to remain Lutheran and the decision of the ruler of Prussia to consolidate the Protestants—Lutheran and Calvinists—into a state church. Those Lutherans who were unwilling to give up their faith for a homogenized church either left the state church to form independent congregations at their own expense, or left the country. The Sorbs of Upper Lusatia who were under Saxon rule had a different religious problem: doctrinal laxity. Rationalism had influenced the clergy, and rationalism had no use for faith. How could people who took their faith seriously find fulfillment in a rationalist context?

Not only were Sorbian and German motives similar, the Sorbs also followed or accompanied the German emigration. Beginning in the 1840s Sorbs, individually or in groups, began leaving Lusatia for Australia, the United States, Canada, South Africa, and some Latin American countries.

## Immigration to the United States

The largest number of Sorbs immigrated to the United States, and the largest single group selected Texas. The Sorbian immigration to Texas began as early as 1849, when some individual Sorbs traveled with some Germans. Four years later a small group of thirty-five followed. In 1854, a party of five hundred under the leadership of a Lutheran pastor, Jan (Johann) Kilian, sailed for Texas.

Kilian had graduated from the University of Leipzig in 1834 and taken a parish at Kotitz in Saxony. There, in addition to composing hymns and writing religious material, he criticized the religious policies of Saxony and neighboring Prussia. In 1848, he accepted a call sent by two independent congregations in Prussia and became the leader of those Lutherans who had abandoned the state church. Six years later, in 1854, he accepted the call from a group of laymen from both Saxony and Prussia who hoped to establish a congregation and community in Texas.

The route used by the Sorbs from Germany to Texas was typical of the 1850s. Wagons first carried them to the nearest railroad station. The train took them to Hamburg; a ship sailed from Hamburg to Hull, on the eastern coast of England; rail again to Liverpool, where they boarded a ship that had recently carried cotton bales to England. In Liverpool some members of the Kilian group con-

tracted cholera, and about seventy died. After the ship arrived at Galveston most of the Sorbs began their journey to the interior, although some remained in Houston. More immigrants followed during succeeding decades and generally settled near the main group or opened neighboring communities.

Sorbs also settled outside of Texas, in Nebraska and Iowa. There were some major differences. They were fewer in number; they immigrated in the 1870s and 1880s; they were from villages in Lower Lusatia; and, even though they were aware of their Slavic heritage at the time of immigration, they had become more absorbed into the German community. The two Nebraska locations are Ster-

A demonstration, using an old mill, shows how the early Sorbian settlers obtained sap from sorghum to produce molasses. Because of adverse growing conditions during the year the photo was taken (1996), the sorghum crop failed and Georgia cane, commonly used for fishing poles, is being used for the demonstration. (*Giddings Times & News*)

ling, in the southeastern part of the state, and Clay Center, near Hastings. In Iowa they settled near State Center.

## Economy

The primary settlement made by Kilian's congregation was in Lee County, between Houston and Austin, where the leaders bought a league (4,254 acres) of land. Several families built homes in the new village of Serbin, but most became farmers and built their homes on scattered sites, as other Texans did. They also adopted Texas agricultural practices. Instead of growing rye, wheat, and flax, as they had in Europe, they became subsistence farmers, producing corn, hogs, cattle, and poultry for their own use and cotton for sale. The Sorbs in Nebraska and Iowa also modified their agricultural practices, in keeping with the farming practices of the Midwest.

## Religion and Expressive Culture

At the center of the Sorbs' community, whether in Texas or the Midwest, was the church and the pastor. In Texas most Sorbs had settled within an area small enough to enable them to travel to a central congregation. Several families who had settled at a greater distance received periodic visits from Kilian. But Kilian also realized the necessity of affiliating with a denomination, so in 1860, he traveled to St. Louis to participate in a national convention of the Lutheran Church—Missouri Synod, a conservative body headed by C. F. W. Walther, an acquaintance from the University of Leipzig. Kilian joined, and the congregation later also affiliated with that same denomination. As the population of Serbin increased, both from natural increase as well as continued immigration, some members of Kilian's flock obtained land at distances too great for continued association, so they formed daughter congregations. They also affiliated with the Missouri Synod and worshiped exclusively in German. The Iowa Sorbs became members of a Missouri Synod congregation, while the Nebraska Sorbs became part of the German Nebraska Synod.

Kilian conducted most church services in Sorbic, but because there were a few Germans in the congregation and most Sorbs were conversant in German, Kilian also preached in German. Kilian recorded the minutes of the congregational meetings in Sorbic, but the official records of the church, such as for baptisms, confirmations, marriages, and deaths, he wrote in German. Kilian also served as the teacher of the parish school, teaching in both languages. Over time, German began replacing Sorbic as the language of the church, school, and home. More and more activities of the church were conducted in German, and finally in 1920, with the death of Herman Kilian, Jan's son and successor, the last scheduled Sorbic service was held in Serbin.

Because the Sorbs made the transition to German, they were destined to repeat the process and change to English. In the 1880s, when German had become the dominant language, English began making inroads. The German-speaking community in Texas, however, was large enough so that change to English was slow, even during World War I. But that generation began to change, and those who did not make the transition in World War I did so after World War II, and soon English church services were held once a month. The Voter's Assembly in Serbin changed to English in 1966, but monthly German services continued into 1996.

The two festivals of the church year that play an important part of the Sorbs' lives are Christmas and Easter. The celebration of Christmas follows German practices, with worship services and a Santa Claus–type person called *Rumplich*. The Texas Easter celebration, however, retains some Sorbian customs associated with water obtained from a brook or stream. Use of the water on Easter morning promises a variety of things, such as beauty and health.

The church also provided the focus for events of the family such as birth, marriage, and death. A mother, returning to church after childbirth, was met at the door of the church and escorted to the altar for prayer. Marriage took place in church before the celebration at the home of the bride, but the planning and direction of the entire event was lead by a person called a *braška*.

Some secular practices remained, such as the celebration of the Birds' Wedding (Vogelhochzeit) on January 25, which involved baking and giving gifts, and featherstripping parties, where young women removed the barbs from the shafts of goose feathers so they could be used in bedding. Home cures also abounded, which ranged from the use of herbs and teas to the use of incantations.

Among individual Sorbs who were not part of a Sorbian community and achieved literary prominence was Mato Kossyk (Kossick). Even though he was a Lutheran pastor, he never became the pastor of a Sorbian congregation. He did, however, visit the two Nebraska settlements and communicated with the Sorbs. His fame rests instead on his poetry. Most of his poetry had been written prior to his departure from Germany, but he continued to write during his life in the American Midwest.

## Sociopolitical Organization

Even though Kilian exerted influence through his sermons and also by virtue of his education, the ultimate control of the congregation rested with the Voters' Assembly. This assembly was composed of adult males who chose to join. Even Kilian, who had opposed the bureaucratic church in Germany, found democracy somewhat burdensome and complained that every voter seemed compelled to "preach" and convince other voters of his opinion. The Voters' Assembly owned the congregational property; paid the salaries; collected the money; and on the advice of the pastors and elders, exercised church discipline, including excommunication—as a last resort. Conflicts were resolved through the application of Matthew 18:15–17:

> Moreover if thy brother shall trespass against thee, go and tell him his fault between thee and him alone: if he shall hear thee, thou hast gained thy brother. But if he will not hear thee, then take with thee one or two more, that in the mouth of two or three witnesses every word may be established. And if he shall neglect to hear them, tell *it* unto the church: but if he neglect to hear the church, let him be unto thee as a heathen man and a publican.

## Ethnic Revival

The Sorbian heritage in Texas, unlike the language, is deeply etched and enjoying a revival. Families are writing their histories and gathering at reunions. The Wendish Heritage Society has a loyal following and supports a museum in Serbin. Each fall they celebrate a Wendish festival day and are now resurrecting customs such as the Birds' Wedding and decorating Easter eggs, practices that had become almost extinct. The Sorbian heritage in Nebraska and Iowa, on the other hand, is a faint memory. Nineteenth-century church records of baptisms and marriages indicate that in the selection of spouses and godparents, the initial immigrants maintained some ethnic ties, but within a generation the bonds were soon broken, and most identified themselves with the German heritage.

*See also:*   GERMANS

## Bibliography

Blasig, A. (1954). *The Wends of Texas*. San Antonio, TX: Naylor.

Caldwell, L. M. (1961). *Texas Wends: Their First Half Century*. Salado, TX: Anson Jones Press.

Nielsen, G. R. (1989). *In Search of a Home: Nineteenth-Century Wendish Migration*. College Station: Texas A & M University Press.

Stone, G. (1972). *The Smallest Slavonic Nation: The Sorbs of Lusatia*. London: Athlone Press.

Wilson, J. B. (1986). "Wendish to German to English: The Texas Wends." In *Texas Country: The Changing Rural Scene*, edited by G. E. Lich and D. B. Reeves-Marquardt. College Station; Texas A & M University Press.

GEORGE R. NIELSEN

# SOUTH ASIAN CHRISTIANS

Christianity is centuries old in South Asia, but South Asian forms of Christianity appeared in the United States only in the late twentieth century. According to an ancient tradition, the Apostle Thomas arrived in India in 52 C.E., preaching and establishing St. Thomas Christianity in South India before dying as a martyr near Madras in 72 C.E. By the fourth century, Indian Christians were in contact with the church in Syria, so that St. Thomas Christians are also called Syrian or Syrian Orthodox Christians. Portuguese explorers arrived in 1498 "seeking Christians and spies," and St. Francis Xavier and other missionaries arrived in 1542 to introduce Roman Catholicism, first in the south and then throughout the Indian subcontinent. Beginning in the eighteenth century, Protestants established many churches, denominations, schools, and hospitals. The result is that many Christian Orthodox, Catholic, and Protestant congregations developed in South Asia that now send members to the United States as part of the post-1965 immigration. Hence it is possible to trace the long history and complexity of Christianity in India in the churches and strategies of adaptation established by these new immigrants from South Asia.

Prior to 1965, few South Asian Christians lived in North America—only a few students at church-related colleges and theological schools. Christian immigrants are part of the general brain drain encouraged by provisions of the Immigration Act—doctors, engineers, scientists—but Christians are unique because of the importance of nurses in the immigration network. Nurses arrived in the United States as professionals in the 1970s for jobs in urban hospitals that desperately needed registered nurses. A survey of several hundred Asian Indian Christians reveals that approximately 70 percent of the adult women are nurses who were attracted to the United States by relatively high wages, security, and status. Indeed, American hospitals actively recruited Indian Christian nurses for employment. Christians are the only South Asian group that arrived in America "on the shoul-

ders" of the women. The women had the green cards, the good jobs, and the high incomes. After having established themselves in America, many brought spouses and children from India as provided for under family reunifications provisions of the law. Or, having gained merit in marriage negotiations, they returned to India for marriage to professionals primed for success in America. Some spouses of nurses were Christian pastors in India and established congregations in America. Others enjoyed professional certifications that were not transferable, so they entered new occupations as pastors, medical technicians, hospital counselors, or entrepreneurs. Within twenty-five years, approximately 125,000 Christians with family roots in India resided in the United States. The numbers increase annually through immigration of family members. They come primarily from four linguistic-ethnic groups of South India—Malayalam-speakers from the state of Kerala, Tamil-speakers from Tamil Nadu, Telugu-speakers from Andhra Pradesh, and Kannada-speakers from Karnataka—but also from other linguistic-ethnic areas of India, especially Gujarati-speakers from the state of Gujarat. They worship in South Asian Christian churches in most American metropolitan areas.

When children reach the age of socialization outside the home, churches and Christian fellowship groups develop. Religion is important for immigrants because it provides a transcendent grounding for the formation and preservation of personal and group identity. The background of immigration shared by so many Americans is one reason why there are so many active churches in North America. Each new immigrant group faces the necessity of establishing its new identity. Each chooses from among several strategies of adaptation in establishing both religious and secular organizations:

1. Individual: The individual carries on religious activities alone or assimilates as an individual in churches of the majority population.
2. Ecumenical: Christians from several ethnic-linguistic groups and from several denomi-

national backgrounds gather into parishes or informal study/prayer groups.

3. Ethnic: Keralites, Gujaratis, Tamils, and other regional-linguistic groups establish their own religious groups.

4. Denominational: Following this strategy, the immigrants establish churches along denominational lines.

Each of these adaptive strategies embodies a large number of decisions about language-use, leadership, ethos, and theology.

## The Churches

*St. Thomas Christians.* Immigrants in both the Indian Syrian Orthodox Church and the Malankara Orthodox Syrian Church trace their history to St. Thomas and to Syriac Christianity. The former accepts the authority of the patriarch of Antioch in Baghdad, who heads the church in Syria. Hence Athanasius Mar Samuel, who had been archbishop for immigrants from Syria since 1949, welcomed and ministered to parishes and congregations of immigrants as they arrived from Kerala. Yuhanon Mar Philoxinos arrived in the United States in 1977 and gathered ten Syrian Orthodox families from India for meetings at Our Lady of Good Counsel Roman Catholic Church on Staten Island, New York. He refers to that church as the "birthplace of Malayalee Syrian Orthodox churches in the United States" and to himself as "the first vicar of the church in the United States." The community grew rapidly in other cities, and seven more churches were established by 1984, one a year, in cities such as Chicago, Dallas, Houston, and Detroit. Lay groups formed ad hoc administrative committees, organized prayer meetings, and observed the Holy Qurbana (Mass) once a month or on special occasions. Priests were called from India to serve the newly established churches. All these parishes had ties in Kerala but were under ecclesiastical control of the Syrian archbishop. The founding priest returned to Kerala in 1984 to be consecrated as a bishop.

In July 1992, a delegates' meeting formally requested that the patriarch establish a new diocese for the Keralite Syrian Orthodox community and consecrate a new bishop for the diocese. The patriarch consecrated bishop Mar Nicholovos Zachariah as bishop in the fall of 1993, and the bishop arrived in the United States in October 1993 to establish residence in a diocesan center in New York and to oversee twenty-three churches in North America, serving approximately 650 families of 3,000 people.

Knanaya Syrian Orthodox Christians form a prosperous business and professional community in both India and the United States that seeks to maintain its identity through participation in an independent Knanaya Orthodox diocese and through in-marriage (endogamy). They marry only among families descending from seventy-two families who emigrated from Cana or Knai to India in the fourth century. The Jacobite Knanaya have exactly the same liturgical practices, prayer books, and discipline as other Syrian Orthodox Christians. Their networks of immigration to America were different because Knanaya women lagged behind other Keralite Christians in taking advantage of the immigration opportunity that nursing provided. Their churches in North America enjoy a separate diocese established in 1988 under their own episcopal authority in Kerala. The Orthodox Knanaya community in North America has approximately 500 families of 2,250 individuals served by eleven priests and three deacons. There are nine parishes (two in New York and one each in Chicago, Philadelphia, Boston, Houston, Dallas, Edmonton, and Toronto), of which three have their own buildings (St. Ignatius Knanaya Church in Yonkers, New York; St. John's Knanaya Church in Houston; and St. Stephen's Church in Boston). The small size of the community in the United States makes it difficult to preserve their separate ethnic identity. They face two immediate problems: (1) to interpret and justify endogamy both to their children and to the general public, and (2) to find appropriate partners for their children. They may, however, intermarry with Knanaya families of the Syro-Malabar Catholic Church.

The Malankara Orthodox Syrian Church of India has a distinct hierarchy, led by the Catholicos of the East in Kottayam, Kerala, and its own separate parishes in America. Thomas Mar Makarios is the founding metropolitan of the North American diocese of the Malankara Orthodox Church. He became metropolitan of the Malankara Diocese of Bombay in 1975, which at that time included Northwest India, the Middle East, North America, the United Kingdom, and Europe. Four years later the North American churches became a separate diocese, and he took up permanent residence as metropolitan in Buffalo, New York. He served for many years as an adjunct professor at Alma College in Alma, Michigan. A second bishop, Mathews Mar Barnabas, arrived in New York in 1992, and a shared leadership of the church developed. By 1995, an estimated 3,000 Malankara Orthodox families resided in the United States, perhaps as many as 13,500 people in fifty-six parishes, of which twenty have their own buildings and forty observe the Holy Qurbana every Sunday. Although the Syrian Orthodox and the Malankara Orthodox are loyal to different hierarchies, their liturgy and church order are the same. Some of the first generation of immigrants can remember when the Holy Qurbana liturgy was translated from Syriac into Malayalam, and in America they now experience a translation from Malayalam into English.

*Catholics.* Other branches of the St. Thomas Christians that were affected by the arrival of Roman Catholic and Protestant missionaries also have congregations and priests in the United

Mass is celebrated in a South Asian Indian church in Chicago. (Mukul Roy)

States. The work of St. Francis Xavier and other Catholic missionary priests, beginning in the sixteenth century, resulted in conversion to Christianity of many people from disadvantaged groups, who generally accepted the Latin rite, liturgy, and hierarchy. Roman Catholic attempts to "purify" the liturgy and practices of St. Thomas Christians led to conflict, division, and eventually to recognition of the Syro-Malabar Catholics as an Oriental rite church in communion with the Roman Catholic Church. A smaller Syro-Malankara also gained recognition from the pope as an ancient Oriental rite church.

Latin rite Catholics from India assimilate into Latin rite parishes in America and support ethnic India Catholic associations in the larger cities. Few Latin rite priests immigrate, but a number of Syro-Malabar rite priests and nuns do serve American Latin rite parishes and institutions. In 1985, the archbishops of Kerala and Chicago established the Syro-Malabar Catholic Mission as well as missions in other cities to preserve the Oriental rite. In 1996, the Synod of Bishops of the Syro-Malabar Church, meeting at the Vatican, made plans to establish eparchy (ecclesiastical structure) with a resident bishop to serve the pastoral needs of Syro-Malabar Catholics. The Knanaya Syro-Malabar Catholics have their own priests, missions, and organization to maintain their ethnic identity. Approximately 8,500 people in 1,800 registered families resided in North America in 1996. Their rituals and discipline are the same as other Syro-Malabar Catholics, but they arrange marriages with Knanaya families, including those in the Syrian Orthodox Church.

Catholic immigrants from India support a third rite in the Syro-Malankara Catholic Church. A bishop from Kerala celebrated the first Syro-Malankara Mass ever held in America during visits to New York and Philadelphia in 1977. Six missions gained recognition in the mid-1980s in New York, Philadelphia, Chicago, Washington, Dallas, and Houston to serve approximately 500 registered Syro-Malankara families. They constitute one of the smallest minorities among American Catholics.

*Protestants.* Protestant missionaries from several countries and many denominations arrived in India in the nineteenth and twentieth centuries, creating even greater diversity within Indian Christianity. That diversity is now represented among the churches South Asian Christians support in America.

The Mar Thoma Church is the strongest and best organized of the churches of the St. Thomas tradition in the United States. It results from the influence of early Anglican missionaries in Kerala, who inspired a reform in 1840 of the Syrian Orthodox Church that introduced Protestant elements in liturgy and discipline. Mar Thoma churches maintain a close relationship with the Episcopal Church in America. Parishes developed from small prayer groups in homes during the 1970s, in the early days served by men studying to be priests in American seminaries. Beginning in the 1980s, the synod appointed to the American congregations nonimmigrant priests to serve three-year terms and then return to Kerala. In 1993, the synod appointed a resident bishop for the North American diocese, Zacharias Mar Theophilus, to serve thirty-seven parishes and two congregations with more than 2,500 families of almost 10,000 members.

South Asian Protestant congregations form along linguistic lines (Malayalam, Telugu, Tamil, Gujarati, and Hindi) and denominational affiliation (Methodist, Baptist, Brethern Assemblies, Church of South India, Pentecostal, and others). By 1995, approximately seventy-five South Asian Methodist pastors, including six women, settled in the United States, but most serve congregations with few if any South Asian members. Overcoming some perceived discrimination and encouraging outreach among the immigrants are reasons given for the formation of the Southern Asian National Caucus of the United Methodists (SANCUM) in 1980. The Church of South India was reluctant to authorize parishes in America because it is a territorial church uniting several denominations; it was founded in 1947. Finally, in 1975, the synod acceded to petitions to authorize American parishes and in 1994 to establish the Zonal Council of the Church of South India in North America for eighteen Malayalam-speaking parishes. More than a hundred small South Asian Pentecostal churches serve immigrants from the Indian Pentecostal Church; the Church of God of Cleveland, Tennessee; the Assemblies of God, the New Testament Church (formerly the Ceylon Pentecostal Mission); and several independent groups. Pentecostal churches are growing rapidly both in India and among immigrants, generally by attracting members from other South Asian churches. Several hundred South Asian Protestant congregations exist across the United States but it is impossible to determine the exact number. Annual summer family conferences are significant gatherings for these various church groups.

## Migration and Economy

South Asian Christians entered the United States as professionals, a large number in the medical professions, and enjoy with other immigrants from India a relatively high economic and professional status. Many spouses of nurses, however, took jobs in manufacturing or sales, providing less wealth or status than their occupations in India or than the nurses enjoyed. Others opened businesses or joined service professions with varied success. Nurses who returned to India for arranged marriage attracted spouses with high professional qualifications. These patterns characterized immigration until the early 1980s. Then the immigration of nurses was restricted and the South Asian Christian community increased only through family reunification by bringing siblings or parents or through births. The arrival of siblings, many of whom lack the professional qualifications of earlier immigrants has gradually changed the community's economic and professional profile.

## Career Selection

Immigrant parents urge their children to excel in their studies and, generally, to prepare for careers in medicine, engineering, business, or the sciences. A 1990 survey of fields of study of second-generation young people showed that medicine was most popular (38% of males and 30% of females), followed by engineering and related fields (25% of males and 16% of females), and business (32% of males and 25% of females). Only 5 percent of men and 29 percent of females studied in other fields. The pressures on young people to excel by standards of both Indian and American society create difficulties for them and tensions between the generations.

## Kinship, Marriage, and Family

Family ties are traditionally very close among South Indians. Indeed, the primary rubric of social relationships is the extended family, whereas, as they perceive it, the primary rubric of social relationships in America is friendship. Only the Knanaya community officially stresses maintenance of family blood ties, but many South Asian congregations consist largely of an extended family. The emotional attachment to family and the accompanying social regulations regarding dating, marriage, and informal social contacts, especially between young men and women, so important to members of the first generation, come into direct conflict with the mores of the society in which members of the second generation are socialized.

The custom is for parents to arrange marriages before the young people are permitted to meet privately. Marriage is viewed as a relationship between families sharing mutual responsibilities for supporting the couple and sustaining the family. Dating is neither necessary nor permitted. American "prom night" is a nightmare for many Indian parents because of the peer pressure their children face to participate in the ritual. Most South Asian Christian families and churches in America discourage dating and encourage some form of family involvement in arranging marriages. A form of semiarranged marriage is common in which a young person becomes acquainted with a potential marriage partner and asks the parents to try to arrange a marriage contract. The relative stability of arranged marriages in the South Asian

South Asian Indians participate in an Easter prayer. (Mukul Roy)

community is contrasted with the perceived instability of "love marriages" in other American groups. It is common for families to take their children, especially sons, back to India for an arranged marriage within the traditional family and regional networks. Increasingly, marriages occur between South Asian Christian families in America, primarily within linguistic-ethnic groups—Malayalees, Tamils, Gujaratis, and others. Although not preferred by parents, some young people enter intercultural or interracial marriages with European Americans, Jews, Hispanics, Koreans, and African Americans. Only the New Testament Church encourages interracial marriages as a sign of the Kingdom of God, but then only within the church. Some priests perform intercultural or interracial marriages, but some churches prohibit sacramental recognition.

## Language and Ethnic Identification

Most South Asian congregations in cities with a large South Asian population are language-specific, drawing membership from a single linguistic group. Both the rituals and social activities are conducted in an Indian language. Language is the primary marker of ethnic identity, but it accompanies other markers, such as cuisine, dress, ritual, leadership style, and ethos. Churches provide a rare location outside the home where immigrants can enjoy, express, value, and transmit these markers of personal and group identity. Churches are also the primary location where immigrants and their children can meet with other families in the same situation to discuss and to negotiate tensions between the generations regarding social and religious customs and identity. Churches gradually change the language of their social activities and then the liturgies from the Indian language to English to attract the young people who lack understanding of either the language or the rituals.

South Asian Christians have established in America diverse forms of Christianity that have long histories in South Asia but that are new to America, thereby changing the religious and cultural landscape.

*See also:* GUJARATIS; MALAYALAM SPEAKERS; TAMILS; TELUGUS

## Bibliography

Agarwal, P. (1991). *Passage from India: Post-1965 Indian Immigrants and Their Children.* Palos Verdes, CA: Yuvati.

Brown, L. W. (1956). *The Indian Christians of St. Thomas: An Account of the Ancient Syrian Church of Malabar.* Cambridge, Eng.: Cambridge University Press.

Chang, J. (1991). "Movement of Self-Empowerment: History of the National Federation of Asian American United Methodists." In *Churches Aflame: Asian Americans and United Methodism,* edited by A. R. Guillermo. Nashville: Abingdon Press.

Christiano, K. J. (1991). "The Church and the New Immigrants." In *Religion and the Social Order: Vatican II and U.S. Catholicism,* edited by H. R. Ebaugh. Greenwich, CT: Jai Press.

Guillermo, A. R., ed. (1991). *Churches Aflame: Asian Americans and United Methodism.* Nashville: Abingdon Press.

Kurian, R. (1979). "Patterns of Emigration from Kerala." *Social Scientist* 78:32–53.

Menachery, G., ed. (1973). *The St. Thomas Christian Encyclopaedia of India.* Trichur, India: The St. Thomas Christian Encyclopaedia of India.

Neill, S. (1984). *A History of Christianity in India: The Beginnings to 1707.* Cambridge, Eng.: Cambridge University Press.

Neill, S. (1985). *A History of Christianity in India: 1707 to 1858.* Cambridge, Eng.: Cambridge University Press.

Pothan, S. J. (1963). *The Syrian Christians of Kerala.* New York: Asia Publishing House.

Thomas, A., and Thomas, T. M. (1984). *Kerala Immigrants in America: A Sociological Study of the St. Thomas Christians.* Cochin, India: Simons Printers.

Williams, R. B. (1988). *Religions of Immigrants from India and Pakistan: New Threads in the American Tapestry.* Cambridge, Eng.: Cambridge University Press.

Williams, R. B. (1996). *Christian Pluralism in the United States: The Indian Immigrant Experience.* Cambridge, Eng.: Cambridge University Press.

RAYMOND BRADY WILLIAMS

# SOUTH ASIANS

*See* BANGLADESHIS; BENGALIS; BURMESE; GUJARATIS; JAINS; MAHARASHTRIANS; MALAYALAM SPEAKERS; NEPALESE; PUNJABIS; SIKHS; SINDHIS; SINHALESE; SRI LANKANS; TAMILS; TELUGUS

# SOUTHEAST ASIANS

*See* BUDDHISTS; CAMBODIANS; CHAM; CHINESE-VIETNAMESE; FILIPINOS; HMONG; INDONESIANS; INDOS; KHMU; LAO; MIEN; THAI

# SOVIET JEWS

*See* JEWS, SOVIET

# SPANIARDS

Spain and its peoples have had an important—although inadequately recognized—influence on the history and culture of North America. There are several reasons for this relative invisibility, but the major one is an American tradition that until recently has placed almost exclusive stress on the history of the original thirteen colonies. In conventional histories, the emergence of the national community is explained in terms of English settlement along the Atlantic seaboard, the growth of these colonies, independence from the British crown, and the westward expansion of the new American republic.

This is a very partial view of the American past. Spanish history in North America predates by several centuries the conventional interpretations found in history books. Simply phrased, there is another frontier, another important sequence of exploration and colonization to consider. But in this case the route of migration and settlement went from south to north, and the people in question were not of British ancestry, but Spaniards and Spanish-speaking inhabitants of what was then the Spanish Empire.

Much of this northward movement was organized, supported, and financed by the colonial authorities, and designed to implement imperial policies. Initially Spanish administrators were particularly interested in controlling and settling the sparsely populated northern Mexican frontier—a territory that would eventually include much of the present-day U.S. Southwest, Texas, and California. In later times, particularly during the eighteenth century, exploration and settlement were fueled by concerns about the growing military power (and territorial ambitions) of Britain and France, Spain's chief imperial rivals in North America and the Caribbean.

## Colonization and Settlement

The process of colonization began very early. Once the Spaniards had firmly established themselves in the Caribbean and conquered the Aztec Empire in 1521, expeditions to the present-day United States departed with regularity from northern Mexico and from Cuba. By the eighteenth century, Spanish institutions and trade touched a vast area that stretched from Florida to California, including much of the Mississippi drainage (the river itself became the western boundary between the United States and Spanish territory in 1783). In the late eighteenth century, Spanish military and scientific expeditions pushed north to explore the entire Pacific coastline as far as Alaska.

This huge space can conveniently be divided into two parts. Close to the Spanish-American heartland of Mexico and the Caribbean are lands that experienced a substantial and enduring Spanish colonial presence. Much of this territory remained under Spanish or Mexican jurisdiction until the nineteenth century. Beyond it lies a zone of former Spanish territorial claims and related trade routes. We can think of this as a colonial periphery more than an area of early settlement.

Spanish colonists brought with them a distinct set of cultural forms based on Old World models. Among them were new crops and systems of water management adapted to arid environments; metallurgy and an extensive inventory of tools; and subsistence techniques, including the whole complex of cattle raising that is now so firmly associated with the American West. But most important of all were social structures that ranged in size and complexity from the cattle ranch to the city.

The Spanish Empire—enormous in size, but poorly connected because communications over such great distances were slow and unreliable—became a network of villages, towns, and cities sharing a common civil pattern. A critical part of this pattern was formal and legal. No settlement was legitimate without a charter, which named the community, placed it under the protection of an appropriate patron saint, and defined the role of municipal government and the rights and obligations of citizens.

Given the importance of municipal life in Spanish and Spanish-American culture, it is not surprising that among the first—and most enduring—markers of the Spanish colonial past in North America is a string of towns and cities across the breadth of the country that still bear their original names: San Antonia, Sante Fe, St. Augustine, San Francisco, Los Angeles, and many others. St. Augustine (San Agustin) in Florida, founded in 1567, is the oldest European colonial city in the continental United States. The town and its fort were built by expeditions from Cuba (1565–1574). Older still is San Juan, the capital of Puerto Rico, chartered in 1521.

Early settlers of the borderlands of the Spanish Empire seldom came directly from Europe, but from other parts of Spanish America. This indirect process has helped obscure the link between Spain and North America. It does, however, point to some very important characteristics shared by Spanish-origin societies in the New World. From

Colonists, measuring with string and digging with shovels and pickaxes, lay out the streets of St. Augustine, Florida, in the seventeenth century. (Library of Congress/Corbis)

the beginning, these societies were something more than European transplants. The cultural forms were predominantly derived from Spain, which is why references to "Latin" or "Hispanic" peoples or societies continue to be used. But Spanish colonial culture changed in the course of the centuries to incorporate local themes and concerns; it became more "American" in the broadest sense of the term. Also, in contrast to the general pattern of racial separation in Anglo America, the populations of these countries have from first contact undergone a great deal of racial mixture. Consequently, the majority of Latin Americans can reasonably claim multiple ancestries that link them

not only to Europe but, depending on the specifics of geography and history, to the native peoples of the Americas; to Africa; and, less frequently, to Asia.

Following the Mexican War of 1846–1848, and later as a consequence of the Spanish-American War of 1898, the United States incorporated vast new lands—and new peoples. The Hispanic world did not come to the United States; an expanding American republic annexed a substantial portion of this cultural sphere. It follows that Puerto Ricans and the descendants of the Old Mexican populations are hardly "immigrants," as the term is commonly understood, but long-settled ethnic groups with historically based claims to culture, language, and identity.

## The Atlantic Migration

Even during the period of modern transatlantic migration (from the middle of the nineteenth century to the early decades of the twentieth), Spain supplied the third largest number of immigrants to New World destinations. The statistics are sketchy before 1880, but it is estimated that about 3.5 million Spaniards made their way to the Americas between 1880 and 1930. Relatively few of these, however, entered the United States directly. In

The interior of Mission San Antonio de Padua, founded in 1771 near Monterey, California. It was the third of twenty-one California missions founded by the Spanish Franciscans. (Richard Cummins/Corbis)

round numbers, more than 250,000 Spaniards have entered the United States directly from Spain since the early nineteenth century, but this is not the whole story.

Modern Spanish transatlantic migration on a large scale is comparatively late and picks up momentum only in the last decades of the nineteenth century. Spanish passenger statistics for 1882 show 40,721 persons traveling to the Americas that year. The majority, 30,730, made their way to Cuba, then still a Spanish colony; 3,245 went to Argentina; 2,247 to Brazil; and only 57 to the United States. It is easy to understand why Spaniards generally selected Latin American countries as destinations of choice. Language was an important consideration, the political and social institutions were based on similar models, and there were homeland populations in place to help the newcomer.

These cultural factors do much to explain the relatively small number of immigrants from Spain reaching the United States. For a more complete understanding of the Spanish immigration pattern, it is also necessary to consider timing, the role of indirect immigration, and the sexual composition of the Spanish immigrant pool. According to U.S. government figures, during the first half of the nineteenth century direct Spanish immigration was low and steady, generally about 200 individuals a year. Numbers pick up in the second half of the century, with 4,419 Spanish immigrants arriving on U.S. shores during the ten-year period 1881–1890, and doubling to 8,731 for the period 1891–1900. Emigration from Spain continues to expand in the first decades of the new century, with the peak decade of 1911–1920 registering the very substantial figure (relative to earlier counts) of 68,611 new arrivals.

But these figures must be considered in the context of overall immigration, particularly that from Europe. Fundamentally, Spanish immigration never managed to make up for a late start. The nearly 70,000 Spaniards who arrived during the decade 1911–1920 represent only a small fraction of a European total of 5.7 million arrivals, a relationship that does not change for the whole

Spanish-American fur trappers and buyers gather on the porch of the Community Store in Delacroix Island, St. Bernard Parish, Louisiana, in 1941 while the furs are being graded for auction. (Library of Congress/Corbis)

period covering the final decade of the nineteenth century and the first thirty years of the twentieth century (see Table 1). These numbers were destined to have important consequences. In 1921, the United States imposed new immigration regulations based on a national-origin quota system. The stated goal of this policy was to restrict immigration so it would better reflect the "stock" or national origin of the resident American population. As late participants in direct immigration to the United States, those categorized by the U.S. Bureau of the Census as of "Spanish stock" (first- and second-generation) came to a mere 80,317 individuals in 1920. The Spanish quota was set at 912 individuals, a figure later reduced to 131. Obviously Spanish Americans did not constitute a nationality or an ethnic group with significant influence on American public policy.

It is also reasonable to assume that the outbreak of the Spanish-American War in 1898, and the years of growing tension between Spain and the United States that preceded the conflict, played a role in reducing Spanish immigration. Again, this is essentially a question of timing. In this respect, it is instructive to look at the situation in Puerto

**Table 1**   Spanish and European Immigration

| Decade | Spaniards | European Total |
|---|---|---|
| 1891–1900 | 8,731 | 3,687,564 |
| 1901–1910 | 27,934 | 8,795,386 |
| 1911–1920 | 68,611 | 5,735,811 |
| 1921–1930 | 28,958 | 4,107,209 |

Rico. The last Spanish census, taken in 1897 (just prior to U.S. annexation), indicates that 2.2 percent of the island's population had been born in Spain. This figure drops drastically following the Spanish-American War, and by 1935 only 0.1 percent of the residents of Puerto Rico could claim a Spanish birthplace. Although these statistics no doubt reflect a number of variables—including, after 1921, the influence of national-origin immigration legislation—the indirect evidence also suggests that a number of potential Spanish immigrants headed instead for Cuba, which became independent in 1902. The tempo of Spanish immigration to Cuba continued to grow until it reached more than 80,000 annual arrivals in the 1917–1921 period.

Two other factors—indirect immigration and the sexual composition of the Spanish immigrant population—need to be considered. Many Spaniards entered the United States from third countries (mostly Latin American republics) and were classified in the immigration statistics by country of last residence. Turning again to Puerto Rico, until travel regulations changed in 1916, Spaniards living in the recently acquired territory could, and did, enter the mainland with no other formality than the purchase of a steamer ticket; presumably they were classified as "Puerto Ricans." Much the same pattern is documented in several other instances, including that of Spanish Basques living in Chile and Argentina. When they were attracted to California by the Gold Rush of 1848, the Basques living in Argentina first had to make their way west to Chile on the Pacific coast. Once there, they then sailed for California, along with the Basques who had already been living in Chile. For this reason, these Spaniards were generally categorized as "Chileans" upon arrival in California.

However, the same ease of movement that led to undercounting Spanish immigrants also caused them to be overcounted. With the introduction of rapid and relatively cheap steamship travel, many single young men made the Atlantic crossing with the intention of returning home after a period of employment, and a substantial number did so. Once more, the statistics are not as good as one would desire, chiefly because American authorities did not begin to collect information on emigration until 1908.

Taken as a whole, the picture of Spanish immigration has some distinctive characteristics. Most obviously the scale has always been modest, particularly when restricted to direct immigration. It continues to be a late immigration. The second major wave of immigration—more than 100,000 arrivals—began in the early 1960s and continued through the late 1990s. This most recent influx is about evenly split between men and women. The 1,886 Spaniards admitted in 1990 is a figure similar to the number of Fijians or Australians entering the United States, but a far cry from the 20,000 Poles arriving the same year.

## Homelands Old and New

Spanish Americans have roots in all the regions of Spain, but at the turn of the twentieth century some parts of Spain accounted for the great majority of immigrants to the New World. Evidence for the specific origins of Spanish immigrants to the United States is fragmentary and indirect, but there is no reason to assume that the patterns typical of Spanish overseas movement did not hold for immigrants headed for the United States. The Canary Islands in the Atlantic off Morocco, experienced very high rates of emigration, particularly to Cuba. Northern Spain, especially the lands fronting the Bay of Biscay (Galicia, Asturias, Cantabria, the Basque country) and farther east, Catalonia, contributed the largest number of immigrants. Spanish sources document the importance of this northern tier of regions. Thus for the 1911–1915 period, of the eight leading emigrant-providing provinces in Spain, six were in the northwest, with Galicia, in the extreme northwest, clearly in the lead. The Bay of Biscay zone accounted for 388,828 of the 602,081 emigrants leaving Spain during the five-year span, a figure that grows to more than 460,000 if Catalonia is added. These statistics mesh with those from receiving countries. Thus, to cite one well-documented example, records from Buenos Aires show that 73 percent of the Spaniards living in the Argentine capital at the turn of the century came from Spain's northern periphery, with Galicia being the place of origin of almost 50 percent of these residents.

Of the regions mentioned, Galicia, Asturias, Cantabria, and the Canaries were impoverished agricultural zones facing rising birthrates—typical of locations where economic conditions force people to look for better livelihoods elsewhere. On the other hand, the Basque country, and especially Catalonia, had begun to industrialize by the end of the nineteenth century and thus were better able to absorb their excess rural populations. Nevertheless, both Catalans and Basques were attracted by overseas opportunities, often as merchants, businessmen, trained craftsmen, professionals, and white-collar workers.

Although immigrants came from both poor and relatively rich regions, many shared the characteristic of coming from non-Castilian-speaking areas. This was true of Galicians, Asturians, Basques, and Catalans. While virtually all immigrants were fluent in Castilian ("Spanish"), they often lacked the powerful emotional attachment to

A man attempts to comfort a crying child during a Spanish-American fiesta in Taos, New Mexico. (Library of Congress/Corbis)

a state language that was not their native tongue. This was particularly true of Basques and Catalans.

This particular ethnic and linguistic mix (especially evident early in the century) was bound to affect patterns of adaptation. An already small emigration from Spain can best be understood as *several* emigrations. Not surprisingly, in the New World Spanish immigrants often come together as members of one or another of Spain's constituent cultures. In the United States, there are Basque, Catalan, and Galician organizations as well as groupings from other regions and Spanish-American cultural associations.

Today, the Spanish ethnic mosaic is influenced by powerful forces within American society. A major element is the role of the large and influential "Hispanic" minority, an emergent identity that can encompass all people of "Spanish origin," including everyone with links to Spain. Hispanic identity is reinforced by the official recognition it receives. Now Spaniards have the option of affiliating with that Hispanic world discussed earlier. Other choices range from a greater or lesser degree of ethnic identity (often ritually expressed at festivals), to incorporation in American society as individuals of general "European origin." There is little indication that Spanish Americans invest a great deal of effort in maintaining a distinctly "Spanish" cultural identity.

There are, however, parts of the country with a significant population of Spanish origin. Until early in the twentieth century, most Spaniards lived in New York, and the city continues to have the largest concentration of Spanish-origin people in the country. There had long been some Spanish presence in Florida, and this increased with the realignment of the Cuban cigar industry following the Spanish-American War. More recently, larger numbers of Cubans of Spanish origin have settled in Florida. Other areas with significant Spanish populations include the mountain states of Idaho and Nevada (areas of Basque settlement), and California.

Beginning about 1960, the most recent immigration of Spaniards brought many young and well-educated people to the United States, often to study or otherwise improve their experience or credentials. Another factor was the desire to live in a democratic society (the Franco dictatorship lasted until 1975). Unlike earlier immigrations, it has tended to draw people from all areas of Spain, particularly the larger cities. A considerable number of these relatively recent arrivals have found employment in the private sector, while others work in the liberal professions (e.g., medicine, law, and education). As a group they generally move comfortably between identities, and there is a high incidence of intermarriage. Language maintenance depends a great deal on context, and in contemporary American society it is much more difficult to transmit Basque or Catalan than to maintain Spanish. Perhaps in part for this reason, academic programs such as the Basque Studies Program at the University of Nevada and the Catalan Studies Program at the University of California at Berkeley have achieved considerable success.

Prospects for Spanish Americans in the United States appear to be good. It is no doubt to their advantage that they are not particularly distinctive, and that few Americans harbor strong feelings about them or their country of origin. Taken as a whole, Spanish Americans tend to be well-educated, innovative, physically mobile, and culturally flexible. As a group with links to some of America's most important global partners—the European Union and the countries of Latin America—their importance is greater than their relatively small numbers suggest.

*See also:* BASQUES; CALIFORNIOS; MEXICANS

## Bibliography

Douglass, W. A., and Bilbao, J. (1975). *Amerikanuak: Basques in the New World*. Reno: University of Nevada Press.

Gómez, R. A. (1962). "Spanish Immigration to the United States." *The Americas* 19:59–77.

Jiménez, A., ed. (1993). *Handbook of Hispanic Cultures in the United States: Vol. 3, History*, edited by N. Kanellos and C. Esteva-Fabregat. Madrid: Agencia Española de Cooperación Internacional and Instituto de Cooperación Iberoamericana; Houston: Arte Público Press.

Jones, O. L., ed. (1974). *The Spanish Borderlands: A First Reader*. Los Angeles: Lorrin L. Morrison.

Nadal, J. (1991). *La población española (Siglos XVI a XX)*. Barcelona: Editorial Ariel.

Nugent, W. (1992). *Crossings: The Great Transatlantic Migrations, 1870–1914*. Bloomington: Indiana University Press.

Sánchez, J. P. (1990). *Spanish Bluecoats: The Catalonian Volunteers in Northwestern New Spain, 1767–1810*. Albuquerque: University of New Mexico Press.

Sánchez-Albornoz, N., comp. (1988). *Españoles hacia América: La emigración en masa, 1880–1930*. Madrid: Alianza Editorial.

U.S. Immigration and Naturalization Service. (1991). *Statistical Yearbook of the Immigration and Naturalization Service, 1990*. Washington, DC: U.S. Government Printing Office.

ORIOL PI-SUNYER
SUSAN M. DIGIACOMO

# SRI LANKANS

Sri Lankans are immigrants from Sri Lanka (formerly known as Ceylon), an island of twenty-five thousand square miles (about the size of West Virginia) off the southeastern tip of India. In this multiethnic island, the majority of the population are the Sinhalese (74%). Sri Lankan Tamils constitute the primary minority at 18 percent. Tamil-speaking Muslims are considered a distinct ethnic and cultural group, and they account for 7 percent of the population. Of the remaining 1 percent, the only group from which immigrants to America have been recruited are the Burghers, descendents of mixed unions between Europeans and the indigenous people.

## Demographics and Settlement History

In the absence of statistics or other public records, there can be no definitive statement about the demography of the Sri Lankan community. An acceptable estimate is 100,000, which can be broken down as follows: California, 40,000; New York City, 24,000; Washington, D.C., 10,000; Chicago,

6,000; Texas, 6,000; and Florida, 4,000. This accounts for 90,000. The remaining 10,000 individuals are scattered elsewhere in the United States. Two observations can be made based on these statistics. First, the Sri Lankans are largely concentrated in large cities. Second, they have settled down in areas where the weather is warm and reminiscent of that of their tropical homeland.

It is obvious that the Sri Lankans are a very small immigrant community. Significant immigration history of the Sri Lankans goes no further back than the 1950s, although there is information about a gem businessman named Salie who arrived in New York in 1908 and a few others who immigrated in the 1930s. From the 1950s on, however, there has been a steady and gradually increasing stream of Sri Lankan immigrants. The most common method of becoming an immigrant for Sri Lankans is through professionalism, either by means of direct recruitment to American jobs on existing qualifications or, more typically, through education in America. Doctors are a good example. Starting in the mid-1960s, large contingents of graduates of Sri Lankan medical schools attended American medical schools and got American qualifications. These doctors have distinguished themselves in their careers and now constitute the largest percentage of professionals among the Sri Lankans in America. In the 1970s, however, there was a lowering of professionalism. This resulted from the recruitment of some of the offspring of the "high professional" category (i.e., doctors, lawyers, engineers, academics, and high bureaucrats) into lower professional jobs and from the increasingly larger number of new immigrants arriving as lower professionals. Regardless of the degree of professionalism involved, almost the entire Sri Lankan immigrant community is comfortably employed. Any destitution or living below the poverty line is rare.

## Ethnicity and Languages

A striking fact in the Sri Lankan immigrant community is that Tamils comprise 50 percent of the Sri Lankan immigrants although they account for only 18 percent of the population in Sri Lanka.

This apparent discrepancy is the result of two circumstances. First, traditionally, due to the greater availability of educational facilities in the Tamil areas, more Tamils were educationally qualified and able to enter the professions, and, as has already been pointed out, it is as professionals that most Sri Lankans became immigrants. Second, after the violent ethnic riots of 1983, a Tamil exodus took place, with many immigrating to America.

More than 49 percent of the Sri Lankan immigrants are Sinhalese, with Muslims and Burghers constituting the remaining fraction of a percentage point. The native language of the Sinhalese is Sinhala (also called Sinhalese); that of the Tamils is Tamil. "Native" is used in a nominal sense here because, especially in relation to the period prior to the 1970s, the large majority of the Sri Lankan immigrants were exclusively educated in English, Sri Lanka having been a British colony from 1815 to 1948, creating a westernized elite. In some segments of this elite, English was adopted as the home language, and in all segments, English proficiency was very high. In general, immigrants who arrived prior to the 1970s, that is, before English was effectively replaced by the indigenous languages in Sri Lanka, are less likely to use the indigenous languages than are those who arrived after that time. In both groups, those who arrived at a very young age as immigrants or those who are born in America are unlikely to be particularly proficient in the indigenous languages. This does not mean a dying out of the old languages in the group, because there is often a conscious attempt to hand down the languages to the younger generations. However, facilities for this process are available only in the major metropolitan areas. Keeping the younger generations proficient in these languages is a difficult task for parents who live outside such areas.

## Kinship, Marriage, and Family

From about 1980, Tamil rebels have been fighting for a separate state in Sri Lanka. This has led partisans of both groups to bring out the separateness of the two communities. In fact, such differences are minimal, and closer observation shows fundamental similarities. Most important, from an ethnological point of view, the near identity of the two systems of kinship and marriage must be noted. Both are bilateral systems, accepting the equality of status of both the paternal and the maternal lines. Both practice putative cross-cousin marriage, with real cross-cousin marriage being the ideal form. Both are caste-based societies, although the hold caste has is stronger among the Tamils than among the Sinhalese. Caste is rarely ignored in marriage, which is "arranged" as opposed to being left to the whims of the two young people concerned. There are exceptions to this system, as when two people express interest in one another. This is particularly so when the choice is a non-Sri Lankan, typically a white American, which may or may not be parentally approved. Especially among Tamils, it is common for immigrants to seek children of other immigrants as the most suitable marriage partners for their children. Sometimes marriage ceremonies provide the occasion for parents to find a partner for their son or daughter. It is likely that in time this traditional framework of marriage will weaken among the older immigrant families, but both the influx of new immigrants and the continuing connections with the old country made possible by frequent travel are likely to ensure that it does not become extinct.

## Religion, Culture, and Social Life

The Sinhalese are Buddhists who follow the orthodox form of Buddhism known as Theravada. The most sacred day is Vesak, the full moon of May, associated with the main events of the Buddha's life. On this day Buddhists intensify their religious and ritual activity. The Sinhalese also observe their most important national holiday, the New Year, which falls on April 13 (14 in leap years), by engaging in religious ceremonies and social activities.

The Tamils are Hindus and thus belong to a much larger religious group, because the overwhelming majority of immigrants from India are Hindus. However, besides common worship and cooperation in carrying out the responsibilities of supporting the temples and so forth, the Sri Lankan Tamil community has little or no social ties with Indians, Tamil or otherwise. They identify themselves more by their loyalties to Jaffna, their cultural center and home in Sri Lanka. They maintain a great interest in the traditional classical dance of South India known as Bharata Natyam, which all girls ideally learn from the age of three or four. While this ideal cannot be conformed to in the same form, Tamil families often give dance instruction to their daughters and hold lavish debuts, known as Arangethram. The two major ritual occasions of the Tamils in Sri Lanka are Thaipongal and the New Year. Thaipongal, a harvest festival, means "January of milk rice" and refers to the central ritual act of the occasion, that of boiling milk, which is done at sunrise. New Year is the same as that of the Sinhalese. Both these occasions are domestic rites, and the second is more likely to be celebrated by the immigrants than the first.

In some major American cities, arts societies have been founded by the Sinhalese for purposes of enjoying music, dance, and other art forms of Sri Lanka. These societies sometimes sponsor performing tours by well-known performers of Sri Lankan music and dance. As in the religious sphere, the Tamils are at a great advantage in this area because of their cultural affinities with Hindu India. However, despite obvious bonds with India and the recent tensions between the Sinhalese and the Tamils, the Sri Lankan Tamil immigrants have a distinctively Sri Lankan identity. This applies to the very few Muslim and Burgher immigrants as well. This identity is best expressed in the love all Sri Lankans share for the colonial game of cricket, a national sport in Sri Lanka. Sri Lankans also have societies formed around loyalty to old schools in the home country. These school-related societies organize cricket games, dinners, and other social activities.

Sri Lankans are very much involved with their culture and way of life. The majority are in touch with their families in Sri Lanka through frequent travel, telephone conversations, and other forms of communication. Despite this they are excellently integrated into the diversity of American social and cultural life.

*See also:* SINHALESE; TAMILS

## Bibliography

De Silva, K. M. (1981). *A History of Sri Lanka.* Delhi: Oxford University Press.

De Silva, K. M. (1986). *Managing Ethnic Tensions in Multi-Ethnic Societies: Sri Lanka, 1880–1985.* Lanham, MD: University Press of America.

Dharmadasa, K. N. O. (1992). *Language, Religion, and Ethnic Assertiveness: The Growth of Sinhalese Nationalism in Sri Lanka.* Ann Arbor: University of Michigan Press.

Ludowyk, E. F. C. (1966). *The Modern History of Ceylon.* London: Weidenfeld and Nicolson.

Ludowyk, E. F. C. (1967). *A Short History of Ceylon.* New York: Praeger.

Nicholas, C. W., and Paranavitana, S. (1961). *A Concise History of Ceylon.* Colombo: Ceylon University Press.

Paranavitana, S. (1967). *Sinhalayo.* Colombo: Lake House.

Perinbanayagam, R. S. (1982). *Karmic Theater.* Amherst: University of Massachusetts Press.

Pieris, R. (1956). *Sinhalese Social Organization.* Colombo: Ceylon University Press.

Russell, J. (1982). *Communal Politics Under the Donoughmore Constitution, 1931–1947.* Dehiwala, Sri Lanka: Tisara Publishers.

H. L. SENEVIRATNE

# SWEDE-FINNS

Swede-Finns in North America (also known as Finland-Swedes, Finlandssvenskar, Finnish-Swede, Swedish-Finns, and Swedo-Finns) derive from the Swedish-speaking minority population of Finland. Prior to achieving national independence in 1917, Finland was for many centuries a frontier of col-onization, military incursion, and conflict between the Swedish and Russian empires. As early as the sixteenth century, the Swedish crown had strong control of colonial Finland, and a modified estate system forced Finnish peasants to participate in the wars of their Swedish lords.

Living primarily in the fertile plains of coastal and insular southwestern Finland (the region supporting the earliest permanent agricultural settlements), Swedish colonists and Swedish-speaking Finns were the source of a ruling elite. Swedish was the language of commerce, the courts, and education until the nationalist movement of the nineteenth century advanced Finnish as an official, written, and cultural language of the majority. Yet, Swedish-speaking Finns, or Swede-Finns, have remained an influential minority, numbering about 349,000, or 12.9 percent of Finland's population in 1900, and about 300,000, or 6 percent of the population in 1987.

The short-lived commercial colony of Nya Sverige (New Sweden), near what is now Wilmington, Delaware, represents the earliest Swedish-Finnish presence in North America. During its brief existence under royal Swedish sponsorship, 1638–1655, the colony attracted several hundred settlers who were primarily involved in trading with the Delaware Indians. While these were Swedish subjects, perhaps half were of Finnish origin. Some were "Forest Finns" from Savo-Karelia who had been burning and clearing pioneer agricultural lands in the forests of west-central Sweden since the late 1500s. Others were Finnish men seeking alternatives to Swedish military service. Yet others were Swedish-speaking Finns from the East Bothnian coast. The Delaware colony ultimately came under Dutch and then English control, but by the end of the 1600s, there were nearly one thousand people of Swedish-Finnish ancestry in the Delaware River valley.

The major tide of Swedish-Finnish immigration to America, and the formation of a distinctive Swede-Finn identity, however, are rather recent phenomena. The period between 1870 and 1914 was a time of heavy emigration from Finland generally. Of the nearly 303,000 total emigrants, more than one-fifth of them, or about sixty-eight thousand were Swede-Finns deriving from the strongholds of Swedish-speaking Finland, primarily the provinces of Vaasa or Ostrobothnia (Osterbotten), Ahvenanmaa (Aland Islands), Uusimaa (Nyland), and Turku and Pori (Aboland). The bulk of these emigrants settled in the United States, but after quota laws were implemented in 1925 another five thousand to ten thousand Swede-Finns settled in Canada, especially in Ontario and British Columbia. By 1930, about eighty-five thousand Swede-Finns had settled in North America, and of these perhaps two-thirds remained in their new homeland.

## Political and Economic History

The great wave of emigration prior to World War I was spurred by a combination of push and pull factors. In Finland there was growing poverty, especially among tenant farmers and landless rural workers and, for many men, fear of conscription into Russian military service (at that time Finland was an autonomous grand duchy under Russia). America, by contrast, offered possibilities of employment, land, freedom from political subjugation, and a new start in life. Swede-Finns quickly filled occupational niches in the rapidly expanding industrial economy. In the northeastern United States they found jobs in furniture and rubber factories, coal mining, and in the bridge-, boat- and shipbuilding trades. Swede-Finns settled in large numbers in the New York metropolitan area, where they became heavily involved in house construction, and in Worcester, Massachusetts, where they worked in tool and metal parts foundries. Work as maids or domestic servants was a common form of employment for Swede-Finn women in many parts of the country.

In the midwestern United States, Swede-Finns gravitated to logging camps and sawmills operated by large timber companies around Lake Superior and Lake Michigan in the 1880s and 1890s. Many who started as loggers or millhands, however, soon became miners in the expanding iron ore mines of "range" towns such as Bessemer, Iron Mountain,

Ironwood, and Negaunee, Michigan, and Eveleth, Hibbing, and Virginia, Minnesota. The drudgery and danger of mining often encouraged families to take up farming, at least on a part-time basis, on small acreages on the cut-over timberlands of the area. Some Swede-Finns settled in the industrial cities of the Midwest as well, particularly Duluth, Minnesota; Chicago and Waukegan, Illinois; and Muskegon, Michigan.

In the decade prior to World War I, Swede-Finns were also active in the burgeoning gold, silver, copper, lead, and zinc mines of the Rocky Mountain states. Eventually many of them moved to the Pacific Coast to work in shipbuilding, farming, commercial fishing, and especially in the lumber and wood products industry. Some Swede-Finns already had been active in harvesting Douglas fir and redwood trees in the Pacific Northwest since the 1880s and 1890s. The logging camps and mining settlements of the Far West were especially fertile grounds for socialist ideas and syndicalist organizations such as the International Workers of the World (IWW). However, most Swede-Finns had been Republicans until the Great Depression in the 1930s spurred a heavy shift to Democratic politics.

With increasing mechanization of the lumber industry after World War I, many Swede-Finns in the Puget Sound area of Washington State pioneered in establishing cooperative businesses. The majority of the shareholder-workers of the Olympia Veneer Company were Swede-Finns. Despite a precarious start in the early 1920s, that firm flourished over several decades and emerged as one of the largest producers of wood veneer products in the United States.

## Social Adaptations and Identity

Prior to 1920, the first generation of Swede-Finn immigrants organized numerous "benefit" and "temperance" societies. The former were meant to provide a context for fellowship and a source of financial aid to cover funeral expenses and to assist sick and disabled members. Per Bhahe of Worcester and Svenk-Finska Sjukhjalpsforbundet av Amerika (originally organized in Michigan) were two notable societies that functioned in this manner. While the temperance societies promoted abstinence from alcohol use, like the benefit societies their local meetings and national conventions provided opportunities for showcasing musical and theatrical skills, achieving leadership and status, and reaffirming ethnic bonds and values while adjusting to the larger host society.

After 1920, the various benefit and temperance societies formally amalgamated into a new association, Runebergorden (Order of Runeberg), with heavy membership in lodges in the western states. One of the two key Swede-Finn newspapers, *Ledstjarnen* (Leading Star), was taken over by the order as well. Choral groups and concert bands, often organized by local lodges, became a vibrant expression of Swede-Finn solidarity and identity in the 1920s and 1930s, and even up to the present in the Pacific Northwest. Membership in the order peaked at eighty-five hundred in 1929 and has steadily declined since that time as Social Security and health legislation as well as changing occupational and social ties have undercut the association's original goals and as the population of first- and second-generation. immigrants itself declines.

Most early Swede-Finn immigrants had been raised in a Lutheran religious tradition in Finland. Accordingly, they founded a network of Lutheran churches across the United States. By 1920, there were at least twenty-five such congregations, with about four thousand members. While independent in many respects, most of these churches adopted the constitution and Confession of Faith of the Swedish-American Augustana Synod. A significant minority of Swede-Finns established Baptist congregations in the United States.

Ethnic newspapers, while sharply reduced in circulation from earlier decades, foster a sense of collective identity for Swede-Finns by reporting local events in far-flung communities as well as national news and political developments in Finland. Known as *Finska Amerikanaren* until 1935, the important weekly paper *Norden* out of Brooklyn, New York, continued for many years to serve as a forum of opinion and common interests among people of Swede-Finn ancestry. In 1987 *Norden* relocated to Manhattan, New York. While its Swedish-language format persists, coverage is heavily slanted to events in Finland. Its current modest circulation of seven hundred subscribers represents a dwindling older generation of Swede-Finns now living in Connecticut, New Jersey, and upstate New York.

## Ethnic Emergence and Decline

The process of ethnic emergence and transformation experienced by Swede-Finns in America reflects their complex and divided past. Although they arrived in the United States mostly as Russian subjects, they had shared a homeland in common with the Finns, a language in common with the Swedes, and a history in common with both. Indeed, some of the earliest Swede-Finn societies had Finnish names, attempted bilingual programs in Swedish and Finnish, or otherwise sought alliances with Finnish immigrant organizations. However, language differences were daunting enough that these early efforts to unite Swede-Finns and Finns soon withered.

At the same time, Swedish-speaking Finns did not build strong ties with Swedish immigrants in the United States. Instead, they developed their own organizations, churches, choral groups, and cultural festivals, signaling the emergence of a separate, distinctive, and uniquely Swede-Finn identity and ethnicity. This process of emergence was well under way and, in many ways, was crystallized by the founding of the Order of Runeberg in 1921. Nonetheless, Swede-Finn ethnicity was forged largely by first-generation immigrants, people with rural and working-class backgrounds who primarily spoke Swedish.

Second-generation Swede-Finns were brought up in Swedish-speaking homes, but through schooling and exposure to mainstream American society they soon acquired English as their primary language. Military service and other experiences during World War II exposed the second generation to a wider world and reinforced their identity as Americans. Moreover, when many second-generation Swede-Finns came of age, they left the industrial, mining, logging, and farming communities of their parents to obtain advanced education and to work in a variety of trades and professions in distant towns and cities. Growing occupational stratification and geographical mobility as well as a high rate of outmarriage starting in the second generation have diminished ties among Swede-Finns. Assimilation in the second mainstream of urban middle-class life continues for the third and suceeding generations. While the 1990 U.S. Census includes some 657,698 people of Finnish ancestry, it is possible that about one-fifth of them (or 131,540) are actually of Swede-Finn background. For many of these people, being Swede-Finn has become a "symbolic identity" of cultural origins or ancestry rather than an indicator of active ethnic associations and ties.

See also:  FINNS; SWEDES

## Bibliography

Acrelius, I. (1874). *A History of New Sweden or, the Settlements on the River Delaware.* Philadelphia: Historical Society of Pennsylvania.

Anderson, C. H. (1970). *White Protestant Americans: From National Origins to Religious Group.* Englewood Cliffs, NJ: Prentice Hall.

Engle, E. (1975). *Finns in North America.* Annapolis MD: Leeward.

Jordan, T. G., and Kaups, M. (1989). *The American Backwoods Frontier: An Ethnic and Ecological Interpretation.* Baltimore, MD: John Hopkins University Press.

Kerkkonen, M. (1976). "Finland and Colonial America." In *Old Friends – Strong Ties,* edited by V. Niitemaa, J. Saukkonen, T. Aaltio, and O. Koivukangas. Turku, Finland: Institute for Migration.

Kero, R. (1974). *Migration from Finland to North America in the Years Between the United States Civil War and the First World War.* Turku, Finland: Institute for Migration.

Koivukangas, O. (1988). "Conferences and Exhibitions Open the Delaware 350th Anniversary." *Siirtolaisuus – Migration* 15:23–40.

Myhrman, A. M. (1976). "The Finland-Swedish Immigrants in the U.S.A." In *Old Friends – Strong Ties,* edited by V. Niitemaa, J. Saukkonen, T. Aaltio, and O. Koivukangas. Turku, Finland: Institute for Migration.

Sandlund, T. (1981). "Patterns and Reasons in the Emigration of Swedish Finns." In *Finnish Diaspora I: Canada, South America, Australia, and Sweden,* edited by M. G. Karni. Toronto: Multicultural History Society of Ontario.

Tarkiainen, K. (1989). "The Emigration of Swedish-Finnish Burnbeaters to Delaware." *Siirtolaisuus – Migration* 16:4–10.

U.S. Bureau of the Census. (1992). *1990 Census of Population and Housing: Characteristics for Congressional Districts of the 103rd Congress.* Washington, DC: U.S. Government Printing Office.

ROBERT JARVENPA

# SWEDES

The Swedes have a long presence in North America. In 1638, Sweden, then a great European power, established a colony on the Delaware River. New Sweden remained under the Swedish flag for only seventeen years, during which its Swedish and Finnish population—Finland then being a part of the Swedish realm—came to fewer than four hundred individuals. They continued to increase, however, under Dutch and, from 1664, under English rule, so that they and their offspring were estimated at about one thousand by 1700. Many Americans are descended in part from them, even if unknowingly. Perhaps the most significant thing about Sweden's seventeenth-century American colony has been the pride it has inspired among later Swedish and Finnish Americans by identifying them with the early colonial history of their new homeland.

## The Great Emigration

*The First Phase.*  Individual Swedes continued to arrive in America during the eighteenth and earlier nineteenth centuries. By 1840, there began to be grave concern over growing impoverishment in Sweden. Much new land had been brought under cultivation since the beginning of the century, and yields had greatly increased with the introduction of improved farming methods. Still, population grew faster, more than doubling between 1800 and 1900, most rapidly among the poorer, landless classes of the countryside. The proportion of the population engaged in farming and related rural occupations meanwhile remained practically constant, at about three-quarters of the total, as late as the 1870s. Available farmland became ever scarcer. Although industrialization increased from midcentury, it was long unable to keep pace with population growth.

Just when the great emigration from Sweden to America may be considered to have properly begun remains open to varying interpretation. In 1838, the five Friman brothers (John, William, Herman, Adolph, and Otto) went out to the Wisconsin frontier. Their letters to their father (Carl) were printed in the widely read liberal Stockholm newspaper *Aftonbladet*, together with reports of the emigration then getting under way from neighboring Norway. In 1841, Gustaf Unonius from Uppsala, together with his bride and three others, established their short-lived "New Upsala" at Pine Lake, Wisconsin. His enthusiastic letters, which likewise came out in *Aftonbladet*, aroused widespread interest, especially in educated circles, encouraging various idealists and restless souls to follow him out to Pine Lake.

Among those who were impressed by Unonius's letters was the miller Peter Cassel, who in 1845 led a group of peasant farmers and their families from Kisa parish, Östergötland Province, in south-central Sweden — twenty-one persons in all — out to Iowa Territory. They established their "New Sweden" in Jefferson County, the first lasting Swedish settlement in the American Midwest. Cassel's letters, widely publicized in the Swedish press, were particularly influential among the Swedish peasantry, coming from a respected man of their own background and experience, while arousing serious concerns among the ruling classes. Beginning in 1846, a growing stream of peasants from Cassel's home region made their way out to Iowa and neighboring northwestern Illinois.

These early immigrants were soon overshadowed by the arrival in 1846 of more than twelve hundred religious dissenters, followers of the self-proclaimed prophet Eric Jansson, mainly from north-central Sweden. At Bishop Hill, in Henry County, Illinois, Jansson's sect established its Utopian community, which survived until 1860, achieving considerable prosperity in the mid-1850s.

Meanwhile, numerous onetime Janssonists left to settle in other northwestern Illinois localities, in turn drawing to them new arrivals from Sweden, many of whom soon moved on in search of available land. Bishop Hill, together with the Swedish Lutheran settlement at Andover, also in Henry County, Illinois, dating from 1847, and Peter Cassel's New Sweden in Iowa would thus be the original "mother colonies" established by emigrants directly from the old country, from which new groups constantly ventured farther west and north to the advancing frontier — mainly in Iowa, Minnesota, Kansas, Nebraska, and the Dakotas. During the 1850s, Swedes, mainly living in the Midwest, also took part in the California Gold Rush, establishing a lasting presence on the Pacific Coast.

Such stage migration resulted in a spreading network of "daughter" colonies, which before the century was over would extend to the Pacific Coast and up into the Canadian prairies. Chicago and the Twin Cities, in Minnesota, meanwhile began to emerge as the main Swedish-American urban centers.

*The Peak Years of Emigration.* Emigration from Sweden reached a first, modest peak in 1854, when it came to more than four thousand persons. Thereafter it fell off during the hard times in America, beginning in 1857 and lasting through the U.S. Civil War (1861–1865) — during which many Swedish immigrants served in the Union forces. Between 1867 and 1869, Sweden was afflicted with serious crop failures. Thanks largely to already established contacts with America, im-

Swedish homesteaders outside their sod house on the Nebraska prairie in 1886. (Nordiska Museet, Stockholm, Sweden)

proved and cheaper transport on steamships and railroads, and the American Homestead Act of 1862, emigration rapidly increased to previously unimaginable proportions, totaling more than thirty-two thousand persons in 1869. An increasingly important factor now was the energetic promotion of emigration by American state governments and land companies, and especially steamship lines and railroads with networks of local agents conveniently dispersed throughout Sweden.

Swedish emigration declined over the next few years, with the return of better times in Sweden and the financial panic of 1873 in the United States. By the late 1870s, however, Sweden, with its overwhelmingly rural population, faced a long-term economic crisis. Steam transport opened up vast new areas overseas, particularly in the American Midwest, to settlement and grain production for export. It thus became increasingly difficult for

Swedish peasant farmers to compete, even at home. Increasing numbers sold their small acreages and departed for America.

Up to this time, most Swedish emigrants had been farmers with land to sell to pay for their families' emigration. By the 1880s, the social composition of the emigration began to change as increasing numbers of poorer persons without means of their own were leaving individually for America. This became ever more possible as the costs of transportation fell and as growing numbers of relatives and friends already there were able to advance money or prepaid tickets to poor persons eager to join them. Emigration from Sweden reached its all-time high in 1888, when more than 45,500 departed.

The increasing numbers of immigrants who could not affort to go directly into farming upon their arrival were largely employed in railroad construction, logging, harvesting, and other types of menial labor. Young unmarried women were in high demand as domestic servants in American homes. After earning enough money to get themselves started, Swedes generally sought in this period to acquire land and become farmers, often following periods of urban residence and employment. Swedish settlement spread to new locations: Texas, the Rocky Mountain states, the West Coast, Alaska, and, in growing numbers, New England and New York State.

This mass exodus aroused both indignation and sorrow in Sweden. It seemed to prove that something was grievously wrong, either with Swedish society or with the Swedes themselves. From the 1860s through the 1880s, there was widespread pessimism that Sweden was virtually helpless in the face of America's overwhelming material attractions. Although some persons urged the outright prohibition of emigration, the government steadfastly rejected this as a violation of fundamental civil rights.

*The End of the Great Emigration.* Emigration remained sizable until America was overtaken by a new, grave economic crisis beginning in 1893. Meanwhile, Sweden entered into a dynamic phase of its own industrial development, stimulating a new optimism that the country both could and should provide adequately for the needs of all its people. By the late 1890s, it appeared that America could no longer offer the same advantages as before and that the great Swedish exodus was at last drawing to a close. However, such hopes proved premature, for emigration rose again, to more than 35,400 in 1903, leading to a full-scale government inquest into its causes and the organization of the National Society Against Emigration, both beginning in 1907.

By now, as good farmland became harder to acquire, growing numbers of Swedes entered nonagricultural occupations in America, frequently in newer areas of settlement — for instance, as factory workers or miners in the Northeast and Great Lakes states, or as lumberjacks in the Pacific Northwest. By 1910, more than half of America's Swedish-born population had become urban dwellers. By now there were sizable concentrations of Swedes in Duluth, Seattle, San Francisco, and Brooklyn, as well as such smaller cities as Rockford and Moline, Illinois; Jamestown, New York; and Worcester, Massachusetts.

World War I brought Swedish emigration practically to a standstill. Emigration increased when peace returned, reaching a final peak of nearly 24,000 in 1923. Thereafter the American immigration quota laws of 1924 and 1927 reduced it, first to 9,561 per year, then to 3,314 per year (not including family members). By the late 1920s, however, even these modest quotas were no longer being filled. The main reasons for the decline were Sweden's own rapid industrialization, urbanization, and comprehensive system of social welfare during the 1920s, which convinced working-class Swedes that their future lay at home. Nonetheless, a limited emigration of Swedes has continued to the present, since World War II consisting mainly of persons in highly qualified occupations.

Even from the beginning of the emigration, there were always some who in time returned permanently to their homeland. Return migration is estimated to have amounted to about 18 percent during the height of the emigration, between 1875 and 1925. During the Great Depression of the 1930s, it became greater still, far surpassing immigration.

## Ethnic Life and Institutions

*The Swedish-American Element.* It has been said that the great emigration created both a "Sweden in America" and an "America in Sweden." It brought approximately 1.25 million Swedes to the United States, some four-fifths of whom stayed. By 1910, it was commonly estimated that one Swede out of five was in the United States. Chicago was then reckoned to be the world's second-largest "Swedish" city, after Stockholm. Only Ireland and Norway had experienced greater emigration in proportion to their total population.

America's "Swedish element," officially described as the first and second generations, peaked in the 1930 U.S. Census at more than 1.5 million. Since then census figures have reflected its aging and numerical decline. However, the number of Americans with at least some Swedish ancestry are estimated in the 1990s at 8 million to 12 million. During the first two generations the great majority married within their own group. Although this has become less common in later generations, they have tended to intermarry primarily with Anglo Americans, other Scandinavian Americans, and German-American Protestants.

*Assimilation Versus Cultural Retention.* As northern European Protestants with closely kindred origins and traditions, Swedish and other Scandinavian immigrants were generally welcomed by the older Anglo-American population, particularly from the 1880s, when growing numbers of southern and eastern Europeans began arriving in the United States. The Swedes were widely praised as the "best Americanizers." Swedish immigrants nonetheless brought with them their own cultural traditions and values, which—adapted to American conditions—found expression not only in their personal lives but also in a multitude of Swedish-American religious organizations, schools and colleges, newspapers, publishing houses, business enterprises, societies, and clubs of every kind.

*Religion.* As Lutheranism was the state religion of Sweden, most church-affiliated Swedish immigrants and their descendants have been Lutherans. In 1860, thirty-six pioneer Swedish and Norwegian congregations formed the Augustana Lutheran Synod. As congregations increased rapidly with rising immigration, the synod divided in 1870 into separate Swedish and Norwegian bodies. From the first years of the immigration, many other Swedish immigrants became Methodists or Baptists, organizing their own Swedish conferences within these denominations. In Sweden, Mormon missionaries made converts who immigrated to Utah. In 1884, a split within Swedish-American Lutheranism led to the establishment of the Swedish Evangelical Mission Covenant, part of which in turn became the Evangelical Free Church. There have also been Swedish-American branches of the Episcopalian and Pentecostal churches, and the Salvation Army. Many Swedish Americans meanwhile joined Anglo-American or in some cases other Scandinavian-American

Swedish carpenters and painters work on a house in Chicago around 1910–1912. (Berton Hansson)

churches or did not formally affiliate with any denomination, even if they occasionally attended services.

*Education.* In 1860, the year of its founding, the Augustana Lutheran Synod established its Augustana College and Seminary in Chicago. With the withdrawal of the Norwegian congregations in 1870, it divided into the present Augustana colleges in Rock Island, Illinois (Swedish), and in Sioux Falls, South Dakota (Norwegian). Thereafter numerous other Swedish-American colleges and academies were founded, many of which have not survived. These now include the Lutheran-affiliated Gustavus Adolphus College in St. Peter, Minnesota, and Bethany College in Lindsborg, Kansas, as well as the Mission Covenant's North Park College in Chicago and the Baptist Bethel College in St. Paul. While some early pioneering settlements organized their own schools to begin with, the Swedes—unlike certain larger immigrant groups, such as the Irish and the Germans (both Lutheran and Catholic)—did not favor ethnic parochial schools. The Swedes did, however, commonly organize congregational summer, or "Swede," schools to prepare children for confirmation and teach them to read and write Swedish. Some of these existed at least into the 1920s.

*Journalism and Literature.* Following *Skandinaven*, briefly published in Swedish, Danish, and Norwegian by a Swede in New York in 1851–1852, the first purely Swedish newspaper in America, *Hemlandet* (The Homeland), was established in 1855 in Galesburg, Illinois, moving soon thereafter to Chicago, which quickly became the center of Swedish-American journalism. It is estimated that some twelve hundred Swedish-language periodicals have been published at various times in the United States, the largest number for any ethnic group except the Germans. The presently surviving Swedish-American newspapers include *Nordstjernan* in New York, *California Veckoblad* in Los Angeles, *Vestkusten* in San Francisco, and *Svenska Amerikanaren-Tribunen* in Chicago, the latter still entirely in Swedish. Numerous devotional works, magazines, yearbooks, practical manuals, and translations from English were published, chiefly

A Swedish-American men's chorus at the statue of Carl Linneaus in Chicago in 1894. (*Valkyrian*)

in Chicago and Rock Island, as well as poetry and prose fiction by both Swedish and a remarkably large number of Swedish-American authors.

*Organizations.* Clubs and societies of every description flourished, for mutual benefits, choral singing, theatricals, sports, literary activities, charity, and for immigrants from particular provinces, all of them involving a lively social life and dedicated, at least in part, to the preservation in the new homeland of Swedish language and culture. In time many joined into broader regional or national federations, such as the Svithiod Order (1880), the Order of Vikings (1890), the American Union of Swedish Singers (1892), and the Vasa Order of America (1896), the last still the largest Swedish-American organization, with some thirty thousand members and with lodges in Canada and Sweden.

*Ethnic Preservation.* Since the end of the great emigration in the 1920s, many of these ethnic institutions—oriented as they were to the cultural needs of Swedish-born and Swedish-speaking immigrants—have gradually died out. Today

Swedish is spoken by few Americans of Swedish origin, as compared with more recent immigrant groups. In 1966, Joshua Fishman rated Swedish thirteenth among non-English "mother tongues" in terms of prospects for maintenance in the United States, behind Norwegian (twelfth) but ahead of Danish (twenty-first).

But loss of the old language has by no means ended the lively interest of Swedish descendants in the land, culture, and traditions of their ancestors. This is amply proven by the constant establishment, from at least the 1920s, of new American-Swedish organizations that foster—now in English—ethnic pride and identification with the old homeland. The Swedish Council of America, founded with three participating societies in 1972, includes well over 160 Swedish-interest groups and continues to grow. Swedish- and Scandinavian-American museums in Philadelphia, Chicago, and Seattle, as well as in certain smaller communities; the American-Swedish Institute in Minneapolis; the Swenson Swedish Immigration Research Center in Rock Island; and the Swedish-American Historical Society in Chicago are of central importance in maintaining the ethnic heritage. Well-preserved Swedish traditions in America include the celebration of St. Lucia Day on December 13, old Christmas customs, Midsummer festivals, and not least the smorgasbord, with its many familiar dishes.

*Social and Occupational Status.* As a long-established element in the American population, Swedish descendants would be described today as predominantly middle-class and comparatively well educated. A relatively high proportion are still rural, engaged in agricultural and related occupations, especially in the upper Midwest; in this regard they are surpassed only by Norwegian and German Americans. Many of those of Swedish descent are in skilled trades (often in construction and precision industries), in business, and in the professions. Historically they have tended to be churchgoers and to identify primarily with the Republican party. The newer immigrants, since World War II, consist mainly of highly trained professionals, technicians, and businesspeople, located in the larger metropolitan areas, especially on the East and West coasts. Frequently they return to Sweden. Culturally they have tended to have relatively little contact with the older working-class immigrants and their descendants.

## Conclusions

The great emigration averted the threat of overpopulation and mass impoverishment in Sweden, allowing both those who left and those who stayed home to attain a more abundant and fulfilling life. Already by the 1880s appeals were heard in the homeland to "bring America to Sweden"—that is, to adopt America's political democracy, social equality, economic and technological skills, optimism, initiative, and work ethic—to counterbalance the fatal lure from across the sea. With time, American values, practices, and innovations have become so strongly rooted there that it is now claimed that the United States is the second-most Americanized country in the world—after Sweden! Materially and culturally, conditions have become ever more similar on both sides of the Atlantic. There nonetheless remains among Americans of Swedish origin a warm sympathy for the old homeland. They value those traits of character and culture they consider to be typically Swedish, and in their families, communities, and organizations, they cherish those customs that have proved adaptable to the American setting and that keep alive their sense of Swedish ethnic identity and pride.

*See also:* SWEDE-FINNS

## Bibliography

Barton, H. A. (1990). *Letters from the Promised Land: Swedes in America, 1840–1914*, revised edition. Minneapolis: University of Minnesota Press.

Barton, H. A. (1994). *A Folk Divided: Homeland Swedes and Swedish Americans, 1840–1940*. Carbondale: Southern Illinois University Press.

Beijbom, U. (1971). *Swedes in Chicago: A Demographic and Social Study of the 1846–1880 Immigration*. Chicago: Chicago Historical Society.

Elmen, P. (1976). *Wheat Flour Messiah: Eric Jansson of Bishop Hill.* Carbondale: Southern Illinois University Press.

Hasselmo, N. (1976). *Swedish America: An Introduction.* New York: Swedish Information Service.

Janson, F. E. (1931). *The Background of Swedish Immigration.* Chicago: University of Chicago Press.

Johnson, A. (1911). *The Swedish Settlements on the Delaware, 1638–1664.* Philadelphia: University of Pennsylvania Press.

Kastrup, A. (1975). *The Swedish Heritage in America.* Minneapolis: Swedish Council of America.

Lindmark, S. (1971). *Swedish America, 1914–1932: Studies in Ethnicity with an Emphasis on Illinois and Minnesota.* Chicago: Swedish Pioneer Historical Society.

Ljungmark, L. (1996). *Swedish Exodus,* 2nd edition. Carbondale: Southern Illinois University Press.

Nelson, H. (1943). *The Swedes and the Swedish Settlements in North America.* Lund, Sweden: Gleerups Förlag.

Ostergren, R. C. (1988). *A Community Transplanted: The Transatlantic Experience of a Swedish Immigrant Settlement in the Upper Middle West, 1835–1915.* Madison: University of Wisconsin Press.

Runblom, H., and Norman, H., eds. (1976). *From Sweden to America: A History of the Migration.* Minneapolis: University of Minnesota Press.

Stephenson, G. M. (1932). *The Religious Aspects of Swedish Immigration.* Minneapolis: University of Minnesota Press.

*Swedish-American Historical Quarterly* (before 1982 the *Swedish Pioneer Historical Quarterly*), published since 1950 by the Swedish-American Historical Society, Chicago.

H. Arnold Barton

# SWISS

Switzerland is a democratic, community-oriented society, specifically with allegiance to the *gemeinde* or *commune* (village or community). All first-generation immigrants to America considered themselves "Swiss," but not in an overtly nationalistic way. Immigrants keep close ties with the family still in Switzerland as well as the community or canton. During World War II, many Swiss males paid their taxes to the "home" canton to maintain citizenship and Swiss military status as a way to avoid the military draft in the United States. However, while return migration has always occurred, it was and is not common.

Old Country differences based on religion and language have been generally lost or submerged in secondgeneration descendants of the immigrants. Early immigrants were more agrarian, but nineteenth- and twentieth-century immigrants were typical of industrial-based capitalism. Family ties are strong, with male-biased legal and custom-based behavior. Descent is reckoned through the male name, and inheritance by the firstborn is favored. Inheritance also favors the children over the surviving female spouse.

## Reasons for Emigration

In examining the history of Swiss immigration to what was the American Colonies and later the United States of America, one must consider not only where the immigrants settled but also where they originated. The evolution of the Swiss Confederation since 1291 has seen the addition of member cantons to the present day. As early as 1525, Anabaptists from Zurich went to Spanish America in search of freedom, and Swiss colonists helped to found Jamestown in 1607. In the eighteenth century, there was an exodus of Swiss from the cantons of Zurich, Bern, and Basel. Less populous cantons such as Schaffhausen, Aargau, Solothurn, and Grabunden (Grisons) together with Luzern and the forest cantons (Schwyz, Uri, Obwalden, and Midwalden) represent the bulk of the confederation before the nineteenth century that was affected by emigration. Protestant as well as Catholic cantons lost population, the latter less so. Early Swiss emigration records have been lost for most cantons, but the surviving records of Bern, Zurich, and Basel give a good picture of the timing demographics, and reasons for emigration.

Even if a Swiss area was not specifically "confederate," such as Ticino, Vaud, Geneva, or Valais, many of these held "associated territory" status prior to the 1800s. They shall be considered Swiss in this entry. From 1474 to 1515, confederation soldiers served in European conflicts as mercenaries. This practice was condemned after the 1515 Battle of Marignano, where Swiss mercenary slew Swiss mercenary. This disastrous result of foreign service for much-needed monies led the confederation to declare neutrality in 1516. While still "neutral" at the end of the War of the Austrian Succession (1740), more than seventy thousand Swiss were in foreign uniforms.

It is instructive to trace the prime motivation for Swiss emigration to the factors that led them afar to fight. Central to the reasons for Swiss social and economic unrest is the fact that for all its modern success as a commercial power, Switzerland is a small, resource-poor nation. It is a beautiful land, but the elements that make it so—high, snowcapped mountains and deep alpine valleys— severely restrict the prospects for agricultural surplus and land for a growing population. Even within Switzerland there has been migration of people from the mountains to the plateau region. More than 60 percent of the modern Swiss population is concentrated in the cities and towns of the plateau.

By the 1600s, class distinctions had set in among the "aristocratic" cantons of Bern, Zurich, Basel, Geneva, Solothurn, Lucerne, and Schaffhausen, while the six democratic cantons retained the social fluidity of the past. Some of the former's attitudes are rooted in a pan-European mind-set not unique to Switzerland. Swiss independence relied on its resistance to this class-consciousness. Still, it existed in Switzerland, along with continued friction between Reform Protestant and Roman Catholic cantons.

## Immigration to America

Immigration to America paralleled that of Swiss to nearer lands, such as to depopulated Germany after the Thirty Years' War. Even immigrants to Alsace and Germany proper may have relocated to America later. Social unrest among peasants in Bern, Luzern, Solothurn, and Basel in 1653 resulted in emigration. By 1710, New Bern was established in North Carolina, led by Christoph von Graffenreid. At least sixty-six persons settled in New Bern.

While Switzerland was neutral as a confederation, Swiss still served in foreign armies. An example is two hundred Swiss recruited by the French to fight in the Louisiana Colony, 1734–1739. Colonel Jean-Pierre de Pury founded Purysburgh in South Carolina in 1732. At least 340 Swiss signed up to relocate to South Carolina, but Purysburgh failed largely because the Swiss considered the climate to be too hot and humid. Population growth, and hence pressure on land and agricultural production, led residents of Basel to emigrate in the eighteenth century. Three hundred emigrants left Zurich in 1734, many of them from Basel; these were generally whole families. After 1736, emigration from Basel was principally to Pennsylvania.

By the mid-eighteenth century, governments in Bern, Zurich, and elsewhere in the confederation were concerned over the loss of population due to emigration. Decrees were issued in the 1740s forbidding immigration to America, but these did little to stem the steady flow. Emigration taxes and obstacles to selling property were imposed. Reasons given to officials for leaving were poverty, lack of employment, and crop failure. From 1753 to 1763, a total of 10,000 people left Bern—4,000 men for foreign service and 6,000 others, both men and women, emigrating. A high tide of Swiss immigration to America from 1733 to 1744 has been estimated at 12,000 people. It is also estimated that a total of 25,000 Swiss left for the American Colonies during the eighteenth century.

U.S. records show a continual increase in Swiss immigration during the nineteenth century; from 1820 to 1920, more than 250,000 Swiss immigrants were allowed into the United States. Although this was a large number relative to the population of the Swiss confederation at that time, it accounted for only a fraction of the entire immigrant population entering the United States.

Townspeople stand on and around haystacks near Little Switzerland, North Carolina. (Library of Congress/Corbis)

Many of these 250,000 individuals, especially those entering the United States between 1888 and 1914, were responding to two basic factors that were stimulating Swiss emigration. The first was limited social mobility with regard to residence within Switzerland; due to political, linguistic, and cultural factors, it was often easier for Swiss to emigrate to another country than to migrate between cantons. For example, it was hard for a German-speaking Swiss to move from Bern to Zurich, and it was harder yet for a French-speaking citizen of Vaud to do the same. The second reason for Swiss emigration during this period was limited professional mobility in Switzerland, which affected those Swiss of the industrial sector even more so than the agrarian Swiss. As Switzerland changed from an agrarian society to a commercial-industrial one, opportunities for Swiss technical workers fluctuated, stimulating emigration.

## Settlements

The settlement of the "German counties" of Pennsylvania included a significant element of Swiss immigrants termed Swiss Mennonites or Anabaptists. They arrived in Pennsylvania in 1710. Swiss Mennonites were particularly disliked by the cantonal authorities because of their refusal to bear arms. To a small country surrounded by aggressive empires, this was tantamount to treason. Bern hoped to get rid of at least sixty Anabaptists in the New Bern enterprise, but these got no farther than Holland, where their Dutch brethren gave them succor. The exact number of Swiss immigrants in 1710 to Lancaster County, Pennsylvania, is in dispute, ranging from several hundred to a few thousand. Most of the Swiss colonists arriving in the then British possessions went to New York. From there they were encouraged to resettle, by

Crown authorities, in the Carolinas, Virginia, and Georgia as well as Pennsylvania. However, the bulk of early Swiss immigrants, particularly religious sects, did not gravitate to Pennsylvania. The largest number of all Swiss immigrants stayed in New York.

While Swiss immigrants initially settled in rural Pennsylvania and urban New York, particularly in the 1820s and 1830s, in the following decades, through and after the Civil War, increasing numbers went West to farms in Ohio, Illinois, Missouri, and Wisconsin. The Swiss expertise in dairy farming and cheese manufacturing must have played a significant role in this new pattern of Swiss-American settlement, because the immigrants were, in large part, farmers and homemakers. In the latter part of the nineteenth century this trend changed, with a growing number of skilled technicians and factory workers beginning to arrive.

Throughout the early twentieth century this industrial trend held, although the total number of immigrants diminished, due in large part to the U.S. Immigration Law of 1921, which set quotas for Swiss and other foreign immigrants. Swiss immigration was also affected by an economic push-pull phenomenon. When times were good in America and economic conditions attractive, the number of Swiss immigrants increased. In less prosperous times, the number of Swiss arriving in America diminished accordingly. The latter point is clearly supported by immigration numbers for the period of the Great Depression (e.g., 1920s Swiss emigrants were 29,676 in number; in contrast, 1930s data showed only 5,512).

In terms of individual states with Swiss-born Americans, California leads New York, New Jersey, and Wisconsin. Illinois and Ohio round out the six states that have absorbed 60 percent of twentieth-century Swiss emigrants.

## Assimilation and Cultural Persistence

The persistence of Swiss cultural traditions and languages has been more evident in rural as compared to urban areas. The speed and ease of integration into larger American society has also been related to the economic affluence of the immigrants. This has been particularly so for immigrants after 1890. Also, there have been no evident difficulties of assimilation into American life.

Economic aspects of Swiss life—watchmaking, dairy, cheese manufacturing, and winemaking—have persisted longer than fashions of dress and house construction. Language, most frequently Swiss-German, was generally lost first in urban settings. The few Swiss-French settlers reported an easy transition. In one of the last twentieth-century strongholds of Swiss-German in America, New Glarus, Wisconsin, the admixture of Glarus and Bernese dialects resisted replacement as daily speech for more than 130 years until there was less community isolation and new Swiss immigrants stopped arriving. As of the mid-1990s, only New Glarus residents born before 1929 retain any fluency in Swiss-German.

In many ways the character of Swiss cultural loss and ultimate assimilation into American culture is reflective of the fact that the number of immigrants from Switzerland never approached the numbers for some other European countries. To some, the Swiss were the "model immigrants," but Swiss immigrants to America ranged from Major Henry Wirz, the Confederate commandant of the infamous U.S. Civil War prison camp at Andersonville, to the Ticino Swiss who introduced winemaking to California's Napa Valley in 1860.

*See also:* MENNONITES

## Bibliography

Arlettaz, G. (1977). "L'integration des Émigrants Suisses aux États-Unis, 1850–1939." *Relations Internationale* 12:307–325.

Bennett, M. T. (1963). *American Immigration Policies: A History.* Washington, DC: Public Affairs Press.

Billigmeier, R. H., and Picard, F. A. (1965). *The Old Land and the New: The Journals of Two Swiss Families in America in the 1820s.* Minneapolis: University of Minnesota Press.

Faust, A. B., and Brumbaugh, G. M. (1925). *Lists of Swiss Emigrants in the Eighteenth Century to the*

*American Colonies*, Vol. 2. Washington, DC: National Genealogical Society.

Fertig, G. (1994). "Transatlantic Migration from the German-Speaking Parts of Central Europe, 1600–1800: Proportions, Structures, and Explanations." In *Europeans on the Move*, edited by N. Canny. Oxford: Clarendon Press.

Grueningen, J. P., von., ed. (1940). *The Swiss in the United States*. Madison, WI: Swiss-American Historical Society.

Handlin, O. (1972). *Pictorial History of Immigration*. New York: Crown.

Kuhn, W. (1976). "Recent Swiss Immigration into Nebraska: An Empirical Study." *Swiss-American Historical Society Newsletter* 12(3):12–20.

Kuhns, O. ([1901] 1971). *The German and Swiss Settlements of Colonial Pennsylvania: A Study of the So-Called Pennsylvania Dutch*. Ann Arbor, MI: Gryphon Books.

Lewis, B. A. (1973). "Swiss German in Wisconsin: The Impact of English." *American Speech* 48(3–4):211–228.

Luck, M. (1985). *A History of Switzerland*. Palo Alto, CA: Society for the Promotion of Science and Scholarship.

Meier, H. K. (1970). *Friendship Under Stress: U.S. Swiss Relations, 1900–1950*. Bern: Herbert Lang.

Morier, C. (1977). "Letters Inédites: Auguste Gouffon." *Schweizerische Zeitschrift für Geschicte* 27(3):324–339.

ERVAN G. GARRISON

# SYRIANS

The Syria of the "Syrians" is a land rich in history and cultural achievement. It embraces geographically what today may be called Syria proper, Lebanon, and Palestine. Traditionally it is defined as a geographic entity bordered by Turkey to the north and west, Iraq to the east, the Gulf of Aqaba to the south, and the Mediterranean to the west. The majority are Arabic-speaking, but there are some strong minorities, such as Armenians, Turkomans, and Kurds, who have preserved their ethnic languages. The land is home to the three great monotheistic faiths and most of their sectarian splinterings. The religion of prominence is Sunni Islam, followed by a number of Shi'a sects and Christians—both Uniates (Jacobites, Maronites, and Melkites) and Orthodox. There is in addition a strong Druze element (originally a derivative sect from Fatimid Ismailism) in the southern regions and a powerful Alawite Shi'a sect (whose members are the dominant political force in the region today) inhabiting mostly northwestern Syria.

The country is rich in history, starting with the third millennium B.C.E., when Canaanites settled the Mediterranean littoral, followed a millennium and a half later by the Aramaeans, who settled east of the Anti-Lebanon range and founded Damascus, the oldest living city in the world. With them came the Hebrews. They engaged largely in trade both inland and on sea, with the Phoenicians establishing the first maritime empire in history. In the Islamic era, the Umayyads, with their capital in Damascus, ruled the largest contiguous empire in history, stretching from China to France. It remained powerful and prosperous until the Crusades, the Mongol invasions, and the Ottoman domination, by which time much of the land's energy and productivity had been sapped. Invasions and civil wars impoverished the land and played a determinative role in the emigrations of the late nineteenth century.

## Immigration History

Emigrants from the Syrian region arrived in the United States in larger numbers only after 1880. The first to reach American shores, in 1854, is said to be Antun Bish'alani, who settled in the Boston area. In the 1870s a few arrived in the United States but soon returned to the Middle East. Before World War I, emigration was primarily from the villages of Mount Lebanon. These people were mostly Christian—Maronite, Melkite, and Greek Orthodox—bringing with them their traditional values, rooted in their faith, in hard work, and in a willingness to sacrifice to succeed. Strong attachment to family and faith enabled the immigrants to withstand the hardships in adjusting to a society whose language they did not speak and whose customs they did not understand.

The principal inducement to immigrate to the United States was economic: the search for a better life. Early immigrants were mostly uneducated single males in their late teens or early twenties. They spoke Arabic and had no knowledge of English. When they first arrived, they tended to head for localities where some relative or acquaintance may already have settled and to participate in activities over which they had a measure of control. Some settled in the industrial centers of the East and Northeast, while most became itinerant merchants crisscrossing the open lands of the Midwest and West, selling from farm to farm. Those who settled in industrial centers worked as laborers in the automobile, mining, or textile industries. They remitted a part of what they earned to needy relatives left behind; the rest they used to build capital for launching independent enterprises. Nearly a third of them returned to their ancestral villages with their savings to strengthen their economic opportunities at home through the purchase of land.

Official estimates reported by the Ottoman embassy in Washington, D.C., to Istanbul placed the number of Ottoman subjects who emigrated by 1906, often surreptitiously, because the sultan did not want to witness a mass exodus of Christian subjects from Syria, at 250,000, of whom 60,000 settled in the United States either temporarily or permanently. This number grew to more than two million by the mid-1990s. The largest number reside in large cities: New York, Detroit, Chicago, Dallas, Houston, Seattle, San Francisco, and Los Angeles. Since World War II, however, they have spread out into smaller metropolitan areas of the Midwest. It is not unusual to find them scattered all over the countryside, given their inclination to self-reliance and self-sufficiency.

## Professional Achievements

These immigrants were attracted at first to clothing and food enterprises. Manufacturing,

A stone pyramid at Quartzsite, Arizona, is topped with a camel and dedicated to Hi Jolly (sic), the Syrian camel driver who served the U.S. military as a scout from his arrival in the United States in 1856 until his death in 1902. (Richard Cummins/Corbis)

wholesaling, and distributing were equally alluring. Those who brought specific skills with them launched manufacturing enterprises. Syrians from Aleppo developed in New York the use of intricate lace in the negligee industry they launched. The Jerros of Aleppo introduced shoe manufacturing concepts and designs that catered to the high-style set nationwide.

Nathan Solomon Farah, who arrived in 1881, established a general store in New Mexico Territory, acquiring vast tracts of land through which the Sante Fe railroad line was laid. He became a developer, building hotels, theaters, and other public facilities that served to foster the growth of

Sante Fe and Albuquerque as major cities. He also served during World War I in the U.S. army that landed in France, rising to the rank of colonel. Others of Syrian origin are known to have served with Theodore Roosevelt's Rough Riders in the invasion of Cuba during the Spanish-American War. Before that, Hajj Ali (Hi Jolly) was brought from the Middle East by the Confederacy to supervise the breeding of camels to be used for transporting war material during the Civil War.

Mansur Farah, who arrived in 1905, launched the pants manufacturing business that grew into one of the largest under the Farah Manufacturing label with his son William, a World War II bomber pilot. They applied the assembly line technique to the art of manufacture, which rendered the product highly competitive and affordable.

Other manufacturing and retailing firms that were launched by Syrian immigrants include Haggar of Dallas, the largest manufacturer of men's apparel in the world today; Azar, also of Texas, in food processing; Maloufs of California, with their Mode-O-Day chain of retail specialty stores; and Gantos Corporation, a nationwide chain of women's boutiques.

The first generation worked hard and sacrificed to be able to afford the education and training needed by their children to enter the rewarding professions. They inculcated their children with strong moral values based on honesty and consideration of others in all transactions—social, economic, and political. Within a generation there sprung up from among them skilled doctors, lawyers, university professors, engineers, and socially conscientious advocates for the public good. They entered public service, becoming governors, judges, mayors, congressmen, and senators. A number of Syrian Americans can also be found in education at all levels. Philip K. Hitti was the founder of the first Arabic Studies program in America (at Princeton University in the 1940s), and his graduates served in high posts in government agencies as well as pioneering work in the field of Middle East studies generally.

Such professional achievements reflect the rapidity with which the first-generation Syrians born in America were able to adjust to the American way of life. Old Country values worked well in the United States. Church and mosque played an important role in conditioning social behavior and respect for elders and others. The extended-family concept provided the cement that bound its members and imbued them with a determination to face the outside world with confidence and anticipation of success.

While the early immigrants were predominantly Christian, there were a number of Druze immigrants. The Druze engaged generally in the same pursuits as their Christian counterparts. The earliest Druze immigrants arrived in 1880, with a larger number entering the United States in 1913. They launched their careers as itinerant merchants; some ventured into the restaurant and food businesses. Amin Fayyad, who settled in Washington, D.C., was the first to start a carryout food service east of the Mississippi. Muslim emigrants followed largely in the post–World War II era, with a heavy contingent being displaced Palestinians. While they had immigrated to the United States initially to acquire higher education, the lack of a home to return to led them to settle, marry, and raise their families in America.

## Identity

In terms of acquiring identities, the transformation paralleled the political fortunes of the homeland. The early immigrants left the Middle East as Ottoman subjects and were referred to as "Turks" when they set foot in America. They tended to call themselves "Awlad Arab" (Arab descendants) at that time, in recognition of their non-Turkish identity. With the breakup of unified Syria during World War I and the emergence of the mandate system, which parceled out Greater Syria between French and British colonialists, they changed over to "Syrian" to denote their land of origin. The auxiliary societies associated invariably from the beginning with their respective churches bore the title "Syrian."

Following the political fragmentation of Greater Syria in 1920, each immigrant or descendant, including those who arrived during the French mandate with French passports, checked the new maps drawn by the French and British authorities. It resulted in the emergence of Lebanese, Syrian, and Palestinian as separate badges of "national identity," albeit religion was the more dominant factor. Greek Orthodox or Maronite supplemented or superseded the national identity of Lebanese, Palestinian, or Syrian.

This is reflected also in the social organizations established. Each church congregation organized concomitantly with the establishment of a church. For Orthodox, Melkite, or Maronite, an auxiliary society bore the name of the denomination—Syrian Orthodox Society, Lebanese Maronite Society, and so on. The same pattern was followed by the Druze, who prefer to call themselves Unitarians rather than to be identified as an offshoot of the Muslim community. Their first society was orga-

nized in 1908 in Detroit and was titled al-Bakura al-Durziyah (First Druze). Its aim was to preserve the Druze identity and uphold the community's cultural heritage and creed. This is reinforced in their annual national conventions, held usually in the Washington, D.C., area, where they have settled in larger numbers.

Early Muslim immigrants formed communities in Detroit; Ross, North Dakota; and Cedar Rapids, Iowa, where the first regular mosque was established in 1911, followed by another in Detroit in 1919. The Muslims, too, developed their own associations to cater to their religious, social, and cultural needs. With the increase in emigration from Syria after World War II, Muslims could be found in all major cities. This led to the expansion of associations promoting welfare services and providing coordination of activities and uniformity. Due to the patronage of wealthy Islamic states,

Syrian children gather together in New York City during the early twentieth century. (Library of Congress/Corbis)

great regular mosques have been constructed in the major cities. The first was built in the 1950s in Washington, D.C. It is the main funneling point for the dissemination of basic information on Islam. Subsequently mosques were built on a large scale in most major cities. With the rapid expansion of the Muslim community, a national council has been organized to coordinate local councils and assist Muslims in fulfilling commitments to their respective communities, Syrian and non-Syrian alike.

When Palestinian refugees who entered the United States to acquire higher education were not able to return to their homes, they settled permanently in America. They were mostly university graduates trained predominantly in the medical and engineering fields. This enabled them to rise rapidly in the professions and to contribute substantially to the advancement of all branches of the sciences. In the wake of the 1967 Arab-Israeli War, they founded the Arab-American Association of University Graduates, a highly professional organization dedicated to fostering an objective awareness in America of both the Arab cultural heritage and the issues of contention with Israel. Other organizations catering to a broader audience and using Arab as the rallying cry include the American Arab Anti-Discrimination Committee and the Arab-American Council, both dedicated to eliminating discrimination on ethnic grounds and promoting better understanding of Arab issues and culture, of which the Syro-Lebanese are equally partaking. They have sponsored scholarly journals published regularly to provide balanced opinions on controversial issues to counter distorted public images of Arabs and Muslims and their faith and culture.

## Clubs and Organizations

In creating local clubs and organizations for men, women, and young adults of both sexes, the Syrians and the Lebanese disagreed about which should be the first member of the compound title, whether it should be "Syrian Lebanese" or "Lebanese Syrian." Even the Palestinians tended to

have their societies titled after the locality from which they derived, such as the Ramallah Association in San Francisco and Jacksonville. The dominant element in a particular locality tended to win out. Nevertheless, the immigrant groups did not hesitate to hold joint annual gatherings to promote solidarity, sometimes in connection with their churches and at other times with the American community at large. The first convention of Syrian clubs was held in Williston, North Dakota, in 1918. With the establishment of the national Federation of Syrian and Lebanese Clubs at the end of World War II, annual conventions became the norm, serving to promote inherited cultural traditions and entertainment. Their social gatherings feature Arabic food, music, and dance and provide opportunities to meet and to exchange ideas on a whole range of subjects of social, economic, and political interest. The young and the old of both sexes mingle and exchange pleasantries, show off their successes, and hope for the right match for those of marriageable age.

The purposes of local and national organizations among the first immigrants were to maintain and further communal ties and to teach children the values the original immigrants brought with them, stressing the honorable ways of the old country. Uncertain of how to relate to non-Syrian women, men preferred to return to their villages for brides once they reached a level of affluence. The pattern changed radically when the "melting pot" absorbed the first generation born in America that had found itself torn between the old and the new countries. The tendency was for them to inculcate second-generation Syrian Americans with what they termed American values, including speaking English and ignoring Arabic, the language of the early immigrants. Acculturation removed inhibitions against marrying outside the ethnic community. The third generation began to yearn for knowledge about their ancestral culture and the great legacies of Arab history, especially when curricula promoting such knowledge were established at leading universities.

Syrians who had been educated before emigrating obtained official positions and quickly became involved in American politics during the Woodrow Wilson era. Samuel Berberi served on political committees and was also an immigration official at Ellis Island. The drive to sustain some Arab cultural identity was reinforced from the beginning when educated immigrants launched Arabic-language newspapers and literary societies in both the New York and Boston areas to encourage poetry and writing, with the aim of keeping alive and enriching the Arabic cultural heritage. What became known as al-Rabitah al-Qalamiyah (League of the Pen) nurtured the careers of some of the most outstanding modern Arabic poets and authors who composed in both English and Arabic. Perhaps the best known among them is Kahlil Gibran, whose work *The Prophet* (1923) has been outprinted only by the Bible.

Between 1892 and 1907, some fifty newspapers were launched, but most were short-lived, especially after the community lost its native-language fluency. Second- and third-generation Syrian Americans were now served by journals and newsletters in English, which disseminated local and regional news. After World War II, the Federation of Lebanese Clubs sponsored the *Lebanese-American Journal*, which became nationally popular for a while in the 1970s. It was designed to cement the Lebanese as distinct from the rest of the erstwhile Syrian community. Those who sought to preserve the "Arabic" label in Portland, Oregon, in the wake of the fragmentation that ensued in the community between Syrians and Lebanese, and with the influx of other Arabic-speaking peoples from the Middle East, decided to accentuate the common ancestry of all in a short-lived publication titled *Awlad Arab*.

## Conclusion

Syrian, Lebanese, or Arab, the descendents of immigrants from the Syrian region continue to excel in all professions. The American Enterprise Institute, founded by the William Baroody of Washington, D.C., is a commitment to the preservation of an American way of life that had benefited them. They are also committed to the principle of justice and fair play, as best exemplified today in Ralph Nader's consumer protection enterprises. They launched and supported charities transcending their own community and serving America at large, an expression of gratitude to a country that has allowed them to fulfill their ambitions and to reward them for their labor. With Danny Thomas as principal benefactor, they established in the early 1960s the Association of Lebanese and Syrian American Charities, which constructed and endowed the St. Jude Hospital and Medical Research Center as a facility for the treatment of all children regardless of ethnic or racial background.

Much of the success achieved by Syrians is due in large part to the rapidity of their integration into the American mainstream. They have been amply rewarded for striving and relying mostly on their own individual talents and resources. Dedication to honesty, integrity, hard work, and fair play has been the mark of their success.

*See also:* LEBANESE CHRISTIANS; LEBANESE MUSLIMS; PALESTINIANS

## Bibliography

Abraham, S., and Abraham, N., eds. (1983). *Arabs in the New World: Studies on Arab-American Communities.* Detroit: Center for Urban Research, Wayne State University.

Abu Laban, B., and Suleiman, M., eds. (1989). *Arab Americans: Continuity and Change.* Belmont, MA: AAUG Press.

Aswad, B., ed. (1974). *Arabic-Speaking Communities in American Cities.* New York: Center for Migration Studies.

El-Kholy, A. (1966). *The Arab Moslems in the United States: Religion and Assimilation.* New Haven, CT: College & University Press.

Hagopian, E., and Paden, A. (1969). *The Arab Americans: Studies in Assimilation.* Willmette, IL: Medina University Press International.

Hitti, P. K. (1924). *Syrians in America.* New York: George Doran.

Hooglund, E., ed. (1985). *Taking Root: Arab-American Community Studies,* Vols. I and II. Washington, DC: American Arab Anti-Discrimination Committee.

Hooglund, E., ed. (1987). *Crossing the Waters: Arabic-Speaking Immigrants to the United States Before 1940.* Washington, DC: Smithsonian Institution.

Hourani, A., and Shehadi, N., eds. (1992). *The Lebanese in the World: A Century of Emigration.* Oxford, Eng.: Centre for Lebanese Studies and I. B. Tauris Press.

Kayal, P. M., and Kayal, J. M. (1975). *The Syrian Lebanese in America: A Study in Religion and Assimilation.* Boston: Twayne.

Mcarus, E., ed. (1994). The Development of Arab-American Identity. Ann Arbor: University of Michigan Press.

Naff, A. (1985). *Becoming American: The Early Arab Immigrant Experience.* Carbondale: Southern Illinois University Press.

Orfalea, G. (1988). *Before the Flame: A Quest for the History of Arab Americans.* Austin: University of Texas Press.

Rizk, S. (1943). *Syrian Yankee.* Garden City, NY: Doubleday Doran.

Sawaie, M., ed. (1985). *Arabic-Speaking Immigrants in the United States and Canada.* Lexington, KY: Mazda Press.

Suleiman, M. W. (1988). *The Arabs in the Mind of America.* Brattleboro, VT: Amana Books.

CAESAR E. FARAH

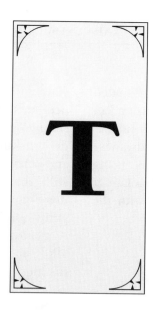

# TAIWANESE

The term "Taiwanese" generally refers to residents of the island of Taiwan off the coast of southeast China after 1949. Taiwan was a late-settled region of the Chinese Empire and has a diverse population. The original inhabitants of the island, speakers of Malayo-Polynesian languages, today include ten aboriginal tribes (collectively called Fan, or barbarians, before 1895; Gaosazhu or hill tribes from 1895 to 1945, during Japanese colonial rule; Gaoshanzhu under the Nationalists from 1945 to 1987; and Yuanzhumin after 1987). Chinese settlers from coastal Fujian and Guangdong provinces began to immigrate to the island after the mid-seventeenth century. They included mainly people from the southern Fujian area, who speak various Minnan (Hokkien) dialects and comprise 80 percent of the immigrants. The Hakka people (or Kejia) from western Fujian and eastern Guangdong provinces make up the other 20 percent. Because of the Minnan speakers' majority status in Taiwan, when the term "Taiwanese" is used, it generally refers to this language group. Finally, in 1949, when the Communists defeated the Nationalists on mainland China, an estimated two million refugees from various parts of China fled to Taiwan. These refugees were mostly soldiers and civilian officials affiliated with the Nationalist government and have been categorized as Mainlanders (Waishenjen, people from other provinces) in Taiwan. Since the Nationalist government had authoritarian and monopolistic control of Taiwanese politics between 1949 and 1987, the Mainlanders are often equated with the Nationalist party and hence are considered the oppressors of residents, including the Minnan-speakers, the Hakkas, and the Yuanzhumin.

Taiwanese thus has three distinct layers of meaning. Linguistically it refers to speakers of Minnan dialects in Taiwan, excluding the Mainlanders, the Hakkas, and the indigenous tribes. Second, from a sociological perspective, Taiwanese refers to all original residents on the island, including the Yuanzhumin, the Hakkas, and the Minnan-speaking people, and their descendents, before the Mainlanders fled to Taiwan in 1949. Third, as used in the U.S. Census, Taiwanese includes all immigrants from Taiwan, including the Minnan-speaking majorities, the Hakkas, the Yuanzhumin, and the Mainlanders. To distinguish themselves from the Nationalist regime, some Taiwanese immigrants also used the term "Formosan" for themselves. The name "Formosa" supposedly originated from Portuguese sailors who first saw the island in the sixteenth century and exclaimed "ha formosa" (the beautiful island). Many opposition Taiwanese groups in the United States insist on using "Formosan". This includes all non-Mainlander Taiwanese, making this term equivalent with the second usage above.

## Immigration History

Immigrants from Taiwan to the United States are composed of three distinct categories. First, there are students who arrived to pursue advanced degrees in the United States after 1949. The emphasis on education, following traditional Confucian teaching, plus the vigorous college entrance exams in Taiwan since 1949, produced highly competent college graduates who sought advanced training in the United States. Even today, Taiwanese students constitute one of the three largest foreign student groups across U.S. campuses. Because of their minority status in Taiwan, and perhaps because of their better family finances, the Mainlanders, in the early years, contributed a disproportionate number of Taiwanese students to the United States. These students initially arrived with nonimmigrant visas. Upon completing advanced degrees, many of them decided to stay, applying for immigrant status and finding employment in the United States. They are generally affiliated with higher education institutions or research centers across the United States and do not form a distinct immigrant community. They are well educated, have well-paid professional jobs, and live in suburbia like other American middle-class professionals. Politically inactive, this group is respected by other Taiwanese immigrants as opinion leaders. Both the Nationalist and the Communist governments have courted and solicited support from this immigrant group.

Second, the 1965 changes in U.S. immigration laws established an annual quota of twenty thousand immigrants from China (including Taiwan and China-born residents outside of mainland China). Eligibility for immigration includes dependents of U.S. legal residents (including their siblings, spouses, parents, and unmarried children), skilled workers, and those talented in arts and science. Since at this point the United States still recognized the Nationalists as the sole, legitimate government of all China, most of the immigrant quotas were filled by Taiwanese in Taiwan. A steady flow of immigrants have arrived since 1965, and they form the main body of the current, distinct Taiwanese immigrant communities. As dependents of the former group, these Taiwanese are very diverse in education and financial status when they arrive. They may range from postcollege-level professionals in Taiwan who speak fluent English, to illiterate country people who must attend entry-level language classes to learn English. Financially they range from entrepreneurs with large amounts of capital to invest internationally, to small bank deposit holders ready to start mom-and-pop stores, to poor laborers performing menial jobs in sweatshops in Chinatowns. When this group settled in the United States, they avoided the established Chinatowns (such as those in San Francisco, New York, or Los Angeles) that are dominated by Cantonese Chinese and have congested streets and stereotyped Chinese professions. New Taiwanese enclaves mushroomed in the San Gabriel Valley in southern California; in the Bay Area around San Francisco; in Dallas, Texas; and in the borough of Queens, New York City. The two most highly concentrated Taiwanese communities are Monterey Park near Los Angeles and Flushing in Queens.

The final group of Taiwanese in the United States are nonlegal immigrants who initially resided in the United States without proper immigrant status. In the 1950s and 1960s Taiwanese sailors often "jumped ship" when harbored in U.S. ports to enter illegally. Many of them sought employment in menial jobs, such as dishwashers and semiskilled laborers, in Chinatowns. They were clear in their intention and worked hard to fulfill their dream of living in the "beautiful nation." Once financially secure, they obtained legal papers through immigration lawyers and brought

U.S. and Taiwanese flags fly from an association hall in San Francisco's Chinatown. (Morton Beebe-S.F./Corbis)

their families to join them. Another group of nonlegal immigrants are more opportunistic. They entered with tourist or business visas and, when they found employment opportunities, extended their stay illegally. They would ultimately seek legal status if their extended stay turned out to be financially rewarding. The last type of nonlegal immigrants are the "little study-abroad students" (*xiao liuxuesheng*). Because of the vigorous college entrance exam in Taiwan, which permits only a small fraction of high school graduates to enter college, plus the conscription of young adult males into the military when they reach eighteen, many Taiwanese parents in the 1970s and 1980s sent their children to the United States at an early age. These children were sent to relatives and friends, specifically in southern California and New York City. While most Taiwanese children have taken advantage of this new opportunity and excel in schoolwork, a small minority have gone "bad" due

to lack of parental supervision and more permissive U.S. school regulations. Their problems, such as drug use and gang activities, have generated outcries in Taiwan and among U.S. Taiwanese communities. However, no viable solutions have been offered thus far, and Taiwanese children continue to arrive in the United States.

## Demography

It is almost impossible to provide an exact count of Taiwanese immigrants or to identify the clearly defined Taiwanese communities in the United States, for two reasons. First, Taiwanese immigrants were categorized as Chinese in U.S. immigration records before 1982, so they were mixed with immigrants from China, who comprise the majority of residents of old Chinatowns, and with Hong Kong immigrants. After 1982, the U.S. Immigration and Naturalization Service separated

Taiwan from China and recorded a total of 102,954 Taiwanese immigrants between 1982 and 1989. This probably represents only a small fraction of the Taiwanese immigrants who had already settled in the United States. Second, socially speaking, many pro-Nationalist Taiwanese regard themselves as Chinese and are ready to mix with Chinese from Hong Kong, China, and other Southeast Asian countries. They shun the term "Taiwanese" for its anti-Nationalist implications. On the other hand, a Minnan-speaking Taiwanese may not consider the Hakkas and the Mainlanders as Taiwanese, since they do not speak that language.

Without an acceptable definition for Taiwanese, it is difficult to draw the boundaries for this ethnic group. A rough estimate of the total number of Taiwanese immigrants is 1 to 1.5 million. According to the 1990 U.S. Census, the highest concentration of Taiwanese/Chinese is in the San Gabriel Valley in southern California, especially in the communities of Monterey Park (21,971 Taiwanese/Chinese, or 36% of the total population), Alhambra (21,303, or 26%), Rosemead (10,832, or 21%), Hacienda Heights (7,839, or 15%), San Gabriel (7,649, or 21%), and Arcadia (7,180, or 15%). The majority of these self-labeled Chinese came from Taiwan, but they also include Chinese from China, Hong Kong, and other Southeast Asian countries. The total Chinese population in Los Angeles County was estimated to be 245,000 in 1990, with the majority from Taiwan. The next Taiwanese concentration area is New York City, especially in Flushing, Queens. A 1986 estimate put the total Chinese population in Flushing at 60,000, with the majority from Taiwan.

## Economic Patterns

Taiwanese immigrants are generally better off in two salient areas than Chinese immigrants who immigrated to the United States before 1949 and who constituted the majority inhabitants of Chinatowns: education and financial status. Besides those Taiwanese who were pursuing advanced degrees, many of the dependent immigrants also have high school or college education and functional English. Language has been less of a barrier for them than it was for the old Chinatown residents. Many Taiwanese had professional jobs in Taiwan and had been exposed to modern living. They are able and very willing to live in a multiethnic society. As to financial status, with an economic boom in Taiwan in the 1980s and 1990s, many immigrants arrived with their own savings or investment capital for new opportunities. The stereotypes of Taiwanese immigrants are brash young couples paying cash for flashy sports cars, motel chains, and exclusive residential properties.

However, sociological research in New York City and in southern California indicates that the majority of new Taiwanese immigrants are not free-spending investors. They work hard to reestablish themselves in this new society. They first look for professional jobs comparable to their former employment in Taiwan. If this approach fails, because of the lack of certification, license, or language capacity, they try to work for established Taiwanese small businesses, such as restaurants, retail grocery stores, launderettes, souvenir shops, and so on. The goal is eventually to establish their own businesses using their own savings as start-up capital. Being a proprietor of an enterprise, no matter how small, is considered being successful in Chinese culture. In this context, the majority of Taiwanese can be considered "entrepreneur elite." There are some Taiwanese who have experienced downward mobility, however, especially those with less education and little investment capital. Without these essential qualifications a few end up working as laborers in Chinatown sweatshops or restaurants.

Most Taiwanese have immigrated to the United States for better economic opportunities. But as the economy in Taiwan has expanded, the margin of difference has narrowed. As employment opportunities in the United States deteriorated in the 1980s and early 1990s, especially for white-collar professionals, there appears to be a reverse immigration taking place. Many laidoff professionals have taken research or teaching positions in

Taiwan's high-tech research institutions or universities, leaving their families in the United States. This reverse immigration has created duolocal families between Taiwan and the United States.

## Housing, Family, and Kinship

Many Taiwanese immigrants arrived in the United States with their families, skills, and capital. This is clearly in sharp contrast to early Chinese immigrants, who were mostly men, came as sojourn laborers, and formed a bachelor society in Chinatowns. While some Taiwanese may reside in or close to Chinatowns for cheap housing or shopping convenience, most Taiwanese consider Chinatowns congested and unclean. While many new immigrants initially find housing in apartments or condominiums, their ultimate goal is to own individual housing in suburbia, like other middle-class Americans. To help pay for rent or mortgages, many new immigrants sublease rooms or part of their houses to other immigrants. Such arrangements often violate city ordinances and create negative images for the immigrants. However, to some extent this merely reflects different perceptions between these two societies regarding space needs and privacy.

Taiwanese are essentially similar to traditional Chinese in emphasizing familial integration and success. Parents work hard and make tremendous sacrifices for their children to succeed. Parents spend a lot of time interrogating their children on schoolwork and grades. Precious family resources are steadily channeled into children's "high class" extracurricular activities: music lessons in piano or violin, ballet, and summer computer or tennis camps. The stereotyped "nerd" who knows nothing other than schoolwork is the ideal, filial child to Taiwanese parents. In social gatherings parents brag about their children's high grades and accomplishments. Annual national high school competitions, such as the Westinghouse Science Contest or the Presidential Merit Scholarships, are the ultimate prizes for the most successful parents. The announcement is anxiously awaited by family members, friends, and relatives of the candidates, and the final list is widely circulated by parents as models for their children to emulate. Parent-child relationships are much closer than among ordinary middle-class Americans, as are mutual expectations. This strong family bond is probably one of the most important factors leading to educational success among Taiwanese children.

Extended kinship beyond the family also plays an important role among Taiwanese immigrants. Many early immigrants sponsored the immigration of their Taiwan siblings, provided temporary housing when they arrived, and arranged initial employment or investment capital for starting up their own businesses. Family members living in different parts of the United States maintain regular contact by telephone calls or visits. Looking after each other's children is considered a natural obligation among kinsmen. Furthermore, mutual trust among close kin also extends to other areas. Monetary loans without collateral or written notes are the norm rather than the exception. Similarly, finding a potential spouse for an unmarried or widowed kinsman is no less an obligation than it was in Taiwan.

Family ties are strong and there a fewer divorces among Taiwanese immigrants compared with mainstream American families. There are, however, signs that this family cohesion seems to be weakening, in part because of open and flexible social relations in the United States. Taiwanese social life is more structured and all-encompassing. The closely knit and sometimes overlapping social relations, including kin, coworkers, former schoolmates, and friends, often serve as deterrents to extramarital relationships. The lack of such overlapping social networks in the United States, plus increased autonomy for women and geographic mobility in general, provide more opportunities for extramarital liaisons. The second reason for weakened family cohesion is familial division between Taiwan and the United States, with one of the parents taking a job on the island. Long-term separation creates conjugal apathy and hence opportunities for marital infidelity and divorce.

## Worldview and Religion

Few Taiwanese students-turned-professionals are true believers in any religion. Some may attend Sunday Bible study when they first arrive, perhaps for more pragmatic reasons such as learning English or socializing than for spiritual renewal. They may go back to Taiwan to attend family rites such as ancestral veneration or funerals, observing traditional Taoist or Buddhist rituals. But seldom do they bring such ritual practices or symbols to the United States.

The arrival of dependent immigrants in the 1970s and 1980s, plus the formation of immigrant enclaves, dramatically changed this aloof attitude toward religion. Various Christian congregations have been formed with bilingual or trilingual pastors to serve the new immigrants. In addition to regular Sunday services and Bible study, some Christian congregations have also organized social services for new immigrants, such as English instruction, medical care, filing income-tax returns, and social gatherings for young and old.

Besides Christianity, many traditional Taiwanese religious activities have also flourished in recent years. Buddhist temples have been built on both coasts and attract a large number of worshipers. Private Taoist/animist religious statues, as well as ancestral tablets, have appeared in private homes. Some private religious altars also have folk religion practitioners who commemorate departed ancestors during death anniversaries; participate in divination of an individual's fate or destination; determine geomancy in selecting house site or direction; and determine auspicious times for a wedding, opening a new business, or traveling.

## Political Participation

Taiwanese immigrants have been more involved in the politics of their home country than in that of their host society, although the situation seems to be changing as second-generation Taiwanese begin to participate in American social life. Before Taiwan lifted martial law in 1987, many Taiwanese political dissidents took refuge in the United States. Sharp lines were drawn between the pro-Nationalist and pro-independence camps. They formed separate groups and associations and competed openly to influence public opinion and American policies. Heated confrontations sometimes resulted in physical violence, which further created chasms and antagonisms among former friends, schoolmates, and even family members. In general, more Mainlander Taiwanese belonged to the pro-Nationalist camp, and more Minnan-speaking Taiwanese joined the opposition. The minority Hakka-speaking Taiwanese and the even more minuscule Yuanzhumin were ambivalent toward this conflict because they tended to be the victims of both groups in Taiwan as well as in the United States.

With democratization in Taiwan after 1988, many Taiwanese activists returned to the home country, and the tension among Taiwanese immigrants was reduced. New opposition political parties in Taiwan have established branches in the United States to maintain their influence over overseas Taiwanese. However, democratization also means demythifying political power. Regular election campaigns in Taiwan have secularized political processes and depoliticized constituents. Apathy toward Taiwanese politics is the reason why many Taiwanese immigrants now pay attention to politics in the United States.

## Assimilation and Cultural Persistence

Large numbers of Taiwanese immigrated to the United States after 1965. The passage of civil rights laws and the establishment of affirmative action programs in the United States minimized the hostility and discrimination these new immigrants encountered. In fact, many Taiwanese immigrants probably benefited from these employment programs because they filled the minority quotas. Coming from a deeply rooted Confucian cultural tradition, which categorizes people more on merit and accomplishments than on race or nationality, most Taiwanese immigrants considered it their natural right to be living in a multiracial, plural society. They took for granted the social benefits they enjoyed, and they were oblivious to the painful struggle of other ethnic minorities during the civil rights movement.

Resentment against Taiwanese immigrants, especially in highly concentrated enclaves such as Monterey Park and Flushing, derived not just from other minority or immigrant groups but even more so from the white, mainstream society. Discriminatory ordinances, even though implicit and local — such as anti-immigration, anti-rezoning and growth, and English only — became hot issues in local elections. Three possible reasons contributed to mainstream antagonism toward this group. First, Taiwanese immigrants do not necessarily consider U.S. culture superior to their own. The United States may have excellent education insti-

tutions and government, but in other spheres of life, such as culinary art, self-discipline, interpersonal relations, and manners, the Taiwanese are not as impressed. Reluctance to abandon their culture can be seen in the persistence of using Taiwan-based language in social gatherings and on street signs. Such noncompliance threatens the host country's self-image as a melting pot for all.

Second, mainstream white Americans resent the fact that many Taiwanese come with good education and ready cash. It seems the Taiwanese immigrants have been ushered into the American dream without a glitch, whereas white Americans remember their immigrant ancestors struggling for two or three generations before entering the middle class.

A man waves a Taiwanese flag to protest a mainland China event taking place across the street in San Francisco during the late 1970s. (Dean Wong/Corbis)

Finally, Taiwanese immigrants are often regarded as greedy and manipulative in business dealings. They are bold in land speculation and real-estate development for quick, personal gain. In so doing they show little concern for community development, aesthetics, and privacy for established inhabitants.

Such interethnic conflicts, however, have not evolved into long-term social cleavages between Taiwanese and the dominant white society. Ethnicity has never been a strong rallying point for educated Taiwanese. Similarly, diverse class interests also hamper the solidarity of the dominant majority. In the meantime, a few Taiwanese leaders have recognized the importance of voluntary associations and individual participation in American politics. More and more Taiwanese immigrants have taken part in local school board or community elections. The development of clearly defined interest groups, such as political party branches, chambers of commerce, and charity organizations, and their articulation with national organizations will ultimately integrate the Taiwanese into American society.

*See also:*   CHINESE

## Bibliography

Chen, H.-S. (1992). *Chinatown No More: Taiwan Immigrants in Contemporary New York.* Ithaca, NY: Cornell University Press.

Chen, H.-S. (1993). "Immigrant Entrepeneurs: Chinese Small Business in Queens, New York." *Bulletin of the Institute of Ethnology* 76:97–136.

Fong, T. P. (1994). *The First Suburban Chinatown: The Remaking of Monterey Park, California.* Philadelphia: Temple University Press.

Kinkead, G. (1992). *Chinatown: A Portrait of a Closed Society.* New York: HarperCollins.

Wong, B. (1988). *Patronage, Brokerage, Entrepreneurship, and the Chinese Community in New York.* New York: AMS Press.

Zhou, M. (1992). *Chinatown: The Socioeconomic Potential of an Urban Enclave.* Philadelphia: Temple University Press.

SHU-MIN HUANG

# TAMILS

Tamils are people whose native language is Tamil, a Dravidian language spoken by about seventy-one million people worldwide. Tamil is the oldest of the Dravidian languages and is principally spoken in the Indian state of Tamilnadu. Other ethnonyms for people of this region include Tamilians, Tamilarkal, Thamizhar, and Thamizharkal. Tamil-speaking people also reside in Sri Lanka, Singapore, Malaysia, Mauritius, Great Britain, Canada, and the United States. Tamil-speaking people in the diaspora tend to keep alive the social distinctions connected with the countries of their origin; thus Tamils from South India do not socialize very much with those from Sri Lanka. Substantial and consistent animosity between South Indian Tamils and Sri Lankan Tamils in the United States is actively seen in World Wide Web Usernet groups, where anonymity allows for frankness of expression. While a substantial majority of the Tamil-speaking people are Hindu, Tamil-speaking Christians and Muslims also have settled in the United States. Various degrees of caste distinctions are retained both by Tamil-speaking Hindus and Christians in the United States, and occasionally Tamil *sangams* and *manrams* (associations) splinter along caste lines in major cities. There are about a dozen major caste groups among Tamils in the United States. There are also distinctions based on sectarian communities, which are distinct from caste differences among the Tamil-speaking people. Some communities are distinguished by the deity they follow; thus there may be Vaishnava (followers of Vishnu) or Saiva Tamils of various castes.

## Immigration Patterns

The first significant number of Tamil-speaking people arrived in the United States on nonimmigrant visa in the late 1940s. These people, whose children became some of the earliest second-generation Tamil-speaking U.S. citizens, were connected with the United Nations and affiliated organizations. However, it was after the loosening of the immigration laws in the 1960s that a new and notably professional wave of Indians began to arrive and settle down in the United States. U.S. Census records show that 90 percent of the Tamil-speaking people in the United States are foreign-born and that immigration increased dramatically in the late 1960s. Many of these Tamils who were professionals (engineers, physicians) and, more recently, computer experts came with a good knowledge of the English language, which has helped in the process of settling down. This group has one of the highest income levels in the United States; 1990 U.S. Census figures show that the mean income of Tamil-speaking families is $66,826 and the median income is $55,311.

## Demographics

There is no official count to record the number of Tamil-speaking people in the United States. Although the 1990 U.S. Census showed that 26,641 people claimed they spoke Tamil at home, on the basis of membership lists from Hindu temples and Tamil sangams it is estimated that the number is 75,000 to 100,000. The discrepancy in numbers, it is believed, results from a number of factors primarily based on the language of the questions. The 1990 U.S. Census questions on language were "Does this person speak a language other than English at home?" "What is this language?" "How well does this person speak English?" Since most Tamils in the United States are bilingual (the percentage of respondents answering the last question as "very well" was very high), many Tamil-speaking people probably reported that they speak English at home. It is also assumed that since many children from Tamil-speaking families are not familiar with their native language, parents communicate with them in English at home and so do not report Tamil as a language spoken at home. Unmarried Tamil-speaking people, especially students, who do not have a family in the United States, would also not reply that they speak Tamil at home. The Tamil population in Canada is much larger (about 100,000 in the Toronto area alone), and most of these new immigrants are from Sri Lanka. Political conditions, including the major civil war between the Tamils and the Sinhalese, has led to an exodus of Tamil-speaking people from Sri Lanka to many parts of the world, especially Canada.

## Economics and Employment

While there is no overt political pressure that brings Tamil people from India to the United States, employment and economic opportunities are significant factors in the emigration of some castes from India. An explicit policy of the Tamil-nadu government is to reserve a quota of all jobs and admissions to professional schools for the "backward castes" and the "scheduled castes and tribes." These quotas have been as high as 69 percent in some years. This official policy of what is dubbed "reverse discrimination" has led to the loss of educational and employment opportunities for what historically had been deemed the "high" caste citizens. In the past, the Brahmans, who were 3 percent of the population in India, had held more than 60 percent of the high-level jobs. The reservation or quota system is said to be an effort to alleviate historical imbalances. Tamils in India also have restricted job opportunities in other Indian states. Many states in India have distinctive languages and cultures. In an effort to preserve college and school spaces, as well as jobs for the people native to an area, many states have adopted what is called the "sons of the soil" policy. This policy is in effect in many states and restricts the number of jobs or educational seats that may be given to people of other states who speak other languages and who have different cultures. The quota system restricts the number of "high"-caste Tamils who can obtain seats in professional colleges and get employment within their home state of Tamilnadu; the "sons of the soil" policy adopted by other states has curbed their chances in other parts of India. Thus it is believed (though there are no records of numbers) that there is a significantly stronger representation of the "higher" castes among the Tamils in the United States than their percentage in the context of the total population in Tamilnadu.

## Marriage and Family

Tamil-speaking people in the United States generally retain conservative attitudes about marriage and family, but many transformations have taken place in the diaspora. Arranged marriages—that is, marriages along caste lines, where the parents of the bride and groom play a predominant role in bringing the couple together—are the norm in India. However, although some caste distinctions are retained in the United States, it is not with the rigor found in India, and the pool of likely brides and bridegrooms is generally enlarged to include many subcastes and parallel castes that would not be considered eligible for matrimonial alliances within India.

Some Tamil families in the United States return to India to get a partner for a child who is ready to be married. In traditional circumstances, especially in the Brahmanical castes, the horoscopes of the prospective bride and bridegroom are matched first before the young couple meet. The young man and woman usually are given a choice after they meet to decide if they want to continue to know each other. If they like each other, the announcement of the engagement is swift. The wedding may take place in India if the older generation of relatives lives there. If the wedding is celebrated in the United States, it is usually in one of the large community halls connected with a Hindu temple. Weddings last several hours, and if one includes the reception, the celebrations usually take the whole day. The bride and bridegroom dress in traditional clothes; the bride may change her heavy silk sari several times during the wedding ritual, and the bridegroom wears a *dhoti* or *veshti* (a gold-laced white cloth) wrapped around his waist.

Although Shyam Selvadurai, a Tamil-speaking Sri Lankan writer, wrote a highly acclaimed fictional work on homosexuality, *Funny Boy*, the subject is not openly discussed by Tamils even in such outspoken forums as electronic usernet groups.

## Food

Unlike other groups from India (such as Gujarati-speaking people), Tamils do not have several generations of people living in the same household. The first generation of Tamil immigrants has not yet reached the stage of retirement in the United States. This generation does not consider American retirement homes as an option. The dietary factor is very important in making these decisions. Many Tamils retain the dietary habits and ethnic cuisine common to South India. Very few castes and communities within the Tamils are vegetarians (all Indian vegetarians consume dairy products), and the cooking style is distinctive and different from that of northern India. Most first-generation Tamils are faithful to the ethnic diet of the Tamilnadu area.

## Associations

Almost all the major cities in the United States have one or two Tamil sangams or manrams, and these societies keep active count of their members. Tamils are justifiably proud of their literary and cultural heritage, and they try to maintain and transmit the awareness of this culture to the younger generation through activities sponsored by Hindu temples as well as by Tamil associations. The New Jersey Tamil sangam, founded in 1989 at Rutgers University and inaugurated by a Hindu religious preacher, now has about five hundred families as members. The goals of the New Jersey Tamil sangam, which are similar to those of other Tamil associations around the country, are to (1) provide a unified forum for Tamils in their area, promote Tamil culture, and celebrate Tamil festivals, (2) organize special projects in Tamilnadu, (3) promote Tamil scholars and artists, (4) help other Tamils, (5) actively participate in the Federation of Tamil Sangams of North America (FeTNA), and (6) make Tamil youths aware of their heritage.

FeTNA, located in North Potomac, Maryland, is an umbrella organization of North American Tamil sangams. It was founded in 1987 by five Tamil sangams and inaugurated in 1988, with more than four hundred families attending the function in Philadelphia. FeTNA was started to help Tamils "spread over the entire country . . . obtain a sense of Tamil Togetherness." The primary objectives of FeTNA are the "preservation and growth of Tamil Language, Culture and Community." FeTNA organizes annual conventions and sponsors one or more Tamil scholars each year. In the 1990s, it has provided support to raise funds for the Tamil Chair at the University of California at Berkeley. Many Tamil sangams routinely celebrate the Tamil New Year (which usually falls between April 13 and 15); Pongal (a Tamil "harvest" festival usually observed on January 14); and other Hindu festivals, such as Deepavali (Diwali), which is celebrated in October and November. They also host drama troupes from India, popular and classical music concerts, classical dances, and showings of Tamil movies. Other associations, such as the Thamizh sangam of Missouri (which lists one hundred Tamil families as members), have Tamil schools for youths, broadcast Tamil songs on radio stations, and conduct *pattimanram*, a traditional form of debating that goes back to about the fourth century C.E. This association prides itself in articulating a line from the famous Tamil poet Subramania Bharati: "One should cause the sweet sounds of Tamil to spread all over the world." Large institutions such as the University of Texas have Tamil students' associations.

## Religion

Tamils tend to socialize with Telugu- and Kannada-speaking people from South India. These South Indian communities also have their own Hindu temples, which are different in architecture and forms of worship from North Indian temples. Cities such as Pittsburgh and Atlanta have both North and South Indian temples. Tamil-speaking people, with the assistance of Alagappa Alagappan

of the United Nations, were responsible for organizing the committees to build the first South Indian temple in the United States, a temple to the Hindu god Ganesha in New York City. The Hindu Temple Society of North America was started in 1970, and the New York temple was consecrated on July 4, 1977. Although this (and other Hindu temples in United States) are not "Tamil temples," they cater heavily to a South Indian population, including Tamils. One unusual temple is the "Tamil Temple," also known as the Thamil Ammai Thirukkoyil, in North Brunswick, New Jersey, where the prayers are all in Tamil. In many Hindu temples the prayers are generally in Sanskrit. While temples are dedicated to the major pan-Indian gods such as Vishnu, Shiva, Ganesha, or the goddess Durga, Vishnu and Ganesha temples are predominant in North America. The Tamil god Murukan (known in other parts of India as Skanda or Kartikeya) is also worshiped in some temples. The Hindu temple in Houston is dedicated to Meenakshi, a Tamil manifestation of the goddess Parvati. The original temple to Meenakshi, a mythical princess of the Pandyan Dynasty, is located in the city of Madurai, Tamilnadu. Meenakshi, therefore, is a uniquely Tamil goddess.

Tamil-speaking Christians also have special church services for Easter and Christmas, and these are generally made known through postings on electronic bulletin boards.

Both Hindu temples and Tamil associations have regular cultural programs, ranging from classical South Indian music (Karnatic music) and classical dance (bharata natyam) to popular entertainment such as film music and drama. Many of the Tamil associations regularly meet on the local temple premises or in university halls. Tamils in the diaspora keep in active touch with the latest Tamil movies from India, and many associations screen them regularly. Many bharata natyam classes were held in the 1970s by Srimati T. Balasaraswati and Srimati Kamala Lakshminarayanan, two famous exponents of the dance form. Hundreds of such classes are now found all over the United States, and Indian newspapers in the

Tamil dancers practice for a performance of traditional dances. (Mukul Roy)

San Francisco Bay Area alone have more than two pages of advertisements for these classes. Young Tamil (and other South Indian) girls and occasionally a few boys are taught this dance form as a way of keeping in touch with the home culture. The lyrics for the dances and classical Karnatic music may be in any one of a half dozen Indian languages, but most of them are in Tamil or Telugu. The bharata natyam dance form has also been used by Tamils in the United States to choreograph the life of Jesus Christ; the show is presented as a dance-drama.

South Indian communities celebrate classical music festivals that commemorate Karnatic music composers. These musical festivals may last as long as a week, as is seen in the Cleveland Thyagaraja Festival. The songs of Thyagaraja, a composer-saint who lived in the eighteenth century in Tamil-nadu, are sung during these days. Although Thyagaraja composed in the Telugu language, more than half (and frequently up to 90 percent)

of performers in these festivals are Tamil people. Other music festivals are more eclectic and are called "Composers Day." The songs of musicians such as the Tamil composer Papanasam Sivan are also sung at these festivals. The music is either vocal or instrumental. Vocalists may be accompanied by the tambura, a background drone, one or two percussions players, and a violin. The festivals in small towns usually rely on local talent, but larger cities such as Chicago and New York feature musicians from India as part of the celebrations. Some Tamils consider exercises such as these music festivals to be entertainment of the Brahmanical castes. Variety entertainments that accompany celebrations of the Tamil New Year or other festivals usually have a few classical dances, some light classical songs, several film songs and dances, and a few Tamil skits.

## Language

Tamil is taught in weekly classes in many South Indian Hindu temples and a few Tamil associations. The written forms of the Tamil language are quite formal and different from the spoken variety. Some higher educational institutions, such as the University of Chicago and the University of California at Berkeley, offer graduate programs in the language. Despite persistent efforts of first-generation Tamils to transmit the language, its knowledge is limited among second-generation immigrants. First-generation Tamils are now making available Tamil classics in electronic form through the World Wide Web. Continued waves of emigration from India and other countries, as well as electronic communication, keep the various communities in touch with the tradition and with changes experienced by Tamils at home and in the diaspora.

*See also:*   SOUTH ASIAN CHRISTIANS; SRI LANKANS

## Bibliography

Hart, G. L., III. (1975). *The Poems of Ancient Tamil: Their Milieu and Sanskrit Counterparts*. Berkeley: University of California Press.

Hart, G. L., III. (1979). *The Poets of the Tamil Anthologies*. Princeton, NJ: Princeton University Press.

Jensen, J. M. (1988). *Passage from India: Asian Immigrants in North America*. New Haven, CT: Yale University Press.

Klein, M. H.; Alexander, A. A.; Miller, M. H.; Haack, L. J.; and Bushnell, N. J. (1986). "Indian Students in the United States: Personal and Professional Issues in Cross-Cultural Education." In *Tradition and Transformation: Asian Indians in America*, edited by R. H. Brown and G. V. Coelho. Williamsburg, VA: Department of Anthropology, College of William and Mary.

Narayanan, V. (1992). "Creating the South Indian Hindu Experience in the United States." In *A Sacred Thread: Modern Transmissions of Hindu Traditions in India and Abroad*, edited by R. B. Williams. Chambersburg, PA: Anima Press.

Ramanujan, A. K. (1967). *Interior Landscape: Love Poems from a Classical Tamil Anthology*. Bloomington: Indiana University Press.

Ramanujan, A. K. (1985). *Poems of Love and War*. New York: Columbia University Press.

Saran, P., and Eames, E., eds. (1980). *The New Ethnics: Asian Indians in the United States*. New York: Praeger.

Singh, J., ed. (1988). *South Asians in North America: An Annotated and Selected Bibliography*. Berkeley: Center for South and Southeast Asia Studies, University of California.

U.S. Bureau of the Census. (1990a). *Language Spoken at Home and Ability to Speak English for United States, Regions, and States: 1990* (CPH-L 133). Washington, DC: U.S. Government Printing Office.

U.S. Bureau of the Census. (1990b). *Social and Economic Characteristics of Selected Language Groups for U.S. and States: 1990* (CPH-L 159). Washington, DC: U.S. Government Printing Office.

VASUDHA NARAYANAN

# TELUGUS

Telugu is a member of the Dravidian family of languages spoken in southern India. Evidence of written materials in Telugu dates back to 633 C.E. A well-established literary tradition in Telugu can be traced from the eleventh century C.E., when the project of translating the *Mahabharata* (a Sanskrit epic) into Telugu was undertaken. Therefore, Telugu can boast of a literary tradition going back almost a thousand years. Telugu shares some similarities with other Dravidian languages such as Tamil and Kannada and has been influenced by Sanskrit, but Telugu is still recognized as distinct from these other languages. Andhra is another name for Telugu, so speakers of the language can therefore be identified as either Telugus or Andhras.

The majority of the Telugu-speakers are concentrated in the state of Andhra Pradesh (one of the largest states of India, ranking fifth in both area and population). A few Telugu-speakers reside in the neighboring states of Tamil Nadu, Karnataka, and Orissa, and some have migrated to the large urban centers in other parts of India to find employment. The number of people who speak Teluga in India is second only to the number of people who speak Hindi, the national language.

Despite the fact that the speakers of a given language often reside in a contiguous area, the political and administrative divisions of the states or provinces of India have not always followed the linguistic divisions. Often, the influence and reach of kingdoms was spread across regions where different languages were spoken. In fact, language as an important political marker of identity did not develop until after India gained independence from British rule in 1947. At that point the Telugus were among the first to make political demands on the basis of linguistic identity, and the reorganization of independent India along linguistic lines was prompted by the Telugu demand for a separate province. In 1953, Andhra was formed as the first linguistic province in India, and, with the addition of other Telugu-speaking areas, the state of Andhra Pradesh, whose official language is Telugu, was formed in 1956. Based on geographical and cultural variations, the state of Andhra Pradesh can be subdivided into the Coastal Region, Rayalaseema, and Telangana.

## Immigration History

During the nineteenth and twentieth centuries, many Telugus emigrated from India to other parts of the world. Their general destinations included Southeast Asia, Mauritius, Fiji, and South Africa. While a few of these Telugu families did immigrate to the United States, the bulk of the Telugu immigrants arrived in America only after the Immigration Act of 1965 went into effect, eliminating national quotas. Most of the early Telugu immigrants came from the Coastal Region of Andhra Pradesh, and that area continues to be the dominant source for new immigrants. However, the number of people emigrating from Rayalaseema and Telangana has increased over the years due to a wider dissemination of opportunities for education and social mobility.

The number of Telugu immigrants in the United States is lower than the number of other Asian Indian immigrant groups, such as Hindi-speakers, Urdu-speakers, Gujarati-speakers, or Punjabi-speakers. However, the number of Telugu immigrants has been rising. Some estimates place the Telugu population in the United States between twenty and twenty-five thousand. This is not a significant portion of the entire Asian Indian population in the United States, especially given the size of the population of Andhra Pradesh, but the Telugu population in the United States is significant when compared to the size of other linguistic groups from southern India such as Kannada-speakers or Oriya-speakers.

The terms of the Immigration Act of 1965 also influenced the composition of arrivals, giving preference to trained personnel. Therefore, a number of Telugus who arrived during the post-1965 period were engineers, physicians, scientists, and professors. This trend has continued with only slight modifications resulting from subsequent immigration laws. Not many Telugu businessmen have emigrated from India, although some successful Telugu professionals in the United States have moved into the business and investment fields and become entrepreneurs. The average income of Telugu immigrants compares favorably with the average income for all Asian Indians in the United

States and tends to be higher than the overall American average. Despite the success of Telugus on the professional level in the United States, there continues to be a feeling among some of them that they cannot reach the top executive positions because of their status as immigrants. This is an important point because material success in the United States has increasingly become the social marker of prestige in the Telugu society back in India. Successful Telugu immigrants are able to provide economic assistance to their families and friends still living in India, and families in Andhra Pradesh are eager to give their children in marriage to successful immigrants in the United States, since such an alliance usually means a huge turnabout in the economic fortunes of those families.

Most Telugu immigrants live in California (where many computer professionals have arrived since the 1980s), New York, Illinois, Texas, Florida, Maryland, Michigan, and Ohio. First-generation immigrants, immigrants who grew up in India, still form the majority in the Telugu immigrant community, and they have tended to remain conservative and traditional in their lifestyle. The overall character of the group is strongly influenced by this factor, resulting in a pattern of cultural persistence rather than assimilation. Relations with other Asian Indian groups are close, but the affinity among the Telugus is stronger. They remain in close touch with one another and maintain close contacts with families still living in India. Most Telugu immigrants are Hindu, and over the years a number of Hindu temples have sprung up across the United States. However, some Telugu immigrants are Christian, and there are instances of church congregations for Asian Indian Christian communities in the United States. It should also be noted that some Telugu immigrants are Muslim.

## Language Maintenance

A number of first-generation immigrants who want their children to learn Telugu commonly lament that the members of the second-generation (most of whom are still children or young adults) are not serious about staying in touch with the language of their ancestry. In fact, few members of the second-generation have learned to speak and write in Telugu, although a great number follow the language when spoken, since the parents continue to speak Telugu at home. Parents, in addition to dealing with their children's lack of enthusiasm for learning Telugu, must deal with the fact that facilities for learning Telugu in the United States are limited. Some temples run summer schools to teach Telugu to the members of the second generation, but only one institution of higher learning in the United States, the University of Wisconsin at Madison, offers an intensive summer course in Telugu.

## Telugu Associations

Local associations have been found wherever Telugu immigrants have settled in significant numbers. Such associations, which generally have cultural orientations, can be found in large cities such as New York, Los Angeles, Chicago, Philadelphia, Houston, and Washington, D.C. Some of these associations have been publishing magazines and journals in Telugu since the 1970s. Participation in Telugu associations allows first-generation immigrants to maintain their strong interests in the literature, culture, and fine arts of the Telugu society. It also allows them to introduce the second generation to the various aspects of their cultural heritage. First-generation immigrants encourage their children, especially their daughters, to learn Karnatic music, classical music of South India, and Kuchipudi and Bharata Natyam, classical dance forms native to the Andhra society. The Telugu associations give active support to individuals who teach music and dance in the United States and often sponsor artists, singers, dancers and other performers from Andhra Pradesh to tour America. Films are also an important part of the Telugu culture. The number of films made in India in Telugu is second only to the number made in Hindi. Watching these movies is a popular pastime in Andhra Pradesh, and the Telugu immigrants have carried the habit with them to the United States. Telugu films, which are popular with the second generation as well as the first generation,

are screened on a regular basis in large cities such as Detroit, but they are also readily available on video cassettes.

The Telugu Association of North America (TANA), which has existed since 1977 and has a number of regional affiliations, is the most important pan-American organization of Telugus in the United States. Every two years, TANA holds conventions that are attended by thousands of Telugu immigrants. Since a number of Telugu immigrants have invested in industries and businesses in Andhra Pradesh, they use the conventions as an opportunity to make important decisions about how they should manage their investments in India. TANA also wields considerable influence with important political parties in Andhra Pradesh, so it is common for leaders of the state government in Andhra Pradesh to attend the TANA conventions in the United States.

## Culture and Conflict

Many of the wives of first-generation Telugus (who, as stated before, generally came from the middle- and upper-classes of Andhra society) did not work for a living in India. The women did not *need* to work for a living because their husbands earned incomes that provided sufficiently for the needs of the entire family, and they were not *encouraged* to work for a living. In the United States, however, these attitudes are changing. The economic benefits resulting from both spouses being employed and the absence of taboos against women working are gradually leading many more Telugu women to seek employment.

Children of the first-generation immigrants are exhibiting significant differences of behavior from those of their parents. The members of the second generation, most of whom were born in the United States, have adopted a number of American values and cultural characteristics. Intergenerational conflicts between Telugu parents and their children occur over a number of issues, including the children's previously mentioned lack of enthusiasm for learning the Telugu language and culture. Another source of conflict is the fact that the first-generation immigrants, who worked hard to be able to immigrate to the United States and be successful upon arrival, find it difficult to inspire in their children the discipline necessary for success. Growing up in relative affluence compared to their parents, second-generation immigrants do not always give the same importance to the value of discipline and education. In addition, the children expect a greater degree of freedom in their personal lives, including dating choices.

The demands for personal freedoms are often difficult for the conservative members of the first-generation to accept because they want their children to marry within the castes or communities of their origin. The parents sometimes succeed in convincing their children, especially their daughters, to marry within the group, and in such cases, the rate of divorce has remained low. While marriages between Telugus and non-Indian racial groups remain rare, there have been an increasing number of marriages occurring between members of different Asian Indian communities and linguistic groups. This new patterns of marriages between different Asian Indian groups has allowed a broader Asian Indian or South Asian identity to emerge in the United States.

Because the society they were emigrating from was quite different from American society, early Telugu immigrants felt isolated and needed time for adjustment when they first arrived in the United States. As the number of immigrant Telugus has gradually increased, however, this feeling of isolation has lessened. In many cases, new immigrants are joining friends or family members already in the United States, providing them with a familiar circle of people who will assist them in adapting to the new culture more quickly. Over the years, due to improvements in communication technology in both the United States and India, it has become far easier for the Telugu immigrants to stay in touch with one another and with friends and families back in Andhra Pradesh. The amount of travel back and forth between the United States and India has also increased, so Telugu immigrants are more likely to have relations from Andhra Pradesh visiting them temporarily or joining them on a more permanent basis.

Communication has also been facilitated by the Internet, which allows Telugus to stay in touch with each other, talk about topics of common interest, stay abreast of current events in Andhra Pradesh, and learn about Telugu literature, film, or music.

## Conclusion

Despite the strong attachment of the first-generation immigrants to the Telugu culture, there is little evidence of any return migration to Andhra Pradesh. Higher income, superior material lifestyle, and the presence of their children in the United States are usually contributing factors to the reluctance of many first-generation immigrants to return to India. However, isolation from the culture of their origin and the need to return have partly been obviated by the improved communications that allow them to stay in touch and make frequent trips to India.

Curiously, these improved communications also make it easier for the first-generation immigrants to imagine that they are only temporarily "away from home," allowing them to persist with their own culture and resist the pressures to assimilate into the mainstream culture. Therefore, it is only very gradually that the members of the second generation are going to be able to make their imprint on the character of the Telugu immigrant community in the United States.

*See also:*    SOUTH ASIAN CHRISTIANS

## Bibliography

Chandrasekhar, S., ed. (1982). *From India to America: A Brief History of Immigration, Problems of Discrimination, Admission, and Assimilation.* La Jolla, CA: Population Review Publications.

Daniels, R. (1989). *History of Indian Immigration to the United States: An Interpretive Essay.* New York: Asia Society.

Jensen, J. M. (1988). *Passage from India: Asian Indian Immigrants in North America.* New Haven: Yale University Press.

Muthanna, I. M. (1982). *People of India in North America: United States, Canada, W. Indies, and Fiji: Immigration History of East-Indians up to 1960*, 2nd ed. Bangalore: Gangarams Book Distributors.

Saran, P. (1985). *The Asian Indian Experience in the United States*. Cambridge, MA: Schenkman.

Saran, P., and Eames, E., ed. (1980). *The New Ethnics: Asian Indians in the United States*. New York: Praeger.

RAJAGOPAL VAKULABHARANAM

# THAI

Thai in the United States are a group of people who came from Thailand and reside in the United States with or without legal documentation. This includes both American-born and naturalized Thai Americans. Thai share a common language and cultural heritage, which serve as their ethnic identification and their natural bonding tie.

## Immigration and Settlement History

Most Thai Americans are part of an Asian-American immigration wave that peaked during the 1960s and 1970s. This is substantially due to the Immigration Act of 1965, which was fully implemented in 1968. Earlier, in 1952, Congress passed the McCarran-Walter Act to nullify the racial restriction of a 1790 naturalization act that specified that only white people could become U.S. citizens. Although the McCarran-Walter Act allowed non-Caucasians to be naturalized, it restricted the number of immigrants by national-origin quota. Only one hundred immigrants from Southeast and East Asian countries could enter the United States each year, whereas immigrants from European countries were allowed to become citizens under a 1924 immigration law. During the 1960s, the civil rights movement was instrumental in raising American consciousness regarding racial equality, which also implied equality for those seeking entry into the United States. Under President Lyndon B. Johnson's leadership, Congress passed the Immigration Act of 1965 to amend the McCarran-Walter Act. The new law eliminated national-origin quotas and provided a legal framework within which Thai joined other Asian groups to constitute more than half of the immigrants who entered the United States during the last quarter of the twentieth century. While the Immigration Act of 1965 repealed the quota system, it introduced seven preferences for countries in the eastern hemisphere. They include preferences for professionals, scientist and artists of "exceptional ability," and for skilled and unskilled workers in occupations in short supply in the United States. A large number of Thai professionals, expecially medical doctors, nurses, scientists, pharmacists, and engineers immigrated between 1968 and 1976, creating a so-called brain drain crisis in Thailand. These professionals also brought with them their immediate families, siblings, and parents. Some were also able to bring their domestic help from Thailand.

Sociopolitical and economic conditions in Thailand during late 1960s and 1970s also played a crucial role in this immigration pattern. The worldwide petroleum crisis had a significant impact on the Thai economy, creating high inflation and job scarcity. Medical doctors, nurses, scientists, and engineers were not paid at the rate they felt their special training deserved. Chances for professional development and mobility appeared to be limited. The country was under a military dictatorship, and there was unrest among students, workers, and farmers. In addition, the Vietnam War and wars in neighboring Laos and Kampuchea (Cambodia) threatened Thai security and stability.

Thai who were already in the United States to study during the 1960s and 1970s also saw an opportunity under the Immigration Act of 1965 and decided to stay permanently. They later applied to have their spouses, minor children, and parents join them.

During the Vietnam War there were several U.S. military bases in Thailand. Some servicemen

A Thai immigrant banana farmer in the Homestead, Florida, area checks the damage resulting from a hurricane. (Raymond Gehman/Corbis)

flew to Thailand on leave. A large number of Thai women who married U.S. servicemen during this period followed their spouses to the United States after the war in Southeast Asia. The 1987 American Homecoming Act, which was passed primarily to allow children born of U.S. military personnel in Vietnam to enter the United States also benefited Thai-American children in Thailand.

Thai who arrived in the United States under the Immigration Act of 1965 were mainly concentrated in California, Texas, Illinois, and New York. They initially stayed with friends, families, or their job contact before moving to establish themselves. Because of their emphasis on close ties to family and community, most Thai choose to live near friends and family, creating ethnic residential communities such as those in the Hollywood area of Los Angeles and Elmhurst, Queens, in New York City.

## Demography

The 1990 U.S. Census lists the number of Thai Americans at 91,275 and classifies them as one of the ten largest Asian groups in the United States. This census also indicates that the majority of Thai Americans reside mostly in five states: California (32,064), New York (6,230), Texas (5,816), Illinois (5,180), and Florida (4,457). California, being located on the West Coast and having a climate similar to that of Thailand, is understandably the state of choice for residence for most Thai. However, the number of Thai Americans listed in the 1990 U.S. Census is significantly lower than the actual number of Thai residing in the United States on a permanent basis. Thai community leaders estimate that more than 100,000 Thai live in California, with the largest concentration in southern California, especially in Los Angeles, and in northern California, around San Francisco. There are more than two hundred Thai restaurants in California alone, and as many as twenty in New York City. A significant number of Thai whose presence is not reflected in the U.S. Census data ignored the census registration, entered the country with or without proper legal documentation, or are changing their residential status.

The immigration and settlement of Thai vary over time. Earlier Thai immigrants were mostly urban or suburban professionals. They were a well-educated, middle-aged group of men and women. Thai immigrants who arrived after 1976 under restricted immigration laws constitute a mixed group of skilled and unskilled male and female workers, young and old, who were seeking economic opportunities. The Thai workers who drew national attention in 1995 because of abusive treatment they received in a sweatshop in El Monte, California, reflect the mixed composition of the later Thai immigrants. Regardless of the level of their labor skills, most Thai concentrate in the metropolitan areas in major cities in the East (New York City), West (Los Angeles, San Francisco, and Seattle) and Midwest (Chicago). The majority of the first generation and first wave of Thai immigrants are entering retirement age. A number of them contemplate returning to Thailand when they retire and when their children finish college. Seeing that Thailand is in a much better economic condition and is more politically stable than when they immigrated to the United States, some have decided to return to start new businesses and/or continue their careers in Thailand. Some leave their families behind, with the intention of visiting them annually.

## Language

There are four dialects spoken in Thailand: the northern, northeastern, central, and southern. In addition, all Thai learn to speak and write the central Thai dialect, which is the official language. Unless one comes from the central part of the country, one is proficient in two dialects. The first wave of Thai immigrants are generally able to communicate in both Thai and English. Most spoke their native language in at least two dialects and struggled to improve their English-language skill when they arrived in the United States. The second generation of Thai Americans are faced with a reverse language proficiency situation. Children of Thai immigrants mostly learn to speak their parents' native language at home. They attend public or private schools with children of other racial groups but largely do not have a written knowledge of Thai. Although there are Thai newspapers published in major cities such as New York, Los Angeles, and San Francisco, their readers are mostly first-generation Thai immigrants or Thai nationals who are in the United States to further their education or to conduct business. Language schools have been organized in Buddhist temples or churches during the weekend to assist younger generations to learn Thai. However, this effort is sporadic and takes place only in cities where there is a big concentration of Thai Americans.

## Cultural Characteristics

*Economic Patterns.* Like other Asian-American groups, Thai immigrants find themselves in a "bipolar occupational structure," meaning a concentration of workers in both low-paid service occupations and high-paying professional occupations, with comparatively few in between. Faced with the issue of survival for themselves and their families, new immigrants have worked in occupations not in their special training categories and at a much lower level than their qualifications. It is common to find university graduates working at gas stations, janitorial and cleaning services, handyman services, or waiting tables in Thai restaurants. Unable to find well-paying employment, those with better financial resources have resorted to self-employment. Many operate car garages, jewelry, grocery, or appliance stores, or shipping and import-export companies targeted to Thai customers. Those with less technological skills usually find domestic work. Highly trained and specialized Thai professionals in health care as well as architects, attorneys, scientists, and engineers, are more fortunate. These individuals are likely to find occupations in their area and to experience the life of professional middle-class Americans. However, like other Asian Americans, they also encounter a "glass ceiling" in their professions, becoming what Edna Bonacich and John Modell typify in *The Economic Basis of Ethnic Solidarity* (1981) as "middlemen minorities." According to Bonacich and Modell, this situation occurs as a result of being excluded from other work and not because of success. The absence of Thai executives in major corporations indicates that the door to top managerial or executive positions is still closed to talented and highly qualified Thai, as it is to members of several other ethnic groups.

*Religion and Worldview.* There is a saying with which most Thai are familiar: "To be a Thai is to be a Buddhist." Thai immigrants brought their cultural and religious beliefs with them. These include in particular a belief in Buddhism, which in practice is a combination of beliefs in Brahmanism, animism, and Theravada Buddhism. In keeping with the tradition of their native country, Thais have built Buddhist temples in cities that have the largest concentration of Thai (New York, Chicago, Dallas, Los Angeles, and San Francisco). There are, for example, at least six temples in southern California. Monks are sent from Thailand to staff the temples, indicating a strong cultural tie that the immigrants still have with their native land. Besides serving as a place to teach Buddhism, celebrate significant religious events, and provide religious services for individuals and families, Buddhist temples also function as centers for spiritual guidance and cultural activities where monks are available to provide counsel and religious services and where Thai-language classes for children are conducted on weekends. In addition, lessons on Thai dance, Thai handicrafts, and Thai cooking are offered at the temples.

A much smaller number of Thai immigrants practice Christianity. There are a few Thai Protestant congregations in southern California, Chicago, Illinois, Houston and Fort Worth, Texas, and

Thai dancers in traditional costumes perform in Chicago. (Mukul Roy)

Brooklyn, New York. Similar to the role the temple plays in the Buddhist community, the church is a center of spiritual, cultural, and social activities for its members. Additionally, it is a place for immigrants to share their stories and concerns.

*Family and Kinship.* Family is the most important social unit in the lives of Thai. Regardless of the rapid change in society and the lesser role the family plays in modern lives, the concept of family remains strong and intact in the Thai social system. Traditionally the Thai family is a unit of an extended-family system. It includes all members in the immediate family, all the in-laws, and all relatives and cousins who share the same family tree. In some cases, everyone in the same village or neighborhood is related. The so-called *yad phiinong*, or relatives, is thus a broad and comprehensive term in understanding Thai social relations. In the United States this concept is extended to include brothers and sisters from Thailand. The term *khon tai muangun* (Thai people) creates a sense of ethnic solidarity among the immigrants. It generates a feeling of being related as a family. Generally, individuals feel obligated to provide for the needs and care of those who share their family tie. This includes providing food, shelter, and financial assistance as well as emotional support. Although their lives in the United States are very different from what they left behind, Thai immigrants gladly assist the new arrivals. In time of personal crisis, illness, or death in the family, the yad phiinong will generally even travel a distance to provide emotional support and fill material needs.

*Marriage.* The traditional way of choosing one's partner has been altered by American lifestyle and influence. Traditionally, Thai have been allowed to decide whom to marry, but parents play a key role in arranging the marriage. In the United States, young people are free to date and marry a person of their choice, although approval of parents and relatives still is a much-wanted blessing. It is no longer expected that once married, a daughter-in-law lives with her spouse and his parents. Divorce among Thai used to be rare, but today separation and divorce occur; the parties are not met with disapproval from family and community, and they feel free to remarry.

*Social and Political Organization.* As members of a racial group in the United States, Thai are concerned with their place, rights, and security in the new country. Thai associations are formed in cities of their highest concentration to provide networks of information, legal services, and support to members. Most immigrants are strongly loyal to their native country and keep in close touch with socioeconomic and political events and trends in Thailand. Like other Asian American groups (i.e., Koreans, Filipinos, and Chinese) in the past, several groups of Thai in the United States organize themselves around issues of political struggle in Thailand. For example, during the 1970s, several Thai-American associations rallied to provide political and financial support for groups in Thailand opposing the military regime there. They wrote letters to members of the U.S. Congress, asking them to protest against the Thai government's treatment of political dissidents and to pressure the government to implement democracy in Thailand.

*See also:* BUDDHISTS; HMONG; KHMU; LAO; MIEN

## Bibliography

Bonacich, E. (1989). "Inequality in America: The Failure of the American System for People of Color." *Sociological Spectrum* 9(1):71–101.

Bonacich, E., and Modell, J. (1981). *The Economic Basis of Ethnic Solidarity.* Berkeley: University of California Press.

Chan, S. (1991). *Asian Americans: An Interpretive History.* New York: Twayne.

Kangvalert, W. (1986). "Thai Physicians in the United States: Causes and Consequences of the Brain Drain." Ph.D. diss., State University of New York at Buffalo.

Kitano, H. H. L., and Daniels, R. (1995). *Asian Americans: Emerging Minorities.* Englewood Cliffs, NJ: Prentice Hall.

Larson, W. (1989). *Confessions of a Mail Order Bride: American Life Through Thai Eyes.* Far Hills, NJ: New Horizon Press.

Reimers, D. M. (1983). "An Unintended Reform: The 1965 Immigration Act and Third World Immigration to the United States." *Journal of American Ethnic History* 3(Fall): 9–28.

Reimers, D. M. (1985). *Still the Golden Door: The Third World Comes to America.* New York: Columbia University Press.

Schaefer, R. T. (1996). *Racial and Ethnic Groups.* New York: HarperCollins.

Takaki, R. T. (1989). *Strangers from a Different Shore: A History of Asian Americans.* Boston: Little, Brown.

NANTAWAN BOONPRASAT LEWIS

# TIBETANS

Tibetans in the United States are one of the smallest ethnic groups in the country, comprised mostly of refugees exiled from their homeland after the Chinese military occupation of Lhasa, the capital city of Tibet, in 1959. The political situation in what is now known as the Tibetan Autonomous Region (TAR) of the People's Republic of China (PRC) has resulted in a global diaspora, and Tibetans (also known as Bhopas) have fled to a number of Asian, European, and North American countries.

Although a comprehensive population census of Tibetan refugees has not been undertaken, some approximate figures have been circulated by the Tibetan Government in Exile in Dharamsala, India. Since 1959, the Department of Information and International Relations of the Central Tibetan Administration (CTA) in Dharamsala estimates that approximately 125,777 Tibetans live in exile. The largest population of "displaced" Tibetans lives in India (approximately 109,320), followed by the Himalayan kingdoms of Nepal (approximately 15,000) and Bhutan (1,457), respectively. Outside of South Asia, the largest community resides in Switzerland, where 2,000 Tibetans have settled since 1960 with the aid of the Swiss Red Cross. The United States ranks next in number. According to 1995 estimates projected by the Tibetan Community Assistance Project in New York City, a total of 1,970 Tibetans have taken up residence in the United States, while 556 live in Canada.

Due to the decades of turmoil in Tibet, it is difficult to speak of a unified Tibetan identity. Tibetans living in exile often comment that those people still residing in the TAR have become "Sinified" to a great extent. Sociological studies conducted in South Asian refugee settlements confirm that ideological and cultural conflicts exist between the indigenous Tibetan population and the diasporic communities established outside of Tibet's border. However, religion and, to a lesser degree, language have provided much common ground for mutual understanding. Faith in the political and spiritual office of His Holiness the Dalai Lama has allowed Tibetans to nurture their cultural identity. The establishment of Tibetan primary schools and higher institutes of learning in exile also have resulted in linguistic retention. Yet Tibetans both in the TAR and in exile have been adapting to the cultures in which they reside. Adaptation has led to a situation of what some researchers have termed "hyphenated" identities, namely the simultaneous display of multiple ethnic, linguistic, and cultural backgrounds as a strategy for coping with acculturation.

More than half of the Tibetans living in the United States arrived as part of a resettlement project initiated by an act of the U.S. Congress in 1990 to allow one thousand Tibetans living in India and Nepal passage to the United States with landed immigrant status. This newest wave of Tibetan immigrants was not able to choose its desired places of residence. Rather, "cluster sites" were designated by the Tibetan U.S. Resettlement Project (TUSRP) in consultation with the CTA and the U.S. State Department. Cluster sites tended to form in areas where religious and cultural centers had been established by Tibetan Buddhist monks and scholars prior to 1990. By far the largest Tibetan population is located in the New York–New Jersey area. However, populations of one hundred or more are thriving in other urban centers, such as Chicago; Los Angeles; Madison, Wisconsin; Minneapolis–St. Paul; Portland, Oregon; San Francisco; and Seattle. Smaller populations exist in a number of other cities in eighteen states throughout the country.

Although it is often contested, mostly on political grounds, the majority of linguists agree that Tibetan belongs to the Sino-Tibetan language family, one of the largest language families in the world, of which Tibetan belongs to the Tibeto-Burman branch. The classical, scriptural language of Tibet, known as Standard Written Tibetan, is transmitted in an alphabet created in the seventh century. The alphabet is derived from a variant of the North Indian brāhmī script, but modified to represent the predominantly monosyllabic language's complex initial consonant clusters. Standard Written Tibetan, however, is quite different from the colloquial language and its numerous dialects, which are arranged into five distinct groups.

The Tibetan diaspora has resulted in numerous modifications in pronunciation and word choice. Moreover, loanwords from the local languages of the host societies in which Tibetan refugees live are being constantly incorporated into spoken Tibetan. Fearing language degeneration and ultimate loss, many exilic Tibetan communities have initiated courses for language study at cultural and religious centers. Most American cities where Tibetans have settled and formed ethnic communities now contain facilities for language instruction.

## History and Cultural Relations

The first Tibetans in the United States arrived as part of a trade delegation sent by the Tibetan government in 1947. The following year a scholar and cleric named Telopa Rinpoche was invited to teach at Johns Hopkins University in Baltimore, Maryland. By 1952, a few other scholars, including the Dalai Lama's elder brother Thubten Norbu, had immigrated to the United States.

After the fall of Lhasa, a number of Tibetans from the regions of Kham and Amdo were brought to Colorado to receive military training under the aegis of the Central Intelligence Agency. Their purpose was to establish a Tibetan guerrilla force on the border between western Nepal and Tibet in the Mustang region. This program existed until 1974, when Richard Nixon established diplomatic relations with the PRC. The U.S. government also commissioned a feasibility study on introducing yak herding in Alaska to create a familiar mode of subsistence for potential Tibetan refugees. The study, which coincided with the initiation of guer-

An interior view of the Wood Valley Temple, a Tibetan Buddhist retreat in Hawaii. (Douglas Peebles/Corbis)

rilla training, suggested that the proposition of herding Tibetan yaks would cause unnecessary competition for scarce resources in the state, and the plan was dropped.

Although the Dalai Lama had established the Office of Tibet in New York in 1964, only a handful of Tibetans lived in the United States during this early period. The American interest in the Tibetan variety of Buddhism led to a slow influx of religious teachers and their entourages. In addition, some Tibetan students from India attended American universities on scholarships arranged by the Office of Tibet. A few American universities also employed learned Tibetans as assistants for classroom instruction on Tibetan culture, religion, and society. As early as 1960, for example, the Inner Asia Project at the University of Washington brought several such "informants" to work in collaboration with American scholars. While many of the clerics became permanent U.S. residents, most of the students returned to India to work for the Tibetan Government in Exile. A limited number of blue-collar settlers also arrived in the United States shortly after the establishment of the Office of Tibet.

A pilot project conceived in 1966 provided unsettled Tibetans with an opportunity to immigrate with jobs as loggers. Their sponsor was the Great Northern Paper Company of Maine, which had brought thirty Tibetans from India by 1970. The Tibetan lumberjacks, who lived and ate together in cabins at the logging camp, managed to retain much of their ethnic identity due to their close quarters, despite the fact that they received informal schooling in English, history, and geography during the evening hours from a tutor named Ruby Searway, a retired schoolteacher from Ashland, Maine. Education, coupled with daily interaction with their American counterparts, enabled the Tibetan lumberjacks to continue learning about local ways of life even as they practiced their own ethnic customs. A recession in the timber industry eventually forced the company to release the immigrants from service in early 1971. Some moved to the Northwest Coast and a few settled in New Jersey. Their dispersal led to gradual assimi-

lation, and the education they received enabled them to participate fully in mainstream American life.

According to the Office of Tibet Census, 524 Tibetans lived in the United States in 1985. By that year, associations for the preservation and revival of Tibetan culture had been established in New York and Portland, Oregan. Tibetans, along with their American supporters, used these associations to campaign actively for Tibetan rights in the homeland. The formation of associations and support groups such as the U.S. Tibet Committee and the Friends of Tibet also roughly corresponds with the establishment of the International Campaign for Tibet, which was formed in 1987 as a response to renewed Chinese suppression of protests in Lhasa. The goal of these organizations was to raise awareness about the plight of Tibetans at home and abroad, as well as to familiarize American audiences with Tibetan culture through museum exhibitions, musical performances, lectures, and other cultural activities. The awareness-raising campaign reaped great benefits, for TUSRP was founded only a few years later, in 1989.

The initial fear and concern by all parties involved at the outset of the project was that Tibetan resettlers would lose their cultural identity after arriving in America. However, after visiting the United States in 1989, the Dalai Lama himself agreed that the maintenance of ethnic and cultural identity in America was indeed possible. After protracted negotiations between Dharamsala and Washington, the U.S. State Department's Bureau of Consular Affairs agreed upon the final regulations for implementing Section 134 of the Immigration Act (allowing one thousand Tibetans to resettle in the United States) by late 1990. TUSRP then quickly established twenty-one cluster sites in eighteen states, securing employment for the potential resettlers, who were to be chosen by a lottery conducted in Dharamsala by the CTA. Finally, on April 16, 1992, the first group of Tibetan resettlers, separated from family and friends, arrived via New York at their designated cluster sites, where they lived with host families until they were able to subsist on their own. Although some still live with their sponsors, many share apartments or communally rent houses to save money to bring their families to the United States after they themselves have become citizens.

## Economy

Earlier Tibetan immigrants in the United States have managed to work their way into the American formal sector economy in diverse ways. Clerics who established or resided in Tibetan religious and cultural centers in the United States were and still are supported by the centers in exchange for their spiritual services. Those who were originally associated with universities as honorary professors, translators, or cultural informants eased into a distinct upper-middle-class or middle-class lifestyle, while others entered the culinary world, opening restaurants in many American cities (e.g., Bloomington, Indiana, has two Tibetan restaurants). Still others have capitalized on the tourist industry by opening curio shops in such fashionable locations as Sante Fe, New Mexico, and Boulder, Colorado. The shops, often supplied by itinerant relatives traveling between South Asia and North America, stock Tibetan art, clothing, and ritual implements used by Western converts to Tibetan Buddhism. Moreover, such institutions and establishments provide employment opportunities for other Tibetans who, feeling dissatisfied and alienated at their original cluster sites, seek employment in other locations.

Because many of the one thousand immigrants who arrived as part of the resettlement program do not have a good command of the English language, they have less lucrative careers, working primarily in low-paying service jobs in hotels, factories, grocery stores, the construction industry, and other occupations that require only a minimal level of skill. Low pay often forces unskilled Tibetans to take a second job. Some even work at three jobs to save for the future. Even those who learned a trade, received college degrees, or practiced a craft prior to their arrival in the United States have been forced to accept menial jobs temporarily. This is most likely due to their recent immigrant status. In a few rare instances, however, Tibetans fluent in English have worked diligently, receiving promotions to management-level positions, line bosses or foremen. The overall income of the resettlement communities, while still much less than that of the previous generation of Tibetan immigrants, is improving steadily due to hard work, thrift, and industriousness as well as generous patronage from American sympathizers.

## Kinship, Marriage, and Family

Traditionally, because of religious beliefs pertaining to spiritual liberation after successive rebirths, the Tibetan family was not viewed as a sacred institution. Rather, the family was perceived to be a biological group, a mundane necessity. But because kinship and descent were tied to land tenure, transmission of a family line as a corporate unit was economically and politically essential at all levels of society. In this sense family integrity superseded the concerns of any given individual in the unit. Kin groups, however, varied according to the family's relative position in the social hierarchy.

Tibetan society was, generally speaking, divided into two hereditary strata: aristocratic lords (*ger-ba*) and serfs (*mi-sey*). The latter were the majority. They were further divided into two classes: taxpayers (*tre-ba*) and small householders (*dü-jung*). The pattern of the serfs' connection to the lord was transmission through parallel descent, where daughters were bonded to the mother's lord and sons to the father's lord. The preferred system of descent in the kinship system was patrilineal and patrilocal, but in a case where all children were female, a groom might move into the bride's family's home and become a legal member of her family.

Marriage customs varied within the different ranks of society. Although monogamy was the general rule, polygamy (one husband, multiple wives) and polyandry (one wife, multiple husbands) were also practiced at different social levels. With the exception of the dü-jung, who chose their own spouses, marriages usually were arranged contractually by a broker for political alliance and social power in the case of the nobility and for economic and ecological stability among the tre-ba. Since the tre-ba were allotted legally inheritable land by their lord, families with more than one son most often attempted to practice polyandry to avoid the partition of the corporate family unit's land. This was not the case with the dü-jung, who held individual plots of land that were uninheritable. Some were also free agents, not bound to one estate. Spatial mobility freed them from the pressure of maintaining an extended family, allowing male children to establish their own nuclear households after marriage. An understanding of marriage patterns in traditional Tibetan society must thus be seen in the context of social stratification and land tenure.

Most of the recent immigrants to the United States do not own land, so the question of inheritance has not been thoroughly researched. Some at cluster sites are devising schemes to pool resources for communal housing, although the legal question concerning how to divide such communal property in future generations has not been adequately addressed.

Marriage patterns have changed considerably in post-1959 Tibet and in the exiled communities scattered throughout the world. In South Asia, where the Tibetan communities are larger, the custom of arranged marriage still takes place on a regular basis. However, the landless nature of the Tibetan refugees in India, for example, has made land tenure a moot point, thereby allowing more flexibility in arranging for suitable partners. In the United States and elsewhere in the West, marriage has adapted to American law and custom. Although many refugees arrive in the United States already married, some choose their own spouses within the refugee community. Intermarriage with other American ethnic groups also is becoming more frequent.

The domestication process has been altered by dislocation, modernization, and acculturation to American life. Many new immigrants who were separated from their families as a result of the lottery tend to live somewhat insulated lives, yearning for the day when they might be able to bring their families to the United States after they themselves have become citizens. Traditional gender roles also have changed, due to occupational shifts. Virtually all Tibetans in the United States work at paid jobs, including women with small children. Unmarried Tibetans tend to adapt very quickly to American ways of life, even though there is a strong tendency in the communities to maintain a modified Tibetan lifestyle.

A good deal of variation exists in patterns of socialization due to class differences. In general, Tibetan families in the United States attempt to nurture values derived from a Buddhist system of morals and ethics. Intermarriage with people of other ethnic backgrounds also has resulted in a blending of American and Tibetan child-rearing practices. Tibetan children born in the United States tend to show an early disinterest in their own ethnic culture in favor of embracing American popular culture. An earlier rejection of their ethnic heritage often leads to a "rediscovery" of tradition during the late teen years.

## Sociopolitical Organization and Control

A traditional type of organization known as *kidu* operates in Tibet and abroad as a mutal aid association. The kidu is a voluntary and egalitarian structure allowing membership to any Tibetan. The function of the kidu is to provide reciprocal services to members at times of crisis and illness. The Tibetan lumberjacks referred to earlier organized a similar type of association in Maine, and after 1991, numerous charitable bodies were established at the cluster sites to assist in the resettlement of new Tibetan immigrants. Many of these organizations are not created for Tibetans only, for American "friends" and sponsors are involved in lending services to the Tibetan community.

Although many people involved with the associations are regionally linked through common affiliations with Tibetan Buddhist temples or centers, others use the associations for activist reasons. Both Tibetans and their American hosts mobilize support for the cause of a "Free Tibet"

Tibetan Americans protest on Tibetan Uprising Day, March 10, 1993, about China's occupation of Tibet. (Alison Wright/Corbis)

through such organizations. Political lobbying, letter-writing campaigns, fundraising, peaceful rallies, and protests against the PRC's claims of sovereignty over Tibet are just some of the activities rooted in these charitable structures. In addition, because Tibetans in exile belong to a "stateless society," most pledge allegiance to the Dalai Lama's Government in Exile. Some more influential members of the Tibetan-American community even maintain transnational links with the Tibetan government in Dharamsala through their overseas involvement with the diasporic political infrastructure.

Tibet, being a "feudal theocracy" prior to 1959, contained a centralized government in Lhasa under the Dalai Lama. It also contained a decentralized element, allowing monasteries and aristocratic estates a great deal of freedom to resolve local conflicts in the most expedient manner. Given the pervasive religious element in Tibetan law and politics, many troubled immigrants in the United States seek advice from a Tibetan monk at the nearest religious center. In some cases, older lay members may also be sought out to resolve a familial dispute or other kinds of social discord within the ethnic community. When a social violation or crime involves non-Tibetans, the American legal system is, of course, used.

Criminal activity within the Tibetan community is reportedly very rare. In a few instances, Tibetans have been involved in confrontations bordering on criminality. Incidents, however, have almost always been connected to demonstrations and skirmishes in the context of organized civil disobedience to raise awareness about the Tibetan political cause.

A Tibetan Buddhist monk creates a sand painting of a mandala. (Morton Beebe-S.F./Corbis)

## Religion and Expressive Culture

Although Bon, an earlier religion based on shamanistic practices, still maintains a following in Tibet and in exile, Tibetan culture has been profoundly influenced by Buddhism. Tibetan Buddhism developed in the seventh century C.E., twelve centuries after the life of its historical founder, Gautama Buddha. Four Buddhist orders emerged in Tibet: Nyingmapa, Kargyu, Sakya, and Gelugpa. The last, established by Tsongkhapa in the fourteenth century, has been central to Tibetan religion especially since the seventeenth century, due to the lineage's innovative institutionalization of the office of the Dalai Lama as a system of spiritual and political succession through incarnation. Moreover, identifying Chenrezig, the patron deity of Tibet and progenitor of the Tibetan people, in the lineage of the country's ruler ulti-

mately allowed for the consolidation of hegemonic control over all of Tibet. These central socioreligious beliefs pervade all Tibetan belief and act as a unifying force for the global community of exiled Tibetans.

Specialists in ritual, prophecy, meditational practices, and a whole range of cultic phenomena existed on the "folk" and monastic levels. Numerous oracles were quite common in Tibet, specializing in predicting the future and exorcizing demons and spirits, which they did by going into a trance and speaking in tongues through an assistant. Shamans also operated in various capacities as healers, exorcists, and ritualists. Buddhist monks, however, were the most visible presence, constituting 20 to 30 percent of the total male population of Tibet. Their role as clerics and spiritual consultants permeated every aspect of Tibetan social life. In exile, monks still serve an important role in Tibetan communities, acting as spiritual guides, ritual specialists, and social workers for the diasporic community.

The Tibetan calendar is filled with a number of special occasions during which both religious and secular performances occur. In addition, such events are occasions for social gatherings and the preparation of special foods. Ceremonies range from celebrating the Dalai Lama's birthday and the day he received the Nobel Peace Prize to the commemoration of the Lhasa Uprising. Perhaps the largest and most important festival, however, occurs on Losar, the Tibetan New Year. Rites of passage such as birth, marriage, and death are also occasions for social gatherings.

Tibet has produced a number of artistic traditions. Perhaps best known in the West is the tradition of religious *thangka* painting. Sacred arts also include a number of other media, such as stonemasonry, carpentry, and metalwork. In addition, a number of religious performing arts exist. These include monastic dances called *cham,* multiphonic changing and singing, stylized verbal debates, and instrumental music. In the secular realm, folktales, songs, and operas known as *Lhamo* thrive. Many Tibetan communities in the United States have established performing groups to perpetuate their rich heritage of expressive traditions. A few professional troupes, whose members were mostly trained at the Tibetan Institute of Performing Arts in Dharamsala, also exist. They tour regularly, offering workshops for amateur troupes and the general public.

Medicine was and still is part of the ecclesiastical sector, since healing practices came from India to Tibet when Buddhism was introduced. It is based on the Ayurveda system used by Buddhists and Hindus in India, combined with indigenous theories of plant and mineral use. The art of healing is thus a complex set of theories using anatomical maps, herbs, fruits, precious minerals, and animal products. Illness is thought to be an imbalance of the "three humors": bile, phlegm, and air. The imbalance is also thought to be directly connected with psychological imbalances. The method employed to heal the individual is thus a psychoreligious one that strives to remove the underlying cause of the patient's imbalance. A number of well-known Tibetan monk-doctors visit the United States frequently, treating Tibetan Americans and the general public regularly.

Buddhists believe in successive reincarnation, ultimately leading to liberation from the cycle of birth and death through adherence to the religion's major tenets embodied in the Four Noble Truths and the Eightfold Path of spiritual practice. However, Tibetans have paid close ritual and philosophical attention to the period between births. The *Bardo Thodol* (Tibetan Book of the Dead) describes the critical forty-nine days between births. Performing the prescribed rituals during this interim period is essential to securing a proper rebirth; otherwise the deceased may come back to life in a fierce form to wreck havoc on human society. Funerary practices ranged from embalming Dalai Lamas and cremating important monks to the unusual practice of what is often termed "sky burial." Sky burials were ritual dismemberments of corpses for consumption by predatory birds. Although these practices still exist in Tibetan communities in South Asia, Tibetan-American communities have had to adapt their funerary practices to accord with American procedures.

*See also:* BUDDHISTS

## Bibliography

Bielmeier, R. (1982). "Problems in Tibetan Dialectology and Language History." *Zentralasiatische Studien* 16(4):404–425.

Calkowski, M. S. (1991). "A Day at the Tibetan Opera: Actualized Performance and Spectacular Discourse." *American Ethnologist* 18(4):643–657.

Fields, R. (1992). *How the Swans Came to the Lake: A Narrative History of Buddhism in America.* Boston: Shambhala.

Goldstein, M. (1971). "Stratification, Polyandry, and Family Structure in Central Tibet." *Southwestern Journal of Anthropology* 27:64–74.

Grunfeld, A. T. (1987). *The Making of Modern Tibet.* London: Zed Books.

Klieger, P. C. (1991). "The Institution of the Dalai Lama as a Symbolic Matrix." *The Tibet Journal* 16:96–107.

Levine, N. E. (1988). *The Dynamics of Polyandry: Kinship, Domesticity, and Population on the Tibetan Border.* Chicago: University of Chicago Press.

Matisoff, J. A. (1991). "Sino-Tibetan Linguistics: Present State and Future Prospects." *Annual Review of Anthropology* 20:469–504.

Messerschmidt, D. A. (1976). "Innovation in Adaptation: Tibetan Immigrants in the United States." *Tibet Society Bulletin* 10:48–70.

Michael, F. (1982). *Rule by Incarnation.* Boulder, CO: Westview Press.

Minority Rights Group. (1983). *The Tibetans, MRG Report No. 49.* London: Author.

Norbu, J., ed. (1986). *Zlos-Gar: Performing Traditions of Tibet.* Dharamsala, India: Library of Tibetan Works and Archives.

Nowak, M. (1984). *Tibetan Refugees: Youth and the New Generation of Meaning.* New Brunswick, NJ: Rutgers University Press.

Samuel, G. (1982). "Tibet as a Stateless Society and Some Islamic Parallels." *Journal of Asian Studies* 41(2):215–229.

Snellgrove, D. (1966). "For a Sociology of Tibetan-Speaking Regions." *Central Asiatic Journal* 11(3): 199–219.

Thurman, R. (1983). "The Dalai Lama of Tibet: Living Icons of a Six-Hundred-Year Millennium." *The Tibet Journal* 8:10–19.

FRANK J. KOROM

# TONGANS

Tongans are Polynesians whose homeland, the Kingdom of Tonga, consists of some 150 raised coral islands in the South Pacific, 36 of which are inhabited by 96,000 people. According to the 1990 U.S. Census, there were 17,600 Tongan Americans residing in the United States. They speak the Tongan language, maintain many core features of their culture and social organization, and share a view of themselves as Tongans or Tongan Americans. Because Tongans are a tiny, little-known minority group, comprising 0.1 percent of the North American population, they are sometimes confused with their more populous Polynesian neighbors, the Samoans and Hawaiians. In fact, it is only since 1980 that Tongans and various other Pacific Islanders have been enumerated in their own right, apart from Asians and Hawaiians.

## Home Country

Polynesia is one of three culture areas in the Pacific, along with Micronesia and Melanesia, whose other major nationalities include Samoans, Fijians, Tahitians, Maori, and Hawaiians. Polynesians traditionally share common cultural characteristics, including close linguistic similarities, adaptations to island environments, hierarchical societies that stress varying degrees of obedience to chiefly authority, and ethics of reciprocity among kindred.

The Kingdom of Tonga is the most conservative and highly stratified of the contemporary Polynesian nations, with three hereditary social classes: the king, a chiefly nobility of thirty-three families, and commoners. Tonga is unique among all the island nations of the Pacific in that it was never colonized by a European power; its constitutional monarchy was created in the nineteenth century by the first Tongan king, and its political affairs have since been controlled by indigenous chiefly elites. Tonga has been Christian—also by chiefly edict—since missionaries consolidated their influence in the mid-nineteenth century. The official state religion today is Wesleyan Methodism, though there are eight other denominations that together comprise the axis along which village life is organized.

Tonga's economy and basic way of life are still primarily agricultural. However, rapid economic development in the capital, Nuku'alofa, supports a growing, overseas-educated middle class rooted in civil service and small business. In addition to universal participation in the market economy, urbanites and villagers alike are steeped in a redistributive economy, consisting of ceremonial exchanges, feasting, and resource-sharing among extended family groups called *kainga*.

Tonga's fragile island ecology and limited educational opportunities cannot support continued population growth and equitable land distribution (a guaranteed eight acres for each man; however, women may now inherit land in Tonga). Outmigration has increasingly come to be a safety valve; in fact, the 1986 Tongan Census indicated that the kingdom's population dropped from more than 100,000 to 96,000 for the first time in its modern history. Emigration from Tonga has accelerated the processes of economic development and social change and also has enabled the system of traditional entitlements to continue to function. Tongans who have resided overseas for a long time without returning, or who have become naturalized U.S. citizens, are legally required to give up their rights to land, and Tongans who remain in Tonga have better chances of inheriting, obtaining, and leasing lands. Additionally, most families in Tonga have at least several members living and working in the United States, New Zealand, or Australia. These overseas relatives send home remittances to defray the increasing cost of living in the islands. In doing this, the U.S. immigrants are contributing to the creation of a class system in which new forms of social status are based not only on traditional lines of descent through chiefs but also on the accumulation of material goods and educational degrees. While Tongan Americans are nostalgic for their homeland and proud of their culture, many if not most choose to remain in the United States, all the while maintaining strong support of home villages, churches, and families, and a distinctly Tongan way of life.

## Immigration and Settlement

Tongans, like all Polynesians, historically have been great travelers. The Tongan archipelago was colonized from Malaysia around 1200 B.C.E. by Polynesian ancestors, who voyaged in canoes over thousands of miles of open ocean in search of habitable islands. A sophisticated voyaging technology enabled the Tongans, who developed an interisland, chiefly political structure, to maintain contact for hundreds of years with their Fijian and Samoan neighbors through warfare, trade, and intermarriage. Tongans have also traveled extensively among their own islands and continue to do so today, visiting kinfolk and friends, attending school in the capital, going to weddings and funerals, seeking marriage partners, and buying and selling produce. Modern modes of travel and communication have made it possible for Tongans to perpetuate this mobile tradition beyond the local and regional levels, on a global scale.

## Location and Demographics

In 1980, Tongan Americans numbered just over 6,200; their 1990 population of 17,600 represented a 184 percent rise in ten years, due to immigration and their natural rate of increase, which at 3.5 children per woman of childbearing age is above the national average.

The Church of Jesus Christ of Latter-Day Saints (Mormon) has probably been the single most significant agent of Tongan immigration, obviating immigration restrictions on Tongans by providing them with student and work visas, employment, and opportunities to meet spouses who are American citizens and naturalized Pacific Islanders. It brought the first Tongan immigrants to Laie, Hawaii, initially in 1916, and then in greater numbers in the 1950s as labor missionaries for the Hawaiian Temple, Church College, and the Polynesian Cultural Center. These families settled permanently in the Laie area, forming the backbone along with Samoans and Hawaiians of a tightly knit, multicultural religious community. Since the mid-1950s, the Mormon Church has also sponsored thousands of Tongan students who attend Brigham Young University in Hawaii and in Provo, Utah; these students have chosen to remain in the United States at a rate of 25 percent. A significant number of these students, along with children of the original settlers, have married Americans and other naturalized Tongans.

The chain migration set in motion in the 1950s and 1960s resulted in movement to the western mainland United States, as more Tongans joined family members and entered certain occupations in the footsteps of their antecedents. Most Pacific Islanders have made California their home; 45 percent of the Tongans live in the Los Angeles and San Francisco Bay regions, mainly in suburban or urban areas. Of the rest, according to the 1990 U.S. Census, 22.2 percent live in Salt Lake City or Provo, Utah; 17 percent in Laie or Honolulu, Hawaii; 3.6 percent in Texas; and 2.5 percent in Seattle. The remainder are scattered throughout Idaho, Oregon, Arizona, and eastern and midwestern states.

While the majority of Tongan Americans originate in Tonga, they have also historically entered the United States through American Samoa, where eight hundred Tongans reside.

Tongans appear to be the youngest Polynesian-American population, with a median age of 18.9 years. Roughly one in five Tongans is a new immigrant. Men and women are present in nearly equal numbers.

## Kinship

Tongan-American communities are loosely knit and flexible, organized around networks of kindred (*kainga*) that can reach across neighbor-

Tongan Americans prepare to participate in an awards ceremony sponsored by the National Tongan-American Society in Salt Lake City, Utah. The ceremony, which was held to honor the 1996 academic achievements of one hundred Utah Tongans (twenty of whom received college degrees and eighty of whom received high school diplomas), featured traditional island dress, music, and dances. (Steve Griffin/*The Salt Lake Tribune*)

hoods, cities, and continents. Ties of descent and marriage are the fundamental orienting principles of Tongan society. All Tongans have a strong sense of their membership in several overlapping descent groups, and ranked placement within a family. Tongans have a complex kinship system coined by anthropologists as double unilineal descent, meaning that they reckon descent through both the mother's and father's lines and have distinctive social obligations to both. Women are symbolically ranked lower socially than their husbands, but ranked higher—more metaphorically, chiefly—than their brothers. Consequently, a brother and his children are especially obligated to support his sisters and their children. In practice, all family members are obligated to provide support on demand.

## Household Composition

Tongans ideally like to own their own homes, which function as family compounds that can accommodate visitors from Tonga and a multigenerational array of children, grandparents, grandchildren, nieces, nephews, and cousins. Statistics show that Tongans, like Samoans, live in large households; fully half of each Tongan household consists of children. While some Tongan-American households are composed of constant numbers of nuclear family members, Tongan residential patterns usually reflect the traditional system, with family members easily changing households for marriage, work, or education. Relatives drop in and out of a person's kinship universe depending on geographic proximity, membership in a household, or joint efforts to raise money. Additionally, Tongans, like all Pacific Islanders, practice high rates of fostercare and adoption of children. In the course of a child's life it is possible that she or he may shift households and experience a variety of caretakers, including parents, grandparents, aunts, and uncles.

## Social Organization

Tongans participate in a variety of associations that crosscut kinship ties: church groups; sports clubs such as rugby, football, and volleyball; alumni association; and community or "cultural" associations. Tongan cultural associations are especially numerous and vital in Hawaii, where they sponsor fund-raisers for student scholarships in the United States and projects in Tonga, dance competitions, school programs, and events for visiting dignitaries. The Tongan-American associations in Hawaii also publish a newspaper for overseas Tongans and produce a local television show. Other mainland Tongan community groups tend to have a short life and few members, apart from those running the organization. Unlike ministers and chiefs, whose authority is traditionally unequivocal, unproven persons who establish themselves as leaders easily arouse suspicion and opposition. This can prove frustrating for those who are working to interest Tongans in the political issues that affect the community, such as bilingual education, community policing, federal immigration policies, and health care.

Tongans typically orient their social activities around their churches, which provide important continuities with tradition. The churches in the United States replicate the round of festivals (Christmas, the Week of Prayer around New Year's, Easter, May Day, Sunday feasts), choir practice, church-sponsored outings, Bible study, women's auxiliary organizations, missionary activities, and fund-raising events found in Tonga. Tongan-speaking Wesleyan churches, Mormon wards, Catholic congregations, and even the indigenous Free Church of Tonga can all be found in the United States.

Aside from the joint efforts required to execute family and community events, men and women spend much of their time in same-sex company. Women visit each other, care for children together, put out organization newsletters, participate in sports such as volleyball and basketball, and organize church activities and fund-raising events.

In addition to competitive sports, work, and other joint masculine activities, Tongan men traditionally socialize around the kava bowl, containing a mildly narcotic drink made from the root of the kava plant, which is carefully cultivated and harvested along with other crops. Each village in

Tonga has several kava clubs, whose members gather together, sometimes every night, to drink, sing, joke, raise money, and discuss social affairs. Kava clubs can also be found in every American town where Tongans live, from garages in San Bruno, California, to living rooms in Kahuku, Hawaii.

Many Tongans express relief that residency in the United States frees them from many of the onerous ceremonial and material obligations to the chiefs who "own" their villages. However, when the chiefs and their families visit the United States, first-generation Tongans feel compelled to express their respect by serving them and presenting them with gifts during their stay, particularly those with ties to the chief's lineage and village. The members of the king's family in particular can expect first-class treatment by their subjects during their frequent visits to Hawaii, California, and Seattle. Such visits activate traditional sentiments that form the cornerstone of Tongan identity: the status that all Tongans derive from tracing their languages to chiefly individuals, and the pride they take in fulfilling their social obligations with all the proper protocol.

### Economic Factors

Tongan culture contains three core values, expressed in the words 'ofa (love), faka'apa'apa (respect), and fuakavenga (responsibility). There are specific ethical norms and practices embodied in these terms, relating to the imperative to engage in economic cooperation among kinfolk. The ethic of sharing economic resources persists nearly as strongly in Tongan-American communities as in Tonga itself and allows families to raise money and labor for important life events such as weddings, funerals, graduation parties, and home-building. Tongans rarely shirk their social obligations; to refuse financial requests from relatives is shameful and disrespectful — "without love." For example, a Tongan man in Oakland, California, must respond to a call from his sister living in Tonga to help finance her daughter's wedding. He might share this obligation with his paternal cousins in Salt Lake City by asking them to donate money as well. The system works to sustain everyone in turn. This

same man may subsequently ask his sister to send tapa cloth and fine mats for his father-in-law's funeral, held in Seattle, the following year. In Tonga, birthdays, weddings, funerals, graduations, and chiefly instatement ceremonies are marked by ceremonial exchanges between families of beautifully painted tapa (bark) cloth, mats woven of pandanus, and feasts. Women produce this ceremonial wealth (koloa), while men provide foodstuffs such as yams, pigs, and root crops. Koloa is not normally hoarded, but circulated — given away at the next funeral or wedding. This presents potential problems to the overseas communities who honor such traditional exchanges but who cannot produce koloa in the American context. They must depend on their relatives in Tonga to send it to them, and these goods are often in short supply. Tongan women have recently created a new tradition — the manufacture and exchange of quilts — that offsets decreased production of traditional koloa in both the United States and Tonga.

### Work

The 1990 U.S. Census shows that the percentage of college-educated Tongans is still quite small — only 9 percent, with men completing four years of college at a slightly higher rate than women. Tongans are pragmatic-minded, hardworking people who value the kind of expertise in both men and women that enhances the fortunes of the group. Many Tongans are less ambitious about education for its own sake than about the kinds of training and degrees that will yield practical results in economic terms. As the U.S. Census attests, most adult Tongans are working-class, with both men and women over sixteen employed at almost the same rate, contributing much of their salaries to the maintenance of households in both Tonga and the United States. About half of working Tongans are employed in service occupations and technical support such as restaurant worker, medical technician, day-care attendent, caretaker of the elderly, teacher's aide, domestic worker, retail salesperson, and secretary; most women hold jobs in these categories. The most common occupational niches filled by men include yardwork, skilled construction, semiskilled labor, mechanical production, and repair. Most Tongan men aspire to operate their own small businesses in these areas, and if they succeed in getting one off the ground, they often employ newly arrived relatives and men from other immigrant groups to work with them. Nine percent of Tongans, the majority of whom have attained advanced degrees at Brigham Young University, obtain work as managers and professionals in a variety of business settings, state agencies, and educational institutions; they are social workers, computer programmers, schoolteachers, professors, physicians, and attorneys. The relatively high rates of poverty noted in the 1990 U.S. Census (20.6 percent of families living below the poverty level) belie a hidden factor that enables Tongans to survive collectively: the flow of money among different households.

## Expressive Culture and the Arts

Tonga has an extremely rich, high tradition of dance, poetry, and music, all of which come together in the *lakalaka*, a line dance performed by men and women. The lakalaka employs elaborate metaphors to commemorate chiefly people, historical events, and places. The dances and songs express and instill great pathos. New ones are also composed and choreographed for special occasions by Tongan poets, both in Tonga and overseas. Tongans sing and play music informally, in another genre called *hiva kakala*, love songs, many of which were composed by Tonga's Queen Salote, who died in 1965. Young women wearing fine mats and elaborate ornaments also perform solo dances to these hiva kakala, called *tau'olunga*, and these are most often seen at fund-raisers. Yet another musical tradition that developed in the nineteenth century is the harmonic singing of hymns. Whether in Texas, Hawaii, or California, Tongan-American voices create the same magnificent harmonies as their Tongan counterparts.

## Assimilation

It is inevitable that successive generations of Tongans will embody an increasingly hybrid version of their culture — culture that somehow encompasses the paradoxes of American individualism and loyalty to the family group; mobility in a class structure and traditional patterns of authority. Despite the fact that the U.S. Census reports Tongans as having the highest degree of native-language maintenance in the household — a figure that reflects the perspective of older heads of household who speak primarily in Tongan — the second generation is in large measure more proficient in English than in Tongan. Most young Tongan Americans have lost the ability to speak in poetry and metaphor, the rich vocabulary and speech conventions of the Tongan language. They are also far less invested in elaborate shows of respect and fulfillment of social obligations. One can glimpse the concern that Tongans feel about this by speaking with family heads and community leaders, who attribute rising dropout rates, crime, drug use, and gang activity by some young people — activities that were unthinkable in previous generations — to the loss of the traditional values of respect and family solidarity.

And yet the Tongans are still on the whole a relatively insulated, conservative group with a distinctly Polynesian style of personhood and means of enforcing social control over their community members. Unmarried people are expected to live with the family and participate in the institutions and activities that reproduce Tongan ethnicity in the American context. Many young people, especially women, know how to do traditional Tongan dances, and perform a repertoire of Tongan songs. Parents regularly send their children to Tonga to visit with family there, "lest they forget" their traditional way of life. Tonga has the highest rate of new immigrant arrivals among Polynesians in the United States, and the community's ties to the homeland, to family, and to tradition are strengthened through this. As long as Tongan Americans continue to hold fast to their language and social institutions and transmit a reflexive consciousness of the *anga fakatonga* (the Tongan way) to their children, the new forms that emerge from the interplay of cultures and generations will remain vital, distinctive, and most important in the Tongan view, adaptive.

*See also:* PACIFIC ISLANDERS IN HAWAII

## Bibliography

Barringer, H. R.; Gardner, R. W.; and Levin, M. J. (1992). *Asians and Pacific Islanders in the United States: The Population of the United States in the 1980s.* New York: Russell Sage Foundation.

Chapman, B. A. (1972). "Adaptation and Maintenance in the Extended Family of Tongan Immigrants." M.A. thesis, University of Utah.

Connell, J. (1983). *Migration, Employment, and Development in the South Pacific Country Report.* Nouméa, New Caledonia: South Pacific Commission.

Grijp, P. v. d. (1993). *Islanders of the South: Production, Kinship, and Ideology in the Polynesian Kingdom of Tonga.* Leiden, Netherlands: KITLV Press.

Herda, P.; Terrell, J.; and Gunson, N.; eds. (1987). *Tongan Culture and History.* Canberra: Australian National University Press.

Kaea, T. A. (1980). "Tongan Diaspora." B.D. thesis, Pacific Theological College, Suva, Fiji.

Latukefu, S. (1974). *Church and State in Tonga.* Canberra: Australian National University Press.

Macpherson, C.; Shore, B.; and Franco, R., eds. (1978). *New Neighbors: Islanders in Adaptation.* Santa Cruz, CA: Center for South Pacific Studies, University of California.

Rutherford, N., ed. (1977). *Friendly Islands: A History of Tonga.* Oxford, Eng.: Oxford University Press.

Spickard, P. R., et al. (1995). *Pacific Islander Americans: An Annotated Bibliography in the Social Sciences.* Laie, HI: Institute for Polynesian Studies, Brigham Young University.

Swartz, M. A. (1995). "Toward Culturally Competent Churches: Analysis of a Tongan-Palangi Experience." D.M. thesis, Austin Presbyterian Theological Seminary.

TAMAR GORDON

# TRAVELERS

Outsiders refer to both the Irish and the Scottish Travelers as "Gypsies" because of their itinerant lifestyles and confusion about their origins. They are also called "Tinkers," after their former occupation of tinsmithing.

The Irish Travelers call themselves "Travelers" or "Traveling People" and identify subgroups by geographical area such as Georgia, Mississippi, or Texas Travelers. They make further distinctions among themselves by clan affiliation: Some of the larger ones are the Sherlocks, Rileys, Carrolls, Costellos, Gormans, McNallys, and O'Haras.

The Scottish Travelers call themselves "Travelers" and "Nawkins." The latter term, of unknown derivation, has become "Naggins" in North America, defined as dealers in horses or "nags" in folk etymology. Within the group, families are known by their clan affiliation; some of the largest clans are the Williamsons, McMillans, Stewarts, Greggs, McDonalds, Watsons, Johnsons, Whites, Reids, and Wilsons. Today "Traveler" is the prevalent designation for both groups.

## Definition

Travelers define themselves primarily by their lifestyle, identifying their itinerancy, business acumen, close-knit families, and a number of other minor traits, as characteristically Traveler. Irishness or Scottishness is a prominant feature of their respective identities, although they clearly distinguish themselves from non-Traveler Irish or Scottish people. In North America the Travelers may be considered immigrant groups. However, since the Scottish Travelers continue to move between Scotland and North America, discussing their immigrant status in terms of when they arrived or how long they have been in the United States is not as meaningful as for immigrants who arrived but once and stayed.

## Immigration History

Travelers are a people primarily of indigenous origin who have adopted a peripatetic lifestyle that most still follow. Over the centuries, they have diverged from the majority population to the extent that they now constitute distinct ethnic groups and not merely subcultures. Some Scottish Traveler families claim affinity with Gypsies and cite a legend that claims Travelers are descendants of landowners who lost their lands and were forced to take to the roads. They were befriended by Gypsies, who taught them to survive using peripatetic strategies.

The ancestors of both Traveler groups began immigrating to North America at about the middle of the nineteenth century, arriving in smaller increments continually into the twentieth century. The Irish landed in New York and then, according to oral tradition, made their way to the environs of Tonawanda, New York; Pittsburgh; Philadelphia; and Washington, D.C. Census records, however, reveal that some small families and members of larger families split from the main group and immediately began traveling throughout the Midwest and even farther, reaching the West Coast by the early 1870s, while the majority headed south. Current population concentrations are in the southern states, but smaller, less well-documented families exist elsewhere. Although much of the group remains seasonally nomadic, living in trailers and mobile homes, many families have established winter home bases in South Carolina, Texas, Tennessee, and elsewhere, where some have built large homes shared by their extended families. In South Carolina a former camping site has developed into an ethnic enclave, Murphy Village, where several hundred families live in close proximity.

The first Scottish Travelers who may have reached America were prisoners ostensibly transported to the colonies during the seventeenth and eighteenth centuries. However, no record of their actually reaching American shores has yet been discovered. The first influx of Scottish Travelers to the United States or Canada for which either oral history or written records exist began in the 1850s; the earliest passenger manifest identified dates from 1858. From 1880 on, census and other records (e.g., city directories) provide some information on the distribution of Travelers and on Traveler-owned businesses. Judging by the birthplace recorded for the children in the 1880 to 1920 censuses, there seems to have been immigration to the United States from Scotland and Canada in the late 1880s and early 1890s.

## Demography

The Irish Traveler population consists of approximately fifty original clans. The bulk of the population is distributed among the above-mentioned enclaves, of which large numbers are traveling at any one time. Although any figures on the group are suspect, the total probably does not exceed seven or eight thousand.

Some law-enforcement officers have tentatively estimated Scottish Travelers to number about ten thousand but admit they do not know all the families. In the 1950s, the Better Business Bureau estimated the Williamson clan alone to have at least two thousand individuals, and more than one hundred Scottish Traveler clans have been identified in the United States, all of which existed as separate clans in Scotland by the 1880s.

Although some Scottish Traveler families travel extensively among the United States, Canada, and Scotland, many are permanently rooted in one of these countries. In the United States some families are concentrated in California and in some southern and southwestern states, such as Florida and Arizona, although the Midwest and the East Coast also get their share of visits each year. Seasonal interstate migration between the South in the winter and the North in the summer has been reported from both coasts and the Midwest.

## Language

All Irish Travelers claimed English as their only language upon their arrival in the United States; none indicated use of Gaelic. In addition to English they also used an argot referred to as Shelta, gammon, or cant. This form of secret speech is based on the substitution or transposition of sounds in English or Gaelic words interspersed at key points of regular speech with normal English syntax. Its function is primarily to hide the gist of Traveler communications from outsiders. Many of the first Scottish Traveler arrivals claimed to be native speakers of Scotch Gaelic, but now most speak English as their first and only language. In eastern Canada many also are fluent in French. In addition, most Scottish Travelers know an argot that contains words from Romany, the language of English Gypsies. Although the argots are still known by most Travelers, their use appears to be decreasing.

## Culture

Upon arriving in America all Travelers first engaged in pursuits they had followed in the old country: tinsmithing, peddling, and horse trading. The Irish Travelers soon changed to horse and mule trading to the exclusion of other activities. When the need for draft animals began to wane, various door-to-door sales again gained prominence. Linoleum, carpets, and lace were reported as favorite sale items. Scottish Travelers relied longer on the wider repertoire of traditional occupations than did the Irish Travelers. Today their occupations range from skilled trades, such as metalworking or blacktopping, to door-to-door hawking. Items sold have included tools, lace, linens, woolens, furs, linoleum, carpets, and a variety of ready-made clothing.

During the 1950s, both groups began specializing in driveway asphalting and seal-coating, although related roof repair and barn painting trades, as well as the sale of recreational vehicles, have also assumed importance.

Travelers migrate to seek work, to visit family and friends, and to explore new territory; in addition, some moves are initiated by the desire to avoid local law enforcement. While traveling, the families stay at motels, hotels, and campgrounds. During the winter the Scottish Travelers use rented houses, apartments, or efficiency units in motels and hotels. The amount of time spent in any locality appears to be related to the season, the purpose of the visit, the amount of work available, and the weather.

Travelers are loosely organized along clan lines, with minimal leadership beyond extended family heads. Kindred get together periodically for holidays and family events such as marriages, funerals, and annual visits to the clan burial grounds on Memorial Day. Most traveling units consist of a single family, or a few related families, who belong to a lineage. Descent is ideally patrilineal, but postmarital residence is ambilocal (i.e., the couple can live with the parents of either the bride or the groom). Household composition is fluid; who might be part of the household at any particular moment is unpredictable. Aside from respected elders there are no spokespersons or leaders of any kind; each family makes its own decisions. Peer pressure is the main form of social control exercised within the group.

Almost all Irish Travelers are devout Roman Catholics. In Murphy Village they even have their own church, which is used for worship, baptisms, marriages, and funerals. Travelers strive to maintain their ethnic distinctiveness by arranging marriages within the group and putting pressure on their members not to associate too much with outsiders. Major social events in the Irish Traveler communities are religious holidays, especially Christmas and Easter, and the World Series, which marks the end of the summer work season.

## Persistence

The Travelers exhibit very strong group cohesion and neither group appears to be in danger of disappearing. Ethnic persistence is partly due to intense socialization to instill ethnic identity and pride in being a Traveler and strong sanctions against interaction with outsiders. Their relationship to the larger society is characterized by the maintenance of social distance; little or no socializing takes place with outsiders, and intermarriages with them are discouraged. However, some do chafe under the strict social control exercised by the group and "escape" to the outside world. Some intermarriages occur among Scottish Travelers, Romnichels (English Gypsies), and Irish Travelers, and also with non-Travelers, but not to the extent that would cause weakening of the ethnic core.

*See also:*   GYPSIES; IRISH; SCOTS

## Bibliography

Andereck, M. E. (1992). *Ethnic Awareness and the School: An Ethnographic Study.* Newbury Park, CA: Sage Publications.

Departmental Committee on Tinkers in Scotland. (1918). *Report of the Departmental Committee on Tinkers in Scotland.* Edinburgh: His Majesty's Stationery Office.

Gmelch, G. (1976). "The Emergence of an Ethnic Group: The Irish Tinkers. *Anthropological Quarterly* 49:225–238.

Harper, J. V. (1969). Irish Traveler Cant: An Historical, Structural, and Sociolinguistic Study of an Argot. M.A. thesis, University of Georgia, Athens.

Harper, J. V. (1971). "Gypsy Research in the South." In *The Not So Solid South: Anthropological Studies in Regional Subcultures,* edited by T. K. Moreland. Athens, GA: *Southern Anthropological Society.*

Harper, J. V. (1977). "The Irish Travelers of Georgia." Ph.D. diss., University of Georgia, Athens.

Kobler, J. (1956). "The Terrible Williamsons." *The Saturday Evening Post,* October 27:26–27, 55–58, 61–62.

Lockwood, W. G., and Salo, S., eds. (1994). *Gypsies and Travelers in North America: An Annotated Bibliography.* Cheverly, MD: Gypsy Lore Society.

Lonergan, S. (1989). "The Rom and the Gypsies." M.A. thesis, University of New Brunswick.

MacRitchie, D. (1894). *Scottish Gypsies Under Stewarts.* Edinburgh: D. Douglas.

McCormick, A. (1906). *The Tinkler Gypsies.* Dumfries, Scotland: J. Maxwell & Son.

Muller, E. (1941). "Roving the South with the Irish Horse Traders." *Reader's Digest,* July:59–63.

Rehfisch, F. (1961). "Marriage and the Elementary Family Among the Scottish Tinkers." *Scottish Studies* 5(2):121–148.

Rehfisch, A., and Rehfisch, F. (1975). "Scottish Travellers or Tinkers." In *Gypsies, Tinkers, and Other Travellers,* edited by F. Rehfisch. London: Academic Press.

Salo, M. T. (1986). "Peripatetic Adaptation in Historical Perspective." *Nomadic Peoples* 21–22:7–36.

MATT T. SALO

# TRINIDADIANS

Trinidad, an island of some two thousand square miles, is the larger of the two islands that constitute the Caribbean nation of Trinidad and Tobago.

Roughly twenty-two miles southwest of Tobago in the Caribbean Sea, Trinidad is the southernmost island of the Lesser Antilles chain and is only twenty-eight miles from the northeastern coast of Venezuela. The ethnic composition of its approximately one million people is 42 percent black, 40 percent East Indian, 2 percent white, and 16 percent from other ethnic groups and mixtures. Trinidad may be characterized as a developing nation and as a society of scarce economic resources. Major sources of income are oil, cocoa, citrus, rice, and sugar, the latter two grown almost exclusively by East Indians. The country's economy is marked by heavy inflation and an extremely high level of unemployment.

Trinidad was first settled by the Spanish in 1498. In 1797, the British took control of the island; it remained British territory until 1962, when it achieved political independence from Britain. Under British control, sugar became the economic mainstay of the island. Blacks were brought from Africa to work on the plantations. This process continued until 1807, when the slave trade to the Caribbean was abolished.

The harsh and often brutal conditions of slavery forcefully restrained expressions of black culture and organization and led to the almost total obliteration of their previous African culture. On the sugar plantations and in a strange land, blacks were left with no alternative but to adopt a slightly different but somewhat similar version of the culture of the British colonialists.

Slavery was abolished in 1838, and freed black slaves refused to continue working on the sugar plantations. In fact, most fled the sugar plantations and took up residence in urban centers. Faced with a shortage of a cheap and constant supply of labor, British plantation owners imported East Indians as indentured laborers. This movement, begun in 1845, is the context in which the history of the present East Indian population in Trinidad must be seen.

During the years from 1845 to 1917, the duration of indenture immigration, roughly 144,000 East Indians arrived in Trinidad. Although the indenture system was somewhat similar to slavery, it differed from the latter in some respects. Due to an elaborate immigration ordinance, and the Protector of Immigrants, who served their interests, East Indians, unlike blacks, were able to retain their culture.

Since their first arrival in Trinidad, East Indians have remained residentially apart from the larger society. Unlike the blacks, they have remained in rural areas, mainly on sugar plantations, and have come to be regarded as a rural and agricultural ethnic group. In fact, relations between the two groups have been strained, and mutual stereotypes have been used in place of communication.

## Immigration History

Following emancipation, many blacks began seeking a more equitable livelihood in developed countries. Many began taking up residence in the United States, especially in Middle Atlantic states. This process continued well past the turn of the twentieth century. It was estimated that in the early 1920s nearly one-third of the population of New York's Harlem were West Indian blacks, with a significant number from Trinidad. However, in the 1920s, owing to the passage of a number of quota laws designed to curb immigration to the United States, the number of blacks who immigrated to the United States decreased significantly. Between the 1920s and the early 1960s, many blacks from Trinidad took up residence in England.

Meanwhile, by the end of World War I, the East Indians in Trinidad were through serving their indenture contracts. Following the end of the indenture system in 1917, many East Indians immigrated to England or Canada. But in 1962, England passed a labor restrictive ordinance, and this forced the East Indians (as well as the blacks) from Trinidad to find another destination abroad.

In the late 1950s and early 1960s, Trinidad was bedeviled with a number of social problems that forced blacks and East Indians to emigrate. Rigidity of the social structure, economic policies, metropolitan domination, job inequality, income imbalance, racial discrimination, unemployment, underemployment, labor unrest, and a host of other problems loomed large in the society at the time. This coincided with the passage of the U.S. Immigration and Nationality Act of 1965, which lifted many of the restrictions imposed by the previous McCarran-Walter Act of 1952, especially the quota laws of the 1920s, and facilitated the movement of large numbers of blacks and East Indians from Trinidad to the United States. Most of the blacks and East Indians from Trinidad living in the United States today immigrated after 1965. It is estimated that well over 200,000 blacks and 75,000 East Indians from Trinidad now have legal status in the United States. In addition, there are an estimated 50,000 illegal immigrants from Trinidad.

In addition to blacks and East Indians, other racial and ethnic groups immigrated from Trinidad to the United States in the post-1967 period. Of all Trinidadians living in the United States today, 1 percent are Chinese; 1 percent are Lebanese, Syrian, or Portuguese; 2 percent are white; and 14 percent are of mixed origin. Most of these groups, especially the lighter-skinned ones, arrived in Trinidad during indentureship or before, and most were exposed to the same socioeconomic and political conditions as their black and East Indian counterparts.

The vast majority of Trinidadian blacks have made Brooklyn, New York, their home. East Indians, meanwhile, have settled mostly in the Richmond Hill–South Ozone Park areas of Queens, New York. Significant numbers of blacks and East Indians can also be found in the Bronx, and relatively insignificant numbers live in Manhattan and Staten Island. Significant numbers of blacks and East Indians also live in New Jersey, and a handful have taken up residence in Connecticut. Today roughly 78 percent of blacks and East Indians from Trinidad have settled in the Northeast, with predominant concentrations in New York, New Jersey, Connecticut, Pennsylvania, and Massachusetts. Blacks and East Indians also have settled in the South, especially in Texas, Louisiana, Florida, Maryland, Virginia, and North Carolina, as well as in the District of Columbia. The lighter-skinned Trinidadians are concentrated mostly in and around New York City.

## Religion

Most Trinidadian blacks in the United States belong to Christian denominations, but the East Indians are mostly Hindus. Broken down by specific denominations, Trinidadians in the United States are about 19 percent Anglican, 3 percent Baptist, 28 percent Hindu, 7 percent Muslim, 6 percent Presbyterian, 28 percent Roman Catholic, 7 percent other Christian sects, and 2 percent non-Christian sects. Trinidadians are a highly religious group; eight out of ten claim affiliation to some organized religion. In addition, religious celebrations in Trinidad are also observed in the United States by the immigrant population. The Christian denominations observe Lent, Easter, and Christmas, among other holy times. The Indian population, which is broken down into Hindus and Muslims, observes such religion occasions as Diwali (the festival of lights) in late October or early November, and Id al-Fitr (the culmination of the revelation of the Koran by God to Muhammad) in late February or early March. Church attendance by Trinidadians in the United States resembles that of other immigrant populations that have come to place a high value on religiosity, and much social life revolves around the church. There are about a dozen distinctly Trinidadian mandirs (Hindu temples) in the United States, most in New York City. In the mandirs the Brahmins have the key roles. The Brahmins form the highest caste and are the priests and teachers. The Khushatriyas (the warrior caste), Vaishyas (the merchant caste), and Sudras (the laboring caste) are subservient to the Brahmins. As in Trinidad, caste still plays a major role among East Indians in the United States. There are also about four distinctly Trinidadian Muslim mosques in the new society. Meanwhile, most of Trinidad's black population in the United States attends Christian churches started by other groups (prior to the former's arrival in the new society), and fewer than six churches can be regarded as distinctly Trinidadian.

## Family and Community Life

Much social life revolves around the family. In *East Indians in Trinidad* (1971), Yogendra Malik notes that East Indian life is more "particularistic" while black life is more "universalistic." This same pattern exists in the United States, where East Indian Trinidadians are more family-oriented. The bonds between and among East Indian family members are strong; the divorce rate is about 1 for every 100 marriages, which is lower than the rate for Irish Catholics (1.8 for every 100 marriages) and Italians (2.0 for every 100 marriages) in the United States. Meanwhile, the divorce rate among the black population from Trinidad in the United States resembles that of the larger population— about two to three of every five marriages. The black family is not as stable as that in Trinidad, owing to both cultural and structural assimilation and the fact that the same kinds of family-related problems that affect other groups in the society are beginning to affect Trinidad's black population in the United States. Such problems as divorce, spousal abuse, and alcoholism are making serious inroads in this group. Likewise, despite the strong sense of family life among the East Indians, they too are beginning to have family problems and this is becoming more pronounced with members of the second and third generations. With increasing time in the United States, problems of the East Indian family might well come to resemble those of other groups in the society.

The "universalistic" and "particularistic" orientations of blacks and East Indians have also affected their social and political involvement in the United States. Blacks have been more mobile politically. Many Black Trinidadians are featured prominently in American politics, among them Shirley Chisholm, Mervyn Dymally, and Stokely Carmichael. Meanwhile, the East Indians have yet to put one of their own in the limelight of American politics. Moreover, the black Trinidadian population in the United States is more socially involved in community-based organizations, while the East Indians' social life tends to revolve more around family and religion.

## Education

Most Trinidadians of the first generation lack the educational credentials to compete effectively in a postindustrial society such as that in the United States. Most do not have any formal schooling beyond high school.

However, the educational level of second-generation blacks and East Indians significantly surpasses that of their parents. Approximately 60 percent of second-generation East Indian men have attended college; 48 percent of East Indian women have a college education, compared with 20 percent of all American women. At the same time, 45 percent of second-generation male blacks from Trinidad have attended college, and 38 percent of their female counterparts are college-educated.

But the Trinidadian population in the United States, both blacks and East Indians, is bedeviled by a number of social problems, especially at the high school level. The black community, in Brooklyn especially, has had to deal with rising levels of drug addiction and violence in the schools. And the East Indian community in Richmond Hill has had to contend with the problem of teenage pregnancy. According to one high school counselor in Queens, who echoes the sentiments of many others, Trinidad's (and Guyana's) East Indian community has one of the highest levels of teenage pregnancy in the Richmond Hill area.

## Employment and Income

Trinidadians in the United States do relatively well, economically. Most members of the first generation are relegated to the working class and engage in work that corresponds with this position because of their lack of education. However, second-generation members are rapidly attaining intergenerational mobility and thus entering the middle class, primarily because of greater educational attainment. Today many second-generation Trinidadians, both black and East Indian, are in the upper middle class; many are doctors, lawyers, college professors, engineers, accountants, or computer scientists. In fact, a Trinidadian who teaches at Boston University, Derek Walcott, received the Nobel Prize for Literature in 1992. Many in the lower-middle class work as bank tellers, salespersons, or real-estate agents.

Unofficial estimates indicate that the median annual income for a Trinidadian middle-class family of four is about $65,000. In addition, relatively few Trinidadians in the United States live below the poverty line (with an income of $14,800 or less); most of those that do are elderly and live on fixed incomes. Also, less than 1 percent of Trinidadians depend on noncontributory benefits such as Aid to Families with Dependent Children (AFDC), Supplementary Security Income (SSI), Medicaid, and food stamps. At the same time, two of every five Trinidadian families in the United States own their own home; this is particularly true of members of the second generation. As more members of the second generation attain college-level education, the percentage of Trinidadians who own their own home will increase.

## Conclusion

Trinidadians in the United States are structurally assimilated, well adjusted, and have attained a fair amount of success in the United States. The rate of crime in the community is relatively low, and blue-collar crime especially, against both the person and property, is virtually confined to a few members of the working class. More recently, however, a few college-educated Trinidadians in the United States have engaged in white-collar crimes such as tax evasion, bribery of public officials, fraud, infringement on copyright laws, and false advertising. Nevertheless, Trinidadians continue to be upwardly mobile in American society. Although they are not fully assimilated culturally and continue to engage in a slightly modified version of a bona fide Trinidadian lifestyle, celebrating such festivals as Carnival and Holi (Hindu Carnival), they have come to regard America as their new home and see themselves as an integral part of it.

See also: AFRICAN AMERICANS; GUYANESE; INDO-CARIBBEANS

## Bibliography

Bahadoorsingh, K. (1968). *Trinidad Electoral Politics: The Persistance of the Race Factor.* London: Institute of Race Relations.

Basch, L. (1978). "Workin' for the Yankee Dollar: The Impact of a Transnational Petroleum Company on Caribbean Class and Ethnic Relations." Ph.D. diss., New York University.

Camejo, A. (1971). "Racial Discrimination in Employment in Trinidad and Tobago." *Social and Economic Studies* 20:294–318.

Gosine, M. (1982). *East Indians and Black Power in the Caribbean: The Case of Trinidad.* New York: Africana Press.

Gosine, M. (1990). *Caribbean East Indians in America: Assimilation, Adaptation, and Group Experience.* New York: Windsor Press.

Gosine, M. (1992). *The Coolie Connection: From the Orient to the Occident.* New York: Windsor Press.

Gosine, M. (1994). *The East Indian Odyssey: Dilemmas of a Migrant People.* New York: Windsor Press.

Gosine, M. (1995). *The Legacy of Indian Indenture: 150 Years of East Indians in Trinidad.* New York: Windsor Press.

Malik, Y. (1971). *East Indians in Trinidad: A Study in Minority Politics.* London: Institute of Race Relations.

Matthews, D. B. (1952). "Crisis in the West Indian Family." *Caribbean Affairs* 1:15–16.

Oxaal, I. (1968). *Black Intellectuals Come to Power.* Cambridge, MA: Schenkman.

Parris, C. (1978). "Revolutionary Changes in the Caribbean: Political Dissidence and Public Policy in Postindependence Jamaica and Trinidad." Ph.D. diss., The New School for Social Research, New York.

Rennie, B. (1974). *History of the Working Class in Twentieth-Century Trinidad and Tobago.* Toronto: New Beginning.

Ryan, S. (1972). *Race and Nationalism in Trinidad and Tobago.* Toronto: University of Toronto Press.

MAHIN GOSINE

# TURKS

Contemporary Turkish Americans form two cohorts. The older cohort includes a few elderly survivors and a few U.S.-born descendants of some twenty-five thousand Turkish- and Kurdish-speaking Muslims who emigrated from the Ottoman Empire between 1900 and 1923 and from the Republic of Turkey between 1923 and the outbreak of World War II. The more recent cohort is composed of individuals and families who have left Turkey since World War II, settling mainly in suburbs throughout the United States. Despite dispersal throughout all regions of the country and segmentation into visiting circles that reflect different social origins in the home country and different educational levels, occupations, and income brackets, the entire community nevertheless is unified by its strong sense of ethnicity based on Turkish cultural traditions and shared historical experience.

## Turkish Identity

Turkish ethnicity is claimed by persons who are descendants of Turkish-speaking Muslim families and acknowledge their Turkish ancestry whether or not they acquire proficiency in the Turkish language or adhere closely to the precepts of Islam. Turks who are agnostics or atheists remain Turks. However, those who convert to Christianity or any other religion forfeit their Turkish identity to become associated with another group. Turkish identity has never been claimed by Greeks, Armenians, Jews, Arabs, or other non-Turkic peoples who emigrated from Turkey or the Ottoman Empire. Different religious traditions and languages often supersede nationality as primary foci of ethnic loyalty among Middle Easterners even today.

Turkish identity is a relatively recent phenomenon stemming from the establishment in 1923 of the Turkish republic, the first secular nation in the predominantly Muslim Middle East. Turks at home and abroad are intensely proud of Turkey's farsighted founder, Mustafa Kemal Atatürk (1881–1938), whose sweeping program of modernization continues to bear fruit. By 1926, Atatürk had abolished the sultanate and caliphate as well as the old religious courts, instituted a parliamentary government, and promulgated a Swiss-style family code that outlaws polygyny and requires civil marriage and divorce (with equal legal rights granted to both spouses). By 1928, all official documents were being written in a new Latin alphabet (rather than Arabic script) designed to render the Turkish language phonetically, thereby promoting literacy among the masses. In 1934, women gained both the right to vote and eligibility to run for parliament. Education was secularized, and public coeducational schools were opened in the larger cities.

## Ottoman Identity

Turkey was once the hub of the Ottoman Empire, which at its peak in the sixteenth century stretched from the walls of Vienna and the banks of the Danube River to the borders of Russia and Iran and across North Africa to Morocco. A major world power, Turkey developed the last great Islamic civilization in the Middle East. Turkish Americans are proud of its many achievements, such as magnificent mosques and public buildings with tile-faced walls bearing bold geometric patterns or gracefully flowing floral designs; fine carpets that have been coveted in the Western World since the fifteenth century; culinary delicacies such as shish kebab, stuffed vegetables, and fine candies; and tulips, introduced to Europe when an Austrian ambassador to the sixteenth-century Ottoman court took some bulbs back home with him. Modern Turkish culture has strong Ottoman roots. Many Turkish-American homes display traditional and contemporary objects of Turkish art, and a few feature an "Ottoman corner," complete with soft cushions, rugs, a copper or brass brazier, and a hanging wall lamp. A rich and varied traditional cuisine is offered to guests and served on holidays.

The Western stereotype of the terrible, incorrigible Turk, which has plagued many Turkish immigrants in the United States, predominated in the nineteenth and early twentieth centuries, when the Ottoman Empire was disintegrating under the pressures of European commercial expansion and political intrigue. The Ottoman Empire's many Christian minorities identified with Christian Europeans and admired the democracies and technological advancements of western Europe. Often fomented by European interest groups, the Christians initiated secessionist movements that evoked severe reprisals from the Ottoman government. In the resulting turmoil, scores of Ottoman Christians immigrated to the United States and Latin America. A trickle of Ottoman Muslims followed in their wake.

## Ottoman Muslims in the United States

Muslims who left Ottoman domain between 1900 and World War I hailed from its most turbulent areas: the eastern provinces (where Armenians were in revolt) and the Balkan provinces (which were embroiled in wars of independence). According to U.S. Immigration and Naturalization Service statistics, 22,085 persons who identified themselves as Turks were admitted to the United States between 1900 and 1925. Of this total, 20,652 (93.1%) were male and 1,433 (6.9%) were female. The majority were between the ages of fourteen and forty-four on arrival. Peak years of Turkish immigration were 1904–1908, 1910, and 1912–1914. However, many Turks, fearing rejection by immigration authorities, gained entry to the United States under the guise of another ethnic identification, and some of the "Turks" were Kurds. The U.S. Ottoman Muslim community cohered as a single ethnic unit despite the different languages its members spoke. About 45 percent spoke Turkish; 45 percent spoke Kurdish, an Indo-European language of Iranian stock; and the rest spoke Albanian, an Indo-European language, or dialects of Arabic, a Semitic language. Ottoman Muslims in the United States formed tiny enclaves in the industrial cities along the eastern seaboard and in the Great Lakes region. Many men went west for a time to work in the mines or build railroads, and others went to Panama to help build the Panama Canal. Detroit boasted the largest Ottoman Muslim community in the United States during the 1920s with at least six thousand persons.

Ottoman Muslim Balkan immigrants to America were displaced persons who entertained little hope of ever returning to their homeland. Mostly Turkish-speaking, they were irrevocably cut off from their kin who remained behind. Equally divided between Turkish- and Kurdish-speakers, emigrants from eastern Ottoman provinces were largely unskilled and illiterate village youths who hoped to get rich in the legendary land where the streets were paved with gold and then return to their homeland when peace was restored and they were too old to be drafted. They dreamed of buying land near their natal villages, hiring others to cultivate it, marrying, having many children, and living splendidly. In actuality, very few of them ever returned to their homeland; they were deterred by the difficulty of leaving the United States during World War I, the chaos in their homeland after the Greeks invaded in 1919, their continuing eligibility for conscription into the Turkish army, the chance to benefit from the American economic boom of the 1920s, sudden job loss and impoverishment during the 1930s, and World War II. By 1945, many of their relatives and friends in the homeland had died. Most of the immigrants earned just enough to support themselves, having been employed chiefly on the assembly lines in Detroit's auto plants, in the steel mills of Gary, Indiana, or Pittsburgh, Pennsylvania, or in various factories in the industrial towns of New England. They looked forward to a retirement sustained by social security checks and small pensions. These incomes allowed them to be self-sufficient and to live in dignity in America, but they were not enough for playing the role of rich man and generous benefactor in postwar Turkey.

Upon arriving in the United States, Ottoman Muslim men took up residence in rooming houses and apartment buildings, some owned by prosperous countrymen, or they cooperatively rented large houses, often sleeping in the same beds in shifts. By the 1920s, Turkish coffeehouses opened in Chicago, Detroit, and the mill towns of the eastern seaboard. There the men would gather after working long hours to relax, play *tavala* (backgammon), listen to recordings of Turkish music, receive mail from home, and discuss politics while they ate. Coffeehouses also served as informal employment agencies where newcomers and men who had been laid off could learn of local job openings from compatriots who worked in large factories. They also served as meeting sites for the voluntary organizations the men founded to meet their needs in an alien land.

In 1921, the American headquarters of Kızıl Ay (Red Crescent), the Muslim wing of the international Red Cross, was established in Detroit; a few years later, a branch was opened in Whiting, Indiana. Contributors to Kızıl Ay eventually were issued booklets from Ankara, the capital of the new Turkish republic, with the regulations of the society printed in Turkish and English. The booklets also included several pages with blocks for the placement of stamps acknowledging receipt of each monthly donation. Unmarried Kızıl Ay members also paid dues into a funeral account to ensure that they received a proper Muslim burial should they die in the United States. Over the years, Kızıl Ay sent money to assist victims of disasters in Turkey. For example, $25,000 was remitted to Ankara in 1924 to help Turkish children orphaned during the War of Independence against the Greeks.

During the 1920s, new national identities came to replace the Ottoman Muslim identity. In 1928, Kurds along Turkey's border with Syria revolted against the secularization of government in the Turkish republic; its failure marked the emergence of Kurdish nationalism. Detroit Kurds and some Turks sympathized with the rebels and sent them money, but most Turks proudly supported the fledgling secular republic. In 1936, the secularist faction quit Kızıl Ay and founded the Türkiye Çocuk Esirgeme (Turkish Orphans Association), with an attached funeral society. It was licensed as a tax-exempt charitable organization by the State of Michigan. Relations between the two Detroit organizations mirrored the oscillating political rifts between Turks and Kurds in Turkey. After the Kurdish revolts subsided in 1938, several Turks and Kurds held memberships in both associations, and the two clubs jointly celebrated Turkish Independence Day and the two important Muslim holidays of Seker Bayram (which concludes Ramadan, the month of fasting) and Kurban Bayram (which commemorates the sacrifice of Abraham). Together, both associations raised thousands of dollars to send to earthquake victims in eastern Turkey in 1938. In the 1950s, the Turkish Orphans Association sent an x-ray machine and ambulance to Elâzığ, a city in Anatolia (Asian Turkey), and contributed to the construction of a new mosque there. In 1953, members of Kızıl Ay purchased a building in Dearborn, Michigan, for the organization's new headquarters. The first floor was converted into a restaurant, which was also used for meetings and various ceremonies such as funeral banquets. The second floor contained sleeping quarters for eight men whose rent payments defrayed the expenses of building upkeep. Dignitaries ranging from Detroit mayors to corporation presidents and visiting Turkish officials often were feted in the building. The Detroit chapter of Kızıl Ay disbanded in 1974 when its membership fell below ten persons; the Dearborn building was sold, and all remaining funds were sent to the central office in Ankara. The Turkish Orphans Association persisted until 1978, mainly as a funeral club for its few surviving elderly members.

Some 95 percent of the Ottoman Turkish and Kurdish male immigrants never married. Most would not risk matrimony with American women, who typically dated many men before marrying and moved freely in public places, unlike women in the immigrants' homeland, and few Muslim women of any ethnicity could be found in the United States before the 1950s. About 75 percent

A Turkish-American woman holds a Turkish flag to celebrate her ethnic heritage during a parade in Chicago. (Sandy Felsenthal/Corbis)

of the men who did marry took American brides, mostly Roman Catholic Euroamericans with working- or middle-class backgrounds. Many Turkish and Kurdish husbands tolerated their wive's faith, although they did not convert to it. A few of the women voluntarily converted to Islam after marriage. Wives usually did not work after marriage, as they and their husbands shared the idea that the husband should be the family breadwinner while the wife took charge of the home. Although many American wives added Turkish recipes to their culinary repertoire, most of them made no effort to learn Turkish or Kurdish, so many mixed couples spoke only English at home. The Turks and Kurds who wed American women became naturalized U.S. citizens and voted in local and national elections, but they still followed politics in Turkey and remained active in the aforementioned ethnic associations. Because a smaller percentage of them became American citizens, the never-married men were less integrated into U.S. political life. Both the married and the never-married men, however, belonged to unions in the workplaces and were active laborers in the U.S. economy. Some men with American wives also joined brotherhoods such as the Masons and Elks and were as comfortable with their many American friends as with their compatriots. A handful of men married before immigrating to the United States and therefore had Muslim wives. A few others were able to contract marriages with Turkish women who had immigrated to the United States with their parents.

Most of the children of the mixed couples had little opportunity to speak Turkish or Kurdish and did not visit Turkey while they were growing up. Few practiced Islam, and most wed Christian Americans. They took little interest in their Middle Eastern heritage and were absorbed easily into the American mainstream. The only exceptions were some sons of couples in which the American wife embraced Islam. Some of the sons resulting from this type of union married Turkish women. Sons of purely Turkish couples maintained pride in their ethnic ancestry; some of them married women in Turkey whom their parents had chosen for them, while others traveled to Turkey to find wives on their own.

The U.S.-born offspring of Ottoman Muslims did not continue their parents' voluntary organizations. Thus, these small but once thriving communities dissolved through attrition (as the elderly bachelors died) and through the Americanization of most of the second generation.

## Post–World War II Communities

Post–World War II immigrants from Turkey contrast sharply with their Ottoman predecessors. The vast majority emigrated from Turkey between the mid-1940s and the late 1960s, arriving as students attending American universities. Most of these immigrants were males who were between the ages of twenty and thirty-five upon arrival, and many of them were already married to Turkish women who either accompanied them or followed within a year. One subgroup among these students consists of the offspring of wealthy merchant and professional families from small towns in Anatolia or of displaced Ottoman Balkan bureaucratic families who settled in Istanbul in the 1920s. These families, who tended to be Western-oriented, committed to secularism, and education-focused, were liberal Muslims or staunch atheists. The male students and many of their wives had earned degrees and professional certificates from Turkish universities and technical institutes prior to their arrival in the United States. Several of the wives also earned undergraduate and graduate degrees from American universities. After earning their degrees, many of these couples decided to remain in the United States to give their children a better education and a better life than would have been possible in Turkey.

The men and women who remained in the United States have gone on to become physicians with various specialties ranging from pediatric endocrinologist to heart surgeon, plastic surgeon, pathologist, and psychiatrists; distinguished university professors of engineering, economics, political science, sociology, and Turkish language and literature; and curators of Middle Eastern collections in American museums. The offspring have followed in their parents' occupational footsteps and been equally successful. Some members of this second generation have become lawyers, stock brokers, accountants, and newspaper reporters. Because they frequently visited relatives in Turkey while they were growing up and were exposed to the luxuries and amenities of modern Turkey, they take pride in and strongly identify with their Turkish heritage. In the suburbs where they matured, neither they nor their parents experienced prejudice or discrimination from their American neighbors. Being Turkish and Muslim has not impeded their professional lives either. Many of the early post–World War II highly educated immigrants have retired to sunbelt states or to Turkey. A few doctors among the latter donate their services and expertise to medical clinics in Turkey. There is also reciprocal visiting between parents and adult offspring who have scattered across the United States as their jobs have required.

Some Turkish male students who were not married when they arrived in the United States later wed Euroamerican women of working- or middle-class background, most of whom were Roman Catholic and a few of whom were Protestant or Jewish. Before marriage, the women worked as nurses, medical technicians, secretaries, and waitresses; after marriage, few continued to work, devoting themselves to home and family. Most mixed couples report satisfaction in their marriages, and divorce rates among them are low. Their children, like their purely Turkish counterparts, have visited Turkey often and are proud of their Turkish heritage. About half of the U.S.-born individuals have wed Turks, and the remainder have wed Americans.

A second group of university students from Turkey was sponsored by the Turkish armed forces under the auspices of the U.S.-Turkish North Atlantic Treaty Organization (NATO) Agreement of 1952. To upgrade the technical training of high-ranking military personnel, each branch of the Turkish armed services sent groups of officers (all male) to America to earn degrees in various engineering fields. The Turkish government paid for their tuition and their textbooks and allotted each student a monthly stipend for living expenses. Moreover, the salary each would have earned, as determined by his current rank, was deposited in a Turkish bank in his name. On completion of his degree, he was expected to resume his commission and serve his remaining years in the military.

Approximately half of the NATO Agreement students were not yet married when they matriculated at American universities, and, for various reasons, about half of those who did not already have a wife married American women. However, the Turkish military code until 1982 forbade any soldiers from marrying foreign women. Excused from further duties and indebted to the Turkish government for the cost of their education, the students who married Americans stayed in the United States to raise their families. A few military men with Turkish wives returned to Turkey, where they were able to get relieved of their responsibilities without incurring a debt, and then they immigrated back to America with their families. The ex-military men worked as engineers in large corporations, established various consulting firms and retail businesses, or went into real-estate sales. They have generally drawn middle- and upper-middle-class incomes, and their college-educated children enjoy similar lifestyles.

The family relations of some mixed, ex-military couples have been troubled, and 75 to 80 percent of the marriages have ended in divorce. This trouble is explained by cultural clashes rooted in the specific backgrounds of the spouses. The military men were from working-class, urban or small town artisan families with conservative views of gender relations. Most of the men envisioned a family in which honor was preserved by virtuous daughters and a faithful, docile wife who was dedicated to the children. The American women were mostly middle-class, Euroamerican, Protestant or Jewish, college-educated, and career- as well as family-oriented. The children of these couples identify with their Turkish fathers' cultural heritage only to the degree that their parents enjoyed a satisfactory marriage. As many of these marriages were unhappy, many of the children have mild to no curiosity about Turkey and its culture; most of them have married Euroamericans and are very Americanized in their values and outlooks.

The third group of post–World War II Turkish immigrants is diverse. It includes small numbers of working-class individuals from both purely Turkish and mixed families who resemble their pre–World War II old community counterparts. Since the 1970s, scattered families and individuals with technical and business skills have settled in America. In that decade, for example, a Turkish physician living in Rochester, New York, sponsored the immigration of Turkish tailors and seamstresses from his hometown. They prospered and built the first Turkish mosque (with an attached school and cultural center) in the United States there. In the 1990s, sundry Turkish tourists and immigrants formed a growing community in the New York City borough of Queens. Newcomers, who include teachers from Turkey's public schools and out-of-work laborers from small export commodity ateliers in Istanbul, are helped by Turkish grocers, roominghouse owners, and taxi drivers to find living quarters, purchase food, and obtain clothing until they obtain a green card, find work, and adjust to life in their new locale. Increasing numbers of Turkish females have enrolled in American universities, and although many of them return home after earning their degrees, some have found remunerative employment in the United States. A few of these women have even married American men.

Voluntary associations have proliferated in post–World War II Turkish-American communities. Local cultural associations were founded mainly by professionals in the 1960s and 1970s. Their activities include celebrations of both Turkish and American national holidays and Islamic holidays, as well as the sponsorship of special lectures by visiting scholars. Overarching national organizations are numerous. The Turkish Cultural Alliance, founded in 1933 in New York City, is the oldest extant Turkish-American organization. It maintains a Turkish cemetery, offers classes in Turkish language and culture for children, and has a multimedia library. The Federation of Turkish-American Associations, established in 1956 in New York City, also maintains a library, publishes a Turkish- and English-language newsletter, and sponsors the annual New York City Turkish-American Day Parade and Turkish Week. The Assembly of Turkish-American Associations, founded in 1978 and located in Washington, D.C., organizes scholarly conferences on Turkish issues in the United States and abroad, publishes a newspaper in Turkish and English for its members, and sends a weekly newsletter to all members of the U.S. Congress. Every American university with a large number of Turkish students boasts a Turkish student organization, and there are two associations that link Turkish professionals throughout the United States: the Society of Turkish Architects, Engineers, and Scientists in America (which was founded in 1970 and publishes a bimonthly bulletin) and the Turkish Physicians Association (which was founded in 1969 and holds an annual convention for the exchange of medical knowledge). In addition, various Turkish-American sports clubs, musical groups, and radio and television programs have been organized over the years. American wives of Turks have also run charitable societies that contribute money and supplies to schools in villages and small towns in Turkey.

## Conclusion

People of Turkish ancestry in the United States number between 100,000 and 150,000. Their largest communities are located in New York City, Washington, D.C., and Detroit, but smaller Turkish-American communities can be found in virtually every state. The contemporary Turkish-American community is diversified economically, but most individuals are members of the upper-middle class, which is successful by American standards.

*See also:* ARMENIANS; GREEKS; JEWS, MIDDLE EASTERN

## Bibliography

Aijian, M. M. (1920). "Mohemmedans in the United States." *The Muslim World* 10:30–35.

Bilgé, B. (1994). "Voluntary Associations in the Old Turkish Community of Metropolitan Detroit." In *Muslim Communities of North America*, edited by Y. Yazbeck Haddad and J. Idleman Smith. Albany: State University of New York Press.

Bilgé, B. (1996). "Turkish-American Patterns of Intermarriage." In *Family and Gender Among American Muslims*, edited by B. C. Aswad and B. Bilgé. Philadelphia: Temple University Press.

Bousquet, G. H. (1935). "Moslem Religious Influences in the United States." *The Muslim World* 25:40–44.

Holmes, M. C. (1936). "Islam in America." *The Muslim World* 26:262–266.

Rankin, L. (1939). "Detroit Nationality Groups." *Michigan History Magazine* 23:165.

BARBARA BILGÉ

# UKRAINIANS

In some ways, the story of the Ukrainian immigrant experience in America is a rags-to-riches narrative with motifs that are similar to those that characterize the mythologies of many other immigrant groups in the United States. Nonetheless, the Ukranian version of "the American dream" includes unique and distinctive elements. Events in the country of origin and issues connected to language and religion are critical factors shaping the Ukrainian-American story. In addition, music, dance, and other aspects of traditional culture are just as crucial to the expression and survival of America's Ukrainian community.

## General Profile

In 1990, according to the U.S. Census, 740,803 Americans identified themselves as partially or exclusively of Ukrainian ancestry. According to unofficial estimates, however, there are 1.5 million Americans of Ukrainian descent in the United States, most of them American-born. The states with the largest Ukrainian populations in 1990 were Pennsylvania, New York, New Jersey, California, Michigan, Ohio, Illinois, Florida, Connecticut,

and Massachusetts. Their heritage has strong links to several other ethnocultural traditions whose histories crosscross over and intertwine with strictly Ukrainian concerns. Strong historic and cultural links with other Slavic and eastern European groups that also immigrated to America (such as Carpatho-Rusyns, Poles, Hungarians, Jews, Romanians, Russians, and Slovaks) often made it difficult for Ukrainians in America to maintain a separate, distinctive identity and consequently to promote their own welfare and interests. In the Old World, geographic proximity and a pervasive Byzantine legacy favored multicultural connections but blurred differences. This duality was transferred to the United States and characterized the culture of America's early communities of Ukrainian and other eastern European immigrants.

The first significant numbers of Ukrainian immigrants to the United States arrived in the late 1870s from Ukrainian ethnic territories ruled by the Austro-Hungarian monarchy in eastern Europe. Most of them were impoverished, illiterate peasants who settled in the industrial regions of Pennsylvania, New York, and New Jersey to find employment in mines and factories. The Reverend Ivan Volansky was one of the pioneering figures

A Ukrainian-American worker tends the cows on a large dairy farm in Waymart, Pennsylvania, in 1949. (UPI/Corbis-Bettmann)

who worked on their behalf during these early years of Ukrainian community life in America. Ukrainians credit him with building their first church and with organizing their first fraternal society, first choir, and first newspaper. Many Ukrainian immigrants stayed in America, while others returned to their homes in the Old World, where they used their earnings to improve their situation in more familiar surroundings.

This first wave brought about half a million immigrants to the United States and ended in 1914 with the outbreak of World War I. Subsequent waves were much less numerous. From 1920 to 1939, immigration quotas limited the total number of Ukrainian immigrants to about fifteen thousand. After World War II, however, approximately eighty-five thousand Ukrainian refugees arrived as "displaced persons" whose experiences in war-torn

Europe had made then acutely politicized and aware of their ethnocultural distinctiveness. In contrast with earlier waves of Ukrainian immigrants, this influx featured many highly skilled professionals who were more comfortable in urban rather than rural settings. Largely as a result of this new influx, figures for 1979 show that Ukrainian Americans enjoyed levels of income and educational and occupational status higher than the American average.

This wave of Ukrainian refugee immigrants introduced a strong element of elitism into the Ukrainian-American community and molded it into a movement committed to the liberation of Ukraine and its transformation into a free nation. Under their tutelage Ukrainian culture in America was transformed from an orally based complex to one more attuned to the demands and style of a modern, technologically driven society. For them, the ancestral language was not only a vehicle for the transmission of Ukrainian culture but was above all a precious cultural resource — an inextricable component of a national Ukrainian ethnos — that had to be preserved as the prime marker of a distinct Ukrainian culture. The new-comers organized literary circles and scholarly associations; they also promoted Ukrainian-lan-guage instruction at all levels of education, from preschool to university graduate studies. A net-work of Ukrainian schooling was developed; in the mid-1970s, for example, the Ukrainian-American community supported twenty-six elementary schools, four high schools, one junior college, two seminaries, and numerous supplementary or "Sat-urday" schools. These efforts culminated in 1973 with the endowment of three "chairs" in Ukrainian studies — in linguistics, history, and literature — and the establishment of the Harvard Ukrainian Research Institute as the most prestigious and principal center of Ukrainian studies in the United States.

Moreover, it became evident that it was only their proficiency in a distinctive language such as Ukrainian that could provide Ukrainian Ameri-cans with the kind of instant recognition accorded other ethnocultural groups in America on the basis of such purely physical characteristics as skin color. In this way for Ukrainians in America, intangible traits rapidly gained importance as ideo-logical factors.

This commitment to language and culture is strongly linked to the drive for recognition on several fronts, in America as well as in Ukraine. Ukraine's historical struggle for statehood, self-rule, and independence were political goals that received aesthetic validation through a set of cul-tural components that emphasized distinction, uniqueness, and separateness. The Ukrainian lan-guage and a church establishment were institu-tionalized as the major supporting factors in this desire and search for ethnocultural and national recognition.

In America, these factors were further com-plicated by the need to adapt to the needs, stan-dards, and pressures of an environment that not only differed from but sometimes clashed with Ukrainian aims and sensibilities. The American focus on individual fortitude threatened Ukrainian traditions of commonality. Efforts to mobilize the community's energies for its own welfare and con-tinuity were consistently jeoparized by factors that threatened the gradual disintegration of the Ukrainian community, which in the opinion of some people had become just another ethnic ghetto. Economic prosperity, increased mobil-ity, intermarriage, and language loss conspired to break the limitations of separateness, confine-ment, and containment. Consequently, vehicles that could bridge the gap between old and new have always been important to the survival of the Ukrainian community in America.

Historically, the Ukrainian immigrant commu-nity in America developed, supported, and relied upon a variety of communication media (stage, print, radio, film, and video) to convey what was perceived as the essence of Ukrainian culture and spirit. Many Ukrainian Americans acted as culture brokers between America and their ancestral homeland until Ukraine's declaration of indepen-dence in 1991 and the end of Communist suprem-acy in eastern Europe. However, a free Ukraine meant that the role of America's Ukrainian com-munity as intermediary became superfluous once the U.S. government recognized the new state of Ukraine. By 1993, a new era of formal relations between the United States and Ukraine began to take shape, and these political developments along with the emergence of a free and independent homeland not only diluted the Ukrainian-Ameri-can community's zeal to preserve Ukrainian cul-ture but also heightened the perennial issue of loyalty conflict faced by many immigrant groups in America. Many Ukrainian Americans continued to see themselves and their communities as exten-sions of a worldwide, inclusive Ukrainian diaspora that pivoted around Ukraine itself. Others, es-pecially the American-born, tried to develop and maintain an independent version of Ukrainian identity that could function as an integral part of a pluralistic America, one not governed by politics in the ancestral homeland. This ideological duality and the issue of cultural dependency are fundamental features that continue to profile the Ukrainian community in America.

The independence of Ukraine in 1991 opened the gates to exchange. Many Ukrainian Americans were able to visit the ancestral homeland for the first time freely and without fear of the political recriminations characteristic of the Communist era in Ukraine. At the same time, a new wave of Ukrainian immigrants entered the United States, many with established, international profiles, such as Oksana Bayul, the champion ice skater whose reputation added luster to the Ukrainian-American community's ongoing efforts to gain general recognition and acceptance.

## Religious Considerations

Church and religion have always been central to the concerns of Ukrainians in America. The strong affiliation with a single faith—Christianity—is rooted in the proclamation of Christianity as the official state religion for Ukraine in 988 C.E. Consequently non-Christian faiths rarely received the preferential treatment accorded the Christian Church. This situation is further complicated by the divisive coexistence of two different but related streams of eastern Christianity: Catholicism (recognizing papal supremacy) and Orthodoxy. Moreover, controversial issues regarding clerical celibacy, the liturgical calendar (Julian versus Gregorian), and language of worship (Old Church Slavic, or Ukrainian, or, especially in America, English) continue to polemicize Ukrainians around the world.

In America, most Ukrainians are Ukrainian Catholics, although in Ukraine itself most Christians belong to non-Catholic, Orthodox denominations. The reason behind this difference lies in the fact that western Ukraine, where Catholicism dominates, is the ancestral homeland for the majority of Ukrainian Americans, who tend to perpetuate old country religious preferences in America. In addition to Catholic and Orthodox denominations, there are several Ukrainian Protestant denominations, the most prominent being the Ukrainian Evangelical Baptist Church.

After the downfall of communism in Ukraine in 1991 and the removal of antireligious laws, many Ukrainian religious groups in America turned their attention to rebuilding religious institutions in the motherland.

## A Political Infrastructure

During the early immigration period, organizational life was frequently racked by factionalism and discord. The Ukrainian National Association, (UNA) founded as a fraternal society in 1894 to meet the insurance needs of the Ukrainian community in America, survives as the leading secular organization for Ukrainians in America. The association's newspaper, *Svoboda* (Freedom), remains the most important publication of its kind outside Ukraine itself. With a head office in Jersey City, New Jersey, the UNA operates throughout the United States and Canada; its members, through their insurance policies with the head office, contribute to various educational and cultural projects that foster the Ukrainian community's aims and development. In 1940, the Ukrainian Congress Committee of America was formed to help coordinate the efforts of all Ukrainian organized groups in the United States.

In the 1990s, a great variety of Ukrainian organizations—educational, political, women's religious, professional, sporting, and cultural—are found in the United States. These organizations reflect a wide range of interests and a continuing dynamism that is important to this group's sense of pride and community. Indeed, some Ukrainian Americans have complained that their community has an excessive number of organizations, making it difficult to attain common goals and diverting attention from a more active role in American politics.

## Defining the Tradition

Before World War II, it was important for the Ukrainian immigrant community in America to develop an understanding of its culture that could bolster its self-esteem as well as offer an image of that culture to non-Ukrainians. Because the community was racked by political and sectarian factionalism, its search for a positive image led to the discovery of cultural accomplishments in apolitical fields. These provided the base that drew together the entire Ukrainian community.

During the early years of Ukrainian settlement in America, rich folkloric resources helped sustain the immigrant community as it struggled to survive on foreign soil. Music-making, rituals, and customs originating in Ukraine functioned as support systems that made the pain of dislocation more tolerable. Early phonograph records were produced in the thousands. These became fixtures in the homes of many homesick Ukrainian immigrants. Traditional festivities associated with weddings, Christmas, and Easter not only brought everyone together but also enhanced the quality of the immigrant experience and provided a framework for community survival in the New World.

A Ukrainian brother and sister perform music on a violin and an accordion upon their arrival in New York City in 1950. (UPI/Corbis-Bettmann)

## Continuity of a Ukrainian Presence

Various forms of cultural expression are used by America's Ukrainian immigrant community to offset the threat of assimilation. These tend to exploit the rich tradition of Ukrainian folklore in combination with venues that allow for the expression of this tradition in a positive, distinctive, and entertaining way. For Ukrainians in America, the appeals of song, dance, and cuisine play dominant roles in the process of cultural continuity and search for general public recognition. These trends have been supported by newspapers and books in Ukrainian and/or English as well as by art and church architecture.

Two influential figures who exemplified these trends were Vasyl Avramenko and Oleksander Koshetz. Avramenko was especially successful as a flamboyant entrepreneur-impresario whose love for Ukrainian folk dance prompted him to use this medium to transform several generations of Ukrainian-American youths into proud and active bearers of Ukrainian tradition. Avramenko staged many Ukrainian pageants and countless performances from coast to coast; sometimes these featured hundreds of participants, as exemplified by the mass participation of Avramenko's folk dance ensembles from Ukrainian communities across America at the Century of Progress Exposition in Chicago in 1933.

The charismatic Oleksander Koshetz gained renown among Ukrainians in America as a conductor whose devotion to Ukrainian choral singing endeared him to all who worked with him. The activities of Avramenko, Koshetz, and their followers set the pattern for cultural activism in many Ukrainian communities for several decades during the middle of the twentieth century.

Other institutions and venues (some of them uniquely Ukrainian-American) developed to help Ukrainian Americans come together and indulge in their common heritage. For example, after World War II many Ukrainian Americans were able to spend holidays and vacations in camps, seasonal resorts, and cottage enclaves that catered exclusively to the Ukrainian-American community.

With their focus on Ukrainian traditions, these venues enabled many urbanite Ukrainian Americans to foster Ukrainian loyalties conveniently. In addition, several Ukrainian museums, libraries, and archives were founded in America after World War II.

In comparison with many other immigrant groups in America, the Ukrainian community in the 1990s is geographically dispersed, relatively young, and small in population. The transformation of its status from an immigrant group into a mature and permanent component of America's ethnocultural mosaic has taken many decades and will continue to evolve in years to come.

*See also:* CARPATHO-RUSYNS; HUNGARIANS; JEWS, SOVIET; POLES; ROMANIANS; RUSSIANS; SLOVAKS

## Bibliography

Isajiw, W. W., ed. (1976). *Ukrainians in American and Canadian Society.* Jersey City, NJ: M. P. Kots.

Klymasz, R. B. (1979). "Ukrainian-American Fiddle and Dance Music, 1926–1936." *Ethnomusicology* 23:485–486.

Kuropas, M. B. (1991). *The Ukrainian Americans: Roots and Aspirations, 1884–1954.* Toronto: University of Toronto Press.

Kuropas, M. B. (1993). "United States of America." In *Encyclopedia of Ukraine,* edited by D. Struk. Toronto: University of Toronto Press.

Magocsi, P. R., ed. (1979). "The Ukrainian Experience in the United States: A Symposium." Cambridge, MA: Harvard Ukrainian Research Institute.

Markus, D., and Wolowyna, O. (1994). "Ukrainians in the United States of America." In *Ukraine and Ukrainians Throughout the World: A Demographic and Sociological Guide to the Homeland and Its Diaspora,* edited by A. L. Pawliczko. Toronto: University of Toronto Press.

Markus, V. (1971). "In the United States." In *Ukraine: A Concise Encyclopaedia,* edited by V. Kubijovic. Toronto: University of Toronto Press.

Subtelny, O. (1991). *Ukrainians in North America: An Illustrated History.* Toronto: University of Toronto Press.

Wolowyna, O., ed. (1986). *Ethnicity and National Identity: Demographic and Socioeconomic Characteristics of Persons with Ukrainian Heritage in the United States.* Cambridge, MA: Harvard Ukrainian Research Institute.

ROBERT B. KLYMASZ

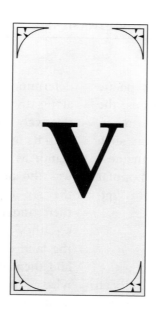

# VIETNAMESE

The Vietnamese have been characterized by their ties to Chinese civilization. These links with China, derived not only from geographic proximity but also from more than a millennium of intensive contact, are reflected in the patriarchally oriented Confucian family system, with its filial piety, cult of ancestors, and an imperial examination system that was based on knowledge of classic literature. Some scholars claim that aspects of these systems existed in Vietnam before the initial entry of the Han Chinese in the first century B.C.E. These economic and social ties and shared values about family structure connect Vietnamese resettling in the United States to overseas Chinese communities.

Like China, Vietnam had a diverse group of coexisting religious systems. In addition to Confucianism these systems included Taoism and the Mahayana system of Buddhism. The latter was imported to Vietnam through China and did not come directly from India, where Buddhism originated. This complexity of religious systems contrasts with the predominant Buddhist faith in Cambodia and Laos, and these differences have resulted in the creation of a variety of Buddhist temples among the Indochinese in the United States, similar to the denominational variations in Christian churches.

Vietnamese share with Chinese some modes of food and dress. But Americans who have had an opportunity to dine in Vietnamese restaurants, (sometimes located in "Chinatowns") are made aware of the differences from Chinese cuisines. At festivals, such as that of Tê't (New Year) or Trung Thu (Mid-Autumn), the traditional costumes are also similar to those of the Chinese. In food, Chinese use more oil, but Vietnamese more frequently boil food. Dress is similar for men, but for Vietnamese women, their dress (áo dài, or long dress) is longer, open on two sides, and always worn with pants.

In language, Vietnamese belongs to the Mon-Khmer group with elements derived from Chinese. There are apparent relationships with Thai languages (including Lao and Thai). Beginning in the thirteenth century, the Vietnamese language was written in modified Chinese characters (Chũ nôm). The switch to the Latin alphabet (Chũ quô'c ngũ) originated with the work of a Catholic priest, Alexandre de Rhodes, in the seventeenth century but was not finalized until the twentieth century. The Vietnamese thus have a long recorded history as well as a well-developed literary and poetic tradition. As with many other ethnic groups, the Vietnamese in the United States struggle to maintain their bilingualism. This is fostered in such diverse ways as religious services in Vietnamese (both Buddhist and Catholic) as well as popular literature, music, and videos imported from Vietnam and a local press in Vietnamese.

## Regional Influences in Vietnam

The Vietnamese (Viêt) have historically been divided into three subcultures. According to the French, these were Tonkin in the North, Annam in the center, and Cochin China in the South. More simply, they were known by the Vietnamese as Bác Kỳ (northern region), Trung Kỳ (middle region), and Nam Kỳ (southern region). Two river systems determine the major population concentrations along the coastal plain and contrast with the relatively sparsely settled mountainous interior with its indigenous tribal peoples. The North, with Hanoi as its major city in the Red River delta, was the original site of Vietnamese culture. For the six centuries after the Vietnamese gained their independence from the Chinese in 939 C.E. they expanded into central Vietnam, taking the land of the kingdom of Champa (the Cham), and then into the South, pushing the Khmer into what is now Cambodia. The South, with Saigon as its major city in the Mekong River delta, was settled in the seventeenth to nineteenth centuries. These historical regions also correspond with differences in dialect, which consist of tone variations and some different vocabulary items. But unlike the case in China, there is mutual

A group of Vietnamese Americans demonstrates in 1994 at the Federal Building in Seattle, Washington, with a hunger strike to protest against human rights abuses in Vietnam. (Dean Wong/Corbis)

intelligibility among these dialects. It is said by the Vietnamese that those from the North are more aggressive but tactful, while individuals from the central area are thought to be more reserved, and people from the South are considered direct and open. These linguistic and cultural distinctions exist within a defined unity. Regional variations remain within the Vietnamese-American community, especially for the older generation. However, these do not inhibit intermarriage and tend to be overridden by religious and class differences.

In Vietnam, there are some important ethnic distinctions within both urban and rural areas. Historically there has been a major Chinese city within Saigon, Cholon. This was the site of the largest Chinese population in Vietnam (divided into regional groups based on place of origin in China). Chinese communities also existed in other urban areas of Vietnam. Known as overseas Chinese throughout Southeast Asia, these communities played a major, even dominant, role in commerce. While Chinese are clearly identifiable both by language and custom from the Vietnamese, there has been intermarriage and mixing of the cultures so that a hinge group of Sino-Vietnamese has emerged between the two societies, the Tàu lai (Chinese mixed blood). The Chinese are respected as hardworking people and are even felt to be more enterprising than the Vietnamese. The Sino-Vietnamese have tended to be incorporated within existing Chinese communities when they immigrated to the United States. Of lower status are the Khmer Krom, the Khmer-Vietnamese who lived mainly in the border regions. Those who have immigrated to the United States are associated with the Khmer-American community. Some attribute this lower status to their darker skin color. This historically low status pertains even more to the mountain peoples formerly known collectively as *moi* (slave) and more recently as *thượng* (mountaineer). They have been pressured by an expanding Vietnamese population. Communities of these people have also resettled in the United States.

The offspring of Franco-Vietnamese unions, the Tây lai (Western mixed blood), have histori-

cally been looked down upon, even though some Vietnamese women from the more prosperous classes considered the children of such unions to be prettier than "pure" Vietnamese. Unlike the case with the children of unions with Chinese, the predominant feeling was that such children were partly of foreign, European, and not Asian blood. More recently, the predominant group in this category has been the Vietnamese Amerasians, generally the offspring of a Vietnamese mother and an American father, the latter being associated with the U.S. war effort in Vietnam between 1965 and 1975. Unlike the Franco-Vietnamese children, who were taken to France when the French military departed in 1954, the Vietnamese Amerasians remained after the collapse of South Vietnam in 1975 and the withdrawal of the Americans. Some were rejected by their mothers, and their low and marginal status was indicated by the term *tre bui dòi* (children, dust of life); these children often lived on the street. In the 1980s, many were officially resettled in the United States.

## History of Immigration

The settlement of the Vietnamese in the United States is the direct result of the disintegration of the French colonial empire after World War II and the subsequent abortive failure of U.S. military intervention against Communist North Vietnam. This followed the defeat of the French colonial armies by the Communist North in 1954 in the first Indochina War. Vietnam became a colony of France only in the nineteenth century even though French Catholic missionaries first appeared in Vietnam in the seventeenth century. French troops entered Dà Nẵng in central Vietnam in 1858, and Vietnam became a protectorate of France in 1886 as part of Indochine Francaise (French Indochina), along with neighboring Cambodia and Laos. French control was interrupted by Japanese occupation in World War II. Perhaps the most lasting effect of French influence was the success of the Catholic Church in Vietnam. Thus about 10 percent of the refugees who entered the United States were Catholic. Many of them or their parents were originally among the approximately one million Catholic refugees from North Vietnam who fled to the South following the French defeat in 1954. However, the overwhelming majority of Vietnamese are Buddhist, and most of the Buddhists are also Confucianist.

The first major wave of emigration from Vietnam consisted of those who left South Vietnam at the time of its collapse in April 1975. This group included the governing elite, those who had worked for the U.S. government, and the high-ranking military with their families. Some ten to fifteen thousand people left in the week before the collapse of the South Vietnamese government. In the beginning this was an orderly departure by scheduled flights. But after the North Vietnamese bombed Saigon's Tan Son Nhut Airport as their forces advanced on the city, the airport closed and the evacuation process became increasingly disorganized. The scenes at the marine-guarded U.S. embassy, where many Vietnamese had assembled following promises made by U.S. officials, became familiar to many American television viewers. Others had assembled and waited at prearranged pickup points in the Saigon area for Americans who never came. An additional eighty thousand were evacuated, mainly by aircraft, during the last part of April. The last group in this wave consisted of those who were picked up by U.S. Navy ships offshore. Altogether some 125,000 arrived in the United States from Vietnam in 1975.

The causes for this chaotic evacuation are many, but certainly the reported unwillingness of the then U.S. ambassador, Graham Martin, to countenance the making of proper plans appears to have been a key contributing factor. Considering this extremely traumatic and inauspicious beginning, the degree of success of subsequent Vietnamese immigration to America is remarkable. While in many ways the Vietnamese are not unlike other immigrant groups, the specifics of this tragic beginning make their immigration history unique. Many other groups have entered the United States fleeing persecution, wars, and traumas in their homeland, but only the Vietnamese, along with their Indochinese neighbors, the Cambodians and

Laotians, have entered the United States as a result of the failure of an American foreign military enterprise. Only recently have these bitter memories begun to recede with the formal establishment of diplomatic ties in 1995 between the United States and Vietnam, with bilateral relations now focusing on family visits, economic affairs, and tourism.

After departure from Vietnam, planned resettlement was mediated through reception camps, mainly in the Philippines. In 1975, this was followed by temporary housing at U.S. Army camps in Arkansas, California, Florida, and Pennsylvania. The refugees were then dispersed throughout the United States with sponsorship by individuals frequently associated with church or other voluntary charitable groups.

The second wave consisted of the now historic "boat people" and was profoundly traumatic. Their subsequent settlement in the United States has also been more problematic. Unlike the well-educated and highly skilled first group, this second wave was more diverse in terms of class origin. Many were semiliterate farmers, fishermen, and small-town merchants with little or no familiarity with large cities. There were also former military and government officials included in this wave. Many were genuine political refugees, but others also saw economic opportunity in leaving an impoverished Vietnam. They put to sea in available boats capable of carrying at least a few dozen people. Some were seaworthy with reliable engines, while others floundered. The lucky individuals were picked up by foreign ships or naval vessels. Other crafts sank at sea or were boarded by Thai pirates, who not only stole but sometimes raped and murdered.

Landing in Malaya or Indonesia, these defenseless boat people were sometimes pushed out to sea again. Since their departure was organized with secrecy and their landfalls were irregular, it was not possible to monitor the losses. Scarcely less dangerous was the overland route of escape through Cambodia to refugee camps on the Thai border. Even more than for the first wave, the experience of escape and ultimate immigration

A Vietnamese American stands in front of a business in the Little Vietnam area of Garden Grove, California. (Joseph Sohm/ChromoSohm Inc./Corbis)

involved trauma they would carry with them for the rest of their lives. Like the first group, they entered the United States after a period of orientation in the Philippines. This experience thus became a personal epic for each individual. Along with other Indochinese such as Cambodians and Hmong, this is a mark of their distinctive history in the American setting—an immigration that was in most respects neither planned nor voluntary. This immigration, which began in 1975, lasted into the 1980s.

Two subsequent programs, bureaucratic in nature, have provided means for Vietnamese to immigrate to the United States. Both of them have involved the cooperation of the Vietnamese government. These included the Orderly Departure Program (ODP), where potential immigrants, including those qualifying for family reunification, received the necessary clearances from both Viet-

namese officials and the U.S. Immigration and Naturalization Service. This program was initially established in 1979 by the Office of the U.N. High Commissioner for Refugees (UNHCR).

In late 1981, Amerasians and their families were included in the ODP program, and they began to arrive in the United States in 1982. While very few of the Amerasians were reunited with their fathers, they do often arrive with their mothers. Unfortunately there has been fraud in this program, where false families have been created, with payment to Amerasians by Vietnamese. Since this program started relatively late, many of the Amerasians have arrived in America as late teens or young adults. By 1993, some eighty thousand Amerasians and their families had entered the United States under the ODP program. They had been marginalized by Vietnamese society, and their educational background was often poor. In the United States they often exist in a confined world of their own, since they usually lack American relatives and have tended to be shunned by the Vietnamese communities. This situation has been particularly true of African-American Amerasians, but it has begun to change as Vietnamese communities become more aware of the multicultural setting in the United States. Some researchers see those who have come under formal Vietnamese-American bilateral governmental programs and others who have arrived with formal immigrant status as a third wave.

Although the history of Vietnamese settlement in the United States is now more than a generation old, one of the outstanding characteristics of the U.S. Vietnamese community, composed of nearly one million, is its heterogeneity. On the one hand, there are the old elite. Some were multilingual at the time of immigration, with advanced university education, previous travel abroad, and substantial economic success. On the other hand, others were relatively uneducated peasants and the urban poor, many not fully literate in Vietnamese. Adaptation to American society has been similarly varied. Some have been very successful in professional and business occupations exemplifying the stereotype of high achievement among Asians. Many of these have been of the old elite and their children. Others of modest background in Vietnam have also done well, obtaining advanced education and rewarding employment. At the opposite extreme, others are welfare clients, and a minority have become gang members and criminals. The latter group has many precedents in American immigration history.

Since the United States only formally recognized Vietnam in 1995, there has not, as yet, been significant return migration, although increasing numbers of Vietnamese Americans go for visits, and some return to set up businesses. There are also those, particularly older people, who have found it difficult to adjust to life in the United States and have returned home to Vietnam. Judging by other immigrant groups, one would think that in future years some Vietnamese Americans will be retiring there.

## Settlement and Adaptation

Initially, in 1975, the intention was, for political reasons, to settle Vietnamese throughout the United States, but like many other Asian-American groups there has been a tendency for communities to concentrate in California. The largest group lives in or near Santa Ana and Westminster, south of Los Angeles. With its shopping malls catering to Vietnamese Americans, this area has come to be known as Little Saigon. Santa Ana alone has an estimated 150,000 Vietnamese, and all Orange County has some 12 percent of the Vietnamese in the United States. Nearby Los Angeles County has another 10 percent. Other areas of Vietnamese population concentration include San Jose and San Francisco in California, Houston and Dallas in Texas, Fairfax County in Virginia, and New York City. Thus, according to available data, it appears that Vietnamese Americans prefer to live in coastal areas. Interestingly, the word *nuóc* in Vietnamese means both *water* and *country*. In the ten states with the largest number of Vietnamese Americans, seven are bordered by the Pacific, the Atlantic, and the Gulf of Mexico. A community of Vietnamese fishermen settled in the Gulf of Mexico were the subject of the film *Alamo Bay*, depicting their initial conflict and ultimate integration with the local population. In the United States, Vietnamese live predominantly in urban and suburban areas.

Regarding achievement, in addition to high class status in Vietnam and extent of formal education, the length of time in the United States has been a critical factor, as has been the availability of family support. Ability in English has also been crucial. Thus, in the early years of immigration, particularly in the late 1970s and early 1980s, bilingual and ESL (English as a second language) classes were very important. These are still used for recent immigrants, but for those born in the United States or who arrived at a young age, complete fluency in English has become the norm.

In contrast to the American-educated doctors, lawyers, and businesspeople are those who are on relief or are gang members. Some of the latter have been involved in murder, and their actions have received considerable publicity. By and large their crimes have been confined to the Vietnamese community and have ranged from small-scale scams to large-scale violent extortion. The actions of these criminals mirror those of earlier immigrant groups. A more positive way of becoming American can be seen, however, in the initial entry of Vietnamese Americans on the political scene, as some gain local office and a few become judges, as in the largest communities in California and Texas.

Given the long and literate history of Vietnamese culture, it seems that the Vietnamese American culture will remain a distinctive part of the American multicultural mosaic but also evolve along with the mainstream. This old American immigrant pattern of maintaining cultural continuity and, at the same time, adapting to mainstream American society is already evident. There have

been modifications in the patriarchal Confucian culture. An important initial factor has been that, especially in the early stages of immigration, it was often easier for the wife, daughter, or son to gain employment than for the family patriarch. There seems to have been a gradual generational and gender realignment of power within the family. Intermarriage appears to be increasing but is clearly affected by religion, class, and ethnicity. Again, these patterns are marked by diversity, as in the case of relationship with or marriage to whites, Hispanics, African Americans, or other Asian Americans.

It is significant that Vietnamese have been the most rapidly increasing segment of the Asian Pacific Islander category, growing some one hundred percent between 1980 and 1990. The rapid growth of the Vietnamese-American population places

A group of Vietnamese teenagers performs a lion dance at Seattle's Sharples Alternative High School. (Dean Wong/Corbis)

them sixth in size within the Asian or Pacific Islander census category, and their numbers have begun to approach those of Asian Indians and Koreans (the next large groups). During the 1980s, Vietnamese businesses, mostly in the service sector, increased more than for any other Asian group. For example, in the Los Angeles–Long Beach area there are more than thirty-five hundred such Vietnamese businesses, the largest concentration in the United States.

Churches, community centers, parks, and even shopping malls, most notably in Little Saigon, south of Los Angeles, provide the setting for celebration of holidays such as Tê't. This holiday, based on the lunar calendar, occurs at the end of January or in February. It marks a time when everyone is considered to be a year older. Celebration of this holiday helps to obtain good fortune for the coming year. In Vietnam this time coincides with the onset of spring, so it is known as a spring festival. It has been a period of rest and enjoyment before beginning hard agricultural labor. In California, the climate adds to the holiday mood. At Tê't the family remembers ancestors, especially parents, and shows them gratitude. There are also visits to relatives and friends and community-sponsored dragon dances. In other parts of the United States, outdoor observances are more difficult because of the weather, but there are always gatherings combined with temple or church services focusing on the deceased. These services are followed by meals at which traditional food for the New Year is served, including square (for Earth) and round (for Heaven) sticky rice cakes (*bánh chừng* and *bánh dày*). The Mid-Autumn festival is special for children. There are sweet "moon cakes" (*bánh trung thu*) and dragon dancers who roam the community collecting gifts of money.

As the Vietnamese Americans look to the future there are different orientations within the community. The older members of the first generation are much concerned with their Vietnamese homeland, its local politics, and the external implications as related to U.S. foreign policy issues. The second generation tends to focus more on internal U.S. issues such as education, civil rights, health, employment, and immigration, although all members of the community share these concerns. Up to now Vietnamese Americans have tended to be inward looking and politically conservative, but after several decades in the United States, there is change. It is estimated that approximately 300,000 Vietnamese are already U.S. citizens. Politically they have already had some success in influencing congressional legislation establishing Radio Free Asia and a Vietnam Human Rights Day Bill. The community is also active in pressing for the release of prisoners in Vietnam.

*See also:*   BUDDHISTS; CHAM; CHINESE-VIETNAMESE

## Bibliography

Butler, R. O. (1992). *A Good Scent from a Strange Mountain.* New York: Penguin Books.

Caplan, N. S.; Whitmore, J. K.; and Choy, M. H. (1989). *The Boat People and Achievement in America: A Study of Family Life, Hard Work, and Cultural Values.* Ann Arbor: University of Michigan Press.

Freeman, J. A. (1989). *Hearts of Sorrow: Vietnamese-American Lives.* Stanford, CA: Stanford University Press.

Halpern, J. M., and Nguyen-Hong-Nhiem, L. (1992). *A Bibliography of Hmong, Lao, and Vietnamese Americans.* Amherst: Asian Studies Program, University of Massachusetts.

Hayslip, L. L., with Wurts, J. (1989). *When Heaven and Earth Changed Places: A Vietnamese Woman's Journey from War to Peace.* New York: Doubleday.

Hickey, G. C. (1964). *Village in Vietnam.* Chicago: Aldine.

Hien, D. D. (1995). "Vietnamese Americans." In *The Asian-American Encyclopedia,* edited by F. Ng. New York: Marshall Cavendish.

Jamieson, N. (1993). *Understanding Vietnam.* Berkeley: University of California Press.

Kibria, N. (1993). *Family Tightrope: The Changing Lives of Vietnamese Americans.* Princeton, NJ: Princeton University Press.

Nakashima, C. (1995). "Vietnamese Amerasians." In *The Asian-American Encyclopedia,* edited by F. Ng. New York: Marshall Cavendish.

Nguyen, C. Q. T. (1993). "The Vietnamese-American Community; A Statistical and Political Perspective."

Washington, DC: Southeast Asia Resource Action Center.

Nguyen, M. H. (1985). "Vietnamese." In *Refugees in the United States: A Reference Handbook,* edited by D. W. Haines. Westport, CT: Greenwood Press.

Nguyen-Hong-Nhiem, L., and Halpern, J. M., eds. (1989). *The Far East Comes Near: Autobiographical Accounts of Southeast Asian Students in America.* Amherst: University of Massachusetts Press.

Pham, V. K. (1987). *Blood Brothers.* New Haven, CT: Council on Southeast Asia Studies, Yale Center for International and Area Studies.

Rutledge, P. J. (1992). *The Vietnamese Experience in America.* Bloomington: Indiana University Press.

LUCY NGUYEN-HONG-NHIEM
JOEL M. HALPERN

# VLACHS

The southeastern European ethnonym "Vlachs" used to designate the descendents of the ancient Balkan population south and north of the lower Danube River Romanized after the Roman conquest of the peninsula. This term (of Slavic origin; cf. Bulgarian Vlah, Russian Volóh, etc.) comes from German (cf. Gothic Walchs; German *walh, walch*) and is related to the English Welch (Welsh, Romanized Briton).

After the emergence of the modern Romanian state in the 1860s, the ethnonym "Vlach" began to be used more restrictedly, mainly for the designation of the Balkan Vlachs. To better distinguish the latter from the North Danubian ones (i.e., from Daco-Romanians), the alternate ethnonym "Macedo-Romanians" was coined in the late nineteenth century. Some Balkan Vlachs call themselves Macedo-Romanians, a term somewhat delusive, since their settlements in the Balkans only partially coincide with the limits of the historical province of Macedonia.

In their own language (known in modern linguistics as Aromanian) Vlachs call themselves Armân'i (with a prothetic *a-*) or Rǎmân'i, a term

derived from the Latin Romanus (Roman). Greeks call them Koutsovlachs, Serbs call them Vlasi or Tsintsari (also spelled Cincari), and Albanians call them Çobani (shepherds). The majority of the Vlach Americans refer to themselves as Vlachs (or some variant thereof).

Vlachs' ethnogenesis has long been a topic of controversy. Some scholars consider them Romanized Thracians or Thraco-Dacians, with a subsequent, mainly Slavic, admixture. However, Greek historians and linguists contend that Vlachs now living in northern Greece and adjacent non-Greek areas and, implicitly, all the Vlachs living abroad (America included) are, for the most part, descendants of Romanized Greeks and therefore view them as being Greek. The dispute has become a political issue.

## Ethnic Identity

Two elements have been inextricably relevant for the ethnic identity of the Vlachs: their religion, Eastern (or Greek) Orthodoxy, and their language, Aromanian (or Macedo-Romanian), which emerged from the fragmentation of what some scholars have called Proto-Romanian. The controversy concerning the status of Aromanian among the other Romance idioms and the nature of its relation to Romanian have created some confusion among the Vlachs both at home, in the Balkans, and in the Vlach diaspora.

Before the Balkan wars of 1912–1913, when northern Greece (Macedonia), Albania, and other parts of the Balkans were under Ottoman rule, Christian immigrants from there were treated as Greek upon their arrival in the United States, solely by virtue of their Orthodox faith. Neither the ethnonym "Vlachs" nor the name of their language (Aromanian) appears in the U.S. immigration and census classifications, although the Vlachs have always been a distinct linguistic group. Subsequently some of the Vlach immigrants integrated into Greek-American communities and have considered themselves rather Greek or fully Greek. However, an important contingent of them have remained more or less attached to their specific ethnic and cultural heritage. The focal point of this heritage for many of them is their language, which has long been looked upon with various degrees of disdain and suspicion by their immediate Balkan neighbors.

## Causes of Emigration

Socioeconomic hardship and backwardness (mainly until 1913) and Communist dictatorship (after 1945) were the leading causes of Vlach (and non-Vlach) emigration from the Balkans. The dream of rapid economic prosperity was also important. An elliptical but telling phrase could be heard from prospective Vlach emigrants before World War II: the thousand and the trip (i.e., I want to earn $1,000 there plus the money to pay for the round trip). Unskilled and unable to speak English, Vlach immigrants found exhausting competition in the American labor market. Some returned home with "the thousand"; many returned overfatigued and sick; and a few managed to establish themselves in America and bring over close family and, not rarely, friends.

## Number and Current Spatial Distribution

A liberal estimate of the foreign-born Vlachs living in America in the 1990s is five thousand. The largest American-Vlach community resides in Bridgeport and Fairfield, Connecticut. Other communities are located in Woonsocket, Rhode Island (sometimes jocularly referred to as the former capital of the American Vlachs); Worcester, Massachusetts; North Grosvenor Dale, Connecticut; and St. Louis, Missouri. Small, dispersed groups of Vlachs live in New York City, New England, and California.

## Organizations

The oldest Vlach organization in America is the Society Fărşărotul, initially Speranţa (Hope), founded in New York City in 1903, with about four hundred active members in 1989. A branch of Speranţa was founded in St. Louis in 1904. The society Perivolea (in New York since 1905), which has an intermittent periodical; the foundation Gramostea (in Princeton, New Jersey); the cultural association Fara Vlahă (the Vlach People, in New York); and the association Armânamea (the Aromanians, in New York) are the best known.

## Language

Along with Greek, first-generation immigrants have spoken Albanian or Bulgarian/Macedonian, according to the regions they had inhibited in the Balkans. With no language maintenance programs in America thus far and with strong motivation to succeed in this country, their second- and particularly third-generation descendants have melded fast into the American English-speaking mainstream. Besides, many Vlachs, mainly belonging to the first and second generation, have socialized with old and recent Romanian immigrants (Vlach Romanians and proper Romanians) and speak Romanian. In addition, a portion of Vlach Americans have been exposed to Greek or Romanian, which are used, along with English, as the liturgical languages in some of the Vlach-American churches. Separate (Greek or Romanian) clergymen and separate churches have led inevitably to separatist views in other areas of concern for the Vlach communities in America.

## Press and Cultural Life

The most important Vlach-American periodical has been *The Newsletter of the Society Fărşărotul*, published in English in Bridgeport with occasional Aromanian insertions. Some American Vlachs subscribe to the periodical *Zborlu a Nostru* (Our Word), published in Aromanian in Frieburg, Germany, since 1985. Classic and contemporary Vlach authors have been published since 1989 by Cartea Aromână [*The Aromanian* (i.e., Vlach) *Book*], a privately supported publishing house in Syracuse, New York. Vlach (Aromanian) books, magazines, and folk music (mainly imported from Greece and Romania) are purchased and circulated. Illiteracy is rare among present-day Vlach

Americans. Although the Gospel is not available in Aromanian, Vlachs value education. There are many autodidacts among them. High school, college, and university graduates are common among second- and particularly third-generation Vlach Americans.

Between 1985 and 1996, six congresses of Vlach language, culture, and civilization were held at Sacred Heart University in Bridgeport under the sponsorship of the Center for Ethnic Studies. Vlachs and non-Vlachs from all over America and from several European countries attended.

## Traditional and New Patterns of Life

Vlachs have shown remarkable adaptability to American economic and cultural patterns but have preserved some of their traditional values and customs, such as frugality, husbandry, and managerial abilities. Alcoholism, violence, and criminality are relatively rare. Mutual help among Vlachs is widespread; it works on the basis and in the spirit of their old saying *Frate, frate, ma caşlu-i cu paradz* (Short accounts make long friends; literally, We certainly are brothers, but my cheese costs money!). Given the assiduity and flexibility of the Vlachs, there has been little room for real poverty among them. If at the start of the twentieth century most of the Vlachs were low-skilled factory workers, at present they can be found in a wide range of professions. The majority of Vlach Americans lead a decent life, with excellent chances for the better.

As many as twelve Vlach folk festivals with Vlach and non-Vlach guests were held at Bridgeport on the first weekend after Labor Day between 1980 and 1996. On such and other occasions the visitor can experience the traditional *pită di caş* (cheese-filled pita), *n'el pi sulă* (lamb on spit), and other dishes and listen to the old Vlach songs with their slightly plaintive tonalities. So common in the old days, marriages negotiated or simply bargained by parents long before the marital age of their children no longer exist. Vlach parents are respected and cherished. Frowned at in the past, non-Vlach spouses are accepted more and more indulgently. As a consequence, children often bear contrasting Vlach last names and Anglo-Saxon first names.

*See also:* ALBANIANS; GREEKS; MACEDONIANS; ROMANIANS

## Bibliography

Balamaci, N. S. (1991). "Can the Vlachs Write Their Own History?" *Journal of the Hellenic Diaspora* 17(1):9–36.

Golab, Z. (1984). *The Arumanian Dialect of Kruševo in SR Macedonia, SFR Yugoslavia.* Skopje: Macedonian Academy of Sciences and Arts.

Kazhdan, A. (1991). "Vlachia" and "Vlachs." *The Oxford Dictionary of Byzantium* 3:2183–2184. Oxford, Eng.: Oxford University Press.

Papahagi, T. (1974). *Dicţionarul dialectului aromân general şi etimologic: Dictionnaire aroumain (macédo-roumain) général et étymologique,* 2nd edition. Bucharest: Editura Academiei.

Stoianivich, T. (1967). *A Study in Balkan Civilization.* New York: Alfred A. Knopf.

Tagliavini, C. (1964). *Le origini delle lingue neolatine,* 4th edition. Bologna: Riccardo Patron.

Wace, A. J. B., and Thomson, M. S. ([1914] 1972). *The Nomads of the Balkans.* London: Methuen.

Winnifrith, T. J. (1987). *The Vlachs: The History of a Balkan People.* London: Duckworth.

Winnifrith, T. J. (1995). *Shattered Eagles: Balkan Fragments.* London: Duckworth.

EMIL VRABIE

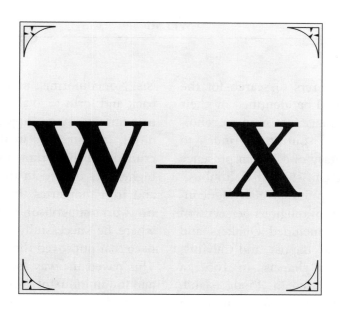

## WELSH

Wales, a rocky, rainy, green, and hilly peninsula of eight thousand square miles west of England in the United Kingdom, has a population of approximately three million persons and is claimed as an ancestral homeland by more than two million citizens of the United States. Known as Cymru in the Welsh language, Wales was originally inhabited by two distinct populations from continental Europe: the Iberians in the Neolithic Period, followed by the Celts in the Bronze Age. The Welsh language (Cymraeg), which was spoken by the majority of the inhabitants of Wales until the middle of the nineteenth century, is related to the languages of the indigenous Celtic populations of Scotland, Ireland, and Brittany. In the 1990s, the highest concentration of Welsh-speakers was in North and West Wales, with the English language more dominant on the eastern border, in South Wales, and on the Pembroke Peninsula.

In recent centuries, many Welsh farmers and agricultural workers participated in seasonal migrations to England to assist with agricultural harvests or to take cattle to market. With the nineteenth-century industrial revolution in South Wales, centered on coal and iron, farmers flocked from other parts of Wales to take up jobs as miners and iron workers. When difficult times came to industry, workers migrated back to their farms. The flexibility of this strategy meant that relatively small numbers of Welsh abandoned their country permanently for life abroad. Other parts of the British Isles contributed larger numbers to the colonizing of America.

### Emigration

The history of Welsh emigration to America can be told in five major phases: the legendary discovery of America, the flight from religious persecution in the Colonial period, the stream of land-hungry farmers, the great influx of industrial workers in the nineteenth century, and the less extensive "brain drain" of the latter half of the twentieth century.

The legendary phase concerns Prince Madoc, son of Owain the Great, king of Gwynedd, who sailed west from Wales in 1170 and left 120 colonists on the shores of a large bay before returning to Wales. He assembled another ten ships and sailed west, never to be seen or heard from again. According to legend, the Welsh colony intermarried with the local Native American population, inspiring later explorers to search for the "Welsh Indians," who could be identified by their light skin and Welsh language. No modern scholarship supports this story, but it continues to nourish the romantic fantasy of a Welsh presence in the New World before Christopher Columbus.

In the seventeenth century, Welsh Nonconformists fled to America from religious persecution under the Stuarts. These included Quakers and members of Congregational, Baptist, and Calvinistic Methodist churches or chapels. In 1667, a congregation of Baptists settled in Rhode Island, the first substantial group of Welsh to arrive in America. After 1680, Welsh Quakers obtained a tract of forty thousand acres from William Penn's colony, intending to establish a Welsh barony or a separate ethnic and religious enclave in which a distinct Welsh culture and legal system could be maintained. This plan was frustrated when Penn was unable to provide a unified tract of land. Another wave of emigrants abandoned their country for America as a result of the Methodist revival in the mid-1700s.

In 1729, Welsh in Philadelphia established the Welsh Society, the oldest ethnic organization in the United States. Books and religious tracts published in Welsh found an eager audience among immigrants who wanted to retain their language and culture. By 1750, Welsh immigrants had settled in communities in other parts of Pennsylvania and as far south as the Carolinas.

The next wave of immigration occurred after the American Revolution and was not a response to religious persecution but to worsening economic conditions and bad harvests in Wales in the 1790s. The flow of immigration to America was moderate during this time and consisted of people of means who saw the opportunity to obtain cheap land in New York, Pennsylvania, and Ohio. During this period most arrived not in organized groups but as individuals, drawn to America by reports from friends and relatives who had preceded them.

Around 1830, skilled industrial workers from the iron and coal industry of South Wales began to arrive, replacing the earlier stream of agricultural-ists. Nonconformist ministers, writing or traveling back and forth to Wales, were active in recruiting new immigrants to supplement the Welsh communities. Industrialists in the United States also recruited skilled workmen who were attracted by the higher pay offered in the fledgling American coal and iron industries. In 1839, David Thomas, an ironworks supervisor, immigrated to Pennsylvania, where he successfully developed a hot blast furnace that improved the quality of iron production. This paved the way for expansion of the industry and for an influx of Welsh miners and ironworkers to the industrial towns of Scranton and Wilkes-Barre. Welsh miners continued to stream into the country, often stopping in the Welsh communities in Pennsylvania before finding work in the new bituminous coalfields as far west as Iowa and Missouri. Quarrymen from North Wales arrived after 1840. Skilled Welsh ironworkers were among the converts to the Church of Jesus Christ of Latter-Day Saints (Mormons) who joined their trek to the Great Salt Lake. In the 1890s, Welsh tinplate workers expanded the new industrial developments in Ohio and Pennsylvania. With the turn of the twentieth century, the demand for Welsh skills began to decline, and emigration from Wales slowed. The Great Depression of the 1930s triggered further migration from Wales to England, but few immigrated to America.

In 1900, Welsh-born residents of the United States were concentrated in nine states: Pennsylvania (35,453) and Ohio (11,481), the heart of the coal mining and steel industry; New York (7,304), with slate mining and farming; and in Illinois (4,364), Wisconsin (3,356), Iowa (3,091), Utah (2,141), Indiana (2,083), and Kansas (2,005), with mining and the agricultural areas. All of the other states had fewer than 2,000 Welsh-born residents at the turn of the century, although the mining states of Colorado and California were near that threshold.

By the last quarter of the twentieth century, the flow of immigrants from Wales became a mere trickle, with only 3,897 persons, 1,763 of them women, entering the United States between 1980 and 1990. This group is highly educated, a part of the "brain drain" of technical and professional workers from the United Kingdom during a period of academic retrenchment. Nearly 23 percent of the Welsh immigrants in that decade had graduate and professional degrees, compared with just under 12 percent for the American-born population of Welsh ancestry. The average family income for these immigrants was $67,671 in 1989, about $8,000 more than for their American-born counterparts.

## Adaptation in America

As is the case for many other immigrant groups, the Welsh have often engaged in chain migration, following in the footsteps of family members, other relatives, friends, or members of their chapel or community who had immigrated to America earlier. Arriving in the United States, they could expect to obtain assistance with food, lodging, and jobs, just as they would in turn be expected to help later immigrants. Jackson and

Gallia counties in southern Ohio drew settlers predominantly from Cardiganshire, re-creating much of the culture of that region of Wales. For several decades these farmers entered the charcoal iron industry and established an ethnic community enterprise in which all of the shareholders and workers were Welsh. One of the recurring themes of the history of Welsh settlement is the desire to establish exclusive ethnic enclaves where the language and culture could be preserved. But in America their ranks were too few and too scattered to maintain this strategy for long.

In addition to smoothing the way for immigrants, chain migration has helped to keep a flow of information from the old country to the new, reinforcing Welsh culture in the new settlements. The *eisteddfod*, a traditional cultural festival for the performance of recitation, oratory, vocal music, and the composition of poetry in ancient forms, was brought to America in 1850 and provided a focus for Welsh culture for the next seventy-five years. The Gymanfa Ganu, a singing festival, re-

A Sunday School group at the Hebron Welsh Church in Chicago around 1912–1915. (*Y Drych*)

placed the eisteddfod in popularity as a consequence of the decline of the Welsh language in America.

Even in areas with the highest concentrations of immigrants, the intensity of Welsh culture did not survive long into the twentieth century. Scranton, for example, which had the largest concentration of Welsh persons outside the United Kingdom, had come to mirror the hierarchy of the surrounding Yankee society by 1850. The Welsh Congregationalists, Baptists, and Wesleyan Methodists promoted a church-centered Protestant culture that contrasted sharply with that of the Irish Catholics, whom they often looked down upon socially. In the early part of the twentieth century, the Irish gained local political control and generally voted Democratic. The Welsh, whether local businesspersons or coal miners, tended to vote Republican. These ethnic distinctions and accompanying prejudices have largely disappeared.

However, while Welsh immigrants and their descendants have generally enjoyed a reputation for hard work and moral rectitude, they have been unfairly associated with the verb "to welsh" or renege on an agreement. The term apparently has no etymological connections with the Welsh. However, in September 1995, President Bill Clinton angered some Welsh Americans by asserting in a speech that as a nation "We don't welsh on our debts." The Twm Sion Cati Welsh-American Legal Defense, Education, and Development Fund requested and received an apology from the White House.

For Americans of Welsh ancestry, ethnic identification is a matter of choice. Given the extensive intermarriage among Americans with European ancestry, many simply do not claim a particular national heritage. For others, ethnic identification is situational, varying with the social context. One might be "British," "Welsh," "Celtic," or "American" in different contexts.

## Cultural Activities

With the anglicization of Welsh Americans, which occurred swiftly when the Welsh language was no longer used in the home, Welsh Americans lost an important cultural connection with their homeland. Welsh-American culture is constructed from a number of activities. These include celebrating St. David's Day (March 1), honoring the patron saint of Wales; participating in the Gymanfa Ganu with its Welsh-language songs and hymns, either on a local level or through meetings of the National Gymanfa Ganu Association of the United States and Canada; worshipping in Welsh churches; compiling information on Welsh and Welsh-American notables such as the seventeen Welsh singers of the Declaration of Independence; reading and writing for publications such as *Y Drych* or *Ninnau*, English-language newspapers that discuss Wales and activities of Welsh Americans; serving a Welsh tea with Welsh cakes; participating in voluntary organizations such as the National Welsh-American Foundation or the Welsh American Genealogical Society; tracing family trees; studying Welsh-language tapes; recording oral histories of elderly members of the Welsh community; participating in the North American Association for the Study of Welsh Culture and History (established in 1994); hosting Welsh guests; visiting Welsh sites on the Internet; and, not least, visiting Wales. Those for whom Welsh identity is very strong may participate in many of these activities; those for whom it is largely symbolic may participate in few or none of these ways of expressing Welshness.

Surveys show that many Americans who claim Welsh ancestry have little knowledge of their family history and lack family records and family stories, usually passed from generation to generation, to trace the link to Wales. Genealogical history, using public records in the United States and in Wales to fill this gap, is a growing industry, however. Still, handicrafts of Welsh origin, sometimes emblazoned with the Welsh dragon, may be the most overt manifestations of ethnic identity in a Welsh-American household.

## Cultural Values

Ethnographers have identified five key cultural values among contemporary Welsh: nostalgia,

A choir from the Welsh church in Delta, Pennsylvania, performs at the Wilkes-Barre National Gymanfa Ganu in 1993. (Cara Keene, *Y Drych*)

egalitarianism, emotionalism, martyrdom, and performance. Apart from nostalgia, these are implicit values that are not consciously articulated. Nostalgia, or a longing for people or places no longer present, is often described by the Welsh term *hiraeth,* inadequately translated as longing or sentimentality. One can feel hiraeth for homeland, culture, loved ones, or even the legendary past. Egalitarian behavior consists of treating all people as social equals, rather than as members of a hierarchy with status differences. Emotionalism means that persons are expected to respond to situations emotionally, rather than coldly and ana-

lytically. Martyrdom, or a willingness to self-sacrifice on behalf of the family or group, is admired. Children are taught to perform, particularly in ways that showcase the expressive culture of the Welsh, in music and poetry. Individuals also recognize that they are performing for others in everyday social life.

When asked about behaviors that incorporate these five values, the Welsh identify them as typical of their culture. These values are sometimes satirized by the English: "Now, the Welsh, as all the English know, are a clannish sort, notoriously hot-blooded, voluble, good at singing, and as fond

A poster promotes Welsh-language courses to encourage bilingual participation in the Welsh-American community. (D. Douglas Caulkins)

of leeks as they are unfond of the truth" ("Watch it, boyo," 1995). The Welsh tend to attribute opposite values to their English neighbors. According to the Welsh stereotype, the English are unsentimental, unemotional, unegalitarian, self-centered, and indifferent performers. This contrast, which reinforces Welsh identity, disappears in the American context.

Without this contrast, and lacking the Welsh language and literature that embody Welsh values, Welsh-American culture might be expected to bear little resemblance to that of Wales. However, a study of Welsh Americans in Iowa reveals substantial similarities between the values and behaviors of the two societies. The Iowa Welsh identified a series of behaviors in which persons displayed emotion, martyrdom, performance, and nostalgia as Welsh behaviors rather than American. The Iowans thought that egalitarianism was typically American behavior and not especially Welsh. Therefore, the cultural behaviors of the Welsh and the Welsh Americans are similar but not identical, and both contrast with the behaviors of the mainstream society—English in one case, and American in the other. The degrees of similarity among Welsh, Welsh-American, and American behaviors can be represented statistically. The correlation between the Welsh and Welsh-American behaviors is +0.834 (very high). In contrast, the correlation between Welsh-American and American behaviors is +0.271 (much lower). In short, although Welsh Americans may differ in their knowledge of their ancestral land and vary in their participation in Welsh-American activities, many are able to recognize implicit Welsh cultural values and behaviors, or at least a version of them. These must be transmitted from generation to generation, perhaps not consciously, through child rearing and adult example.

## Social Position and Family Structure

As a group, the two million Americans who claim Welsh ancestry have been economically successful. Median family income for this group in 1989 was $42,170, with a per-capita income of $21,258. Only 3.4 percent of the families that claim Welsh ancestry had incomes below the poverty level in 1989. Educational attainment for the group has been substantial, according to the 1990 U.S. Census. Nearly 32 percent of those twenty-five years old or over have bachelor's, professional, or advanced degrees. Of those employed, 38 percent work in managerial and professional specialties, with 31.5 percent (42.9% for women) in technical jobs or sales. Fewer than 10 percent of the group are in service occupations (12% for women), and a similar percentage are in precision production work. Slightly fewer are operators or laborers. Mining and farming, occupations traditionally associated with Welsh immigrants, now account for less than 3 percent of those employed.

Most of the employed (74%) are wage or salary earners in the private sector, while 17 percent are employed in government. Fewer than 9 percent are self-employed small-business persons.

Marital status for Welsh Americans, according to the 1990 U.S. Census, is generally conventional. Seventy-two percent were married, separated, or widowed; 20 percent never married; and 8 percent were divorced. Fertility rates were relatively low, with 1,727 births per 1,000 women. Average household size was 2.5 persons. The majority (84.2%) of children under age eighteen were living in a two-parent household. Only 8 percent of households were female-headed, with no husband present.

The 2,033,893 persons who selected Welsh as their ethnic identity in the 1990 U.S. Census were concentrated in the following ten states: California (238,134), Pennsylvania (221,964), Ohio (165,494), New York (103,679), Florida (103,115), Texas (95,447), Washington (69,094), Michigan (55,588), Virginia (54,891), and Utah (48,070).

## Bibliography

Berthoff, R. T. (1953). *British Immigrants in Industrial America, 1790–1950.* Cambridge, MA: Harvard University Press.

Conway, A. (1973). "Welsh Emigration to the United States." *Perspectives in American History* 7:175–271.

Davies, J. (1993). *A History of Wales.* New York: Penguin Books.

Gray, D. J. (1991). "Shadows of the Past: The Rise and Fall of Prejudice in an American City." *American Journal of Economics and Sociology* 50(1):33–43.

Hartman, E. G. (1967). *Americans from Wales.* Boston: Christopher.

Holt, C. W. (1993). *Welsh Women: An Annotated Bibliography of Women in Wales and Women of Welsh Descent in America.* Metuchen, NJ: Scarecrow Press.

Jones, W. D. (1993). *Wales in America: Scranton and the Welsh, 1860–1920.* Scranton, PA: University of Scranton Press.

Knowles, A. K. (1993). "Charcoal Iron and Welsh in Southern Ohio, 1850–1880." *Historical Geography* 23(1–2):33–43.

Lieberson, S., and Waters, M. C. (1988). *From Many Strands: Ethnic and Racial Groups in Contemporary America.* New York: Russell Sage Foundation.

Murray, L. (1990). "Unique Americans: The Welsh-American Ethnic Group in the Philadelphia Area." In *Encounters with American Ethnic Cultures,* edited by P. L. Kilbride, J. C. Goodale, and E. R. Ameisen. Tuscaloosa: University of Alabama Press.

Trosset, C. (1993). *Welshness Performed.* Tucson: University of Arizona Press.

"Watch it, boyo." (1995). *The Economist* 336(7934):28.

Williams, G. A. (1979). *Madoc: The Making of a Myth.* London: Eyre Methuen.

D. DOUGLAS CAULKINS

# WEST INDIANS

*See* BARBADIANS; CUBANS; DOMINICANS; GRENADIANS; GUYANESE; HAITIANS; INDO-CARIBBEANS; JAMAICANS; PUERTO RICANS; TRINIDADIANS

# XIAO LIUXUESHENG

*See* TAIWANESE

# YEMENIS

Yemeni Americans trace their ancestry to the Middle Eastern country of Yemen, now the Yemen Arab Republic, which is located on the southwestern corner of the Arabian Peninsula. A large majority of Yemeni immigrants originated in the mountainous north-central regions of Yemen, especially the province of Ibb. A smaller number originated in southern Yemen, especially the city of Aden. Alternate names for the group include Yemenites and Adenites.

Yemenis consider themselves ethnically Arab. As such, they identify with attributes that bind Arabs throughout the world: a common language (Arabic) and a tightly knit extended family unit with modes of behavior that govern private and public interaction as well as relationships between siblings and their parents, maternal and paternal grandparents, cousins, and other members of their lineage. Yemenis and other Arabs also hold in high regard the cherished values associated with honor, respect, and hospitality.

Yemenis further define their identity in terms of a common Arab history and cultural heritage, which consists of rich literary, musical, and artistic traditions. In addition to adherence to the broader definition of Arab ethnicity and identity, Yemenis are proud of their unique national culture, including a folkloric tradition that recounts the glory of the ancient southern Arabian kingdoms as well as the biblical story of Queen Sheba. Yemeni material culture (associated notably with the production of jewelry and textiles) its architectural achievements, and mocha coffee are renowned worldwide.

Yemen was the first nation to embrace Islam, and Yemenis are devout Muslims, belonging to the Zaidi branch of Shi'ism. Islam forms the core of the Yemenis' identity and regulates the émigrés ethical and moral framework as well as their spiritual quest within the larger setting of Arab and Muslim society in the United States.

## Immigration and Settlement History

Yemeni immigration to America, while relatively small in numbers, is part of a broad movement of workers wordwide that continues to affect both the sending country and the host country. The magnitude of Yemeni emigration has been profound. At one point in the 1970s, it is estimated that nearly one-third of Yemen's adult male population, mostly young single men, were employed abroad—in Saudi Arabia, England, and the United States.

Attracted by the prospects of work in the powerful economies of the West, Yemenis began to arrive on American shores in the 1960s. At the outset most were sojourning labor migrants—single men who planned to work in America's industrial and agricultural heartlands for a temporary period of several years. During this span of time the Yemeni workers would send their hard-earned wages back to their families in Yemen. Most settled in Detroit, where they worked on the automobile assembly lines and ancillary plants. Others headed to California and labored as farmworkers, in canneries and food processing plants, and in the service industry. Yemenis also settled in New York City, where many are self-employed in groceries and convenience stores.

Economic recession in the United States and spiraling inflation in Yemen were some of the factors that brought the sojourning pattern of Yemeni immigration to an end as the workers either returned to Yemen or settled permanently in the United States. Immigration laws permitting family reunification brought the workers' wives and children together, and many have become residents and citizens of the United States. In California their arrival also signified a change in occupation—from farmworking, which often involved a transient lifestyle, to a more sedentary existence suited for family life.

## Demography

The Yemeni-American community, estimated at fifty thousand, is concentrated primarily in three states: Michigan, California, and New York. In Michigan, the Yemenis reside in South Dearborn adjacent to the Ford River Rouge plant, in Hamtramck, and in Coldwater and other blue-collar communities supporting automobile production. In California, the largest concentration is located in Oakland, while the farmworker community is dispersed, with the majority residing in Delano, Bakersfield, Modesto, and the various towns along Highway 99. The Yemeni presence in New York extends from Buffalo, where a small community of Yemenis is employed in the steel factories, to New York City, especially the boroughs of Brooklyn and Queens.

## Language

Most Yemeni immigrants have arrived in the United States with little familiarity with the English language. Like other immigrant groups with limited English-language skills, they have sought the comfort of compatriots and residential areas where Arabic is spoken. While Yemeni Arabic is used in most of the immigrant homes, English has been accepted readily, especially by school-age children and adolescents, workers on assembly lines, and Yemenis involved in public service jobs and stores.

Bilingualism is a common practice for both foreign- and native-born Yemenis. In Detroit, with its large community of Arab Americans, opportunities to learn Arabic are available at schools with sizable Arab-American student populations and in classes offered by community organizations, such as the Arab-American Community Center for Economic and Social Services (ACCESS), or by educational centers at mosques.

## Cultural Characteristics

The family unit and the religious community remain the cornerstone of the Yemeni-American identity. This bond is reinforced at special events such as the celebrations of birthdays, marriages, and other rites of passage that often combine religious and ethnic overtones. Notably, marriage contracts are embedded in Islam and kinship. These festive occasions also provide opportunities to showcase Yemeni and Arab culture through musical expression and communal dance.

The observance and celebration of religious holidays, especially the fast of Ramadan, also provide a context for highlighting Yemeni cultural traits, especially its cuisine. Traditional meals are prepared at the evening break of the month-long fasting period, and a feast is prepared at its con-

A Yemeni-American employee listens to a customer's order in an Arab grocery store in Brooklyn, New York. (Steven J. Gold)

clusion. Yemeni-American culture is also highlighted during holidays commemorating Yemeni independence and unification. These occasions are marked by visitations among families and friends. Caring for the elderly and the ill further preserves the cohesiveness of the community.

The harmonious relations that the community seeks to maintain are sometimes disrupted by the clash of Yemeni and American cultures. Intergenerational conflict can flare over the nature of authority and the expected boundaries of behavior. Although most incidents are resolved civilly, some have resulted in tragic consequences over accusations of disobeying traditional authority figures or bringing shame or dishonor to the family.

Most Yemenis operate within the familiar networks established by families and linkages. Provincial and village ties are maintained. In Detroit and elsewhere, coffeehouses and restaurants provide forums for interaction, discussion, and per-

petuating pan-Yemeni sentiments among compatriots. A national association of Yemeni immigrants has sought to deal with the concerns of the community at large — from issues related to immigration and naturalization, to working conditions and cultural preservation.

## Assimilation and Cultural Persistence

Throughout their history, Yemenis have maintained a distinct identity that finds its roots in their religion, culture, and in the great love for their ancestral homeland. In the United States this identity is challenged as Yemenis face the dilemma of two-tier assimilation. The first is into the broader Arab-American and Muslim community, and the other is into American society.

In some cases, Yemenis have attempted to maintain their subethnic identity by establishing mosques and educational centers specifically (but not exclusively) geared toward their members, such as the formative effort made by the Yemeni community in San Francisco. A pervasive tendency, evident in New York and Detroit, points, however, to the absorption and integration of Yemenis within established religious institutions that serve Arab immigrants and their descendants, as well as African-American Muslims and Muslims at large.

For the increasing number of American-born Yemenis, assimilation into the mainstream culture has been fashioned in great part by the public education system and the electronic media. Whether they reside in urban or rural settings, assimilation into the culture of the majority has fostered close contact and ties between Yemenis and the large Hispanic populations in the ethnically diverse neighborhoods of New York City and Oakland, or in the many agricultural towns of the San Joaquin Valley and central California. Fearing wholesale assimilation and what some perceive as the corrosive elements of American society and culture, Yemeni families continue to send their children on extended visits to family members still in Yemen. Concerns for safety and modesty have also restricted the exposure of tradition-bound women to mainstream American culture and public life, and some Yemeni women remain sheltered in their homes. These protective measures have been problematic especially for pregnant women who require the services of public health agencies for prenatal care and counseling.

Living in America has also meant assuming the status of an ethnic and religious minority. As a result, Yemenis have felt the brunt of discrimination and hostility that flare during political and military confrontations between the United States and adversaries in the Middle East. Incidents of violence were perpetrated against Yemenis during the 1973 oil embargo, the hostage crisis of the 1980s, and the Gulf War (in which Yemen sided with Iraq). Yemenis have also suffered the consequence of nationalistic fervor and backlash during incidents of domestic and international terrorism that were blamed on Arabs and Muslims.

Unlike many other small immigrant groups, Yemeni Americans have initially been able to hold to their ethnic identity, navigating amidst the constant forces of assimilation. It remains uncertain, however, whether this perseverance can be maintained in the twenty-first century.

## Bibliography

Abraham, N. (1983). "The Yemeni Immigrant Community in Detroit: Background, Emigration, and Community Life." In *Arabs in the New World: Studies on Arab-American Communities,* edited by S. Y. Abraham and N. Abraham. Center for Urban Studies, Wayne State University.

Aswad, B., ed. (1974). *Arab-Speaking Communities in American Cities.* New York: Center for Migration Studies of New York.

Friedlander, J., ed. (1985). *Sojourners and Settlers: The Yemeni Immigrant Experience.* Salt Lake City: University of Utah Press.

Haddad, Y. Y., and Smith, J. I., eds. (1994). *Muslim Communities in North America.* Albany: State University of New York Press.

Zogby, J. (1990). *Arab America Today: A Demographic Profile of Arab Americans.* Washington, DC: Arab-American Institute.

JONATHAN FRIEDLANDER

# YORUBA

Two-thirds of all African immigrants currently in the United States arrived after 1980. The two countries contributing the most people in the post-1980s to that influx were Ghana and Nigeria, and Yoruba make up a large part of the Nigerian portion of the African immigrant population. Statistical information on Yoruba immigration is buried within the African immigration statistics. Only since 1990 has the African immigrant population been separated out and reported as a distinct unit within the U.S. Census categories. Presumably they were counted previously as black, or as foreign born but without designation as African.

Yoruba comprise one of the largest ethnic groups in Nigeria and in sub-Saharan Africa as a whole. Estimates of the group's size range from thirteen to sixteen million in Nigeria alone, not including Yoruba populations existing in the nations of western Africa (Togo, Dahomey, and Sierra Leone). Yoruba traders appear in the market towns of every country in western Africa, and Yoruba descendants who identify as Yorubas and speak the Yoruba language exist in the diasporas of Cuba, Brazil, Belize, Trinidad, and the United States.

## Geographical Origins

The overwhelming majority of Yorubas immigrating to the United States come from southwestern Nigeria. Yorubas are urbanites who, when they farm, go to their farms during the day and return to the city at night. These are dense cities that in some cases date back to the sixteenth century and have contemporary populations in the hundreds of thousands. More than half of Nigeria's population is Yoruba, and they are the dominant group in the country's educated elite. Although they, together with the Igbo, were major forces in Nigerian nationalism, after independence Yoruba became a minority party second to the coalition between the Igbo and Hausa groups. Nonetheless Yoruba still remain an important element in Nigeria politics.

Nigeria's state and provincial boundaries were redrawn between 1992 and 1993, but for a discussion of Yoruba immigrants, it is more helpful to locate their homelands geographically using the old provincial names. Within Nigeria there are prominent, if not predominant, Yoruba populations in the southwestern provinces of Oyo, Ibadan, Abeokuta, Ijebu, and Ondo (these areas are usually referred to as Yorubaland proper); most of the remaining Nigerian Yoruba live in Lagos and the northern provinces of Illorin and Kabba. A geographically and culturally marginal group, the Itsekiri, lives in the southeastern province of Warri.

Traditionally the Yoruba had no general term that referred to the group as a whole; instead, people identified with their subgroups, the names of which were often derived from the indigenous kingdoms and city-states that governed their areas, the largest being Oyo. The term "Yoruba" was one that was used by other groups in western Africa, the Fulani and Hausa, to refer to people of the Oyo subgroup and supposedly meant "cunning." Similar terms such as "Nago," "Anago," "Lucumi," and "Aku" (terms used in Dahomey, Brazil, Cuba, and Sierra Leone, respectively) seem to have originated in the same way, that is, as terms outsiders used to refer to the people without regard to subgroup. "Yoruba" only became accepted generally as a term referring to the group as a whole due to its early and continuing use in mission schools. Indeed, some older people still do not recognize it and deny being Yoruba, asserting the subgroup identity instead. The Nigerian Yoruba subgroups are the Ana, Shabe, Ketu, Awori, Egbado, Egba, Oyo, Ife, Ijesha, Ondo, Owo, Ilaje, Ekiti, Igbomina, Yagba, Bunu, Aworo, and Itsekiri; those in Togo and the borderlands of Nigeria and the Republic of Benin include the Isha, Idasha, and Ifonyin (also known as Nago, Anago, Dje, and Ahori).

Aside from ethnically distinctive facial scarifications, the most obvious cultural characteristic differentiating Yoruba from other Nigerians is language. Within Yoruba territories, however, there is considerable local variation in language and custom. A Ketu Yoruba may have trouble understanding the speech of someone from the Bunu subgroup at first, but they can still communicate. There is a popular proverb about this local variation in custom: "What may be tradition in my house may be taboo in someone's else's."

## Religious Influences

The worldview of the Yoruba is deeply influenced by religion, and religious adherence is a major source of variation within the group. The majority of Yoruba are nominally adherents to either Christianity or Islam, but at the individual level they often hold tenaciously to beliefs and practices indigenous to their own culture. Africans tend to see other religions as supplementing rather than replacing their own, and the Yoruba are no exception. For many Yoruba, then, attendance at a church or mosque is not inconsistent with traditional religious and social practices, regardless of what Christian ministers or Muslim clerics may say.

Yoruba traditional religion includes belief in a somewhat distant Supreme Being and a number of lesser deities called orisha, who are more concerned with the affairs of everyday life; the practice of ancestor veneration; witchcraft and sorcery beliefs, as well as belief in reincarnation within family lines; and recourse to divination and a variety of herbal and ritual healing techniques. Traditional worship is highly participatory and features ritual dance, call and response chants to complex drumming, ceremonial spirit possession, and, on occasion, animal sacrifice. Lay traditionalists carry out a round of private rites at their homes, while priests and priestesses perform rituals, provide healing, and counsel believers at temples and shrines. The cycle of lavishly colorful annual festivals involves the entire local community. Yoruba traditional religion is not a salvation religion nor a revealed religion; it is human-centered, Earth-centered, and concerned primarily with ethics and the problems of daily life. The traditional religion should not be looked at as a body of beliefs, doctrines, and rituals. Rather, it should be viewed as the ongoing manifestation of a basic attitude toward life that is expressed in a variety of ways, in a variety of contexts (from the obviously religious to the artistic, economic, and political), and in a variety of patterns of interpersonal interaction. There is considerable variation from town to town and between regions in the deities who are worshipped and in details of ideology and ritual practice. Aside from regional or local deities there are also deities (orisha) specific to particular families and passed down family lines. The traditional attitude toward religion is basically instrumental—that is, "if it works for you, believe it"—and generally tolerant of change, innovation, and other religions.

Interaction of the traditional religion with Islam and Christianity has tended to follow two paths. In the first path, people blend or fuse the new beliefs with the old. This is a path that has been relatively unimportant and had minimal impact among the Yoruba. The second (and predominant) tendency has been to emphasize those aspects of Islam and Christianity that are most in line with traditional patterns. In this way the Yoruba have adapted Islam and Christianity to meet their needs, maintained their own cultural identity to a great extent, and joined contemporary vitality to continuity with the past.

Christianity and Islam are about equal in strength among the Yoruba, but the two religions differ in their attractions. Islam existed in Nigeria much earlier than Christianity and is better adapted to Yoruba social structure because it permits a man to have more than one wife. Islam and the traditional religion also offer divination, healing techniques, and protection against witches. On the other hand, Christianity has an almost total monopoly on Western-style education at the primary and secondary levels, the main gateway to upward mobility in Nigerian society.

While many families are now wholly Christian or wholly Muslim, the spread of these two religions has been rapid enough for there to be many households in which one sibling might be a Christian and another a Muslim, while the parents are both traditionalists. While they attempt to accommodate the religious differences and live together

amicably, Yoruba Christians and Muslims are tending more and more often to marry partners from within their respective religions.

The two main Yoruba Islamic brotherhoods are the Qadiriyya and the Tijaniyya. These are Sufi brotherhoods. The predominant school of Islamic law followed by Muslim Yoruba is the Maliki school. Islamic law has had little influence on social structure, and the tendency is for Yoruba customary law to predominate. Likewise, Yoruba religious specialists have often incorporated some traditional ritual and magical practices into their variety of Islam.

Their separate tradition of learning and scholarship has made Muslims a distinct group among the Yoruba. Relations of Muslim religious leaders with Yoruba Christians have tended to be friendly while their relations with traditionalists often are not. Few primary or secondary schools are under Muslim control. Instead Islamic instruction is based in study circles gathered around individual teachers, scholars, and divines. Students often leave these circles before age sixteen, to seek a career or further schooling, so knowledge of or fluency in Arabic is often faulty. A major problem for Muslim Yoruba is how to combine Western-style education—still sponsored mainly by Christian mission—with Islamic adherence. In the meantime, elite status is still closely linked with Western education, and the pursuit of Western-style college or graduate degrees is a major force impelling many Yoruba to go abroad. Nonetheless, Muslim Yoruba probably constitute a very small fraction of Yoruba immigrating to the United States.

The Church Missionary Society (CMS), representing the Church of England, was the first missionary organization to make Christian converts and have an impact in Nigeria. CMS arrived in 1842 and seems very much to have had the field to itself until the end of the nineteenth century, when other missions appeared in short order: the Methodists in the late 1880s; Catholics in the 1890s; Baptists in the early years of the twentieth century; the Salvation Army and Seventh-Day Adventists in the 1920s.

The American Southern Baptist Convention probably has had more impact on Yoruba immigration to the United States than any other missionary group, except possibly the Methodists. In the era when college and university education in the United States was almost entirely racially segregated, particularly in the 1950s and 1960s, the Baptist and Methodist missions funneled Yoruba students into historically Black colleges and universities. Most of these institutions had a strong Baptist or Methodist religious orientation. Yorubas—mainly males in the beginning—studied at Morehouse College, Howard University, Lincoln University, Wilberforce, Hampton Institute, and Fisk University, sometimes remaining in the United States to pursue graduate study at predominantly white institutions in the North or Midwest.

Upon returning to Africa, many of these graduates found that the Nigerian academic and professional elite remained strongly British-oriented, even after independence, and would not recognize American degrees, preferring instead the British system, upon which they had patterned their own system of higher education. Nigeria was already producing more highly trained technical and academic people than it could employ, so many American-trained Yoruba professionals returning to Nigeria in the 1960s and 1970s were forced either to work in Nigeria in a career other than the one in which they had been trained or to go abroad once more.

## Immigration Factors

Nigeria's 1970s oil boom made it possible for the elite and upwardly mobile working-class Nigerians to immigrate to the United States without missionary sponsorship, and affirmative action and the desegregation of federally funded education in the United States broadened the range of institutions African students could attend. There were also increased opportunities for graduate or postgraduate training of people who had British degrees. The oil boom also made it possible for Nigerians who were not students to visit the United States as tourists, work seekers, and businessmen.

The Nigerian oil price shock of the early 1970s, the mid-1970s droughts, the boom and bust in Nigerian oil in the late 1970s, followed by worldwide recession made it more difficult for Nigeria to support its professionals, whether trained at home or returning from abroad. The inability of the Nigerian economy to absorb all the professionals it produced, the instability and corruption of Nigerian politics, and the general strikes and closure of government agencies and the universities for years at a time all contributed to producing a Yoruba population in the United States that has been selected largely from the elite and the upwardly mobile segments of the Nigerian middle class.

The Yoruba immigrant population in the United States comes mainly from families who have regular employment in Nigeria for wages and salaries. This is a small, wealthy, highly educated group that constitutes the power elite: senior army and police officers, senior civil servants, university staff, secondary school teachers, managers in large firms, professionals, and the judiciary. Parallel to immigrants from this background are those from the upwardly mobile segments of the middle class. Many of these immigrants are in transit to elite status via education. They have secondary or technical school educations and are from the families of primary school teachers, clerical workers, middle-level army and police personnel, and skilled manual workers in supervisory positions. This group has a good level of upward mobility, and an important vehicle for that mobility is Western-style education and even education in foreign countries, a major reason for their immigration to the United States.

## U.S. Settlement and Demography

Although there are significant Yoruba communities in the United States (e.g., in New York City; Newark, New Jersey; Washington, D.C.; Chicago; Atlanta; and Los Angeles), they can only be reported on within the context of the larger African immigrant community because of past census categorizations.

The African immigrant community is largely male. However, the trend has been for increasing numbers of African females to immigrate to the United States, causing the male-female ratio to go from 1.5 males per female in 1980 to 1.3 males per female in 1990. The African immigrant community is also relatively young, with 62 percent of the population falling between the ages of twenty-five and forty-four.

The average household income for African immigrants is $38,794 a year, with an elite segment, about 6 percent of the households, earning more than $100,000 a year. It should be noted that non-citizen African immigrants tend to have significantly lower incomes than African immigrants who have become U.S. citizens.

The African immigrant population is concentrated in managerial and professional work (35%); technical, sales, and administrative employment (29%); or in service occupations (18%). The traditional Yoruba entrepreneurial streak has become evident in the business districts of African-American enclaves through Yoruba involvement in retail trade (especially as arts and crafts retailers), in hair braiding, and as clothiers.

Female employment is fairly high; 56 percent of all female African immigrants over sixteen are in the work force. They also tend to concentrate in the same areas as the males. African females constitute 28 percent of African immigrant managers and professionals; 41 percent of the technical, sales, and administrative personnel; and 41 percent of African immigrant service workers. Although women in Nigeria often ask younger kin to assist with children and some hire professional child care while they are at work, this can become a problem in the United States since the cost of such hired help is often more than the women can afford.

## Family

Housing patterns in the United States affect the kinds of arrangements and exchanges that usually exist in Yoruba families and extended families. Because apartments are too small, descent groups members are often scattered. Even in households where there are subfamilies (i.e., descent group members, married or unmarried, with or without children) living with a married couple, it is but a pale semblance of the living arrangements in a traditional Yoruba compound, where one or more wives might have their own rooms for themselves and their children surrounded by those of their husband's male and female relatives all encircling a courtyard where people gather to cook and/or eat together.

Of the African immigrant population that lives in households rather than group quarters (587,741), about 25 percent live in married couple families with or without children of their own. Approximately 4 percent of African immigrant households are headed by single women, with or without children. About 25 percent of African immigrant households consist of a person living alone (which may well reflect the high proportion of students and unmarried people in search of careers or intending to return home—adults and young adults in transition). The proportion of unmarried partner households (male-female) likewise is small, with only 1.4 percent of all households conforming to this pattern.

Ties with the home country remain close, with those able to afford it returning frequently, at least once a year or once every other year. It is common, especially for professionals, to send a portion of their earnings home to Nigeria, either for maintaining relatives or for investments in personal projects. These remittances are the main benefit Nigeria derives from Yoruba presence in the United States.

In Nigeria, Yoruba society is quite patriarchal, but women are also extremely independent. It is a mildly hierarchial society with an elaborate etiquette expressing differences in status between males and females; youngsters and elders; and priests, chiefs, and other title holders. The differences are often manifested in greetings, seating arrangements, the order of serving food, kneeling, bows, prostrations, and curtsies. In the United

States, some of this deference still occurs in the more traditional households, but generally it is not displayed in public settings.

Male circumcision is universal among Yoruba, usually done within a week to nine days after birth as part of a naming-day ceremony. Clitoridectomy, much less widespread, was performed mainly as a preliminary to marriage. In modern Nigeria, excision is most often done in childhood or infancy, if it is done at all, and is uncommon in elite families. Naming-day ceremonies continue among Yoruba parents in the United States; a traditional diviner may even be brought in to give the name and divine for the child's future. Facial scarifications have become less common in educated families, and when they are done it is usually at the behest of older people who want to have their marks perpetuated. In general, the practice is not to anglicize their names. Yorubas generally acquire a series of names across their lifetime. These names frequently are metaphors and fragments of proverbs or poetry and do not readily translate into viable English names, so the tendency has been to keep them as is. English first names acquired in mission schools are sometimes used at work or school, but generally they do not replace the Yoruba names anywhere else.

## Language

Yoruba is a written language with a system of writing based on English. There does not seem to be an ethnic Yoruba-language press based in the United States, but Yoruba language papers are sometimes obtained from Nigeria. Yoruba, however, are involved as writers and journalists in African-oriented magazines published in English. These often short-lived efforts are sometimes published as collaborations with Nigerians from other ethnic groups and with Ghanaians. Yoruba also make up a good portion of the readership of English-language magazines published out of Africa and Europe that deal with the business, politics, and culture of western Africa. Most adult immigrants speak Yoruba at home and may alternate between Yoruba and English freely. (It should be

remembered that most Yoruba immigrants have been educated in an environment in which being bilingual in Yoruba and English is not only common but normal.) However, the children of these immigrants often have a very poor knowledge of the Yoruba language and are primarily English-speakers.

## Religious Organization

Although Yoruba are sometimes involved in African-American Baptist and Methodist denominations, they have also been establishing indigenized Christian churches of their own. These are branches of independent churches that arose as prophetic movements under African leadership in Nigeria, churches such as the Cherubim and Seraphim, the Christ Apostolic Church, and the Church of the Lord (Aladura), which incorporate a traditional African flavor into their distinctively Yoruba version of Christianity.

Yoruba have also established a number of cultural centers and cultural associations promoting African culture in the United States. These are more often associated with the traditional religion rather than Christianity or Islam. Since the founders of these centers are often musicians, as well as priests (priestesses) in the traditional religion or the children of traditional healers, the general emphasis of the activities is on Yoruba music, song, and dance, along with the Orisha religion. The traditional religion serves as one context within which Yoruba interact intensively with Latinos and African Americans who are adherents of African- and Yoruba-based religions such as Santeria, Voodoo, or Orisha-Voodoo. In this context, they work together to provide religious exchange and instruction and to gain societal recognition of their common religion and religious practices.

## Conclusion

Many Yoruba immigrated to the United States because they were highly skilled and highly trained individuals who could not obtain jobs in Nigeria that made use of their expertise and education. Others immigrated to study and, for any of a number of reasons, have not been able to complete their education. Once in the United States, many Yoruba find that their Nigerian credentials are automatically evaluated as substandard or are not recognized at all. Furthermore, many of them, despite the cachet that used to be attached to being a black foreigner, find they are subject to the same discrimination that black Americans face and, in many situations, are treated the same way. As a result some Yoruba men who could or would be among the professional elite or middle rank in Nigeria are found driving taxicabs in cities across the United States.

*See also:* AFRICAN AMERICANS; IGBO

## Bibliography

Apraku, K. K. (1991). *African Emigres in the United States*. New York: Praeger.

Bascom, W. R. (1969). *The Yoruba of Southwestern Nigeria*. New York: Holt, Rinehart and Winston.

Brandon, G. (1993). *Santeria from Africa to the New World: The Dead Sell Memories*. Bloomington: Indiana University Press.

Eades, J. S. (1980). *The Yoruba Today*. Cambridge, Eng.: Cambridge University Press.

Ikeri, M. (1992). "The Other Racism." *Essence* 22:124.

Lloyd, P C.; Mabogunje, A. L.; and Awe, B., eds. (1967). *The City of Ibadan*. Cambridge, Eng.: Cambridge University Press.

Speer, T. (1994). "The Newest African Americans." *American Demographics* 16:9–10.

Thompson, R. F. (1983). *Flash of the Spirit: African and Afro-American Art and Philosophy*. New York: Random House.

U.S. Bureau of the Census. (1990). *Characteristics of the Foreign-Born Population in the United States*. Washington, DC: U.S. Government Printing Office.

GEORGE BRANDON

# ZOROASTRIANS

Zoroastrians are a small population, originating in Iran, who are followers of the prophet Zoroaster (Zarathustra) and the Zoroastrian religion. Estimated at between two and five thousand, the Iranian Zoroastrian population in the United States is too small in number to be counted by the U.S. Census. Even in their homeland, Iran (formerly Persia), Zoroastrians constitute less than 0.1 percent of the population, although Zoroastrianism was once the official religion of the Sasanian Persian Empire (third to seventh centuries C.E.). Unknown to most Americans, Zoroastrianism is nonetheless considered a world religion and is also important for its influence on early Greece, Judaism, and Christianity.

## Religious Background

The Zoroastrian religion was founded in eastern Iran by Zoroaster; the date of its founding is variously estimated as 1200 or 600 B.C.E. Zoroaster's words are recorded in the Gathas, which are a key part of the Zoroastrian scriptures, the *Avesta*. Zoroastrian youth in America often explain their religion with reference to the Avestan phrase "good words, good thoughts, good deeds" (*humat, hukht, huvarest*), which sometimes is worn by Zoroastrians on a medallion. Some Zoroastrian organizations call themselves Mazdayasna or worshipers of Mazda, which refers to the one God, Ahura Mazda. Other key elements of the Zoroastrian religion often repeated by its modern-day followers include that all men and women should open their eyes and choose the right path toward Truth and Justice embodied in Ahura Mazda; that one should actively resist the "Lie" and Ahriman (the embodiment of evil); and that resisting evil is very specifically meant to include keeping elements of nature — earth, water, fire, and air —free from pollution. As part of this concept, the dead are not to be buried in the earth but should be set out in a large tower, the *dachme*. Although this particular practice is no longer performed, the concern with purity of natural elements remains. Fire, representing light and the truth, is kept pure and ever burning in Zoroastrian temples.

The Zoroastrian faith was practically destroyed by the Arab conquest of Persia in the seventh century C.E. The new Arab rulers pressured the Persians to convert to Islam, and within two to three centuries after the conquest the vast majority of Zoroastrians had become Muslims. What was left of the once great Zoroastrian Empire were a few Zoroastrians who fled to India to continue their religion there, and a few communities of Zoroastrians who remained stalwart in their Persian homeland. Those who escaped to India are known as Parsis. Their population increased, and in the late twentieth century numbered more than 120,000 in India and other countries. The Zoroastrians who remained in Iran lived primarily in remote areas but still faced pressures to convert to Islam. They were required to pay a special head tax, and they faced periods of persecution and discrimination. At times they were ordered to wear special clothing and were prohibited from traveling abroad, going to school, wearing glasses, building their homes higher than the reach of a Muslim hand, or riding a donkey in the presence of a Muslim. They were often branded as fire-worshipers because of their use of fire as a symbol representing light, truth, and justice. Called "people without a book," they were deemed ritually unclean by many Muslims, and for many centuries were forbidden to touch the food or clothing of Muslims. When it rained they were told to stay home lest the water carry their pollution to others. Their daughters were sometimes kidnapped, converted to Islam, and married to Muslim men. However, despite persecution, a few thousand persisted, holding on to their religion, rituals, ethics, ways of dress, and a regional language called Dari.

## Zoroastrian Persistence

In the late nineteenth and early twentieth centuries, conditions improved. A number of Parsis had become very wealthy in India and worked on behalf of their brethren in Iran, leading eventually to the abolition of the head tax and the establishment of Zoroastrian schools. Furthermore, Zoroastrians were able to enter the increasingly active trade among India, Iran, and European nations. A number of Zoroastrians became business entrepreneurs, professionals, and political figures. Westernization and secularization under the rule of Reza Shah (1922–1941), and later under

A Zoroastrian fire temple. (Janet Kestenberg Amighi)

his son Mohammad Reza Shah (1941–1978), led many Iranians to discard earlier prejudices. Furthermore, Mohammad Reza Shah attempted to raise pride in Persian nationalism and legitimize his own power by tracing a line of continuity from the Persian Empire under Cyrus and Darius, both probably Zoroastrians, to the present. This enhanced the image of the Zoroastrians further as representatives of true (i.e., pre-Muslim) Iranian identity. In fact, in the 1970s, a time of widespread Westernization, a number of Muslims sought to convert to Zoroastrianism.

Despite greatly reduced discrimination and pressure to convert to Islam, there was concern that Zoroastrianism would die out. In 1974, a Zoroastrian periodical, *Hukht*, estimated that there were only 12,500 Zoroastrians in all of Iran. Would the Zoroastrian community continue in an age of secularization and Westernization? Zoroastrians of 1970s Iran were very much part of the Persian culture. They spoke Persian, ate Persian food, and enjoyed a Persian identity. However, Zoroastrians still shared kinship ties, celebration of distinct rituals, and distinct cultural practices; in contrast to Muslims, they were strictly monogamous, their women had greater freedom of movement and were not required to wear a veil; divorce and remarriage of widows was rare. They saw themselves as having modest personalities, a shared sense of vulnerability, a common descent, and a shared commitment to Zoroastrian ethics.

## Immigration

In the United States, the issue of Zoroastrian persistence has become an even greater concern. In the 1960s and 1970s, it became increasingly popular and financially possible for Iranians to study abroad. Many Zoroastrian families who could afford it sent their sons, and more rarely daughters, to the United States (and Europe) for a university education. Some men married American women and settled permanently in the United States, but quite a few returned after their studies, seeking reconnection to family and the good jobs that Iran offered in the 1970s. Those who remained, mostly men, mostly professionals, settled primarily in large cities such as Chicago, New York, and Los Angeles. Where they lived usually depended on where they found jobs or where the family of an American spouse lived. Very few in number, scattered in widespread locales, they rarely formed communities or Zoroastrian organizations. In contrast to many other immigrant groups, many of these settlers came as students, learned English fluently, developed professions, and settled in dispersed locales. In fact, those men who married American women often raised children who did not learn to speak either Dari (lost by most of their parents' generation) or Persian. These scattered families rarely practiced their Zoroastrian religion. Although they retained their identities as Iranians and secondarily as Zoroastrians, many of these early immigrants do not dispute the suggestion that they were becoming highly assimilated.

During the difficult time following the Islamic Revolution (1979), immigration of Zoroastrians from Iran to North America began to increase dramatically. Wealthier Zoroastrian families were the first to leave Iran. They were uncertain how they would be treated by the new Islamic regime. Families who had supported the shah were being singled out for retribution. Another religious minority, the Baha'is, were openly persecuted, and Zoroastrians felt that they, too, would either lose their jobs and their businesses or be more actively persecuted. At first they emigrated legally, taking their families and some wealth. Then, when emigration became more difficult, many young men left illegally, smuggled across the border into Afghanistan and then into India, where a Parsi organization helped those who could demonstrate their Zoroastrian identity.

At least two-thirds, if not more, of the present-day Iranian Zoroastrian immigrants to the United States arrived after the Islamic Revolution in Iran. The wave of immigrants who followed the revolution differed from earlier immigrants in significant ways. Whereas the earlier Zoroastrian immigrants arrived in America freely seeking economic benefits, the second group were refugees from a lost homeland. Many immigrated to America hoping that the war with Iraq would end soon, that the revolution would evolve into a more secular state, and that they could then return home. They gathered in Persian nightclubs together with recent Muslim Irananian immigrants who also were refugees from the restrictive regime. They listened to songs about their Iranian homeland and cried over the way of life that had been lost to them. Zoroastrians, like other Iranians, went through a period of shock and numbness. Their place in America did not feel permanent. In addition, many faced an American population who were angry about the American embassy staff being taken hostage in 1979 by Iranian students in Tehran. Anti-Iranian sentiment across the United States was high from at least late 1979 to late 1980. Most Americans did not distinguish between Iranian refugees in America and the Islamic regime in Iran. Thus many Zoroastrians felt twice victimized, by Iran and by the United States.

The postrevolution wave of immigration brought many more families than single individuals, and even the single men who arrived often had kin already living in the United States. Furthermore, although the new immigrants were still fairly well educated, many did not speak English fluently. Thus they were more isolated from American friendships and more involved in family and ethnic life. For a while at least, families spoke Persian at home and encouraged their children to retain Persian and Zoroastrian identities.

## Community Organization

When it became apparent that a return to Iran was unlikely, many sought some connection with other Iranians in the United States and more specifically with other Zoroastrians. These connections developed in two ways. As new immigrants arrived, they often settled near family members so that in certain regions, particularly California and New York, some extended families were reestablished. New immigrants rekindled interest in Persian/Zoroastrian identity among earlier immigrants.

This was not a one-way trend, however, since many families still lived far away from other Zoroastrians, and some relatives, particularly non-English-speaking elders, chose to return to Iran. Outside of the California and New York regions, most Zoroastrians remained fairly isolated from kin or other coreligionists. Thus there was considerable variation from region to region.

With the help of the Rostam Giv Foundation (an Iranian Zoroastrian charitable organization), several Zoroastrian temples (in Toronto; Chicago; New Rochelle, New York; and Los Angeles) were opened, and centers for celebration of Zoroastrian holidays and Zoroastrian studies were established. These Zoroastrian temples are managed and used jointly by Iranian Zoroastrians and the more numerous Parsis. The Parsis provide the priests (*mobeds*) and generally set the tone for the religious celebrations.

There are more than twenty-two Zoroastrian organizations in continental North America. In Los Angeles, for example, there are several organizations: the Zoroastrian Center (mostly Iranian), the Zoroastrian Association of California (mostly Parsi), the Zoroastrian Assembly, and the traditional Mazdayasnan Zoroastrian Association of orthodox families. Other large Iranian Zoroastrian organizations exist in New York (Zagny), northern California, and Canada. Quite a few others are Parsi-dominated, with a small to medium percentage of Iranian Zoroastrian members.

Where Iranian Zoroastrians exist in sufficient numbers, they sometimes split off from the Parsi groups. Cultural and religious differences often outweigh the shared aspects of their religion. Indian food is spicy, while Iranian food is mild. Iranian Zoroastrians enjoy speaking Persian together, while Parsis speak English. The two groups also clash over the calender and dates of rituals, the way rituals are to be conducted, burial practices, the behavior of the congregation (Iranian Zoroastrians talk right through the rituals), and other philosophical issues (e.g., the acceptance of converts or children of a non-Zoroastrian father). A small but outspoken group of Parsis opposes both conversion and intermarriage, while Iranian Zoroastrians tend to be less adamant on the issue and more open to outsiders. Because Iranian Zoroastrians are so few in number, the intermarriage rate of the younger generation is high. There is some pressure for young people to marry within the faith, particularly in the case of women, but by and large the majority of Iranian Zoroastrians accept children of mixed marriages as Zoroastrian and are open to converts. Rayna Writer, a Parsi researcher, found that Parsis tend to be more focused on rituals and rules, while Iranian Zoroastrians focus more on philosophy. These differences notwithstanding, cooperation continues in most locations and permits the sponsorship of large-scale events such as the Zoroastrian Youth Congress.

Although many people today are concerned about the future of Zoroastrians in America, almost everywhere where even two or three Zoroastrian families are found, some kind of formal or informal organization has been established. Stanford University hosts a Zoroastrian Students' Club. In some locales, such as Detroit, Denver, and the Raleigh/Durham area of North Carolina, Zoroastrians in small numbers have formed alliances with Muslim Iranians who are also interested in the celebration of their ancient Iranian heritage. Celebrations include the fall festival, Jashne Mehregan; the winter fire ceremony, Jashne Sadeh; and the spring New Year, Now Ruz.

## Conclusion

In America, Persian culture in general and Zoroastrian culture in particular survive in an environment that is fairly tolerant of ethnic differences. While the new generation often does not speak Persian fluently, does not always cook Iranian food for dinner, and does not always participate in Zoroastrian holidays and rituals, there are quite a number of young people seeking both an American identity and an Iranian Zoroastrian connection.

For most Zoroastrians, being Zoroastrian is an ethnic identity and a belief in a common descent, which distinguishes them from Muslims, links them to their families and Iran, engages them in special celebrations, and suggests a strong commitment to the truth. Although many Zoroastrian families are nonpractitioners of their religion, it is difficult to forget that one is a member of a minority so small that each case of intermarriage out of the faith and each child not brought up Zoroastrian represent significant steps toward extinction of a religion/community that has existed for more than twenty-five hundred years.

*See also:* IRANIANS

## Bibliography

Boyce, M. (1977). *A Persian Stronghold of Zoroastrianism.* Oxford, Eng.: Clarendon Press.

Boyce, M. (1991). *Zoroastrianism.* New York: Mazda.

Browne, E. G. (1926). *A Year Amongst the Persian: 1887–1888.* Cambridge, Eng.: Cambridge University Press.

Frye, R. (1963). *The Heritage of Persia.* New York: New American Library.

Kestenberg Amighi, J. (1990). *The Zoroastrians of Iran.* New York: AMS Press.

Malandra, W., ed. and trans. (1983). *An Introduction to Ancient Iranian Religion.* Minneapolis: University of Minnesota Press.

Mehr, F. (1991). *The Zoroastrian Tradition.* Rockport, MA: Element.

Writer, R. (1993). *Contemporary Zoroastrians: An Unstructured Nation.* Lanham, NY: University Press of America.

Yarshater, E., ed. (1983). *The Cambridge History of Iran,* Vol. 3: *The Seleucid, Parthian, and Sasanian Periods.* Cambridge, Eng.: Cambridge University Press.

Zaehner, R. C. (1961). *The Dawn and Twilight of Zoroastrianism.* New York: Putnam.

JANET KESTENBERG AMIGHI
AFRUZ SHARRON AMIGHI

# Appendix

# MAPS

One of the most common factors used in defining a distinct ethnic group is its ancestral homeland. This identification refers in many cases simply to a country of origin, but it should be remembered that the political borders of individual countries have been subject to change throughout history. For example, in a discussion of Austrians it becomes necessary to determine relevant geographical boundaries and time periods for discussion of a group of people at the center of the vast Austro-Hungarian Empire, an empire that at times included Poles, Serbs, Croats, Slovenes, Slovaks, Hungarians, and "Austrians" among its population. Another consideration in determining geographical origins for an ethnic group is that some groups are identified solely on the basis of their religious beliefs, which are not necessarily restricted by political boundaries.

With these complex issues of precise geographical identification in mind, the following maps can be used to obtain a better understanding of the origins of the individual ethnic groups included in this publication. The world map provided below identifies the sections of the world covered by the eight region-specific maps that follow. This world map provides a general means of evaluating the global relationship between the United States and the homelands of various immigrant groups. The eight region-specific maps that follow provide general geographic identifications of the ancestral homelands of the ethnic groups discussed in this publication. These maps provide not only a visual means of identifying the geographical regions from which various immigrant cultures originated but also a way of showing which ethnic groups originally lived in close proximity to each other.

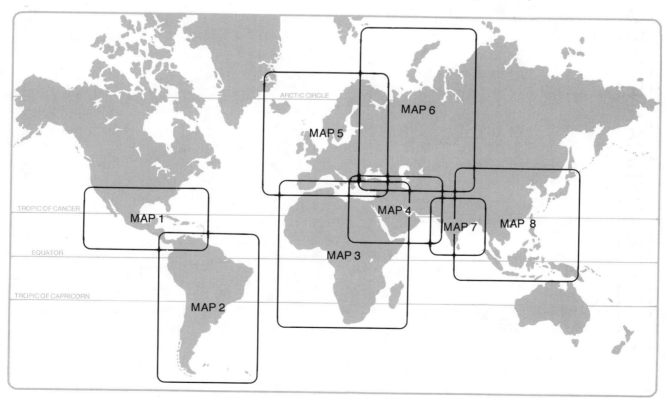

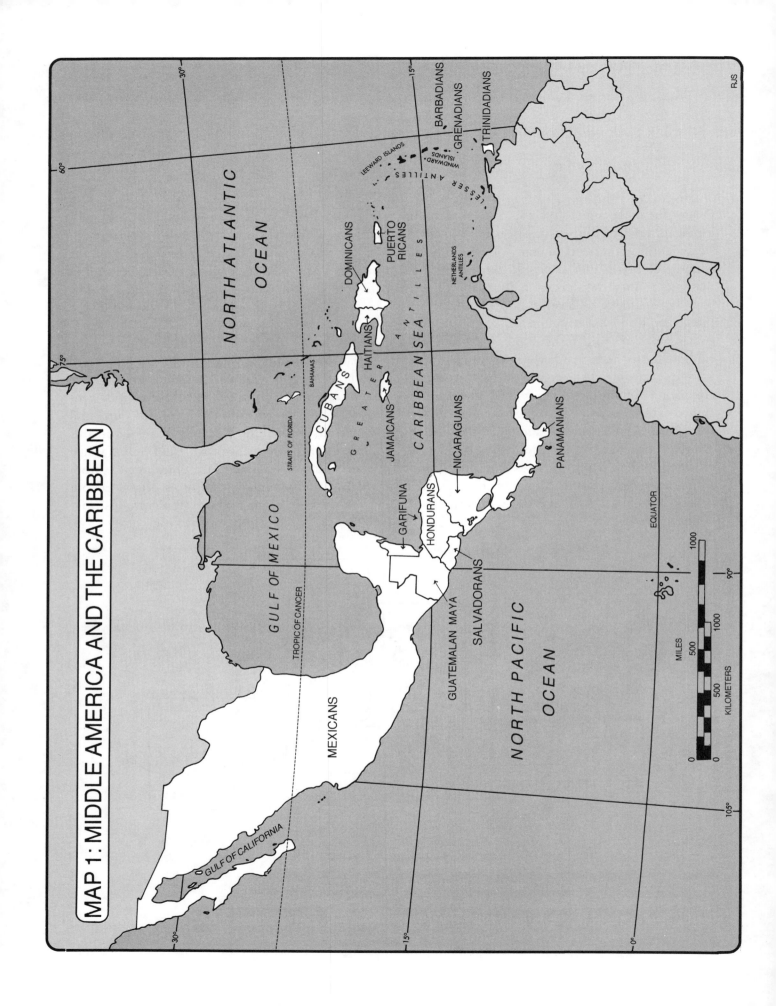

# MAP 1: MIDDLE AMERICA AND THE CARIBBEAN

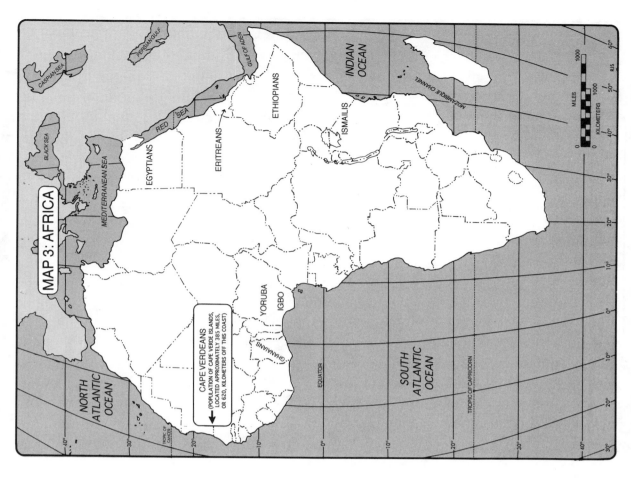

MAP 3: AFRICA

MAP 2: SOUTH AMERICA

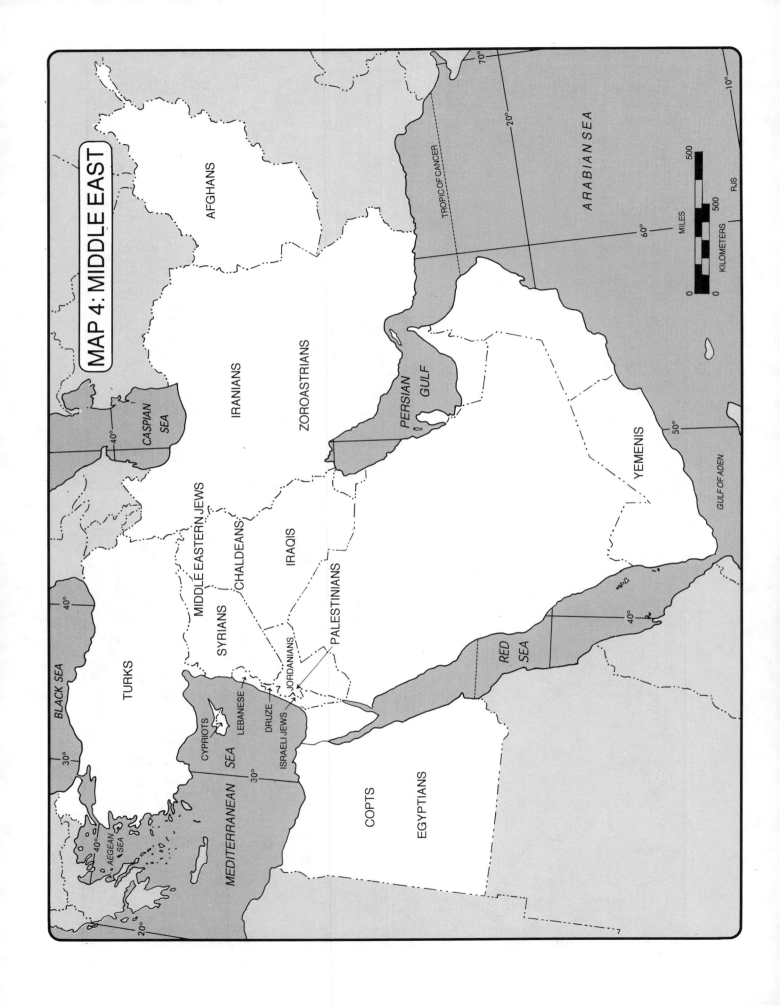

MAP 4: MIDDLE EAST

# MAP 5: EUROPE

ARCTIC OCEAN

ICELANDERS

ARCTIC CIRCLE

NORWEGIAN SEA

NORTH ATLANTIC OCEAN

FINNS
SWEDE-FINNS

NORWEGIANS

SWEDES

BALTIC SEA

SCOTS

NORTH SEA

SCOTCH-IRISH

TRAVELERS

IRISH

DANES

KASHUBIANS

POLES

FRISIANS

DUTCH

WELSH

ENGLISH

CORNISH

BELGIANS

GERMANS

MENNONITES

HASIDIC JEWS

EUROPEAN JEWS

CZECHS

SORBS

SLOVAKS

AMISH

HUTTERITES

GYPSIES

BAY OF BISCAY

FRENCH

SWISS

AUSTRIANS

HUNGARIANS

ROMANIANS

CROATIANS

SERBS

SLOVENES

BOSNIAN MUSLIMS

BASQUES

ITALIANS

ADRIATIC SEA

BULGARIANS

BLACK SEA

PORTUGUESE

SPANIARDS

MONTENEGRINS

MACEDONIANS

ALBANIANS

VLACHS

GREEKS

AEGEAN SEA

SARDINIANS

TYRRHENIAN SEA

IONIAN SEA

MEDITERRANEAN SEA

SICILIANS

MILES
0          500

KILOMETERS
0          500

RJS

# MAP 6: EURASIA

ARCTIC    OCEAN

ARCTIC CIRCLE

BALTIC SEA

RUSSIAN
OLD BELIEVERS

ESTONIANS

LATVIANS

LITHUANIANS

BELARUSANS

RUSSIANS

CARPATHO-RUSYNS

SOVIET JEWS

GERMANS
FROM RUSSIA

UKRAINIANS

CIRCASSIANS

RUSSIAN MOLOKANS

KALMYKS

BLACK SEA

ARAL
SEA

GEORGIANS

CASPIAN
SEA

ARMENIANS

MILES    500

KILOMETERS    500

RJS

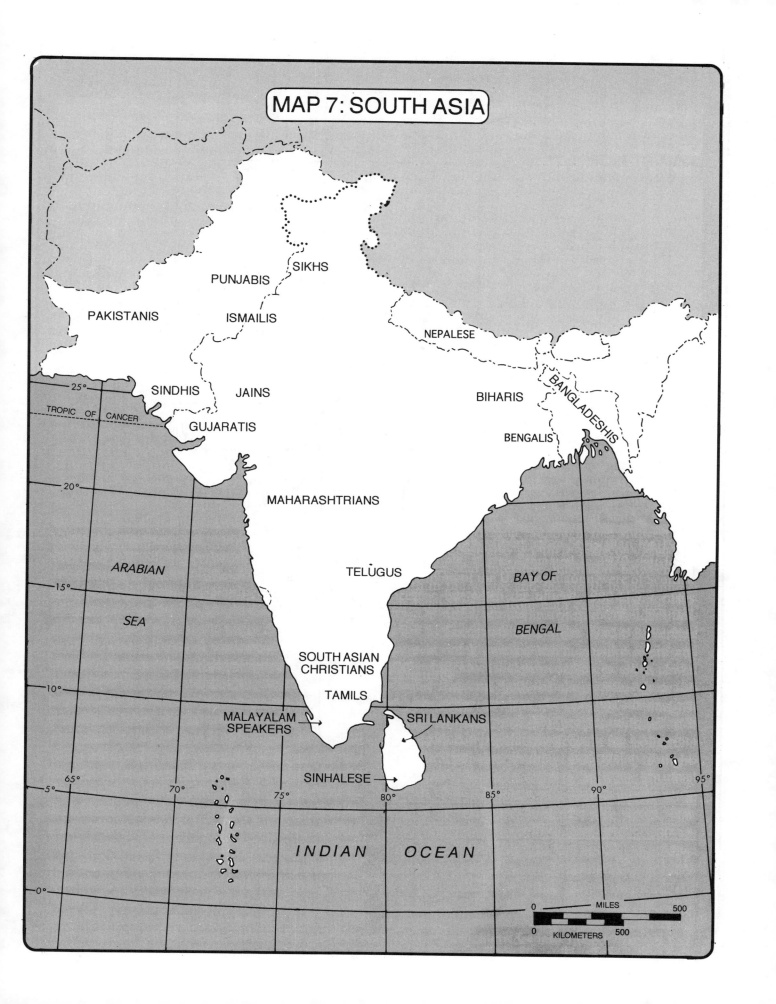

# MAP 7: SOUTH ASIA

PAKISTANIS

PUNJABIS

SIKHS

ISMAILIS

NEPALESE

BANGLADESHIS

SINDHIS

JAINS

BIHARIS

TROPIC OF CANCER

GUJARATIS

BENGALIS

25°

20°

MAHARASHTRIANS

ARABIAN

TELUGUS

BAY OF

15°

SEA

BENGAL

SOUTH ASIAN
CHRISTIANS

10°

TAMILS

MALAYALAM
SPEAKERS

SRI LANKANS

SINHALESE

65°

70°

75°

80°

85°

90°

95°

5°

INDIAN   OCEAN

0°

```
0          MILES          500
0        KILOMETERS       500
```

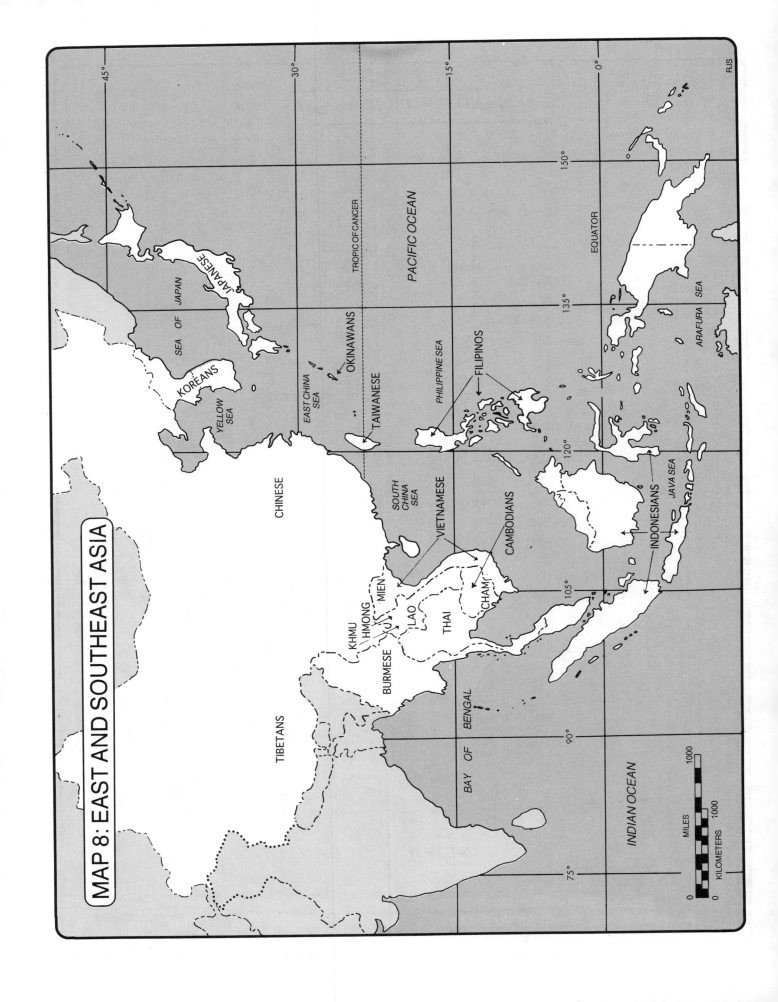

# ANCESTRY STATISTICS

The following tables are compiled from 1990 U.S. Census statistics included in *Detailed Ancestry Groups for States*, published by the U.S. Bureau of the Census (1992). Some of the ancestry group headings used in these tables, which are those reported by the U.S. Bureau of the Census, do not coincide with the enthnonyms adopted for general use by the editors of this publication. The census data were obtained through voluntary self-identification responses to the ancestry section of the 1990 census questionnaire. While the questionnaire provided no prelisted categories and allowed for a maximum of two ancestry responses, almost 10 percent of the population did not complete the ancestry question, and less than 30 percent provided a second ancestry response.

Interpretation of the data is complicated by the fact that the listing of an ethnic group as an individual's ancestry does not reflect the degree of attachment to that ethnic group. For example, a response of "Irish" might reflect complete involvement in the Irish community or only a memory of distant Irish ancestors. In fact, since 1980, the ethnic data have been gathered without regard to the number of generations an individual is removed from the country of origin. Prior to 1980, ethnic information was based on questions concerning the country of birth of persons and their parents; ancestry statistics, therefore, reflected the circumstances of only the foreign-born or of native persons of foreign or mixed parentage.

While there were significant inconsistencies observed between the 1980 and the 1990 results from the open-ended ancestry response question, there were also strong consistencies. For groups such as Italian, French, Polish, Dutch, Swedish, Welsh, Danish, Swiss, Austrian, and Lebanese, there was reasonable consistency between 1980 and 1990. On the other hand, there were groups that show inconsistent reporting. Persons of German ancestry substantially increased from 1980 to 1990. In contrast, persons reporting English ancestry declined from 1980 to 1990. Reports of Scottish and Irish ancestry also declined, but not as dramatically.

For these reasons, the following tables must be read with caution. To assist with quick comparisons of the total responses for each ancestry, Table 1 presents an alphabetical arrangement of the ethnic groups reported in response to the ancestry question in the 1990 U.S. Census. The table also includes a breakdown of the number of individuals reporting the ethnic group as a first response and the number reporting it as a second response, along with the percentages represented by these response divisions in relation to the total number of individuals reporting a given ethnic ancestry. To facilitate a detailed study of individual ethnic groups, Table 2 presents a state-by-state distribution for the responses concerning each ancestry; this table does not distinguish between first ancestry responses and second ancestry responses.

**TABLE 1** Ancestry Reports for 1990

| Ethnic Group | Persons Who Reported At Least One Specific Ancestry | | | Percent of Total Per Ancestry | |
| --- | --- | --- | --- | --- | --- |
| | Total | Reported as First Ancestry | Reported as Second Ancestry | First Ancestry | Second Ancestry |
| Acadian/Cajun | 668,271 | 597,729 | 70,542 | 89.4 | 10.6 |
| Afghanistan | 31,301 | 30,600 | 701 | 97.8 | 2.2 |
| African | 245,845 | 224,740 | 21,105 | 91.4 | 8.6 |
| Afro-American | 23,777,098 | 23,541,280 | 235,818 | 99.0 | 1.0 |
| Albanian | 47,710 | 38,361 | 9,349 | 80.4 | 19.6 |
| Aleut | 15,816 | 13,232 | 2,584 | 83.7 | 16.3 |
| Algerian | 3,215 | 2,537 | 678 | 78.9 | 21.1 |
| Alsatian | 16,465 | 9,683 | 6,782 | 58.8 | 41.2 |
| Amerasian | 15,523 | 15,449 | 74 | 99.5 | 0.5 |
| American | 12,395,999 | 12,395,999 | 0 | 100.0 | 0.0 |
| American Indian | 8,708,220 | 4,864,263 | 3,843,957 | 55.9 | 44.1 |
| Arab | 127,364 | 112,411 | 14,953 | 88.3 | 11.7 |
| Argentinean | 63,176 | 54,324 | 8,852 | 86.0 | 14.0 |
| Armenian | 308,096 | 267,975 | 40,121 | 87.0 | 13.0 |
| Asian | 107,172 | 98,776 | 8,396 | 92.2 | 7.8 |
| Asian Indian | 570,322 | 549,669 | 20,653 | 96.4 | 3.6 |
| Assyrian | 51,765 | 46,099 | 5,666 | 89.1 | 10.9 |
| Australian | 52,133 | 36,290 | 15,843 | 69.6 | 30.4 |
| Austrian | 864,783 | 542,138 | 322,645 | 62.7 | 37.3 |
| Bahamian | 21,081 | 18,752 | 2,329 | 89.0 | 11.0 |
| Bangladeshi | 12,486 | 11,901 | 585 | 95.3 | 4.7 |
| Barbadian | 35,455 | 33,178 | 2,277 | 93.6 | 6.4 |
| Basque | 47,956 | 37,842 | 10,114 | 78.9 | 21.1 |
| Bavarian | 4,348 | 2,833 | 1,515 | 65.2 | 34.8 |
| Belgian | 380,498 | 239,439 | 141,059 | 62.9 | 37.1 |
| Belizean | 22,922 | 21,205 | 1,717 | 92.5 | 7.5 |
| Belorussian | 4,277 | 3,471 | 806 | 81.2 | 18.8 |
| Bermudan | 4,941 | 4,007 | 934 | 81.1 | 18.9 |
| Bolivian | 33,738 | 31,035 | 2,703 | 92.0 | 8.0 |
| Brazilian | 65,875 | 57,108 | 8,767 | 86.7 | 13.3 |
| British | 1,119,154 | 867,255 | 251,899 | 77.5 | 22.5 |
| British West Indian | 37,819 | 35,446 | 2,373 | 93.7 | 6.3 |
| Bulgarian | 29,595 | 20,894 | 8,701 | 70.6 | 29.4 |
| Burmese | 8,646 | 7,196 | 1,450 | 83.2 | 16.8 |
| Cambodian | 134,955 | 132,157 | 2,798 | 97.9 | 2.1 |
| Canadian | 549,990 | 354,656 | 195,334 | 64.5 | 35.5 |
| Cantonese | 25,020 | 24,926 | 94 | 99.6 | 0.4 |
| Cape Verdean | 50,772 | 46,552 | 4,220 | 91.7 | 8.3 |

**TABLE 1** *(Continued)*

| Ethnic Group | Persons Who Reported At Least One Specific Ancestry | | | Percent of Total Per Ancestry | |
| --- | --- | --- | --- | --- | --- |
| | Total | Reported as First Ancestry | Reported as Second Ancestry | First Ancestry | Second Ancestry |
| Carpath Rusyn | 7,602 | 6,927 | 675 | 91.1 | 8.9 |
| Celtic | 29,652 | 22,966 | 6,686 | 77.5 | 22.5 |
| Central American | 10,310 | 9,755 | 555 | 94.6 | 5.4 |
| Central European | 5,604 | 5,434 | 170 | 97.0 | 3.0 |
| Chamorro | 4,427 | 4,065 | 362 | 91.8 | 8.2 |
| Chilean | 61,465 | 54,842 | 6,623 | 89.2 | 10.8 |
| Chinese | 1,505,245 | 1,404,634 | 100,611 | 93.3 | 6.7 |
| Colombian | 351,717 | 329,160 | 22,557 | 93.6 | 6.4 |
| Cornish | 3,991 | 2,237 | 1,754 | 56.1 | 43.9 |
| Costa Rican | 51,771 | 45,601 | 6,170 | 88.1 | 11.9 |
| Croatian | 544,270 | 409,458 | 134,812 | 75.2 | 24.8 |
| Cuban | 859,739 | 805,204 | 54,535 | 93.7 | 6.3 |
| Cypriot | 4,897 | 4,678 | 219 | 95.5 | 4.5 |
| Czech | 1,296,411 | 769,427 | 526,984 | 59.4 | 40.6 |
| Czechoslovakian | 315,285 | 240,489 | 74,796 | 76.3 | 23.7 |
| Danish | 1,634,669 | 980,868 | 653,801 | 60.0 | 40.0 |
| Dominican | 505,690 | 484,893 | 20,797 | 95.9 | 4.1 |
| Dutch | 6,227,089 | 3,475,410 | 2,751,679 | 55.8 | 44.2 |
| Dutch West Indian | 61,530 | 33,473 | 28,057 | 54.4 | 45.6 |
| Ecuadorian | 197,374 | 182,904 | 14,470 | 92.7 | 7.3 |
| Egyptian | 78,574 | 73,097 | 5,477 | 93.0 | 7.0 |
| English | 32,651,788 | 21,834,160 | 10,817,628 | 66.9 | 33.1 |
| Eritrean | 4,270 | 4,231 | 39 | 99.1 | 0.9 |
| Eskimo | 52,920 | 48,523 | 4,397 | 91.7 | 8.3 |
| Estonian | 26,762 | 20,996 | 5,766 | 78.5 | 21.5 |
| Ethiopian | 30,581 | 29,637 | 944 | 96.9 | 3.1 |
| Eurasian | 14,177 | 13,553 | 624 | 95.6 | 4.4 |
| European | 466,718 | 444,107 | 22,611 | 95.2 | 4.8 |
| Fijian | 7,472 | 6,928 | 544 | 92.7 | 7.3 |
| Filipino | 1,450,512 | 1,333,521 | 116,991 | 91.9 | 8.1 |
| Finnish | 658,870 | 465,070 | 193,800 | 70.6 | 29.4 |
| Flemish | 14,157 | 8,636 | 5,521 | 61.0 | 39.0 |
| French | 10,320,935 | 6,194,501 | 4,126,434 | 60.0 | 40.0 |
| French Canadian | 2,167,127 | 1,698,394 | 468,733 | 78.4 | 21.6 |
| German | 57,947,374 | 45,555,748 | 12,391,626 | 78.6 | 21.4 |
| German Russian/Volga | 10,153 | 9,833 | 320 | 96.8 | 3.2 |
| Ghanian | 20,066 | 19,695 | 371 | 98.2 | 1.8 |
| Greek | 1,110,373 | 921,782 | 188,591 | 83.0 | 17.0 |

**TABLE 1** *(Continued)*

| Ethnic Group | Persons Who Reported At Least One Specific Ancestry | | | Percent of Total Per Ancestry | |
|---|---|---|---|---|---|
| | Total | Reported as First Ancestry | Reported as Second Ancestry | First Ancestry | Second Ancestry |
| Guamanian | 39,237 | 33,053 | 6,184 | 84.2 | 15.8 |
| Guatemalan | 241,559 | 229,479 | 12,080 | 95.0 | 5.0 |
| Guyanese | 81,665 | 75,765 | 5,900 | 92.8 | 7.2 |
| Haitian | 289,521 | 280,874 | 8,647 | 97.0 | 3.0 |
| Hawaiian | 256,081 | 205,802 | 50,279 | 80.4 | 19.6 |
| Hispanic | 1,113,259 | 1,059,910 | 53,349 | 95.2 | 4.8 |
| Hmong | 84,823 | 81,194 | 3,629 | 95.7 | 4.3 |
| Honduran | 116,635 | 108,364 | 8,271 | 92.9 | 7.1 |
| Hong Kong | 5,774 | 4,541 | 1,233 | 78.6 | 21.4 |
| Hungarian | 1,582,302 | 997,545 | 584,757 | 63.0 | 37.0 |
| Icelander | 40,529 | 27,171 | 13,358 | 67.0 | 33.0 |
| Indonesian | 43,969 | 27,936 | 16,033 | 63.5 | 36.5 |
| Iranian | 235,521 | 220,714 | 14,807 | 93.7 | 6.3 |
| Iraqi | 23,212 | 20,657 | 2,555 | 89.0 | 11.0 |
| Irish | 38,735,539 | 22,695,454 | 16,040,085 | 58.6 | 41.4 |
| Israeli | 81,677 | 69,018 | 12,659 | 84.5 | 15.5 |
| Italian | 14,664,550 | 11,246,781 | 3,417,769 | 76.7 | 23.3 |
| Jamaican | 435,024 | 410,933 | 24,091 | 94.5 | 5.5 |
| Japanese | 1,004,645 | 908,599 | 96,046 | 90.4 | 9.6 |
| Jordanian | 20,656 | 19,657 | 999 | 95.2 | 4.8 |
| Kenyan | 4,639 | 4,460 | 179 | 96.1 | 3.9 |
| Khmer | 2,979 | 2,979 | 0 | 100.0 | 0.0 |
| Korean | 836,987 | 798,595 | 38,392 | 95.4 | 4.6 |
| Laotian | 146,930 | 142,640 | 4,290 | 97.1 | 2.9 |
| Latin American | 43,521 | 39,446 | 4,075 | 90.6 | 9.4 |
| Latvian | 100,331 | 75,747 | 24,584 | 75.5 | 24.5 |
| Lebanese | 394,180 | 309,578 | 84,602 | 78.5 | 21.5 |
| Liberian | 8,797 | 8,309 | 488 | 94.5 | 5.5 |
| Lithuanian | 811,865 | 526,089 | 285,776 | 64.8 | 35.2 |
| Luxemburger | 49,061 | 28,846 | 20,215 | 58.8 | 41.2 |
| Macedonian | 20,365 | 16,113 | 4,252 | 79.1 | 20.9 |
| Malaysian | 27,800 | 25,317 | 2,483 | 91.1 | 8.9 |
| Maltese | 39,600 | 30,292 | 9,308 | 76.5 | 23.5 |
| Manx | 6,317 | 3,806 | 2,511 | 60.3 | 39.7 |
| Mexican | 11,586,983 | 11,165,939 | 421,044 | 96.4 | 3.6 |
| Micronesian | 3,406 | 3,171 | 235 | 93.1 | 6.9 |
| Middle Eastern | 7,656 | 6,654 | 1,002 | 86.9 | 13.1 |
| Mongolian | 3,507 | 2,554 | 953 | 72.8 | 27.2 |

**TABLE 1** *(Continued)*

| Ethnic Group | Persons Who Reported At Least One Specific Ancestry | | | Percent of Total Per Ancestry | |
|---|---|---|---|---|---|
| | Total | Reported as First Ancestry | Reported as Second Ancestry | First Ancestry | Second Ancestry |
| Moravian | 3,781 | 2,660 | 1,121 | 70.4 | 29.6 |
| Moroccan | 19,089 | 15,015 | 4,074 | 78.7 | 21.3 |
| Nepali | 2,516 | 2,369 | 147 | 94.2 | 5.8 |
| Newfoundland | 5,412 | 3,636 | 1,776 | 67.2 | 32.8 |
| New Zealander | 7,742 | 5,997 | 1,745 | 77.5 | 22.5 |
| Nicaraguan | 177,077 | 167,395 | 9,682 | 94.5 | 5.5 |
| Nigerian | 91,688 | 86,875 | 4,813 | 94.8 | 5.2 |
| North American | 12,618 | 12,618 | 0 | 100.0 | 0.0 |
| Northern European | 65,993 | 64,758 | 1,235 | 98.1 | 1.9 |
| Northern Irish | 4,009 | 2,832 | 1,177 | 70.6 | 29.4 |
| Norwegian | 3,869,395 | 2,517,760 | 1,351,635 | 65.1 | 34.9 |
| Nova Scotian | 5,489 | 3,320 | 2,169 | 60.5 | 39.5 |
| Okinawan | 10,554 | 8,498 | 2,056 | 80.5 | 19.5 |
| Other Asian | 2,185 | 1,887 | 298 | 86.4 | 13.6 |
| Other Central and South American | 1,217 | 1,078 | 139 | 88.6 | 11.4 |
| Other Eastern European and Soviet Union | 132,332 | 123,717 | 8,615 | 93.5 | 6.5 |
| Other Groups and Not Classified | 3,389,599 | 3,088,188 | 301,411 | 91.1 | 8.9 |
| Other Hispanic | 5,259 | 3,940 | 1,319 | 74.9 | 25.1 |
| Other North African and Southwest Asian | 10,670 | 9,225 | 1,445 | 86.5 | 13.5 |
| Other North American | 309 | 185 | 124 | 59.9 | 40.1 |
| Other Pacific Islander | 8,674 | 7,258 | 1,416 | 83.7 | 16.3 |
| Other South Asian | 116 | 116 | 0 | 100.0 | 0.0 |
| Other Subsaharan African | 20,607 | 19,182 | 1,425 | 93.1 | 6.9 |
| Other Western European | 2,005 | 1,328 | 677 | 66.2 | 33.8 |
| Other West Indian | 4,139 | 3,405 | 734 | 82.3 | 17.7 |
| Pacific Islander | 11,330 | 10,289 | 1,041 | 90.8 | 9.2 |
| Pakistani | 99,974 | 95,301 | 4,673 | 95.3 | 4.7 |
| Palestinian | 48,019 | 44,651 | 3,368 | 93.0 | 7.0 |
| Panamanian | 88,649 | 76,829 | 11,820 | 86.7 | 13.3 |
| Paraguayan | 5,415 | 4,916 | 499 | 90.8 | 9.2 |
| Pennsylvania German | 305,841 | 246,461 | 59,380 | 80.6 | 19.4 |
| Peruvian | 161,866 | 147,504 | 14,362 | 91.1 | 8.9 |
| Polish | 9,366,106 | 6,542,844 | 2,823,262 | 69.9 | 30.1 |
| Polynesian | 10,854 | 8,303 | 2,551 | 76.5 | 23.5 |

**TABLE 1** *(Continued)*

| Ethnic Group | Persons Who Reported At Least One Specific Ancestry | | | Percent of Total Per Ancestry | |
| --- | --- | --- | --- | --- | --- |
| | Total | Reported as First Ancestry | Reported as Second Ancestry | First Ancestry | Second Ancestry |
| Portuguese | 1,153,351 | 900,060 | 253,291 | 78.0 | 22.0 |
| Prussian | 25,469 | 19,184 | 6,285 | 75.3 | 24.7 |
| Puerto Rican | 1,955,323 | 1,813,122 | 142,201 | 92.7 | 7.3 |
| Rom | 5,693 | 3,353 | 2,340 | 58.9 | 41.1 |
| Romanian | 365,544 | 235,774 | 129,770 | 64.5 | 35.5 |
| Russian | 2,952,987 | 2,115,232 | 837,755 | 71.6 | 28.4 |
| Ruthenian | 3,776 | 3,010 | 766 | 79.7 | 20.3 |
| Salvadoran | 499,153 | 479,977 | 19,176 | 96.2 | 3.8 |
| Samoan | 55,419 | 49,503 | 5,916 | 89.3 | 10.7 |
| Saudi Arabian | 4,486 | 4,257 | 229 | 94.9 | 5.1 |
| Saxon | 4,519 | 2,658 | 1,861 | 58.8 | 41.2 |
| Scandinavian | 678,880 | 480,646 | 198,234 | 70.8 | 29.2 |
| Scotch-Irish | 5,617,773 | 4,334,197 | 1,283,576 | 77.2 | 22.8 |
| Scottish | 5,393,581 | 3,315,306 | 2,078,275 | 61.5 | 38.5 |
| Serbian | 116,795 | 89,583 | 27,212 | 76.7 | 23.3 |
| Sicilian | 50,389 | 40,034 | 10,355 | 79.4 | 20.6 |
| Sierra Leonean | 4,627 | 4,441 | 186 | 96.0 | 4.0 |
| Singaporean | 2,419 | 2,230 | 189 | 92.2 | 7.8 |
| Slavic | 76,931 | 43,301 | 33,630 | 56.3 | 43.7 |
| Slovak | 1,882,897 | 1,210,652 | 672,245 | 64.3 | 35.7 |
| Slovene | 124,437 | 87,500 | 36,937 | 70.3 | 29.7 |
| South African | 17,992 | 15,347 | 2,645 | 85.3 | 14.7 |
| South American | 10,867 | 9,075 | 1,792 | 83.5 | 16.5 |
| Soviet Union | 7,729 | 6,080 | 1,649 | 78.7 | 21.3 |
| Spaniard | 360,935 | 312,865 | 48,070 | 86.7 | 13.3 |
| Spanish | 2,024,004 | 1,625,866 | 398,138 | 80.3 | 19.7 |
| Sri Lankan | 14,448 | 13,541 | 907 | 93.7 | 6.3 |
| Sudanese | 3,623 | 3,341 | 282 | 92.2 | 7.8 |
| Swedish | 4,680,863 | 2,881,950 | 1,798,913 | 61.6 | 38.4 |
| Swiss | 1,045,495 | 607,833 | 437,662 | 58.1 | 41.9 |
| Syrian | 129,606 | 95,155 | 34,451 | 73.4 | 26.6 |
| Taiwanese | 192,973 | 187,012 | 5,961 | 96.9 | 3.1 |
| Thai | 112,117 | 102,941 | 9,176 | 91.8 | 8.2 |
| Tirol | 5,748 | 3,718 | 2,030 | 64.7 | 35.3 |
| Tongan | 16,019 | 14,971 | 1,048 | 93.5 | 6.5 |
| Trinidadian and Tobagonian | 76,270 | 71,720 | 4,550 | 94.0 | 6.0 |
| Turkish | 83,850 | 66,492 | 17,358 | 79.3 | 20.7 |

**TABLE 1** (*Continued*)

| Ethnic Group | Persons Who Reported At Least One Specific Ancestry | | | Percent of Total Per Ancestry | |
| --- | --- | --- | --- | --- | --- |
| | Total | Reported as First Ancestry | Reported as Second Ancestry | First Ancestry | Second Ancestry |
| Ugandan | 2,681 | 2,475 | 206 | 92.3 | 7.7 |
| Ukrainian | 740,803 | 514,085 | 226,718 | 69.4 | 30.6 |
| United States | 643,561 | 643,561 | 0 | 100.0 | 0.0 |
| Uruguayan | 14,641 | 13,418 | 1,223 | 91.6 | 8.4 |
| U.S. Virgin Islander | 7,621 | 6,831 | 790 | 89.6 | 10.4 |
| Venezuelan | 40,331 | 34,046 | 6,285 | 84.4 | 15.6 |
| Vietnamese | 535,825 | 519,200 | 16,625 | 96.9 | 3.1 |
| Welsh | 2,033,893 | 1,038,603 | 995,290 | 51.1 | 48.9 |
| Western European | 42,409 | 41,664 | 745 | 98.2 | 1.8 |
| West German | 3,885 | 3,509 | 376 | 90.3 | 9.7 |
| West Indian | 159,167 | 138,521 | 20,646 | 87.0 | 13.0 |
| White | 1,799,711 | 1,799,711 | 0 | 100.0 | 0.0 |
| Windish | 3,189 | 1,935 | 1,254 | 60.7 | 39.3 |
| Yemeni | 4,011 | 3,497 | 514 | 87.2 | 12.8 |
| Yugoslavian | 257,994 | 184,952 | 73,042 | 71.7 | 28.3 |
| Total* | 298,559,710 | 224,788,502 | 73,771,208 | | |

*Ancestry was not reported by 23,921,371 persons.

**Table 2**  State Populations Broken Down By Ancestry

| State | Ancestry | | | | | | | | |
|-------|----------|--|--|--|--|--|--|--|--|
| | Acadian/ Cajun | Afghanistan | African | Afro- American | Albanian | Aleut | Algerian | Alsatian | Amerasian |
| Alabama | 5,780 | 19 | 3,120 | 838,689 | 26 | 29 | 2 | 31 | 130 |
| Alaska | 852 | 0 | 361 | 18,834 | 197 | 10,244 | 11 | 12 | 100 |
| Arizona | 2,459 | 220 | 2,073 | 91,580 | 189 | 57 | 0 | 251 | 343 |
| Arkansas | 5,237 | 58 | 1,125 | 307,292 | 36 | 44 | 0 | 68 | 110 |
| California | 18,337 | 13,018 | 32,413 | 1,784,171 | 2,261 | 1,091 | 579 | 1,865 | 3,022 |
| Colorado | 2,528 | 456 | 1,566 | 115,008 | 198 | 67 | 108 | 215 | 331 |
| Connecticut | 784 | 131 | 3,064 | 189,181 | 2,745 | 0 | 38 | 368 | 143 |
| Delaware | 247 | 30 | 774 | 94,890 | 123 | 0 | 0 | 77 | 21 |
| District of Columbia | 167 | 42 | 4,750 | 315,318 | 60 | 29 | 26 | 68 | 96 |
| Florida | 12,114 | 196 | 13,065 | 1,194,537 | 1,812 | 131 | 169 | 805 | 633 |
| Georgia | 7,893 | 503 | 10,212 | 1,420,631 | 202 | 17 | 133 | 155 | 494 |
| Hawaii | 800 | 44 | 308 | 23,864 | 63 | 86 | 0 | 76 | 153 |
| Idaho | 374 | 6 | 80 | 3,190 | 21 | 41 | 0 | 28 | 48 |
| Illinois | 3,175 | 557 | 10,106 | 1,425,762 | 2,837 | 61 | 89 | 888 | 301 |
| Indiana | 1,860 | 129 | 3,108 | 370,476 | 255 | 11 | 10 | 286 | 290 |
| Iowa | 498 | 37 | 926 | 41,013 | 86 | 0 | 15 | 138 | 185 |
| Kansas | 1,474 | 175 | 1,628 | 121,451 | 66 | 35 | 10 | 100 | 202 |
| Kentucky | 2,086 | 18 | 1,601 | 222,428 | 53 | 7 | 0 | 133 | 108 |
| Louisiana | 432,549 | 9 | 5,604 | 1,097,499 | 81 | 38 | 36 | 133 | 207 |
| Maine | 2,365 | 304 | 168 | 4,882 | 597 | 9 | 0 | 41 | 49 |
| Maryland | 2,298 | 488 | 12,107 | 965,573 | 429 | 21 | 128 | 308 | 448 |
| Massachusetts | 1,162 | 214 | 5,841 | 170,439 | 7,710 | 33 | 283 | 444 | 264 |
| Michigan | 1,954 | 217 | 6,219 | 1,099,751 | 4,955 | 22 | 63 | 342 | 223 |
| Minnesota | 645 | 225 | 2,129 | 78,891 | 148 | 68 | 40 | 204 | 283 |
| Mississippi | 11,097 | 0 | 2,459 | 774,950 | 23 | 1 | 10 | 38 | 138 |
| Missouri | 3,074 | 158 | 4,607 | 469,075 | 531 | 6 | 12 | 228 | 231 |
| Montana | 235 | 0 | 36 | 2,071 | 45 | 80 | 0 | 8 | 18 |
| Nebraska | 483 | 275 | 740 | 51,226 | 50 | 15 | 0 | 40 | 100 |
| Nevada | 1,278 | 196 | 1,045 | 67,797 | 158 | 42 | 7 | 46 | 249 |
| New Hampshire | 257 | 9 | 239 | 5,181 | 849 | 9 | 0 | 49 | 55 |
| New Jersey | 1,047 | 659 | 10,922 | 750,914 | 3,339 | 94 | 94 | 717 | 366 |
| New Mexico | 1,308 | 223 | 872 | 25,288 | 30 | 163 | 0 | 156 | 166 |
| New York | 2,219 | 4,675 | 41,452 | 1,620,890 | 10,628 | 133 | 523 | 1,977 | 777 |
| North Carolina | 4,478 | 118 | 7,650 | 1,227,936 | 191 | 10 | 62 | 165 | 420 |
| North Dakota | 49 | 0 | 66 | 3,082 | 15 | 3 | 0 | 19 | 92 |
| Ohio | 2,614 | 100 | 8,035 | 997,269 | 1,107 | 120 | 116 | 868 | 471 |
| Oklahoma | 3,957 | 11 | 1,604 | 194,597 | 22 | 55 | 64 | 47 | 135 |
| Oregon | 1,061 | 272 | 1,109 | 38,914 | 139 | 439 | 36 | 292 | 286 |
| Pennsylvania | 1,649 | 561 | 8,367 | 893,892 | 2,538 | 25 | 69 | 607 | 475 |
| Rhode Island | 96 | 0 | 1,179 | 21,098 | 223 | 23 | 0 | 49 | 43 |
| South Carolina | 5,086 | 46 | 3,390 | 869,786 | 52 | 9 | 7 | 86 | 173 |
| South Dakota | 65 | 0 | 133 | 2,613 | 0 | 0 | 4 | 9 | 32 |
| Tennessee | 5,498 | 120 | 2,980 | 674,249 | 187 | 25 | 8 | 141 | 168 |
| Texas | 105,982 | 1,145 | 13,629 | 1,720,618 | 539 | 89 | 264 | 2,673 | 1,056 |
| Utah | 519 | 29 | 488 | 9,288 | 137 | 25 | 0 | 29 | 104 |
| Vermont | 74 | 7 | 210 | 1,611 | 101 | 6 | 0 | 48 | 23 |
| Virginia | 4,581 | 4,814 | 7,112 | 969,899 | 533 | 69 | 121 | 456 | 667 |
| Washington | 2,504 | 696 | 2,795 | 125,060 | 339 | 2,165 | 64 | 292 | 834 |
| West Virginia | 377 | 2 | 423 | 47,174 | 12 | 0 | 5 | 33 | 72 |
| Wisconsin | 593 | 65 | 1,845 | 214,538 | 772 | 67 | 9 | 344 | 168 |
| Wyoming | 452 | 24 | 110 | 2,732 | 0 | 2 | 0 | 12 | 20 |

| | | | | | Ancestry | | | | | |
|---|---|---|---|---|---|---|---|---|---|---|
| American | American Indian | Arab | Argentinean | Armenian | Asian | Asian Indian | Assyrian | Australian | Austrian | Bahamian |
| 687,394 | 236,720 | 757 | 63 | 353 | 738 | 3,686 | 42 | 442 | 2,497 | 167 |
| 22,350 | 50,506 | 148 | 54 | 138 | 288 | 466 | 0 | 197 | 1,695 | 20 |
| 96,176 | 255,131 | 1,600 | 413 | 2,519 | 1,273 | 4,642 | 302 | 869 | 12,212 | 70 |
| 305,459 | 228,070 | 303 | 15 | 185 | 393 | 1,202 | 111 | 95 | 1,746 | 14 |
| 658,879 | 838,458 | 27,688 | 18,390 | 151,340 | 34,715 | 112,560 | 15,736 | 12,006 | 104,645 | 398 |
| 91,998 | 107,287 | 1,394 | 391 | 1,686 | 1,232 | 2,764 | 106 | 786 | 16,568 | 24 |
| 70,810 | 40,309 | 815 | 1,407 | 5,218 | 966 | 8,866 | 1,212 | 976 | 20,333 | 154 |
| 27,697 | 16,278 | 250 | 43 | 294 | 170 | 1,518 | 0 | 96 | 2,203 | 48 |
| 10,639 | 7,331 | 493 | 300 | 369 | 290 | 1,150 | 62 | 129 | 2,533 | 48 |
| 678,601 | 426,108 | 7,233 | 8,356 | 7,424 | 3,760 | 22,240 | 414 | 2,791 | 63,932 | 13,668 |
| 804,672 | 292,003 | 1,198 | 455 | 1,122 | 1,858 | 9,868 | 101 | 1,065 | 9,396 | 462 |
| 7,013 | 14,835 | 254 | 89 | 478 | 1,903 | 719 | 9 | 409 | 1,943 | 5 |
| 41,831 | 42,043 | 183 | 68 | 147 | 104 | 382 | 59 | 375 | 2,759 | 8 |
| 301,671 | 254,707 | 10,468 | 1,759 | 8,431 | 5,655 | 45,778 | 13,759 | 1,539 | 49,970 | 286 |
| 373,498 | 246,891 | 1,513 | 199 | 1,052 | 1,012 | 6,093 | 398 | 826 | 8,330 | 64 |
| 82,295 | 57,866 | 391 | 79 | 304 | 525 | 2,438 | 0 | 231 | 4,516 | 68 |
| 112,285 | 122,760 | 579 | 75 | 358 | 714 | 3,280 | 66 | 645 | 6,541 | 44 |
| 586,090 | 208,938 | 569 | 112 | 258 | 557 | 2,367 | 3 | 475 | 2,945 | 32 |
| 272,108 | 154,511 | 1,271 | 392 | 530 | 1,095 | 4,385 | 78 | 350 | 3,445 | 50 |
| 84,120 | 48,617 | 156 | 96 | 908 | 165 | 449 | 11 | 191 | 1,910 | 2 |
| 167,320 | 121,765 | 2,160 | 1,432 | 3,076 | 2,358 | 21,262 | 157 | 1,251 | 18,028 | 295 |
| 150,550 | 67,157 | 2,782 | 1,421 | 28,714 | 1,944 | 13,603 | 663 | 1,198 | 20,733 | 192 |
| 316,566 | 282,695 | 14,842 | 595 | 14,263 | 2,688 | 18,100 | 14,724 | 1,388 | 24,899 | 250 |
| 63,517 | 70,252 | 751 | 132 | 714 | 1,012 | 5,308 | 66 | 607 | 16,361 | 66 |
| 317,021 | 114,236 | 160 | 14 | 158 | 463 | 1,793 | 46 | 162 | 1,171 | 50 |
| 316,691 | 306,254 | 1,090 | 318 | 1,058 | 981 | 4,030 | 70 | 763 | 11,764 | 71 |
| 22,699 | 55,858 | 52 | 17 | 158 | 64 | 213 | 9 | 268 | 5,556 | 0 |
| 30,722 | 31,998 | 310 | 119 | 210 | 200 | 948 | 15 | 140 | 3,152 | 37 |
| 39,377 | 55,723 | 553 | 415 | 1,224 | 909 | 1,236 | 66 | 576 | 4,401 | 97 |
| 48,993 | 30,114 | 307 | 43 | 2,710 | 149 | 1,871 | 0 | 241 | 2,851 | 21 |
| 156,379 | 88,728 | 5,311 | 5,789 | 14,664 | 4,234 | 54,039 | 845 | 1,573 | 58,912 | 562 |
| 46,290 | 144,936 | 712 | 116 | 525 | 346 | 1,566 | 13 | 129 | 3,299 | 4 |
| 426,740 | 271,105 | 12,884 | 12,087 | 23,590 | 9,117 | 80,430 | 680 | 3,688 | 156,994 | 1,986 |
| 752,901 | 265,777 | 1,348 | 410 | 1,060 | 1,521 | 7,091 | 14 | 698 | 6,859 | 114 |
| 9,669 | 26,597 | 26 | 0 | 174 | 33 | 428 | 6 | 25 | 1,178 | 23 |
| 512,979 | 383,689 | 5,340 | 544 | 2,948 | 2,006 | 17,633 | 159 | 1,489 | 29,810 | 154 |
| 257,655 | 468,588 | 790 | 162 | 401 | 764 | 3,810 | 14 | 410 | 3,379 | 68 |
| 98,355 | 141,079 | 866 | 251 | 1,308 | 680 | 2,726 | 139 | 1,429 | 9,582 | 71 |
| 287,304 | 166,847 | 2,893 | 1,206 | 6,763 | 2,232 | 19,769 | 322 | 1,483 | 63,060 | 218 |
| 19,137 | 12,731 | 380 | 153 | 6,345 | 325 | 1,227 | 57 | 170 | 2,695 | 5 |
| 347,488 | 117,321 | 608 | 107 | 455 | 670 | 3,500 | 55 | 379 | 3,166 | 147 |
| 12,191 | 46,998 | 49 | 14 | 82 | 102 | 214 | 26 | 85 | 1,390 | 5 |
| 653,143 | 302,454 | 1,085 | 189 | 540 | 990 | 4,551 | 107 | 478 | 3,714 | 265 |
| 880,681 | 815,112 | 7,067 | 2,448 | 3,183 | 7,585 | 40,506 | 453 | 2,677 | 23,447 | 336 |
| 54,004 | 43,145 | 404 | 332 | 928 | 263 | 1,306 | 16 | 1,372 | 3,903 | 3 |
| 31,178 | 28,443 | 55 | 50 | 419 | 147 | 259 | 9 | 93 | 1,913 | 2 |
| 549,672 | 201,613 | 4,122 | 1,350 | 4,078 | 3,696 | 14,937 | 220 | 1,651 | 14,886 | 237 |
| 161,521 | 190,713 | 1,725 | 486 | 2,269 | 2,957 | 6,973 | 211 | 2,012 | 18,430 | 93 |
| 259,573 | 109,517 | 256 | 19 | 139 | 344 | 1,925 | 20 | 211 | 1,993 | 0 |
| 72,625 | 76,294 | 1,139 | 181 | 2,771 | 909 | 4,133 | 114 | 821 | 25,396 | 77 |
| 17,472 | 21,112 | 34 | 20 | 55 | 70 | 82 | 0 | 173 | 1,742 | 0 |

**Table 2** *(Continued)*

| | Ancestry | | | | | | | | |
|---|---|---|---|---|---|---|---|---|---|
| State | Bangladeshi | Barbadian | Basque | Bavarian | Belgian | Belizean | Belorussian | Bermudan | Bolivian |
| Alabama | 116 | 64 | 82 | 59 | 290 | 8 | 15 | 97 | 70 |
| Alaska | 0 | 6 | 245 | 0 | 172 | 0 | 0 | 0 | 42 |
| Arizona | 85 | 26 | 1,316 | 74 | 1,651 | 154 | 30 | 0 | 198 |
| Arkansas | 12 | 22 | 104 | 29 | 359 | 9 | 23 | 20 | 41 |
| California | 1,256 | 1,160 | 19,122 | 634 | 10,229 | 10,848 | 368 | 176 | 7,989 |
| Colorado | 40 | 36 | 937 | 43 | 2,055 | 44 | 24 | 7 | 179 |
| Connecticut | 75 | 972 | 319 | 42 | 1,196 | 82 | 71 | 127 | 182 |
| Delaware | 27 | 74 | 13 | 0 | 219 | 0 | 18 | 32 | 36 |
| District of Columbia | 67 | 102 | 37 | 33 | 147 | 0 | 27 | 70 | 764 |
| Florida | 425 | 1,770 | 1,189 | 227 | 4,636 | 1,334 | 232 | 400 | 2,904 |
| Georgia | 165 | 287 | 128 | 29 | 1,099 | 63 | 15 | 203 | 352 |
| Hawaii | 24 | 30 | 169 | 13 | 171 | 31 | 8 | 56 | 8 |
| Idaho | 0 | 0 | 5,587 | 34 | 310 | 3 | 0 | 0 | 41 |
| Illinois | 233 | 195 | 445 | 184 | 13,131 | 2,118 | 627 | 92 | 1,423 |
| Indiana | 98 | 62 | 190 | 102 | 5,180 | 129 | 42 | 22 | 154 |
| Iowa | 46 | 6 | 59 | 48 | 2,997 | 10 | 12 | 7 | 55 |
| Kansas | 109 | 21 | 70 | 126 | 1,719 | 33 | 0 | 7 | 145 |
| Kentucky | 62 | 28 | 94 | 29 | 309 | 10 | 0 | 21 | 53 |
| Louisiana | 23 | 87 | 226 | 26 | 1,203 | 331 | 0 | 3 | 131 |
| Maine | 15 | 8 | 36 | 8 | 250 | 0 | 35 | 47 | 24 |
| Maryland | 487 | 626 | 268 | 116 | 1,152 | 150 | 239 | 168 | 2,879 |
| Massachusetts | 256 | 3,393 | 337 | 41 | 2,263 | 102 | 99 | 390 | 717 |
| Michigan | 250 | 128 | 236 | 79 | 22,559 | 80 | 189 | 126 | 226 |
| Minnesota | 0 | 50 | 130 | 172 | 6,328 | 20 | 33 | 15 | 196 |
| Mississippi | 26 | 12 | 28 | 16 | 134 | 6 | 18 | 37 | 0 |
| Missouri | 55 | 3 | 151 | 116 | 1,930 | 29 | 10 | 29 | 276 |
| Montana | 0 | 0 | 469 | 5 | 994 | 0 | 8 | 0 | 6 |
| Nebraska | 15 | 0 | 45 | 8 | 1,017 | 5 | 0 | 0 | 65 |
| Nevada | 22 | 25 | 4,840 | 32 | 469 | 61 | 0 | 7 | 165 |
| New Hampshire | 17 | 32 | 53 | 0 | 688 | 14 | 24 | 58 | 10 |
| New Jersey | 548 | 1,687 | 534 | 70 | 2,978 | 304 | 629 | 529 | 1,052 |
| New Mexico | 63 | 26 | 502 | 18 | 283 | 50 | 0 | 5 | 67 |
| New York | 5,989 | 22,298 | 1,300 | 227 | 5,115 | 5,520 | 703 | 1,050 | 4,406 |
| North Carolina | 69 | 211 | 119 | 97 | 813 | 74 | 45 | 110 | 127 |
| North Dakota | 0 | 0 | 11 | 18 | 441 | 0 | 0 | 5 | 0 |
| Ohio | 191 | 114 | 203 | 226 | 3,085 | 10 | 146 | 88 | 153 |
| Oklahoma | 108 | 31 | 105 | 57 | 589 | 18 | 19 | 7 | 108 |
| Oregon | 16 | 26 | 2,257 | 92 | 1,862 | 23 | 99 | 11 | 132 |
| Pennsylvania | 293 | 761 | 250 | 213 | 4,804 | 161 | 233 | 246 | 284 |
| Rhode Island | 16 | 72 | 24 | 0 | 554 | 47 | 24 | 47 | 361 |
| South Carolina | 20 | 75 | 48 | 31 | 247 | 58 | 0 | 37 | 65 |
| South Dakota | 0 | 8 | 30 | 24 | 621 | 0 | 0 | 0 | 0 |
| Tennessee | 73 | 18 | 91 | 53 | 595 | 6 | 16 | 37 | 47 |
| Texas | 528 | 466 | 1,248 | 204 | 3,285 | 793 | 39 | 132 | 1,499 |
| Utah | 27 | 12 | 1,422 | 12 | 425 | 6 | 0 | 8 | 224 |
| Vermont | 2 | 6 | 2 | 23 | 175 | 0 | 0 | 13 | 17 |
| Virginia | 363 | 315 | 403 | 151 | 1,564 | 89 | 45 | 237 | 5,385 |
| Washington | 14 | 50 | 1,770 | 140 | 2,862 | 60 | 44 | 107 | 272 |
| West Virginia | 60 | 14 | 9 | 40 | 399 | 7 | 7 | 16 | 15 |
| Wisconsin | 100 | 40 | 101 | 327 | 25,345 | 22 | 61 | 39 | 186 |
| Wyoming | 0 | 0 | 602 | 0 | 160 | 0 | 0 | 0 | 7 |

Ancestry

| Brazilian | British | British West Indian | Bulgarian | Burmese | Cambodian | Canadian | Cantonese | Cape Verdean | Carpath Rusyn | Celtic |
|---|---|---|---|---|---|---|---|---|---|---|
| 188 | 19,913 | 62 | 197 | 22 | 363 | 2,650 | 11 | 0 | 0 | 500 |
| 64 | 3,012 | 33 | 110 | 3 | 75 | 1,440 | 0 | 20 | 0 | 107 |
| 617 | 18,034 | 80 | 431 | 79 | 958 | 9,644 | 110 | 104 | 60 | 590 |
| 18 | 9,383 | 22 | 54 | 0 | 81 | 1,306 | 19 | 67 | 14 | 205 |
| 9,357 | 151,050 | 994 | 5,277 | 3,636 | 63,431 | 86,341 | 13,457 | 2,433 | 128 | 5,420 |
| 307 | 19,730 | 43 | 591 | 18 | 929 | 6,191 | 103 | 29 | 40 | 746 |
| 2,489 | 17,547 | 493 | 181 | 0 | 1,217 | 13,768 | 37 | 3,047 | 262 | 529 |
| 89 | 4,378 | 22 | 13 | 23 | 65 | 1,248 | 27 | 0 | 0 | 57 |
| 524 | 3,803 | 298 | 57 | 77 | 92 | 603 | 63 | 145 | 0 | 76 |
| 7,788 | 76,630 | 3,678 | 1,396 | 267 | 1,347 | 43,958 | 274 | 718 | 220 | 1,172 |
| 742 | 39,724 | 341 | 205 | 50 | 1,860 | 6,425 | 73 | 204 | 10 | 738 |
| 67 | 2,882 | 24 | 137 | 145 | 133 | 1,699 | 394 | 50 | 0 | 114 |
| 129 | 5,121 | 0 | 80 | 14 | 73 | 2,323 | 0 | 0 | 0 | 122 |
| 1,729 | 34,734 | 191 | 2,136 | 482 | 2,720 | 12,794 | 748 | 111 | 75 | 564 |
| 419 | 24,749 | 11 | 944 | 40 | 277 | 6,451 | 49 | 53 | 78 | 470 |
| 153 | 7,960 | 16 | 437 | 11 | 586 | 2,385 | 56 | 0 | 0 | 228 |
| 243 | 10,028 | 29 | 219 | 28 | 662 | 2,793 | 22 | 69 | 11 | 252 |
| 98 | 18,006 | 41 | 106 | 0 | 190 | 2,200 | 67 | 60 | 0 | 354 |
| 290 | 10,837 | 76 | 124 | 30 | 173 | 2,435 | 63 | 84 | 6 | 281 |
| 113 | 6,646 | 56 | 95 | 9 | 809 | 13,648 | 0 | 57 | 0 | 280 |
| 2,551 | 28,992 | 1,196 | 588 | 513 | 1,798 | 6,606 | 186 | 484 | 146 | 689 |
| 7,483 | 28,905 | 1,268 | 532 | 237 | 11,821 | 66,007 | 952 | 29,326 | 36 | 792 |
| 887 | 31,204 | 296 | 2,232 | 85 | 687 | 47,488 | 232 | 85 | 174 | 721 |
| 403 | 11,596 | 65 | 635 | 31 | 2,981 | 4,495 | 29 | 37 | 82 | 372 |
| 120 | 8,537 | 5 | 50 | 27 | 14 | 1,357 | 0 | 12 | 7 | 208 |
| 254 | 18,492 | 29 | 361 | 14 | 695 | 4,359 | 76 | 36 | 6 | 404 |
| 7 | 2,135 | 2 | 246 | 3 | 6 | 1,469 | 0 | 0 | 0 | 73 |
| 103 | 3,997 | 5 | 123 | 0 | 125 | 1,077 | 9 | 21 | 0 | 126 |
| 408 | 5,368 | 106 | 206 | 40 | 290 | 3,354 | 84 | 22 | 0 | 165 |
| 289 | 6,716 | 24 | 2 | 25 | 289 | 12,913 | 5 | 114 | 0 | 230 |
| 7,482 | 27,217 | 1,857 | 815 | 196 | 476 | 12,783 | 632 | 436 | 614 | 784 |
| 184 | 6,397 | 8 | 61 | 29 | 59 | 1,643 | 10 | 21 | 0 | 186 |
| 11,145 | 58,197 | 23,799 | 2,208 | 970 | 3,326 | 45,274 | 5,366 | 1,099 | 1,038 | 1,920 |
| 469 | 34,868 | 149 | 240 | 112 | 1,493 | 6,621 | 0 | 211 | 38 | 517 |
| 36 | 853 | 0 | 175 | 0 | 74 | 438 | 0 | 0 | 0 | 45 |
| 531 | 41,342 | 128 | 2,408 | 250 | 2,165 | 13,508 | 40 | 214 | 620 | 1,028 |
| 235 | 11,932 | 30 | 277 | 3 | 451 | 2,306 | 10 | 44 | 15 | 176 |
| 394 | 19,028 | 9 | 768 | 72 | 2,255 | 10,553 | 196 | 19 | 2 | 1,048 |
| 1,512 | 36,845 | 625 | 1,010 | 184 | 4,155 | 11,325 | 290 | 346 | 3,701 | 895 |
| 529 | 3,181 | 77 | 105 | 19 | 3,417 | 5,338 | 103 | 10,080 | 0 | 117 |
| 298 | 15,548 | 42 | 117 | 7 | 248 | 3,438 | 24 | 78 | 0 | 199 |
| 6 | 1,040 | 2 | 109 | 10 | 54 | 504 | 0 | 0 | 0 | 60 |
| 236 | 24,044 | 113 | 183 | 42 | 953 | 3,970 | 5 | 81 | 0 | 566 |
| 2,147 | 76,861 | 999 | 867 | 285 | 5,659 | 17,117 | 575 | 264 | 41 | 2,258 |
| 386 | 24,527 | 22 | 275 | 63 | 1,050 | 4,287 | 32 | 20 | 0 | 268 |
| 57 | 2,798 | 0 | 38 | 4 | 33 | 3,923 | 8 | 23 | 0 | 132 |
| 1,382 | 49,823 | 268 | 355 | 311 | 3,761 | 9,597 | 159 | 387 | 103 | 1,109 |
| 614 | 35,509 | 146 | 969 | 129 | 10,074 | 21,862 | 331 | 51 | 48 | 1,262 |
| 59 | 7,073 | 4 | 155 | 25 | 24 | 1,021 | 16 | 0 | 46 | 235 |
| 233 | 9,961 | 35 | 547 | 24 | 444 | 4,425 | 77 | 10 | 7 | 246 |
| 11 | 2,001 | 0 | 148 | 2 | 37 | 630 | 0 | 0 | 0 | 16 |

**Table 2**   *(Continued)*

| State | Central American | Central European | Chamorro | Chilean | Chinese | Colombian | Cornish | Costa Rican | Croatian |
|---|---|---|---|---|---|---|---|---|---|
| Alabama | 19 | 96 | 8 | 95 | 3,529 | 574 | 8 | 177 | 5,336 |
| Alaska | 3 | 8 | 0 | 138 | 1,549 | 421 | 0 | 47 | 518 |
| Arizona | 148 | 43 | 61 | 655 | 12,542 | 1,517 | 86 | 441 | 6,769 |
| Arkansas | 22 | 16 | 0 | 68 | 1,575 | 270 | 36 | 21 | 3,145 |
| California | 5,712 | 874 | 1,851 | 16,124 | 641,250 | 39,427 | 681 | 16,379 | 47,822 |
| Colorado | 39 | 93 | 64 | 466 | 9,117 | 810 | 93 | 325 | 6,437 |
| Connecticut | 3 | 120 | 35 | 1,183 | 10,217 | 7,098 | 55 | 942 | 2,669 |
| Delaware | 0 | 0 | 0 | 98 | 1,813 | 369 | 0 | 67 | 542 |
| District of Columbia | 29 | 22 | 0 | 316 | 2,574 | 822 | 14 | 128 | 547 |
| Florida | 548 | 449 | 94 | 8,856 | 28,787 | 78,183 | 109 | 7,130 | 18,020 |
| Georgia | 35 | 53 | 69 | 441 | 11,180 | 3,308 | 62 | 510 | 9,651 |
| Hawaii | 24 | 25 | 416 | 55 | 95,899 | 244 | 4 | 84 | 679 |
| Idaho | 0 | 4 | 2 | 106 | 1,469 | 120 | 10 | 36 | 981 |
| Illinois | 285 | 266 | 18 | 1,580 | 44,077 | 9,747 | 160 | 1,000 | 61,284 |
| Indiana | 19 | 13 | 30 | 237 | 6,128 | 667 | 28 | 241 | 18,633 |
| Iowa | 0 | 36 | 0 | 129 | 3,727 | 200 | 44 | 111 | 5,295 |
| Kansas | 0 | 3 | 13 | 172 | 4,298 | 505 | 0 | 159 | 8,511 |
| Kentucky | 11 | 23 | 49 | 76 | 3,137 | 678 | 24 | 143 | 3,140 |
| Louisiana | 175 | 27 | 13 | 341 | 5,321 | 1,421 | 0 | 628 | 5,081 |
| Maine | 0 | 4 | 2 | 45 | 1,269 | 219 | 2 | 24 | 645 |
| Maryland | 205 | 207 | 69 | 2,231 | 26,479 | 4,332 | 45 | 762 | 5,869 |
| Massachusetts | 105 | 210 | 24 | 1,493 | 47,245 | 7,795 | 49 | 1,739 | 2,535 |
| Michigan | 35 | 171 | 6 | 545 | 17,100 | 1,623 | 292 | 313 | 29,356 |
| Minnesota | 2 | 101 | 32 | 268 | 8,850 | 1,295 | 55 | 115 | 11,020 |
| Mississippi | 0 | 7 | 0 | 90 | 2,532 | 201 | 0 | 59 | 7,428 |
| Missouri | 0 | 187 | 3 | 307 | 8,006 | 1,011 | 15 | 144 | 16,519 |
| Montana | 0 | 0 | 0 | 24 | 811 | 49 | 6 | 0 | 3,119 |
| Nebraska | 0 | 25 | 0 | 143 | 1,908 | 124 | 41 | 42 | 3,283 |
| Nevada | 53 | 35 | 22 | 374 | 7,001 | 1,262 | 52 | 443 | 2,560 |
| New Hampshire | 2 | 4 | 0 | 99 | 2,218 | 436 | 16 | 103 | 682 |
| New Jersey | 369 | 454 | 26 | 4,640 | 47,068 | 47,809 | 48 | 4,612 | 8,173 |
| New Mexico | 0 | 53 | 12 | 306 | 2,400 | 469 | 13 | 90 | 1,842 |
| New York | 1,300 | 913 | 43 | 10,288 | 236,876 | 99,935 | 104 | 7,939 | 20,517 |
| North Carolina | 31 | 44 | 202 | 456 | 8,078 | 1,707 | 29 | 433 | 8,189 |
| North Dakota | 0 | 4 | 0 | 4 | 364 | 152 | 0 | 0 | 246 |
| Ohio | 107 | 183 | 49 | 409 | 16,829 | 1,584 | 99 | 423 | 59,315 |
| Oklahoma | 14 | 16 | 27 | 121 | 5,178 | 780 | 52 | 138 | 2,592 |
| Oregon | 25 | 37 | 131 | 448 | 14,796 | 722 | 110 | 381 | 3,804 |
| Pennsylvania | 21 | 266 | 29 | 923 | 25,908 | 5,124 | 158 | 712 | 78,750 |
| Rhode Island | 0 | 18 | 0 | 146 | 3,037 | 4,617 | 0 | 13 | 461 |
| South Carolina | 0 | 49 | 41 | 165 | 2,872 | 888 | 20 | 127 | 4,585 |
| South Dakota | 0 | 17 | 0 | 62 | 410 | 44 | 0 | 9 | 281 |
| Tennessee | 19 | 8 | 25 | 158 | 5,048 | 452 | 2 | 94 | 4,677 |
| Texas | 824 | 81 | 172 | 2,442 | 55,023 | 15,669 | 100 | 2,664 | 15,742 |
| Utah | 0 | 22 | 39 | 649 | 5,487 | 666 | 46 | 233 | 1,446 |
| Vermont | 0 | 30 | 0 | 11 | 572 | 140 | 3 | 25 | 249 |
| Virginia | 94 | 75 | 132 | 2,195 | 20,857 | 4,078 | 27 | 870 | 7,543 |
| Washington | 16 | 110 | 590 | 896 | 33,954 | 1,091 | 236 | 324 | 10,430 |
| West Virginia | 0 | 0 | 0 | 103 | 1,248 | 127 | 25 | 17 | 4,215 |
| Wisconsin | 16 | 102 | 24 | 288 | 7,147 | 910 | 922 | 354 | 22,391 |
| Wyoming | 0 | 0 | 4 | 0 | 485 | 25 | 10 | 0 | 746 |

Ancestry

| Cuban | Cypriot | Czech | Czechoslo-vakian | Danish | Dominican | Dutch | Dutch West Indian | Ecuadorian | Egyptian | English |
|---|---|---|---|---|---|---|---|---|---|---|
| 1,260 | 0 | 3,031 | 1,109 | 5,180 | 326 | 76,037 | 583 | 150 | 279 | 479,499 |
| 366 | 10 | 2,834 | 878 | 5,993 | 394 | 14,365 | 51 | 20 | 0 | 76,600 |
| 2,314 | 44 | 18,043 | 5,374 | 36,859 | 383 | 95,326 | 782 | 364 | 568 | 586,458 |
| 331 | 34 | 4,175 | 1,115 | 5,014 | 183 | 72,670 | 2,679 | 32 | 43 | 290,462 |
| 64,152 | 324 | 88,286 | 35,510 | 262,101 | 7,032 | 591,618 | 3,841 | 28,698 | 19,597 | 3,645,975 |
| 2,049 | 0 | 24,184 | 6,662 | 42,801 | 547 | 100,024 | 421 | 456 | 489 | 581,886 |
| 5,377 | 36 | 10,682 | 6,162 | 16,739 | 4,253 | 37,183 | 89 | 3,212 | 735 | 462,919 |
| 649 | 13 | 1,449 | 736 | 1,732 | 245 | 14,956 | 14 | 41 | 221 | 122,759 |
| 911 | 22 | 1,034 | 483 | 1,264 | 1,568 | 3,768 | 0 | 688 | 291 | 34,266 |
| 541,011 | 330 | 35,993 | 15,085 | 46,654 | 36,116 | 279,077 | 903 | 16,377 | 3,119 | 1,845,667 |
| 6,530 | 55 | 7,199 | 2,817 | 10,404 | 1,301 | 112,322 | 600 | 778 | 1,043 | 889,698 |
| 314 | 9 | 1,553 | 703 | 3,455 | 259 | 9,839 | 46 | 176 | 125 | 71,569 |
| 140 | 0 | 5,252 | 1,260 | 40,297 | 19 | 35,881 | 176 | 32 | 40 | 290,516 |
| 14,625 | 177 | 131,503 | 23,927 | 70,586 | 2,518 | 264,339 | 232 | 9,009 | 2,407 | 1,140,917 |
| 1,537 | 68 | 11,582 | 3,458 | 14,918 | 426 | 198,589 | 256 | 272 | 571 | 767,070 |
| 388 | 8 | 58,690 | 6,142 | 84,202 | 162 | 175,769 | 79 | 70 | 221 | 389,466 |
| 1,111 | 0 | 21,629 | 3,564 | 18,878 | 108 | 99,645 | 476 | 537 | 228 | 405,709 |
| 931 | 25 | 2,832 | 1,073 | 3,888 | 502 | 79,575 | 434 | 526 | 147 | 552,802 |
| 6,048 | 52 | 3,883 | 1,666 | 5,713 | 657 | 43,259 | 339 | 781 | 269 | 335,620 |
| 262 | 0 | 1,833 | 746 | 6,979 | 190 | 15,416 | 1 | 67 | 14 | 372,042 |
| 5,254 | 231 | 18,130 | 6,686 | 12,563 | 3,342 | 80,433 | 178 | 2,632 | 1,817 | 670,915 |
| 6,468 | 120 | 9,285 | 4,569 | 18,172 | 29,065 | 53,062 | 100 | 2,437 | 2,197 | 920,850 |
| 3,890 | 193 | 40,242 | 14,485 | 51,184 | 1,053 | 560,792 | 212 | 471 | 1,785 | 1,315,444 |
| 1,116 | 37 | 87,718 | 11,466 | 98,373 | 186 | 103,757 | 48 | 192 | 760 | 356,574 |
| 309 | 0 | 1,271 | 400 | 2,454 | 211 | 31,860 | 225 | 63 | 141 | 253,741 |
| 1,845 | 11 | 24,529 | 4,550 | 20,695 | 314 | 153,961 | 778 | 467 | 520 | 743,232 |
| 145 | 7 | 7,607 | 1,967 | 16,752 | 29 | 27,018 | 37 | 24 | 37 | 137,181 |
| 383 | 0 | 90,043 | 7,871 | 59,860 | 105 | 46,237 | 97 | 53 | 186 | 208,616 |
| 5,430 | 7 | 5,518 | 1,615 | 19,170 | 429 | 30,751 | 169 | 286 | 253 | 207,010 |
| 641 | 12 | 1,693 | 799 | 4,156 | 756 | 14,238 | 0 | 129 | 185 | 265,668 |
| 72,373 | 659 | 23,473 | 13,686 | 27,703 | 51,138 | 159,165 | 152 | 27,486 | 11,704 | 702,504 |
| 772 | 7 | 4,245 | 1,811 | 7,122 | 246 | 29,401 | 899 | 101 | 143 | 188,934 |
| 64,741 | 1,734 | 50,014 | 28,402 | 47,058 | 337,867 | 369,807 | 1,153 | 89,040 | 15,211 | 1,566,019 |
| 3,296 | 17 | 6,156 | 2,355 | 9,848 | 999 | 147,469 | 550 | 1,008 | 903 | 986,683 |
| 70 | 0 | 15,298 | 1,565 | 10,801 | 2 | 10,459 | 32 | 28 | 28 | 39,015 |
| 2,826 | 74 | 67,389 | 15,864 | 21,602 | 840 | 310,765 | 539 | 515 | 1,654 | 1,449,303 |
| 905 | 0 | 15,215 | 3,451 | 9,938 | 254 | 140,457 | 23,465 | 163 | 328 | 441,391 |
| 1,197 | 6 | 16,470 | 5,202 | 47,806 | 186 | 118,089 | 604 | 148 | 255 | 575,183 |
| 6,365 | 129 | 29,528 | 16,453 | 20,875 | 4,236 | 354,656 | 152 | 1,453 | 2,071 | 1,274,665 |
| 811 | 0 | 1,262 | 640 | 1,978 | 8,902 | 6,933 | 21 | 457 | 306 | 161,001 |
| 1,204 | 29 | 3,183 | 1,087 | 5,307 | 544 | 55,860 | 220 | 292 | 279 | 436,149 |
| 34 | 7 | 18,593 | 1,383 | 23,456 | 10 | 36,844 | 27 | 6 | 63 | 68,345 |
| 1,602 | 29 | 4,876 | 1,524 | 7,449 | 393 | 125,571 | 2,139 | 166 | 453 | 691,508 |
| 17,758 | 76 | 166,814 | 23,731 | 47,655 | 3,875 | 324,375 | 16,713 | 4,033 | 3,146 | 2,023,901 |
| 497 | 0 | 3,373 | 1,108 | 163,048 | 114 | 55,770 | 81 | 159 | 94 | 749,665 |
| 209 | 10 | 1,555 | 551 | 2,386 | 71 | 9,923 | 0 | 37 | 55 | 147,384 |
| 5,851 | 234 | 13,555 | 5,144 | 18,374 | 2,318 | 117,477 | 217 | 2,564 | 2,462 | 1,050,605 |
| 1,723 | 53 | 23,873 | 7,922 | 82,215 | 457 | 179,310 | 366 | 485 | 588 | 897,190 |
| 256 | 0 | 1,936 | 851 | 1,332 | 187 | 74,877 | 233 | 62 | 122 | 269,798 |
| 1,444 | 8 | 104,155 | 8,887 | 80,791 | 359 | 162,466 | 80 | 125 | 421 | 410,016 |
| 18 | 0 | 3,745 | 790 | 10,889 | 13 | 15,648 | 41 | 6 | 0 | 101,398 |

**Table 2**   *(Continued)*

| | | | | | Ancestry | | | | |
|---|---|---|---|---|---|---|---|---|---|
| State | Eritrean | Eskimo | Estonian | Ethiopian | Eurasian | European | Fijian | Filipino | Finnish |
| Alabama | 0 | 50 | 110 | 0 | 133 | 8,769 | 8 | 2,305 | 1,759 |
| Alaska | 0 | 42,024 | 95 | 0 | 40 | 3,598 | 2 | 8,584 | 3,773 |
| Arizona | 0 | 263 | 323 | 43 | 291 | 8,645 | 31 | 10,069 | 10,395 |
| Arkansas | 0 | 133 | 33 | 0 | 53 | 3,422 | 0 | 2,166 | 983 |
| California | 1,438 | 1,854 | 4,101 | 315 | 5,728 | 89,777 | 5,866 | 709,599 | 64,302 |
| Colorado | 34 | 303 | 391 | 0 | 193 | 10,921 | 43 | 7,270 | 8,632 |
| Connecticut | 21 | 24 | 1,088 | 0 | 176 | 3,689 | 13 | 6,272 | 7,486 |
| Delaware | 0 | 8 | 123 | 0 | 27 | 906 | 0 | 1,479 | 872 |
| District of Columbia | 180 | 0 | 48 | 11 | 34 | 1,777 | 0 | 2,035 | 479 |
| Florida | 91 | 319 | 1,501 | 14 | 691 | 22,179 | 30 | 37,531 | 25,031 |
| Georgia | 163 | 147 | 236 | 32 | 190 | 14,216 | 33 | 7,527 | 4,978 |
| Hawaii | 0 | 237 | 48 | 0 | 289 | 1,622 | 371 | 176,370 | 1,422 |
| Idaho | 0 | 202 | 71 | 0 | 16 | 3,757 | 0 | 1,586 | 3,937 |
| Illinois | 129 | 254 | 1,164 | 14 | 488 | 14,040 | 0 | 66,984 | 20,636 |
| Indiana | 0 | 184 | 315 | 21 | 55 | 7,263 | 6 | 5,354 | 4,470 |
| Iowa | 0 | 24 | 93 | 0 | 21 | 4,071 | 0 | 2,156 | 2,401 |
| Kansas | 0 | 155 | 78 | 4 | 38 | 6,333 | 8 | 2,974 | 1,717 |
| Kentucky | 0 | 71 | 71 | 9 | 75 | 7,385 | 0 | 2,587 | 1,405 |
| Louisiana | 82 | 98 | 55 | 0 | 54 | 2,820 | 9 | 5,981 | 1,590 |
| Maine | 8 | 41 | 86 | 5 | 7 | 1,443 | 0 | 1,438 | 6,326 |
| Maryland | 419 | 77 | 1,487 | 53 | 407 | 9,881 | 50 | 21,086 | 5,547 |
| Massachusetts | 120 | 128 | 977 | 26 | 335 | 6,787 | 20 | 8,024 | 31,529 |
| Michigan | 106 | 150 | 478 | 77 | 300 | 10,523 | 35 | 16,086 | 109,357 |
| Minnesota | 137 | 240 | 558 | 33 | 155 | 6,247 | 0 | 5,210 | 103,603 |
| Mississippi | 0 | 65 | 0 | 7 | 11 | 3,563 | 0 | 2,120 | 1,250 |
| Missouri | 16 | 335 | 155 | 0 | 45 | 9,436 | 46 | 7,181 | 3,583 |
| Montana | 0 | 131 | 66 | 0 | 13 | 2,652 | 7 | 908 | 7,324 |
| Nebraska | 0 | 44 | 58 | 0 | 49 | 2,271 | 0 | 1,699 | 1,651 |
| Nevada | 20 | 161 | 148 | 12 | 164 | 2,626 | 0 | 12,734 | 3,582 |
| New Hampshire | 0 | 34 | 128 | 0 | 0 | 1,481 | 0 | 1,304 | 8,294 |
| New Jersey | 33 | 71 | 2,623 | 26 | 335 | 9,531 | 52 | 51,821 | 8,343 |
| New Mexico | 0 | 31 | 67 | 7 | 38 | 3,229 | 4 | 2,539 | 2,266 |
| New York | 192 | 388 | 3,982 | 74 | 715 | 27,446 | 68 | 64,202 | 21,288 |
| North Carolina | 0 | 95 | 304 | 9 | 123 | 11,253 | 7 | 6,181 | 3,830 |
| North Dakota | 0 | 15 | 115 | 0 | 3 | 327 | 0 | 934 | 3,807 |
| Ohio | 196 | 231 | 852 | 2 | 210 | 10,902 | 0 | 12,726 | 21,044 |
| Oklahoma | 20 | 195 | 47 | 19 | 93 | 5,156 | 9 | 3,689 | 1,844 |
| Oregon | 11 | 694 | 641 | 6 | 284 | 16,311 | 256 | 9,114 | 22,977 |
| Pennsylvania | 37 | 197 | 727 | 16 | 309 | 10,705 | 38 | 14,474 | 8,612 |
| Rhode Island | 9 | 79 | 56 | 0 | 40 | 1,017 | 0 | 2,032 | 1,562 |
| South Carolina | 0 | 47 | 194 | 0 | 83 | 4,958 | 0 | 6,028 | 1,849 |
| South Dakota | 0 | 86 | 10 | 0 | 17 | 915 | 0 | 824 | 3,468 |
| Tennessee | 0 | 105 | 110 | 6 | 76 | 8,043 | 0 | 3,901 | 2,488 |
| Texas | 196 | 339 | 642 | 6 | 499 | 23,825 | 47 | 40,053 | 12,634 |
| Utah | 0 | 173 | 107 | 0 | 189 | 11,711 | 18 | 2,983 | 3,718 |
| Vermont | 0 | 19 | 93 | 5 | 20 | 2,080 | 0 | 405 | 1,968 |
| Virginia | 355 | 212 | 461 | 59 | 346 | 14,593 | 0 | 35,605 | 6,770 |
| Washington | 223 | 1,982 | 1,255 | 23 | 600 | 23,897 | 395 | 49,222 | 44,110 |
| West Virginia | 0 | 43 | 19 | 0 | 26 | 1,511 | 0 | 1,624 | 452 |
| Wisconsin | 34 | 146 | 336 | 10 | 71 | 5,310 | 0 | 4,942 | 35,118 |
| Wyoming | 0 | 16 | 36 | 0 | 22 | 1,898 | 0 | 594 | 2,408 |

| | | | | Ancestry | | | | | | |
|---|---|---|---|---|---|---|---|---|---|---|
| Flemish | French | French Canadian | German | German Russian (Volga) | Ghanian | Greek | Guamanian | Guatemalan | Guyanese | Haitian |
| 68 | 93,104 | 9,185 | 430,442 | 23 | 17 | 6,895 | 141 | 108 | 133 | 188 |
| 35 | 23,844 | 5,335 | 127,103 | 24 | 5 | 1,665 | 234 | 56 | 72 | 91 |
| 219 | 155,951 | 25,248 | 878,088 | 283 | 148 | 12,799 | 571 | 1,359 | 42 | 319 |
| 53 | 75,026 | 5,981 | 400,234 | 47 | 45 | 2,734 | 175 | 137 | 0 | 39 |
| 2,130 | 1,032,843 | 156,625 | 4,935,147 | 1,563 | 1,681 | 125,792 | 19,820 | 143,017 | 2,671 | 5,054 |
| 304 | 148,950 | 21,859 | 1,063,694 | 469 | 84 | 11,999 | 697 | 640 | 85 | 198 |
| 190 | 260,064 | 110,426 | 450,247 | 116 | 375 | 26,646 | 82 | 1,304 | 698 | 5,004 |
| 39 | 19,190 | 2,990 | 138,128 | 40 | 6 | 3,203 | 21 | 59 | 38 | 242 |
| 96 | 8,566 | 1,717 | 39,218 | 85 | 168 | 2,279 | 31 | 1,053 | 757 | 937 |
| 634 | 508,205 | 110,221 | 2,410,257 | 145 | 415 | 66,861 | 935 | 12,137 | 4,497 | 105,495 |
| 315 | 155,250 | 20,430 | 810,165 | 59 | 531 | 14,795 | 545 | 962 | 530 | 1,183 |
| 63 | 21,674 | 3,176 | 102,714 | 40 | 17 | 1,589 | 1,954 | 60 | 49 | 215 |
| 44 | 45,801 | 7,529 | 278,615 | 29 | 0 | 2,525 | 148 | 92 | 0 | 32 |
| 849 | 355,629 | 47,059 | 3,326,248 | 464 | 1,167 | 93,046 | 410 | 15,263 | 679 | 4,597 |
| 414 | 209,181 | 20,094 | 2,084,667 | 167 | 111 | 18,978 | 113 | 203 | 81 | 316 |
| 144 | 103,265 | 11,030 | 1,394,542 | 67 | 51 | 6,233 | 27 | 132 | 60 | 50 |
| 115 | 109,945 | 11,512 | 968,078 | 659 | 94 | 3,986 | 257 | 336 | 5 | 85 |
| 132 | 92,588 | 8,033 | 798,001 | 101 | 59 | 4,060 | 180 | 159 | 47 | 276 |
| 123 | 550,440 | 86,569 | 507,453 | 77 | 68 | 5,964 | 307 | 1,890 | 80 | 633 |
| 32 | 223,653 | 110,209 | 108,859 | 8 | 7 | 5,341 | 85 | 75 | 0 | 157 |
| 357 | 125,278 | 21,206 | 1,218,257 | 90 | 2,502 | 32,203 | 390 | 4,042 | 3,106 | 3,837 |
| 414 | 634,833 | 310,636 | 497,462 | 86 | 661 | 81,769 | 256 | 5,866 | 541 | 23,692 |
| 692 | 652,465 | 174,138 | 2,666,179 | 338 | 330 | 42,678 | 216 | 475 | 126 | 614 |
| 278 | 236,268 | 46,719 | 2,020,975 | 385 | 181 | 8,924 | 140 | 227 | 414 | 237 |
| 52 | 84,955 | 7,487 | 224,674 | 0 | 0 | 2,215 | 83 | 85 | 5 | 80 |
| 166 | 268,116 | 17,860 | 1,843,299 | 202 | 59 | 13,294 | 216 | 259 | 79 | 414 |
| 41 | 43,073 | 7,780 | 285,385 | 30 | 0 | 1,920 | 44 | 46 | 27 | 0 |
| 72 | 54,459 | 6,503 | 794,911 | 172 | 16 | 3,266 | 145 | 27 | 28 | 55 |
| 47 | 60,172 | 9,662 | 279,693 | 89 | 19 | 6,490 | 245 | 852 | 23 | 128 |
| 97 | 205,455 | 118,857 | 118,033 | 3 | 68 | 15,507 | 40 | 103 | 39 | 281 |
| 272 | 157,195 | 30,768 | 1,407,956 | 328 | 1,466 | 60,899 | 363 | 6,694 | 6,697 | 18,854 |
| 90 | 43,970 | 6,260 | 234,000 | 88 | 8 | 3,108 | 249 | 681 | 33 | 66 |
| 801 | 625,459 | 155,531 | 2,898,888 | 598 | 6,158 | 159,876 | 775 | 20,293 | 56,462 | 107,207 |
| 299 | 141,803 | 20,308 | 1,110,581 | 179 | 205 | 14,927 | 380 | 471 | 308 | 542 |
| 20 | 27,901 | 4,194 | 324,929 | 228 | 0 | 608 | 14 | 14 | 0 | 25 |
| 442 | 360,151 | 38,709 | 4,067,840 | 441 | 215 | 49,496 | 209 | 770 | 476 | 703 |
| 125 | 118,804 | 10,961 | 714,184 | 222 | 215 | 4,451 | 329 | 277 | 70 | 208 |
| 373 | 160,967 | 29,161 | 878,555 | 127 | 24 | 8,535 | 746 | 992 | 60 | 195 |
| 351 | 263,960 | 31,007 | 4,314,762 | 313 | 400 | 55,158 | 367 | 636 | 619 | 2,253 |
| 62 | 134,128 | 72,747 | 73,425 | 0 | 67 | 6,208 | 11 | 3,463 | 69 | 958 |
| 70 | 87,527 | 9,923 | 500,089 | 67 | 103 | 8,119 | 230 | 118 | 73 | 300 |
| 19 | 24,490 | 3,288 | 355,102 | 37 | 0 | 905 | 33 | 12 | 0 | 8 |
| 80 | 113,713 | 11,272 | 724,059 | 45 | 76 | 7,061 | 322 | 125 | 98 | 166 |
| 755 | 571,175 | 60,277 | 2,949,686 | 333 | 925 | 31,048 | 2,117 | 10,732 | 904 | 1,673 |
| 127 | 53,902 | 5,607 | 299,414 | 24 | 11 | 10,439 | 69 | 612 | 0 | 63 |
| 61 | 132,574 | 33,049 | 59,090 | 0 | 4 | 1,842 | 18 | 15 | 2 | 64 |
| 595 | 178,732 | 33,641 | 1,186,056 | 289 | 1,048 | 23,390 | 1,006 | 3,850 | 660 | 1,398 |
| 477 | 265,350 | 52,725 | 1,389,914 | 595 | 172 | 18,275 | 3,280 | 560 | 139 | 228 |
| 50 | 40,125 | 3,296 | 468,927 | 15 | 5 | 4,325 | 12 | 13 | 0 | 64 |
| 818 | 239,004 | 55,442 | 2,630,680 | 343 | 79 | 14,366 | 120 | 204 | 83 | 97 |
| 55 | 21,762 | 2,885 | 158,469 | 20 | 0 | 1,681 | 55 | 3 | 0 | 0 |

**Table 2** *(Continued)*

| State | | | | | Ancestry | | | | |
| --- | --- | --- | --- | --- | --- | --- | --- | --- | --- |
| | Hawaiian | Hispanic | Hmong | Honduran | Hong Kong | Hungarian | Icelander | Indonesian | Iranian |
| Alabama | 436 | 1,151 | 0 | 278 | 0 | 4,117 | 210 | 110 | 1,118 |
| Alaska | 985 | 1,232 | 0 | 40 | 0 | 2,200 | 131 | 56 | 144 |
| Arizona | 2,324 | 50,573 | 24 | 693 | 24 | 22,433 | 759 | 506 | 2,351 |
| Arkansas | 318 | 919 | 0 | 90 | 0 | 2,300 | 95 | 64 | 343 |
| California | 43,418 | 303,271 | 42,843 | 26,834 | 2,761 | 159,121 | 6,512 | 21,767 | 108,871 |
| Colorado | 1,931 | 53,798 | 1,080 | 209 | 36 | 16,861 | 939 | 608 | 2,105 |
| Connecticut | 353 | 12,428 | 0 | 593 | 31 | 49,508 | 444 | 323 | 1,669 |
| Delaware | 96 | 1,229 | 0 | 55 | 8 | 3,468 | 29 | 50 | 254 |
| District of Columbia | 121 | 1,147 | 0 | 365 | 35 | 2,518 | 91 | 223 | 1,144 |
| Florida | 3,075 | 54,960 | 22 | 21,682 | 141 | 99,822 | 1,348 | 1,211 | 6,088 |
| Georgia | 1,156 | 4,071 | 320 | 789 | 11 | 13,418 | 353 | 340 | 3,279 |
| Hawaii | 156,812 | 1,133 | 0 | 161 | 76 | 2,631 | 127 | 474 | 352 |
| Idaho | 695 | 3,018 | 0 | 74 | 10 | 2,455 | 408 | 97 | 366 |
| Illinois | 1,535 | 22,248 | 483 | 3,212 | 197 | 68,439 | 981 | 723 | 6,458 |
| Indiana | 1,008 | 3,287 | 134 | 224 | 27 | 40,828 | 224 | 406 | 1,230 |
| Iowa | 430 | 1,547 | 325 | 208 | 2 | 3,710 | 310 | 270 | 787 |
| Kansas | 631 | 4,895 | 483 | 174 | 35 | 4,058 | 169 | 236 | 1,155 |
| Kentucky | 539 | 1,255 | 0 | 145 | 0 | 5,819 | 108 | 307 | 962 |
| Louisiana | 779 | 4,325 | 0 | 8,268 | 0 | 5,722 | 81 | 224 | 1,123 |
| Maine | 276 | 363 | 0 | 30 | 0 | 3,234 | 110 | 41 | 143 |
| Maryland | 986 | 5,999 | 0 | 1,910 | 63 | 26,726 | 425 | 770 | 9,644 |
| Massachusetts | 637 | 13,516 | 90 | 3,155 | 244 | 19,989 | 719 | 808 | 4,659 |
| Michigan | 1,333 | 10,461 | 2,013 | 525 | 24 | 109,178 | 756 | 876 | 3,117 |
| Minnesota | 493 | 2,437 | 16,785 | 204 | 80 | 12,349 | 3,165 | 164 | 1,922 |
| Mississippi | 303 | 635 | 0 | 122 | 0 | 1,462 | 84 | 39 | 235 |
| Missouri | 1,202 | 2,752 | 0 | 224 | 6 | 14,843 | 304 | 268 | 2,208 |
| Montana | 269 | 553 | 123 | 36 | 0 | 2,750 | 334 | 22 | 106 |
| Nebraska | 342 | 2,083 | 117 | 97 | 6 | 3,318 | 226 | 92 | 479 |
| Nevada | 2,060 | 5,022 | 13 | 384 | 0 | 7,100 | 342 | 180 | 1,118 |
| New Hampshire | 308 | 369 | 0 | 204 | 0 | 4,093 | 166 | 47 | 499 |
| New Jersey | 1,260 | 26,265 | 16 | 7,241 | 133 | 141,627 | 522 | 916 | 5,804 |
| New Mexico | 583 | 105,892 | 0 | 87 | 6 | 4,337 | 149 | 175 | 667 |
| New York | 1,876 | 78,843 | 184 | 23,014 | 1,090 | 186,898 | 1,427 | 3,680 | 18,183 |
| North Carolina | 1,428 | 2,795 | 551 | 457 | 19 | 12,749 | 245 | 273 | 2,094 |
| North Dakota | 86 | 287 | 5 | 65 | 0 | 3,005 | 3,161 | 33 | 117 |
| Ohio | 1,225 | 7,884 | 243 | 503 | 74 | 218,145 | 590 | 659 | 3,399 |
| Oklahoma | 983 | 3,847 | 76 | 359 | 13 | 3,797 | 155 | 313 | 2,494 |
| Oregon | 3,437 | 6,957 | 516 | 404 | 65 | 10,776 | 1,200 | 1,239 | 2,208 |
| Pennsylvania | 1,900 | 15,632 | 359 | 822 | 112 | 152,863 | 523 | 746 | 3,214 |
| Rhode Island | 158 | 1,537 | 970 | 152 | 11 | 2,902 | 185 | 52 | 378 |
| South Carolina | 799 | 1,307 | 6 | 322 | 12 | 6,111 | 127 | 57 | 570 |
| South Dakota | 155 | 429 | 0 | 19 | 0 | 1,361 | 209 | 25 | 150 |
| Tennessee | 885 | 1,438 | 26 | 234 | 17 | 7,349 | 176 | 155 | 1,902 |
| Texas | 4,136 | 254,202 | 133 | 9,614 | 262 | 31,884 | 1,147 | 1,555 | 13,639 |
| Utah | 2,102 | 6,708 | 155 | 216 | 10 | 2,944 | 2,970 | 288 | 1,458 |
| Vermont | 54 | 151 | 0 | 43 | 6 | 3,102 | 44 | 56 | 144 |
| Virginia | 1,901 | 7,779 | 7 | 1,561 | 26 | 25,178 | 814 | 894 | 9,858 |
| Washington | 7,207 | 14,834 | 779 | 320 | 59 | 16,797 | 5,976 | 1,088 | 3,629 |
| West Virginia | 180 | 352 | 0 | 47 | 0 | 9,248 | 106 | 46 | 362 |
| Wisconsin | 639 | 3,405 | 15,942 | 135 | 42 | 25,385 | 809 | 404 | 1,261 |
| Wyoming | 236 | 2,038 | 0 | 35 | 0 | 1,374 | 44 | 13 | 61 |

## Ancestry

| Iraqi | Irish | Israeli | Italian | Jamaican | Japanese | Jordanian | Kenyan | Khmer | Korean | Laotian |
|---|---|---|---|---|---|---|---|---|---|---|
| 45 | 617,065 | 135 | 52,969 | 814 | 3,516 | 287 | 11 | 5 | 3,969 | 746 |
| 0 | 74,322 | 14 | 14,467 | 186 | 3,009 | 0 | 0 | 0 | 4,349 | 233 |
| 243 | 529,575 | 966 | 159,140 | 1,005 | 8,430 | 195 | 5 | 0 | 7,300 | 581 |
| 47 | 464,287 | 26 | 30,199 | 180 | 1,586 | 13 | 23 | 0 | 1,470 | 2,004 |
| 6,080 | 3,425,089 | 20,651 | 1,439,778 | 19,237 | 353,251 | 5,503 | 942 | 1,317 | 260,822 | 59,976 |
| 158 | 537,945 | 423 | 155,844 | 819 | 15,198 | 71 | 21 | 12 | 12,490 | 1,771 |
| 85 | 613,765 | 1,320 | 628,232 | 20,219 | 5,000 | 57 | 28 | 9 | 5,427 | 2,720 |
| 39 | 139,180 | 162 | 63,467 | 118 | 989 | 24 | 9 | 0 | 1,463 | 122 |
| 44 | 34,392 | 146 | 11,662 | 3,184 | 1,260 | 16 | 33 | 0 | 943 | 33 |
| 696 | 1,898,822 | 5,518 | 784,770 | 86,231 | 15,401 | 615 | 76 | 7 | 14,722 | 2,365 |
| 90 | 970,713 | 415 | 111,940 | 6,262 | 9,450 | 300 | 134 | 6 | 16,580 | 3,306 |
| 0 | 65,473 | 74 | 21,535 | 443 | 262,113 | 0 | 6 | 0 | 28,887 | 1,554 |
| 26 | 141,901 | 45 | 23,736 | 78 | 3,865 | 7 | 4 | 0 | 1,214 | 430 |
| 1,638 | 1,860,989 | 2,528 | 729,000 | 7,734 | 26,579 | 1,833 | 171 | 3 | 42,167 | 4,191 |
| 47 | 965,080 | 521 | 124,581 | 1,368 | 6,338 | 170 | 12 | 0 | 6,298 | 699 |
| 30 | 527,428 | 125 | 45,213 | 104 | 2,189 | 130 | 31 | 25 | 4,959 | 2,860 |
| 74 | 435,784 | 137 | 44,528 | 442 | 3,360 | 103 | 62 | 0 | 5,406 | 2,049 |
| 17 | 695,853 | 136 | 55,423 | 600 | 3,275 | 229 | 20 | 0 | 4,264 | 308 |
| 98 | 518,124 | 184 | 196,904 | 1,105 | 2,681 | 123 | 0 | 37 | 3,643 | 862 |
| 0 | 217,226 | 76 | 51,397 | 198 | 1,202 | 9 | 5 | 0 | 1,225 | 44 |
| 468 | 769,312 | 2,254 | 252,428 | 15,456 | 10,067 | 467 | 408 | 83 | 29,471 | 639 |
| 383 | 1,570,742 | 2,899 | 843,524 | 11,990 | 10,662 | 326 | 166 | 528 | 12,878 | 3,953 |
| 6,668 | 1,320,458 | 1,150 | 409,573 | 3,777 | 13,309 | 1,441 | 53 | 0 | 17,738 | 2,753 |
| 80 | 573,755 | 452 | 88,812 | 696 | 5,330 | 111 | 102 | 21 | 12,922 | 7,252 |
| 9 | 392,864 | 83 | 36,304 | 318 | 1,576 | 37 | 0 | 0 | 1,610 | 54 |
| 119 | 1,037,658 | 566 | 161,173 | 1,202 | 6,233 | 122 | 59 | 0 | 6,452 | 637 |
| 18 | 138,828 | 24 | 21,322 | 26 | 1,391 | 19 | 0 | 0 | 842 | 171 |
| 23 | 272,185 | 172 | 35,014 | 158 | 2,307 | 15 | 0 | 0 | 2,600 | 675 |
| 30 | 199,772 | 339 | 86,785 | 369 | 5,111 | 33 | 54 | 0 | 4,693 | 950 |
| 51 | 232,409 | 51 | 81,310 | 324 | 1,153 | 0 | 12 | 0 | 1,635 | 475 |
| 632 | 1,415,489 | 6,569 | 1,457,013 | 26,690 | 19,948 | 1,234 | 493 | 12 | 38,087 | 526 |
| 31 | 163,690 | 144 | 36,204 | 261 | 3,482 | 41 | 20 | 0 | 1,756 | 444 |
| 2,814 | 2,800,128 | 24,091 | 2,837,904 | 186,429 | 39,859 | 2,408 | 272 | 153 | 93,145 | 2,658 |
| 124 | 841,276 | 253 | 111,983 | 2,639 | 8,069 | 265 | 87 | 92 | 8,572 | 1,731 |
| 28 | 53,678 | 13 | 4,255 | 67 | 560 | 26 | 0 | 0 | 687 | 42 |
| 267 | 1,896,231 | 1,158 | 637,143 | 3,841 | 13,999 | 723 | 245 | 41 | 13,041 | 2,053 |
| 74 | 641,733 | 167 | 44,951 | 332 | 4,272 | 153 | 7 | 0 | 5,459 | 821 |
| 104 | 466,887 | 249 | 83,093 | 223 | 14,142 | 43 | 109 | 5 | 9,355 | 3,287 |
| 299 | 2,255,867 | 2,722 | 1,372,904 | 10,191 | 10,151 | 431 | 96 | 104 | 25,800 | 1,928 |
| 9 | 213,653 | 194 | 199,028 | 483 | 1,010 | 78 | 9 | 8 | 1,293 | 2,040 |
| 11 | 485,804 | 198 | 56,291 | 1,135 | 3,279 | 118 | 0 | 0 | 3,198 | 393 |
| 32 | 87,657 | 9 | 6,110 | 29 | 458 | 16 | 0 | 0 | 686 | 89 |
| 149 | 875,155 | 244 | 73,079 | 1,150 | 4,735 | 203 | 54 | 0 | 5,063 | 2,494 |
| 495 | 2,368,863 | 2,114 | 312,294 | 7,500 | 23,729 | 1,498 | 531 | 113 | 35,281 | 9,157 |
| 43 | 136,645 | 134 | 45,857 | 102 | 8,455 | 66 | 0 | 6 | 3,215 | 1,678 |
| 0 | 100,839 | 93 | 32,428 | 113 | 536 | 0 | 0 | 0 | 798 | 137 |
| 570 | 888,908 | 856 | 207,023 | 4,975 | 12,385 | 660 | 162 | 128 | 32,362 | 2,321 |
| 202 | 768,293 | 448 | 156,943 | 1,482 | 43,378 | 235 | 94 | 236 | 32,918 | 5,370 |
| 13 | 348,448 | 33 | 71,684 | 260 | 1,257 | 8 | 0 | 10 | 955 | 45 |
| 9 | 612,358 | 390 | 144,249 | 1,443 | 4,235 | 194 | 13 | 18 | 6,499 | 5,297 |
| 0 | 72,941 | 6 | 13,084 | 36 | 875 | 0 | 0 | 0 | 378 | 6 |

**Table 2** *(Continued)*

| | Ancestry | | | | | | | |
|---|---|---|---|---|---|---|---|---|
| State | Latin American | Latvian | Lebanese | Liberian | Lithuanian | Luxemburger | Macedonian | Malaysian | Maltese |
| Alabama | 58 | 252 | 3,672 | 33 | 1,809 | 113 | 18 | 202 | 107 |
| Alaska | 0 | 179 | 279 | 0 | 1,267 | 79 | 2 | 62 | 15 |
| Arizona | 358 | 1,029 | 6,296 | 0 | 9,353 | 924 | 243 | 245 | 435 |
| Arkansas | 70 | 198 | 817 | 0 | 1,456 | 104 | 21 | 170 | 63 |
| California | 15,631 | 13,652 | 49,776 | 639 | 63,871 | 3,487 | 1,498 | 9,755 | 8,029 |
| Colorado | 339 | 1,772 | 3,544 | 23 | 7,232 | 629 | 122 | 132 | 144 |
| Connecticut | 410 | 2,389 | 8,612 | 83 | 41,747 | 234 | 285 | 498 | 280 |
| Delaware | 20 | 438 | 533 | 22 | 2,695 | 7 | 13 | 14 | 40 |
| District of Columbia | 176 | 552 | 1,070 | 101 | 1,789 | 72 | 38 | 89 | 61 |
| Florida | 4,188 | 5,725 | 24,322 | 199 | 41,713 | 1,259 | 583 | 904 | 2,190 |
| Georgia | 327 | 1,035 | 5,792 | 563 | 6,751 | 192 | 74 | 426 | 182 |
| Hawaii | 73 | 224 | 504 | 0 | 1,411 | 162 | 6 | 634 | 41 |
| Idaho | 70 | 47 | 285 | 0 | 831 | 207 | 74 | 40 | 28 |
| Illinois | 1,338 | 6,978 | 8,299 | 282 | 109,417 | 9,249 | 1,264 | 972 | 314 |
| Indiana | 433 | 1,622 | 3,610 | 39 | 11,098 | 685 | 3,210 | 421 | 121 |
| Iowa | 140 | 965 | 2,180 | 9 | 3,090 | 6,153 | 17 | 132 | 80 |
| Kansas | 121 | 384 | 2,937 | 32 | 2,079 | 361 | 17 | 315 | 49 |
| Kentucky | 123 | 240 | 3,153 | 0 | 1,726 | 83 | 61 | 63 | 114 |
| Louisiana | 444 | 285 | 6,705 | 19 | 1,899 | 59 | 33 | 120 | 61 |
| Maine | 9 | 455 | 2,623 | 0 | 4,678 | 42 | 3 | 33 | 30 |
| Maryland | 488 | 3,398 | 5,771 | 720 | 23,608 | 340 | 198 | 400 | 184 |
| Massachusetts | 535 | 6,479 | 29,700 | 385 | 68,447 | 326 | 181 | 310 | 401 |
| Michigan | 579 | 5,485 | 39,673 | 312 | 38,384 | 907 | 4,106 | 503 | 13,446 |
| Minnesota | 160 | 2,612 | 6,096 | 452 | 7,033 | 5,898 | 115 | 76 | 104 |
| Mississippi | 95 | 116 | 3,177 | 0 | 569 | 70 | 15 | 198 | 88 |
| Missouri | 118 | 760 | 4,973 | 54 | 6,283 | 417 | 265 | 535 | 98 |
| Montana | 9 | 223 | 816 | 0 | 915 | 216 | 36 | 42 | 0 |
| Nebraska | 35 | 869 | 1,682 | 17 | 3,557 | 922 | 42 | 173 | 45 |
| Nevada | 228 | 278 | 2,219 | 0 | 2,722 | 225 | 145 | 223 | 193 |
| New Hampshire | 6 | 713 | 3,777 | 0 | 7,953 | 90 | 31 | 51 | 84 |
| New Jersey | 934 | 5,393 | 12,261 | 952 | 49,870 | 425 | 460 | 718 | 1,252 |
| New Mexico | 144 | 257 | 1,974 | 0 | 1,943 | 132 | 62 | 118 | 11 |
| New York | 2,843 | 12,038 | 31,089 | 1,422 | 70,397 | 915 | 1,570 | 2,471 | 8,245 |
| North Carolina | 213 | 843 | 5,619 | 220 | 5,602 | 83 | 29 | 203 | 268 |
| North Dakota | 6 | 64 | 563 | 0 | 383 | 419 | 9 | 14 | 36 |
| Ohio | 381 | 3,973 | 27,226 | 251 | 29,840 | 867 | 3,452 | 861 | 294 |
| Oklahoma | 132 | 338 | 4,308 | 49 | 2,090 | 253 | 38 | 322 | 55 |
| Oregon | 236 | 1,197 | 2,611 | 9 | 4,341 | 606 | 135 | 192 | 107 |
| Pennsylvania | 552 | 4,847 | 19,234 | 364 | 103,272 | 401 | 808 | 397 | 388 |
| Rhode Island | 29 | 377 | 2,666 | 611 | 4,580 | 65 | 66 | 72 | 104 |
| South Carolina | 91 | 252 | 3,732 | 20 | 2,673 | 108 | 28 | 176 | 87 |
| South Dakota | 0 | 115 | 717 | 0 | 256 | 1,242 | 17 | 98 | 19 |
| Tennessee | 188 | 623 | 2,837 | 87 | 3,252 | 141 | 21 | 454 | 88 |
| Texas | 9,909 | 2,279 | 21,934 | 404 | 14,034 | 704 | 279 | 1,650 | 702 |
| Utah | 136 | 172 | 1,534 | 0 | 1,118 | 39 | 0 | 40 | 84 |
| Vermont | 24 | 179 | 1,359 | 2 | 1,579 | 5 | 34 | 19 | 45 |
| Virginia | 660 | 1,806 | 10,692 | 382 | 13,375 | 564 | 150 | 1,117 | 360 |
| Washington | 302 | 2,926 | 3,784 | 0 | 8,530 | 1,171 | 177 | 762 | 237 |
| West Virginia | 11 | 168 | 4,178 | 0 | 2,225 | 22 | 45 | 15 | 7 |
| Wisconsin | 137 | 3,003 | 2,827 | 40 | 16,790 | 7,288 | 256 | 324 | 163 |
| Wyoming | 12 | 127 | 142 | 0 | 332 | 99 | 13 | 39 | 21 |

| | | | | | Ancestry | | | | | |
|---|---|---|---|---|---|---|---|---|---|---|
| Manx | Mexican | Micronesian | Middle Eastern | Mongolian | Moravian | Moroccan | Nepali | New Zealander | Newfoundland | Nicaraguan |
| 28 | 7,556 | 5 | 18 | 6 | 19 | 73 | 13 | 12 | 6 | 137 |
| 13 | 6,888 | 28 | 0 | 44 | 0 | 5 | 0 | 32 | 0 | 113 |
| 67 | 520,009 | 104 | 99 | 49 | 13 | 163 | 30 | 117 | 23 | 606 |
| 37 | 10,835 | 21 | 2 | 0 | 8 | 20 | 26 | 35 | 7 | 102 |
| 1,048 | 5,322,170 | 615 | 1,836 | 828 | 260 | 2,981 | 224 | 2,460 | 186 | 64,285 |
| 102 | 198,902 | 101 | 55 | 82 | 95 | 118 | 84 | 144 | 12 | 244 |
| 22 | 7,555 | 0 | 53 | 21 | 47 | 187 | 15 | 92 | 62 | 420 |
| 0 | 2,515 | 0 | 0 | 0 | 0 | 74 | 6 | 0 | 0 | 41 |
| 17 | 2,361 | 0 | 43 | 0 | 0 | 353 | 8 | 25 | 23 | 850 |
| 351 | 134,161 | 31 | 324 | 66 | 134 | 1,400 | 67 | 368 | 288 | 70,374 |
| 85 | 37,267 | 41 | 82 | 60 | 21 | 89 | 21 | 134 | 43 | 694 |
| 4 | 10,720 | 999 | 35 | 42 | 0 | 24 | 79 | 137 | 0 | 101 |
| 149 | 35,591 | 49 | 8 | 5 | 5 | 10 | 0 | 36 | 3 | 127 |
| 634 | 557,536 | 10 | 283 | 106 | 438 | 690 | 16 | 160 | 88 | 1,366 |
| 78 | 60,593 | 6 | 23 | 40 | 21 | 138 | 13 | 65 | 37 | 101 |
| 95 | 21,255 | 0 | 58 | 7 | 27 | 44 | 27 | 63 | 2 | 103 |
| 81 | 65,729 | 77 | 75 | 0 | 90 | 81 | 0 | 74 | 10 | 117 |
| 32 | 6,823 | 0 | 20 | 55 | 13 | 49 | 0 | 7 | 7 | 95 |
| 20 | 21,046 | 50 | 59 | 19 | 27 | 58 | 3 | 67 | 21 | 3,635 |
| 9 | 1,990 | 0 | 2 | 13 | 18 | 37 | 15 | 18 | 107 | 19 |
| 113 | 14,948 | 33 | 266 | 76 | 47 | 1,303 | 241 | 201 | 58 | 3,279 |
| 103 | 11,421 | 0 | 256 | 52 | 50 | 550 | 197 | 206 | 2,333 | 591 |
| 343 | 118,424 | 50 | 161 | 53 | 114 | 758 | 167 | 144 | 87 | 237 |
| 206 | 28,512 | 21 | 116 | 13 | 30 | 70 | 25 | 36 | 48 | 158 |
| 19 | 4,900 | 0 | 29 | 6 | 2 | 27 | 22 | 8 | 0 | 74 |
| 133 | 35,860 | 76 | 85 | 20 | 54 | 437 | 0 | 46 | 65 | 240 |
| 87 | 7,037 | 7 | 2 | 48 | 1 | 34 | 11 | 45 | 0 | 37 |
| 67 | 25,814 | 29 | 13 | 5 | 179 | 43 | 15 | 0 | 6 | 44 |
| 45 | 72,281 | 27 | 0 | 83 | 0 | 214 | 25 | 96 | 20 | 957 |
| 23 | 2,334 | 5 | 0 | 0 | 3 | 12 | 4 | 39 | 257 | 31 |
| 57 | 24,703 | 9 | 491 | 362 | 65 | 811 | 36 | 219 | 201 | 3,663 |
| 32 | 215,576 | 0 | 44 | 37 | 7 | 61 | 0 | 34 | 12 | 270 |
| 130 | 71,284 | 3 | 1,618 | 301 | 118 | 4,043 | 441 | 386 | 688 | 10,036 |
| 50 | 24,685 | 39 | 45 | 21 | 71 | 124 | 123 | 107 | 51 | 408 |
| 21 | 2,311 | 8 | 25 | 0 | 4 | 5 | 0 | 7 | 1 | 3 |
| 632 | 50,725 | 11 | 96 | 84 | 98 | 449 | 76 | 54 | 69 | 370 |
| 57 | 53,069 | 8 | 42 | 10 | 24 | 66 | 20 | 25 | 0 | 100 |
| 208 | 71,680 | 297 | 67 | 8 | 47 | 142 | 88 | 250 | 25 | 412 |
| 124 | 20,913 | 52 | 176 | 311 | 82 | 1,097 | 101 | 153 | 201 | 723 |
| 6 | 1,994 | 0 | 6 | 11 | 25 | 41 | 0 | 15 | 38 | 130 |
| 7 | 8,316 | 18 | 39 | 0 | 7 | 180 | 0 | 17 | 19 | 151 |
| 0 | 2,951 | 0 | 0 | 6 | 14 | 0 | 0 | 48 | 9 | 0 |
| 0 | 11,997 | 37 | 99 | 28 | 21 | 18 | 0 | 50 | 18 | 200 |
| 245 | 3,403,368 | 161 | 469 | 277 | 1,209 | 554 | 113 | 346 | 58 | 7,562 |
| 108 | 45,675 | 69 | 0 | 0 | 9 | 89 | 2 | 390 | 0 | 115 |
| 18 | 635 | 10 | 10 | 11 | 23 | 16 | 0 | 25 | 12 | 7 |
| 135 | 28,375 | 38 | 248 | 148 | 57 | 1,076 | 55 | 331 | 143 | 2,821 |
| 292 | 128,472 | 260 | 122 | 38 | 61 | 97 | 38 | 353 | 58 | 502 |
| 16 | 2,157 | 0 | 0 | 12 | 0 | 8 | 0 | 8 | 0 | 18 |
| 158 | 51,339 | 1 | 50 | 43 | 123 | 165 | 69 | 54 | 10 | 386 |
| 10 | 13,725 | 0 | 6 | 0 | 0 | 5 | 0 | 3 | 0 | 22 |

**Table 2**   (*Continued*)

| | | | | | Ancestry | | | | |
|---|---|---|---|---|---|---|---|---|---|
| State | Nigerian | North American | Northern European | Northern Irish | Norwegian | Nova Scotian | Okinawan | Other Asian | Other Central and South American |
| Alabama | 1,401 | 334 | 777 | 12 | 8,489 | 14 | 64 | 0 | 0 |
| Alaska | 53 | 35 | 611 | 0 | 23,087 | 17 | 10 | 0 | 0 |
| Arizona | 557 | 139 | 1,081 | 73 | 70,940 | 13 | 237 | 21 | 0 |
| Arkansas | 894 | 163 | 348 | 22 | 8,778 | 23 | 0 | 16 | 0 |
| California | 10,027 | 1,712 | 14,188 | 538 | 411,282 | 369 | 1,799 | 709 | 233 |
| Colorado | 730 | 202 | 2,131 | 51 | 75,646 | 39 | 110 | 51 | 0 |
| Connecticut | 803 | 79 | 670 | 159 | 19,004 | 107 | 8 | 0 | 0 |
| Delaware | 231 | 14 | 38 | 0 | 3,036 | 0 | 0 | 9 | 0 |
| District of Columbia | 1,762 | 13 | 167 | 0 | 2,620 | 0 | 9 | 9 | 0 |
| Florida | 2,922 | 741 | 1,920 | 285 | 90,375 | 406 | 142 | 28 | 247 |
| Georgia | 5,040 | 515 | 732 | 39 | 21,388 | 83 | 114 | 13 | 7 |
| Hawaii | 13 | 6 | 170 | 0 | 9,054 | 0 | 5,998 | 48 | 0 |
| Idaho | 96 | 18 | 785 | 6 | 32,956 | 0 | 17 | 0 | 0 |
| Illinois | 4,455 | 433 | 1,807 | 118 | 167,003 | 9 | 77 | 15 | 0 |
| Indiana | 720 | 374 | 1,078 | 52 | 25,978 | 13 | 75 | 11 | 0 |
| Iowa | 423 | 63 | 1,250 | 26 | 152,084 | 30 | 0 | 7 | 0 |
| Kansas | 344 | 126 | 689 | 79 | 21,878 | 42 | 23 | 64 | 0 |
| Kentucky | 445 | 193 | 198 | 79 | 7,355 | 21 | 22 | 14 | 0 |
| Louisiana | 1,430 | 164 | 685 | 59 | 9,510 | 485 | 0 | 0 | 0 |
| Maine | 44 | 29 | 161 | 39 | 7,256 | 182 | 27 | 19 | 0 |
| Maryland | 6,515 | 254 | 1,070 | 48 | 22,520 | 61 | 61 | 40 | 0 |
| Massachusetts | 1,620 | 200 | 1,249 | 360 | 30,726 | 2,206 | 17 | 23 | 32 |
| Michigan | 2,103 | 286 | 2,153 | 141 | 72,261 | 41 | 67 | 20 | 0 |
| Minnesota | 1,714 | 83 | 2,871 | 56 | 757,212 | 48 | 34 | 4 | 0 |
| Mississippi | 1,225 | 249 | 122 | 5 | 4,052 | 7 | 71 | 0 | 0 |
| Missouri | 1,644 | 252 | 798 | 55 | 29,531 | 22 | 66 | 8 | 0 |
| Montana | 67 | 31 | 588 | 5 | 86,460 | 28 | 0 | 8 | 0 |
| Nebraska | 466 | 62 | 472 | 0 | 30,533 | 0 | 21 | 5 | 0 |
| Nevada | 188 | 60 | 427 | 16 | 23,229 | 11 | 53 | 14 | 0 |
| New Hampshire | 49 | 48 | 270 | 9 | 8,401 | 267 | 9 | 0 | 0 |
| New Jersey | 4,330 | 207 | 1,010 | 175 | 46,991 | 32 | 45 | 39 | 45 |
| New Mexico | 95 | 50 | 710 | 0 | 13,936 | 7 | 18 | 5 | 0 |
| New York | 9,610 | 517 | 2,854 | 411 | 90,158 | 113 | 78 | 271 | 489 |
| North Carolina | 2,083 | 689 | 920 | 87 | 20,184 | 23 | 150 | 137 | 17 |
| North Dakota | 147 | 0 | 219 | 6 | 189,106 | 3 | 2 | 0 | 0 |
| Ohio | 2,329 | 327 | 1,271 | 112 | 31,911 | 60 | 162 | 29 | 5 |
| Oklahoma | 1,132 | 174 | 509 | 1 | 17,401 | 16 | 54 | 6 | 8 |
| Oregon | 541 | 102 | 2,724 | 20 | 124,216 | 76 | 92 | 55 | 0 |
| Pennsylvania | 1,984 | 215 | 1,153 | 276 | 31,146 | 84 | 117 | 14 | 24 |
| Rhode Island | 508 | 33 | 161 | 31 | 4,010 | 83 | 0 | 6 | 0 |
| South Carolina | 1,582 | 425 | 406 | 45 | 9,170 | 5 | 26 | 5 | 0 |
| South Dakota | 128 | 19 | 797 | 8 | 106,361 | 0 | 7 | 0 | 0 |
| Tennessee | 1,082 | 689 | 862 | 50 | 12,098 | 8 | 0 | 5 | 0 |
| Texas | 13,153 | 1,048 | 2,840 | 95 | 94,096 | 190 | 275 | 97 | 59 |
| Utah | 280 | 57 | 935 | 27 | 36,178 | 21 | 10 | 7 | 0 |
| Vermont | 13 | 10 | 447 | 8 | 3,537 | 33 | 4 | 0 | 0 |
| Virginia | 2,210 | 696 | 1,643 | 199 | 35,815 | 52 | 178 | 31 | 9 |
| Washington | 772 | 200 | 5,772 | 100 | 333,521 | 84 | 164 | 293 | 35 |
| West Virginia | 247 | 159 | 141 | 3 | 2,598 | 6 | 0 | 0 | 0 |
| Wisconsin | 1,379 | 115 | 853 | 13 | 416,271 | 49 | 41 | 29 | 7 |
| Wyoming | 102 | 8 | 260 | 10 | 18,047 | 0 | 0 | 0 | 0 |

| | | | | | Ancestry | | | | | |
|---|---|---|---|---|---|---|---|---|---|---|
| Other Eastern European and Soviet Union | Other Groups and not Classified | Other Hispanic | Other North African and Southwest Asian | Other North American | Other Pacific Islander | Other South Asian | Other Subsaharan African | Other West Indian | Other Western European | Pacific Islander |
| 368 | 27,612 | 31 | 36 | 0 | 8 | 0 | 95 | 22 | 13 | 40 |
| 337 | 8,091 | 2 | 7 | 8 | 48 | 0 | 20 | 0 | 28 | 188 |
| 1,017 | 49,752 | 11 | 239 | 0 | 183 | 0 | 260 | 51 | 32 | 242 |
| 120 | 27,446 | 0 | 36 | 0 | 54 | 0 | 44 | 10 | 10 | 0 |
| 18,469 | 331,630 | 471 | 2,168 | 39 | 2,031 | 34 | 2,377 | 315 | 343 | 4,869 |
| 1,335 | 42,904 | 38 | 151 | 25 | 102 | 0 | 270 | 0 | 72 | 163 |
| 3,347 | 36,781 | 60 | 78 | 0 | 34 | 0 | 314 | 139 | 21 | 49 |
| 342 | 8,097 | 0 | 22 | 0 | 17 | 0 | 93 | 8 | 0 | 23 |
| 1,272 | 5,539 | 5 | 50 | 0 | 33 | 0 | 662 | 23 | 0 | 21 |
| 5,900 | 179,096 | 2,644 | 621 | 12 | 264 | 0 | 786 | 861 | 164 | 340 |
| 1,699 | 55,318 | 125 | 195 | 18 | 113 | 0 | 931 | 41 | 37 | 53 |
| 95 | 6,182 | 0 | 33 | 0 | 1,887 | 0 | 33 | 0 | 0 | 691 |
| 53 | 21,968 | 0 | 0 | 0 | 101 | 0 | 16 | 0 | 0 | 65 |
| 4,901 | 154,153 | 117 | 330 | 2 | 148 | 0 | 675 | 32 | 68 | 397 |
| 549 | 142,902 | 23 | 117 | 18 | 31 | 0 | 201 | 17 | 53 | 44 |
| 226 | 24,282 | 21 | 77 | 2 | 10 | 0 | 225 | 0 | 26 | 10 |
| 371 | 29,779 | 0 | 57 | 0 | 74 | 0 | 100 | 2 | 21 | 0 |
| 256 | 60,667 | 9 | 93 | 13 | 60 | 0 | 103 | 11 | 9 | 57 |
| 472 | 35,710 | 219 | 93 | 0 | 47 | 0 | 102 | 32 | 21 | 32 |
| 405 | 23,291 | 0 | 0 | 0 | 37 | 0 | 25 | 6 | 12 | 43 |
| 6,577 | 63,168 | 82 | 359 | 5 | 141 | 0 | 1,929 | 249 | 71 | 101 |
| 8,381 | 94,050 | 107 | 341 | 0 | 41 | 9 | 601 | 35 | 17 | 56 |
| 2,376 | 127,760 | 41 | 310 | 11 | 179 | 0 | 556 | 50 | 51 | 227 |
| 1,049 | 29,622 | 18 | 170 | 0 | 83 | 0 | 280 | 9 | 55 | 101 |
| 107 | 36,803 | 11 | 48 | 0 | 11 | 0 | 19 | 9 | 11 | 7 |
| 1,275 | 67,918 | 12 | 178 | 52 | 58 | 0 | 283 | 5 | 34 | 55 |
| 97 | 12,369 | 0 | 0 | 0 | 19 | 0 | 19 | 0 | 16 | 6 |
| 151 | 14,494 | 0 | 7 | 6 | 14 | 7 | 53 | 0 | 19 | 2 |
| 315 | 20,711 | 18 | 51 | 0 | 219 | 0 | 56 | 0 | 9 | 150 |
| 511 | 14,963 | 0 | 33 | 0 | 10 | 0 | 31 | 0 | 0 | 9 |
| 11,075 | 105,831 | 77 | 359 | 6 | 92 | 27 | 734 | 320 | 23 | 353 |
| 243 | 16,118 | 53 | 42 | 0 | 81 | 0 | 29 | 12 | 14 | 27 |
| 34,778 | 431,474 | 334 | 1,338 | 0 | 302 | 7 | 3,408 | 1,330 | 154 | 188 |
| 913 | 63,639 | 130 | 72 | 17 | 103 | 8 | 686 | 51 | 29 | 117 |
| 8 | 2,636 | 0 | 59 | 0 | 16 | 0 | 0 | 0 | 6 | 10 |
| 2,876 | 219,731 | 12 | 336 | 7 | 163 | 6 | 309 | 35 | 31 | 121 |
| 95 | 40,140 | 4 | 85 | 4 | 64 | 0 | 131 | 22 | 27 | 100 |
| 871 | 61,015 | 0 | 310 | 0 | 460 | 0 | 164 | 25 | 69 | 234 |
| 9,212 | 138,575 | 94 | 248 | 0 | 84 | 0 | 898 | 67 | 12 | 76 |
| 519 | 11,329 | 0 | 8 | 0 | 0 | 0 | 108 | 0 | 15 | 8 |
| 356 | 27,035 | 29 | 17 | 0 | 101 | 0 | 96 | 20 | 25 | 136 |
| 14 | 5,421 | 0 | 7 | 0 | 10 | 0 | 29 | 0 | 4 | 8 |
| 522 | 64,718 | 33 | 310 | 0 | 53 | 0 | 89 | 47 | 4 | 81 |
| 2,444 | 209,466 | 274 | 608 | 33 | 252 | 0 | 1,252 | 137 | 142 | 502 |
| 178 | 21,845 | 0 | 73 | 10 | 133 | 0 | 47 | 0 | 0 | 140 |
| 545 | 11,622 | 0 | 16 | 0 | 0 | 0 | 12 | 0 | 0 | 5 |
| 2,957 | 58,132 | 98 | 434 | 0 | 188 | 12 | 772 | 84 | 26 | 333 |
| 1,293 | 80,898 | 17 | 234 | 12 | 439 | 6 | 380 | 32 | 124 | 757 |
| 84 | 34,696 | 12 | 19 | 7 | 4 | 0 | 18 | 0 | 7 | 31 |
| 960 | 27,298 | 27 | 195 | 2 | 56 | 0 | 286 | 30 | 61 | 39 |
| 16 | 4,922 | 0 | 0 | 0 | 16 | 0 | 0 | 0 | 19 | 23 |

**Table 2** *(Continued)*

| State | Pakistani | Palestinian | Panamanian | Paraguayan | Pennsylvania German | Peruvian | Polish | Polynesian | Portuguese |
|---|---|---|---|---|---|---|---|---|---|
| Alabama | 365 | 367 | 540 | 36 | 395 | 119 | 21,907 | 43 | 1,408 |
| Alaska | 21 | 15 | 203 | 0 | 354 | 246 | 12,294 | 152 | 1,628 |
| Arizona | 549 | 497 | 733 | 30 | 2,645 | 950 | 102,405 | 189 | 7,338 |
| Arkansas | 226 | 144 | 219 | 9 | 682 | 65 | 17,600 | 48 | 1,337 |
| California | 17,729 | 11,566 | 13,015 | 634 | 12,742 | 42,322 | 578,256 | 3,545 | 356,495 |
| Colorado | 666 | 489 | 1,272 | 66 | 3,569 | 1,264 | 82,257 | 171 | 4,654 |
| Connecticut | 1,301 | 322 | 543 | 133 | 904 | 3,897 | 312,587 | 23 | 43,098 |
| Delaware | 217 | 94 | 341 | 75 | 2,396 | 39 | 38,286 | 0 | 1,127 |
| District of Columbia | 228 | 186 | 581 | 165 | 59 | 933 | 9,879 | 0 | 870 |
| Florida | 3,835 | 2,786 | 10,907 | 269 | 9,451 | 21,784 | 410,666 | 390 | 32,345 |
| Georgia | 1,665 | 420 | 2,133 | 60 | 1,027 | 1,581 | 67,171 | 154 | 4,925 |
| Hawaii | 192 | 10 | 241 | 0 | 149 | 143 | 11,795 | 1,083 | 57,125 |
| Idaho | 92 | 23 | 93 | 3 | 930 | 170 | 11,540 | 53 | 2,717 |
| Illinois | 11,237 | 5,534 | 1,903 | 207 | 7,208 | 4,821 | 962,827 | 103 | 6,810 |
| Indiana | 1,035 | 471 | 567 | 46 | 9,684 | 273 | 179,501 | 123 | 2,476 |
| Iowa | 356 | 165 | 304 | 18 | 6,580 | 95 | 32,502 | 40 | 1,097 |
| Kansas | 623 | 270 | 444 | 77 | 5,042 | 256 | 34,844 | 76 | 1,414 |
| Kentucky | 228 | 231 | 531 | 0 | 818 | 180 | 24,487 | 74 | 1,275 |
| Louisiana | 485 | 454 | 982 | 14 | 469 | 410 | 22,456 | 60 | 2,988 |
| Maine | 16 | 67 | 79 | 13 | 374 | 51 | 23,838 | 19 | 4,523 |
| Maryland | 3,342 | 1,038 | 2,243 | 483 | 3,581 | 4,396 | 200,570 | 85 | 6,898 |
| Massachusetts | 1,814 | 903 | 1,497 | 157 | 1,025 | 2,817 | 359,677 | 66 | 289,424 |
| Michigan | 2,524 | 2,695 | 638 | 44 | 10,758 | 487 | 889,527 | 48 | 4,203 |
| Minnesota | 446 | 368 | 358 | 79 | 2,185 | 338 | 238,039 | 69 | 1,386 |
| Mississippi | 99 | 92 | 236 | 0 | 181 | 78 | 10,645 | 42 | 1,306 |
| Missouri | 908 | 291 | 585 | 1 | 3,013 | 476 | 95,900 | 211 | 3,086 |
| Montana | 28 | 23 | 75 | 0 | 1,040 | 62 | 15,736 | 56 | 1,421 |
| Nebraska | 145 | 14 | 143 | 0 | 3,709 | 197 | 61,199 | 28 | 744 |
| Nevada | 380 | 57 | 361 | 28 | 752 | 430 | 33,591 | 130 | 8,246 |
| New Hampshire | 217 | 8 | 45 | 10 | 355 | 119 | 48,767 | 19 | 10,199 |
| New Jersey | 7,053 | 2,367 | 3,063 | 413 | 7,886 | 22,962 | 626,506 | 52 | 63,188 |
| New Mexico | 203 | 112 | 434 | 13 | 664 | 175 | 19,523 | 46 | 1,768 |
| New York | 19,163 | 4,098 | 26,491 | 1,552 | 10,503 | 30,011 | 1,181,077 | 339 | 44,090 |
| North Carolina | 787 | 894 | 1,890 | 34 | 1,747 | 462 | 59,722 | 183 | 4,970 |
| North Dakota | 59 | 20 | 42 | 0 | 518 | 12 | 17,320 | 36 | 256 |
| Ohio | 1,683 | 2,436 | 814 | 66 | 24,872 | 1,080 | 442,226 | 178 | 6,151 |
| Oklahoma | 610 | 181 | 711 | 18 | 1,810 | 486 | 29,519 | 95 | 2,612 |
| Oregon | 333 | 317 | 346 | 13 | 3,556 | 612 | 48,414 | 292 | 11,369 |
| Pennsylvania | 1,924 | 821 | 1,384 | 77 | 143,008 | 1,442 | 882,348 | 126 | 12,770 |
| Rhode Island | 116 | 44 | 170 | 0 | 182 | 440 | 47,227 | 25 | 94,650 |
| South Carolina | 182 | 140 | 625 | 21 | 797 | 192 | 29,762 | 110 | 2,252 |
| South Dakota | 71 | 24 | 115 | 0 | 773 | 9 | 9,139 | 10 | 422 |
| Tennessee | 470 | 464 | 505 | 0 | 1,160 | 306 | 35,325 | 119 | 2,002 |
| Texas | 8,921 | 2,944 | 5,566 | 240 | 3,808 | 6,135 | 237,557 | 658 | 13,304 |
| Utah | 132 | 105 | 258 | 35 | 329 | 829 | 14,832 | 831 | 1,954 |
| Vermont | 87 | 12 | 30 | 2 | 148 | 49 | 17,475 | 7 | 1,859 |
| Virginia | 5,278 | 2,170 | 3,000 | 218 | 3,033 | 6,105 | 115,121 | 119 | 10,818 |
| Washington | 715 | 451 | 1,054 | 38 | 4,490 | 1,196 | 95,828 | 482 | 13,215 |
| West Virginia | 367 | 76 | 39 | 0 | 988 | 41 | 30,864 | 5 | 487 |
| Wisconsin | 722 | 735 | 266 | 18 | 2,691 | 306 | 505,808 | 37 | 1,769 |
| Wyoming | 129 | 8 | 34 | 0 | 801 | 17 | 9,764 | 4 | 882 |

Ancestry

| Prussian | Puerto Rican | Rom | Romanian | Russian | Ruthenian | Salvadoran | Samoan | Saudi Arabian | Saxon | Scandinavian |
|---|---|---|---|---|---|---|---|---|---|---|
| 167 | 2,659 | 11 | 816 | 5,157 | 0 | 80 | 34 | 33 | 35 | 2,845 |
| 77 | 1,623 | 0 | 549 | 6,032 | 0 | 161 | 533 | 0 | 0 | 4,814 |
| 569 | 6,840 | 112 | 5,714 | 35,508 | 28 | 1,697 | 374 | 143 | 47 | 16,735 |
| 97 | 1,069 | 130 | 427 | 2,595 | 0 | 179 | 36 | 128 | 6 | 2,343 |
| 3,430 | 113,548 | 1,213 | 57,417 | 447,752 | 270 | 300,102 | 26,444 | 517 | 527 | 102,310 |
| 707 | 6,020 | 89 | 3,211 | 36,134 | 19 | 595 | 295 | 224 | 45 | 17,002 |
| 368 | 93,608 | 57 | 6,359 | 79,884 | 65 | 1,018 | 48 | 93 | 48 | 5,029 |
| 18 | 5,246 | 0 | 680 | 6,839 | 16 | 115 | 0 | 11 | 0 | 966 |
| 17 | 1,089 | 0 | 987 | 12,353 | 0 | 8,547 | 8 | 75 | 0 | 736 |
| 1,270 | 174,445 | 306 | 29,675 | 232,298 | 65 | 10,502 | 602 | 324 | 258 | 20,057 |
| 558 | 11,512 | 30 | 3,850 | 29,235 | 57 | 1,783 | 332 | 45 | 56 | 6,978 |
| 126 | 16,432 | 29 | 610 | 5,246 | 16 | 111 | 14,971 | 11 | 30 | 1,748 |
| 162 | 512 | 115 | 470 | 4,155 | 6 | 114 | 130 | 13 | 2 | 10,349 |
| 1,093 | 121,871 | 275 | 23,202 | 144,656 | 120 | 5,951 | 136 | 157 | 68 | 23,446 |
| 455 | 13,164 | 147 | 7,725 | 18,288 | 67 | 156 | 164 | 49 | 147 | 6,528 |
| 273 | 762 | 24 | 917 | 7,669 | 21 | 299 | 25 | 33 | 25 | 13,221 |
| 588 | 2,342 | 34 | 940 | 16,484 | 0 | 306 | 268 | 7 | 12 | 4,700 |
| 157 | 2,692 | 41 | 1,081 | 6,435 | 2 | 96 | 181 | 0 | 91 | 2,696 |
| 297 | 4,089 | 70 | 858 | 7,328 | 5 | 1,118 | 98 | 38 | 22 | 2,774 |
| 77 | 939 | 10 | 421 | 8,122 | 6 | 78 | 23 | 0 | 19 | 2,217 |
| 584 | 13,004 | 114 | 7,672 | 95,964 | 137 | 16,449 | 87 | 84 | 86 | 7,012 |
| 421 | 103,792 | 56 | 7,809 | 133,080 | 29 | 7,835 | 115 | 106 | 44 | 8,804 |
| 1,130 | 13,698 | 145 | 24,832 | 76,121 | 137 | 345 | 148 | 178 | 126 | 16,514 |
| 662 | 2,668 | 99 | 4,903 | 31,945 | 79 | 315 | 72 | 74 | 27 | 91,712 |
| 29 | 880 | 77 | 445 | 1,892 | 7 | 85 | 56 | 40 | 43 | 1,755 |
| 633 | 2,894 | 114 | 3,733 | 27,516 | 7 | 232 | 621 | 75 | 35 | 7,156 |
| 109 | 368 | 20 | 572 | 7,776 | 8 | 34 | 91 | 0 | 31 | 9,971 |
| 183 | 916 | 48 | 900 | 10,136 | 46 | 192 | 87 | 59 | 45 | 5,988 |
| 286 | 3,829 | 53 | 1,745 | 13,241 | 0 | 3,121 | 384 | 0 | 29 | 6,112 |
| 77 | 2,528 | 17 | 937 | 11,066 | 0 | 88 | 0 | 6 | 0 | 2,428 |
| 487 | 219,942 | 284 | 21,177 | 229,449 | 330 | 14,766 | 147 | 46 | 76 | 7,921 |
| 153 | 2,183 | 34 | 713 | 7,912 | 3 | 498 | 100 | 54 | 29 | 4,098 |
| 1,366 | 762,429 | 225 | 66,977 | 596,875 | 277 | 40,992 | 335 | 46 | 76 | 17,092 |
| 373 | 10,161 | 12 | 2,007 | 17,688 | 16 | 863 | 390 | 68 | 77 | 6,678 |
| 53 | 263 | 18 | 339 | 18,544 | 0 | 30 | 16 | 0 | 0 | 11,074 |
| 1,075 | 35,644 | 224 | 25,950 | 81,618 | 417 | 615 | 106 | 75 | 1,147 | 9,046 |
| 364 | 3,444 | 143 | 860 | 7,580 | 15 | 312 | 128 | 83 | 65 | 4,305 |
| 540 | 2,180 | 206 | 4,439 | 28,735 | 0 | 800 | 488 | 152 | 57 | 28,021 |
| 827 | 97,817 | 226 | 17,755 | 215,841 | 1,235 | 925 | 206 | 240 | 378 | 7,499 |
| 48 | 8,366 | 13 | 1,102 | 12,412 | 0 | 826 | 0 | 21 | 0 | 924 |
| 197 | 4,282 | 16 | 936 | 6,483 | 15 | 119 | 108 | 0 | 46 | 3,874 |
| 179 | 259 | 17 | 226 | 7,322 | 0 | 12 | 0 | 41 | 0 | 7,790 |
| 288 | 3,112 | 169 | 1,361 | 10,622 | 19 | 90 | 236 | 57 | 102 | 4,437 |
| 1,388 | 37,517 | 246 | 7,564 | 55,602 | 59 | 53,077 | 748 | 413 | 246 | 22,201 |
| 377 | 1,656 | 0 | 943 | 4,401 | 31 | 629 | 1,854 | 0 | 23 | 34,106 |
| 24 | 437 | 2 | 412 | 5,743 | 3 | 9 | 27 | 5 | 6 | 1,044 |
| 581 | 17,453 | 57 | 4,633 | 42,578 | 92 | 21,170 | 442 | 363 | 129 | 10,366 |
| 1,046 | 6,816 | 275 | 5,124 | 41,395 | 22 | 1,314 | 3,635 | 185 | 107 | 64,179 |
| 49 | 470 | 45 | 749 | 5,022 | 23 | 122 | 12 | 30 | 13 | 958 |
| 1,367 | 15,493 | 31 | 2,651 | 33,289 | 6 | 256 | 52 | 72 | 38 | 24,491 |
| 67 | 360 | 14 | 169 | 2,969 | 0 | 24 | 26 | 12 | 0 | 3,830 |

## Table 2 (Continued)

| State | Ancestry | | | | | | | | |
|---|---|---|---|---|---|---|---|---|---|
| | Scotch-Irish | Scottish | Serbian | Sicilian | Sierra Leonean | Singaporean | Slavic | Slovak | Slovene |
| Alabama | 127,826 | 76,020 | 182 | 297 | 0 | 0 | 162 | 5,022 | 247 |
| Alaska | 12,850 | 16,996 | 274 | 124 | 0 | 0 | 254 | 1,895 | 97 |
| Arizona | 82,552 | 93,835 | 1,772 | 1,157 | 0 | 4 | 1,456 | 21,335 | 1,104 |
| Arkansas | 67,388 | 36,231 | 155 | 142 | 0 | 0 | 146 | 3,752 | 76 |
| California | 546,496 | 646,674 | 10,605 | 8,654 | 275 | 890 | 10,803 | 101,328 | 5,546 |
| Colorado | 95,012 | 100,952 | 1,271 | 763 | 0 | 27 | 2,225 | 24,257 | 3,194 |
| Connecticut | 45,742 | 82,319 | 374 | 991 | 26 | 74 | 1,106 | 49,891 | 864 |
| Delaware | 13,847 | 16,796 | 183 | 101 | 0 | 0 | 193 | 4,697 | 79 |
| District of Columbia | 5,943 | 8,194 | 163 | 29 | 167 | 17 | 73 | 1,378 | 169 |
| Florida | 320,217 | 316,732 | 4,082 | 2,887 | 210 | 35 | 3,136 | 74,335 | 2,733 |
| Georgia | 192,187 | 141,833 | 558 | 538 | 146 | 20 | 755 | 13,110 | 726 |
| Hawaii | 10,628 | 13,784 | 188 | 157 | 0 | 47 | 164 | 2,087 | 73 |
| Idaho | 26,230 | 39,890 | 161 | 127 | 0 | 0 | 207 | 2,582 | 112 |
| Illinois | 173,035 | 176,096 | 15,503 | 2,824 | 17 | 70 | 3,658 | 120,400 | 11,743 |
| Indiana | 113,568 | 111,535 | 8,418 | 716 | 19 | 8 | 1,252 | 44,412 | 1,495 |
| Iowa | 64,500 | 53,694 | 639 | 182 | 0 | 16 | 454 | 10,599 | 397 |
| Kansas | 74,643 | 57,460 | 454 | 102 | 0 | 0 | 479 | 8,085 | 1,085 |
| Kentucky | 89,822 | 65,638 | 333 | 159 | 8 | 5 | 241 | 5,017 | 321 |
| Louisiana | 79,491 | 40,417 | 236 | 874 | 0 | 15 | 364 | 5,133 | 166 |
| Maine | 41,310 | 72,320 | 85 | 219 | 0 | 0 | 195 | 3,518 | 67 |
| Maryland | 89,223 | 108,427 | 1,196 | 849 | 975 | 47 | 1,398 | 33,597 | 1,018 |
| Massachusetts | 108,407 | 199,489 | 595 | 1,908 | 156 | 56 | 957 | 16,321 | 393 |
| Michigan | 157,483 | 252,104 | 7,439 | 2,636 | 53 | 31 | 3,713 | 84,864 | 3,002 |
| Minnesota | 52,423 | 63,996 | 3,292 | 351 | 78 | 16 | 4,169 | 31,190 | 6,614 |
| Mississippi | 88,052 | 35,921 | 115 | 195 | 0 | 0 | 323 | 2,319 | 66 |
| Missouri | 129,228 | 94,211 | 1,285 | 949 | 19 | 0 | 1,084 | 17,261 | 515 |
| Montana | 25,369 | 27,904 | 522 | 139 | 0 | 0 | 556 | 3,907 | 264 |
| Nebraska | 34,701 | 26,278 | 443 | 301 | 0 | 0 | 342 | 9,156 | 190 |
| Nevada | 27,950 | 32,601 | 871 | 740 | 0 | 22 | 475 | 6,311 | 238 |
| New Hampshire | 27,747 | 56,864 | 68 | 386 | 0 | 0 | 131 | 2,671 | 80 |
| New Jersey | 86,869 | 132,882 | 1,718 | 2,284 | 384 | 82 | 4,171 | 117,562 | 972 |
| New Mexico | 33,977 | 29,082 | 307 | 174 | 0 | 0 | 384 | 4,469 | 189 |
| New York | 165,952 | 266,312 | 3,534 | 5,968 | 710 | 315 | 5,969 | 118,045 | 2,619 |
| North Carolina | 343,345 | 177,699 | 639 | 434 | 103 | 57 | 751 | 12,313 | 537 |
| North Dakota | 8,262 | 8,557 | 27 | 46 | 0 | 33 | 85 | 1,557 | 24 |
| Ohio | 217,478 | 224,351 | 15,545 | 3,274 | 150 | 50 | 4,165 | 273,380 | 49,598 |
| Oklahoma | 95,508 | 59,409 | 160 | 142 | 0 | 8 | 298 | 5,781 | 215 |
| Oregon | 95,336 | 110,314 | 466 | 688 | 10 | 34 | 917 | 8,939 | 343 |
| Pennsylvania | 270,299 | 223,544 | 19,913 | 1,936 | 211 | 11 | 8,654 | 447,384 | 14,584 |
| Rhode Island | 13,638 | 24,144 | 7 | 162 | 0 | 0 | 192 | 2,231 | 73 |
| South Carolina | 159,534 | 77,111 | 262 | 210 | 0 | 42 | 382 | 6,926 | 290 |
| South Dakota | 9,980 | 8,472 | 22 | 46 | 0 | 24 | 78 | 1,788 | 22 |
| Tennessee | 197,942 | 100,080 | 354 | 260 | 24 | 38 | 345 | 7,417 | 256 |
| Texas | 495,886 | 306,854 | 2,181 | 1,452 | 416 | 176 | 2,120 | 48,463 | 2,254 |
| Utah | 24,292 | 89,463 | 220 | 151 | 0 | 9 | 532 | 4,167 | 289 |
| Vermont | 12,286 | 30,588 | 55 | 207 | 0 | 0 | 206 | 1,641 | 45 |
| Virginia | 195,722 | 166,959 | 1,563 | 554 | 405 | 34 | 1,446 | 31,604 | 1,125 |
| Washington | 154,566 | 182,690 | 1,195 | 803 | 39 | 22 | 2,592 | 18,892 | 1,132 |
| West Virginia | 54,222 | 34,173 | 1,365 | 151 | 6 | 0 | 255 | 11,267 | 423 |
| Wisconsin | 43,582 | 58,589 | 5,715 | 1,926 | 20 | 77 | 2,597 | 45,769 | 6,478 |
| Wyoming | 15,227 | 17,097 | 85 | 24 | 0 | 7 | 321 | 2,872 | 295 |

| | | | | Ancestry | | | | | | |
|---|---|---|---|---|---|---|---|---|---|---|
| South African | South American | Soviet Union | Spaniard | Spanish | Sri Lankan | Sudanese | Swedish | Swiss | Syrian | Taiwanese |
| 78 | 49 | 2 | 631 | 366 | 26 | 57 | 18,235 | 4,107 | 270 | 1,003 |
| 0 | 0 | 0 | 442 | 4,252 | 14 | 0 | 17,716 | 2,902 | 76 | 193 |
| 265 | 126 | 78 | 6,385 | 44,059 | 171 | 85 | 92,248 | 16,700 | 1,820 | 1,704 |
| 19 | 21 | 0 | 501 | 5,668 | 0 | 0 | 16,168 | 5,280 | 301 | 342 |
| 4,299 | 2,134 | 1,262 | 74,787 | 434,759 | 3,827 | 305 | 587,772 | 140,351 | 15,803 | 79,658 |
| 227 | 126 | 147 | 14,052 | 121,029 | 184 | 40 | 125,097 | 20,288 | 801 | 1,062 |
| 496 | 168 | 107 | 3,599 | 23,222 | 234 | 50 | 79,374 | 10,558 | 1,843 | 1,127 |
| 36 | 27 | 7 | 291 | 2,514 | 92 | 7 | 7,659 | 1,860 | 202 | 444 |
| 129 | 24 | 67 | 529 | 3,628 | 110 | 126 | 3,531 | 1,632 | 116 | 278 |
| 1,379 | 1,031 | 350 | 78,656 | 201,059 | 422 | 47 | 171,780 | 37,877 | 8,225 | 4,509 |
| 700 | 167 | 65 | 2,703 | 21,116 | 73 | 8 | 39,612 | 9,210 | 1,032 | 2,364 |
| 13 | 43 | 0 | 1,332 | 12,998 | 186 | 0 | 10,396 | 1,948 | 152 | 1,632 |
| 43 | 0 | 11 | 767 | 8,159 | 14 | 0 | 52,892 | 12,680 | 145 | 82 |
| 599 | 253 | 322 | 6,845 | 41,586 | 405 | 147 | 374,965 | 47,057 | 3,367 | 7,163 |
| 109 | 19 | 91 | 1,246 | 11,734 | 267 | 9 | 69,619 | 44,511 | 1,773 | 1,168 |
| 35 | 17 | 14 | 367 | 4,211 | 53 | 18 | 120,470 | 18,886 | 660 | 1,025 |
| 18 | 22 | 76 | 1,067 | 10,046 | 152 | 38 | 79,188 | 18,105 | 450 | 1,246 |
| 59 | 14 | 11 | 591 | 5,810 | 57 | 6 | 16,447 | 10,901 | 639 | 356 |
| 58 | 69 | 11 | 4,099 | 65,125 | 129 | 24 | 15,908 | 4,217 | 1,659 | 968 |
| 33 | 7 | 0 | 119 | 2,947 | 24 | 0 | 24,131 | 2,227 | 490 | 48 |
| 568 | 272 | 362 | 3,326 | 22,255 | 844 | 170 | 40,456 | 14,405 | 1,845 | 5,303 |
| 750 | 311 | 513 | 3,812 | 32,495 | 297 | 57 | 143,841 | 10,670 | 7,552 | 4,401 |
| 360 | 195 | 128 | 2,426 | 26,094 | 158 | 82 | 194,063 | 27,146 | 7,656 | 2,892 |
| 119 | 12 | 27 | 584 | 7,584 | 497 | 22 | 536,203 | 25,524 | 1,114 | 1,179 |
| 19 | 84 | 0 | 588 | 8,555 | 35 | 13 | 8,629 | 2,237 | 314 | 297 |
| 88 | 41 | 41 | 1,351 | 13,993 | 136 | 23 | 69,039 | 26,697 | 1,230 | 1,500 |
| 0 | 12 | 0 | 229 | 3,351 | 7 | 0 | 36,784 | 5,754 | 164 | 16 |
| 58 | 5 | 32 | 406 | 4,686 | 55 | 7 | 99,263 | 10,408 | 749 | 378 |
| 8 | 24 | 63 | 2,435 | 20,156 | 99 | 0 | 31,301 | 7,392 | 789 | 605 |
| 25 | 16 | 56 | 247 | 3,051 | 9 | 5 | 25,464 | 2,608 | 628 | 200 |
| 716 | 547 | 469 | 23,666 | 71,596 | 898 | 158 | 72,647 | 25,402 | 11,722 | 11,391 |
| 106 | 20 | 12 | 24,861 | 190,700 | 61 | 0 | 19,999 | 4,281 | 269 | 476 |
| 1,884 | 3,168 | 2,150 | 42,309 | 156,310 | 1,923 | 1,221 | 165,333 | 46,873 | 18,201 | 21,956 |
| 217 | 153 | 28 | 1,620 | 15,957 | 180 | 23 | 35,861 | 10,716 | 1,114 | 2,076 |
| 0 | 0 | 0 | 47 | 1,158 | 0 | 0 | 35,933 | 2,036 | 204 | 127 |
| 630 | 94 | 127 | 2,056 | 26,408 | 341 | 37 | 87,475 | 88,523 | 6,145 | 3,032 |
| 52 | 39 | 9 | 1,329 | 13,880 | 26 | 0 | 32,638 | 7,474 | 732 | 1,010 |
| 116 | 38 | 43 | 1,745 | 18,692 | 211 | 14 | 124,620 | 30,984 | 1,350 | 939 |
| 649 | 303 | 484 | 4,003 | 35,494 | 713 | 241 | 126,255 | 68,919 | 12,591 | 4,625 |
| 14 | 18 | 90 | 301 | 3,679 | 26 | 0 | 22,373 | 1,459 | 2,796 | 300 |
| 149 | 123 | 18 | 817 | 8,497 | 24 | 45 | 18,534 | 5,546 | 637 | 450 |
| 0 | 0 | 0 | 117 | 1,296 | 0 | 0 | 33,421 | 3,431 | 300 | 53 |
| 202 | 29 | 20 | 939 | 9,242 | 54 | 0 | 27,552 | 10,252 | 700 | 1,266 |
| 1,786 | 375 | 119 | 31,226 | 186,758 | 649 | 92 | 155,193 | 32,304 | 5,322 | 13,080 |
| 93 | 103 | 8 | 2,804 | 21,075 | 33 | 17 | 103,715 | 31,737 | 315 | 567 |
| 3 | 9 | 26 | 125 | 2,525 | 0 | 0 | 10,113 | 1,902 | 173 | 93 |
| 437 | 316 | 146 | 3,600 | 30,357 | 405 | 307 | 56,040 | 19,451 | 2,248 | 3,527 |
| 236 | 174 | 112 | 3,488 | 33,319 | 124 | 49 | 257,953 | 36,795 | 1,189 | 3,541 |
| 10 | 24 | 6 | 292 | 4,921 | 41 | 0 | 6,856 | 3,956 | 806 | 292 |
| 102 | 32 | 19 | 648 | 9,265 | 156 | 65 | 159,216 | 65,915 | 878 | 985 |
| 0 | 13 | 0 | 529 | 7,367 | 6 | 8 | 20,885 | 3,401 | 49 | 44 |

**Table 2** *(Continued)*

| State | Thai | Tirol | Tongan | Trinidadian and Tobagonian | Turkish | U.S. Virgin Islander | Ugandan | Ukrainian | United States |
|---|---|---|---|---|---|---|---|---|---|
| Alabama | 674 | 15 | 0 | 225 | 592 | 28 | 13 | 1,585 | 18,179 |
| Alaska | 432 | 0 | 121 | 41 | 66 | 0 | 0 | 962 | 615 |
| Arizona | 1,800 | 14 | 244 | 250 | 772 | 67 | 0 | 8,471 | 5,177 |
| Arkansas | 368 | 0 | 2 | 24 | 166 | 0 | 8 | 870 | 8,582 |
| California | 33,654 | 138 | 7,056 | 3,100 | 12,929 | 517 | 436 | 56,211 | 48,851 |
| Colorado | 1,645 | 78 | 0 | 58 | 792 | 71 | 45 | 6,984 | 4,410 |
| Connecticut | 710 | 64 | 0 | 899 | 1,329 | 63 | 20 | 23,711 | 5,598 |
| Delaware | 270 | 161 | 0 | 158 | 327 | 9 | 17 | 4,950 | 1,373 |
| District of Columbia | 335 | 0 | 0 | 1,012 | 309 | 131 | 26 | 1,082 | 999 |
| Florida | 6,295 | 93 | 136 | 7,500 | 5,809 | 1,353 | 41 | 33,792 | 45,577 |
| Georgia | 2,224 | 28 | 0 | 616 | 1,478 | 213 | 143 | 4,967 | 31,997 |
| Hawaii | 1,753 | 22 | 3,283 | 63 | 229 | 6 | 8 | 1,234 | 553 |
| Idaho | 279 | 8 | 78 | 43 | 103 | 0 | 0 | 906 | 1,419 |
| Illinois | 5,963 | 26 | 9 | 444 | 2,778 | 53 | 137 | 38,414 | 16,966 |
| Indiana | 1,056 | 28 | 26 | 157 | 842 | 63 | 30 | 6,379 | 21,625 |
| Iowa | 1,305 | 0 | 33 | 31 | 301 | 2 | 31 | 1,356 | 4,396 |
| Kansas | 1,073 | 4 | 43 | 71 | 205 | 0 | 69 | 2,075 | 6,242 |
| Kentucky | 625 | 9 | 10 | 111 | 290 | 25 | 10 | 1,582 | 23,512 |
| Louisiana | 1,032 | 0 | 0 | 349 | 449 | 110 | 0 | 1,391 | 7,871 |
| Maine | 221 | 11 | 2 | 40 | 152 | 0 | 0 | 1,328 | 2,677 |
| Maryland | 3,202 | 153 | 0 | 4,493 | 2,366 | 277 | 317 | 15,872 | 11,126 |
| Massachusetts | 1,996 | 55 | 23 | 2,590 | 2,336 | 281 | 211 | 17,500 | 10,519 |
| Michigan | 1,803 | 79 | 8 | 294 | 1,776 | 38 | 46 | 43,914 | 15,615 |
| Minnesota | 883 | 60 | 39 | 63 | 597 | 75 | 99 | 10,691 | 2,884 |
| Mississippi | 283 | 0 | 0 | 24 | 206 | 0 | 0 | 480 | 11,006 |
| Missouri | 1,433 | 23 | 56 | 54 | 632 | 27 | 0 | 4,766 | 12,952 |
| Montana | 126 | 0 | 0 | 0 | 52 | 0 | 14 | 1,478 | 1,458 |
| Nebraska | 525 | 0 | 0 | 8 | 218 | 4 | 0 | 1,161 | 1,323 |
| Nevada | 2,408 | 8 | 177 | 73 | 404 | 0 | 0 | 2,434 | 1,799 |
| New Hampshire | 285 | 0 | 0 | 53 | 379 | 9 | 0 | 2,434 | 1,985 |
| New Jersey | 2,284 | 287 | 4 | 4,245 | 7,579 | 338 | 0 | 73,935 | 13,853 |
| New Mexico | 655 | 1 | 18 | 16 | 336 | 0 | 9 | 1,512 | 3,771 |
| New York | 6,991 | 385 | 25 | 42,973 | 19,325 | 2,743 | 231 | 121,113 | 41,497 |
| North Carolina | 1,982 | 9 | 0 | 391 | 1,046 | 71 | 64 | 4,897 | 34,210 |
| North Dakota | 159 | 0 | 0 | 0 | 80 | 0 | 0 | 3,634 | 325 |
| Ohio | 1,965 | 141 | 14 | 469 | 2,147 | 65 | 133 | 43,569 | 27,685 |
| Oklahoma | 1,087 | 0 | 7 | 179 | 459 | 30 | 0 | 1,969 | 8,559 |
| Oregon | 1,144 | 0 | 181 | 4 | 673 | 17 | 23 | 6,220 | 4,895 |
| Pennsylvania | 1,889 | 3,496 | 55 | 1,509 | 2,430 | 106 | 48 | 129,753 | 22,295 |
| Rhode Island | 348 | 15 | 0 | 147 | 399 | 6 | 5 | 3,530 | 1,824 |
| South Carolina | 965 | 8 | 0 | 189 | 828 | 47 | 112 | 2,266 | 15,882 |
| South Dakota | 138 | 7 | 8 | 10 | 70 | 0 | 0 | 391 | 336 |
| Tennessee | 784 | 8 | 0 | 189 | 529 | 49 | 0 | 2,063 | 27,690 |
| Texas | 7,930 | 35 | 512 | 2,018 | 3,273 | 429 | 138 | 13,094 | 58,877 |
| Utah | 831 | 58 | 3,630 | 6 | 317 | 0 | 8 | 1,062 | 3,207 |
| Vermont | 49 | 0 | 13 | 17 | 74 | 0 | 0 | 978 | 945 |
| Virginia | 3,997 | 100 | 9 | 737 | 2,673 | 216 | 109 | 12,321 | 27,923 |
| Washington | 3,269 | 18 | 184 | 168 | 1,683 | 49 | 46 | 10,814 | 9,629 |
| West Virginia | 343 | 0 | 0 | 0 | 368 | 0 | 5 | 1,514 | 8,304 |
| Wisconsin | 539 | 58 | 13 | 159 | 649 | 33 | 29 | 6,783 | 3,933 |
| Wyoming | 110 | 45 | 0 | 0 | 28 | 0 | 0 | 405 | 625 |

Ancestry

| Uruguayan | Venezuelan | Vietnamese | Welsh | West German | West Indian | Western European | White | Windish | Yemeni | Yugoslavian |
|---|---|---|---|---|---|---|---|---|---|---|
| 16 | 221 | 2,136 | 18,809 | 50 | 692 | 524 | 60,705 | 0 | 0 | 656 |
| 0 | 20 | 429 | 5,774 | 0 | 140 | 187 | 7,445 | 0 | 0 | 1,374 |
| 70 | 363 | 4,511 | 38,340 | 35 | 649 | 419 | 37,431 | 0 | 18 | 4,869 |
| 0 | 63 | 1,788 | 12,436 | 20 | 211 | 401 | 37,817 | 0 | 0 | 450 |
| 1,837 | 4,575 | 242,946 | 238,134 | 514 | 9,136 | 8,666 | 267,505 | 55 | 525 | 53,442 |
| 75 | 391 | 6,679 | 41,520 | 58 | 409 | 1,167 | 27,241 | 0 | 0 | 4,840 |
| 216 | 599 | 3,671 | 19,018 | 98 | 3,842 | 399 | 11,125 | 9 | 0 | 2,786 |
| 0 | 18 | 475 | 9,759 | 19 | 289 | 114 | 2,910 | 3 | 0 | 364 |
| 80 | 104 | 663 | 2,477 | 14 | 1,164 | 86 | 2,258 | 0 | 16 | 386 |
| 2,039 | 12,362 | 14,586 | 103,115 | 360 | 13,350 | 1,327 | 62,393 | 16 | 152 | 9,462 |
| 254 | 697 | 6,864 | 37,811 | 53 | 2,064 | 1,255 | 82,402 | 16 | 8 | 1,317 |
| 15 | 45 | 5,277 | 4,596 | 0 | 268 | 168 | 13,442 | 6 | 13 | 678 |
| 0 | 4 | 572 | 20,746 | 38 | 53 | 387 | 9,138 | 0 | 0 | 1,137 |
| 183 | 654 | 8,550 | 63,144 | 174 | 2,093 | 1,330 | 29,455 | 13 | 25 | 19,145 |
| 15 | 191 | 2,420 | 42,004 | 116 | 494 | 735 | 32,446 | 0 | 0 | 4,214 |
| 29 | 21 | 2,128 | 29,060 | 35 | 75 | 680 | 9,644 | 8 | 0 | 1,047 |
| 10 | 285 | 6,001 | 27,031 | 16 | 326 | 632 | 17,117 | 0 | 0 | 1,425 |
| 5 | 65 | 1,340 | 21,128 | 74 | 315 | 339 | 42,777 | 0 | 0 | 860 |
| 0 | 481 | 14,696 | 12,408 | 0 | 829 | 283 | 34,343 | 0 | 0 | 1,818 |
| 5 | 45 | 809 | 10,124 | 21 | 156 | 147 | 7,603 | 0 | 0 | 339 |
| 316 | 1,257 | 7,809 | 47,236 | 156 | 5,424 | 921 | 18,457 | 18 | 156 | 2,505 |
| 525 | 1,403 | 13,101 | 26,621 | 27 | 7,271 | 907 | 18,700 | 0 | 23 | 2,390 |
| 87 | 589 | 5,229 | 55,588 | 108 | 1,357 | 1,206 | 38,556 | 0 | 840 | 15,878 |
| 151 | 119 | 8,698 | 22,753 | 18 | 498 | 561 | 8,890 | 0 | 35 | 7,765 |
| 0 | 142 | 3,340 | 8,611 | 12 | 274 | 211 | 44,108 | 0 | 0 | 952 |
| 49 | 215 | 3,652 | 40,516 | 109 | 394 | 879 | 34,484 | 6 | 40 | 2,668 |
| 0 | 66 | 239 | 9,704 | 24 | 10 | 174 | 3,669 | 11 | 0 | 3,355 |
| 9 | 46 | 1,242 | 11,998 | 30 | 117 | 195 | 3,766 | 0 | 0 | 483 |
| 36 | 150 | 1,978 | 14,266 | 12 | 238 | 328 | 9,093 | 20 | 0 | 2,483 |
| 142 | 62 | 281 | 7,868 | 13 | 147 | 284 | 7,417 | 0 | 0 | 359 |
| 3,297 | 2,130 | 5,480 | 47,015 | 238 | 8,935 | 759 | 11,325 | 29 | 141 | 12,682 |
| 5 | 95 | 1,374 | 11,275 | 28 | 179 | 251 | 29,880 | 0 | 9 | 903 |
| 3,742 | 5,559 | 12,116 | 103,679 | 322 | 80,075 | 1,693 | 33,624 | 31 | 1,564 | 30,455 |
| 58 | 430 | 4,406 | 36,229 | 92 | 1,634 | 1,103 | 76,652 | 7 | 0 | 1,315 |
| 0 | 6 | 256 | 1,697 | 0 | 18 | 55 | 661 | 0 | 0 | 272 |
| 13 | 416 | 4,121 | 165,494 | 99 | 1,499 | 1,092 | 45,819 | 17 | 42 | 13,172 |
| 38 | 233 | 6,248 | 21,894 | 77 | 414 | 204 | 53,971 | 9 | 0 | 652 |
| 16 | 148 | 8,130 | 40,781 | 29 | 357 | 1,361 | 27,747 | 0 | 34 | 4,968 |
| 85 | 658 | 14,126 | 221,964 | 206 | 3,427 | 1,104 | 23,122 | 2,827 | 77 | 10,446 |
| 32 | 162 | 587 | 3,253 | 9 | 332 | 37 | 3,308 | 0 | 15 | 251 |
| 22 | 146 | 1,379 | 17,190 | 41 | 752 | 337 | 40,027 | 7 | 7 | 769 |
| 0 | 0 | 389 | 4,034 | 0 | 16 | 26 | 1,685 | 0 | 9 | 360 |
| 28 | 244 | 1,921 | 28,745 | 38 | 594 | 627 | 66,823 | 0 | 46 | 694 |
| 629 | 3,295 | 60,649 | 95,447 | 202 | 4,513 | 3,435 | 249,937 | 66 | 73 | 4,943 |
| 97 | 147 | 2,540 | 48,070 | 27 | 86 | 629 | 15,055 | 0 | 7 | 3,095 |
| 0 | 28 | 177 | 7,081 | 8 | 63 | 196 | 4,809 | 0 | 0 | 233 |
| 315 | 912 | 20,271 | 54,891 | 89 | 2,787 | 1,343 | 56,228 | 6 | 90 | 2,523 |
| 67 | 281 | 17,004 | 69,094 | 115 | 877 | 2,271 | 50,460 | 9 | 32 | 12,726 |
| 6 | 26 | 133 | 16,896 | 4 | 67 | 214 | 14,295 | 0 | 14 | 887 |
| 27 | 143 | 2,324 | 29,895 | 50 | 245 | 595 | 8,118 | 0 | 0 | 6,177 |
| 0 | 19 | 84 | 6,674 | 7 | 12 | 165 | 3,828 | 0 | 0 | 1,024 |

# HOLIDAYS

The following selective account of holidays and festivals celebrated around the world provides a sampling of events that were of significance to individuals in their countries of origin and might still be observed after immigration to the United States. The degree to which a given holiday is celebrated after immigration varies according to the importance of the person being honored or the event being commemorated. In general, these world holidays fall into two major categories: national and religious.

National holidays are generally intended to encourage patriotism in the citizenry. They honor the heroic figures of a given nation's past and mark pivotal events in its history. These national holidays frequently are tied to a country's struggle for independence, with the declarations, battles, and prominent military leaders given special attention. In addition, individuals who have made meaningful contributions to the cultural fabric of a nation are often honored.

Religious observations have long been a part of the lives of people around the world. They have provided opportunities to fight evil spirits and welcome the assistance of the compassionate ones. Religious festivals have provided the opportunity to mark the changing seasons and celebrate bountiful harvests and continued good health. Religious holidays have also served as times for honoring the accomplishments of prominent individuals of given religions and for commemorating significant religious events.

Celebration of these world holidays after immigration to the United States is complicated by the fact that different nations and religions use different calendars to divide up the solar year (365.242199 days) into meaningful periods. These calendars fall into three main types: lunar, solar, and lunisolar.

A lunar calendar is based on the length of the lunar month (29.5 days, the time from one new moon to the next) and disregards the length of the solar year. The Islamic calendar, which is a lunar calendar, contains the following twelve lunar months (some with 29 days and some with 30 days, supplying an average of 29.5 days):

Muharram (the sacred month)
Safar (the month that is void)
Rabi I (the first spring)
Rabi II (the second spring)
Jumada I (the first month of dryness)
Jumada II (the second month of dryness)
Rajab (the revered month)
Shaban (the month of division)
Ramadan (the month of great heat)
Shawwal (the month of hunting)
Dhu al-Qadah (the month of rest)
Dhu al-Hijja (the month of pilgrimage).

These twelve months, however, provide a lunar year of only 354.367056 days. Because the lunar year is 10.875143 days shorter than the solar year, the months regress (move backward) each solar year, causing the seasons to occur at earlier and earlier dates. In fact, any given month of the Islamic calendar will have regressed through an entire solar year in 33.585 solar years. Another complicating factor is that the decimal value of the length of a lunar year (which amounts to about 11.012 days in 30 lunar years) is unaccounted for in the Islamic calendar. Instead, 11 days are intercalated (inserted) once every thirty years to restore the accuracy with respect to the moon.

A solar calendar ignores the lunar cycle and adheres to the set length of the solar year, with this period divided into twelve set months. There are four critical periods in the solar cycle: two equinoxes and two solstices. The accuracy of a solar calendar can be judged based on the accuracy with which these four events occur on the same days each year. The two most relevant solar calendars are the Julian calendar and the Gregorian calendar. The Julian calendar was the result of an order by Julius Caesar to convert from the Roman lunar calendar to a solar calendar in 46 B.C.E. This conversion involved an intercalation of 90 days (23 days after February, and two months of 34 and 33 days added between November and December) to correct for a discrepancy that had been growing between the seasons and the calendar periods in which they had traditionally fallen. The intercalation meant that 46 B.C.E. had a total of 445 days, but thereafter, Caesar ordered that the normal length of the year would be 365 days, with one day added to February every four years to adjust for the true length of the solar year. However, this meant that a solar year would be calculated as 365.25 days, which exceeds the true solar year of 365.242199 days by 11 minutes and 14 seconds. This might seem to be a small discrepancy, but over time the calendar once again began to fall out of synchronization with the seasons. To correct for this discrepancy, Pope Gregory XIII instituted two alterations to the Julian calendar: (1) 10 days were dropped from the calendar of 1582, so the day after October 4 became October 15, a change that restored the vernal equinox date to March 21, and (2) century years were changed to common years (rather than leap years), unless the century year was divisible by 400. These modifications of the Julian calendar to create the Gregorian calendar restored the synchronization between the months and the seasons. Although the Gregorian calendar has become the most widely used of the two solar calendars, the Julian calendar is still used by Orthodox Christian churches.

A lunisolar calendar is generally a compromise between following a lunar calendar and the need to synchronize dates and the seasons. This type of calendar traditionally follows the lunar cycle but intercalates an additional month as necessary to maintain synchronization. Two examples of lunisolar calendars are the Jewish calendar and the Hindu calendar. The Jewish calendar contains the following twelve calendar months, which alternate between 30 and 29 days in length:

Tishri (September–October)
Heshvan (October–November)
Kislev (November–December)
Tevet (December–January)
Shevat (January–February)
Adar (February–March)
Nisan (March–April)
Iyyar (April–May)
Sivan (May–June)
Tammuz (June–July)
Av (July–August)
Elul (August–September).

A thirteenth month is intercalated into the Jewish calendar in the third, sixth, eighth, eleventh, fourteenth, seventeenth, and nineteenth years of a nineteen-year cycle. The standard months of the Hindu lunisolar calendar are as follows:

Asvina (September–October)
Karttika (October–November)
Margasirsa (November–December)
Pausa (December–January)
Magha (January–February)
Phalguna (February–March)
Caitra (March–April)
Vaisakha (April–May)
Jyaistha (May–June)
Asadha (June–July)
Sravana (July–August)
Bhadrapada (August–September).

A thirteenth month is intercalated in the Hindu calendar every sixty months.

## National Holidays

January 1
Haiti Independence Day: Honors Jean-Jacques Dessalines's 1804 proclamation of independence.
Independence Day for Western Samoa: Honors the 1962 declaration of independence from New Zealand.

Liberation Day in Cuba: Celebrates the end of Spanish rule in 1899.

New Year's Day: Marks the first day of the year according to the Gregorian calendar.

Taiwan Foundation Day: Commemorates the founding of the Republic of China in 1912.

January 2

Berchtoldstag: Observed in Switzerland in honor of the twelfth-century Duke Berchtold V, who founded the city of Bern.

Granada Day in Spain: Commemorates the recapture of Granada from the Moors in 1492.

January 4

Burma Independence Day: Commemorates the 1948 establishment of Burma as a free nation.

January 11

Albanian Republic Day: Commemorates the 1946 establishment of the republic.

Hostos Day: Marks the anniversary of the 1839 birth of Eugenio Maria de Hostos, a Puerto Rican philosopher and patriot.

January 22

Ukrainian Day: Marks the 1918 proclamation of the free Ukrainian Republic.

January 25

Burns Day: Commemorates the 1759 birth of Robert Burns, the national poet of Scotland.

January 26

Duarte Day: A holiday in the Dominican Republic honoring Juan Pablo Duarte, a founder of the republic and a leader in its fight for liberation from Haiti.

India's Republic Day (Basant Panchmi): Commemorates the proclamation of the republic in 1950.

January (movable)

Sankranti: Harvest Festival commemorated in several states of southern India.

January (movable; third Monday)

Martin Luther King Jr. Day: Celebrates the 1929 birth of the civil rights leader who was assassinated in 1968.

January–February (movable)

Lunar New Year: The celebrations throughout Asia of the Lunar New Year vary from country to country, but they all include offerings to household gods, house-cleaning and new clothes, large banquets, and ancestor worship. The Chinese festival, known as Chun Chieh (Spring Festival), is characterized by bright colors and loud noises to scare away evil spirits. The Vietnamese celebration, which is the most important festival of the year, is known as Tet (an abbreviation of Tet Nguyen Dan, "first day") and is marked by paying homage to ancestors, wiping out debts, and enjoying family reunions. The Korean New Year, known as Je-sok, is brought in with the lighting of torches and a night-long vigil to guard against evil spirits.

February 4

Sri Lanka Independence Day: Celebrates the 1948 granting of independence of the former British colony, which changed its name from Ceylon to Sri Lanka in 1972.

February 5

Mexican Constitution Day: Honors the anniversaries of the constitutions of 1857 and 1917.

Runeberg's Day: Commemorates the 1804 birth of Johan Ludvig Runeberg, Finland's leading poet.

February 7

Grenada Independence Day: Honors the attainment of complete independence in 1974.

February 11

Japanese National Foundation Day: Celebrates the founding of the nation of Japan in 660 B.C.E. by the first emperor.

February 12

Burma Union Day: Commemorates the 1947 conference leading to the formation of the Union of Burma.

February 14

Fjortende Februar (Fourteenth of February): Traditional day for the exchange of tokens and gifts among schoolchildren in Denmark.

February 21

Shaheel Day: Observed in Bangladesh as the national day of mourning.

February 23

Guyana Republic Day: Commemorates the 1970 establishment of Guyana as a sovereign democratic state in South America and within the British Commonwealth.

**February 24**

Estonia National Day: Honors the 1920 peace treaty that confirmed Estonian independence.

**February 25**

Fiesta sa EDSA (People Power Anniversary): Commemorates the bloodless People Power Revolution that toppled the Marcos regime in the Philippines in 1986.

**February 27**

Independence Day in the Dominican Republic: Honors the independence obtained with the 1844 withdrawal of the Haitians.

**February (movable; third Monday)**

Presidents' Day: Jointly honors the birthdays of George Washington and Abraham Lincoln but is generally considered to be a day to honor all former presidents of the United States.

**February–March (movable)**

Prajatantradivasa: Celebrated on the seventh day of the month of Phalguna (according to the Hindu calendar) to commemorate the victory of the Nepalese people over the Panchayat and Rana autocratic regimes in Nepal.

**March 1**

Independence Day in South Korea: Celebrates the anniversary of demonstrations in 1919 protesting Japanese occupation, although independence did not occur until the Japanese surrender in 1945 at the end of World War II.

Pinzón Day: Marks the return of Martín Pinzón to Spain, bringing the news of the discovery of the New World.

**March 3**

Bulgaria Liberation Day: Marks the anniversary of Bulgaria's release from Ottoman domination by the 1878 Treaty of San Stefano.

**March 6**

Discovery Day in Guam: Commemorates the 1521 discovery of Guam by Ferdinand Magellan.

Ghana Independence Day: Commemorates the establishment of the former British Crown Colony of the Gold Coast as a sovereign nation in 1957.

**March 8**

Syrian Revolution Day: Marks the anniversary of the 1963 assumption of political power by the National Council of Revolution.

**March 9**

Amerigo Vespucci Day: Honors the fifteenth-century Italian navigator for whom the Americas were named.

Taras Shevchenko Day: Marks the anniversary of the 1814 birth of the foremost Ukrainian poet of the nineteenth century.

**March 13**

National Day in Grenada: Commemorates the bloodless revolution of 1979, which was led by the Joint Endeavor for Welfare, Education, and Liberation (JEWEL).

**March 20**

Lajos Kossuth Day: Marks the anniversary of the 1894 death of Lajos Kossuth, the symbol of Hungarian nationalism.

**March 21**

Juárez Day: Commemorates the 1806 birth of Benito Pablo Juárez, the first Mexican president of Amerindian descent.

Now Ruz: The first day of this thirteen-day celebration of the Iranian New Year begins at the vernal equinox, which coincides with the first day of spring.

**March 23**

Pakistan Republic Day: Commemorates the establishment of Pakistan in 1956.

**March 25**

Greek Independence Day: Honors the day in 1821 when the Greek flag was first raised against Ottoman domination.

**March 26**

Bangladesh Independence Day: Marks the anniversary of the 1971 proclamation establishing Bangladesh.

**March 27**

Resistance Day: Honors the movement of guerrilla forces in Burma to oppose invaders during World War II.

**March 30**

Land Day: Observed by Palestinians since 1976 to commemorate the confiscation of Palestinian land by Israeli authorities.

**March (movable; second Sunday)**

Commonwealth Day: Honors the British Empire and was formerly known as Empire Day and British Commonwealth Day.

March–April (movable)

Ugadi: Marks the Telugu New Year's Day.

April 4

Liberation Day in Hungary: Commemorates the defeat of the Germans in 1945 and their departure from Hungary.

April 6

Chakri Day: Commemorates the enthronement of Rama I, who founded the Chakri Dynasty in Thailand in 1782.

April 14

Pan-American Day: Commemorates the 1890 founding of the Organization of American States, which includes Argentina, Bolivia, Brazil, Chile, Colombia, Costa Rica, Cuba, The Dominican Republic, Ecuador, El Salvador, Guatemala, Haiti, Honduras, Mexico, Nicaragua, Panama, Paraguay, Peru, The United States, Uruguay, and Venezuela.

April 16

De Diego Day: Marks the anniversary of the 1867 birth of Puerto Rican patriot José de Diego.

April 17

Evacuation Day in Syria: Commemorates the withdrawal of French troops from Syria in 1946.

Flag Day in American Samoa: Commemorates the 1900 signing the Instrument of Cession by the seven high chiefs at the invitation of President Theodore Roosevelt and the establishment of the Samoan constitutional government in 1960.

April 21

Tiradentes Day in Brazil: Commemorates the execution of the dentist José da Silva Xavier, a conspirator in the 1789 revolt against the Portuguese.

April 24

Armenian Martyrs' Day: Memorializes the Armenian victims of the killings in Turkey in 1915–1916.

April 25

Italian Liberation Day: Celebrated to commemorate the Allied victory in World War II.

Liberation Day in Portugal: Marks the anniversary of the 1974 coup that led to the downfall of the Salazar-Caetano dictatorship that had lasted for forty-two years.

April 30

Walpurgis Night: Observed since ancient times in Germany, Finland, and the Scandinavian countries to ward off witches, warlocks, and demons.

April (movable)

Festival of the Tombs: Observed on the third day of the third moon as a day for the Chinese to honor their dead.

April (movable; first Thursday)

Glarus Festival: Swiss commemoration of the 1388 defeat of the Austrians by the men of Glarus, Switzerland.

April–May (movable)

Naya Varsha: Observed on the first day of the month of Vaisakha (according to the Hindu calendar) as the Nepalese New Year.

May 1

International Labor Day: Day set aside by many countries to honor workers.

May Day: The traditional day of flower festivals.

May 3

Japanese Constitution Day: Celebrates the 1947 establishment of a democratic form of government under parliamentary rule.

Polish Constitution Day: Commemorates the Polish constitution of 1791.

May 5

Cinco de Mayo: Mexican holiday celebrating the defeat of the French at the Battle of Puebla in 1867.

Dutch Liberation Day: Commemorates the expulsion of German forces from Holland by the Allies in 1945.

May 6

Dukhnovych Day: Commemorates the 1803 birth of Aleksander Dukhnovych, the "National Awakener of the Carpatho-Rusyns."

May 8

French Liberation Day: Commemorates the expulsion of German forces from France at the end of World War II.

May 9

Carpatho-Rusyn National Day: Commemorates the day in 1919 when Rusyns living south of the Carpathians voluntarily united with

Czechoslovakia to form their own autonomous province of Subcarpathian Rus.

May 12

Snellman Day: Finnish observation of the anniversary of the birth of J. V. Snellman, journalist, statesman, and leader of the Nationalist movement.

May 17

Constitution Day in Norway: Marks the adoption of the constitution in 1814 and the gaining of independence from Sweden by Norway in 1905.

May 18

Haitian Flag Day: Honors the flag that bears the country's national arms.

May 19

Flag Day of the Army: Honors those who died to preserve Finland's freedom.

Youth and Sports Day: Turkish holiday commemorating the day Mustafa Kemal Atatürk landed in Samsun and began his national movement for independence.

May 20

Botev Day: Marks the anniversary of the death of Khristo Botev, Bulgarian poet and hero in the revolutionary movement against the Turks.

May 21

Chilean Navy Day: Commemorates the Battle of Iquique in 1879.

The Anasternarides Feast: Macedonian celebration in accordance with classic traditions.

May 22

Haitian National Day: Observed as a day to celebrate Haitian culture.

Sri Lanka Republic Day (Heroes' Day): Honors the ratification of the constitution in 1972.

May 24

Bulgarian Day of Slavonic Letters (Culture Day): Pays tribute to Bulgarian culture, education, and communications.

Independence Battle Day: Commemorates the Battle of Pinchincha, which liberated Ecuador from Spanish rule in 1822.

May 25

Argentine National Day: Marks the anniversary of the beginning of the 1810 revolution in Argentina.

Jordan Independence Day: Honors the 1946 treaty that gave Jordan autonomy and set up a monarchy.

May 26

Guyana Independence Day: Commemorates the agreement that gave independence to the former British colony in 1966.

Independence Day in Georgia: Marks the declaration of independence of the first Georgian Republic, which lasted from 1918 to 1921.

May 28

Armenian Independence Day: Commemorates the founding of the First Republic in 1918.

May 30

Croatian Independence Day: Marks the 1991 declaration of independence.

May (movable; Monday preceding May 25)

Victoria Day: Canadian celebration honoring the birth of Queen Victoria.

May (movable; last Monday)

Memorial Day: Honors all U.S. citizens who have died in war, although the observance was originally known as Decoration Day and was created to honor Union soldiers who died in the U.S. Civil War.

May–June (movable)

Dragon Boat Festival: Celebrated on the fifth day of the fifth moon with the sending out of boats in a reenactment of the search for the body of Chu'u Yuan (328–298 B.C.E.), a Chinese poet and statesman of the Chou Dynasty who drowned himself in Tungting Lake to protest the corruption and injustice of Prince Huai's court.

June 2

Italian Republic Day: Commemorates the proclamation of the republic established by referendum in 1946, in which a majority vote was cast for the republic as opposed to the retention of the monarchy.

Seaman's Day: Honors the sailors and fishermen of Iceland, who represent the lifeline of the country's economy.

June 4

Flag Day of the Finnish Armed Forces: Commemorates the 1867 birth of Marshall Carl

Gustaf Mannerheim, Finland's great military leader.

**June 5**

Denmark Constitution Day: Honors the 1849 constitution and the new constitution signed in 1953.

**June 6**

Constitution and Flag Day in Sweden: Recognizes the adoption of the Swedish constitution in 1809 and the ascension of Gustavus I to the throne in 1523.

**June 10**

Portugal National Day: Commemorates the 1580 death of the Portuguese poet Luíz Vaz de Camoëns.

**June 11**

King Kamehameha Day: Commemorates the victories of Kamehameha I, who unified the Hawaiian islands in the eighteenth century.

**June 12**

Helsinki Day: Commemorates the founding of the city of Helsinki, Finland, in 1550.

Philippine Independence Day: Commemorates the 1898 declaration of independence from Spain.

**June 15**

Flag Day in Denmark: Honors the first appearance of the Danish flag in 1219, when, according to legend, a red banner with a white cross floated down from the sky during a battle to conquer Estonians and convert them to Christianity; a voice from the clouds promised that the Danes would win if they raised the banner before their enemies.

Magna Charta Day: Marks the anniversary of King John's signing in 1215 of the "great charter," the foundation of England's constitutional monarchy.

**June 17**

Iceland Independence Day: Commemorates the reestablishment of an independent republic in 1944.

Okinawa Day: Marks the anniversary of the 1971 treaty between the United States and Japan that returned Okinawa, which had been seized by the United States during World War II, to Japan.

**June 18**

Evacuation Day in Egypt: Marks the anniversary of the 1956 departure of the last British troops from the Suez Canal bases.

Waterloo Day: Marks Napoleon's 1815 defeat at the Battle of Waterloo.

**June 20**

Argentina Flag Day: Honors the history of the country's flag, which dates back to 1812.

**June 24**

Bannockburn Day in Scotland: Commemorates Robert Bruce's winning of independence for Scotland in 1314 by expelling the English.

Battle of Carabobo Day: Commemorates the battle fought at Carabobo (west of Caracas) in 1821, a battle that assured Venezuela's independence.

Day of the Indian: Celebrated in Peru and other Latin American countries to honor and preserve native customs, music, folklore, and poetry.

San Juan Day: Puerto Rican holiday commemorating the Battle of San Juan, which ended in victory for the Americans over the Spanish. The island was ceded to the United States at the end of the Spanish-American War.

**June 26**

United Nations Charter Day: Commemorates the signing of the charter in five official languages, Chinese, English, French, Russian, and Spanish, in 1945.

**June 30**

Guatemala Army Day: Commemorates the 1871 Guatemalan revolution for agrarian reform.

**July 1**

Canada Day (Dominion Day): Commemorates the confederation of the provinces of Canada into the Dominion of Canada under the terms of the British North America Act of 1867.

Ghana First Republic Day: Commemorates the 1960 change from dominion status to that of a republic in the British Commonwealth.

**July 2**

Bahia Independence Day: Commemorates the consolidation of Brazilian independence in the state of Bahia with the 1823 defeat of Portuguese troops.

July 4

Caricom Day: Celebrates the Caribbean Community and Common Market, which was founded in 1973 to promote cooperation among the Caribbean states.

Garibaldi Day in Italy: Commemorates the 1807 birthday of Giuseppi Garibaldi, an important figure in the nineteenth-century unification of Italy.

Independence Day in the United States: Celebrates the signing of the Declaration of Independence in 1776.

July 5

Independence Day in Cape Verde: Commemorates the country's 1975 independence from Portugal's colonial rule.

Independence Day in Venezuela: Commemorates the 1811 declaration of independence from Spanish rule.

July 7

The Fiesta de San Fermin: Includes the famous running of the bulls in Pamplona, Spain.

July 9

Independence Day in Argentina: Marks the 1816 declaration of independence from Spain.

July 12

Orangeman's Day (Battle of the Boyne Day): Dedicated to the anniversary of the 1690 Battle of the Boyne; a statutory public holiday in Northern Ireland.

July 13

Night Watch (La Retraite aux Flambeaux): French holiday celebrating the eve of the fall of the Bastille.

July 14

Bastille Day (Fête Nationale): French holiday commemorating the storming of the Bastille in 1789 and the release of political prisoners.

Iraq 1958 Revolution Day: Commemorates the revolution ending Hashemite rule.

July 17

Constitution Day in South Korea: Commemorates the adoption of the constitution in 1963.

July Revolution Day in Iraq (Peaceful Revolution Day): Commemorates the Iraqi revolts of 1968.

Muñoz Rivera Day: Marks the anniversary of the 1859 birth of Luis Muñoz Rivera, Puerto Rican patriot and journalist.

July 18

Constitution Day in Uruguay: Commemorates the adoption of the 1951 constitution.

July 19

Sandinista Day: Commemorates the revolution ending the rule of the Samoza regime in Nicaragua.

July 20

Independence Day in Colombia: Celebrates the 1810 declaration of independence from Spanish rule.

July 21

Belgium Independence Day: Commemorates the accession of the first Belgian king, Leopold I, following separation from the Netherlands in 1831.

Liberation Day in Guam: Honors the freeing of the island from the Japanese in 1944.

July 22

Manifesto Day: Commemorates the anniversary of the issuance of Catherine the Great's 1763 manifesto urging foreign colonists to settle in the Russian Empire, a date considered by many to be the "birthday" of the Germans from Russia.

Polish National Liberation Day: Honors the end of World War II in 1944 and the enactment of a constitution in 1952.

July 23

Egyptian Revolution Anniversary Day: Commemorates the 1952 revolutionary command terminating the Egyptian royal government and declaring the nation to be a republic.

July 24

Bolívar Day: Celebrated in Ecuador and Venezuela to honor Simon Bolívar, known as the "George Washington of South America."

July 25

Constitution Day: Honors the 1952 proclamation of Puerto Rico's constitution.

July 26

Bellman Day: Honors the memory of Sweden's

Carl Michael Bellman, an eighteenth-century troubadour.

Cuban Revolution Day: Commemorates Fidel Castro's "26th of July Movement" of 1953 against the Batista military dictatorship.

July 27

Barbosa Day: Honors the 1857 birth of José Celso Barbosa, black physician and political hero of nineteenth-century Puerto Rico.

Sovereignty Day in Belarus: Marks the anniversary of the declaration of sovereignty in Belarus in 1990.

July 28

Peruvian Independence Day: Commemorates the declaration of independence from Spain in 1821, which led to war and complete freedom in 1824.

July 30

Marseillaise Day: Commemorates the first singing of the French national anthem, which took place in 1792 at the port city of Marseilles.

August 1

Swiss Confederation Day: Celebrates the 1291 founding of the Swiss Confederation.

August 2

Constitution Day in Iceland: Marks the anniversary of the granting of a constitution to the country in 1874 by the Danish king and commemorates the 874 settlement, according to legend, of the first Norwegians in Iceland.

Freedom Day in Guyana: Commemorates the enactment of the Emancipation Act of 1837, which freed the slaves in the then colony of British Guiana.

August 7

Battle of Boyacá Day: Colombian holiday commemorating the victory of the South American insurgents over Spanish forces in 1819.

August 10

Ecuador Independence Day: Commemorates the 1809 proclamation of independence.

August 14

Pakistan Independence Day: Commemorates the establishment of Pakistan as a free nation in 1947.

August 15

Independence Day in India: Commemorates the day the Indian Independence Act went into effect in 1947.

Republic Day in South Korea: Commemorates the 1945 liberation of South Korea from Japanese occupation and the 1948 proclamation of the Republic of South Korea.

August 16

Cyprus Independence Day: Marks the anniversary of the 1960 agreement between the British and the Greek and Turkish Cypriots to provide independence for Cyprus.

Dominican Restoration Day: Commemorates the restoration of the Dominican Republic's independence in 1963.

August 17

Indonesia Independence Day: Honors the proclamation of independence made by the Indonesian Revolutionaries in 1945, although full independence for Indonesia did not come until in 1949.

San Martín Day: Commemorates the 1850 death of José Francisco de San Martín, Argentinean soldier and statesman.

August 20

Constitution Day in Hungary: Commemorates the institution of the country's constitution in 1949.

August 23

Romanian Liberation Day: Commemorates the 1944 coup that deposed the Fascist Iron Guard dictatorship.

August 25

Independence Day in Belarus: Marks the anniversary of the declaration of the independence of Belarus in 1991.

August 30

Victory Day in Turkey: Honors the memory of those individuals who died in the 1922 Battle of Dumlupinar, the final battle for Turkish independence.

August 31

Merdeka Day: Celebrates Malaysia's achievement of the status of an independent member of the British Commonwealth in 1957; full independence was gained in 1963.

Trinidad and Tobago Independence Day: Commemorates the independence achieved in 1962 within the British Commonwealth of Nations.

August (movable)

Pjodhatid: Commemorates the granting of Iceland's constitution on July 1, 1874, which permitted the nation, formerly under Danish control, to handle its own domestic affairs.

August (movable; first Monday)

Jamaican Independence Day: Commemorates the achievement of independence in 1962.

August–September (movable)

Mid-Autumn Festival: Asian celebration on the fifteenth day of the eighth moon to honor the moon goddess and mark the harvest time with a day of thanksgiving.

September 3

Cromwell's Day: Commemorates the day in 1650 when Oliver Cromwell lead the British to victory in the Battle of Dunbar, the day in 1651 when he lead the victory at the Battle of Worcester against the Scots, and the day in 1658 on which he died.

Treaty of Paris Day: Marks the anniversary of the 1783 signing of the treaty between the United States and England ending the American Revolution.

September 7

Brazilian Independence Day: Honors Dom Pedro's 1822 proclamation of independence from Portugal.

September 9

Bulgarian National Day: Memorializes the 1944 joining of the Bulgarian partisans and Soviet troops to drive out the Nazis.

September 11

Enkutatash (Ethiopian New Year): Marks the first day of the Ethiopian month of Maskarem, which coincides with the end of the rainy season.

Jinnah Day: Marks the anniversary of the 1948

death of Quaid-i-Azam Mohammed Ali Jinnah, the founder of a free and independent Pakistan.

September 12

National Day in Ethiopia: Commemorates the 1974 termination of the Ethiopian Empire and the deposing of Haile Selassie.

September 14

Battle of San Jacinto Day: Commemorates the Nicaraguan defeat of foreign invaders in 1856.

September 15

Central American Independence Day: Observed in El Salvador, Guatemala, Honduras, and Nicaragua to commemorate the overthrow of Spanish rule in 1821.

September 16

Mexican Independence Day: Commemorates the country's establishment of independence.

September 18

Independence Day in Chile: Commemorates the declaration of independence from Spain, although complete independence was not gained until February 12, 1818.

September 19

Chilean Armed Forces Day: Celebrated as part of the independence festivities.

September 21

Armenian Independence Day: Commemorates the founding of the Second Republic in 1991.

September (movable)

Odwira: Celebrates the national identity of the Asante people of Ghana.

September (movable; first Monday)

Labor Day: Established as a national holiday in Canada and the United States to honor the worker.

September–October (movable)

Festival of the Kites: Observed on the ninth day of the ninth moon as a Chinese family-remembrance day to honor ancestors with visits to their graves and to go to the hills for picnics and kite-flying, since kites are believed to carry misfortune into the skies.

Oktoberfest: First celebrated in honor of the 1810 marriage of Crown Prince Ludwig of Bavaria to Princess Therese von Saxe-Hildburghausen, Oktoberfest now serves as a celebration of German ancestry.

**October 1**

National Day in China: Commemorates the establishment of the People's Republic of China in 1949.

**October 2**

Ghandi Day: Commemorates the 1869 birth of Mahatma Gandhi, a dominant political figure in India's struggle for independence.

**October 3**

Leyden Day: Celebration in the Netherlands commemorating the lifting of the Siege of Leyden in 1574 through a storm that carried the Spanish fleet out into the ocean.

Morazán Day: Honors Francisco Morazán, an early nineteenth-century Honduran statesman whose dream was a unified Central America.

**October 5**

Portuguese Republic Day: Honors the proclamation of the republic in 1910.

**October 6**

Armed Forces Day in Egypt: Marks the surprise attack on Israel that began the October War of 1973.

**October 9**

Day of National Dignity: Marks the anniversary of the Peruvian government's seizure of the oil fields on behalf of the Peruvian nation; often regarded as a second Independence Day.

Guayaquil Independence Day: Marks the 1820 declaration of the Ecuadorian city's independence.

Leif Ericson Day: Celebrated in Iceland and Norway to honor the landing of the Norsemen in Vinland around 1000 C.E.

**October 10**

Aleksis Kivi Day: Honors the 1834 birth of the "Father of the Finnish novel and drama."

National Day in Taiwan: Commemorates the anniversary of the Proclamation of the Republic in 1911.

**October 11**

Beginning of Independence Wars Day: Honors the guerrilla wars of the 1950s that were led by Fidel Castro to overthrow the Batista regime.

Panama Revolution Day: Commemorates the 1968 revolt.

Pulaski Day: Honors Count Casimir Pulaski who, upon being forced to flee Poland because of his efforts to preserve Polish independence, fought in the American Revolution and died in a 1779 battle to free Savannah, Georgia, from British control.

**October 12**

Dia de la Raza (Day of the Race): Celebration in Latin American countries paying tribute to the contributions of Spanish civilization to the American continent.

National Day in Spain: Honors the landfall of Christopher Columbus in the New World.

**October 14**

Yemen National Day: Honors the revolts of 1962.

**October 17**

Dessalines Day: Commemorates the 1806 death of Jean Jacques Dessalines, a revolutionist who was proclaimed emperor of Haiti in 1805.

**October 20**

Guatemala Revolution Day: Commemorates the revolution of 1944.

**October 21**

Honduras Army Day: Commemorates the 1956 revolt.

**October 23**

Chulalongkorn Day: Commemorates the 1868 birth of Rama V, a progressive ruler who abolished slavery in Thailand (then still called Siam) and introduced numerous reforms.

Revolution Day in Hungary: Marks the anniversary of the 1956 revolution.

**October 24**

United Nations Day: Commemorates the 1945 founding of the United Nations in the wake of World War II.

**October 26**

Austria National Day: Commemorates the passing of the neutrality law by the Austrian parliament in 1955.

**October 28**

Greek National Day: Commemorates the anniversary of Greece's successful resistance to Italian aggression in 1940.

October 29

Turkey's Republic Day: Commemorates the 1923 proclamation of the republic.

October 31

Halloween (All Hallows' Eve): Ancient Celtic harvest festival.

October (movable; second Monday)

Canadian Thanksgiving Day: Commemorates the arrival of the fall harvest.

November 1

Day of the Awakeners (Den na Buditelite): Commemorates the patriots, writers, and revolutionaries who helped foster the spirit of Bulgarian nationalism.

November 2

Balfour Declaration Day: Celebration, observed particularly by Jews in Israel, to mark the 1917 establishment of a Jewish national home.

November 3

Cuenca Independence Day: Marks the 1820 declaration of the Ecuadorian city's independence.

Independence Day in Panama: Commemorates the 1903 declaration establishing Panama's independence from Colombia.

November 4

Panama Flag Day: Celebrated in conjunction with the country's independence festivities.

Victory of Vittorio Veneto: Honors the Italian Unknown Soldier.

November 5

First Cry for Independence Day: Commemorates the first battle for El Salvador's freedom from Spain.

Guy Fawkes Day: Marks the anniversary of the 1605 "Gunpowder Plot" to blow up England's parliament and the king.

November 6

Gustavus Adolphus Day: Honors the Swedish king who laid the foundations of the modern Swedish state, turned the country into a major European power, and died in battle in 1632.

November 7

Bangladesh Revolution Day: Marks the anniver-

sary of the 1975 takeover of the government by the military.

November 9

Crystal Night: Marks the anniversary of the street riots of November 9 and 19, 1938, when Nazi storm troopers raided Jewish homes and synagogues; the name comes from the shattering of glass in Jewish homes and stores.

Iqbal Day: Marks the anniversary of the 1877 birth of Muhammad Iqbal, Pakistan's philosopher-poet.

November 11

Independence Day in Poland: Commemorates the restoration of Polish independence in 1918.

Veterans' Day: Originally called Armistice Day and observed to commemorate the signing of the 1918 armistice between the Allied and Central Powers that marked the end of World War I, it was later renamed Veterans' Day and expanded to honor those who served their countries in other wars as well.

November 15

Republic Day in Brazil: Honors the 1889 proclamation that dethroned Dom Pedro II.

November 18

Vertières Day: Commemorates the 1803 defeat of the French by the Haitian army in the Battle of Vertières.

November 19

Settlement Day: Commemorates the arrival of Garifuna in Belize but is observed in the United States as a day of ethnic celebration for Garifuna of all nationalities.

November 20

Mexico Revolution Day: Marks the anniversary of the Mexican Revolution of 1910.

November 22

Lebanese Independence Day: Celebrates Lebanon's achievement of independence in 1943.

November 28

Albanian Independence Day: Commemorates the 1912 proclamation of independence, issued at the end of the Balkan War that terminated Turkish rule.

November 29

Albanian Liberation Day: Celebrates the 1944 withdrawal of foreign troops.

November 30

Barbados Independence Day: Commemorates the island's becoming an independent member of the British Commonwealth of Nations in 1966.

Bonifacio Day (National Heroes' Day): Commemorates the birth of Andres Bonifacio, the Philippine patriot who led the 1896 revolt against the Spanish.

November (movable; fourth Thursday)

U.S. Thanksgiving Day: Commemorates the Pilgrims' 1621 harvest feast that celebrated the completion of their first year in the Plymouth Colony.

December 1

Iceland National Day: Marks the anniversary of the 1918 treaty recognizing Iceland as an independent state under the Danish crown.

December 1

National Day in Romania: Commemorates the unification in 1918 of Romania and Transylvania and the formation of the Romanian State.

December 2

Republic Day in Laos: Commemorates the founding of the Lao People's Democratic Republic in 1975.

December 6

Finnish Independence Day: Commemorates the 1917 declaration of freedom from Russia.

December 10

Thailand Constitution Day: Commemorates the 1932 constitution, the first for the Thai.

December 11

Scaling Day (Escalade): Honors the night in 1602 when the citizens of Geneva, Switzerland, routed the Savoyards, who were scaling the walls of the city.

December 16

Bangladesh Victory Day: Commemorates the end of the 1971 conflict with Pakistan.

Nepal Constitution Day: Honors the 1962 adoption of a constitution for the Kingdom of Nepal.

December 25

Taiwan Constitution Day: Honors the 1946 adoption of the constitution.

December 26

Boxing Day: Customary day for distributing gifts to public servants and employees.

Kwanzaa: Marks the first day of a seven-day celebration of oneness in the African-American community that honors the seven principles of unity, self-determination, collective work and responsibility, cooperative economics, purpose, creativity, and faith.

December 30

Rizal Day: Commemorates the 1896 death of José Mercado Rizal, Philippine doctor and author whose books denouncing the Spanish administration were an inspiration to the Philippine nationalist movement.

December 31

Evacuation Day: Celebrated the withdrawal of French troops from Lebanon in 1946.

## Baha'i Holidays

February 26

Ayyam-i-Ha: Marks the first of the four (five in leap years) intercalary days in the Baha'i calendar, a calendar made up of nineteen months of nineteen days each; Ayyam-i-Ha is followed by a nineteen-day fasting period (from March 2 through March 20), which in turn is followed by the Baha'i New Year's Day (Now Ruz) on March 21.

April 21

Feast of Ridvan: Marks the first day of the twelve-day celebration commemorating the 1863 declaration by Mirza Husain Ali Nuri (Baha Allah), the founder of the Baha'i religion, that he was God's messenger for the age.

May 23

Declaration of the Bab: Celebrates the announcement by Mirza Ali Muhammad Shirazi, that he was the "gate" (the Bab) to the coming of the promised one of all religions, a proclamation considered to be the beginning of the Baha'i religion.

May 29

Ascension of Baha Allah: Marks the anniversary of the 1892 death of Mirza Husain Ali Nuri, the founder of the Baha'i religion.

July 9

Martyrdom of the Bab: Commemorates the 1850 execution of Mirza Ali Muhammad Shirazi, the first prophet of the Baha'i religion.

October 20

Birth of the Bab: Celebrates the 1819 birth of Mirza Ali Muhammad Shirazi, who was the founder of the Babi faith and considered by those in the Baha'i religion to be the herald whose chief task was to announce the advent of the dispensation of Baha Allah (the founder of the Baha'i religion).

November 12

Birth of Baha Allah: Marks the anniversary of the 1817 birth of Mirza Husain Ali Nuri, the founder of the Baha'i religion.

November 26

Day of the Covenant: Commemorates the covenant that Baha Allah, the founder of the Baha'i religion, made with humanity and his followers, appointing his eldest son, Abd al-Baha, to be the head of the Baha'i religion and interpret Baha'i teachings.

November 28

Ascension of Abd al-Baha: Commemorates the 1921 death of Abbas Effendi, the eldest son of the founder of the Baha'i religion, Mirza Husain Ali Nuri.

## Buddhist Holidays

Margasirsa (the nineteenth day)

Birthday of the Goddess of Mercy: Honors Kuan Yin, the goddess of infinite compassion and mercy.

Magha (full moon)

Magha Puja: Commemorates the occasion when 1,250 followers ordained by the Buddha arrived by coincidence at Veluvan Monastery in Rajagriha, India, to hear him lay down monastic regulations and predict his own death.

Phalguna (the sixth day)

Airing the Classics: Commemorates the time when the boat carrying the Buddhist scriptures from India to China was upset at a river crossing and all the books had to be spread to dry.

Vaisakha (full moon)

Vesak (Buddha Purnima): Commemorates the Buddha's birth, enlightenment, and attainment of Nirvana.

Jyaistha (full moon)

Poson: Commemorates the bringing of Buddhism to Sri Lanka in the third century B.C.E.

Asadha (the twenty-fifth day)

Ganden Ngamcho (Festival of Lights): Commemorates the birth and death of Tsongkhapa (1357–1419), a saintly scholar and teacher in Tibetan Buddhism, whose successors became the Dalai Lamas.

Asadha to Asvina

Waso (Buddhist Lent): Three-month period of abstinence and meditation, the day prior to which commemorates the Buddha's first sermon to his five disciples, forty-nine days after his enlightenment.

## Christian Holidays

January 1

St. Basil's Day: Celebrated in Greece to honor the fourth-century bishop of Caesarea.

January 5

Twelfth Night: Celebrated the evening before Epiphany as the traditional end to the Christmas season.

January 6

Feast of the Epiphany: Commemorates the worshipping of Jesus by the Three Kings (emphasized in Roman Catholic and Protestant churches) and the baptism of Jesus (emphasized in Eastern Orthodox churches), the first two occasions on which Christ was manifested. Epiphany is observed on January 19 by the Eastern Orthodox churches, which base religious observations on the Julian calendar.

January 8

St. Gudula's Day: Honors the patron saint of Brussels.

January 13

St. Knut's Day: Observed as the Swedish day for dismantling Christmas trees.

Tyvendedagen: Celebrates the official end of the Yuletide in Norway.

January 15

Feast of Christ of Esquipulas (The Black Christ Festival): Observed at Esquipulas in Guatemala and named after a figure of Christ that was carved out of dark brown balsam.

January 19

St. Henry of Uppsala's Day: Honoring the patron saint of Finland.

January 21

St. Altagracia's Day: Celebrated in the Dominican Republic with a pilgrimage to the St. Altagracia shrine.

January 26

St. Nino's Day: Honors St. Nino of Cappadocia, who introduced Christianity to Georgia in the fourth century.

January 27

St. Sava's Day: A Serbian children's festival in honor of St. Sava, a king's son who built schools and monasteries all over Serbia.

January 30

St. Charles's Day: Observed in commemoration of the 1649 execution of King Charles I for his defense of the Anglican Church.

February 1

St. Bridget's Day: Honors the patron saint of Ireland who established the first Irish convent, around which the city of Kildare eventually grew.

February 2

Candlemass (Feast of the Purification of the Blessed Virgin Mary): The blessing of candles is a great tradition of the Roman Catholic and Anglican observance that is particularly popular in Mexico and other Latin American countries.

February 2–March 8 (movable)

Shrove Monday: Observed the Monday before Ash Wednesday as a preparation day for Lent.

February 3

St. Anskar's Day: Honors the patron saint of Denmark, who was a missionary to Denmark, Sweden, Norway, and northern Germany.

February 3–March 9 (movable)

Shrove Tuesday (Mardi Gras): Celebrated the day before Ash Wednesday as the last day of preparation for Lent.

February 4–March 10 (movable)

Ash Wednesday: Marks the first day of Lent, the forty-day period of abstinence before Palm Sunday, recalling the fasts of Moses, Elijah, and Jesus.

February 14

St. Cyril and St. Methodius's Day: Honors the two brothers from Thessalonica who became the "Apostles of the Slavs" and created the Glagolithic alphabet (from which the Cyrillic alphabet was later derived) to aid in their mission. (This feast day is observed on May 24 by Eastern Orthodox churches, which calculate religious dates according to the Julian calendar.)

March 1

St. David's Day: Honors the patron saint of Wales, who founded many churches in southern Wales in the sixth century and moved the seat of ecclesiastical government from Caerleon to Mynyw, the present cathedral city of Saint David's.

March 4

St. Casimir's Day: Honors the patron saint of Poland and Lithuania.

March 15–April 18 (movable)

Palm Sunday: Celebrated on the Sunday preceding Easter to commemorate the arrival of Jesus in Jerusalem, where palm branches, the symbol of victory, were spread before him by the people who viewed him as the leader who would deliver them from the domination of the Roman Empire.

March 17

St. Patrick's Day: Honors the patron saint of Ireland who, after becoming a bishop, returned to Ireland about 432 as a missionary to the pagans.

March 18–April 21 (movable)

Spy Wednesday: Observed on the Wednesday before Easter to commemorate the betrayal of Jesus by Judas Iscariot in the Garden of Gethsemane.

March 19

St. Joseph's Day: Honors the patron saint of Belgium and Colombia.

March 19–April 22 (movable)

Maundy Thursday: Celebrated the Thursday before Easter to commemorate Jesus Christ's institution of the Eucharist in the Last Supper.

March 20–April 23 (movable)

Good Friday: Observed on the Friday before Easter to commemorate the crucifixion of Jesus.

March 21–April 24 (movable)

Holy Saturday: Celebrated on the day before Easter, bringing the season of Lent to a close.

March 22

St. Nicholas von Flüe's Day: Honors the patron saint of Switzerland.

March 22–April 25 (movable)

Easter: Celebrated the first Sunday after the first full moon on or following the vernal equinox to commemorate the anniversary of Jesus Christ's resurrection from the dead.

March 25

Feast of the Annunciation (Lady Day): Celebrates the appearance of the Archangel Gabriel to the Virgin Mary announcing that she was to become the mother of Jesus.

April 2

Martyrdom of Blessed Diego Luis de San Vitores: Commemorates the 1672 death of the priest who introduced Catholicism to Guam.

April 23

St. George's Day: Honors the patron saint of England, Canada, Portugal, Germany, Genoa, and Venice.

May 10–June 13 (movable)

Pentecost (Whitsunday, Pinkster Day): Celebrated on the seventh Sunday (fifty days) after Easter to commemorate the Holy Spirit's visit to the Apostles, giving them the gift of tongues that allowed them to preach about Jesus Christ to people from all over the world.

May 15

St. Isidore the Husbandman's Day: Honors the patron saint of Madrid.

May 18

St. Eric of Sweden's Day: Honors the patron saint of Sweden.

May 30

St. Joan's Day: Honors Joan of Arc, who helped save the French city of Orleans from the British in the fifteenth century.

May (movable)

Ascension Day (Holy Thursday): Celebrated forty days after Easter to commemorate Jesus Christ's ascension to heaven.

May (third week)

Carabao Festival: Honors San Isidro Labrador (St. Isidore the Farmer), the patron saint of the Filipino farmer.

June 5

St. Boniface's Day: Honors the patron saint of Germany.

St. Euphrosynia of Polack's Day: Honors the patron saint of Belarus.

June 9

St. Columba's Day: Honors the patron saint of Ireland who went into self-imposed exile on the island of Iona, where he founded a monastery and school from which he and his disciples preached the Gospel.

June 13

St. Anthony of Padua's Day: Honors the patron saint of Portugal.

June 24

Feast of the Nativity of St. John the Baptist: Celebration, especially by the French in Canada, of the birth of the cousin of Jesus.

June 28

St. Vitus's Day: Commemorates the Serbian defeat by the Turks at Kosovo in 1389.

July 8

St. Elizabeth's Day: Honors the saint who was the mother of John the Baptist and a cousin of the Virgin Mary.

July 25

St. James the Great's Day: Honors the patron saint of Chile and Spain.

July 26

St. Anne's Day: Honors the patron saint of Canada.

July 28

St. Prince Vladimir of Kiev's Day: Honors (with celebrations of the Russian culture involving lectures, readings, and concerts) the saint who introduced Christianity to ancient Rus in 988.

July 29

St. Olav's Day: Commemorates the death of Olav Haraldsson (the second King Olav), who brought Christianity to Norway and was later killed in the Battle of Stiklestad in 1030.

August 15

Feast of the Assumption: Commemorates the belief that when Mary, the mother of Jesus, died, her body did not decay but was assumed into heaven and reunited there with her soul.

August 25

St. Louis's Day: Honors the patron saint of France.

August 30

Rose of Lima Day: Honors the patron saint of South America and the Philippines.

September 8

Feast of the Nativity of the Blessed Virgin Mary: Celebrates the birth of Mary, the mother of Jesus.

September 14

Feast of the Exaltation of the Cross: Commemorates the finding of the cross on which Jesus was crucified, the dedication of a basilica built in 335 on the supposed site of Christ's crucifixion on Golgotha, and the recovery in 629 of the relic of the cross that had been stolen by the Persians.

September 28

St. Vaclav's Day: Honors the patron saint, widely known as Good King Wenceslas, of the Czech Republic.

September 29

Michaelmas: Honors St. Michael, traditionally

viewed as the leader of the heavenly host of angels.

October 4

St. Francis of Assisi's Day: Honors the patron saint of Italy.

October 9

St. Denis's Day: Honors the patron saint of France.

October 15

St. Teresa of Avila's Day: Honors the patron saint of Spain.

October 18

El Señor de los Milagros Day: Honors the patron saint of Peru with special services and foods, as well as the wearing of purple, the symbolic color of the saint.

October 26

St. Demetrius's Day: Honors the patron saint of Greece.

November 1

All Saints' Day: Celebration of all Christian saints, particularly those that do not have special feast days of their own.

November 2

All Souls' Day: Commemorates the souls of all the faithful departed.

November 8

Saints, Doctors, Missionaries, and Martyrs Day: Celebrated in England in memory and commemoration of the "unnamed saints of the nation."

November 11

Beggar's Day in the Netherlands: Honors St. Martin with children dressing as beggars and going from door to door.

November 30

St. Andrew's Day: Honors the patron saint of Scotland, Russia, and Greece.

November (movable; Sunday closest to November 30)

Advent: Marks the beginning of the Christian year and consists of a period varying in length from twenty-two to twenty-eight days, beginning on the Sunday nearest to St. Andrew's Day and encompassing the next three Sundays, ending on Christmas Eve.

December 4

St. Barbara's Day: Celebrated in parts of France, Germany, and Syria as the beginning of the Christmas season.

December 6

St. Nicholas's Day: Honors the patron saint of Russia and children.

December 12

Festival of Our Lady of Guadalupe: Religious ceremony commemorating the appearance of the Blessed Virgin to an Indian boy in Mexico in 1531.

December 13

St. Lucia's Day: Swedish celebration of the festival of lights honoring St. Lucia, the "Queen of Light."

December 16

Posadas: Marks the first day of a nine-day celebration in Mexico commemorating the journey Mary and Joseph took from Nazareth to Bethlehem, where Jesus was born.

December 25

Christmas Day: Christian celebration of the birth of Jesus. Christmas is celebrated on January 7 by Eastern Orthodox churches, which base religious observations on the Julian calendar.

December 26

St. Stephen's Day: Honors the patron saint of Hungary.

December 28

Holy Innocents' Day: Commemorates the massacre of all male children under two years of age ordered by King Herod in an attempt to kill the baby Jesus.

December 31

St. Sylvester's Day: Honors the saint who was pope in 325, the year Emperor (Constantine declared the pagan religion of Rome abolished in favor of Christianity.

## Confucian Holiday

September 28

Confucius's Birthday: Commemorates the birth in the sixth century B.C.E. of the Chinese philosopher and teacher.

## Hindu Holidays

Karttika (fifteenth day of the waning moon)

Diwali (Deepavali, Festival of Lights): Commemorates Rama's rescue of Sita from Ravana, an important episode in the *Mahabrahata*, and marks the Hindu New Year.

Phalguna (fourteenth day of the waxing moon)

Holi: A Hindu spring festival marking the triumph of Good over Evil with celebrants throwing red and yellow powder over one another and lighting bonfires to remember the burning of the demoness Holika.

Phalguna (full moon)

Dol Purnima: Commemorates the birthday of Chaitanya Mahaprabhu (1486–1534), also known as Gauranga, the sixteenth century Vishnavite saint and poet of Bengal who is regarded as an incarnation of Krishna.

Phalguna (full moon)

Meenakshi Kalyanam: Honors the marriage of the goddess Meenakshi, an incarnation of Parvati, and the Lord Shiva.

Phalguna (thirteenth day of the waning moon)

Shivaratri: Commemorates the night Lord Shiva, the god of destruction and the restorer, danced the Tandav, his celestial dance of creation, preservation, and destruction.

Caitra

Hanuman Jayanti: Honors Hanuman, the Monkey-God and central figure in the Hindu epic *Ramayana*.

Caitra (ninth day of the waxing moon)

Ramanavami (Ram Navami): Honors the birth of Rama, the seventh incarnation of Lord Vishnu.

Jyaistha

Ganga Dussehra: Honors the healing power of the Ganges River, which originally flowed only in heaven but was brought down to earth in the form of the goddess Ganga by King Bhagiratha to purify the ashes of his ancestors.

Jyaistha (sixth day of the waxing moon)

Sithinakha: Honors the birthday of Kumara, the Hindu god of war and the first-born son of Lord Shiva.

Sravana (waxing moon)

Naag Panchami: Honors the sacred serpent Ananta, on whose coils Lord Vishnu rested while he created the universe.

Sravana (fourteenth day of the waning moon)

Ghanta Karna: Commemorates the death of Ghanta Karna, who caused death and destruction wherever he went until a god in the form of a frog persuaded him to leap into a well, after which the people beat him to death and dragged his body to the river for cremation.

Bhadrapada (waxing moon)

Ganesh Chathurthi: Honors Ganesh, the elephant-headed Hindu god of wisdom and success.

Bhadrapada (waning moon)

Indra Jatra: Eight-day celebration to pay homage to the recently deceased and to honor the Hindu god Indra and his mother Dagini so they will bless the coming harvest.

Bhadrapada (new moon)

Janmashtami (Krishnastami; Krishna's Birthday): Celebrates the birthday of Lord Krishna, the eighth incarnation of Vishnu.

Asvina (waxing moon)

Durga Puja: Honors Durga, one aspect of the Mother Goddess and the personification of energy, who rides a lion and destroys demons.

## Igbo Holidays

April

Awuru Odo Festival: Celebrated among the Igbo people of Nigeria in honor of the biannual visit of the Odo (the spirits of the dead).

August–September

Agwunsi Festival: Honors the god of healing and divination among the Igbo people of Nigeria.

September

Okpesi Festival: Ceremony of the Igbo people of Nigeria honoring their ancestors.

## Islamic Holidays

Muharram (first ten days)

Ashura: Commemorates the death of Muhammad's grandson Hussein in the year 680 C.E.

during a battle between Sunnis and the group of Shi'ite supporters with whom he was traveling.

Rabi I (the twelfth day)

Mawlid al-Nabi (Prophet's Birthday): Honors the birth of the Prophet Muhammad, the founder of Islam, who was born in Mecca in 570 C.E.

Rajab (the twenty-seventh day)

Laylat al Miraj: Commemorates the ascent of the Prophet Muhammad into Heaven.

Shaban (night of the fifteenth)

Shab-Barat: A period of intense prayer in preparation for Ramadan during which individuals ask Allah to forgive the people who they know have died.

Ramadan

Ramadan: The holiest period of the Islamic year commemorates the time when the Koran, the Islamic holy book, was revealed to the Prophet Muhammad. Devout Muslims abstain from food, drink, smoking, sex, and gambling from sunrise to sunset during this period.

Ramadan (last ten days)

Laylat al-Qadr: Commemorates the night in 610 C.E. when Allah revealed the entire Koran to Muhammad.

Shawwal (first day)

Id al-Fitr (Feast of Fast-Breaking): Marks the end of the month-long fasting period of Ramadan.

Dhu al-Hijjah (between the eight and thirteenth days)

Hajj (Pilgrimage to Mecca): A fundamental duty of each Muslim to be completed at least once in a lifetime.

Dhu al-Hijjah

Id al-Adha (Feast of Sacrifice): Three-day feast serving as the concluding rite for those performing a pilgrimage to Mecca and, for those not performing a pilgrimage, as a commemoration of Ibrahim's (Abraham) near sacrifice of his son.

## Jain Holidays

Caitra (thirteenth day of the waxing moon)

Mahavir Jayanti: Honors Vardhamana Jnatrputra, who lived during the fifth century B.C.E. and is regarded by the Jains as the twenty-fourth and last in a series of Tirthankaras (Enlightened Teachers).

Bhadrapada

Paryushana: A festival to focus on the ten cardinal virtues (i.e., forgiveness, charity, simplicity, contentment, truthfulness, self-restraint, fasting, detachment, humility, and continence) by individuals asking those whom they may have offended for forgiveness and restoring lapsed friendships.

## Jewish Holidays

Tishri (the first day)

Rosh Hashanah: Marks the first day of the two-day observance of the Jewish New Year, which are also the first two days of the ten High Holy Days that conclude with Yom Kippur, the Day of Atonement.

Tishri (the third day)

Tsom Gedaliah (Fast of Gedaliah): Fast to commemorate the assassination of Gedaliah ben Ahikam, the Jewish governor left in charge by King Nebuchadnezzar to administer the affairs of Judah after the destruction of Jerusalem and the fall of the First Temple in 586 B.C.E.

Tishri (the tenth day)

Yom Kippur (Day of Atonement): The holiest and most solemn day in the Jewish Calendar and the last of the ten High Holy Days (Days of Penitence) that begin with the Jewish New Year (Rosh Hashanah).

Tishri (the fifteenth day)

Sukkot: Marks the first day of the eight-day commemoration of the forty years after the Exodus that Jews wandered in the desert under the leadership of Moses.

Tishri (the twenty-first day)

Hoshana Rabbah: Considered to be the last possible day on which one can seek forgiveness for the sins of the preceding year.

Tishri (the twenty-second day)

Shemini Atzeret (Eighth Day of Solemn Assembly): Marks the eighth day of the festival of Sukkot but is celebrated as a separate holiday dedicated to the love of God.

Tishri (the twenty-third day)

Simhat Torah: Celebrates the annual completion of the public reading of the Torah, the first five books of the Bible.

Kislev (the twenty-fifth day)

Hanukkah: Marks the first day of an eight-day celebration to commemorate the successful rebellion of the Jews against the Syrians in the Maccabean War of 162 B.C.E. and the associated miracle of a small bottle of consecrated oil for the menorah (perpetual lamp) lasting eight days until more could be obtained.

Tevet (the tenth day)

Asarah be-Tevet (Tenth of Tevet): Fast day commemorating the beginning of the siege of Jerusalem by the Babylonians under King Nebuchadnezzar in 586 B.C.E. that was a prelude to the destruction of the First Temple.

Nisan

Hagodol: Observed on the Sabbath just prior to Passover to commemorate the Sabbath before the Exodus from Egypt that ended more than four hundred years of slavery.

Nisan (the fifteenth day)

Passover: Marks the first day of the eight-day celebration of the deliverance of the Jews from slavery in Egypt.

Nisan (the twenty-seventh day)

Yom Hashoah (Holocaust Day): Observed, as a memorial to the six million Jews killed by the Nazis between 1933 and 1945, on the anniversary of the date on which the Allied troops liberated the first Nazi concentration camp, Buchenwald, in Germany, in 1945.

Sivan (the sixth day)

Shavuot: Observed fifty days after Passover to mark the end of the barley harvest and the beginning of the wheat harvest and to celebrate the return of Moses from the top of Mt. Sinai with the Ten Commandments, the fundamental laws of the Jewish faith.

Tammuz (the seventeenth day)

Shivah Asar be-Tammuz (Fast of the Seventeenth of Tammuz): Commemorates the breaching of the walls of Jerusalem in 586 B.C.E., when the Babylonians conquered Judah, destroyed the First Temple, and carried most the Jewish population off into slavery.

Av (the ninth day)

Tishah be-Av (Fast of Av): A twenty-four-hour period of fasting, lamentation, and prayer in memory of the destruction of both the First Temple (586 B.C.E.) and the Second Temple (70 C.E.) in Jerusalem.

## Zoroastrian Holidays

January 30

Joshne Sadeh: Celebration of the fire building festival with people saying prayers as they circle large bonfires.

March 16

Pange Porse Hamagoni: Observed on the first of the five days preceding New Year's day as the second of the two days of the year for commemoration of all deaths.

March 27

Tavalode Zartosht: Observed six days after Now Ruz (the Iranian New Year) to commemorate Zoroaster's birthday and the day he was named the prophet.

April 3

Sizda be Dar: Observed on the thirteenth day after the New Year with traditional picnics and the throwing out of the greens (from the New Year's table), which helps a young woman find a mate.

June 14

Ziarat Pir Sabz: A pilgrimage to Pir Sabz, a shrine (the most important of all shrines for most Zoroastrians) near Yazd in Iran.

June 19

Porse Hamagoni: The first of two celebrations commemorating all deaths together.

July 1

Tirgan: Celebration of the water (or rain) festival.

September 2

Joshne Mehregan: Celebration of the fall festival.

# INDEX

Pages numbers in **boldface** refer to the main entry on a subject.
Page numbers in *italics* refer to tables and illustrations.

Kalmyk immigration to, 544
Macedonian emigration from, 600
Yugoslavians
ancestry reports for 1990, 975
population by state, 995
Yunus, Muhammad, 90

**Z**

Zachariah, Mar Nicholovos, 830
Zaibei Okinawa Kenjinkai (Association of the People of Okinawa Prefecture in America), 665
Zaibei Okinawa Seinenkai (Association of Young Okinawans in America), 664
*Zajednicar* (Fraternalist)

(publication), 193
Zaldastani, Guivy, 314, 315
Zaldastani, Othar, 315
Zarechnak, Dimitry, 147
Zastava (Flag), 820
Zayek, Francis (Bishop), 581
*Zborlu a Nostru* (Our Word) (periodical), 932
Zenbat Gara dance group, 74
*Zeri i Shqiperise* (Voice of Albania), 30
Zhatkovich, Gregory I., 145
Ziarat Pir Sabz, 1017
Zibergs (Sieberg), Jekabs, 574
*Živena* (Giver of Life) Beneficial Society, 814
Zonal Council of the Church of South India in North America, 832–833

Zora (Dawn) (Slovene singing society), 820
Zoroastrian Assembly (Los Angeles), 956
Zoroastrian Association of California, 956
Zoroastrian Center (Los Angeles), 956
Zoroastrians, **953–957**
Gujarati, 359
Iranian, 446
map, 964
religion, 953–954
temples, 956
Zoroastrian Youth Congress, 956
Zotti, Frank, 193
Zuk, Alexandra. *See* Dee, Sandra
Zul (Feast of Lights), 547
Zvorykin, Vladimir V., 752